Contents

*The **Michelin maps** which accompany this guide are:*

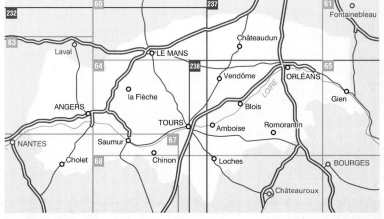

Principal sights

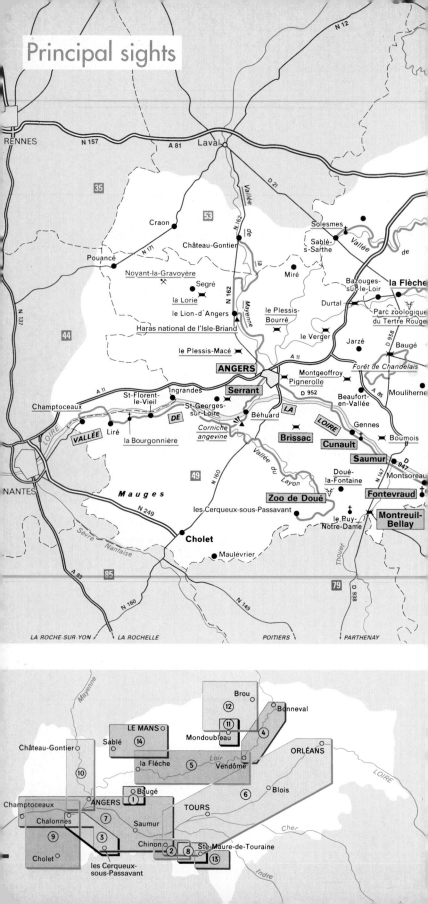

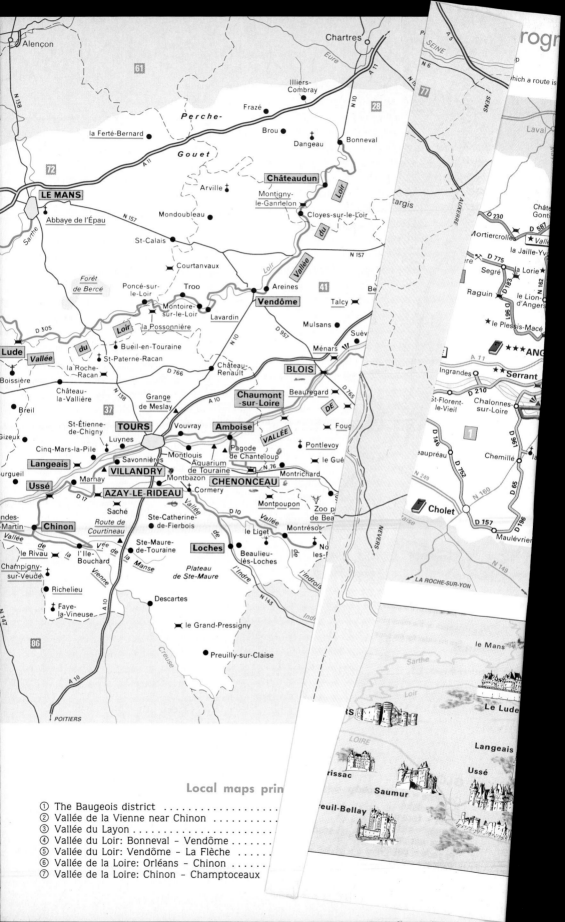

Local maps prin

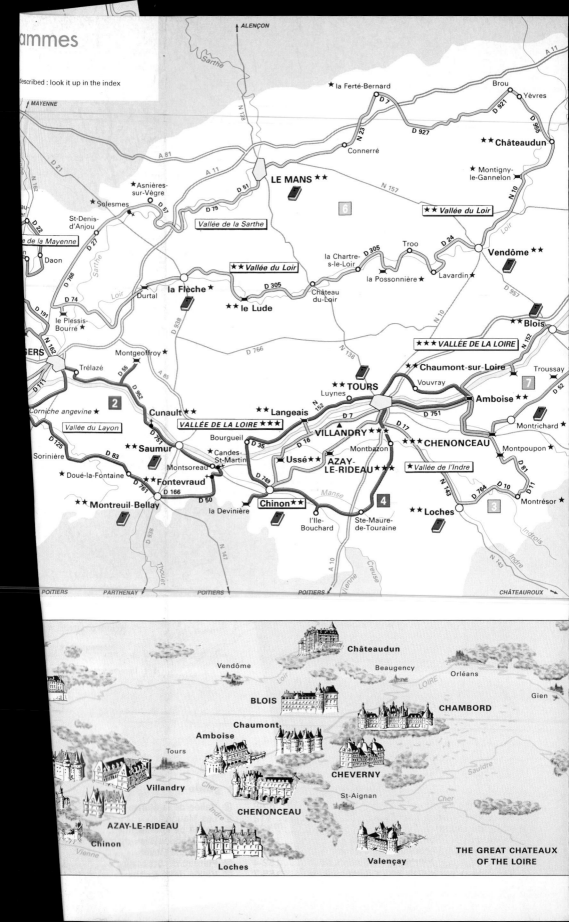

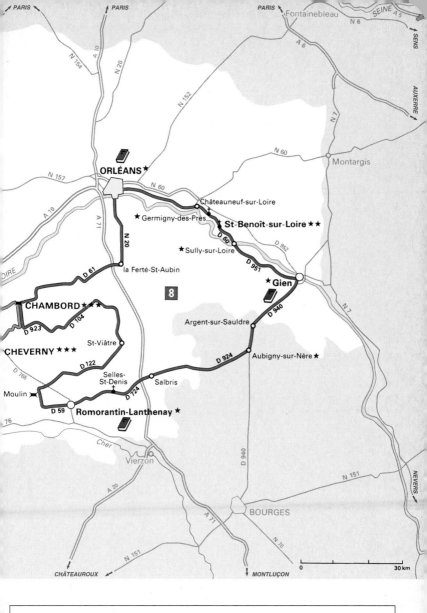

1	Anjou – Les Mauges: 250km/155mi
2	Anjou – Saumurois: 250km/155mi (vineyards, megaliths and troglodyte dwellings)
3	Châteaux and gardens of Touraine: 250km/155mi
4	Great wines of Touraine: 200km/125mi
5	Slate country, Upper Anjou, the Segréen region and Vallée de la Mayenne: 200km/125mi (ending with a tour of the Musée de l'Ardoise in Trélazé near Angers)
6	Vallée de la Sarthe and Vallée du Loir: 400km/250mi
7	The great Châteaux of the Loire (beginning at Blois): 150km/95mi
8	Sologne – Vallée de la Loire: 350km/220mi

Places to stay

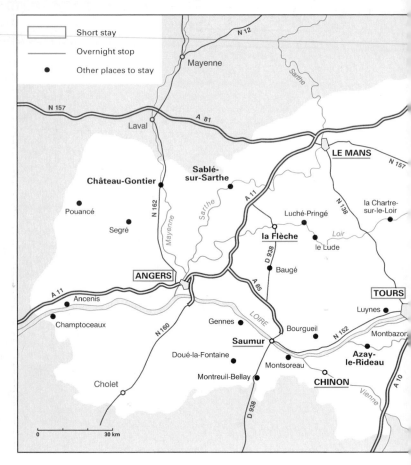

Choosing where to stay

The map above shows a number of "overnight stops" – largish towns which deserve a visit and which offer many opportunities for accommodation. Angers, Le Mans, Tours and Orléans are all ideal destinations for a short break on account of their influence, their myriad sights and museums and the important events they stage. Besides the hotels and camp sites mentioned in the Michelin guides, these places offer other forms of accommodation (furnished rooms, country cottages, board and lodging for live-in residents); apply to the local Tourist Information Centre to ask for a list of possibilities.

Accommodation

The **Michelin Red Guide France** of hotels and restaurants and the **Michelin Guide Camping Caravaning France** are annual publications which give details of a selection of hotels, restaurants and camp sites. The final listing is based on regular on-the spot enquiries and visits. Both the hotels and camp sites are classified according to the standard of comfort of their amenities. Establishments which are notable for their setting, their décor, their quiet and secluded location and their warm welcome are indicated by special symbols. The Michelin Red Guide France also gives the addresses and telephone numbers of the local Tourist Information Centres *(syndicat d'initiative/office de tourisme).*

Route planning, sports and recreation

The **Michelin 1:200 000 maps** in the series 51 to 90 and 230 to 246 cover the whole of France. Those which can be used with this guide are shown in the diagram on p 1. The maps help you see at a glance the general surroundings of a given place. In addition to information about the roads, the maps show beaches, bathing places on lakes and rivers, swimming pools, golf courses, race-courses, gliding-grounds, aerodromes, forest roads, long-distance footpaths etc.

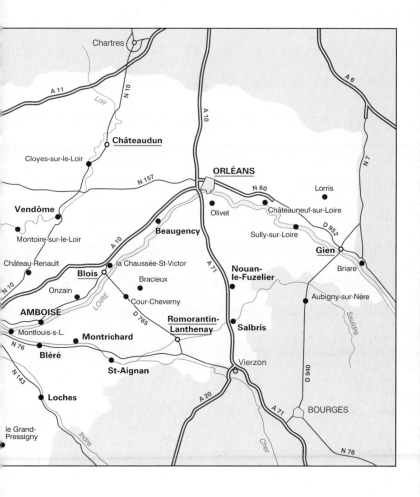

CHÂTEAUX OF THE LOIRE – FROM CHAMBORD TO CHINON
THE MICHELIN GREEN GUIDE
NOW ON VIDEO!

Sit back and enjoy a glimpse of the splendours of the Loire Valley from the comfort of your home.
The majestic course of the Loire from Chambord to Chinon evokes the history of the French kings who, charmed by its natural beauty, had magnificent châteaux built in which they installed the colourful pageantry – and intrigue – of their courts, bringing the ideas and aesthetics of the Renaissance to France.
To echoes of sumptuous court banquets the Loire takes us past the richly stocked game parks of Chambord and Chinon, which once rang to the sound of the hunt, and the famous vineyards and orchards which have earned the Touraine region its reputation as "the garden of France". Mouthwatering images of local gastronomic delights complete this voyage of discovery, ideally suited both as a tempting preview and as a colourful reminder of your holiday in the Loire Valley.

Château de Chenonceau

Introduction

Description of the country

GEOLOGICAL FORMATION

The Loire region is enclosed by the ancient crystalline masses of the Morvan, Armorican Massif and Massif Central and forms part of the Paris Basin.

In the Secondary Era the area invaded by the sea was covered by a soft, chalky deposit known as **tufa**, which is now exposed along the valley sides of the Loir, Cher, Indre and Vienne. A later deposit is the limestone of the sterile marshlands (**gâtines**) interspersed with tracts of sands and clays supporting forests and heathlands. Once the sea had retreated, great freshwater lakes deposited more limestone, the surface of which is often broken down into loess or silt. These areas are known as **champagnes** or *champeignes*.

During the Tertiary Era the folding of the Alpine mountain zone created the Massif Central, and rivers running down from this new watershed were often laden with sandy clays which when deposited gave rise to areas such as the Sologne and the forest of Orléans. Later subsidence in the west permitted the ingress of the **Faluns Sea** as far as Blois, Thouars and Preuilly-sur-Claise, creating a series of shell marl beds *(falunières)* on the borders of Ste-Maure plateau and the hills to the north of the Loire. Rivers originally flowing northwards were attracted in a westerly direction by the sea, thus explaining the great change in the direction of the Loire at Orléans. The sea finally retreated for good, leaving an undulating countryside with the river network the most important geographical feature. The alluvial silts (**varennes**) deposited by the Loire and its tributaries were to add an extremely fertile light soil composed of coarse sand. The limestone terraces which provided shelter and the naturally fertile soil attracted early human habitation, of which there are traces from the prehistoric era through the Gallo-Roman period (site of Cherré) to the Middle Ages (Brain-sur-Allonnes). This substratum is immediately reflected in the landscape; troglodyte dwellings in the limestone layers, vineyards on the slopes, cereals on the silt plateaux, vegetables in the alluvial silt; the marshy tracts of the Sologne were for many centuries untilled since they were unhealthy and unsuitable for any sort of culture.

LANDSCAPE

The landscapes described by Du Bellay, Balzac, Alain-Fournier or Genevoix have not lost their essential characteristics but have been modified by post-war urbanisation and the growth of industrial and commercial estates on the outskirts of towns.

The garden of France – From whatever direction one approaches the Loire region – across the immense plains of the Beauce, over the harsher Berry countryside or through the green wooded farmland *(bocage)* of the Gâtine Mancelle – one is always welcomed by the sight of vineyards, white houses and flowers. For many foreigners this peaceful, fertile countryside is a typically French landscape. But make no mistake, the "Garden of France" is not simply a sort of Eden full of fruit and flowers. The historian Michelet once described it as a "homespun cloak with golden fringes", meaning that the valleys – the golden fringes – in all their wonderful fertility bordered plateaux whose harshness was only tempered by occasional fine forests.

Northern Berry – This region lying between the Massif Central and the Loire country includes the **Pays Fort**, an area of clay soil sloping down towards the Sologne. The melancholy atmosphere of the landscape is described by Alain-Fournier in his novel *Le Grand Meaulnes*. Between the Cher and the Indre is the **Champeigne**, an area of limestone silt pockmarked with holes *(mardelles)*.

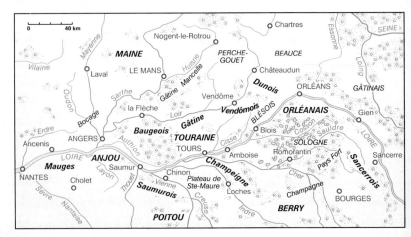

Touraine Landscape

Orléanais and Blésois – Below Gien the valley opens out, the hills are lower and a refreshing breeze makes the leaves tremble on the long lines of poplars and willows. This is the gateway to the Orléanais which covers the Beauce, the Loir valley (ie the Dunois and Vendômois), the Sologne and Blésois (Blois region). In the vicinity of St-Benoît the valley, commonly known as the **Val**, is a series of meadows; beyond, horticulture predominates with the growing of seedlings and rosebushes on the alluvial deposits known locally as *layes*. There is a proliferation of greenhouses, some with artificial heating. Orchards and vineyards flourish on the south-facing slopes. From Orléans to Chaumont along its northern bank, the Loire eats into the Beauce limestone and then into the flinty chalkland and tufa. On the south the river laps the alluvial sands brought down by its own waters, which, besides growing asparagus and early vegetables, are covered in dense brushwood, where the kings of France once used to hunt. The great châteaux then begin: Blois, Chambord, Cheverny, Chaumont...

The **Beauce**, the granary of France, a treeless plain covered with a thin layer (2m/6ft maximum) of fertile silt or loess, extends into the area between the Loire and Loir known as the Petite Beauce where silt gives way to clay in Marchenoir forest. In the **Sologne** and the **Forest of Orléans** meagre crops alternate with lakes and woodland.

Touraine – The comfortable opulence of the **Loire valley** will delight the visitor already charmed by the luminous beauty of the light. The blue waters of the Loire, which flow slowly between golden sandbanks, have worn a course through the soft tufa chalk. Channels abandoned by the main river are divided into backwaters *(boires)* or occupied by tributary streams such as the Cher, Indre, Vienne and Cisse.

From Amboise to Tours the flinty chalk soil of the valley slopes is clad with vineyards producing the well-known Vouvray and Montlouis wines. **Troglodyte** houses have been carved out of the white tufa. The **Véron**, lying between the Loire and the Vienne, is a patchwork of small fields and gardens bordered by rows of poplars.

The **Gâtine** of Touraine, between the Loir and Loire, was once a great forest; the area is now under cultivation, although large tracts of heath and woodland still exist (Chandelais and Bercé forests). The main features of the Touraine **Champeigne**, where the fields are studded with walnut trees, are the Forests of Brouard and Loches and the Montrésor Gâtine. The plateaux of Montrichard and Ste-Maure are similar in many ways to the Champeigne.

Anjou – Anjou, like the Touraine, has little physical unity but is typified more easily by the gentleness of its countryside, so lovingly described by the poet Du Bellay. The north bank of the Loire consists of a fertile alluvial plain **(varenne de Bourgueil)** where spring vegetables flourish surrounded by the famous vineyards planted on the warm, dry gravels lying at the foot of the pine-covered hills. Between the Loire and the Authion, which is lined with willows, green pastures alternate with rich market gardens growing vegetables, flowers and fruit trees. The land below Angers is covered with vineyards, especially the famous Coulée de Serrant vineyard.

The pleasant **Saumurois**, which lies south of the Loire and extends from Fontevraud and Montsoreau to Doué-la-Fontaine and the Layon valley, has three differing aspects: woods, plains and hillsides; the slopes are often clad with vineyards, which produce excellent wine including the white wine to which the town of Saumur has given its name. The many caves in the steep, tufa valley sides of the Loire

13

around Chênehutte-les-Tuffeaux are now used for mushroom growing. North of the river lies the sandy **Baugeois**, an area of woods (oak, pine and chestnut) and arable land. Angers marks the border between the schist countryside of Black Anjou and the sharply contrasting limestone of White Anjou. The countryside is greener, heralding an area of wooded farmland – le Bocage Segréen and **les Mauges** – which is characterised by a patchwork of small fields surrounded by hedge-topped banks crisscrossed by deep lanes leading to small farmsteads. Around Angers, nursery and market gardens specialise in flowers and seedlings.

Maine – Only the southern part of this region is included in the guide.
The Lower Maine **(Bas-Maine)** otherwise known as Black Maine, is a region of sandstones, granites and schists and wooded farmland. Geographically this area is part of the Breton Armorican Massif. The Upper Maine **(Haut-Maine)**, covering the Sarthe and Huisne basins, is known as the White Maine because of its limestone soils.

ECONOMY

Activities of the past – Many of the traditional local activities have disappeared: namely the growing of saffron in the Gâtinais; of anise, coriander and liquorice in Bourgueil; of madder; and the silk industry based on the mulberries and silkworms introduced to Touraine by Louis XI. The once-familiar fields of hemp around Bréhémont and Béhuard have dwindled in number as have the dependent ropeworkers. Gone also are the blacksmiths' forges. The coal of the Layon Basin is no longer mined. The drastic decline in river traffic on the Loire has resulted in the closure of the boatyards at Angers and the sail-making factories at Ancenis. There is however still a demand for slates from Trélazé but the very fine white tufa stone from Bourré and Pontlevoy, which characterizes the houses of Touraine, is no longer quarried. The only quarries still being worked are St-Cyr-en-Bourg and Louerre which supply workshops with stone for restoration.
Nowadays it is only in the museums that the old trades can be observed (flintstone museum at Meung-sur-Loire; slate museums at Trélazé and Renazé, the Mine Bleue at Noyant-la-Gravoyère, and the local museum at Montjean-sur-Loire).

Agriculture

A well-disposed lie of the land, fertile soil and temperate climate make the Loire valley ideal for the cultivation of trees and market gardens. Fruit and vegetables make a significant contribution to the economy of the Centre and Pays de Loire regions, representing about 20% of national production. The cultivation of many of the varieties to be found in the Loire valley dates from as early as Roman rule, while others introduced to the region during the Renaissance continue to thrive.

Fruit – Ripening well in the local climate, the succulent fruits of the region are renowned throughout France. The most common are apples, pears and more recently blackcurrants. Many have a noble pedigree: the *Reine-Claude* greengages are named after Claude de France, the wife of François I, the *Bon-chrétien* pears originated from a cutting planted by St Francis of Paola in Louis XI's orchard at Plessis-lès-Tours. They were introduced into Anjou by Jean Bourré, Louis XI's Finance Minister. Rivalling the latter are the following varieties: *de Monsieur, William*, a speciality of Anjou, *Passe-Crassane* and autumn varieties such as

Conference, Comice and *Beurré Hardy*. Melons were introduced to the region by Charles VIII's Neapolitan gardener. Already in the 16C the variety and quality of the local fruit and vegetables were much praised by Ronsard among others. The walnut and chestnut trees of the plateaux yield oil and much-prized wood (in the former case) and edible chestnuts (in the latter), often roasted during evening gatherings. Alongside traditional varieties like the Reinette apple from Le Mans are more prolific varieties better adapted to market demands such as the Granny Smith and Golden Delicious.

Early vegetables – A wide variety of vegetables is grown in the Loire valley. There are two main areas of production: the stretch of valley between Angers and Saumur and the Orléans region. Vegetables cultivated under glass or plastic include tomatoes, cucumbers and lettuce, especially around Orléans. Early vegetables are a speciality in the Loire valley since, in general, they are ready two weeks before those of the Paris region. Asparagus from Vineuil and Contres, potatoes from Saumur, French beans from Touraine, onions and shallots from Anjou and Loiret and artichokes from Angers are despatched to Rungis, the main Paris market. One of the region's more unusual crops is mushrooms; over 60% of French button mushrooms come from the Loire valley. They are grown in the former tufa quarries near Montrichard, Montoire, Montsoreau, Tours and particularly in the Saumur area.

Flowers and nursery gardens – Pots of geraniums or begonias, borders of nasturtiums and climbing wistaria with its pale mauve clusters adorn the houses. The region of Orléans-la-Source, Olivet and Doué-la-Fontaine is famous for its cultivated flowers – roses, hydrangeas, geraniums and chrysanthemums – which are grown under glass. Tulips, gladioli and lilies are grown (for bulbs) near Soings. Nursery gardens proliferate on the alluvial soils of the Loire. The lighter soils of Véron, Bourgueil and the Angers district are suitable for the growing of artichokes, onions and garlic for seed stock. The medicinal plants that were cultivated in the Chemillé region during the phylloxera crisis are attracting renewed interest.

Livestock

Cattle, sheep and pigs – Dairy stock are generally reared in the fields outside, except in winter, when they are kept indoors and given corn silage. However, in the case of beef cattle, the animals spend most of the year feeding on pastures in the Maine, Anjou and Touraine valleys. The main dairy cattle breeds are Prim'Holstein, Normandy and Pie-Noire, while the best known beef breeds are Normandy, Maine-Anjou and especially Charolais. Dairy production is concentrated in Maine, Anjou, the Mayenne valley, Les Mauges and in the west of the Sarthe valley. Sheep rearing is confined to the limestone plateaux of the Upper Maine where the black-faced Bleu du Maine and Rouge de l'Ouest prosper.

Pigs can be found everywhere but particularly in Touraine, Maine and Anjou; the production of potted pork specialities – *rillettes* and *rillons* – is centred in Vouvray, Angers, Tours and Le Mans. Recently, in the Sarthe *département* a *label rouge* (red label), guaranteeing the highest quality, was awarded to free-range pigs raised on farms. The ever-growing demand for the well-known goats' cheeses, in particular the Appellation d'Origine Contrôlée (AOC) brands "Selles-sur-Cher" and, more recently, "Sainte-Maure", have led to an increase in goat keeping. Market days in the west country are colourful occasions: the liveliest are the calf sales in Château-Gontier and the cattle and goat sales in Cholet and Chemillé.

Poultry – Poultry rearing, firmly-established in the Loire region, has developed quite considerably; its expansion is linked to the food industry and local co-operatives. This sector has two main characteristics: the high quality of its produce, thanks to many labels, in particular the most prestigious ones recommending the free-range poultry of Loué, and variety: chickens, capons, ducks, guinea fowl, turkeys, geese, poulards, quails, pigeons and, generally speaking, all game birds.

Horses – Numerous stud farms continue to rear pure-bred horses, race horses and draught horses; the Percheron remains an important breed in the Maine area. Traditions of horsemanship are perpetuated by the École Nationale d'Équitation (National Riding School) and Cadre Noir at St-Hilaire-St-Florent near Saumur. A great many small towns still have their own racecourse and local riding clubs and schools keep alive the interest in horses and horseriding.

Industry

Recent industrial growth has affected most large towns in the Val de Loire, particularly in the case of non-polluting activities such as research, electronics, high technology, pharmaceuticals, cosmetics, fashion etc. At the same time, the region has seen the expansion of industries derived from the processing of agricultural and dairy produce. These food-related industries are extremely prosperous today: *rillettes* at Connerre, meat at Sablé, hamburger meat packaging at the SOCOPA plant in Cherré, mushroom canning at Saumur, vegetable canning in the Orléanais. With the exception of Châteaudun, Pithiviers and Vendôme, the main industrial centres are to be found along the Loire river at Gien, Sully, St-Denis-de-l'Hôtel, Orléans, Beaugency, Meung-sur-Loire, Mer, Blois, Amboise, Tours and Angers. The recent industrialisation process, which is not confined to cities, has therefore helped to stimulate the economy in rural areas, for instance the region around Cholet. Michelin tyre factories have been set up at Orléans, Tours and Cholet. Nuclear power stations for producing electricity are in operation at Avoine-Chinon, Belleville-sur-Loire, Dampierre-en-Burly and St-Laurent-des-Eaux.

Service industries – Insurance, mainly in Le Mans, conferences, a speciality of Tours and Orléans, as well as the decentralisation of financial institutions, health services and prestigious business and administrative schools, and the great tourist potential are all factors in the attraction of investment into the region.

The cultural heritage, the forests, the 570km/354mi of navigable water for leisure craft and the proliferation of leisure parks all play their part in the local economy.

Historical table and notes

Gallo-Roman Era and the Early Middle Ages

52 BC	*Carnutes revolt. Caesar conquers Gaul.*
AD 1C-4C	*Roman occupation of Gaul.*
313	*Constantine grants freedom of worship to Christians (Edict of Milan).*
372	St Martin, Bishop of Tours (dies at Candes in 397).
573-594	Episcopacy of Gregory of Tours, author of *the History of the Franks.*
7C	Founding of the Benedictine Abbey of Fleury, later to be named St-Benoît.
late 8C	Alcuin of York's school for copyists *(TOURS)*; Theodulf, Bishop of Orleans.
768-814	*Charlemagne.*
840-877	*Charles the Bald.*
9C	Vikings invade Angers, St-Benoît and Tours. Rise of Robertian dynasty.

The Capets (987-1328)

987-1040	Fulk Nerra, Count of Anjou.
996-1031	*Robert II, the Pious.*
1010	Foundation of the Benedictine abbey at Solesmes.
1060-1108	*Philippe I.*
1101	Foundation of Fontevraud Abbey.
1104	First Council of Beaugency.
1137-1180	*Louis VII.*
1152	Second Council of Beaugency; Eleanor of Aquitaine marries Henry Plantagenet.
1154	Henry Plantagenet becomes King of England as Henry II.
1180-1223	*Philippe-Auguste.*
1189	Death of Henry II Plantagenet at Chinon. *Struggle between Capets and Plantagenets.*
1199	Richard the Lionheart dies at Chinon and is buried at Fontevraud.
1202	John Lackland loses Anjou. Last of the Angevin kings, he dies in 1216.
1215	*Magna Carta.*
1226-1270	*Louis IX (St Louis).*
1285-1314	*Philippe IV, the Fair.*
1307	Philippe the Fair suppresses the Order of the Knights Templars.

The Valois (1328-1589)

1337-1453	*Hundred Years War: 1346 Crécy; 1356 Poitiers; 1415 Agincourt.*
1380-1422	*Charles VI.*
1392	The King goes mad *(Le MANS).*
1409	Birth of King René at Angers.
1418	The Massacre at Azay-le-Rideau.
1422-1461	*Charles VII.*
1427	The Dauphin Charles establishes his court at Chinon.
1429	Joan of Arc delivers Orléans; but is tried and burnt at the stake two years later *(CHINON, ORLÉANS).*
1453	Battle of Castillon: final defeat of the English on French soil.
1455-1485	*Wars of the Roses: Margaret of Anjou leader of Lancastrian cause.*
1461-1483	*Louis XI.*
1476	*Unrest among the powerful feudal lords.* *Royal marriage at Montrichard.*
1483	Death of Louis XI at Plessis-lès-Tours.
1483-1498	*Charles VIII.*
1491	Marriage of Charles VIII and Anne of Brittany at Langeais.
1494-1559	*The Campaigns in Italy.*
1496	Early manifestations of Italian influence on French art *(AMBOISE).*
1498	Death of Charles VIII at Amboise.
1498-1515	*Louis XII.* He divorces and marries Charles VIII's widow.
1515-1547	*François I.*
1519	French Renaissance: Chambord started; Da Vinci dies at Le Clos-Lucé.
1539	*Struggle against the Emperor Charles V.* He visits Amboise and Chambord.
1547-1559	*Henri II.*
1552	The sees of Metz, Toul and Verdun join France; treaty signed at Chambord.
1559-1560	*François II.*
1560	Amboise Conspiracy; François II dies at Orléans.
1560-1574	*Charles IX.*
1562-1598	*Wars of Religion.*
1562	The Abbey of St-Benoît is pillaged by the Protestants; battles at Ponts-de-Cé and Beaugency.

1572	The St Bartholomew's Day Massacre in Paris.
1574-1589	Henri III.
1576	Founding of the Catholic League by Henri, Duke of Guise to combat Calvinism. Meeting of the States-General in Blois.
1588	The murder of Henri, Duke of Guise and his brother, the Cardinal of Lorraine (BLOIS).

The Bourbons (1589-1702)

1589-1610	Henri IV.
1589	Vendôme retaken by Henry IV.
1598	Edict of Nantes. Marriage of César de Vendôme (ANGERS).
1600	Henri IV marries Marie de Medici.
1602	Maximilien de Béthune buys Sully.
1610-1643	Louis XIII.
1619	Marie de Medici flees Blois.
1620	Building of the college by the Jesuits at La Flèche.
1626	Gaston d'Orléans, brother of Louis XIII, is granted the County of Blois.
1643-1715	Louis XIV.
1648-1653	Civil war against Mazarin, the Fronde.
1651	Anne of Austria, Mazarin and young Louis XIV take refuge in Gien.
1669	Première of Molière's play Monsieur de Pourceaugnac at Chambord.
1685	Revocation of the Edict of Nantes by Louis XIV at Fontainebleau.
1715-1774	Louis XV.
1719	Voltaire exiled at Sully.
1756	Foundation of the Royal College of Surgeons at Tours.
1770	The Duke of Choiseul in exile at Chanteloup.

The Revolution and First Empire (1789-1815)

1789	Storming of the Bastille.
1792	Proclamation of the Republic.
1793	Execution of Louis XVI. Vendée War. Fighting between the Republican "Blues" and Royalist "Whites" (CHOLET, Les MAUGES).
1803	Talleyrand purchases Valençay.
1804-1815	First Empire under Napoleon Bonaparte.
1808	Internment of Ferdinand VII, King of Spain, at Valençay.

Constitutional Monarchy and the Second Republic (1815-1852)

1814-1824	Louis XVIII.
1824-1830	Charles X.
1830-1848	July Monarchy: Louis-Philippe.
1832	The first steamboat on the Loire.
1832-1848	Conquest of Algeria.
1848	Internment of Abd El-Kader at Amboise.
1848-1852	Second Republic. Louis Napoleon-Bonaparte, Prince-President.

The Second Empire (1852-1870)

1852-1870	Napoleon III as Emperor.
1870-1871	Franco-Prussian War.
1870	Proclamation of the Third Republic on 4 September in Paris. Frederick-Charles of Prussia at Azay-le-Rideau. Defence of Châteaudun. Tours made headquarters of Provisional Government.
1871	Battle of Loigny.

The Third Republic (1870-1940) and up to the Present

1873	Amédée Bollée completes his first car, l'Obéissante (Le MANS).
1908	Wilbur Wright's early trials with his aeroplane.
1914-1918	First World War.
1919	Treaty of Versailles.
1923	The first Twenty-four Hour Race at Le Mans.
1939-1945	Second World War.
1940	Defence of Saumur; historic meeting at Montoire.
1945	Armistice of Reims.
1946	Fourth Republic.
1952	First son et lumière performances at Chambord.
1958	Fifth Republic.
1963	France's first nuclear power station at Avoine near Chinon.
1970	Founding of the University of Tours.
1989	Inauguration of the TGV (high-speed train) Atlantique.
1993	Opening of the International Vinci Congress Centre in Tours.

(1) Events of general historical import are printed in italics.

The rich history of the Loire

Antiquity and the Early Middle Ages

During the Iron Age the prosperous and powerful people known as the **Cenomanni** occupied a vast territory extending from Brittany to the Beauce and from Normandy to Aquitaine. They minted gold coins and put up a long resistance to both barbarian and Roman invaders.

The Cenomanni reacted strongly to the invasion of Gaul by the Romans and in 52 BC the **Carnutes**, who inhabited the country between Chartres and Orléans, gave the signal, at the instigation of the Druids, to raise a revolt against Caesar. It was savagely repressed but the following year Caesar had to put down another uprising by the Andes, under their leader Dumnacos.

Peace was established under Augustus and a period of stability and prosperity began. Existing towns such as Angers, Le Mans, Tours and Orléans adapted to the Roman model with a forum, theatre, baths and public buildings. Many agricultural estates *(villae)* were created or extended as the commercial outlets developed. They reached their peak in the 2C. By the end of the 3C instability and danger were so rife that cities had been enclosed behind walls.

At the same time Christianity was introduced by St Gatien, the first bishop of Tours; by the end of the 4C it had overcome most opposition under **St Martin**, the greatest bishop of the Gauls, whose tomb later became a very important place of pilgrimage (St Martin's Day: 11 November).

In the 5C the Loire country suffered several waves of invasion; in 451 Bishop Aignan held back the Huns outside Orléans while waiting for help. Franks and Visigoths fought for domination until the Frankish king Clovis was finally victorious in 507.

His successors' endless quarrels, which were recorded by Gregory of Tours, dominated the history of the region in the 6C and 7C while St Martin's Abbey was establishing its reputation. In 732 the Saracens, who were pushing north from Spain, reached the Loire before they were repulsed by Charles Martel. The order achieved by the Carolingians, which was marked by the

Alcuin and Rabanus Maurus
(National Library, Vienna)

activities of **Alcuin** and **Theodulf**, did not last. In the middle of the 9C the Vikings came up the river and ravaged the country on either side, particularly the monasteries (St Benoît, St Martin's). **Robert**, Count of Blois and Tours, defeated them but they continued their depredations until 911 when the Treaty of St-Clair-sur-Epte created the Duchy of Normandy.

During this period of insecurity the Robertian dynasty (the forerunner of the Capet dynasty) gained in power to the detriment of the last Carolingian kings. A new social order emerged which gave rise to feudalism.

Princely power

The weakness of the last Carolingian kings encouraged the independence of turbulent and ambitious feudal lords. Although Orléans was one of the favourite royal residences and the Orléans region was always Capet territory, Touraine, the county of Blois, Anjou and Maine became independent and rival principalities. This was the age of powerful barons, who raised armies and minted money. From Orléans to Angers every high point was crowned by an imposing castle, the stronghold of the local lord who was continually at war with his neighbours.

The counts of Blois faced a formidable enemy in the counts of Anjou, of whom the most famous was **Fulk Nerra**. He was a first-class tactician; little by little he encircled Eudes II, Count of Blois, and seized part of his territory. His son, Geoffrey Martel, continued the same policy; from his stronghold in Vendôme he wrested from the house of Blois the whole county of Tours. In the 12C the county of Blois was dependent on Champagne which was then at the height of its power.

At the same period the counts of Anjou reached the height of their power under the Plantagenets; when Henri, Count of Anjou, became King Henry II of England in 1154 his kingdom stretched from the north of England to the Pyrenees. This formidable new power confronted the modest forces of the kings of France but they did not quail under the threat of their powerful neighbours and skilfully took advantage of the quarrels which divided the Plantagenets.

In 1202 King John of England, known as John Lackland, lost all his continental possessions to Philippe-Auguste; the Loire country returned to the French sphere of interest.

In accordance with the wishes of his father Louis VIII, when Louis IX came to the throne he granted Maine and Anjou as an apanage to his brother Charles, who abandoned his French provinces, including Provence, and tried to establish an Angevin kingdom in Naples, Sicily and the Near East, as did his successors. Nonetheless, Good **King René**, the last Duke of Anjou, earned himself a lasting place in popular tradition.

The Cradle of Feudalism

Feudalism flourished in France in the 11C and 12C in the region between the Seine and the Loire under the **Capet** monarchy. The system was based on two elements: the **fief** and the lord. The fief was a "beneficium" (benefice), usually a grant of land made by a lord to a knight or other man who became his vassal.

The numerous conflicts of interest which arose from the system in practice produced a detailed code of behaviour embodying the rights of the parties. During the 12C the services due were defined, such as the maximum number of days to be spent each year in military service or castle watch. Gradually the fiefs became hereditary and the lord retained only overall ownership. In the case of multiple vassalage, liege homage was paid to one lord and this was more binding than homage to any other.

An almost perfect hierarchical pyramid was created descending from the king to the mass of simple knights. The more important vassals had the right of appeal to the king in case of serious dispute with their suzerain; it was by this means that King John (John Lackland) was deprived of his French fiefs by Philippe-Auguste early in the 13C.

All the inhabitants of an estate were involved in the economic exploitation of the land; the estate had evolved from the Carolingian method of administration and was divided into two parts: the domain, which was kept by the lord for himself, and the holdings, which were let to the tenants in return for rent. The authority exercised by the lord over the people who lived on his estate derived from the royal prerogative of the monarch to command his subjects which passed into the hands of powerful lords who owned castles. This unlimited power enabled them to impose military service, various duties (road mending, transport etc) and taxes on their tenants.

Joan of Arc

The Hundred Years War (1337-1453) brought back the English, who became masters of half the country and besieged Orléans; if the town had surrendered, the whole of the rest of the kingdom would probably have passed into the enemy's hands. Then **Joan of Arc** appeared and proclaimed her intention of "driving the English out of France"; national pride was awakened. The shepherdess from Domrémy persuaded Charles VII to give her a command *(see CHINON)*. With her little army she

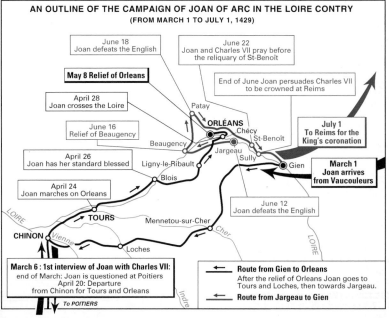

AN OUTLINE OF THE CAMPAIGN OF JOAN OF ARC IN THE LOIRE CONTRY
(FROM MARCH 1 TO JULY 1, 1429)

June 18
Joan defeats the English

June 22
Joan and Charles VII pray before the reliquary of St-Benoît

May 8 Relief of Orleans

End of June Joan persuades Charles VII to be crowned at Reims

April 28
Joan crosses the Loire

Patay

ORLÉANS

June 16
Relief of Beaugency

Chécy

St-Benoît

**July 1
To Reims for the King's coronation**

Beaugency

Jargeau

April 26
Joan has her standard blessed

Ligny-le-Ribault

Sully

Gien

**March 1
Joan arrives from Vaucouleurs**

April 24
Joan marches on Orleans

Blois

June 12
Joan defeats the English

TOURS

Mennetou-sur-Cher

Cher

CHINON

Vienne

Loches

March 6 : 1st interview of Joan with Charles VII:
end of March: Joan is questioned at Poitiers
April 20: Departure
from Chinon for Tours and Orleans

← **Route from Gien to Orleans**
After the relief of Orleans Joan goes to Tours and Loches, then towards Jargeau.

← **Route from Jargeau to Gien**

To POITIERS

Indre

LOIRE

19

entered beleaguered Orléans, stormed the English strongholds and freed the city *(see ORLÉANS)*. The retreating English forces were defeated on the Loire, at Jargeau, and in the Beauce, at Patay, and in spite of the betrayal of Compiègne and the stake at Rouen, Joan had fulfilled her vow and assured their total defeat.

16C: Royal munificence and religious tumult

The 16C saw in the Renaissance, and with it an explosion of new ideas in art and architecture, resulting in one of the liveliest periods in the history of the Loire region.

The Renaissance – The University of Orléans with its long-established reputation attracted a number of **humanists**: Nicolas Béraud, Étienne Dolet, Pierre de l'Estoille, Anne du Bourg. The world of ideas was greatly extended by the invention of printing – the first printing press in the Loire valley was set up in Angers in 1477 – which made learning and culture more accessible. In the middle of the century the **Pléiade** was formed in the Loire valley and attracted the best local talent.

By choosing Touraine as their favourite place of residence the kings made a significant contribution to the artistic revival of the region. The chief instigators of the great French Renaissance were **Charles VIII** and even more so **Louis XII** and **François I**, who had all travelled in Italy. These monarchs transformed the Loire valley into a vast building site where the new aesthetic ideals flourished at Amboise, Blois and especially Chambord. The great lords and financiers followed suit and built themselves most elegant houses (Azay-le-Rideau, Chenonceau) while graceful mansions were erected in the towns.

The Renaissance was the expression of a new way of thinking which redefined man's place in the world and presented a radically different view from that which had been held in the past; this gave rise to the desire for harmony and the cult of beauty in all fields: poetry, music, architecture as an expression of nature shaped by man.

Religious tumult – The Renaissance excited not only intellectual activity but also the need for a moral and religious revival. De-

François I in 1525, by Jean Clouet

spite several local experiments (eg Le Mans), the Roman Church did not succeed in satisfying these aspirations. Naturally the ideas of **Luther** and **Calvin** (who was in Orléans between 1528 and 1533) were well received in cultivated circles. In 1540 the Church responded with repression; several reformers died at the stake but the Reform movement continued to grow; nor was support confined to the elite but extended to the mass of the people, craftsmen and tradesmen. The dispute between Protestants and Roman Catholics inevitably led to armed conflict. In 1560 the **Amboise Conspiracy** failed disastrously and ended in bloodshed. Catherine de' Medici tried to promote conciliation by issuing edicts of tolerance but in April 1562 the Huguenots rose up, committing numerous acts of vandalism: damaging places of worship and destroying statues, tombs and relics.

The Roman Catholics under Montpensier and Guise regained the upper hand and exacted a terrible vengeance, particularly in Angers. From 1563 to 1567 there was relative peace, but in 1568 the armed struggle broke out anew; the Catholic and Protestant armies, the latter under Condé and Coligny, indulged in regular waves of violence. The inhabitants of Orléans suffered their own **massacre of St Bartholomew** with nearly a thousand deaths. During the last quarter of the century the Reformed Churches had become much weaker and **Henri III's** struggle with the Catholic League came to the fore. In 1576 Touraine, Anjou and Berry were granted to François d'Alençon, the king's brother and head of the League, as a conciliatory gesture but the Guises would not compromise and conspired against the king who, seeing no other solution, had them assassinated at Blois in December 1588. The population divided into Royalists and Leaguers, who were powerful in the Loire region. Henri III, who had been forced to withdraw to Tours, allied himself with Henri of Navarre and was marching on Paris when he himself was assassinated on 2 August 1589. It took Henri IV nearly 10 years to restore peace to the region. The brilliant period in the history of the Loire valley, which coincided with the last years of the Valois dynasty, ended in tragedy.

17C and 18C: Peace is restored

The Loire country ceased to be at the centre of political and religious ferment. There were admittedly a few alarms during the minority of Louis XIII and the Fronde uprising, in which the indefatigable conspirator, Gaston d'Orléans, played a significant role. Order was however restored under Louis XIV with centralisation under the crown stifling any sign of autonomy: the districts of Orléans and Tours were administered by energetic treasury officials while the towns lost the right to self-government.

As far as religious life was concerned, the Roman Catholic Church re-established itself: a growth in number of convents and seminaries, the reform of the old monastic foundations and the suppression of sorcery went hand in hand with the improvement in the intellectual level of the clergy. Protestantism had a struggle to survive, except in Saumur thanks to the Academy, and was dealt a devastating blow by the **Revocation of the Edict of Nantes** in 1685.

A developing economy – Human enterprise benefited from the general stability. Agriculture developed slowly: cereals in the Beauce, raw materials for textiles (wool, linen, hemp), market gardening together with fruit growing and wine making in the Loire valley were a considerable source of wealth while cattle raising remained weak. Rural crafts played an important role together with urban manufacturing: hemp cloth round Cholet, cheesecloth in the district of Le Mans, sheeting in Touraine and Anjou, bonnets in Orléanais. The silk weavers of Tours earned themselves a good reputation.

Nevertheless in the 18C, except for sheets from Laval and Cholet, the textile industry went into decline. Orléans, the warehouse of the Loire, specialised in sugar refining and the finished product was distributed throughout the kingdom. The Loire, under the control of the "community of merchants" *(see the Vallée de la LOIRE: Boats and Boatmen)*, was the main axis for trade; wine from Touraine and Anjou, wool from the Berry, iron from the Massif Central, coal from the Forez, wheat from the Beauce, cloth from the Touraine and cargoes from exotic countries – everything travelled by water. On the eve of the Revolution these activities were in decline but the region had about two million inhabitants and several real towns: Orléans (population 40 000), Angers (population 30 000), Tours (population 20 000) and Le Mans (population 17 000).

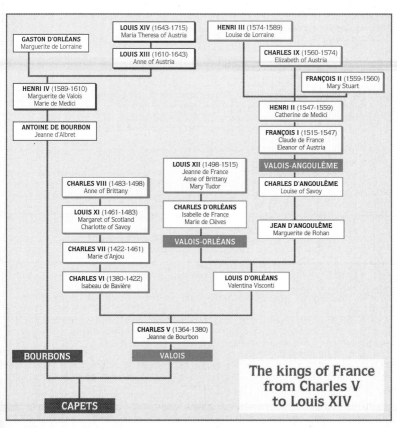

The kings of France
from Charles V
to Louis XIV

The Revolution

The Touraine and Orléanais regions accepted the Revolution but Maine and Anjou rose in revolt.

Social conflict – At first it was social conflict in which the country peasants were opposed to the townspeople and the weavers from the villages. The townspeople, who had been won over by the new ideas, were enthusiastic about the new political order while the peasants became increasingly disillusioned. Religious reform upset parish life and the administrative reforms provoked criticism and discontent because they favoured the townspeople. The national guards in their blue uniform were increasingly disliked: they were sent out from the towns to impose revolutionary decisions on the populace, if necessary by force. The decree imposing mass conscription in March 1793 was seen as an unacceptable provocation in rural areas and the peasants rose in a body. Les Mauges in particular was immediately in the forefront of the battle.

The Vendée War – The Angevin rebels appointed leaders from among their own class, countrymen like **Stofflet** and **Cathelineau**, as well as noblemen like **Bonchamps**. For four months their armies won several important engagements in support of the Church and the king; they captured Cholet, Saumur and then Angers. The Convention, the Republican government of France between September 1792 and November 1795, replied by sending in several army units. The royalist Whites were severely defeated at Cholet on 17 October by General Kléber and General Marceau and had to retreat. As they fled they were pitilessly massacred and the remnants of the "great Catholic and royal army" were exterminated in the Savenay Marshes beyond Nantes. By way of reprisal against the local population the Convention appointed General Turreau in January 1794 to "clean up" the country. From February to May his "**infernal columns**" converged on the centre, killing women and children and setting fire to villages.

The Chouans – The war was followed by sporadic outbursts of guerrilla activity: daring exploits, ambushes and even assassinations. Jean **Cottereau**, also known as Jean Chouan, was the leading figure who gave his name to the movement. The country people maintained a relentless resistance. At the end of August a faint peacemaking gesture was made under the authority of General **Hoche**. Charette and Stofflet, who continued the struggle, were arrested and shot in February and March 1796. The insurrection in the Vendée came to an end under the Consulate, a triumvirate including a certain General Bonaparte set up in 1799 to provide stronger government than the existing Republican regime with its divided factions. The war left in its wake widespread ruin and an entrenched bitterness which was revealed later in the very rigid political attitudes of the people of Maine and Anjou.

From war to war

October 1870 – January 1871 – After the fall of the Empire, France recovered its balance under the stimulus of Gambetta who arrived in Tours by balloon on 9 October, having escaped the Paris siege. The Bavarians, who were victorious at Artenay, had already captured Orléans (11 October) and indicated that they would link up with the Prussian army at Versailles via the Beauce. Châteaudun put up a heroic resistance for 10 hours on 18 and 19 October and was bombarded and set on fire in reprisal.

The army of the Loire was formed under the command of **General d'Aurelle de Paladines**; two corps, the 15th and 16th (Chanzy), formed in the Salbris camp, set out from Blois for Orléans. The engagement took place at Marchenoir and then at Coulmiers on 9 November: the French were victorious and General Von der Thann was forced to evacuate Orléans. Meanwhile the 18th and 20th corps tried to check the advance of the Duke of Mecklenburg on Le Mans and Tours but they were beaten on 28 November at Beaune-la-Rolande by Prince Frederick-Charles who had hastened south from Metz. On 2 December the 16th and 17th corps were defeated at Patay and Loigny where the Zouaves under Lt Col de Charette, the great-nephew of the famous Vendéen Royalist, fought with distinction. Although cut in two the first army of the Loire survived. Orléans had to be abandoned while the government retreated to Bordeaux (8 December).

A second Loire army was formed under **General Chanzy**; it resisted every enemy attack and then retrenched on the Loir. On 19 December the Prussians captured Château-Renault and two days later arrived in front of Tours but did not besiege the town. The decisive battle was fought between 10 and 12 January on the Auvours plateau east of Le Mans. Chanzy was forced to retreat towards Laval; Tours was occupied and Prince Frederick-Charles took up residence at Azay-le-Rideau. The armistice was signed on 28 January 1871.

1917-18 – The Americans set up their headquarters in Tours while the first "Sammies" disembarked at St-Nazaire and were billeted along the Loire.

1940-44 – On **10 June 1940** the French Government moved to Tours, and Cangé Château, on the southeast edge of the town, became the temporary residence of the President of the Republic. On 13 June the Franco-British Supreme Council met in Tours; at Cangé the Council of Ministers decided to transfer the government to Bordeaux. During that week of tragedy the bridges over the Loire were machine-gunned and bombarded; floods of refugees choked the roads. The towns were badly damaged. Two thousand cadets from the Cavalry School at Saumur excelled themselves by holding up the German advance for two days along a 25km/15mi front *(see SAUMUR)*. On 24 October 1940 Marshal Pétain met Hitler at **Montoire**, and agreed to his demands; collaboration was born. The Gestapo in Angers unleashed a reign of terror in the region.

The Resistance was born in 1941; the information and sabotage networks, the underground forces and the escape agents (the demarcation line followed the River Cher and ran between Tours and Loches) hampered the movements of the occupying forces who responded with torture, deportation and summary execution. In August and September 1944 the American army and the forces of the Resistance achieved control of the area with heavy losses.

BIRTH AND EVOLUTION OF THE CHÂTEAUX

The first châteaux (5C to 10C) – In the Merovingian period the country was protected by isolated strongholds: some had evolved from Gallo-Roman "villas" (country estates) which had been fortified; others were built on high ground (Loches, Chinon). Generally they covered a fairly large area and served several purposes: residence of important people, place of worship, a place for minting money, an agricultural centre and a place of refuge for the population. This type of stronghold continued under the Carolingians but the growing insecurity in the second half of the 9C introduced a wave of fortification in an attempt to counter the Viking threat. The early castles, which were built in haste, rested on a mound of earth surrounded by a wooden palisade; sometimes a central tower was erected as an observation post. The structure contained very little masonry. Until the 10C castle building was a preroga-tive of the king but thereafter the right was usurped by powerful lords; small strongholds proliferated under the designation "towers"; the keep had been invented.

The motte castle (11C) – The motte was a man-made mound of earth on which was erected a square wooden tower, the **keep**. An earth bank protected by a ditch supported the perimeter fence, which consisted of a wooden palisade and enclosed an area large enough to contain the people of the neighbourhood. The keep was built either as the last place of refuge or at the weakest point in the perimeter fence; some castles had more than one motte. In several of the Angevin castles built by Fulk Nerra the keep protected a residential building erected at the end of a promontory, as at Langeais, Blois and Loches, which are typical of the Carolingian tradition.

The stone castle (12C-13C) – By the 11C some castles had defensive works built of stone. The keep was still the strongest point and took the form of a massive quadrangular structure. The keeps at Loches, Langeais, Montbazon, Chinon (Coudray) and Beaugency are remarkable examples of 11C architecture.

The 12C keep overlooked a courtyard which was enclosed by a stone **curtain wall**, gradually reinforced by turrets and towers. Within its precincts each castle comprised private apartments, a great hall, one or more chapels, soldiers' barracks, lodgings for the household staff and other buildings such as barns, stables, storerooms, kitchens etc.

The tendency grew to rearrange the buildings more compactly within a smaller precinct. The keep comprised a storeroom on the ground floor, a great hall on the first and living rooms on the upper floors. The compact shape and the height of the walls made it difficult to besiege and only a few men were needed to defend it.

In the 13C, under the influence of the crusades and improvements in the art of attack, important innovations began to make their presence felt. Castles were designed by experts to be even more compact with multiple defensive features so that no point was unprotected. The curtain wall bristled with huge towers and the keep was neatly incorporated into the overall design.

A circular plan was adopted for the towers and keep; the walls were splayed at the base; the depth and width of the moat were greatly increased. Sometimes a lower outer rampart was built to reinforce the main rampart; the intervening strip of level ground was called the lists. Improvements were made to the arrangements for launching missiles: new types of loophole (in a cross or stirrup shape), stone machicolations, platforms, bratticing etc. The 13C castle, which was more functional and had a pronounced military character, could be built anywhere, even in open country. At the same time a desire for indoor comfort began to express itself in tapestries and draperies and furniture (chests and beds), which made the rooms more pleasant to live in than they had been in the past.

The late medieval castle – In 14C and 15C castle-building the accent moved from defence to comfort and decoration. The living quarters were more extensive; large windows to let in the light and new rooms (state bedrooms, dressing rooms and lavatories) appeared; decoration became an important feature.

In the military sphere there were no innovations, only minor improvements. The keep merged with the living quarters and was surmounted by a watchtower; sometimes the keep was suppressed altogether and the living quarters took the form of a rectangular block defended by huge corner towers. The entrance was flanked by two semicircular towers and protected by a barbican (a gateway flanked by towers) or by a separate fort. The top of the curtain wall was raised to the height of the towers which were crowned by a double row of crenellations. In the 15C the towers were capped by pointed, pepper-pot roofs.

Other fortified buildings – Churches and monasteries, which were places of sanctuary and therefore targets of war, were not excluded from the fortification movement, especially during the Hundred Years War. The towns and some of the villages also turned their attention to defence and built ramparts round the residential districts. In 1398, 1399 and 1401 Charles VI issued letters and ordinances enjoining the owners of fortresses and citizens to see that their fortifications were in good order.

From the end of the 13C fortified houses were built in the country districts by the lords of the manor; they had no military significance but are similar in appearance to the smaller châteaux.

The Renaissance château – In the 16C military elements were abandoned in the search for comfort and aesthetic taste: moats, keeps and turrets appeared only as decorative features as at Chambord, Azay-le-Rideau and Chenonceau. The spacious attics were lit by great dormer windows in the steep pitched roofs. The windows were very large. The spiral turret stairs were replaced with stairs that rose in straight flights in line with the centre of the main façade beneath coffered ceilings. The gallery – a new feature imported from Italy at the end of the 15C – lent a touch of elegance to the main courtyard.

Whereas the old fortified castle had been built on a hill, the new château was sited in a valley or beside a river where it was reflected in the water. The idea was that the building should harmonise with its natural surroundings, although these were shaped and transfigured by human intervention; the gardens, which were laid out like a jewel casket, were an integral part of the design. Only the chapel continued to be built in the traditional style with ogive vaulting and Flamboyant decoration.

The classical style, which dominated the 17C and 18C, introduced a rigorous sense of proportion. The château became a country house set in a beautiful garden (Cheverny and Ménars).

SIEGE WARFARE IN THE MIDDLE AGES

The siege – The attackers' first task was to besiege the enemy stronghold. The defences they constructed (moat, stockade, towers, forts or blockhouses) were intended both to prevent a possible sortie by the besieged and to counter an attack from a relief army. In the great sieges a fortified town grew up in its own right to encircle the site under attack. In order to make a breach in the defences of the besieged place the attackers used mines, slings and battering rams. For this they had specialist troops who were experts in siege operations.

Sapping – When the ground was suitable the attackers would dig tunnels under the ramparts and curtain walls. The cavity would be shored up with wooden props which were set on fire when the attackers withdrew; the tunnel and the wall above then collapsed. The defenders would respond by digging another gallery intersecting the

Ballista

The projectile is placed in ① and launched by the action of the spring ② on the release of the lever ③, which has been drawn back by the winch ④

first and the combatants would fight underground. When they could no longer defend the breaches, the besieged would withdraw to the keep.

Projectiles – The machines used for launching projectiles worked on a spring or a counterbalance. The most usual were the **ballista**, the crossbow mounted on a tower, the trebuchet, the mangonel and the stone sling.

The large **mangonels** could launch stones of over 100kg/220lbs which would travel up to 200m/654ft on an average trajectory. These rocks could smash the merlons, shake the walls or enlarge the breaches made by the battering ram. Other projectiles were used: grape shot, incendiary arrows (Greek fire), flaming faggots and even carrion to spread disease. The crossbow fired shafts 5m/16ft long which could fell a whole file of soldiers.

The siege tower – This was the most highly developed weapon of attack. It was built of wood – the Middle Ages had marvellous carpenters – and covered with hide; it was about 50m/160ft tall and could shelter hundreds of men.

To advance it to the foot of a wall it was necessary to fill in a section of moat and build a wooden slipway. The huge structure was placed on rollers and moved with hoisting gear.

The battering ram – The ram complemented the work of the projectiles. It was manned by a hundred soldiers who maintained the to-and-fro movement of the beam. For breaking down gates there was a smaller version

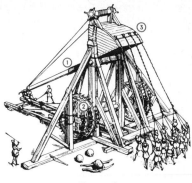

Mangonel

The lever ① is brought to ground level by the winch ②. When it is released it returns sharply to the perpendicular by the action of the counterweight ③ and the men pulling on the ropes. The projectile is launched by the catapult at the end of the lever.

which could be manœuvred by a dozen strong men. The force of the large rams was very great; to cushion the blow the defenders would try to interpose bales of wool. The ram was protected by a stout wooden shield covered with hide which the defenders tried to pierce with stones and flaming faggots.

The assault – The siege towers were equipped with drawbridges which were let down on to the ramparts so that the soldiers could flood over the curtain walls while others rushed in through the breaches. Scaling ladders were erected against the walls. The more agile men threw grappling irons over the battlements and hauled themselves up hand over hand by rope. The defenders unleashed a hail of arrows and projectiles and tried to cut the ropes or throw down the ladders. Boiling pitch and quicklime were poured on the heads of the assault troops. If the attackers succeeded in breaching the walls they still had to capture a succession of individual defences (gates, towers and keep). A determined defence could hold out for a long time by means of narrow twisting stairs, false entrances, traps, chicanes, loopholes and internal machicolations.

The era of the cannon – The bombard increased in effectiveness. Towards the middle of the 15C under the influence of the Bureau brothers, the French royal artillery became the best in the world. In one year Charles VII recaptured from the English 60 places which had resisted sieges of from four to ten months. Siege technique was altered and adapted. The place being besieged was encircled by a ring of fortified camps linked to one another by trenches. The artillery was then drawn up into position and the gunners were protected behind a bank or stockade. The firing rate was not very high and the aim was even less accurate. The defenders also used artillery and made sorties to spike the enemy's guns. Military architecture was completely transformed; towers were replaced by low thick bastions and curtain walls were built lower but much thicker. This new system of defences was perfected by Vauban.

MEDIEVAL CHÂTEAU LIFE

One living room – In the 10C and 11C life in a castle was primitive. The whole family lived, ate and slept in the same room on the first floor of the keep. Furniture was sparse and tableware rudimentary.

A lonely life – The owner of a castle had to be self-sufficient and lived in an atmosphere of great insecurity. When the lord was out hunting or fighting his neighbours or off on a crusade, his lady would take over the administration of his affairs.

MEDIEVAL PALACE LIFE

The Great Hall – In the 13C living quarters began to improve. In the Near East the crusaders experienced a comfortable way of life and acquired a taste for it. From this period on public and private life were conducted in separate rooms. The finest room in the castle was the Great Hall, where the lord held audience and dispensed justice, and where feasts and banquets were held. The earlier loopholes were replaced by windows, fitted with panes and shutters. The walls were hung with paintings and tapestries, the floor tiles were covered with rush mats or carpets on which one could sit or lie; flowers and greenery were strewn on the floor and, in summer, in the fireplaces.

The bedchamber – The bedchamber opened off the Great Hall. Except in royal or princely households, a married couple slept in the same room. Over the centuries the furnishings grew richer; the bed was set on a dais and surrounded with rich curtains; there were Venetian mirrors, tapestries, costly drapes, benches with backs, a princely chair, a prie-dieu, library steps and cushions, a dresser, a table, chests, a cupboard. To entertain the ladies there was an aviary, often with a parrot. Mourning lasted for two weeks during which the ladies hung their rooms with black and stayed in bed with the shutters closed. For a birth the shutters were also closed; the room was lit with candles and decorated with flowers and the most precious objects which were set on the dresser.

Near to the bedchamber there was a study which was also used for private audiences, a council chamber and an oratory or chapel. A special room was set aside for the guards. In the larger houses there was also a state room where the ceremonial clothes were on display. After an initial toilette in his bedchamber among the close members of his household, the prince would repair to the bed in the reception room and finish the process of getting dressed among a different group of people. This practice evolved into the solemn and lengthy procedures for getting up – "levées" – of Louis XIV.

Food – Food at court was good and the meals gargantuan. When eaten in private, meals were served in the bedchamber or in the Great Hall. Before and after eating, basins and ewers of scented water were provided for the diners to rinse their hands since fingers often took the place of forks. The plates were of silver. At banquets the diners sat along one side of a great table since the central area was used by the jugglers, acrobats and musicians who provided entertainment in the intervals.

Bathing and hygiene – Near the bedchamber or in a separate building was the bath house. Until the 14C bathing was the fashion in France. The common people used to go to the public baths once a week; the upper classes often took a daily bath. The bath house contained a sort of pool which was filled with warm water and a chamber for the steam bath and massage. A barber or a chambermaid was in attendance, for it was the fashion to be clean shaven.

In the absence of a bath house, baths were taken in a tub made of wood or bronze or silver. Often people took supper together while bathing. Before a meal guests would be offered a bath. Men and women bathed together without being thought immoral.

These habits of cleanliness disappeared from the Renaissance until the Revolution. The preachers inveighed against the communal baths which they asserted had become places of debauchery. In the 13C there were 26 public baths in Paris; by the time of Louis XIV's reign there were only two. In other respects medieval castles were well enough provided with conveniences.

Entertainment – Castle life had always had plenty of idle hours and a variety of distractions had developed to fill them. Indoors there was chess, spillikins, dice, draughts and, from the 14C, cards. Outdoors there was tennis, bowls and football, wrestling and archery. Hunting with hounds or hawks and tournaments and jousts were the great sports of the nobles. The women and children had dwarfs to entertain them; at court the jester was free to make fun of people, even the king. There were frequent festivities. Performances of the Mystery Plays, which sometimes lasted 25 days, were always a great success.

qui non abyit in consilio
impiorum et in via peca

Troubadours – Peterborough Psalter (1390)

THE COURT IN THE LOIRE VALLEY

A bourgeois court – The court resided regularly in the Loire valley under Charles VII whose preference was for Chinon and Loches. These visits ended with the last of the Valois, Henri III. Owing to the straitened circumstances to which the King of France was reduced Charles VII's court was not particularly glittering; but the arrival of Joan of Arc in 1429 won the castle of Chinon a place in the history books. Louis XI disliked pomp and circumstance. He installed his wife, Charlotte of Savoy, at Amboise but he himself rarely went there. He preferred his manor at Plessis-lès-Tours where he lived in fear of an attempt on his life. According to Commines, his only interests were hunting and dogs. The queen's court consisted of 15 ladies-in-waiting, 12 women of the bedchamber and 100 officers in charge of various functions including the saddler, the librarian, the doctor, the chaplain, the musicians, the official tasters and a great many butlers and manservants. The budget amounted only to 37 000 *livres*, of which 800 *livres* were spent on minor pleasures: materials for needlework and embroidery, books, parchments and illuminating. Charlotte was a deep-thinking

Porcupine (Louis XII) – Cominus et eminus
(*Hand to hand and out of hand's reach* – in reference to different ways of fighting)

woman and a great reader; her library contained over 100 volumes, a vast total for that time. They were works on religious thought, ethics, history, botany and domestic science. A few lighter works, such as the *Tales of Boccaccio*, relieved this solemnity. In fact, compared with Charles the Bold, the royal lifestyle seemed homely rather then princely.

A luxurious court – In the late 15C, Charles VIII acquired a considerable amount of furniture and numerous other decorative objects in order to embellish the interior of Amboise château. He installed hundreds of Persian carpets, Turkish woollen pile carpets, Syrian carpets, along with dozens of beds, chests, oak tables and dressers. The rooms and sometimes the courtyards (in the case of prestigious events) were hung with sumptuous tapestries from Flanders and Paris. He also endowed the château with an extensive collection of beautifully-crafted silverware, and a great many works of art, mainly from Italy. The Armoury (note the inventory dating back to 1499) contains several sets of armour and outstanding weapons having once belonged to Clovis, Dagobert, St Louis, Philip the Fair, Du Guesclin and Louis XI.

A gallant court – Louis XII, who was frugal, was the "Bourgeois King" of Blois. But under François I (1515-47) the French court became a school of elegance, taste and culture. The Cavalier King invited men of science, poets and artists to his court. Women, who until then had been relegated to the Queen's service, were eased by the king into a more prominent role in public life as focal points of a new kind of society. He expected them to dress perfectly and look beautiful at all times – and gave them the wherewithal to do so. The King also took care that these ladies were treated with courtesy and respect. A gentleman who had permitted himself to speak slightly of one of them escaped the ultimate penalty only by flight – "So great was the King's anger," a contemporary historian records, "he swore that whoever reflected on the honour of these ladies would be hanged." A code of courtesy was established and the court set an example of good manners.

The festivals given by François I at Amboise, where he spent his childhood and the first years of his reign, were of unprecedented brilliance. Weddings, baptisms and the visits of princes were sumptuously celebrated. Sometimes the festivities took place in the country, as on the occasion when the reconstruction of a siege was organised; a temporary town was built to be defended by the Duke of Alençon while the King led the assault and capture. To increase the sense of realism, the mortars fired huge balls. Hunting, however, took pride of place; 125 people

Salamander (François I) – Nitrusco et extinguo
(*I nourish the good and destroy the bad*)

were employed in keeping the hounds at a cost of 18 000 *livres* per year while 50 looked after the hawks at a cost of 36 000 *livres*.

The Last Valois – Under Henri II and his sons, Blois remained the habitual seat of the court when it was not at the Louvre palace in Paris. It was Henri III who drew up the first code of etiquette and introduced the title "His Majesty", taken from the Roman Emperors. The Queen Mother and the Queen had about

100 ladies-in-waiting. Catherine de' Medici also had her famous "Flying Squad" of pretty girls, who kept her informed and assisted her in her intrigues. About 100 pages acted as messengers. In addition there were 76 gentlemen servants, 51 clerks, 23 doctors and 50 chambermaids.

The King's suite included 200 gentlemen-in-waiting and over 1 000 archers and Swiss guards. There was a multitude of servants. Princes of the blood and great lords also had their households. Thus, from the time of François I, the royal entourage numbered about 15 000 people. When the court was on the move, 12 000 horses were needed. By way of comparison, in the 16C only 25 towns in the whole of France had more than 10 000 inhabitants!

QUEENS AND GREAT LADIES

Whether they were queen or the current royal mistress, women at court played an increasingly important political role, while the lively festivities with which they surrounded themselves made a major contribution to the sphere of cultural and artistic influence of the royal court.

Agnès Sorel graced the court of Charles VII at Chinon and at Loches. She gave the King good advice and reminded him of the urgent problems facing the country after the Hundred Years War, while the Queen, Marie d'Anjou, moped in her castle.

Louise of Savoy, mother of François I, was a devout worshipper of St Francis of Paola. This religious devotion, mingled with the superstitions of her astrologer Cornelius Agrippa, was barely enough to keep her insatiable ambition in check however. She lived only for the accession of her son to the throne and to this end she upset the plans of **Anne of Brittany** by making him marry Claude, daughter of Louis XII.

The love life of François I featured many women, including Françoise de Châteaubriant and the **Duchess of Étampes**, who ruled his court until his death.

Diane de Poitiers, the famous favourite of Henri II, was a remarkably tough woman. She retained her energy, both physical and mental, well into old age, to the amazement of her contemporaries. She made important decisions of policy, negotiated with the Protestants, traded in Spanish prisoners, distributed honours and magistracies and, to the great humilia-

Ermine (Anne of Brittany) – Potius mori quam foedari
(Better to die than betray)

tion of the Queen, saw to the education of the royal children. Such was her personality that almost every artist of the period painted her portrait.

The foreign beauty of **Mary Stuart**, the hapless wife of young King François II, who died at the age of 17 after a few months' reign, lent an all too brief lustre to the court in the middle of the 16C. She is recalled in a drawing by Clouet and some verses by Ronsard.

A different type altogether was **Marguerite de Valois**, the famous Queen Margot, sister of François II, Charles IX and of Henri III. Her bold eyes, her exuberance and her amorous escapades caused a great deal of concern to her mother, Catherine de' Medici. Her marriage to the future King Henri IV did little to calm her down and was in any case later annulled.

Catherine de' Medici married the Dauphin Henri in 1533 and was a prominent figure at court for 55 years under five different kings. Although eclipsed for a while by the beautiful Diane de Poitiers, she had her revenge on the death of Henri II by taking Chenonceau from her.

With the accession of Charles IX she became regent and tried to uphold the authority of the monarchy during the Wars of Religion by manœuvring skilfully between the Guises and the Bourbons, making use of diplomacy, marriage alliances and family intrigue. Under Henri III her influence waned steadily against that of younger women.

The Michelin Green Guide France...
makes tourism in France easier and more enjoyable
by highlighting the outstanding natural features and the works of man.
Never visit France without a Michelin guide.

Famous names from the Loire

LITERATURE

The French language, with its balance and clarity, has found some of its finest expression in the Loire valley, where the peace and beauty of the countryside have fostered many leading French writers.

Middle Ages – In the 6C, under the influence of St Martin, Tours became a great centre of learning. Bishop **Gregory of Tours** wrote the first history of the Gauls in his *Historia Francorum* and **Alcuin of York** founded a famous school of calligraphy at the behest of Charlemagne, while art in the 11C came under the influence of courtly life in the Latin poems of **Baudri de Bourgueil**. At the beginning of the 13C Orléans witnessed the impact of the popular and lyrical language of the *Romance of the Rose*, a didactic poem by two successive authors – the mannered **Guillaume de Lorris**, who wrote the first 4 000 lines, and the realist **Jean de Meung**, who added the final 18 000. The poem was widely translated and exerted tremendous influence throughout Europe. **Charles d'Orléans** (1391-1465) discovered his poetic gifts in an English prison. He was a patron of the arts and author of several short but elegant poems; at his court in Blois he organised poetic jousts, of which one of the winners was **François Villon** in 1457.

Hitherto a princely pastime, poetry in the hands of Good King René of Anjou became an aristocratic and even mannered work of art. In Angers **Jean Michel**, who was a doctor and a man of letters, produced his monumental *Mystery of the Passion*; its 65 000 lines took four days to perform.

Renaissance and Humanism – When the vicissitudes of the Hundred Years War obliged the French court to move from Paris to Touraine, new universities were founded in Orléans (1305) and Angers (1364). They very soon attracted a vast body of students and became important centres in the study of European humanism. Among those who came to study and to teach were Erasmus and William Bude, Melchior Wolmar, a Hellenist from Swabia, and the reformers Calvin and Theodore Beza; **Étienne Dolet**, a native of Orléans, preached his atheist doctrines for which he was hanged and burned in Paris.

François Rabelais (1494-1553), who was born near Chinon, must be about the best known product of the Touraine. After studying in Angers, he became a learned Benedictine monk and then a famous doctor. In the adventures of Gargantua and Pantagruel he expressed his ideas on education, religion and philosophy. He was very attached to his native country and made it the setting for the Picrocholine war in his books. His comic and realistic style, his extraordinarily rich vocabulary and his universal curiosity made him the foremost prose writer of his period.

The Pléiade – A group of seven poets from the Loire founded a new school, named after a cluster of stars in the Taurus constellation, which was to dominate 16C French poetry; they aimed to develop their language by imitating Horace and the Ancients. Their undoubted leader was **Ronsard**, the Prince of Poets from near Vendôme, but it was **Joachim du Bellay** from Anjou who wrote the manifesto of the group, *The Defence and Illustration of the French Language*, which was published in 1549. The other members of the group were Jean-Antoine de **Baif** from La Flèche, Jean Dorat, Étienne Jodelle, Marot and Pontus de Tyard who all held the position of Court Poet; their subjects were nature, women, their native country and its special quality, *"la douceur angevine"*.

Classicism and the Age of Enlightenment – At the end of the Wars of Religion, when the king and the court returned north to the Paris region (Ile-de-France), literature became more serious and philosophical. The **Marquis de Racan** composed verses on the banks of the Loir and the Protestant Academy in Saumur supported the first works of **René Descartes**. In the following century, **Néricault-Destouches**, from Touraine, followed in Molière's footsteps with his comedies of character; Voltaire stayed at Sully; Rousseau and his companion Thérèse Levasseur lived at Chenonceau; Beaumarchais, who wrote *The Barber of Seville*, settled at Vouvray and visited the Duke of Choiseul in exile at Chanteloup.

Romanticism – The pamphleteer **Paul-Louis Courier** (1772-1825) and the songwriter **Béranger** (1780-1857), both active during the second Bourbon restoration, were sceptical, witty and liberal in politics. **Alfred de Vigny** (1797-1863), a native of Loches who became a soldier and a poet, painted an idyllic picture of Touraine in his novel, *Cinq-Mars*.

The greatest literary genius of Touraine was however **Honoré de Balzac** (1799-1850). He was born in Tours and brought up in Vendôme; he loved the Loire valley and used it as a setting for several of the numerous portraits in his vast work, *The Human Comedy*.

Contemporary writers – The poet, **Charles Péguy**, born in Orléans, wrote about Joan of Arc and his beloved Beauce. **Marcel Proust** also returned to the Beauce in his novel *Remembrance of Things Past*. Another poet, **Max Jacob** (1876-1944), spent many years in work and meditation at the abbey of St-Benoît-sur-Loire.

The Sologne calls to mind the young novelist, **Alain-Fournier**, and his famous work, *Le Grand Meaulnes (The Lost Domain)*. The character of Raboliot the poacher is a picturesque evocation of his native country by the author **Maurice Genevoix** (1890-1980), a member of the Academy. The humorist **Georges Courteline** (1858-1929) was born in Touraine which was also the retreat of several writers of international reputation: Maeterlinck (Nobel prize in 1911) at Coudray-Montpensier; Anatole France (Nobel prize in 1921) at La Béchellerie; Bergson (Nobel prize in 1927) at La Gaudinière. **René Benjamin** (1885-1948) settled in Touraine where he wrote *The Prodigious Life of Balzac* and other novels.

Balzac (Musée des Beaux-Arts. Tours)

Angers was the home of **René Bazin** (1853-1932), who was greatly attached to the traditional virtues and his home ground, and of his great-nephew, **Hervé Bazin** (1911-96), whose violent attacks on conventional values were directly inspired by his home town.

FINE ARTS

Clément Janequin (1480-1565), a master of religious and secular music, became an Angevin by adoption and was for many years head of the Angers Cathedral Choir School. **Jean Clouet** from Flanders, who was attached to Louis XII and François I, and his son **François**, who was born in Tours, produced some very fine portraits. In the 19C the sculptor and engraver, **David d'Angers** (1788-1856), achieved fame through the hundreds of medallions which record the profiles of the celebrities of his period.

Painters

Jean Fouquet (c 1420-80). Portraitist and miniaturist, born in Tours; his landscape backgrounds evoke the Loire valley.

The Master of Moulins (late 15C). His charm and purity of line are characteristic of the French school. Identified by some with Jean Perréal (Jehan de Paris, c 1455-1530).

Jean Bourdichon (c 1457-1521). Miniaturist who painted Anne of Brittany, with a fluid and seductive style.

Leonardo da Vinci (1452-1519). Invited to settle in the Loire valley from 1516 by François I; died at Amboise.

François Clouet (1520-72). Born in Tours, and became portrait painter to the Valois kings.

Jean Mosnier (1600-56). Interior decorator and author of religious works. Worked mainly at Cheverny and Beauregard and also in the neighbourhood.

Sculptors

Michel Colombe (c 1430-1514?). Head of an important studio in Tours; he combined Gothic tradition with Italian novelty.

Fra Giocondo (c 1433-1515). Famous monk from Verona, humanist and engineer who settled in Amboise in 1499.

Guido Mazzoni (c 1450-1518) or Il Paganino. Italian who specialised in terracotta.

Domenico da Cortona (1470-1549). Italian architect. called Il Boccadoro (Golden Mouth), in France from 1495.

The Justes (16C). Florentine family descended from Antoine Juste (1479-1519) who was naturalised in 1513 and settled in Tours in 1515.

Girolamo della Robbia (1488-1566). Arrived in the Orléans region from Florence in 1518 and produced terracotta medallions.

Michel Bourdin (1585-1645). From Orléans; a realist in style.

SCIENCE

The Royal School of Surgery, now the Faculty of Medicine and Pharmacy, was founded in Tours in 1756. Also in Tours, **Bretonneau** (1778-1862) taught and did research on infectious diseases; his work was continued by his pupils **Trousseau** and **Velpeau**. **Denis Papin** (1647-1714), physicist and inventor, was born near Blois. **Charles** (1746-1823), born in Beaugency and also a physicist, collaborated with the Montgolfier brothers and in 1783 made the first ascent in a hydrogen balloon in Paris.

The inhabitants of the Loire valley

The character of the people in the Loire valley is apparently best illustrated by the following legend which is still related in Touraine. The holy relics of St Martin were being carried from Auxerre to Tours. The route was crowded with invalids and cripples who were instantly cured as the relics passed by. Two cripples who lived on alms suddenly heard the terrible news – terrible because for them it meant ruin. To escape the miracle which threatened them, they fled as fast as their poor limbs would carry them but they were too slow; the procession overtook them and they were cured. They had to abandon their crutches and begging bowl and work for their living. There was no point in lamenting their lot; it was better to profit from their cure. They went off along the banks of the Loire, praising the Lord and his saint with such enthusiasm that they were able to found a rich chapel and a village, La Chapelle-sur-Loire, near Langeais.

The region where the "best French" is spoken – Since the Loire valley was the cradle of France, it is here that old France is recalled in the sayings which have shaped the French language. It is said that the best French is spoken in the Touraine region. This does not mean that one hears nothing but the most sophisticated, high-brow language, however; the local dialect is as unintelligible to the untuned ear as any other.

RURAL ARCHITECTURE

The various types of local houses to be found in the Loire valley are determined by local building materials, needs and customs.

On the plateaux and in the wooded plains – In the **Beauce**, a wheat-growing plain, the farms are built round a closed courtyard with an imposing entrance. In the towns the houses are rough-cast and roofed with flat tiles.

In the **Dunois** and the **Vendômois** the houses are decorated with a chequered pattern of alternating stone and flint. The long low cottages of the **Sologne** are roofed with thatch or flat tiles; the older houses are built of timber frames filled with cob while the more modern are of brick.

On the plateaux between the Cher, the Indre and the Vienne country houses are often surrounded by clumps of walnut or chestnut trees. Flat tile roofs predominate in the country while slate roofs are more common in town. The old landlord's house in a particular area is usually recognisable by its hipped roof. Between the Sologne and the Loire there are numerous pretty red brick buildings with white tufa facings.

In **Anjou** there are two distinct types of building: those constructed of limestone in White Anjou in the east and those constructed of schist in Black Anjou in the wooded farmland of les Mauges, Craonnais and Segréen. The fine blue-black slates are found throughout the province except in les Mauges.

In **Maine** the houses are built of limestone in White Maine on the River Sarthe and of granite or schist in Black Maine in the Mayenne valley.

In the river valleys – In the valleys of the Loire and its tributaries the typical wine-grower's house consists of the living quarters, the storeroom and the stable under one roof with an external oven and an outside stair beneath which is the entrance to the cellar.

A peculiarity of the valleys is the **troglodyte dwelling** which is hollowed out of the limestone tufa cliff and has a chimney protruding at ground level. Often decorated with flowers and trellises and sheltered from the wind, it is cool in summer and warm in winter.

Normandy is Normandy, Burgundy is Burgundy, Provence is Provence; but Touraine is essentially France. It is the land of Rabelais, of Descartes, of Balzac, of good books and good company, as well as good dinners and good houses. ... Touraine is a land of old châteaux – a gallery of architectural specimens and of large hereditary properties. ... This is, moreover, the heart of the old French monarchy; and as that monarchy was splendid and picturesque, a reflection of that splendour still glitters in the current of the Loire. Some of the most striking events of French history have occurred on the banks of that river, and the soil it waters bloomed for a while with the flowering of the Renaissance.

Henry James *A Little Tour in France*

Art

Ecclesiastical architecture

LE MANS – Ground plan of St-Julien cathedral (12C-15C)

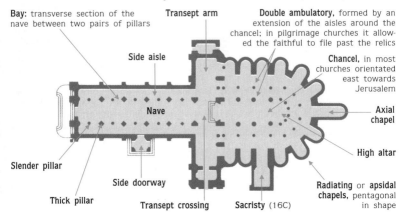

Bay: transverse section of the nave between two pairs of pillars

Transept arm

Double ambulatory, formed by an extension of the aisles around the chancel; in pilgrimage churches it allowed the faithful to file past the relics

Side aisle

Chancel, in most churches orientated east towards Jerusalem

Nave

Axial chapel

Slender pillar

High altar

Side doorway

Thick pillar

Transept crossing

Sacristy (16C)

Radiating or **apsidal chapels,** pentagonal in shape

ST-AIGNAN – Longitudinal section of the collegiate church (11C-12C), transept and chancel

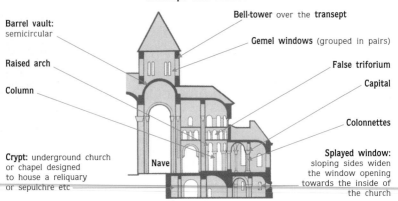

Barrel vault: semicircular

Bell-tower over the **transept**

Gemel windows (grouped in pairs)

Raised arch

False triforium

Column

Capital

Colonnettes

Crypt: underground church or chapel designed to house a reliquary or sepulchre etc

Nave

Splayed window: sloping sides widen the window opening towards the inside of the church

ANGERS – Vaulting of St-Serge church (early 13C)

This type of domical vaulting is known in France as **Angevin** or **Plantagenet vaulting**. It is curved so that the central keystone is higher than the supporting arches, unlike ordinary Gothic vaulting where they are at the same level. Towards the end of the 12C, Angevin vaulting became lighter, with slimmer, more numerous ribs springing from slender round columns. Early in the 13C, church interiors became higher, beneath soaring lierne vaulting decorated with elegant sculptures.

Quarter or **cell,** in brick

Keystone

Rib

Lierne: auxiliary rib

Capital

Rib vault

Pillar or **column**

R. Corbel

ST-BENOÎT-SUR-LOIRE – Basilique Ste-Marie (11C-12C)

Romanesque church. Ground plan with double transept is rare in France; the small, or false, transept crosses the chancel.

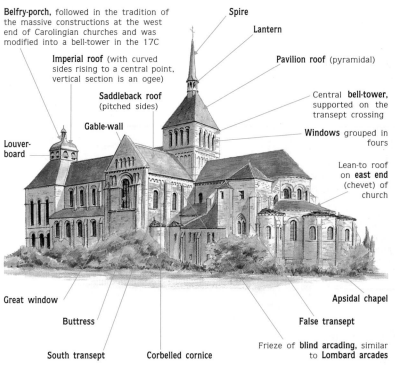

Belfry-porch, followed in the tradition of the massive constructions at the west end of Carolingian churches and was modified into a bell-tower in the 17C

Imperial roof (with curved sides rising to a central point, vertical section is an ogee)

Saddleback roof (pitched sides)

Gable-wall

Louver-board

Spire

Lantern

Pavilion roof (pyramidal)

Central **bell-tower,** supported on the transept crossing

Windows grouped in fours

Lean-to roof on **east end** (chevet) of church

Great window

Buttress

South transept

Corbelled cornice

Apsidal chapel

False transept

Frieze of **blind arcading,** similar to **Lombard arcades**

LE MANS – Chevet of St-Julien cathedral (13C)

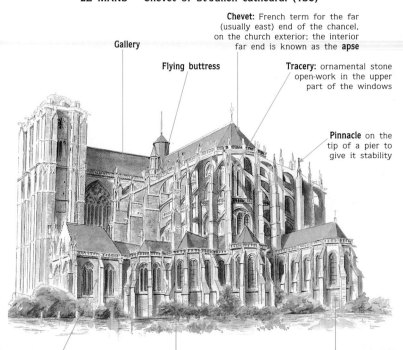

Gallery

Flying buttress

Chevet: French term for the far (usually east) end of the chancel, on the church exterior; the interior far end is known as the **apse**

Tracery: ornamental stone open-work in the upper part of the windows

Pinnacle on the tip of a pier to give it stability

Buttress: external support for a wall, built against it or projecting from it

Pier: solid masonry support structure absorbing the thrust of the arches

Apsidal chapel. In churches not dedicated to Our Lady, this chapel in the main axis of the building is often consecrated to her (Lady Chapel)

R. Corbel

33

TOURS – Façade of St-Gatien cathedral (13C-16C)

St-Gatien is a fine example of a harmonious combination of styles: Romanesque at the base of the towers, Flamboyant Gothic on the façade, and Renaissance at the top of the bell-towers which are crowned with **lantern-domes**.

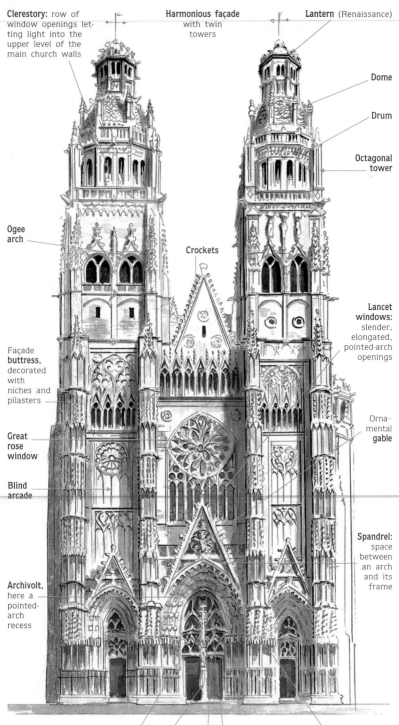

Clerestory: row of window openings letting light into the upper level of the main church walls

Harmonious façade with twin towers

Lantern (Renaissance)

Dome

Drum

Octagonal tower

Ogee arch

Crockets

Lancet windows: slender, elongated, pointed-arch openings

Façade buttress, decorated with niches and pilasters

Orna-mental gable

Great rose window

Blind arcade

Spandrel: space between an arch and its frame

Archivolt, here a pointed-arch recess

Engaged piers or **jambs:** vertical side of a doorway/window, here supporting the archivolt

Open-work tympanum

Pier, usually adorned with a statue

Doorway

Architraves: concentric arch mouldings covering an arch recess, making up the **archivolt**

R. Corbel

34

LORRIS — Organ case (15C) in Notre-Dame church

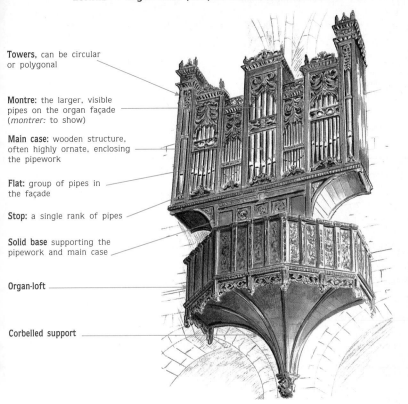

Towers, can be circular or polygonal

Montre: the larger, visible pipes on the organ façade (*montrer:* to show)

Main case: wooden structure, often highly ornate, enclosing the pipework

Flat: group of pipes in the façade

Stop: a single rank of pipes

Solid base supporting the pipework and main case

Organ-loft

Corbelled support

ANGERS — Monumental 19C pulpit in St-Maurice cathedral

This work by Abbé René Choyer is a pastiche (1855) of 13C Gothic art. As a whole, the pulpit embodies an in-depth knowledge of medieval architecture and sculpture.

Finial: detached formal ornament in the shape of a stylised flower adorning the top of a pinnacle

Canopy: richly ornate baldaquin above a statue or an altar etc

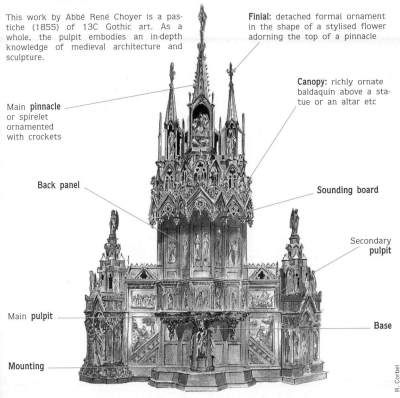

Main **pinnacle** or spirelet ornamented with crockets

Back panel

Sounding board

Secondary pulpit

Main **pulpit**

Base

Mounting

Military architecture

LOCHES – Porte des Cordeliers (11C and 13C fortified gateway)

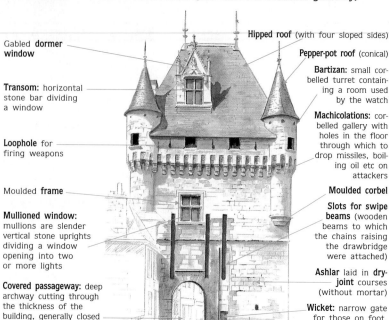

Gabled dormer window

Transom: horizontal stone bar dividing a window

Loophole for firing weapons

Moulded **frame**

Mullioned window: mullions are slender vertical stone uprights dividing a window opening into two or more lights

Covered passageway: deep archway cutting through the thickness of the building, generally closed off at either end by carriage gates

Hipped roof (with four sloped sides)

Pepper-pot roof (conical)

Bartizan: small corbelled turret containing a room used by the watch

Machicolations: corbelled gallery with holes in the floor through which to drop missiles, boiling oil etc on attackers

Moulded corbel

Slots for swipe beams (wooden beams to which the chains raising the drawbridge were attached)

Ashlar laid in **dry-joint** courses (without mortar)

Wicket: narrow gate for those on foot, easily defended in case of attack

Civil architecture

BLOIS – Château, François-1er staircase (16C)

The spiral stairway is built inside an octagonal staircase half set into the façade. It opens onto the main courtyard in a series of balconies which form loggias. The king and his court would view all sorts of entertainment from here: the arrival of dignitaries, jousting, hunting or military displays.

Candelabrum: an ornamental torch-shaped spike on top of a tower, chimney etc

Chimney stack

Ornate **gable** over dormer window

Cornice of shell motifs, very common ornamentation under François I

Sculpted stone **corbels**

Stone canopy: **baldaquin** decorated with tiny arches and pinnacles, designed to protect statues standing against the building

Field: plain background to decorative motif

Plain surface left bare of ornamentation

Medallion: sculpted portrait or other subject in a circular frame

Gargoyle: drain in the shape of an imaginary and often grotesque animal, through whose mouth rainwater would be projected away from the castle walls

Balustrade

Sculpted **parapet** (filled-in protective wall)

Rampant arch: arch with ends springing from different levels

Sculpted **bracket** (projecting support, smaller than a corbel)

Crowned salamander: decorative motif of François I, sculpted in low relief

R. Corbel

36

SERRANT – Château (16C-17C)

Brown schist, white tufa and grey-blue slate lend great character to this luxurious residence in which Renaissance and Classical styles are harmoniously combined.

Imperial dome (pointed dome, vertical section of which is an ogee)

Œil-de-bœuf window: small and circular ("bull's-eye")

Main building, or *corps-de-logis*

Balustrade: low protective wall composed of balusters

Corner tower

Attic: small extra upper storey

Dormer window surmounted by a broken pediment

Triangular **pediment**

Lantern

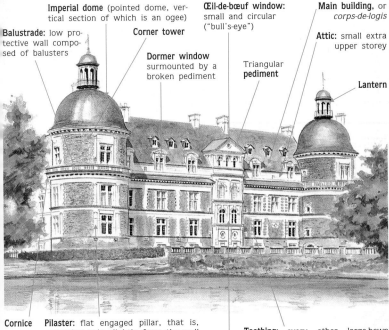

Cornice

Pilaster: flat engaged pillar, that is, projecting only slightly from the wall behind it

Toothing: every other large-hewn stone is left projecting from the stonework framing the windows for a more solid – and more decorative – bond with the adjoining schist walls

Avant-corps: part of a building projecting from the rest of the façade for the entire height of the building, roof included

VILLANDRY — Layout of the Jardins d'Amour (Renaissance style)

The four gardens on the theme of love consist of box borders punctuated by clipped yews and filled with flowers. Each box parterre is laid out in the form of symbolic images: tragic love is represented by sword blades and daggers; unfaithful love by cuckolds' horns, ladies' fans and love letters etc

Monumental fountain in a niche against the wall

Arbour: trellised row of clipped hornbeams

Viewing terrace: commanding a view of the gardens

Mall: tree-lined avenue originally used for games of pall-mall, a precursor of croquet

Espalier wall

Hedge formed by clipped shrubs

Canal

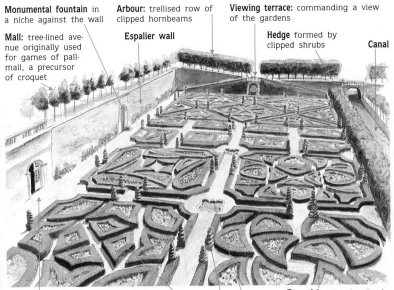

Path covered in *mignonnette* (sand from the Loire which resembles coarse-ground pepper, hence its name)

Box-edged **bed**

Basin

Box edging: low box border (basic element of topiary art)

Topiary: free-standing clipped shrub. Topiary art involves clipping and trimming trees and shrubs to create figurative or geometric shapes verging on sculpture.

R. Corbel

SECULAR ARCHITECTURE

Gothic period

In addition to the castles built for the Dukes of Anjou, such as Saumur, manor houses and mansions were constructed in the 14C for merchants who had grown rich through trade. The 15C saw a proliferation in the lively ornate Gothic style of châteaux built of brick with white stone facings, such as the château at Lassay, of manor houses such as Le Clos-Lucé near Amboise, of town mansions with projecting stair turrets and high dormers, and of half-timbered houses. The finest examples of Gothic houses are to be found in Le Mans, Chinon and Tours.

Gardens – Monastic gardens, such as those belonging to the abbeys in Bourgueil, Marmoutier and Cormery, consisted of an orchard, a vegetable patch with a fish pond and a medicinal herb garden.
In the 15C they were succeeded by square flower beds which were created by King René at his manor houses in Anjou and by Louis XI at Plessis-lès-Tours. A fresh note was introduced with shady arbours and fountains where the paths intersected; entertainment was provided by animals at liberty or kept in menageries or aviaries.

Renaissance period

The Renaissance did not spring into being at the wave of a magic wand at the end of the Italian campaigns. Before the wars in Italy, Italian artists had been made welcome at the French court and the court of Anjou; Louis XI and King René had employed sculptors and medallion makers such as Francesco Laurana, Niccolo Spinelli and Jean Candida. New blood, however, was imported into local art by the arrival of artists from Naples in 1495 at the behest of Charles VIII.
At Amboise and Chaumont and even at Chenonceau, Azay or Chambord, the châteaux still looked like fortresses but the machicolations assumed a decorative role. Large windows flanked by pilasters appeared in the façades which were decorated with medallions; the steep roofs were decorated with lofty dormers and carved chimneys. The Italian influence is most apparent in the low-relief ornamentation. At Chambord and Le Lude the décor was refined by local masters such as Pierre Trinqueau.

Renaissance Decoration

Château d'Azay-le-Rideau
Grand staircase frieze

① Shell – ② Urn
③ Scroll – ④ Dragon
⑤ Putto – ⑥ Cupid
⑦ Horn of plenty
⑧ Satyr

The Italian style is most obvious in the exterior of the François I wing at Blois where Il Boccadoro copied Bramante's invention, the rhythmic façade composed of alternating windows and niches separated by pilasters. Later, as in Beaugency town hall, came semicircular arches and superimposed orders, then the domes and pavilions which mark the birth of Classical architecture.
The Italians created new types of staircases: two spirals intertwined as at Chambord, or straight flights of steps beneath coffered ceilings as at Chenonceau, Azay-le-Rideau and Poncé.
The Renaissance also inspired a number of towns halls – Orléans, Beaugency, Loches – and several private houses – Hôtel Toutin in Orléans, Hôtel Gouin in Tours and the Hôtel Pincé in Angers.

Gardens – In his enthusiasm for Neapolitan gardens. Charles VIII brought with him from his kingdom in Sicily a gardener called **Dom Pacello de Mercogliano**, a Neapolitan monk, who laid out the gardens at Amboise and Blois; Louis XII entrusted him with the royal vegetable plot at Château-Gaillard near Amboise.
Pacello popularised the use of ornate flower beds bordered with yew and fountains with sculpted basins. The gardens of Chenonceau and Villandry give a good idea of his style.
The extraordinary vegetable garden at Villandry, which is laid out in a decorative pattern in the style popular during the Renaissance, still has certain traditional medieval and monastic features; the rose trees, planted in a symmetrical pattern, symbolise the monks, each digging in his own plot.

Classical period (17C-18C)

Following the removal of the court to the Paris region (Ile-de-France), architecture in the Loire valley fell into decline. Handsome buildings were still constructed but the designers came from Paris. In the more austere climate of the 17C the pompous style of the Sun King displaced the graceful fantasy of the Renaissance and the picturesque asymmetry of the medieval buildings. The fashion was for pediments, domes (Cheverny) and the Greek orders (Gaston-d'Orléans wing at Blois). Tower structures were abandoned in favour of rectangular pavilions containing huge rooms with monumental fireplaces decorated with caryatids and painted ceilings with exposed beams; the pavilions were covered with steep roofs in the French style.

There was a new wave of château building – Ménars. Montgeoffroy – but the main legacy of the 18C is in the towns. Great terraces were built in Orléans. Tours and Saumur with long perspectives aligned on the axis of magnificent bridges which had level roadways.

RELIGIOUS ARCHITECTURE

Romanesque art (11C-12C)

Orléanais – The church in Germigny-des-Prés, which dates from the Carolingian period, and the Benedictine basilica of St-Benoît are particularly fine examples of Romanesque art in the Orléans area. There are two pretty churches in the Cher valley at St-Aignan and Selles.

Touraine – Various influences from Poitou are evident: apses with column buttresses, domed transepts, doorways without pediments. The bell-towers are unusual: square or octagonal with spires surrounded at the base by turrets.

Anjou – The Angevin buildings are clustered in the region round Baugé and Saumur. The church in Cunault shows the influence of Poitou in the ogive-vaulted nave buttressed by high aisles with groined vaulting. The domes roofing the nave of the abbey church at Fontevraud and the absence of aisles are features of the Aquitaine school.

From Romanesque to Gothic

The **Plantagenet style**, which is also known as **Angevin**, takes its name from Henry Plantagenet. It is a transitional style which reached the height of its popularity early in the 13C and died out by the century's end.

Angevin vaulting – Unlike standard Gothic vaulting in which all the keystones are at the same level, Angevin vaulting is domical so that the central keystones are higher than the supporting arches. The best example is the cathedral of St-Maurice in Angers. This type of vaulting evolved to feature an ever finer network of increasingly fragile-looking ribs, which were eventually adorned with sculptures.

The Plantagenet style spread from the Loire valley into the Vendée, Poitou, Saintonge and the Garonne valley. At the end of the 13C it was introduced by Charles of Anjou to southern Italy.

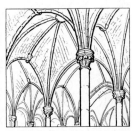

Angevin vaulting

Mid 12C — Late 12C — Early 13C

Cathédrale St-Maurice, Angers — Chancel of St-Serge in Angers

Gothic art (12C-15C)

Gothic art is characterised by the use of intersecting vaults and the pointed arch. The triforium, which originally was blind, is pierced by apertures which eventually give way to high windows *(illustrations overleaf)*. The tall, slender columns, which were topped by capitals supporting the vaulting, were at first cylindrical but were later flanked by engaged columns. In the final development the capitals were abandoned and the roof ribs descended directly into the columns.

The **Flamboyant style** follows this pattern; the diagonal ribs are supplemented by other, purely decorative, ribs called liernes and tiercerons.

The Flamboyant style (15C) of architecture is to be found in the façade of La Trinité in Vendôme and of St-Gatien in Tours, in Notre-Dame de Cléry and in the Sainte-Chapelle at Châteaudun.

Renaissance and classical styles (16C-17C-18C)

Italian influence is strongly evident in the decoration of **Renaissance** churches: basket-handle or round-headed arches, numerous recesses for statues. Interesting Montrésor examples at Ussé, Champigny-sur-Veude and La Bourgonnière.

In the **classical** period (17C-18C) religious architecture was designed to create a majestic effect, with superimposed Greek orders, pediments over doorways, domes and flanking vaulting. The church of Notre-Dame-des-Ardilliers in Saumur has a huge dome; the church of St-Vincent in Blois is dominated by a scrolled pediment.

Romanesque, Gothic and Renaissance elevations

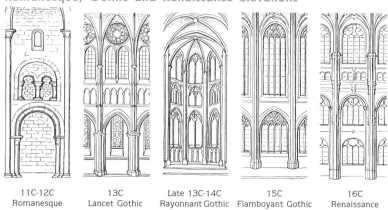

11C-12C	13C	Late 13C-14C	15C	16C
Romanesque	Lancet Gothic	Rayonnant Gothic	Flamboyant Gothic	Renaissance

STAINED GLASS

A **stained-glass window** is made of pieces of coloured glass fixed with lead to an iron frame. The perpendicular divisions of a window are called **lights.** Metal oxides were added to the constituent materials of white glass to give a wide range of colours. Details were often drawn in with dark paint and fixed by firing. Varied and surprising effects were obtained by altering the length of firing and by the impurities in the oxides and defects in the glass. The earliest stained-glass windows were made in the 10C but none has survived.

13C stained-glass window (detail)
(Cathédrale St-Maurice, Angers)

Pélissier/VLOO

12C-13C – The colours were vivid with rich blues and reds predominating; the glass and leading were thick and smoothed down with a plane; the subject matter was naïve and confined to superimposed medallions.

The Cistercians favoured grisaille windows which were composed of clear-to-greenish glass with foliage designs on a cross-hatched background which gives a greyish (grisaille) effect.

14C-15C – The master-glaziers discovered how to make a golden yellow; lighter colours were developed, the leading became less heavy as it was produced using new tools and techniques, the glass was thinner and the windows larger. Gothic canopies appeared over the human figures.

16C – Windows became delicately coloured pictures in thick lead frames, often copied from Renaissance canvases with strict attention to detail and perspective; there are examples at Champigny-sur-Veude, Montrésor and Sully-sur-Loire.

17C-19C – Traditional stained glass was often replaced by vitrified enamel or painted glass without lead surrounds. In the cathedral of Orléans there are 17C windows with white diamond panes and gold bands and 19C windows depicting Joan of Arc.

20C – The need to restore or replace old stained glass stimulated a revival of the art. Representational or abstract compositions of great variety emerged from the workshops of the painter-glaziers: Max Ingrand, Alfred Manessier and Jean Le Moal.

MURAL PAINTINGS AND FRESCOES

In the Middle Ages the interiors of ecclesiastical buildings were decorated with paintings, motifs or morally and spiritually uplifting scenes. A school of mural painting akin to that in Poitou developed in the Loire region. The surviving works of this school are well preserved owing to the mild climate and low humidity. The paintings are recognisable by the weak matt colours against light backgrounds. The style is livelier and less formalised than in Burgundy or the Massif Central while the composition is more sober than in Poitou. Two techniques were used: **fresco work**, which was done with watercolours on fresh plaster thus making it impossible to touch it up later; and **mural painting**, where tempera colours were applied to a dry surface, producing a less durable work of art.

Romanesque period – The art of fresco work with its Byzantine origins was adopted by the Benedictines of Monte Cassino in Italy, who in turn transmitted the art to the monks of Cluny in Burgundy. The latter used this art form in their abbeys and priories, from where it spead throughout the country.

The technique – The fresco technique was the one most commonly used, although beards and eyes were often added once the plaster was dry with the result that they are now usually no longer visible. The figures, drawn in red ochre, were sometimes highlighted with touches of black, green and the sky-blue so characteristic of the region.

The subject matter – The subjects, which were often inspired by smaller-scale works, were intended to instruct the faithful in religious truths and also to instil in them a fear of sin and Hell. The most common theme for the oven-vaulting was Christ the King enthroned, majestic and severe; the reverse of the façade (ie at the opposite end of the church from the apse) often carried the Last Judgement; the walls depicted scenes from the New Testament while the Saints and Apostles adorned the pillars. Other subjects portrayed frequently are the Conflict of the Virtues and Vices, and the Labours of the Months.

The most interesting examples – Good examples of fresco painting are to be found throughout the Loir valley in Areines, Souday, St-Jacques-des-Guérets, Lavardin and best of all in the chapel of St-Gilles at Montoire. There is also a fine work in St-Aignan in the Cher valley. The crypt of the church in Tavant in the Vienne valley is decorated with lively paintings of high quality.

In Anjou a man called Fulk seems to have supervised the decoration of the cloisters in St-Aubin's abbey in Angers. His realistic style, although slightly stilted in the drawing, seems to spring from the Poitou school. More characteristic of the Loire valley are the Virgin and Christ the King from Ponginé in the Baugé region.

Gothic period – It was not until the 15C and the end of the Hundred Years War that new compositions were produced on themes which were to remain in fashion until the mid 16C. These were really more mural paintings than frescoes and new subjects were added to the traditional repertoire; a gigantic St Christopher often appeared at the entrance to a church (*see AMBOISE*), while the legend of the Three Living and Three Dead, represented by three proud huntsmen meeting three skeletons, symbolized the brevity and vanity of human life.

The most interesting examples – In the Loire valley such paintings are to be found in Alluyes, Lassay and Villiers. Two compositions with strange iconography adorn the neighbouring churches in Asnières-sur-Vège and Auvers-le-Hamon.

Renaissance – In the 16C paintings in churches became rarer. There are however two surviving examples from this period: the Entombment in the church in Jarzé and the paintings in the chapter-house of Fontevraud abbey.

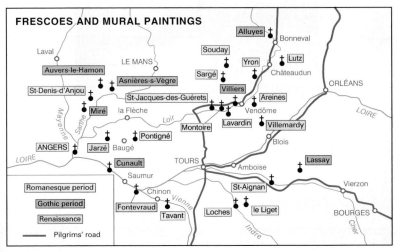

FRESCOES AND MURAL PAINTINGS

GEMMAIL

Gemmail is a modern art medium consisting of assembling particles of coloured glass over a light source. The inventor of this art form was **Jean Crotti** (1878-1958). The Malherbe-Navarre brothers, an interior decorator and a physicist, provided the technical expertise; they discovered a bonding agent which did not affect the constituent elements.

TAPESTRIES FROM THE LOIRE WORKSHOPS

Hanging tapestries, which had been in existence since the 8C to exclude draughts or divide up huge rooms, became very popular in the 14C. The weavers worked from cartoons or preparatory sketches using wool woven with silk, gold or silver threads on horizontal (low warp – *basse-lisse*) or vertical (high warp – *haute lisse*) looms.

Religious tapestries – Their value made tapestries ideal for use as investments or diplomatic gifts; as well as those commissioned for châteaux or even specific rooms, some were hung in churches or even in the streets. The most famous is the 14C Apocalypse tapestry *(see ANGERS)*.

Mille-fleurs – The *mille-fleurs* (thousand flowers) tapestries evoke late medieval scenes – showing an idealized life of enticing gardens, tournaments and hunting scenes – against a green, blue or pink background strewn with a variety of flowers, plants and small animals. These are attributed to the Loire valley workshops (c 1500). Good examples can be seen in Saumur. Langeais and Angers.

Renaissance to 20C – The use of cartoons (full-scale designs, usually in reverse) instead of paintings, and more sophisticated weaving techniques and materials render greater detail possible. The number of colours increases and panels are surrounded by wide borders. In the 18C the art of portraiture is introduced into tapestry work.

In the 20C **Jean Lurçat**, originally a tapestry renovator, recommends the use of natural dyes. Contemporary weavers experiment with new techniques to create relief and three dimensional effects.

Le Chant du Monde by Jean Lurçat, 1958
(Musée Jean-Lurçat, Angers)

Food and wine

The Loire valley is a region renowned for its simple healthy cooking, enjoyable wines and relaxed way of making the most of life.
The following menu lists some ot the local specialities and the best wines to accompany them.

Hors-d'œuvre: various types of potted pork *(rillons, rillettes);* sausage stuffed with chicken meat *(boudin blanc).*

Fish: pike, salmon, carp or shad with the famous *beurre blanc* (white butter) sauce; small fried fish from the Loire, rather like whitebait *(friture);* stuffed bream and casserole of eels simmered in wine with mushrooms, onions and prunes (in Anjou).

Main course: game from Sologne; pork with prunes; veal in a cream sauce made with white wine and brandy; casserole of chicken in a red wine sauce or in a white wine and cream sauce with onions and mushrooms; spit-roasted capon or pullet.

Vegetables: green cabbage with butter; Vineuil asparagus; mushrooms – stuffed or in a cream sauce; lettuce salad with walnut oil dressing.

Menu

HORS-D'ŒUVRE
Vouvray - Sancerre

Les rillons de Touraine.
Les rillettes du Mans, de Tours ou d'Angers.
Le boudin blanc bourré non de mie, mais de blanc de poulet.

POISSONS
Vouvray - Saumur - Montlouis - Sancerre - Rosés d'Anjou

Le brochet, le saumon, la carpe ou l'alose au beurre blanc.
La friture de Loire.
La brème farcie et surtout la matelote d'anguille au vin vieux.

VIANDES
Bourgueil - Chinon - Saumur-Champigny

Le gibier de Sologne.
Le carré ou la noisette de porc aux pruneaux.
Le cul-de-veau à l'angevine.
Le coq au vin du pays ou la fricassée de poulet.
Le chapon ou la poularde du Mans à la broche.

LÉGUMES
Les choux-verts au beurre.
Les asperges de Vineuil.
Les champignons farcis ou à la crème.
La salade à l'huile de noix.

FROMAGES
Bourgueil - Chinon

Crottins de Chavignol ; Olivet à la cendre.
St-Benoît ; Valençay ; Selles-sur-Cher ; Ste-Maure ; Vendôme.
St-Paulin ; crémets d'Anjou.

FRUITS
Les prunes et pruneaux de Tours, les melons de Tours.
Les fraises de Saumur, les abricots et les poires d'Angers.
Les Reinettes du Mans.

DESSERTS
Vouvray pétillant, Vouvray, Crémant de Loire
Saumur - Coteaux du Layon - Montlouis

Les macarons de Cormery.
Les chaussons aux pommes et toute la cohorte des cotignacs,
des confitures d'Orléans et des pâtisseries de Tours ; les tartes des demoiselles Tatin.
Pour digérer : d'excellents marcs, des liqueurs de fruits dont Angers a le secret.

Fried fish from the Loire

Cheese: St-Benoît, Vendôme and St-Paulin are made from cows' milk. Chavignol, Valençay, Selles-sur-Cher, Ste-Maure and *crémets d'Anjou* are made from goat's milk (the latter are small fresh cream cheeses); Olivet is factory-made with a coating of charcoal.

Fruit: plums and prunes from Tours; melons from Tours; strawberries from Saumur; apricots and pears from Angers; Reinette apples from Le Mans.

Dessert: macaroons from Cormery; apple pastries; quince and apple jelly *(Cotignac);* preserves from Orléans and pastries from Tours; caramelised upside-down apple tart *(Tarte Tatin).*

Liqueurs: there are excellent *marcs* and fruit liqueurs, notably those from Angers.

Marcs: pure white spirit obtained from pressed grapes.

Tarte Tatin

(Caramelised Upside-down Apple Tart)

Ingredients:

225g/8oz plain flour	1 egg
5 tbsp castor sugar	1 tbsp cold water
pinch of salt	6-8 large crisp apples
225g/8oz unsalted butter	(such as Coxes)

Method:

Make up pastry base using the flour, 1 tbsp of sugar, 140g/5oz of butter, pinch of salt and the egg, and adding the water if necessary. Cover dough ball and leave in a cool place for a couple of hours.

Preheat the oven to 200ºC (400ºF/Gas 6). Grease a 20-25cm/9-10in baking tin (fairly deep) with some of the remaining butter, and sprinkle some of the sugar over the bottom.

Peel, core and slice the apples, and arrange them in a couple of neat layers on the bottom of the tin. Dot the top with knobs of the remaining butter and cover with the rest of the sugar.

Roll out the pastry into a fairly thin (about 0.5cm/0.25in thick) circle and place over the apples, trimming it to fit just inside the rim of the tin. Cut some air holes with the tip of a sharp knife.

Bake for 30-45min in the upper half of the oven. When cooked, turn out onto a serving dish so that the layers of apple are on top (which is why they should have been arranged neatly!) and place under a red-hot grill for a few minutes to caramelise the top.

Serve warm, with lashings of crème fraîche.

WINE

Local wines – The vestiges of an early stone wine-press were discovered at Cheille, near Azay-le-Rideau, testifying to the existence of wine-making in the Loire valley under Roman rule, towards AD 100. It is believed that the great St Martin himself ordered vines to be planted on the slopes of Vouvray in the 4C. From then onwards, this activity became firmly established in the area. Over the centuries, Anjou, Touraine and the Orléanais have adopted a number of grape varieties coming from different natural regions, which accounts for the great diversity of the *cépages*. The best-known white wines are from Vouvray, a dry, mellow wine tasting of ripe grapes, and Montlouis, with a delicate fruity flavour. Both are made from the Chenin Blanc grape, known locally as the **Pineau de la Loire**.

The best-known red wine, known as Breton, is made from the Cabernet Franc grape which came originally from Bordeaux and produces the fine, light wines of Bourgueil and those from Chinon which have a stronger bouquet; the same grape is used to make a dry rosé which has charm and nobility. Among the wines of Anjou are the rouge de Cabernet and the Saumur-Champigny which have a fine ruby glow and the subtle taste of raspberries. The Cabernet de Saumur is an elegant dry rosé with a good flavour. Another red wine comes from the Breton vines grown on the Loudun slopes. The wines of Sancerre, on the eastern fringe of the châteaux country, are made from the Sauvignon grape and are known for their "gun-flint" flavour. Less famous wines are the *gris meuniers* from the Orléanais and the *gascon*, which are pale and have a low alcohol content.

The slopes of the Loir produce a dry white and an acid-tasting red which improve with keeping. A light and pleasant white wine is made from the Romorantin grape which is grown only in the Sologne. The slopes of the Loire produce 15% of the entire *Muscadet* crop. The Ancenis-Gamay wine, made from Burgundy Gamay vines, is less well-known than the Gros Plant from Nantes as it is produced in smaller quantities. This light, dry, fruity wine, a perfect accompaniment to cooked pork meats, is produced in an area of about 350ha/865 acres around Ancenis.

The character of the region is most apparent in the wine cellars which are often old quarries hollowed out of the limestones slopes at road level. They are therefore easily accessible so that the owner can drive his vehicles straight in. The galleries often extend for several hundred metres. Some open out into chambers where local societies hold their meetings and festivities.

The wine cellars also host meetings of the *confréries vineuses* which preserve the tradition of good wine in the Loire valley and joyously initiate new members (*chevaliers*) to their brotherhoods: *Les Sacavins* in Angers, *les Bons Entonneurs rabelaisiens* in Chinon, *la Chantepleure* in Vouvray and *Côterie des Closiers de Montlouis*.

In the temple of Bacchus – Picture the scene... The prospective wine-buyer, stands in front of barrel of the latest vintage, firmly propped on their stands. The owner of the vineyard fills the glasses and the ruby-red nectar is held up to the light. The tumblers have no stem or foot so they cannot be set down until they are drained. The wine should be savoured first for its bouquet and then, after a knowing glance at one's neighbour, tasted in small sips. On enptying the glass, a simple click of the tongue is enough to signal appreciation. The owner, his eyes shining, will say *"ça se laisse boire..."*.

Once inside the celler, all round, projecting from recesses in the rock, are coloured bottle tops – red, yellow, blue and white: full-bodied Sancerre; Vouvray which "rejoices the heart"; heady Montlouis; Chinon with its aftertaste of violets; Bourgueil with its hint of raspberries or wild strawberries; and their Angevin brothers, sparkling Saumur, lively and spirited, white Saumur, dry and sprightly, wines from La Coulée de Serrant and the Layon.

For the vintage years see the list printed in the current Michelin Red Guide France.

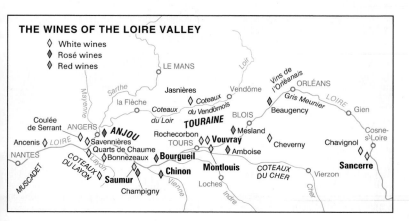

THE WINES OF THE LOIRE VALLEY

Château de Chambord

Sights

AMBOISE★★

Population 10 982
Michelin map 64 fold 16 or 238 fold 14
Local map see Vallée de la LOIRE: Orléans-Chinon

The town of Amboise, which lies on the south bank of the Loire below the proud remains of its castle, appears at its most picturesque when seen from the bridge or the north bank of the river.

★★ CHÂTEAU

Son et lumière – *See the Practical information section at the end of the guide.*

The rock spur above the town, on which the château ruins stand, has been fortified since the Gallo-Roman period. Before long a bridge was built which brought in revenue from tolls on the passage of goods and increased the strategic importance of Amboise *(1)*

For a period in the 11C there were two fortresses on the heights and one down in the town; all three were engaged in perpetual warfare. Eventually the Counts of Amboise gained the upper hand and held the domain until it was confiscated by Charles VII (1422-61).

The golden age of Amboise was the 15C when the château was enlarged and embellished by Louis XI and Charles VIII. Although the end of the century (1496) marks the beginning of Italian influence on French art, there is little to see at Amboise, since the new building was by then well advanced. The Italian style was to gain in popularity under Louis XII and flourish under François I.

Charles VIII's taste for luxury – Charles VIII, who was born and grew up in the old castle, had since 1489 dreamed of enlarging and redecorating it in accordance with his taste for luxury.

Work began in 1492 and during the next five years two ranges of buildings were added to the older structure. Hundreds of workmen laboured continuously, if necessary by candlelight, to satisfy the king's desire to move into his new residence without delay. In the interim the king visited Italy where he was dazzled by the artistic standards and the luxurious lifestyle. He returned to France in 1495 laden with furniture, works of art, fabrics etc. He also recruited to his service a team of scholars, architects, sculptors, decorators, gardeners and tailors... even a poultry breeder who had invented the incubator.

Charles VIII was particularly impressed by Italian gardens: "They lack only Adam and Eve to make an earthly paradise". On his return he instructed Pacello to design an ornamental garden on the terrace at Amboise. Among the architects whom he employed were Fra Giocondo and Il Boccadoro; the latter, a leading figure in the introduction of Renaissance ideas into France, had worked at Blois and Chambord and on the Hôtel de Ville in Paris.

A tragic death – In the afternoon of 7 April 1498 Charles VIII was escorting the Queen to watch a game of real tennis in the castle moat when they passed through a low doorway in the outer wall. Although not tall, the King hit his head on the lintel. Apparently unscathed, he chatted unconcernedly as the game progressed. Suddenly, however, he fell back unconscious. He was laid on a bed of straw in an evil-smelling chamber and such was the consternation caused by his collapse that he was left there until 11 o'clock in the evening when he died.

Chapelle St-Hubert

The Château d'Amboise in the 16C
Only the parts shown in black are extant

---

(1) In the Middle Ages there were only seven bridges between Gien and Angers. Troops then moved very slowly and the possession or loss of a bridge had a great influence on operations. Towns at bridgeheads drew great profit from the passage of merchandise.

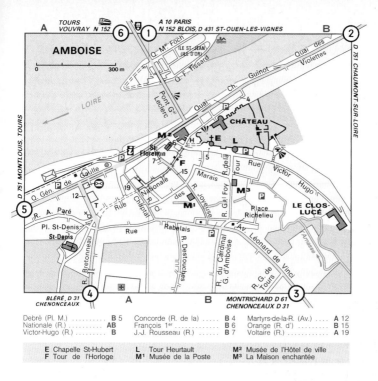

AMBOISE

CHÂTEAU

LE CLOS-LUCÉ

| E | Chapelle St-Hubert | L | Tour Heurtault | M² | Musée de l'Hôtel de ville |
| F | Tour de l'Horloge | M¹ | Musée de la Poste | M³ | La Maison enchantée |

The whirl of gaiety under François I – François d'Angoulême, the future François I, was only seven when he came to Amboise with his mother, Louise of Savoy, and his sister, who was to become the famous and learned Margaret of Navarre. At Amboise, which Louis XII had appointed as his residence near to his own château at Blois, the young François, who was heir apparent to the throne, was given a thorough intellectual, sporting and military education. He continued to live at the château during the first three years of his reign and this was the most brilliant period in the life of Amboise. Magnificent festivities were organised to celebrate his engagement to Claude de France, his departure for Italy, the birth of the Dauphin etc. Balls, tournaments, masquerades and wild beast fights followed one another in endless days given over to luxury and pleasure. A bevy of prostitutes was hired by the king to add to the enjoyment of the young noblemen of the court.

The wing of the château begun by Louis XII was completed by François I and his mother between 1517 and 1520 at a cost of 230 000 *livres*. Such was the king's passion for the arts that he invited Leonardo da Vinci to live at Le Clos-Lucé. After 1519 he grew tired of Amboise and stayed there only for brief periods, as for example on his return from captivity in Italy in 1526.

On 18 October 1534 Amboise was involved in the "affair of the placards": a pamphlet inveighing against "the terrible gross and intolerable abuses of the papal Mass" was fixed to the door of the royal chamber. François I was furious and decided to take repressive measures; the religious dispute became acrimonious.

François returned to Amboise on 8 December 1539 where he received his old adversary, Emperor Charles V, with great pomp and ceremony.

Towards the end of his life François preferred to live at Chambord or Fontainebleau.

Amboise Conspiracy (1560) – This conspiracy was one of the bloodier episodes in the château's history. During the turbulent years leading up to the Wars of Religion a Protestant aristocrat, **La Renaudie**, gathered a body of reformists round him in Brittany. These were dispatched to Blois in small groups to request of the young king, François II, the freedom to practise their religion. While they were there, the intention was that they should also try to lay hands on the Guises, bitter enemies of the Huguenots.

The plot was uncovered and the court promptly withdrew from Blois, which was indefensible, to Amboise where the king signed an edict of pacification in an attempt to calm things down. The conspirators persisted, however, and on 17 March they were arrested and killed as fast as they arrived. La Renaudie also perished. The conspiracy was mercilessly suppressed; some of the conspirators were hanged from the balcony of the château, some from the battlements, others were thrown into the Loire in sacks, the noblemen were beheaded and

49

quartered. In 1563 there was a truce followed by an Act of Toleration, signed at Amboise, which brought an end to the first War of Religion. The country settled down for the time being to four years of peace.

Destruction – Together with Blois, Amboise passed into the hands of Gaston d'Orléans, Louis XIII's brother and a great conspirator *(see BLOIS)*; during one of his many rebellions, the château was captured by royalist troops and the outer fortifications were razed in 1631. It reverted to the crown and was used as a prison where Fouquet, his financial adviser, and the Duke of Lauzun, the lady-killer, were imprisoned by Louis XIV.

Later Napoleon granted the château to Roger Ducos, a former member of the Directory. As there were no subsidies for its upkeep, he had a large part of it demolished. The château now belongs to the St-Louis Foundation which was set up by the Count of Paris to preserve the French national heritage.

Tour ⊘ *45min*

Terrace – The château is entered by a ramp which opens on to the terrace overlooking the river. From here there is a magnificent **view★★** of the Loire flowing lazily through the rich green valley, and of Amboise town's pointed roofs and walls. The silhouette of the Tour de l'Horloge (15C belfry) can be seen rising above the rooftops not far from the old town walls, and to the west that of the imposing church of St-Denis with its squat bell-tower, while Le Clos-Lucé can be glimpsed to the southeast.

In the time of Charles VIII the terrace was entirely surrounded by buildings. Festivals were held in this enclosed courtyard: tapestries adorned the walls, and a sky-blue awning decorated with sun, moon and stars gave protection from the weather.

Chapelle St-Hubert (B E) – Curiously set astride the fortified town walls this jewel of Flamboyant Gothic architecture is all that remains of the buildings which once lined the ramparts.

The chapel, with its harmonious proportions and finely sculpted decoration, crowned by a delicate spire, is the work of Flemish masters who were brought to Amboise by Louis XI; they were also employed by Charles VIII before his admiration turned to Italian art. Built in 1491 it was Anne of Brittany's oratory. The transept houses the tomb thought to contain the body of the great artist Leonardo da Vinci, who died at Amboise.

Outside, admire the Gothic door panels and the finely carved lintel: on the left **St Christopher** carries the Infant Christ while on the right **St Hubert**, the patron saint

of hunting, is depicted prostrating himself before a glowing cross which has appeared between the antlers of a stag he was hunting.

Logis royal – The royal apartments are the only part of the château which escaped demolition between 1806 and 1810. The Gothic wing, which overlooks the ramparts above the Loire, was built by Charles VIII (1483-98), as was the adjacent Tour des Minimes. The Renaissance wing set at right angles to it, on the other hand, was constructed by Louis XII and had another storey added to it under François I.

The tour begins in the lower storey of the Gothic wing, where the guards kept watch. The **Salle des gardes nobles**, or guardroom, recently opened to the public, is roofed with vaulting supported on a single column, forming a Gothic "palm-tree" of ribs.

M. Desjardins/TOP

Amboise – Chapelle St-Hubert

A spiral staircase leads up to the **Salle des tambourineurs** (named after the drummers who accompanied the king on royal visits), where Charles VIII sequestered himself from the public gaze. The room contains some interesting pieces of furniture (Cardinal Georges d'Amboise's pulpit) and a beautiful Brussels tapestry (16C) on the wall depicting *Homage to Alexander the Great*. Leading on from the Salle des tambourineurs is the Salle du Conseil, also known as the **Salle des États** (Hall of State). This features a double stone vault supported by a line of columns down the centre of the room, which is liberally adorned with motifs of the Kingdom of France and the Duchy of Brittany, the fleur-de-lis and ermine. It was here that the king presided over the State Council which decided on policies of the realm. Continue the visit in the second wing, built at the beginning of the 16C and furnished in early French Renaissance style: wine-waiter's sideboard, a Gothic piece with a distinctive linen-fold motif, carved extendable tables and chests in walnut. In Henri II's bedchamber, *trompe-l'œil* decoration is continued onto furniture and wall hangings. On the first floor three adjoining rooms, the suite of apartments fitted out for Louis-Philippe, contain a collection of furniture and portraits of the d'Orléans family, including a grand piano (1842), armchairs bearing the manufacturer's stamp of Jacob and paintings from the workshop of German master painter Winterhalter.

> The wars of religion have left here the ineffaceable stain which they left wherever they passed. An imaginative visitor at Amboise to-day may fancy that the traces of blood are mixed with the red rust on the crossed iron bars of the grim-looking balcony, to which the heads of the Huguenots executed on the discovery of the conspiracy of La Renaudie are rumoured to have been suspended. There was room on the stout balustrade – an admirable piece of work – for a ghastly array.
>
> **Henry James** *A Little Tour in France*

Tour des Minimes ou des Cavaliers – This round tower adjoining the Logis royal is famous for its wide ramp which horsemen could ride up, ensuring easy access for the provisioning of supplies from the outbuildings in the gardens. The ramp spirals round an empty core which provides air and light. From the top (40m/130ft above the Loire) there is a sweeping view★★ of the Loire valley, the Gothic wing of the château and, to the left, the balcony from which several of the conspirators of 1560 were hung.

Gardens – These pleasant gardens, redesigned in the 19C under Louis-Philippe, lie within the rampart walls where parts of the château once stood. Most of the park is laid out in the informal English style and a border of lime trees has replaced the Italian Renaissance garden of the 16C. A bust of Leonardo da Vinci stands on the site of the collegiate church, where the master of the Renaissance was originally buried.

Tour Heurtault (B L) – This tower set in the château's south wall features a spiral ramp like the Tour des Minimes, to which it forms a counterpart. The detail on the sculpted corbels supporting the rib vaulting is particularly interesting. The tower leads directly to the town of Amboise.

★ LE CLOS-LUCÉ (B) ⏱ 1hr

Le Clos-Lucé, a manor house of red brick relieved by tufa dressings, was acquired by Charles VIII in 1490. François I, Margaret of Navarre and their mother, the regent Louise of Savoy, also resided here. In 1516, François I invited **Leonardo da Vinci** to Amboise and lodged him at Le Clos-Lucé where the great artist and scholar organised the court festivities and lived until his death on 2 May 1519 at the age of 67.

The wooden gallery in the courtyard, all that remains of a medieval construction, gives a good view of the manor's main façade. On the first floor is the bedroom, restored and furnished, where Da Vinci died, as well as his studio. This is where he would have worked on schemes such as his project for the draining of the Sologne or his design for a palace at **Romorantin** for Louise of Savoy.

Self-portrait of Leonardo da Vinci

The ground floor includes the oratory built by Charles VIII for Anne of Brittany, the salons with 18C wainscots where Da Vinci probably had his workshops, the Renaissance reception room and the kitchen with its monumental chimneypiece. In the basement is the museum of Leonardo's **"fabulous machines"**, a collection of models made by IBM based on the designs of this polymath who was painter, sculptor, musician, poet, architect, engineer and scholar all in one, and whose ideas were four centuries ahead of his time. Note the entrance to the secret passageway which the King used on his visits to Da Vinci.

The grounds include gardens laid out in Renaissance style, from the terrace of which there is a view back to the château and over the river.

For visitors who wish to know more about Leonardo, there is a video of his life and works, portraying not only the artist but also the humanist who considered the spiritual dimension in his scientific work.

A short stroll in the park down to the river is an ideal way of rounding off the visit.

ADDITIONAL SIGHTS

Musée de la Poste (B M¹) ⊙ – Housed in the early 16C Hôtel Joyeuse, the post office museum has fascinating collections tracing the development of postal services in France. On the ground floor is a display of models of coaches, **badges**, postilions' uniforms, including the legendary "seven-league boots" and various documents dating back to the days of horse-drawn carriages and inns founded by Louis IX, when mail was exclusively "royal". The early 18C *Guide classique du voyageur en France et en Belgique*, listing the addresses of the roadhouses and the approximate distance between them, and offering information on regional geography, towns and sights, is a reminder that the post office book was the ancestor of the modern travel guide. The upper floors are devoted to the history of the letter post, a distribution network accessible to one and all, and to that of air mail and maritime services. Note the famous Boules de Moulins – zinc globes containing messages that were floated along the river from the capital to the provinces during the Paris siege in 1870-71. The carriage room contains the famous pistols used by the Russian poet Pushkin in the duel that was to end his life in 1837.

A room on the second floor presents wireless radio sets and pays tribute to the Gody establishment, France's most long-standing manufacturer, who invented the first radio set functioning with tubes in 1919. Based in Amboise between 1912 and 1955, this "thriving hive of radio electronics" often made reference to the historical and architectural heritage of the Val de Loire when advertising its products.

Musée de l'Hôtel de ville (B M²) ⊙ – *Entrance on rue François-1ᵉʳ.*
The former town hall, which was built early in the 16C for Pierre Morin, treasurer to the King of France, now houses a museum containing examples of the royal signature, a 14C carving of the Virgin Mary, Aubusson tapestries, portraits of the Duke of Choiseul and six rare 18C gouaches of the Château de Chanteloup, depicting it at the height of its splendour.

Tour de l'Horloge (B F) – The clock tower, which is also known as the Amboise belfry and has recently been restored, was built in the 15C at the expense of the inhabitants on the site of a town gateway called l'Amasse. It spans a busy pedestrian street.

Nearby on the old town ramparts stands a church, the **église St-Florentin (B)**, built at the behest of Louis XI.

Église St-Denis (A) – This compact little church dates mostly from the 12C. Inside there are Angevin vaults and, in the nave, fine Romanesque capitals. The south aisle has a 16C Entombment, the recumbent figure known as the Drowned Woman *(Femme noyée)* and an interesting 17C painting of *Charles VIII welcoming St Francis of Paola to Amboise.*

La Maison Enchantée (B M³) ⊙ – The magic atmosphere of this "enchanted house" is probably due to the exuberant yet studied sense of disorder that reigns in the rooms, bringing to mind the carefree memories of childhood. The various exhibits – dolls, puppets, large mannequins and automata – are arranged with humour (the dentist's surgery and its waiting room, the "saloon"), sensitivity ("sitting on the bench", the toys in the attic) and refinement (the fashion parade, the "animals' ball").

Mini-Châteaux ⊙ – *South of town, along the Chenonceaux road (D 81).*
This 2ha/5 acre park is home to 60 or so models (scale 1:25) of great châteaux and smaller manor houses of the Loire valley, displayed in a setting commensurate with their size (bonsai trees, miniature TGV railway and boats on the river etc). By night, fibre-optical illuminations lend a fairy-tale atmosphere to the scene.

Le fou de l'âne ⊙ – *South of town, along the Chenonceaux road (D 81).*
Donkey-lovers will be interested in this park which is home to about 60 donkeys of various types, in reconstructions of their natural habitat. Besides admiring the donkeys themselves, visitors can look at the collection of saddles, harnesses and other equipment, as well as assorted literature on the subject of donkeys.

EXCURSION

★ **Aquarium de Touraine** ⊙ – *8km/5mi west along D 751; on leaving Lussault-sur-Loire, take D 283 and follow the signposted route.*
Devoted exclusively to European freshwater fish, this aquarium has the particularity of presenting the 70 species forming its stock in open-air basins. The advantage of this new technique is that it allows the fish to live according to the seasons, just as they would in their natural environment. Visitors, however, are always under shelter.
Each of the 38 aquariums has been designed to present a specific natural setting. One evokes a mountain torrent, peopled with fish belonging to the *Salmonidae* family (rainbow trout, Fario, grayling), another shows rivers and streams of the Upper Loire, teeming with minnows, stickleback, gudgeon and various types of loach, yet another resembles a series of small lakes, home to numerous carp, pike, bream, roach, tench and perch. Note the pike-perch and crucian carp swimming along a carefully-reconstituted bank of the Loire river. The most impressive aquarium is no 20, a 40 000 litre/8 800 gallon basin accommodating giant sturgeon, also known as *acipenser baeri* or *transmontanus*.

Leonardo da Vinci on CD-ROM

On his death at Le Clos-Lucé in 1519, Leonardo da Vinci left several thousands of pages of manuscript, executed in his unique mirror-writing to preserve his ideas from the prying eyes of potential competitors. His writings, illustrated with diagrams, cover a wide range of subjects – engineering, music, sculpture, painting, science – in keeping with the universal scope of his genius. This valuable legacy became the property of Francesco Melzi, one of Leonardo's students. When Melzi died in 1570, the collection was divided by his heirs. The manuscripts were bound into volumes, or codices, the largest of which is the *Codex Altanticus* comprising 1 119 leaves, now kept at the Biblioteca Ambrosiana in Milan.
The *Codex Leicester*, formerly the *Codex Hammer*, is the smallest of these volumes, with 36 folios (72 pages) setting out some of Leonardo's thoughts on hydrology, paleontology and cosmology. It is the only manuscript of Leonardo's to be privately-owned – by none other than Bill Gates, since November 1994. It cost the founder and president of Microsoft over 30 million dollars at Christie's in New York, breaking all previous records for the price fetched at auction by a manuscript. Gates became the latest in a long line of owners of the manuscript, but he is the only one not to have given it his name, preferring it to retain the name of the British family who owned it from the early 18C to 1980. Following his purchase, Gates organised exhibitions of the *Codex Leicester* in Rome, New York and Paris. The fragile state of the manuscripts make it difficult to display them for any but the most superficial of viewings, so a CD-ROM version has been brought out by Gates and his computer graphics company Corbis for those seeking to read the manuscripts in any detail. The *Codex Leicester* is now on show back in Seattle, prior to being transferred for safe-keeping to a specially designed cabinet in the library of Gates's magnificent new home there. *(For further information on the Codex Leicester, look in the Corbis.com website on the Internet).*

ANGERS★★★

Conurbation 206 276
Michelin maps 63 fold 20 and 64 fold 11 or 232 fold 31
Local maps see Vallée de la LOIRE: Chinon-Champtoceaux
and Vallée de la MAYENNE
Plan of the conurbation in the current Michelin Red Guide France

The former capital of Anjou stands on the banks of the Maine, formed by the confluence of the Mayenne and the Sarthe, 8km/5mi before it flows into the Loire. Modern Angers is a lively town, with a youthful population thanks to its university (25 000 students). Quality of life here is renowned for its excellence even by French standards, and with about 42m²/450ft² of undeveloped land per head of population the town is one of the prettiest in France, with numerous parks and gardens bright with flowers in season. The attraction of the distinctive local architecture lies not least in its striking combination of pale tufa and dark slate.

Angers can boast a flourishing trade based on Anjou wines, liqueurs (Cointreau), early fruit and vegetables, seeds, flowers, medicinal plants and other horticultural products (it is home to a highly reputed horticultural centre which is at the forefront of research in this field). High-tech industries also thrive here (electronics and car accessories). Home to the famous medieval *Apocalypse tapestry* and its modern replica, the *Chant du Monde*, as well as to the **Jean-Lurçat museum of contemporary tapestry**, Angers has become an international centre for the art of tapestry-making.

The **Anjou festival** *(see Calendar of events)*, with its many and varied entertainments (drama, music, dancing, poetry, art etc), takes place in July throughout the Maine-et-Loire *département* and draws large appreciative audiences with the quality of its performances. Angers also offers a programme of cultural events and entertainment during the summer months.

HISTORICAL NOTES

In the 1C BC Angers was at the centre of a community of hunters and fishermen. Their chief was Domnacus, who took to the heaths and forests and never submitted to the Romans who captured the city.

From Romans to Vikings – Angers-Juliomagus, the capital of the Andes tribe, covered 80ha/200 acres and flourished in the 2C AD. Unfortunately few archeological traces of this brilliant past have survived. In the Late Empire the city went into decline and was obliged to confine itself to a small area (9ha/20 acres) on a slope above the River Maine; under the combined effect of the threat of invasion by Germanic tribes and general impoverishment the population level dropped. Christianity, on the other hand, continued to gain influence and in 453 AD a church council met in Angers. Bishop Thalaise was one of the important ecclesiastical figures of the period, a scholar who protected and defended his city.

Angers's religious rise was not affected by the bloody quarrels of the Merovingian succession; the abbeys of St-Aubin and St-Serge were founded in the 6C and 7C and soon attracted new settlements. Under the Carolingians the town recovered but was soon destabilised by the revolts of the nobility and Viking invasions. In December 854 the Vikings pillaged Angers but then withdrew. In 872 they returned and held the town for over a year. Charles the Bald, assisted by the Duke of Brittany, laid siege to the invaders and succeeded in dislodging them; a more or less legendary tradition says that Charles dug a canal intending to divert the waters of the Maine and when the Vikings realised that their ships would be grounded they fled in panic.

First House of Anjou (10C-13C) – Under the early Counts, who were called Fulk, Angers flourished.

The founders – The weakness of the throne at the end of the 9C encouraged the emergence of independent principalities. The first Angevin dynasty was established in 898 by Fulk the Red, Viscount and then Count of Angers, a title which he handed down to his descendants. Fulk II the Good extended his territory into Maine showing scant regard for the King of France, delicate Louis IV of Outre-Mer, whom he openly despised, while Geoffrey I Grisegonelle exacted homage from the Count of Nantes. The Angevins also played a more subtle game manoeuvring between the Robertians (ancestors of the Capets), who were well established in the region, and the Carolingians whose power continued to wane.

Fulk Nerra and his successors – The rise of the Angevin dynasty to the height of its power in the 11C and 12C was due to its members' exceptional political skill, uninhibited by any scruples, remarkable ability in warfare and keen eye for alliances through marriage. **Fulk III Nerra** (987-1040) was the most formidable of this line of feudal giants. Hot-blooded and aggressive, he was always making war to extend his territory; one by one he obtained Saintonge as fief of the Duke of Aquitaine, annexed les Mauges, extended his boundaries to Blois and Châteaudun, captured Langeais and Tours (he was expelled from the latter by Robert the Pious), intervened in the Vendômois, took Saumur etc. Ambitious, predatory, covetous, brutal and criminally violent, Fulk Nerra ("the Black" owing to his very dark complexion) was typical of the great feudal lord in the year 1000. From time to time he had sudden fits of Christian humility and penitence when he would shower gifts on churches and abbeys or take up the pilgrim's staff and depart for Jerusalem.

His son Geoffrey II (1040-60) continued his father's work consolidating the conquest of Maine and Touraine but died without issue. The succession was divided between his two nephews who lost no time in quarrelling. Fulk IV, the Morose, finally gained the upper hand over Geoffrey III, at the cost of the Saintonge, Maine and Gâtinais which he was too lazy to try to recover. In 1092 his second wife, the young and beautiful Bertrade de Monfort, was seduced, abducted and married by King Philip I. For this scandalous behaviour the King was excommunicated *(see BEAUGENCY)*. The family's fortunes were salvaged by Geoffrey IV Martel, killed in 1106, and most of all by **Fulk V the Younger** (1109-31), who took advantage of Anglo-French rivalry and made judicious marriage alliances. He recovered Maine through his own marriage in 1109; two years later with the family's approval he married his two daughters to the kings of France and England. His greatest success however was the marriage in 1128 of his son Geoffrey to Mathilda of England, daughter and heir to Henry I and widow of the German Emperor Henry V. His ultimate achievement concerned himself: in 1129, by then a widower, he married Melisand, daughter of Baldwin II and heir to the kingdom of Jerusalem. He founded a new Angevin dynasty in the Holy Land and consolidated the position of the Frankish kingdoms.

Geoffrey V (1131-51), known as Plantagenet because he wore a sprig of broom *(genêt)* in his hair, ruled with a rod of iron over "Greater Anjou" (Anjou, Touraine and Maine) and tried to exercise his wife's rights over Normandy, which he annexed in 1144, and England, where Stephen of Blois had been king since 1135. Geoffrey died in 1151.

Plantagenets and Capets

In 1152 **Henry Plantagenet**, son of Geoffrey and Mathilda, married Eleanor of Aquitaine whom Louis VII had recently divorced. He already held Anjou, Maine, Touraine and Normandy; by his marriage he acquired Poitou, Périgord, the Limoges and Angoulême regions, Saintonge, Gascony and suzerainty of the Auvergne and the County of Toulouse. In 1153 he forced Stephen of Blois to recognise him as his heir and the following year he succeeded him on the throne of England. He was now more powerful than his Capet rival. Henry II of England spent most of his time in France, usually at Angers. "He was a redhead, of medium height, with a square, leonine face and prominent eyes, which were candid and gentle when he was in a good humour but flashed fire when he was irritated. From morning to night he was involved in matters of state. He was always on the go and never sat down except to eat or ride a horse. When he was not handling a bow or a sword, he was closeted in Council or reading. None was more clever or eloquent than he; when he was free from his responsibilities he liked to engage in discussion with scholars." (M. Pacaut).

For the next 50 years there was war between the Plantagenets and the Capets. In the end it was the latter who were victorious: by relying on the subtleties of feudal law, they played upon the separatist tendencies of the individual provinces brought together in the Anglo-Angevin empire and the dissension dividing the Plantagenets. Philippe-Auguste inflicted a harsh blow when he captured the French territory of King John in 1205; this meant that Anjou and Touraine ceased to belong to the English crown but England and France continued to fight one another for supremacy until the end of the Hundred Years War.

Successive Anjou Dynasties (13C-15C)

During the regency of Blanche of Castille, Anjou was again lost as a result of the barons' revolt when Pierre de Dreux surrendered the province to Henry III. Taking advantage of a truce in 1231 Blanche and her son Louis began to build the impressive fortress of Angers.

Anjou returned to the Capet sphere of influence and in 1346 St Louis gave it, together with Maine, to his younger brother Charles as an apanage. In 1258 it was confirmed as a French possession by the Treaty of Paris. In 1360 Anjou was raised to a duchy by John the Good for his son Louis. From the 13C to the 15C Anjou was governed by the direct line of Capet princes and then by the Valois. The beginning and end of this period were marked by two outstanding personalities, Charles I and King René.

Charles of Anjou – Charles was an unusual character – deeply religious and at the same time madly ambitious. At the request of the Pope, he conquered Sicily and the Kingdom of Naples and established his influence over the rest of the Italian peninsula. Intoxicated with his success he dreamed of adding the Holy Land, Egypt and Constantinople to his conquests but the Sicilian Vespers awoke him rudely to reality: on Easter Monday 1282 the Sicilians revolted and massacred 6 000 Frenchmen half of whom were Angevins.

Good King René – The last of the dukes was Good King René – titular monarch of Sicily. He had one of the most cultivated minds of his day; having mastered Latin, Greek, Italian, Hebrew and Catalan, he also painted and wrote poetry, played and composed music and was knowledgeable about mathematics, geology and law. He was an easy-going, informal ruler who liked to talk to his subjects; he organised popular festivities and revived the old games of the age of chivalry. He loved flower gardens and introduced the carnation and the Provins rose. At 12 he married Isabelle de Lorraine and was devoted to her for 33 years until her death, shortly after which, at the age of 47, he married Jeanne de Laval who was only 21. Despite the odds, this was also a happy marriage. Towards the end of his life René accepted the annexation of Anjou by Louis XI philosophically. As he was also Count of Provence he left Angers, which he had greatly enriched, and ended his days in Aix-en-Provence at the age of 72 (1480). During the period of the Duchy a university was founded in Angers which flourished with 4 000 to 5 000 students from 10 nations.

Henri IV to the present – The Wars of Religion took on a bitter twist at Angers where there was a strongly entrenched Calvinist church; a dispute on 14 October 1560 brought death to numerous townspeople. Thereafter confrontations grew more frequent and in 1572 the town experienced its own St Barthlomew's Day massacre. It was at the château of Angers in 1598 that Henri IV finally brought the fomenting discontent of the Catholic League to an end by promising his son César *(see VENDÔME)* to Françoise de Lorraine, daughter of the Duc de Mercœur, the leader of the Catholic party. The marriage contract was signed on 5 April, when the bride and groom were six and three years old. A week later the Edict of Nantes came into force; the Protestants had obtained freedom of worship. In 1652, although held by the forces of the Fronde, Angers had to submit to Mazarin; in 1657 the town lost its right to elect its local magistrates. After his arrest in Nantes Louis XIV's Finance Minister, **Fouquet**, spent three weeks in the château in the governor's apartments, guarded by d'Artagnan. By then the town had about 25 000 inhabitants and was only slightly industrialised.

At the outbreak of the Revolution in 1789, Angers declared enthusiastically for the reformers. The cathedral was sacked and turned into a temple of Reason. In 1793 the defection of the Girondin administration allowed the Royalist Vendée party to capture the town between 20 June and 4 July. The Republicans lost no time in retaking it and the Terror claimed many victims.

In the early 19C Angers dozed until awakened by the arrival of the railway line from Paris to Nantes: the station was opened in 1849 by Louis-Napoléon. Modern development had begun and, apart from a brief lull early in the 20C, it has continued to expand during recent decades.

★★★ CHÂTEAU (AZ) ⏱ *2hr*

The **fortress**, which incorporates the former Plantagenet fief, was built by St Louis between 1228 and 1238 and is a fine specimen of feudal architecture in dark schist alternating with courses of white stone. The castle moats are now laid out as splendid gardens. The 17 round towers, strung out over 1km/0.5mi, are 40-50m/131-164ft high.

Château d'Angers

The towers were originally one or two storeys taller and crowned with pepper-pot roofs and machicolations. They were reduced to the level of the curtain walls under Henri III during the Wars of Religion. The original order had been to demolish the fortress entirely, but the governor simply removed the tops of the towers and laid down terraces there, to give defenders a clear field of fire. The king then died, thus saving the rest of the building from destruction. From the top of the highest tower, the **Tour du Moulin** (Mill Tower), on the north corner, there are interesting **views★** over the town, the cathedral towers and St-Aubin, the banks of the Maine and the gardens laid out at the foot of the castle, and, in the castle precincts, the series of towers on the curtain wall, the sophisticated design of the gardens interspersed with topiary arches, the chapel and the **Logis royal** (Royal Apartments), residence of the Dukes of Anjou in the 15C.

Follow the **rampart walk** along the east side where a charming medieval garden is laid out with lavender, marguerites and hollyhocks growing in profusion near a vine like those which King René loved to plant.

★★★ Apocalypse tapestry – Housed in a specially designed building this famous tapestry is the oldest and largest to survive until the present. It was commissioned by Nicolas Bataille for Duke Louis I of Anjou and probably made in Paris at the workshops of Robert Poinçon between 1373 and 1383, after cartoons by Hennequin of Bruges based on an illuminated manuscript belonging to King Charles V. It was used at the marriage of Louis II of Anjou to Yolande of Aragon in Arles in 1400 and then at religious festivals until the end of the 18C when King René bequeathed it to the cathedral. It was later discarded as a piece of no value, but one of the cathedral canons had it restored between 1843 and 1870.

Originally 133m/436ft long and 6m/20ft high, it consisted of six sections of equal size, each with a main character sitting under a canopy, their eyes turned towards two rows of seven pictures, the alternating red and blue backgrounds of which form a chequered design. Two long borders represent heaven, filled with angel-musicians, and earth, strewn with flowers (first part missing).

The 76 scenes which have survived form a superb piece of work; the biblical text corresponding to each scene appears opposite the tapestries together with a reproduction of the reverse side.

One cannot remain unmoved by the scale of the work, its rigorously disciplined composition, as well as its great decorative value and purity of design. The tapestry closely follows the text of the Apocalypse as recounted in the Revelation of John, the last book of the New Testament, in which a divine revelation foretells the coming of a "new Jerusalem", or Christ's kingdom on earth. To rekindle the hope of Christians shattered by violence and persecution all around them, the artist depicts the ultimate victory of Christ in the form of prophetic visions and, after many ordeals, the triumph of his Church.

Chapelle et Logis royal – These 15C buildings, which house the chapel and Royal Apartments, stand inside the rampart wall. In the vast and well-lit chapel, note the finely sculptured Gothic leaves of the door, the small separate ducal chapel with a fireplace and, on a keystone, an image of the Anjou cross *(see BAUGÉ)*. The adjacent staircase, the work of King René, leads to the upper floor of the apartments.

★★ Passion and Mille-fleurs tapestries – The Royal Apartments house a beautiful collection of 15C and 16C tapestries including the four hangings of the late-15C **Passion tapestry**, which are wonderfully rich in colour, and several *mille-fleurs* tapestries. Among these is the tapestry entitled **Angels carrying the Instruments of the Passion**, which is unusual in that it has a religious theme, the admirable 16C **Lady at the Organ** and a fragment showing **Penthesilea**, the Queen of the Amazons, from a hanging of the Nine Heroines, women with chivalrous virtues.

Angers – Passion Tapestry:
Angel carrying Pilate's ewer

★ **OLD TOWN** *allow half a day*

Start from the château entrance and take small rue St-Aignan.

Hôtel du Croissant (AY B) – This 15C mansion, with mullion windows and ogee arches, housed the registrar of the Order of the Crescent (Ordre du Croissant), a military and religious chivalrous order founded by King René. The blazon on the façade bears the coat of arms of St Maurice, patron of the order, a 4C Christian legionary put to death because he refused to kill his fellow Christians. Opposite stand picturesque half-timbered houses.

Continue to Montée St-Maurice, a long flight of steps which leads to the cathedral square (fine view of the cathedral).

★★ **Cathédrale St-Maurice (BY)** ⊘ – The cathedral is a fine 12C and 13C building. The Calvary standing to the left of the façade is by David d'Angers.

Façade – This is surmounted by three towers, the central tower having been added in the 16C. The **doorway** was damaged by the Protestants and the Revolutionaries, and in the 18C by the canons, who removed the central pier and the lintel to make way for processions. Notice the fine statues on the door splays. The tympanum portrays Christ the King surrounded by the symbols of the Four Evangelists; the graceful folds of the garments show skilful carving.

Above at the third-storey level are eight niches containing roughly carved, bearded figures in 16C military uniforms: St Maurice and his companions.

CATHÉDRALE ST-MAURICE

Interior – The single nave is roofed with one of the earliest examples of Gothic vaulting which originated in Anjou in the mid 12C. This transitional style known as Angevin or Plantagenet vaulting *(see Introduction: Art)* has the characteristic feature that the keystones of the diagonal (ogive) arches are at least 3m/10ft above the keys of the transverse and stringer arches giving a more rounded or domical form. In Gothic vaulting all the keys are at roughly the same level. The vaulting of St-Maurice covers the widest nave built at that time measuring 16.38m/54ft across, whereas the usual width was 9-12m/30-40ft; the capitals in the nave and the brackets supporting the gallery with its wrought-iron balustrade feature remarkable carved decoration. The gallery is supported by a relieving arch at each bay. The Angevin vaulting in the transept is of a later period than that in the nave, with more numerous and more graceful ribs. The evolution of this style was to continue along these lines.

The chancel, finished in the late 12C, has the same Angevin vaulting as the transept. Its 13C stained glass has particularly vivid blues and reds.

The church is majestically furnished: 18C great organ (**A**) supported by colossal telamones, monumental 19C pulpit (**B**), high altar (**C**) surmounted by marble columns supporting a canopy of gilded wood (18C), 18C carved stalls (**D**) in front of which is a marble statue of St Cecilia (**E**) by David d'Angers. The walls are hung with tapestries, mostly from Aubusson.

St-Maurice's **stained-glass windows**★★ allow visitors to follow the evolution of the art of the master glaziers from the 12C to the present. *Detailed printed description of the windows in the church; they are best examined through binoculars.*

1 St Catherine of Alexandria (12C).
2 Dormition and Assumption of the Virgin (12C).
3 The martyrdom of St Vincent of Spain (12C).
4 Transept rose windows (15C): to the left Christ showing his wounds and to the right Christ in Majesty.
5 North transept side windows (15C): St Rémi and Mary Magdalene.
6 Chancel windows (13C) – from left to right: life of St Peter and St Eloi; St Christopher (16C); St Lawrence; the Tree of Jesse; St Julian; the life of Christ, and the lives of Saints Maurille, Martin, Thomas Becket and John the Baptist.

The modern stained-glass windows of the Chapelle Notre-Dame-de-Pitié (Our Lady of Mercy) and the south aisle bear witness to a revival of this art which had been in decline since the 16C.

Walk past the Bishop's Palace (Évêché) to reach rue de l'Oisellerie.

At nos 5 and 7, there are two lovely half-timbered houses dating from the 16C.

Take the first road on the right.

Out and about in Angers

Tourist information – Brochures in English on the town of Angers and on three waymarked walks around town *(see below)* are available from the local tourist office, which also produces a small brochure in French entitled *Angers: simplifiez-vous la ville* with detailed information for visitors.

Exploring on foot – Three themed walks are waymarked around town, with information panels along the way, on the town and outskirts of Angers, façades and gardens and the Doutre district. Accompanying leaflets are available in English from the tourist office.

Taking the tourist train – Several trips are operated, leaving from the tourist office opposite the château; some combine the trip with a visit to a museum or a boat cruise on the Maine.

Local specialities – "Quernons d'ardoise" (chocolate and nougatine tinted to look like chunks of local slate), Cointreau and, of course, local Anjou wines!

Entertainment – Addresses include: Auditorium du Centre des Congrès, ☎ 02 41 93 40 40; Nouveau théâtre d'Angers, ☎ 02 41 87 80 80; Théâtre musical d'Angers, ☎ 02 41 60 40 40; Théâtre Chanzy, ☎ 02 41 24 16 30.

Dates for your diary – **January:** European close-shot cinema festival; **February:** Loire wine fair; **July:** Anjou festival; **August/September:** Haut-Anjou music festival; **November:** Journalism festival.

★ **Maison d'Adam** (**BYZ D**) – This picturesque 16C half-timbered house has posts decorated with numerous carved figures. It owes its name to the apple tree which appears to hold up the corner turret and which was flanked by statues of Adam and Eve until the Revolution. By chance, in the 18C this house was inhabited by a magistrate called Michel Adam.

Continue along rue Toussaint.

No 37 (**BZ L**) has a classical doorway, once the entrance to the abbey of Toussaint (All Saints'). It leads to an elegant little courtyard flanked by a turret on a squinch to the right.

★ **Galerie David d'Angers** (**BZ E**) ⊘ – *33 bis rue Toussaint.*
The gallery in this restored 13C abbey church houses practically the complete collection of plaster casts donated by the sculptor David d'Angers to his native town. The Plantagenet vaulting has been replaced by a vast iron-framed glass roof, so that weather conditions play a major part in the lighting of the exhibition.
The well-displayed collection comprises monumental statues (King René, Gutenberg, Jean Bart whose bronze statue stands in Dunkerque), funerary monuments (eg of General Bonchamps whose tomb is in the church of **St-Florent-le-Vieil**), busts of famous people of the time (Chateaubriand, Victor Hugo, Balzac), and medallions in bronze of the artist's contemporaries.
The chancel with its square east end lit by a rose window added in the 18C contains a display of terracotta studies, drawings and sketch books as well as the graceful *Young Greek Girl* which adorned Markos Botzaris's tomb. In a windowed recess stands the *Young Shepherd*, set off to perfection against the greenery of the gardens of the modern public library.
To the south of the church are the 18C cloisters with two remaining galleries *(restored).*

Go round the east end of the church to reach Logis Barrault.

Logis Barrault (**BZ**) ⊘ – This beautiful late-15C residence housing a **Fine Arts Museum** was built by Olivier Barrault, the King's Secretary, Treasurer to the Brittany States and Mayor of Angers. In the 17C it was taken over by the seminary, whose pupils included **Talleyrand** *(see VALENÇAY)*, the future Bishop of Autun.
On the first floor are the collections belonging to the archeological museum, evoking the history of Anjou from the 12C to the 14C (enamels, carved wooden works, statuary etc). Note the 12C reliquary-cross, the fine 13C mask on the recumbent statue and the 16C terracotta **Virgin of Tremblay**. A display case devoted to "precious arts" exhibits splendid ivories and painted enamels.
The second floor is devoted to paintings: lovely primitive works, two remarkable small portraits of Charles IX as a young man and Catherine de' Medici after Clouet; 17C paintings (Philippe de Champaigne, Mignard) and above all the 18C French School (Chardin, Fragonard, Watteau, Boucher, Lancret, Greuze)

ANGERS

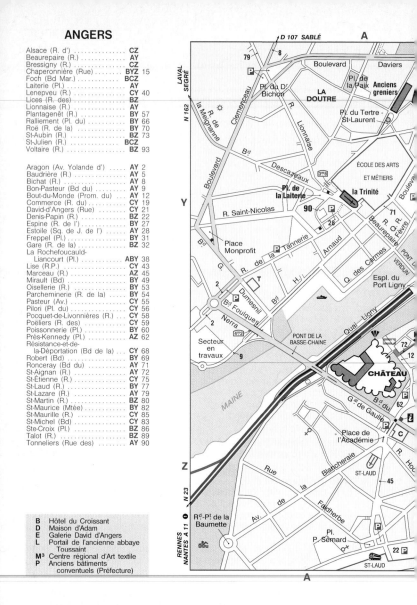

together with sculptures by Lemoyne, Houdon and Falconet; and 19C works including sketches by David, Ingres, Géricault, Delacroix, landscapes by Corot and Jongkind. There are also canvases by the local painters Lenepveu and Bodinier, and pastels (separate room) by Alexis Axilette, who was born at Durtal.

Tour St-Aubin (BZ) – This is the belfry (12C) of the former abbey of St-Aubin, a wealthy Benedictine abbey founded in the 6C. The tower takes its name from St Aubin, Bishop of Angers (538-550), who was buried here.

★ **Monastery buildings (BZ P)** ⊙ – The abbey buildings, extensively restored in the 17C and 18C, are now local government offices. On the left side of the courtyard is a glazed-in **Romanesque arcade**★★, part of the cloisters, with sculptures of remarkably refined craftsmanship. The door with sculpted arch mouldings led to the chapter-house; the arcades support a gallery from which those monks who had no voice in the chapter could listen to the proceedings; decorating the twin bay on the right of the door is a Virgin in Majesty with two censing angels while on the archivolt a multitude of angels bustle about; beneath this is painted the scene of the Three Wise Men: on the left Herod is depicted sending his men to massacre the innocents, while on the right the star is guiding the Wise Men.

The last arch on the right has the best preserved scene of all: in the centre the unequal combat between David armed with his sling and the giant Goliath in his coat of chain-mail is about to start; on the right the victorious David is cutting off the head of the vanquished giant and on the left he is offering his trophy to King Saul.

Take rue St-Martin to reach Place du Ralliement.

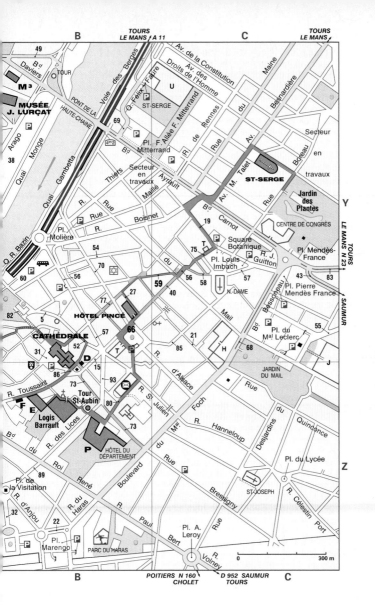

Place du Ralliement (**BY 66**) – This lively square marks the centre of town. Its shops are dominated by the monumental façade of the theatre, embellished with columns and statues.

Walk from the square into rue Lenepveu and then take the first street on the left, rue l'Espine.

★ **Hôtel Pincé** (**BY**) ⊘ – The Hôtel Pincé is a Renaissance mansion built for a Mayor of Angers and bequeathed to the town in 1861. It houses the **musée Turpin-de-Crissé**, originally based on the fine personal collection of this local painter (1772-1859) who was chamberlain to the Empress Josephine and a member of the Institut de France.

There are Greek and Etruscan vases on the ground floor and an Egyptian collection on the first floor. But the principal attraction is on the second floor, a beautiful collection of Japanese ceramics, masks and engravings, the bequest of the Count of St-Genys, nephew of Turpin de Crissé, as well as a Chinese collection (ceramics, bronzes, fabrics).

St-Laud district – The small rue St-Laud (**BY 77**) is the axis of a pleasant pedestrian and shopping district, where a number of very old façades can be admired: particularly good examples include no 21 rue St-Laud (15C) and no 9 rue des Poëliers (16C) (**CY 59**).

Take rue St-Étienne and rue du Commerce, then cross boulevard Carnot to reach the church of St-Serge.

★ **Église St-Serge** (CY) – Until 1802 this was the church of the Benedictine abbey of the same name founded in the 7C. The 13C **chancel**★★ is remarkably wide, elegant and well-lit, a perfect example of the Angevin style, with its lierne vaulting descending in feathered clusters onto slender columns. In contrast, the 15C nave seems narrower because of its massive pillars. At the end the high windows are filled with graceful 15C stained glass with monochrome backgrounds depicting the Prophets *(north side)* and the Apostles *(south side)*. On the rear wall of the chancel is a Flamboyant sacrarium where relics were kept. Beneath the organ-loft, a mural painting depicting St Christopher, which dates from the late 15C but which was covered over with white paint in the 18C, was uncovered in 1991.

Jardin des Plantes (CY) – Located behind the Centre des Congrès and opposite the old conventual buildings (18C) of St-Serge abbey church, this botanical garden is home to some beautiful, rare species of tree (such as the *Davidia*, or "handkerchief tree"). There is a pool in the lower part of the garden. Parrots can be heard squawking in the aviary. The small Romanesque church of St-Samson, restored in the 16C and 17C, used to be the parish church of the old town of St-Serge.

NORTH BANK OF THE RIVER MAINE *1hr*

★★ **Musée Jean-Lurçat et de la Tapisserie contemporaine** (ABY) ⊘ – This museum of contemporary tapestry is housed in the **Ancien hôpital St-Jean**★, a hospital founded in 1174 by Étienne de Marçay, Seneschal to the Plantagenet King Henry I, which provided treatment and care for the sick until 1854.

The vast hospital ward has Angevin vaulting resting on slender columns; to the right of the entrance is the 17C **dispensary**★ with glazed earthenware jars and trivets on the wooden shelves. In the central recess stands a splendid pewter vessel (1720) which once contained treacle, an antidote to snake bites.

The room is hung with Lurçat's famous series of tapestries called the **Chant du Monde**★★ (Song of the World). Jean Lurçat (1892-1966), who was largely responsible for reviving the art of tapestry, had discovered the *Apocalypse tapestry* *(see p. 57 above)* in 1938 and had been profoundly impressed by it, declaring it to be one of the masterpieces of western art. Nineteen years later he began work on the tapestry series displayed here, which constitutes his masterpiece. It consists of 10 compositions with a combined length of 80m/260ft, the fruit of years of research carried out by the artist himself; it is coarsely woven and characterized by an almost total lack of perspective and deliberate restriction of the range of colours. Evoking the joys and agonies of humanity in the face of Life and Death, it is an extraordinary synthesis of forms, colours and rhythms.

The doorway in the west wall leads to the Romanesque cloisters and a little garden containing a collection of stonework. The adjacent chapel has Angevin vaulting and a Baroque high altar and gallery. Further west still is the former **granary** with its twin bays. An annexe contains the Simone Lurçat bequest of paintings, ceramics and other tapestries made by her husband.

One of the rooms is devoted to tapestries constituting the Thomas Gleb donation. The ground floor is used for temporary exhibitions.

A short distance away, at no 3 boulevard Daviers, the **Centre régional d'Art textile** (BY M³) ⊘, which consists of a group of workshops for about 20 warp-weavers, organises guided tours and introductory training courses in the art of tapestry. The weavers here produce remarkable creations, displayed at national and international exhibitions, which can be subsequently bought or hired.

★ **La Doutre district** (AY) – The district "the other side of the Maine" *(d'outre Maine)* has kept its old timber-framed houses in good repair: in pretty place de la Laiterie (AY), in rue Beaurepaire which runs from the square to the bridge (note in particular no 67, the house of the apothecary Simon Poisson, which is ornamented with statues and dates from 1582) and along rue des Tonneliers (AY 90).

The church of **La Trinité** (AY) is a 12C building with a 16C belfry.

EXCURSIONS

Distillerie Cointreau ⊘ – *Take the Le Mans road, northeast on the town plan; then turn right onto boulevard de la Romanerie to the St-Barthélemy-d'Anjou industrial area.*

The famous clear, orange-flavoured liqueur was invented by the Cointreau brothers in 1849. Various attempts to fake it are on display in the museum of this distillery, as is the firm's own publicity material.

There is an audio-visual presentation *(12min)* and then visitors are taken round the production area with its stills as well as the maturing floors. The annual output of the plant amounts to some 28 million litres, three-quarters of which is exported.

★ **Château de Pignerolle** – *8km/5mi east of Angers on D 61, just past St-Barthélemy-d'Anjou.*

This château, which stands in a large public park of over 70ha/170 acres, is a replica of the Petit Trianon in Versailles. It was built in the 18C by an Angevin architect, Bardoul de la Bigottière, for Marcel Avril, King's Equerry and Master of the Riding Academy of Angers. During the Second World War the castle served successively as the seat of the Polish government in exile, the headquarters of the German admiral Doenitz, who made it his radio communications centre with the submarine fleet, and, after the liberation of France, the quarters for American units under General Patton.

The château now houses the **Musée européen de la Communication**★★ (European Museum of Communication) ⊙. The rich collection of scientific apparatus displayed in an instructive and lively manner traces the fascinating history of communication, the major steps in its development and the various modes of expression employed "from the tom-tom to the satellite". The ground floor, dedicated to Leonardo da Vinci, shows the origins of communication – language, the written word, the measurement of time, music, the invention of printing (through which cultural exchanges took place for the first time), the history of electricity, and the advent of telegraphy with its impact on man from a sociological and cultural point of view. A modern sculpture composed of several elements representing locomotion recalls this other aspect of communication. On the first floor is an extensive retrospective from wireless to radio – which made instantaneous communication possible – (an entire room is devoted to radio sets from 1898 to 1960) and television (there is a reconstruction of a 1950s recording studio). The second floor displays reconstructions of the salon in Jules Verne's *Nautilus* and Armstrong's landing on the moon. The imaginary future is represented by a couple of beings from Venus.

Musée européen de la communication, Angers

Musée européen de la Communication.
Aeroplane radio receiver (1918)

The well-designed and well-kept château grounds are a pleasant place for a stroll.

St-Sylvain-d'Anjou – *8km/5mi northeast on the Le Mans road.*

Archeologists and master carpenters have worked closely together to reconstruct as faithfully as possible a medieval **motte-and-bailey** ⊙, like those which made an appearance at the beginning of the feudal period.

At the end of the 10C and during the 11C and 12C, these wooden strongholds built on a steep man-made earthen mound (the *motte*) with a lower courtyard (the bailey or ward), were a common defensive feature. The feudal lord and his family, together with the chaplain and some guardsmen, would live in the keep. The rest of the soldiers, craftsmen and servants would live in buildings down in the bailey, which was enclosed by a ditch and a bank of earth surmounted by a palisade. Other buildings to be found in the bailey included stables, byres, barns, ovens and occasionally an oratory.

Les Ponts-de-Cé – *7km/4mi to the south on N 160.*

This is a straggling town about 3km (a couple of miles) long; its main street crosses a canal and several arms of the Loire, affording some fine views from its four bridges. The history of this small town includes many bloody episodes. Under Charles IX 800 camp-followers were thrown into the Loire; when the château was taken from the Huguenots in 1562, any surviving defenders were treated to a similar fate. In 1793 numerous Royalists were shot on the island that surrounds the château.

On the edge of the road, overlooking the Loire, stand the remains of a château, an ancient 15C fortress crowned with machicolations.

The Gothic church of **St-Aubin** has recently been restored after being gutted by fire in 1973. Some interesting furnishings survived the fire: altarpieces and statues (note the Christ in Captivity).

Trélazé – *7km/4mi east, on the road to Saumur.*

Trélazé is famous for its **slate** which has been quarried since the 12C. When the Loire was still a commercial highway, the blue-grey slates were transported upstream by boat to provide roofs for all the châteaux, manor houses and more modest residences which lined the banks of the river.

A slate museum, the **Musée de l'Ardoise** ⊙, has been set up on a 3ha/7-acre site near a disused quarry and presents the geological formation of slate, the traditional methods used in quarrying, the life of the men who worked in the quarries and finally something on modern quarrying techniques.

There is a demonstration of old-style slate splitting given by former "slate-men".

AREINES

Population 555
Michelin map 64 fold 6 or 238 fold 2 – 3km/2mi east of Vendôme
Local map see Vallée du LOIR: Bonneval-Vendôme

Areines, a village in the Loir plain, was an important town in the Roman era.

Church ⊙ – The plain façade is adorned by a 14C Madonna; the church itself is 12C. The interior is decorated with a group of interesting **frescoes**, executed with graceful draughtsmanship and a fresh palette.

On the oven vault of the apse is a majestic figure of Christ surrounded by symbols of the Evangelists: note the lion of St Mark, in stylised Byzantine manner; below are the Apostles with sky-blue haloes, typical of Loire valley art *(see p. 41)*; in the central window are warrior saints also with haloes.

The chancel vault shows the Lamb adored by angels; on the sides are the Annunciation and the Visitation, elegantly depicted, and a somewhat damaged Nativity scene. The frescoes on the walls of the chancel seem to be of a later period: the Marriage of the Virgin is on the right.

ARGENT-SUR-SAULDRE

Population 2 525
Michelin map 65 north of fold 11 or 238 northwest of fold 19

Print works, clothing factories, potteries and brickworks contribute to the commercial activity of this little town on the River Sauldre in the Sologne.

Château – The château was built on the banks of the Sauldre by the Sully family in the 13C; it was modified in the 15C and again in the 18C and now houses two interesting museums.

Musée des Métiers et Traditions de France ⊙ – The collections displayed in this Trades and Traditions Museum illustrate the life of country people from the 18C onward. There are reconstructed workshops (shoemaker, coppersmith, cooper) as well as agricultural implements, tools and household objects as made and used in the various regions of France. Leisure activities are also evoked with displays devoted to seasonal festivities. Particularly of interest are a late-19C sorcerer's chair from Berry and a compass elaborately decorated with the suits from playing cards. The museum also houses a large collection of late-19C Gien faience.

Église St-André – The former château chapel is entered through a stout belfry-porch (16C) with a spire rebuilt in the 17C. On the keystone of the chancel vault is the crucified figure of St Andrew, to whom the church is dedicated, while the baptismal chapel houses a stunning 16C group of the Trinity.

EXCURSIONS

★ **Étang du Puits to Cerdon** – *16km/10mi northwest. Cross the Sauldre and turn left onto D 176.*

★ **Étang du Puits** – This large and shining expanse of water covers 175ha/330 acres at the heart of an oak and pine forest; there is a fine view from the road along the retaining dyke. There are facilities for regattas as well as a beach, pedal-boats, rowing boats and a playground. There is good fishing, as the lake has plentiful resident carp, bream and pike which can weigh up to 15 pounds. The reservoir feeds the Sauldre canal.

Go round the reservoir on D 765 and then continue to Cerdon.

Cerdon – A peaceful, well-kept village in the Sologne. In the 15C church are several paintings and some fine modern stained glass in the chancel.

★ **Blancafort** – *8km/5mi southeast on D 8. See BLANCAFORT.*

ARVILLE

Population 122
Michelin map 60 southwest of fold 16 or 237 fold 37
Local map see MONDOUBLEAU

The D 921 running south from Le Gault-Perche gives a good view of the Templar Commandery which later passed to the Knights of St John of Jerusalem. The ironstone building in its rural setting makes an attractive picture.

La Commanderie ⊙ – The 12C chapel housing the Commandery is crowned by a gable belfry which is linked to a flint tower, once part of the town walls. The town gateway (late 15C) is decorated with two brick turrets with unusual conical roofs made of chestnut slats.

The Templars

The Order, which was both military and monastic, was founded in 1119 near the site of Solomon's Temple in Jerusalem. The members wore a white mantle bearing a red cross and were bound by their vows to defend the Holy City from the Muslims and protect all Christians making a pilgrimage to Jerusalem. To this end they built fortified commanderies on the main roads. A pilgrim would deposit a sum of money at his local commandery before setting out and in exchange for the receipt could draw the same sum on arrival in the Holy Land; thus the commanderies came to serve as banks in the 13C.

The Templars lent money to the Popes and to kings and princes, and grew rich and powerful. Early in the 14C the Order of Templars numbered 15 000 knights and 9 000 commanderies. It had its own judicial system, paid no tax and took its authority directly from the Pope. Such wealth and independence created many enemies and brought about the Order's downfall. In 1307 Philip the Fair persuaded the Pope that the Templars should be brought to trial; he had every member of the Order in France arrested on the same day. The Grand Master, Jacques de Molay, and 140 knights were imprisoned in Chinon castle; the follow-

Arville – La Commanderie

ing year they were brought to Paris. A trial was held in which they were accused of denying Christ by spitting on the Cross in their initiation ceremonies; 54 of them, including Jacques de Molay, were burned alive on one of the islets in the Seine. This was a particularly brutal punishment even considering the occasional lapses into immoral behaviour to which the Order had been prone.

ASNIÈRES-SUR-VÈGRE★

Population 338
Michelin map 64 northwest of fold 2 or 232 northeast of fold 20

Asnières lies in an attractive setting, deep in the picturesque Vègre valley. The road (D 190) from Poillé gives a pretty view over the old houses with their steeply-pitched roofs, the church and a mansion called the Cour d'Asnières.

Bridge – This medieval humpback structure provides a charming **view**★ of the river, of the old mill – still operational – against a backdrop of fine trees, and of the elegant mansion with its turret and dormer windows on the right bank. Close to the mill stands a château known as the Moulin Vieux dating from the 17C and 18C.

Church ⊙ – The interior is decorated with Gothic **wall paintings**★ – 13C in the nave and 15C in the chancel. The most famous, on the inside wall of the main façade, depicts Hell. On the left Christ is preparing to release the souls trapped in Limbo by attacking the three-headed dog, Cerberus, with a lance; in the centre Leviathan is swallowing up the Damned; finally canine-headed demons are stirring a cauldron of the Damned in which the wimple of the lady of the manor and the bishop's mitre can be seen.

The scenes on the north wall of the nave portray the Adoration of the Magi, the Presentation of Jesus in the Temple and the Flight into Egypt. Note in the chancel a Baptism of Christ, a Flagellation and a Crucifixion.

Cour d'Asnières – Standing a little to the south of the church is a large, elongated Gothic building, with pretty paired windows. It was here that the canons of Le Mans, the one-time lords of Asnières, exercised their seigneurial rights, hence the name *cour* meaning court.

Château de Verdelles – *2.5km/1.5mi on D 190 towards Poillé.*
This late-15C château has remained unaltered since its construction by Colas Le Clerc, Lord of Juigné. It marks the transition between the feudal castle and the stately home; four towers grouped closely together surround the central part of the château which has moulded windows. Note the attractive hanging turret decorated with Gothic arcades.

AUBIGNY-SUR-NÈRE★

Population 5 803
Michelin map 65 fold 11 or 238 folds, 18, 19
Town plan in the current Michelin Red Guide France

On the borders of Berry and the Sologne, little Aubigny is a busy place on the River Nère which here flows partly underground. Local activity centres on the fairs, the electric motor and precision instrument factories and the sports ground.

The Stuart City – In 1423 Charles VII gave Aubigny to a Scotsman, John Stuart, his ally against the English. He was succeeded by Béraud Stuart, who effected a reconciliation between Louis XI and his cousin, the future Louis XII, and then by Robert Stuart, known as the Marshal of Aubigny, who fought in Italy under François I.
Gentlemen and craftsmen from Scotland settled here. They established glass-making and weaving using the white wool from the Sologne. Before the 19C the importance of cloth manufacture was so great that the town was known as Aubigny-les-Cardeux or Carders' Aubigny. Rue des Foulons recalls the days when cloth was dressed by fulling in the waters of the Nère.

SIGHTS

★ **Old houses** – A number of early-16C half-timbered houses have survived. The oaks used in their construction were given by Robert Stuart from the nearby Forest of Ivoy. There are several along rue du Prieuré and its continuation, rue des Dames, charming and busy streets hung with shop signs from the town hall to the church, as well as in rue du Charbon and place Adrien-Arnoux. No 10 rue du Pont-Aux-Foulons is the only house to have survived the fire of 1512. In rue du Bourg-Coutant stands the **Maison du Bailli**★ with its carved beams, and almost opposite, at the corner of rue de l'Église, the pretty **Maison François I**.

Église St-Martin ⊙ – The church is built in Gothic style, marking the arrival of influences from the Paris region (Ile-de-France) in Berry. At the entrance to the chancel two 17C painted statues represent a charming Virgin and Child and a dramatic Christ Reviled, while in the chancel a 16C stained-glass window depicts the life of St Martin. In the third chapel to the right there is an admirable 17C wood *Pietà*.

Ancien château des Stuarts ⊙ – This 16C building was the work of Robert Stuart. It was subsequently altered by Louise de Kéroualle, Duchess of Ports-mouth, and now serves as Aubigny's town hall. The entrance gatehouse, dating from the time of Robert Stuart, is flanked by attractive brick bartizans; the keystone of the vault is emblazoned with the Stuart coat of arms. Pass into the charming irregular courtyard with its mullioned windows and round or polygonal turreted staircases. One of the rooms of the château houses a small museum devoted to the life and work of **Marguerite Audoux** (1863-1937), the local writer whose novel about a shepherdess, *Marie-Claire*, is based on her own childhood.

Ramparts – The line of the old town wall, built originally by Philippe-Auguste, is marked by the streets enclosing the town centre and the two round towers overlooking the Mall which runs parallel to the Nère spanned by footbridges.

The Practical information section at the end of the guide lists :
   – information on travel, motoring, accommodation, recreation
   – local or national organisations providing additional information;
   – calendar of events
   – admission times and charges for the sights described in the guide.

AZAY-LE-RIDEAU

Population 3 053
Michelin map 64 fold 14 or 232 fold 35
Local map see Vallée de la LOIRE: Orléans-Chinon

Strategically sited at a bridging point on the Indre on the main road from Tours to Chinon, Azay was soon fortified. It is named after one of its lords, Ridel or Rideau d'Azay, who was knighted by Philippe-Auguste and built a strong castle.

The most tragic incident in its history was a massacre which occurred in 1418. When Charles VII was Dauphin he was insulted by the Burgundian guard as he passed through Azay. Instant reprisals followed. The town was seized and burnt and the Captain and his 350 soldiers were executed. Azay was called Azay-le-Brûlé (Azay the Burnt) until the 18C.

★★★ CHÂTEAU

A financier's creation (16C) – When it rose from its ruins Azay became the property of **Gilles Berthelot**, one of the great financiers of the time. He had the present delightful mansion built between 1518 and 1527. His wife, **Philippa Lesbahy**, directed the work, as Catherine Briçonnet had directed that of Chenonceau.

But under the monarchy, fortune's wheel turned quickly for financiers. The rich Beaune-Semblançay ended his career on the gibbet at Montfaucon. Berthelot saw the fatal noose drawing nearer, took fright, fled home and country and later died in exile. François I confiscated Azay and gave it to one of his companions in arms from the Italian campaigns, **Antoine Raffin**.

In the 19C one of the many subsequent owners rebuilt the great north tower and added a corner tower on the east.

Château d'Azay-le-Rideau

In 1870, when Prince Frederick-Charles of Prussia was staying in the château, one of the chandeliers crashed down on to the table. The Prince thought that his life was being threatened and Azay barely escaped further retribution. In 1905 the château was bought by the French State for 200 000 francs.

Son et lumière – *See the Practical information section at the end of the guide.*

Tour ⊙ *45min*

A tree-clad setting on the banks of the Indre provides the backdrop for the château of Azay-le-Rideau, one of the gems of the Renaissance. Similar to Chenonceau, but less grandiose, its lines and dimensions suit the site so perfectly that it gives an unforgettable impression of elegance. Though Gothic in outline, Azay is forward-looking in its bright appearance and the handsome design of its façades.

The medieval defences are purely symbolic and testify only to the high rank of the owners. The massive towers of earlier periods have given way to harmless turrets with graceful outlines. Dormer windows spring from the corbelled sentry walk, the machicolations lend themselves to ornament and the moats are mere placid reflecting pools.

Partly built over the Indre, the château consists of two main wings at right angles. The decoration shows the influence of the buildings erected by François I at Blois: pilasters flank the windows, double entablatures separate the storeys but here there is a strict symmetry throughout the design of the building.

The château's most striking feature is the **grand staircase** with its three storeys of twin bays forming loggias opening onto the courtyard and its elaborately decorated pediment. At Blois the staircase is still spiral and projects from the façade; at Azay it is internal with a straight ramp.

The reflections in the water add to the gentle melancholy of the site and, together with the rows of houses and gardens along the River Indre, make excellent subjects for photographs.

The interior is lavishly decorated and furnished with some pieces of truly outstanding beauty: late 15C oak canopy-throne, fine brocade bed dating from the late 17C, credence tables, cabinets, etc. A splendid collection of 16C and 17C **tapestries★** are exhibited on the walls: *verdures* (landscapes dominated by flower and plant motifs) from Antwerp and Tournai, lovely compositions woven in Oudenaarde (scenes from the Old Testament) and Brussels (*Story of Psyche* series), and the fine *Tenture de Renaud et Armide*, executed in the Parisian workshops of the Faubourg-St-Marcel after cartoons by Simon Vouet.

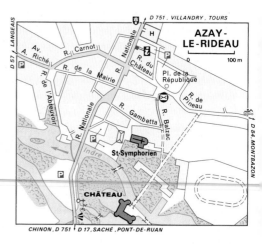

ADDITIONAL SIGHT

Église St-Symphorien – This curious 11C church, altered in the 12C and 16C, has a double gabled **façade★**. Embedded to the right are remains of the original 5C and 6C building: two rows of statuettes and diapered brickwork. To the left above the basket-handle arched porch, there is a Flamboyant window (restored) which dates from the 16C.

EXCURSIONS

★ Marnay: Musée Maurice-Dufresne ⊙ – *6km/4mi west of Azay-le-Rideau on D 57, then D 120.*

This museum, set up in a former paper mill, is largely devoted to locomotion. It displays all kinds of machines over an area of 7 000m²/8 400yd²: some are unique pieces, but all share the common characteristic of being driven by some form of mechanism. The exhibits were painstakingly gathered over 30 years, restored and painted in their original bold colours. Presented with informative cards explaining how and where they were discovered, they take the visitor on an unexpected and unusual tour through the ages: American, German and French military vehicles from the First and Second World Wars, converted into farming machinery, gipsy caravans from the turn of the century, the first French machine used for making draught beer, a Blériot monoplane, identical to

Musée Dufresne. Laffly pavement cleaner and sweeper

the one that crossed the Channel in July 1909... Each presentation enlightens us on the history of mankind: the famous "presidential" Laffly pavement cleaner and sweeper (1911), used for hosing down roads when the Head of State went on official visits, a small Bauche tractor found in an attic, entirely dismantled to escape being requisitioned, a Hanomag mine extractor-excavator which helped to erect the "Wall of the Atlantic", or one of the several hundred Fordson tanks that landed in Arromanches on 6 June 1944.

The large paddle wheel and the hydraulic turbine of the mill, dating from 1876-77, are in perfect working order and can be operated in front of visitors.

Vallée de l'Indre from Azay to Pont-de-Ruan

Round tour of 26km/16mi east - about 2hr

Leave Azay going south by the bridge over the Indre which gives an attractive view of the château through the trees of the park.

Bear left immediately onto D 17 and then right onto D 57.

Villaines-les-Rochers – Wickerwork has always been the mainstay of the village. In the 19C Balzac wrote from the neighbouring Château de Saché: "We went to Villaines where the local baskets are made and bought some very attractive ones". The black and yellow water-willow and green rushes are cut in winter and steeped in water until May when they are stripped and woven. This craft is traditionally handed down from father to son who work in troglodyte workshops (several troglodyte houses can be seen).

The **Société coopérative agricole de Vannerie** ⊘ of Villaines, which was founded in 1849 by the parish priest, numbers about 80 families; several basketwork workshops have been set up where young craftsmen are trained. The workshops can be visited and the craftsmen's work is on sale.

Rejoin D 17 via D 217 which runs beside the River Villaine.

Saché – *See SACHÉ.*

Pont-de-Ruan – A beautiful scene is revealed as the road crosses the Indre: two windmills, each on an island, set among trees. The site is described at length by Balzac in *Le Lys dans la Vallée.*

Return to Azay on D 84.

MICHELIN GUIDES

The Red Guides (hotels and restaurants)
Benelux – Deutschland – España Portugal – Europe – France –
Great Britain and Ireland – Italia – Switzerland

The Green Guides (fine art, historical monuments, scenic routes)
Austria – Belgium and Luxembourg – Berlin – Brussels – California – Canada –
Chicago – Europe – Florida – France – Germany –
Great Britain – Greece – Ireland – Italy – London – Mexico – Netherlands –
New England – New York City – Portugal – Quebec – Rome –
Scandinavia-Finland – Scotland – Spain – Switzerland – Tuscany –
Venice – Vienna – Wales – Washington – West Country of England
...and the collection of regional guides for France.

BAUGÉ

Population 3 748
Michelin map 64 folds 2 and 12 or 232 fold 21

Baugé, a peaceful town with noble dwellings, is the capital and market town of the surrounding region, a countryside of heaths, forests and vast clearings. There is a good view of the town with its ruined walls from rue Foulques-Nerra to the west.

Under the sign of the Cross of Anjou – Baugé, which was founded in 1000 by Fulk Nerra, became one of the favourite residences of Yolanda of Aragon, Queen of Sicily, and her son, King René, in the 15C. Yolanda, who was a faithful supporter of Charles VII and Joan of Arc, repulsed the English from Anjou at the battle of Vieil-Baugé (1421) in which Sir Guérin de Fontaines distinguished himself at the head of the Angevins and Scottish mercenaries.

René painted, wrote verses and hunted the wild boar in its lair *(bauge)* in the adjacent forests; he also prayed before the relic of the True Cross which was venerated at the abbey of La Boissière.

Once Louis XI had gained possession of Anjou, Baugé went into decline: the saying "*Je vous baille ma rente de Baugé*" (I'll give you my rent from Baugé) means "I can give you nothing".

SIGHTS

Château (Z) ⊘ – This 15C building now serves as a tourist information centre and museum (collections of weapons, porcelain and old coins).

In 1455 King René himself supervised the building of the turrets, dormer windows and the oratory as well as the bartizan on the rear façade, where the master masons are portrayed.

An ogee-arched doorway gives access to the **spiral staircase** which terminates with a magnificent palm tree vault, decorated with the Anjou-Sicily coat of arms and other emblems: angels, tau crosses (T-shaped), symbols of the cross of Christ and stars which, in the Apocalypse, represent the souls of the blessed in eternity.

Chapelle des Filles-du-Cœur-de-Marie (Z **B**) ⊘ – Formerly part of an 18C hospice, the chapel now houses a particularly valuable piece of treasure.

★★ Cross of Anjou – The cross with two transoms (the upper one carried the inscription), which was also known as the Cross of Jerusalem, was venerated as a piece of the True Cross by the Dukes of Anjou and in particular by King René. At the end of the 15C after the Battle of Nancy in which René II Duke of Lorraine, a descendant of the Dukes of Anjou, defeated Charles the Bold, the Lorraine troops adopted the Cross of Anjou as their own symbol in order to

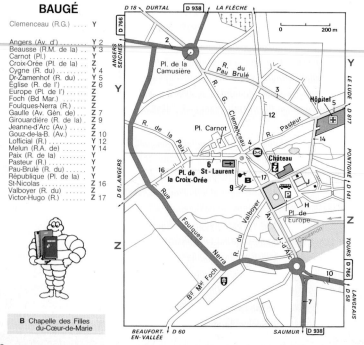

BAUGÉ

B Chapelle des Filles du-Cœur-de-Marie

recognize one another in battle and the cross became known henceforward as the Cross of Lorraine. It is supposed to be made from a piece of the True Cross, brought back from the Holy Land after the crusade in 1241; it is a marvel of the goldsmith's craft, set with precious stones and fine pearls and was created at the end of the 14C for Louis, first Duke of Anjou, by his brother Charles V's Parisian goldsmith. It is unusual in that it has a figure of Christ on both sides.

Hôpital public (Y) – The hospice, which was founded in 1643, was run by the nuns of the St Joseph Order of Hospitallers.

The **dispensary★** ⊙ with its original parquet floor and wall panelling displays a collection of herb jars which match the colours of the ceiling, glass and pewter vessels and 16C-17C faience pots from Lyon and Narbonne with Italian or Hispano-Moorish decoration. It is best to visit on a bright day as the exhibits cannot be subjected to electric light. Across the corridor is the Chapel; the altarpiece with a gilt wood ciborium is 17C.

Hôtels (Z) – The quiet streets of old Baugé are lined with noble mansions *(hôtels)* with high doorways: rue de l'Église, rue de la Girouardière and place de la Croix-Orée.

Église St-Laurent (Z) ⊙ – Late - 16C to early – 17C church; the organ, dating from 1644, was restored in 1975.

THE BAUGEOIS

38km/24mi – about 1hr Leave Baugé on D 141 east along the Couasnon valley.

Dolmen de la Pierre Couverte – *Leave the car at the side of the road 3.5km/2mi from Baugé.* A signposted path leads to the dolmen standing in a forest clearing. *By car again, take D 141 towards Pontigné.* There are fine views to the right of the Couasnon valley and the forested massif of Chandelais.

Pontigné – The church ⊙, dedicated to St Denis, whose effigy is above the Romanesque portal, is crowned by an unusual twisting spiral bell-tower. Inside, Angevin vaulting covers the nave while the capitals of the transept sport monstrous heads and water-lily leaf motifs and the charming central apse is supported by a complex network of radiating tori.

In the apsidal chapels 13C-14C **mural paintings★** depict Christ the King and the Resurrection of Lazarus on one side and the Virgin Enthroned, surrounded by the Annunciation, the Nativity and the Adoration of the Shepherds on the other. *Follow the road behind the church and turn right onto D 766.*

The road affords a fine view of the orchards in the valley. *Bear left and then turn right in the direction of Bocé.*

★ **Forêt de Chandelais** – This is a magnificent State-owned forest, covering 800ha/2 000 acres. The splendid fully-grown oak and beech trees are replanted every 210 years. *Follow the forest road to the central crossroads before turning right in the direction of Bocé. Then take D 939 to the left towards Cuon.*

Cuon – Behind the church with the curious conical spire is a charming 15C manor house.

Opposite the church an old inn still bears the inscription "Au Soleil d'Or" (The Golden Sun) where travellers on foot or on horseback could find lodging. *From Cuon take the road to Chartrené.*

The wooded park on the left marks the site of the Château de la Grafinière. *Beyond Chartrené turn left onto D 60. After 4.5km/3mi follow D 211 to the right, crossing heaths and woodlands, to reach Fontaine-Guérin.*

Fontaine-Guérin – The belfry of the much-altered Romanesque church is crowned by a twisting spire.

Inside, the 15C roof is decorated with 126 painted panels (15C-16C) with secular themes.

The D 211 towards St-Georges-du-Bois leads to an artificial lake with facilities for swimming, sailboarding and picnicking. A "Threshing Festival" with processions in traditional costume is held on the second Sunday in August.

Follow the Couasnon valley, taking D 144 in the direction of Le Vieil-Baugé and passing within sight of ruins of the Château de la Tour du Pin.

Le Vieil-Baugé – Le Vieil-Baugé is the site of a battle in 1421 when the English were defeated by an Angevin army supported by Scottish mercenaries led by John, the Earl of Buchan. He was rewarded with the baton of High Constable of France.

The old village crowns a hilltop overlooking the valley of the Couasnon.

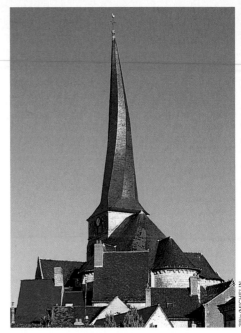

Le Vieil-Baugé – Twisted spire

St-Symphorien, the church, has a slim twisted spire which leans as a result of the distortion of the internal wooden framework. The nave is partially 11C and the handsome **chancel**★ is 13C with Angevin vaulting.

The façade and the south transept are by the Angevin architect, Jean de Lespine, and date from the Renaissance.

BAZOUGES-SUR-LE-LOIR

Population 1 088
Michelin map 64 fold 2 or 232 fold 21

From the bridge there is a charming **view** ★ of the river with its washing places, the castle and the water mill, the church and its tower in the square and the gardens mounting to the roofs of Bazouges.

Château ⊙ – The château of Bazouges, together with its water mill, was built on an attractive site on the banks of the Loir in the 15C and 16C by the Champagne family, one of whom, Baudoin (Baldwin), was chamberlain to Louis XII and François I.

The entrance is flanked by two massive towers, with machicolations and pepper-pot turrets; one of them contains the 15C chapel which is decorated with Angevin vaulting and two old statues of St Barbara and St John.

The guard-room over the gateway leads to the sentry walk. Another more imposing guard-room with a stone chimneypiece is on view as well as the 18C state rooms and the formal French park which is planted with cypresses and yew trees and surrounded by water.

Church ⊙ – The building dates from the 12C. A solid tower rises above the crossing. The nave vaulting, which is made of oak shingles, is painted with 24 figures (12 Apostles and 12 angels) separated by trees each bearing an article from the Creed (early 16C).

For a quiet place to stay

Consult the annual Michelin Red Guide France (hotels and restaurants)
and the Michelin Guide Camping Caravaning France
which offer a choice of pleasant hotels and quiet camp sites
in convenient locations.

BEAUFORT-EN-VALLÉE

Population 5 364
Michelin map 64 fold 12 or 232 folds 32, 33
Local map see Vallée de la LOIRE: Chinon-Champtoceaux

Beaufort is set in the middle of the rich plains of the Anjou valley. In the 18C-19C it was one of the largest manufacturers of sailcloth in France. The town is dominated by the ruins of the **château**, which was built in the 14C by Guillaume Roger, Count of Beaufort and father of Pope Gregory XI. One of the towers was rebuilt in the 15C by King René. From the top of the bluff on which the ruins stand there is a charming **view** of the surrounding country.

> **Church** – This was largely restored in the 19C and has a fine belfry built by Jean de Lespine and completed in 1542 over the 15C transept.
> The interior contains a 17C Adoration of the Shepherds, a carved wooden altar (1617) and the earlier high altar, made of marble, which is now under the great window in the transept.

EXCURSION

> **Blou** – *16km/10mi on N 147 towards Longué and D 206.*
> The Romanesque **church** ⊘ with its massive buttresses has curious 11C diapering on its north transept. A 13C bell-tower rises above the transept crossing.

BEAUGENCY★

Population 6 917
Michelin map 64 fold 8 or 238 fold 4
Local map see Vallée de la LOIRE: Orléans-Chinon

Beaugency recalls the Middle Ages. It is best to enter the town from the south, crossing the River Loire by the age-old multi-arched bridge *(attractive view)*. The oldest parts of the bridge date from the 14C but there was an earlier bridge as a toll was already in existence in the 12C.

The Two Councils of Beaugency (12C) – Both councils were called to deal with the marital problems of Philippe I and Louis VII.
While visiting **Fulk IV** in Tours, Philippe seduced his host's wife, the Countess Bertrade, and shortly afterwards repudiated Queen Bertha. The King thought that he would easily obtain the annulment of his marriage by raising a vague claim of consanguinity but Pope Urban II refused him. The King persisted and was excommunicated so that he was unable to join the First Crusade (1099). Eventually the excommunication was lifted by the Council of Beaugency in 1104 and four years later the King died at peace with the church. He was buried according to his wishes at St-Benoît-sur-Loire.

BEAUGENCY

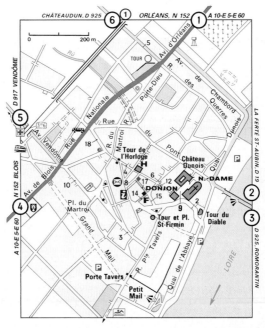

Cordonnerie (R. de la)	6
Maille-d'or (R. de la)	10
Martroi (Pl. du)	
Pont (R. du)	
Puits-de-l'Ange (R. du)	14
Abbaye (R. de l')	2
Bretonnerie (R. de la)	3
Change (R. de)	4
Châteaudun (R. de)	5
Dr-Hyvernaud (Pl.)	8
Dunois (Pl.)	9
Pellieux (Passage)	12
Sirène (R. de la)	15
Traîneau (R. du)	17
Trois-Marchands (R. des)	18

F Maison des Templiers
H Hôtel de ville

BEAUGENCY

Much more important was the Council of 1152 which annulled the marriage of Louis VII and **Eleanor of Aquitaine**. The beautiful and seductive Eleanor, who was the daughter and heir of the Duke of Aquitaine, had married Louis in 1137. For 10 years the royal couple lived in perfect harmony, Eleanor exercising great influence over her husband. In 1147 they set out together on the Second Crusade but once in Palestine their relationship deteriorated.

Louis grew jealous of Eleanor's partiality for Raymond of Poitiers. They had a quarrel and returned to France separately. Divorce became inevitable and on 20 March 1152 the Council of Beaugency officially dissolved the union of Louis and Eleanor for prohibited kinship: both were descended from Robert the Pious.

Eleanor was not without suitors; almost immediately she married **Henry Plantagenet**, the future King of England, so that her dowry, a large part of southwest France, passed to the English crown.

This event, one of the most important in the Middle Ages, was to lead to many centuries of Anglo-French rivalry.

A disputed town – Beaugency commanded the only bridge that crossed the Loire between Blois and Orléans before modern times. For this reason the town was often attacked *(see note 1 under AMBOISE)*. During the Hundred Years War (1337-1453) it fell into English hands four times: in 1356, 1412, 1421 and 1428. It was delivered by Joan of Arc in 1429.

The town was then caught up in the turmoil of the Wars of Religion (1562-98). Catholic Leaguers and Protestants held it by turns. At the time of the fire started by the Huguenots in 1567, the abbey was burnt down, the roof of Notre-Dame collapsed and so did that of the keep.

During the 1870-71 war against the Prussians there was fierce fighting not far from the town which was held by General Chanzy.

SIGHTS

★ **Église Notre-Dame** – The Romanesque church was built in the 12C as part of an abbey and has been restored. In the chancel a series of twinned arches alternates with the windows and larger arches; the huge round columns in the nave with their massive carved capitals represent the calm strength of the purest Romanesque art, despite the false wooden vaulting in the nave which was put up after the fire in 1567.

Near the church are the 18C buildings of the old abbey. At the bottom of the narrow rue de l'Abbaye stands the Tour du Diable (Devil's Tower) which was part of the fortifications defending the bridgehead; in the Middle Ages the Loire flowed at its foot.

Place Dunois, the square in front of the abbey church and the keep, and **place St-Firmin** make a picturesque combination. Lit by old lanterns, the two squares are equally attractive after dark.

★ **Donjon** – This keep is a fine example of 11C military architecture. At this period, keeps were rectangular and buttressed; later they became circular. The interior is in ruins.

Hôtel de Ville, Beaugency – Detail of the façade

Château Dunois – This began life as a medieval fortress and was transformed into a typical 15C residence, with mullion windows, a stair turret and an arcaded courtyard, by Dunois, Lord of Beaugency.

★ **Musée Régional de l'Orléanais** ⊘ – The rooms of the Château Dunois now house a fine collection of furniture and costumes from the Orléans district. Traditional arts and crafts are on display as well as souvenirs of local celebrities: **Charles**, the physicist (1746-1823), Eugène Sue, the writer (1804-57). From the loft one can see the 15C timberwork of the roof.

Tour St-Firmin – A street used to run under this tower, which is the sole remaining feature of a 15C church destroyed during the Revolution. You can hear the chimes of the Angelus bell at 8am, noon and 7pm.

Maison des Templiers (**F**) – This Templars' house has fine Romanesque windows.

Hôtel de Ville (**H**) ⊘ – The elegant Renaissance façade of the town hall can be admired from place de la Poste. The Council Chamber on the first floor is hung with eight beautiful pieces of **embroidery**★, executed with incomparable skill. Four of them, depicting the four continents then known, are 17C; the others (gathering mistletoe and pagan sacrifices) are 18C. They belonged to the last but one Abbot of Notre-Dame, who came from a family of shipbuilders in Nantes, which had grown rich importing sugar cane from the West Indies; the sugar cane was shipped up the Loire and processed around Beaugency and Orléans.

Tour de l'Horloge – This was originally the Exchange Tower, then in the 12C it became one of the gateways in the town wall.

Petit mail – This little tree-lined avenue overlooks the River Loire. Fine view of the valley.

Porte Tavers – This gateway is part of the old town walls.

BEAULIEU-LÈS-LOCHES

Population 1 864
Michelin map 68 fold 6 or 238 fold 14

This old village contains the ruins of a famous abbey founded in 1004 by Fulk Nerra, who was buried there at his request.

Église abbatiale ⊘ – The abbey church is dominated by a majestic square Romanesque tower, surmounted by an octagonal spire.
The arms of the transept also date from the Romanesque period but the nave and chancel were rebuilt in the 15C after being destroyed by the English in 1412; beyond the chancel are a few traces of the original Romanesque apse.
The interior is adorned with a 15C *Pietà*, some 18C terracotta statues in the chancel and some 17C portraits and a low-relief carving of the Last Supper in the sacristy.
A curious outdoor pulpit adjoins the old abbot's lodgings on the site of the old cloisters to the right of the church.

Ancienne église St-Laurent – This old church has a Romanesque tower and three fine aisles roofed with Angevin vaulting.

BEAUNE-LA-ROLANDE

Population 1 877
Michelin map 61 fold 11 or 237 fold 42

Beaune-la-Rolande in the Gâtinais takes its name from the River Rolande west of the town. It is a market town where sugar-beet and cereals have replaced saffron and vines.

Church – The building is 15C-16C and features an elegant north side in the Renaissance style: there are pilasters bearing medallions, recesses and doorways with pediments decorated with busts.
To the left is the gate to the former cemetery with a "thought for the day" on the lintel. The aisles are almost as wide and high as the nave, so that the building resembles the hall-churches of the German Late Gothic period.
At the back of the left aisle there is a painting of the Mystic Marriage of St Catherine by Frédéric Bazille, who fell in the Battle of Beaune-la-Rolande in 1870.
The last side chapel on the left contains a 17C gilt wood altar with panels depicting biblical scenes and a statue of St Vincent de Paul earlier than the stereotyped 19C representations.

Château de BEAUREGARD★

The château stands in a vast park laid out on geometric lines. The building has kept its Renaissance appearance despite 17C additions and the 20C roof extension.

TOUR ⏱ 45min

★★ **Galerie des Illustres** – Above the ground floor arcade is a portrait gallery which was decorated for Paul Ardier, Lord of Beauregard at the beginning of the 17C and Treasurer of the Exchequer under Louis XIII. The long room has retained its old Delft tiling depicting an army on the march: cavalry, artillery, infantry, musketry... The panelling and the ceiling were painted by Pierre Mosnier. The most interesting feature of the gallery is the collection of over 300 historical portraits. They are arranged in bays, each devoted to a different reign making a complete succession of monarchs from the first Valois, Philippe VI, to Louis XIII. Round the portrait of each king are grouped the queen, the chief courtiers and important foreign contemporaries; thus, next to Louis XII are Isabella of Castille, her daughter Joan the Mad and Amerigo Vespucci, the Florentine explorer who gave his name to America. Each reign is complete with its dates and the king's emblem.

Galerie des Illustres

★ **Cabinet des Grelots** – The work of Scibec de Carpi who was also active at Fontainebleau and Anet, this charming little room was fitted out towards the middle of the 16C for Jean du Thiers, Secretary of State to Henri II and then Lord of Beauregard. His coat of arms, azure with three spherical gold bells *(grelots)*, decorates the coffered ceiling; the bells reappear as a decorative motif on the oak panelling which lines the room and conceals the cupboards where the château archives are kept.

The huge 16C kitchen with two fireplaces is also on show.

BÉHUARD★

Population 94
Michelin map 63 fold 20 or 232 fold 31
Local map see Vallée de la LOIRE: Chinon-Champtoceaux

Béhuard island has accumulated round a rock on which stands the little church. In the pagan era there was a shrine on the island dedicated to a marine goddess, which was replaced in the 5C by a small oratory where prayers were said for sailors "in peril on the Loire". In the 15C Louis XI who believed he had been saved from a shipwreck by the intercession of the Virgin Mary, built the present church which became an even more popular place of pilgrimage than in the past and was dedicated to the Virgin Mary, the protector of travellers, since she herself had experienced the dangers of travel during the Flight into Egypt.

The old **village**★ with its 15C and 16C houses makes a picturesque ensemble.

Église Notre-Dame – The church, which is dedicated to the Virgin Mary, faces the souvenir shop which stands on the site of the old **King's Lodging** (Logis du Roi) built in the 15C, so it is said, for the visits of Louis XI; a small stairway leads to the church.

Part of the nave is composed of the island rock. Votive chains, presented by a lucky man who escaped from the barbarian galleys, hang in the chancel; the 16C stalls have misericords carved with delightfully malicious images. The statue of Our Lady of Béhuard stands in a niche in the chancel. The late-15C window of the Crucifixion in one of the aisles shows the donor, Louis XI *(left)*. Behind the entrance door there is an old medieval chest.

Walk – It is well worth exploring such an attractive site; a short path, beside the Calvary where religious ceremonies take place, leads down to the Loire and a broad sandy beach.

BELLEGARDE

Population 1 442
Michelin map 61 fold 11 or 237 fold 42

The colour-washed houses of Bellegarde are grouped round a huge square and surrounded by rose nurseries, market gardens and wheat fields.
The town was called Choisy-aux-Loges until 1645 when it was bought by the Duke of Bellegarde. In 1692 it passed to Louis-Antoine de Pardaillan, **Duc d'Antin.**

Courtier and patron of the arts – D'Antin was the son of Madame de Montespan and the Surveyor to the King. He was a model courtier; Voltaire wrote that he had a talent for flattery, not only in words but in actions.
During a visit to Petit-Bourg Château, near Paris, Louis XIV complained about a row of chestnut trees which, although very fine from the garden, obscured the view from the royal apartments. D'Antin had the trees felled during the night and all trace of the work cleared away; on waking, the King was astonished to find the view unobstructed.
D'Antin collected works of art and acted as a patron to artists. His mother was a frequent visitor to Bellegarde where he erected a series of brick buildings (1717-27).

SIGHTS

★ **Château** – At the centre of this unusual and picturesque group of buildings stands the square keep, quartered with bartizans and cut off by a moat, which was built in the 14C by Nicolas Braque, Finance Minister to Charles V.
The brick **pavilions** with stone dressings which surround the courtyard were built by D'Antin to house the château staff and his guests; from left to right they comprise the Steward's pavilion surmounted by a pinnacle turret, the Captain's massive round brick tower, the kitchen pavilion, the Salamander pavilion, which houses the town hall – **Hôtel de ville** ⊘ – and contains a salon with Regency wood panelling, and, on the other side of the gate, the D'Antin pavilion with a mansard roof. A **rose garden** has been laid out round the moat.
A drive skirting the rose garden leads to the stables *(private property)*; the pediment is decorated with three horses' heads sculpted by Coysevox.
Turn left to reach the church in place du Marché.

Church – The façade of this Romanesque building is a remarkable combination of balanced proportion and harmonious decoration. Note the ornamentation of the central doorway: wreathed and ringed engaged piers support carved capitals depicting imaginary foliage and animals.
The nave contains an interesting collection of 17C **paintings**: *St Sebastian* by Annibale Carracci and *The Infant Louis XIV as St John the Baptist* by Mignard (right wall) and *The Descent from the Cross* by Lebrun (right chapel); Louise de la Vallière may have been the model for the two female characters in these pictures.

EXCURSION

Boiscommun – *7.5km/5mi northwest on D 44.*
Of the castle only two towers and other ruins remain and these can be seen from the path which now follows the line of the former moat.
The interesting 13C **church** with its Romanesque doorway has a Gothic nave with a majestic elevation. It is relatively easy to discern the different periods of construction by looking at the changes in the capitals, the form of the high windows and openings of the triforium.
At the end of the aisle, above the sacristy door, is a late-12C stained-glass window showing the Virgin and Child. On leaving glance at the organ loft, ornamented with eight painted figures (16C) in costumes of the period; the figure of Roland, hero of a 12C epic poem, is identified by the inscription.

Forêt de BERCÉ

Michelin map 64 fold 4 or 232 folds 22, 23

Bercé forest is all that remains of the great Le Mans forest which used to extend from the River Sarthe to the River Loir; its foliage covers a fine plateau (5 391ha/13 322 acres) incised by small valleys and natural springs.

The magnificent trees – immensely tall sessile oaks mixed with chestnuts and slim beeches – provide cover for a herd of deer.

In the 16C Bercé forest was crown property; it is now carefully exploited for high quality oak. The trees, which are felled on a rotation of between 200 and 240 years, yield a pale yellow wood with a fine grain much in demand in cabinet-making (veneers) and for export throughout Europe.

Pines (maritime, Scots) and larches predominate on the poorer soil to the west of the forest.

TOUR ⊙ 45min
16km/10mi from St-Hubert to La Futaie des Clos

The trees which are destined to be felled are marked on the trunk; those with a number (oaks and beeches) are to be retained.

Fontaine de la Coudre – The spring, which is the source of the River Dinan, a tributary of the Loir, flows slowly under the tall oaks known as La Futaie des Forges.

A path is marked with instructive notices for children explaining the uses of the forest.

★ **Sources de l'Hermitière** – A deep valley thick with towering oaks and beeches hides the pure waters of these springs.

★ **Futaie des Clos** – This is the finest stand of oaks in the forest. Two violent storms in 1967 caused great gaps among the trees. While some of the giant oaks (300 to 340 years old) are very decrepit, others are splendid specimens.

Park in the car park under the trees.

A path leads to the Boppe oak, or rather to its stump, protected by a roof, since the ancient tree was struck by lightning in 1934 at the venerable age of 262; its circumference was 4.77m/15ft 9in at 1.3m/4ft from the ground. Its neighbour – Roulleau de la Roussière – is still flourishing after 340 years; it has grown to a height of more than 43m/141ft.

BLANCAFORT★

Population 991
Michelin map 65 north of fold 11 or 238 fold 19

This pretty village is clustered round the church which has an unusual belfry-porch.

★ **Château** ⊙ – The 15C château is built of red brick and has a uniform and rather plain façade. The courtyard which is flanked by two pavilions was added in the 17C. The tour of the château includes a visit to the library with its Regency panelling and the dining room with its walls covered in Flemish leather, painted, gilded and embossed; there is a fine display of pewter.

The park is a pleasant place for a walk among the scroll-like flower beds laid out in the French style near the château or along woodland paths beside the river where the scents of the garden are strongest at dusk.

EXCURSION

Take D 8 towards Concressault; follow the signposted route.

Musée de la Sorcellerie ⊙ – This Witchcraft Museum is set up in a 19C barn in the north of the Berry, a region known for its strong connections with sorcery. Around 20 scenes, some involving video animation and special effects, and many explanatory panels present this mysterious world of the imagination (Merlin, imps and goblins, dragons, trials of the Inquisition). The first floor, decorated and furnished in the Sologne tradition, evokes the tales of witchcraft that the locals used to tell each other during the long winter evenings, with reproductions of sorcerers and their *birettes* (strange, headless white shapes with no hands, characteristic of the Berry region).

The length of time given in this guide
    – for touring allows time to enjoy the views and the scenery
    – for sightseeing is the average time required for a visit.

Conurbation 65 132
Michelin map 64 fold 7 or 238 fold 3
Local map see Vallée de la LOIRE: Orléans-Chinon

Blois is situated on the Loire between the Beauce to the north of the river and the Sologne to the south. It is the commercial centre of an agricultural region producing mainly wheat in the Beauce and in the valley wine, strawberries, vegetables and flower bulbs. King of the vegetables is asparagus, which was originally cultivated at Vineuil and St-Claude in the Blois region; it is now grown as far as Contres in the south and in the Sologne where the soil is light.

Blois is built on the north bank of the Loire, on the hillside overlooking the river; many of the medieval streets still remain, steep and twisting and occasionally linked by flights of steps. The terracing of the houses produces the characteristic tricoloured harmony of Blois, the white façades of its buildings contrasting with their blue slate roofs and red brick chimneys.

> Seated on the north bank of the Loire, it presents a bright, clean face to the sun, and has that aspect of cheerful leisure which belongs to all white towns that reflect themselves in shining waters. It is the water-front only of Blois, however, that exhibits this fresh complexion; the interior is of a proper brownness, as befits a signally historic city.
>
> **Henry James** *A Little Tour in France*

HISTORICAL NOTES

From the Counts of Blois to the Dukes of Orléans

In the Middle Ages the Counts of Blois were powerful lords with two estates: Champagne and the region of Blois and Chartres. Despite the repeated attacks of their neighbours and rivals, the Counts of Anjou, particularly the mighty **Fulk Nerra**, who whittled down their Blois territory, they founded a powerful dynasty.

The Count of Blois married the daughter of William the Conqueror and their son, Stephen, became king of England in 1135. At this period the House of Blois was in the ascendant under Thibaud IV. After his death in 1152, attention was concentrated on Champagne, and the Loire land was somewhat abandoned together with England, where the Plantagenets took over in 1154.

In 1234 Louis IX bought a lease on the County of Blois from the Count of Champagne. In 1392 the last Count, Guy de Chatillon, sold the county to Louis, Duke of Orléans and brother of Charles VI. Thereafter the court of Orléans was held at Blois. Fifteen years later Louis d'Orléans was assassinated in Paris on the orders of the Duke of Burgundy, John the Fearless. His widow, Valentina Visconti, retired to Blois where she expressed her disillusion by carving on the walls: *Rien ne m'est plus, plus ne m'est rien* ("Nothing means anything to me any more"); she died inconsolable the following year.

An aristocratic poet: Charles d'Orléans (1391-1465)

Charles, the eldest son of Louis d'Orléans, inherited the castle and spent some of his youth there. At 15 he married the daughter of Charles VI, but she died in childbirth. At 20 he married again but soon departed to fight the English. He proved a poor general at the Battle of Agincourt where he was wounded and taken prisoner but his poetic gift helped him to survive 25 years of captivity in England. He returned to France in 1440 and being once more a widower he married, at the age of 50, Marie de Clèves, who was then 14. The château of Blois was his favourite residence. He demolished part of the grim old fortress and built a more comfortable mansion. Charles formed a little court of artists and men of letters. Great joy was granted to him in old age: at 71 he had a son and heir, the future Louis XII. He died at Amboise in 1465.

The Golden Age of the Renaissance

Louis XII was born at Blois in 1462 and succeeded Charles VIII in 1498. Blois became the royal residence rather than Amboise. The King and his wife, **Anne of Brittany**, liked Blois and embarked on considerable improvements: the construction of a new wing and the laying out of huge terraced gardens, designed by the Italian gardener, Pacello, who also worked at Amboise. These gardens covered the modern place Victor-Hugo and extended towards the railway station. Queen Anne had a large suite (ladies-in-waiting, pages, equerries and guards) and lived in high style. She died on 9 January 1514; the King was soon married to a 16-year-old English princess but he died on 1 January 1515 in Paris without a male heir. While at Blois he had drawn up the Customs of France, a code of law.

François I divided his time between Amboise and Blois. He commissioned the architect, Jacques Sourdeau, to build a new wing at Blois; it is the most beautiful part of the château and bears the King's name. His wife, **Claude de France**, was the daughter of the late king and was very attached to Blois, where she was brought up and where she died in 1524, barely 25 years old, having borne seven children in eight years. As François I was away fighting in Italy, her funeral was not held until November 1526. After that the king came to Blois no more.

Assassination of the Duke of Guise (1588) – The historical interest of the château reached its peak under **Henri III**. The States-General twice met at Blois. The first time was in 1576, when there was a demand for the suppression of the Protestant Church. In 1588 **Henri de Guise**, the Lieutenant-General of the kingdom and all-powerful head of the League in Paris, supported by the King of Spain, forced Henri III to call a second meeting of the States-General, which was then the equivalent of Parliament. Five hundred deputies, nearly all supporters of Guise, attended. Guise expected them to depose the King. The latter, feeling himself to be on the brink of the abyss, could think of no other means than murder to get rid of his rival. The assassination took place in the château itself, on the second floor *(see below)*. Relieved of the threat, Henry III exclaimed "Now, I am king!". Eight months later he himself succumbed to the dagger of Jacques Clément.

A conspirator: Gaston d'Orléans (17C) – In 1617 **Marie de Medici** was banished to Blois by her son, Louis XIII. A little court in exile grew up in the château; the leading figure was **Richelieu**, the Queen Mother's confidant and cardinal-to-be, but he became involved in intrigues and decided to flee to Luçon hoping for a more favourable occasion to pursue his ambition.

On 22 February 1619 the Queen Mother escaped; despite her size, she climbed down a rope ladder into the moat in the dark. After such a feat she and her son were reconciled… through the mediation of Richelieu!

In 1626 Louis XIII gave the country of Blois and the duchies of Orléans and Chartres to his brother, **Gaston d'Orléans**, who was scheming against Cardinal Richelieu. However, Gaston soon grew bored with his new estates and turned to conspiracy again, but his inconstancy prevented him from carrying any project to its conclusion: one day he would talk of killing Richelieu, the next day he would be reconciled with him. He went into exile, returned to France, started a new conspiracy and then left again. He was reconciled with the King in 1634 and was at last able to devote himself to his residence in Blois for which he had grandiose schemes. He sent for Mansart and commissioned a vast new building which would have entailed the destruction of the old château. Between 1635 and 1638 a new range of buildings was erected but then work had to stop owing to lack of funds. The birth of the Dauphin released Richelieu from the need to humour the King's brother so the latter returned to his old ways. In 1642 he was a party to the plot hatched by the Duc de Bouillon and the Marquis de Cinq-Mars. He escaped conviction but was deprived of his claim to the throne. From 1650-53 he played an active part in the Fronde against Mazarin and was banished to his estates; after this further failure he finally settled down. He lived in the François-I wing, embellishing the gardens, until his death in 1660.

★★★ CHÂTEAU ⊘ *2hr*

Son et lumière – *See the Practical information section at the end of the guide.*

Place du Château – This vast esplanade was once the "farmyard" of the château. Slightly below, the terraced gardens offer a wide view of the bridge over the Loire beyond the rooftops and place Louis XII at the foot of the retaining wall; to the right are the spires of St-Nicolas church and to the left the cathedral with its Renaissance tower.

Feudal Period:
① Salle des États-généraux (13C)
② Tour du Foix (13C)
Gothic – Renaissance Transitional Period:
③ Galerie Charles-d'Orléans (late 15C-early 16C)
④ Chapelle St-Calais (1498-1508)
⑤ Aile Louis-XII (1498-1501)
Renaissance period:
⑥ Aile François-I: Façade des Loges (1515-1524)
Classical period:
⑦ Aile Gaston-d'Orléans (1635-1638)

Château de Blois

The **façade** of the château – "one of the most beautiful and elaborate of all the old royal residences of this part of France" (Henry James) – on the esplanade has two main parts: the pointed gable of the Salle des États-généraux (Chamber of the States-General – **1**), relic of the former feudal castle (13C), on the right and then the pretty building of brick and stone erected by Louis XII (**5**). In keeping with the endearing whimsicality which characterizes buildings of the Middle

Ages, this has a random, assymetrical arrangement of window openings. Two windows on the first floor have balconies. That on the left opened from Louis XII's bedroom. His Minister, the Cardinal d'Amboise, lived in a neighbouring mansion, which was destroyed in June 1940 and has since been rebuilt with only moderate success. When the King and the Cardinal took the air on their balconies they were able to exchange pleasantries.

The great Flamboyant gateway is surmounted by an alcove containing an equestrian statue of Louis XII, a modern copy (made in 1857 by Seurre) of the original. The window consoles are adorned with spirited carvings. The coarse humour of the period is sometimes displayed with great candour (first and fourth windows to the left of the gateway).

The inner courtyard – Cross the courtyard to reach the delightful terrace (good **view** of St-Nicolas church and the Loire) on which stands the **Tour du Foix (2)**, a tower which formed part of the medieval fortified wall.

Return to the courtyard lined with buildings from a succession of periods, which together make up the château.

Chapelle St-Calais (4) – Of the King's private chapel which was rebuilt by Louis XII, only the Gothic chancel remains. Mansart demolished the nave when he built the Gaston d'Orléans wing. The modern stained-glass windows depicting the life of St Calais are by Max Ingrand.

Galerie Charles-d'Orléans (3) – Although called after Charles d'Orléans this gallery probably dates from the Louis XII period. Until alterations were made in the 19C the gallery was twice its present length and connected the two wings at either end of the courtyard. Note the unusual basket-handle arches.

Aile Louis-XII (5) – The corridor or gallery serving the various rooms in the wing marks a step forward in the search for more comfort and convenience. Originally rooms opened into one another. At each end of the wing a spiral staircase gave access to the different floors. The decoration is richer and Italianate panels of arabesques adorn the pillars.

Aile François-Ier (6) – The building extends between the 17C Gaston d'Orléans wing and the 13C Salle des États-généraux (chamber of the States-General – **1**). Only 14 years passed between work finishing on the Louis-XII wing and beginning on the François-Ier wing, but in this time an important milestone had been passed, heralding the triumphant arrival of the Italian decorative style.

French originality, however, persisted in the general composition. The windows were made to correspond with the internal arrangement of the rooms, without regard for symmetry; they could be close together in some places and far apart in others; their mullions might be double or single; and pilasters might flank the window openings or occupy the middle of the opening. A magnificent **staircase** was added to the façade. Since Mansart demolished part of the wing to make room for the Gaston d'Orléans buildings, this staircase is no longer in the centre of the façade. It climbs spirally in an octagonal well, three faces of which are recessed in the building. This masterpiece of architecture and sculpture was evidently designed for great receptions. The well is open between the buttresses and forms a series of balconies from which members of the court could watch the arrival of important people.

The sculptured decoration is varied and elaborate. The royal insignia are used together with all the customary themes of the Renaissance.

Château de Blois – François I staircase

Aile Gaston-d'Orléans (7) – This wing designed by François Mansart between 1635 an 1638 in the classical style is in sharp contrast to the rest of the building. Inside, a projecting gallery runs round the base of the cupola crowning the grand staircase, lavishly decorated on all but the lower level with trophies, garlands and masks.

Royal apartments (aile François-Iᵉʳ) – The François I staircase leads up to the royal apartments on the first floor where a succession of rooms containing splendid fireplaces, tapestries, busts, portraits and furniture can be seen. The interior decoration was restored by Duban in the 19C. The smoke from the open fireplaces, candles and torches used during the years the château served as a royal residence would have blackened the décor in no time.

First floor – The most interesting room is that of Catherine de' Medici. It still has its 237 carved wood panels concealing secret cupboards which may have been used to hide poisons, jewels or State papers, or may simply have been made to cater for the then prevalent taste for having wall cupboards in Italian-style rooms. They were opened by pressing a pedal concealed in the skirting board.

Second floor – This is the scene of the **murder of the Duke of Guise**. The rooms have been altered and the old cabinet demolished to make way for the Gaston-d'Orléans wing. It is therefore rather difficult to follow the phases of the assassination on the spot. The floor plan below shows the layout of the rooms at the time of the murder. The narrative is based on the accounts of contemporary witnesses.

It is 23 December 1588, about 8 o'clock in the morning. Of the 45 impoverished noblemen who are Henri III's men of action, 20 have been chosen to deal with the Duke. Eight are waiting in the Chambre du Roi (king's chamber), with daggers hidden under their cloaks, sitting on chests and seeming innocently to be swapping yarns. The 12 others, armed with swords, are in the Cabinet vieux (old cabinet). Two priests are in the oratory of the Cabinet neuf (new cabinet), where the king is making them pray for the success of his enterprise. The Duke of Guise is in the Salle du Conseil (council chamber) with various dignitaries. He has been up since 6 o'clock, after spending the night with one of the girls from Catherine de' Medici's "Flying Squad" *(see Introduction, p 000)*, and is cold and hungry. First he warms himself at the fire and eats a couple of the prunes in

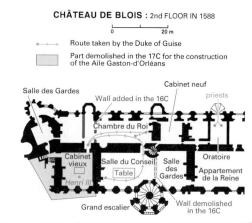

CHÂTEAU DE BLOIS : 2nd FLOOR IN 1588

0   20 m

→ ─ ─ →   Route taken by the Duke of Guise

▨   Part demolished in the 17C for the construction of the Aile Gaston-d'Orléans

Cabinet neuf

priests

Salle des Gardes

Wall added in the 16C

Chambre du Roi

Cabinet vieux

Salle du Conseil

Table

Henri III

Salle des Gardes

Oratoire

Appartement de la Reine

Grand escalier

Wall demolished in the 16C

his comfit box. Then the Council begins. Henri III's secretary tells Guise that the King would like to see him in the old cabinet.

To reach this room Guise has to go through the king's chamber as, only two days previously, the door between the council chamber and the old cabinet had been walled up. The Duke enters the king's chamber and is greeted by the men there as if nothing were amiss. He turns left towards the old cabinet but, as he opens the door leading into the corridor outside it, he sees men waiting for him with swords drawn in the narrow passage. He tries to retreat but is brought up short by the eight, now obviously assassins, in the king's chamber. They fall upon their victim, seizing him firmly by his arms and legs and trapping his sword in his cloak.

The Duke, who is an exceptionally strong man, manages to strike down four of his assailants and wound a fifth with his comfit box. He gives his murderers a run for their money for the entire length of the king's chamber, but with the odds so heavily stacked against him his valiant efforts are in vain and he finally collapses, riddled with stab wounds, by the king's bed, gasping, "Miserere mei Deus". Henri III emerges from behind the wall hanging where he has been hiding and ventures up to the corpse of his rival. According to some accounts, he slapped his face, marvelling at the dead man's size and commenting that he seemed almost bigger now than he did when alive. The dead man's pockets are found to contain a letter with the observation, "It costs 700 000 *livres* every month to sustain a civil war in France".

Afterwards, Henri III is reported to have gone down to his mother, Catherine de' Medici, and told her joyfully, "My comrade is no more, the king of Paris is dead!" To which his mother is said by some to have replied, "God grant that you have not become king of nothing at all", while other accounts suggest she remained silent. His conscience apparently clear, Henri goes to hear Mass in the chapel of St-Calais as an act of thanksgiving.

The next day, the Duke of Guise's brother, the Cardinal de Lorraine, imprisoned immediately after the murder, is also assassinated. His body is put with Guise's somewhere in the château – speculation surrounds the precise location of the room where the bodies were kept. Finally, the bodies are burned and the ashes thrown into the Loire. The Queen Mother does not long survive these dramatic events; she dies about 12 days later.

Take the grand staircase down to the first floor and cross the guard-room.

Salle des États-généraux (1) – This is the oldest (13C) part of the château, the feudal hall of the old castle of the Counts of Blois. From 1576 to 1588 the States-General, the French Parliament, used to convene in this hall. The twin barrel vaults are supported on a central row of columns.

Go out into the courtyard.

Musée archéologique ⊙ – *Ground floor of the François-Ier wing on the right of the grand staircase.*
The archeological museum has displays of prehistoric remains from the Loir-et-Cher. Five rooms contain stone tools, pottery, glassware, weapons and sarcophagi dating from the Paleolithic to the Merovingian periods, shown in chronological order.

Salle Robert-Houdin – The gallery is devoted to the famous local conjurer (1805-71), who was also a clock-maker, scholar, writer and pioneer in the art of Son et Lumière. He invented electric clocks including a master clock (Horloge-mère, 1850) which was exhibited with the "puzzle" clock (Pendule mystérieuse, 1839), a fine piece with three elements whose workings are a bit of a mystery – moving hands with a glass clock-face and column (a clock of this type can be seen at Cheverny château).

To the left of the grand staircase there is an **audio-visual presentation** on the château.

★ **Musée des Beaux-Arts** ⊙ – *First floor in the Louis-XII wing.*
The main interest of this recently restored fine arts museum lies in the 16C and 17C paintings and portraits. The portrait gallery contains paintings from the châteaux of St-Germain-Beaupré (Creuse *département*) and Beauregard. In the gallery of 17C and 18C works, there is an outstanding collection of 50 terracotta medallions by Jean-Baptiste Nini. The Guise gallery houses several works on the theme of the events of 1588, such as *Meeting of the Duke of Guise and Henri III* by Pierre-Charles Comte. Finally, the wrought-iron and locksmithing gallery contains the Frank collection in which one of the star exhibits is the remarkable fire-pan destined for the Count of Chambord made by local ironsmith Louis Delcros.

Façade des Loges and Façade Gaston-d'Orléans – During 1997 these façades are being restored to the colours added to them by architect Duban in the middle of the 19C. The façades themselves are best admired at the beginning of the walk through Old Blois which is described below.

★ **OLD BLOIS** *2hr – route shown on town plan opposite*

★ **Pavillon Anne-de-Bretagne (Z)** ⊙ – This graceful little building of stone and brick is now the tourist centre. Note the cable mouldings which emphasize the corners, and the open-work sculptured stone balustrade with the initials of Louis XII and Anne of Brittany, his wife. Originally the pavilion was in the middle of the château gardens (avenue Jean-Laigret was later opened up) and the royal couple often went to say novenas in the small oratory, hoping to win God's blessing in the shape of a son.

On the right along avenue Jean-Laigret, the pavilion extends into a long half-timbered wing, also built under Louis XII, which was later used as an **orangery.** Walk along place Victor-Hugo, which is lined on the north by the façade of the 17C church of **St-Vincent (Z)** built in the style known as Jesuit, and on the south by the beautiful Façade des Loges of the château.

Jardin du Roi – This small terraced garden, overlooking place Victor-Hugo, is all that remains of the vast château gardens, which were once directly accessible from the François-I wing by a footbridge over the moat, and which stretched as far as the railway station. From near the balustrade there is an excellent **view**★ to the left over the high slate roof topping the Pavillon Anne-de-Bretagne which was built in these gardens, as was the neighbouring orangery, and to the right over the church of St-Vincent and place Victor-Hugo; in the background is the massive square silhouette of Beauvoir tower, and to its right is the cathedral steeple; on the right rises the Façade des Loges (François-Ier wing of the château) and the end pavilion of the Gaston-d'Orléans wing.

E Hôtel d'Alluye
H Hôtel de ville
K Hôtel de la Chancellerie
N Fontaine Louis-XII
Q Maison Denis-Papin
V Maison des Acrobates

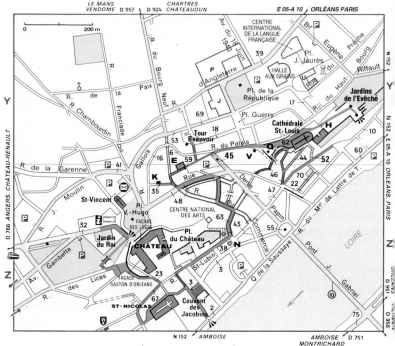

Façade des Loges – The interior part of François I's first construction backed on to the medieval rampart wall and had no outside view. This troubled the King and so he decided to add a second building with as many openings as possible against the outside of the ramparts. Since from here it is a sheer drop into the gully, the new building had to be shored up on a stone substructure. The two storeys of loggias *(loges)* and the upper gallery of the resulting façade make it very different from other parts of the building. It has a certain air of the Italian palazzo about it. However, the asymmetry of the windows, watchtowers, balconies, pilasters and the foundations is very typically French.

There is an impressive row of gargoyles above the upper floor of the loggias.

Returning to place des Lices, one can take in at a glance the majestic **Gaston-d'Orléans façade** which overlooks the moat, its classical style no longer comparing unfavourably with the lively Renaissance façades.

★ **Église St-Nicolas** (**Z**) – A beautiful building of the 12C and 13C, of great unity, the church was once part of the Benedictine abbey of St-Laumer whose sober monastic buildings, in classical style, extend as far as the Loire. The layout is characteristically Benedictine, with a large chancel surrounded by an ambulatory and radiating chapels. Note the lovely historiated capitals in the chancel and the unusual 15C altarpiece dedicated to St Mary of Egypt to the left.

Couvent des Jacobins (**Z**) – *Rue Anne-de-Bretagne.*

The convent building dates from the 15C-16C. On the first floor is the **musée d'Art religieux** ⊘, with religious art collections, and on the second floor, beneath a fine timber roof, is the **muséum d'Histoire naturelle** ⊘, with good displays on the wildlife of the region.

There is a fine view of the J-Gabriel bridge from the banks of the Loire.

Fontaine Louis-XII (**Z N**) – This fountain is a copy of the monument which was erected by Louis XII in the Flamboyant Gothic style; the original, which is badly damaged, is kept in the château.

Hôtel de la Chancellerie (Z K) – This late-16C mansion is one of the largest in Blois. Behind the 17C carriage entrance note the superb staircase with straight banisters at the back of the courtyard.

Hôtel d'Alluye (YZ E) – *At no 8 rue St-Honoré.*
This fine private mansion was built in 1508 for **Florimond Robertet**, Treasurer successively to Charles VIII, Louis XII and François I. When accompanying Charles VIII on his expedition to Naples, the financier took a liking to Italian art. Behind the façade of the mansion with its delicate Gothic Renaissance sculptures, a large **courtyard** ⊙ opens up with pure Renaissance Italianate **galleries★**. The building now houses the head office of a group of insurance companies founded in 1820.

Tour Beauvoir (Y) – This square keep (12C) belonged to a separate fief from the château and was later incorporated into the town's fortifications.
Old half-timbered façades line rue Beauvoir (nos 3, 15 and 21), surrounding a 15C stone house (no 19).

Escaliers Denis-Papin (Y 45) – At the top of this flight of steps a long view suddenly opens up towards the south. Dominating the view is the statue of **Denis Papin**, recognized as the father of the steam machine.
Born in Chitenay *(12km/8mi south of Blois)* in 1647, Papin was forced into exile by the Revocation of the Edict of Nantes and published his memorandum on "How to soften bones and cook meat quickly and cheaply" in England; his "digester" known as Papin's cooking pot, thus became the forerunner of today's pressure cooker. In Germany, under the patronage of the Landgrave of Hesse, Papin discovered "a new way of raising water by the use of fire"; in 1706 in Kassel he carried out public tests demonstrating the motive power of steam. After the death of his patron, he died in poverty in 1714.

Maison des Acrobates (Y V) – *At no 3 place St-Louis.*
This is a typical medieval house, with its half-timbered façade, its two corbelled storeys, and posts carved with acrobats, jugglers etc.

Cathédrale St-Louis (Y) – Rebuilt in the 16C and flanked by a high Renaissance tower with a lantern, the cathedral was almost entirely destroyed in 1678 by a hurricane. Thanks to the intervention of Colbert, whose wife was a native of Blois, it was rapidly rebuilt in the Gothic style. In the nave, above the large arches, one can still see the projecting stones which were to be sculptured like those in the bays of the chancel. The base of the tower (12C) is part of the original collegiate church built by St Solenne, bishop of Chartres in the 5C, who taught Clovis his catechism and assisted at his baptism by St Rémy. The **crypte St-Solenne** ⊙ *(entrance to the right of the chancel)* dates from the 10C and was enlarged in the 11C to accommodate the crowds of pilgrims; it was the largest of its day and contained the tomb of St Comblée.

Hôtel de Ville (Y H) and Jardins de l'Évêché – *Access through the gate to the left of the cathedral.*
Situated behind the cathedral, the town hall is in the former bishop's palace, built at the beginning of the 18C by Jacques-Jules Gabriel, father of the architect of place de la Concorde in Paris.
Further towards the east, the gardens of the bishop's palace form a terrace overlooking the Loire, with a lovely **view★** *(stand near the statue of Joan of Arc)* over the river, its wooded slopes and the roofs of the town; to the south is the pinnacle of the church of St-Saturnin, and to the right on the north bank, the pure spires of the church of St-Nicolas. Lovely view also of the cathedral chevet.

Maison Denis-Papin (Y Q) – Also called Hôtel de Villebresme, this lovely Gothic house at the top of rue Pierre-de-Blois spans the road with a timber-framed footbridge.
At the bottom of rue Pierre-de-Blois on the left a fine Renaissance door stands out bearing the Latin inscription *"Usu vetera nova"* which can be translated "through use, the new becomes old" or vice versa "the old becomes new again". Go down rue des Juifs: at no 3 is the 16C-17C Hôtel de Condé, with its classical courtyard. Lower down on the left, bordering a half-timbered house, is the crossroads of rue des Papegaults (16C houses at nos 4, 10 and 14) and rue du Puits-Châtel.

Rue du Puits-Châtel (Y 52) – Many interior courtyards are worth a glance through half-open entrance doors.
At no 3 there is an outside staircase with a half-timbered balcony (16C); at no 5 the staircase turret is in stone and there are vaulted galleries and sculptured balconies on the landings (early 16C); next door at no 7 the Hôtel Sardini has a courtyard with Renaissance arcades, and above the door of the staircase turret is Louis XII's porcupine.

ADDITIONAL SIGHTS

Haras national ⊙ – *East of town, 62 avenue du Maréchal Maunoury.*
This stud farm, which has occupied an old Carmelite convent since 1810, is home to about 30 blood stallions, in particular the Selle Français breed, and 20 or so draught stallions most of which are Percherons. From March to July these horses are divided between the 11 riding centres in the Cher, Eure-et-Loir, Indre, Indre-et-Loire, Loir-et-Cher and Loiret *département*. While visiting the handsome 19C buildings, there will be opportunities of meeting technicians and national agents.

Cloître St-Saturnin ⊙ – *Entrance indicated on the quai Villebois-Mareuil.*
This former cemetery with timber-roofed galleries, was built under François I. The cloisters serve as a lapidary museum, containing fragments of sculptures from the houses of Blois destroyed in 1940.

Basilique Notre-Dame-de-la-Trinité – *Northeast of the plan. Take rue du Prêche.*
This basilica designed by the architect Paul Rouvière, built between 1937 and 1949, has some fine stained glass and a Stations of the Cross sculpted out of cement by Lambert-Rucki. The 60m/200ft high campanile affords an extensive view of the surrounding countryside *(240 steps)*. The carillon consists of 48 bells, the largest weighing over 5 tonnes. It is one of the best in Europe.

EXCURSION

Orchaise – *9km/6mi west on D 766.*
The **church** (restored) has a Romanesque bell-tower. Inside, there is a fresco by Denys de Solère. The **priory botanical gardens** ⊙, covering an area of 3ha/7 acres, boast a superb collection of rhododendrons, azaleas, camellias and peonies, as well as numerous evergreen plants.

Maves ⊙ – *19km/12mi north.* 15C post windmill.

La BOISSIÈRE

Michelin map 64 south of fold 3 or 232 fold 22

The name of La Boissière is linked with a precious relic: the Cross of Anjou *(see BAUGÉ)*. The cross was brought from the Middle East in the 13C by a crusader and given to the Cistercians at La Boissière who built a chapel for it. During the Hundred Years War the cross was kept in Angers château. It returned to La Boissière in about 1456 and remained there until 1790 when it was transferred to Baugé.

Abbaye de la Boissière ⊙ – In the 18C the abbey buildings were converted into a château; the 12C church was reduced to the chancel: note the altarpiece and Gothic recumbent figures.

Chapelle de la Vraie Croix – The 13C Chapel of the True Cross *(restored)* on the road to Dénezé features three bays of Angevin vaulting inside.

BONNEVAL

Population 4 420
Michelin map 60 fold 17 or 237 fold 38
Local map see Vallée du LOIR: Bonneval-Vendôme

Bonneval grew up in the Middle Ages round the 9C Benedictine monastery of St-Florentin on the Loir. The old town walls are reflected in the waters of the surrounding moat.

Ancienne abbaye – A specialist hospital centre now occupies the old abbey buildings. The beautiful 13C **fortified gateway**★ with its pointed archway was integrated into the abbot's lodging, which was built by René d'Illiers, bishop of Chartres in the late 15C. The lodge is an attractive building of chequered stonework, flanked by two machicolated towers and capped with pinnacled gables over the dormer windows. In front of the abbey stretches the **Grève**, a large shaded square beside the moat. For an attractive view of the old towers and the church spire go to the end of rue des Fossés-St-Jacques to the west of the town.

Église Notre-Dame – The early-13C church was built in the pure Gothic style: a fine rose window above the flat chevet, an elegant triforium in the nave, fine woodwork behind the font and a 17C figure of Christ.
From the nearby bridge, rue de la Résistance, there is a picturesque view.

Porte St-Roch and Tour du Roi – Several pointed arches mark the old houses which line rue St-Roch, the street which leads to St-Roch gate with its two round towers. Beside it stands the "King's Tower", the old keep, pierced by loopholes and capped with a pepper-pot roof. This part of the town wall was built in the 15C when the Fossés du Mail moat was dug to cut the town in two since the length of the walls made it difficult to defend.

Porte Boisville and Pont du Moulin – To the west of the town, between the railway and the by-pass, stands the Boisville gate (13C); the only remaining part of the first town wall, it was reduced in size in the 15C.

EXCURSION

Alluyes – *7km/5mi northwest.*
Once one of the five baronies of Le Perche-Gouet, Alluyes belonged to **Florimond Robertet** at the end of the 15C. All that is left of the old **castle** is the great round tower of the keep and a fortified gate across the moat.
On the east bank of the river stands the **church** ⊘ (15C-16C); the south side features a series of pointed gables corresponding to the bays of the south aisle – a common architectural feature in this region. On the left wall of the nave are two Gothic murals depicting *St Christopher* and the *Legend of the Three Living and the Three Dead*. On the left of the nave is a 16C Virgin Mary bearing a representation of the Trinity on her breast and the arms of Florimond Robertet at her feet.

Château de BOUMOIS★

Michelin map 64 fold 12 or 232 fold 33 – 7km/4mi northwest of Saumur

The **Château de Boumois** ⊘ is hidden among the trees some 300m from the road (D 952). The apparently feudal exterior of the 16C château conceals an elegant residence in the Flamboyant and Renaissance styles.
The drive leads to the main entrance; on the left stands a 17C dovecot still with its rotating ladder and nesting-places for 1 800 birds. A massive gate leads into the main courtyard which is protected by a fortified wall, formerly reinforced by a moat.

The house itself, which is late 15C, is flanked by two huge machicolated towers. The entrance to the stair turret in the inner courtyard is closed by a door with detailed Renaissance motifs and the original and most unusual wrought-iron lock.

The armoury on the first floor displays a collection of 15C and 16C weapons (mostly Germanic in origin), a marble effigy of Marguerite de Valois, a full-length portrait of Elizabeth I of England and an Indian screen from Coromandel. The tour also takes in a second-floor room with a wooden ceiling, the parapet walk and a chamber containing a fine 16C bed from the Vosges. In the beautiful Flamboyant chapel is a *Virgin and Child* by Salviati and a 15C Burgundian sculpture of the Holy Family.

Château de Boumois

D'après photo Karquel

Boumois was the birthplace in 1760 of Aristide Dupetit-Thouars. This highly experienced naval officer took part in the French expedition to Egypt. In the course of the Battle of the Nile, fought between the British (commanded by Nelson) and the French off Aboukir, Dupetit-Thouars preferred to die a hero's death on the quarterdeck of his ship, the *Tonnant*, rather than haul down his flag.

A Map of Touring Programmes
is given at the beginning of the guide.
To plan a special tour
use the preceding Map of Principal Sights.

Chapelle de la BOURGONNIÈRE★

*Michelin map 63 fold 18 or 232 fold 29, 30 – 9km/6mi southeast of Ancenis
Local map see Vallée de la LOIRE: Chinon-Champtoceaux*

South of D 751, between Bouzillé and Le Marillais, is the modest entrance to La Bourgonnière chapel.

★ **Chapelle St-Sauveur** ⊘ – Towers, turrets and buttresses adorn the chapel which is decorated with shells, the initials LC and tau-crosses (T-shaped) – all symbols of the Antonians, properly known as the Hospital Brothers of St Anthony. The order was protected by Charles du Plessis and Louise de Montfaucon who had the sanctuary built between 1508 and 1523. The Antonians nursed people afflicted with ergotism, a violent fever, also known as St Anthony's Fire since St Anthony was invoked to relieve the suffering.

The beautiful doorway is surmounted by a sculpted lintel and the door panels are marked with tau-crosses. The star vaulting above the nave is ornamented with coats of arms and pendants. The oratory *(right)* contains a rare feudal bench decorated with 16C Italianate grotesques. Above the high altar is a remarkable statue of the Virgin, attributed to Michel Colombe, between St Sebastian and St Anthony the Hermit.

The **altarpiece**★ *(left)*, decorated with foliated scrolls and cherubs, as well as the central altarpiece, is probably the work of an Italian artist. There is a remarkable Christ in Majesty, clothed in a long tunic, crowned and nailed to a cross, against a painted background depicting the Angels bearing the instruments of the Passion, as well as Charlemagne and St Louis, the patrons of the donors.

BOURGUEIL

*Population 4 001
Michelin map 64 fold 13 or 232 fold 34
Local map see Vallée de la LOIRE: Chinon-Champtoceaux*

Bourgueil is well situated in a fertile region between the Loire and the Authion at the eastern end of the Anjou valley where the hillsides are carpeted with vines. French poet **Pierre de Ronsard** (1524-85) was a frequent visitor and it was there that he met the "Marie" of his love songs. Nowadays the little town's renown derives from the full-bodied red wines produced by the ancient Breton vines found only in that area. Rabelais mentions them in his works. The great French actor **Jean Carmet** (1921-94) was a native of this region, and he was particularly fond of these wines.

Church – Illuminated by lancet windows, the large Gothic chancel of this parish church is divided into three and covered with Angevin vaulting of equal height. Its width contrasts with the narrow and simple 11C Romanesque nave.

Market – Opposite the church backing on to the old town hall is the elegant covered market place *(halles)* with stone arcades.

Abbey ⊘ – *East of town on the road to Restigné.*
The abbey was founded at the end of the 10C by the Benedictines and was one of the richest in Anjou. Its vineyards stretched over the entire hillside and its woods reached down to the Loire. In the 13C and 14C it was fortified and surrounded by a moat. The elegant building by the roadside containing the **cellar** and **granary** dates from the same period; the gable is flanked by two turrets surmounted by an octagonal stone spire. The wine cellars were on the ground floor and the abbey's grain was stored on the floor above.

The tour includes the building constructed in 1730: dining room with 18C panelling, monumental staircase with wrought-iron banisters and huge vaulted hall. On the first floor the monks' cells have been made into a museum with displays of costumes, bonnets and tools from the early years of this century.

Musée Van Oeveren ⊘ – This small museum on the art of fencing, duelling and hand-to-hand fighting occupies the Château des Sablons (19C). The splendid armoury is where the château owner gives fencing lessons.

Moulin bleu ⊘ – *2km/1.3mi north.*
The Blue Windmill is of a similar type to the one at La Herpinière near Turquant *(see MONTSOREAU)*; a wooden cabin is perched on top of a cone made of ashlar-work supported by a vaulted substructure, so that the top can pivot to bring the sails into the wind. The tannin obtained from grinding the bark of the chestnut tree was used in the tanneries in Bourgueil.

From the terrace, there is a fine **view** down on to the vineyards of Bourgueil and south to the Loire valley.

Cave touristique de la Dive Bouteille ⊘ – The cool chamber (12°C/54°F), hollowed out of the rock, contains a collection of old presses – one of which dates from the 16C – and of photographs of the vineyard. Wine tasting.

EXCURSIONS

Restigné – *5km/3mi east.*
The wine-growing village lies just off the main road clustered round the church. The façade is decorated with a diaper pattern and the lintel of the south doorway is carved with fantastic beasts and Daniel in the lion's den. The Angevin Gothic chancel ending in a flat chevet is similar to that in Bourgueil; the keystones in the high vaults are decorated. The 11C nave is roofed with 15C timberwork; the beams are decorated with the heads of monsters.

Les Réaux – *4km/2.5mi south.*
In the 17C this charming **château** ⊙ dating from the late 15C belonged to Tallement des Réaux, who wrote a chronicle, *Historiettes*, of early 17C French society. The château is surrounded by a moat and the entrance pavilion is flanked by two machicolated towers; the defensive features have however been subordinated to the decorative ones: chequerwork in brick and stone; gracefully carved ornamentation in the shell-shaped dormer windows; the salamander above the entrance; soldiers for weather vanes.

Chouzé-sur-Loire – *7km/4mi south.*
The attractive village on the north bank of the Loire was once a busy port; the deserted dockside where the mooring rings are rusting and the **Musée des mariniers** (Nautical Museum) ⊙ recall the past. The charming 15C **manor house** in rue de l'Église is where Marie d'Harcourt, wife of Dunois, the famous Bastard of Orléans *(see CHÂTEAUDUN)*, died on 1 September 1464.

Varennes – *15km/9mi southwest.*
From the old river port on the Loire there is a very attractive **view** of the château of **Montsoreau**. The towpath makes a pleasant place for a walk.

Brain-sur-Allonnes – *10km/6mi west.*
Excavations in a 14C house have uncovered the medieval site of the **Cave Peinte** (Painted Cellar) ⊙. Some beautiful faience tiles are displayed in the adjoining **museum** ⊙.

BREIL

Population 303
Michelin map 64 fold 13 or 232 fold 34 – 6km/4mi southeast of Noyant

The path to Breil through Baugeois woods makes a pleasant walk.

Church – The semicircular apse and the tall stone spire above the nave are characteristically Romanesque exterior features; note the fine Plantagenet vaulting in the chancel.

Château de Lathan ⊙ – Opposite the church stands the château with its 17C formal park *(currently being restored)*, featuring charming arbours, a long sweep of green lawn adorned with clipped yews and a double avenue of lime trees. There is a delightful view along the ornamental canal with an elegant 18C pavilion at the end of it.

BRIARE

Population 6 070
Michelin map 65 fold 2 or 238 fold 8

Briare stands on the banks of the Loire at the mouth of a canal which links the great French river with another, the Seine. This delightful town boasts a marina with excellent facilities catering for a variety of leisure activities.
At the beginning of the 20C, Briare was a thriving manufacturing centre of buttons and beads, made of porcelain and jet, and of ceramic mosaic floor coverings known as *Émaux de Briare (see museum below).*

Briare canal – Work on the canal, instigated by Sully and carried out by the Compagnie des seigneurs du canal de Loyre en Seine, was begun in 1604, and it was completed by 1642. It is the first junction canal to have been built in Europe. Stretching for 57km/36mi, it connects the Loire lateral canal with the Loing canal. The reach separating the Loire and Seine basins runs between Ouzouer-sur-Trézée and Rogny-les-Sept-Écluses (seven locks which form a sort of aquatic staircase).

BRIARE

SIGHTS

★★ Pont-Canal – This aqueduct, begun in 1890 and inaugurated in 1896, is a work of art as well as an engineering feat which carries the Loire lateral canal over the river to flow into the Briare canal. The canal duct is made of metal plates held together by millions of rivets. It is 662m long, 11m wide (including the towpaths) and 2.2m deep (2 172ft x 37ft x 7ft) and is supported on 15 stonework piers constructed by the Société Eiffel. Steps lead down the the banks of the Loire, from where the magnificent metal structure of the aqueduct can be admired in all its splendour.

Musée de la Mosaïque et des Émaux ⊘ – This museum is housed on the premises of the button factory, which is still in production, and traces the meteoric career of **Jean-Félix Bapterosses**. This man was the inventor of the first machine to produce buttons on an "industrial" scale, beating France's old rival England where factory equipment was capable of punching out only one button at a time. A huge variety of buttons made by Bapterosses's invention is on display in the museum. This skilled engineer kept abreast of technological development and thought of a number of new manufacturing processes. He diversified into making beads, and myriad examples of beads produced not only for the European market, but also for that of Africa and Asia, are on display here. In 1882, the mosaic floor tiles known as *Émaux* made their debut. One of the precursors of Art Nouveau, Eugène Grasset, was called upon to assist with the design of the decoration on these, and many examples of his talented work can be admired in the museum collection. To complement their visit to the museum, visitors may be interested in having a look at the floor of the church in Briare, which is covered with mosaic tiles representing the river Loire.

Château de BRISSAC★★

Michelin map 64 fold 11 or 232 fold 32
Local map see Vallée de la LOIRE: Chinon-Champtoceaux

The château is set in a fine park shaded by magnificent **cedar trees★**. The building is unusual both because it is exceptionally tall, and because it comprises two juxtaposed buildings one of which was intended to replace the other, rather than stand next to it.
The main façade is flanked by two round towers with conical roofs, ringed by elegantly sculpted machicolations, traces of the medieval castle which was built c 1455 by Pierre de Brézé, minister to Charles VII and then to Louis XI.

Château de Brissac

90

The castle was bought by René de Cossé in 1502 and has remained in the family ever since. It was severely damaged during the Wars of Religion. René's grandson, **Charles de Cossé**, Count of Brissac, was one of the leaders of the League, the Catholic party which supported the Guises *(see BLOIS)* in the 16C; in 1594, as Governor of Paris, he handed the keys of the city to Henri IV who had arrived newly converted to Roman Catholicism at the city gates; in gratitude the King raised him to the status of duke. The new Duke began to rebuild his house following the plans of **Jacques Corbineau**, the architect responsible for the Port-Louis citadel at Lorient in Brittany; work was brought to a halt by his death in 1621 and the château has been left unaltered ever since.

TOUR ⊙ *1hr*

The château has an incomplete main façade flanked by medieval towers. The central pavilion and the left wing are abundantly ornamented with pilasters and statues in niches. The right wing, which would have replaced the Gothic tower, was never built.

The French **ceilings**, often embellished with sculptures, are still adorned with their original 17C paintings; the walls are hung with superb **tapestries** and the rooms are full of fine furniture.

The dining room has a large painting of the old Bercy château and park in Paris and in the grand salon there are fine 18C furnishings, Venetian crystal chandeliers and a pastel portrait of the 8th Duke of Brissac by Elisabeth Vigée-Lebrun.

The Louis XIII staircase leads to the imposing guard-room on the first floor, as well as to the bedchamber where Louis XIII and his mother, Marie de Medici, were at least temporarily reconciled after the Battle of Ponts-de-Cé in 1620, and to the Hunt Room (Chambre des Chasses) hung with magnificent 16C Flemish tapestries from the collection of Louis-Philippe.

Beyond the picture gallery, with its portrait of the famous Widow Clicquot in the company of her grand-daughter Anne de Mortemart, is the chapel; here there is a moving low-relief by David d'Angers as well as finely-worked choir-stalls in the Italian Renaissance style.

On the second floor there is a delightful 17C-style theatre (restored), built in 1883 by the Vicomtesse de Trédern, who had a beautiful pure soprano voice. The tour ends in the cellars of the château.

North of Brissac, alongside the road to Angers, there is a fine corn mill.

EXCURSION

Centre Piscicole de Brissac ⊙ – *Take D 748 south of Brissac-Quincé and follow the signposted route.*

This fish-breeding centre, pleasantly located on the banks of Montayer lake, enlightens visitors on the river and the action taken by local fishermen to protect it. Besides viewing fish typical of the Loire basin, visitors can watch the various stages involved in the breeding of pike, from the hatching of eggs to the growing of young fry in basins, learning as they do so the problems that beset the fish breeding in the natural environment. A botanical trail reveals the flora characteristic of shores and wetlands. A pretty footpath around the lake shore is a good way to round off the visit.

The key inside the front cover explains the abbreviations and symbols used in the text or on the maps.

BROU

Population 3 803
Michelin map 60 fold 16 or 237 folds 37, 38

Although Brou was once a barony in Le Perche-Gouet, it is more characteristic of the rich and fertile agricultural region of the Beauce; it is a market town centred on its market place where poultry and eggs are the main commerce.

There are many old street names which have remained unchanged since the Middle Ages.

Place des Halles – On the corner of Rue de la Tête-Noire stands an old house with projecting upper storeys, which dates from the early 16C; the timberwork is decorated with carved motifs.

In Rue des Changes near the market place there is another 16C house with a curved façade; the corner post bears the figures of St James and a pilgrim, since Brou is on the old pilgrimage route from Chartres to Santiago de Compostela in Spain.

EXCURSIONS

Yèvres – *1.5km/1mi east.*
The **church** ⊙ dates mainly from the 15C and 16C. The elegant Renaissance doorway is framed by carved pilasters (instruments of the Passion) and surmounted by a double pediment.

The interior contains some remarkable classical **woodwork**★: the pulpit which is decorated with effigies of the Virtues, the retable on the high altar, the altars in the side chapels and an eagle lectern. The door into the baptismal chapel is beautifully carved with scenes of the martyrdom of St Barbara and the baptism of Christ.

There is a fine carved wood ceiling and the original cupboards in which the oil for Holy Unction is kept. Behind the churchwardens' pew there is a collection of 18C and 19C vestments.

The sacristy contains Louis XIII woodwork and collections of 18C and 19C sacred vessels.

Frazé – *See FRAZÉ.*

Tour of Le Perche-Gouet – *See Le PERCHE-GOUET.*

BUEIL-EN-TOURAINE

Population 341
Michelin map 64 fold 4 or 232 fold 23

Set above the valley of the River Long, Bueil-en-Touraine is the cradle of the Bueil family which has supplied France with an admiral, two marshals and a poet, Honorat de Bueil, Marquis de Racan.

At the top of the hill there is a curious group of buildings formed by the juxtaposition of the church of St-Pierre-aux-Liens (left) and the collegiate church of St-Michel.

Église St-Pierre-aux-Liens – The church is built against a large but incomplete square tower; steps lead up to the door. Inside, there is a remarkable **font** in the Renaissance style, with small statues of Christ and the Apostles in the panels. At the end of the nave there are traces of early 16C frescoes and old statues. A door leads into the collegiate church.

Collégiale Sts-Innocents-St-Michel – The church was built by the Bueil family to contain their tombs. The recumbent figures of the Lords of Bueil and their ladies are laid in the recesses: the first wife (right) of John V of Bueil is wearing a local head-dress *(hennin)* and an emblazoned surcoat.

CANDES-ST-MARTIN★

Population 244
Michelin map 64 southwest of fold 13 or 232 fold 33
Local map see Vallée de la LOIRE: Chinon-Champtoceaux

The village of Candes stands on the south bank of the Vienne at its confluence with the Loire; the church was built on the spot where St Martin died in 397 and it was from here that the Saint's body was taken on its miraculous journey up the Loire to Tours *(see TOURS).*

★ **Church** – The building was erected in the 12C and 13C and equipped with defence features in the 15C. The roadside façade is remarkable for its combination of military architecture and rich decoration. The vault of the porch is supported by a central pillar to which the ribs fall in a cluster. The doorway is framed by sculptures (damaged).

Inside, the nave is buttressed by aisles of the same height. The Angevin vaulting rests on soaring piers; the whole structure gives an impression of tremendous lightness. The nave was built at an angle to the older chancel.

On leaving the church look up at the west façade which is also fortified.

A narrow path on the right of the church leads to the top of the slope *(15min on foot there and back)*; fine **view** of the confluence of the rivers.

Another walk along rue St-Martin, below the church, and then rue du Bas ends near a plaque showing the distances between the various ports on the Loire, recalling how much the river was used for transporting goods in days gone by.

Château de CHAMBORD★★★

"Chambord is truly royal – royal in its great scale, its grand air, its indifference to common considerations" (Henry James). This château, the largest by far of the Loire châteaux, is built on a scale foreshadowing that of the château at Versailles. It comes into sight suddenly, at the end of a long avenue, and as the view of its white mass gradually expands on approaching, its detail becoming ever clearer, it makes a striking impression on the viewer, even more so at sunset. This magnificent building owes its impact also to its fine architectural unity, sumptuous Renaissance decoration, dating from the period when this style was at its most splendid, and finally two particularly outstanding features: the great staircase and the roof terrace.

HISTORICAL NOTES

Grandiose creation of François I (16C) – The Counts of Blois had built a small castle in this isolated corner of the forest of Boulogne, which was excellent hunting country only four leagues from their capital. As a young man François I liked to hunt in the forest and in 1518 he ordered the old castle to be razed to make room for a sumptuous palace.

Several designs were put forward and no doubt Leonardo da Vinci, the King's guest at Le Clos-Lucé, drew up a plan which was made into a model by Il Boccadoro. In 1519 the surveyor, François de Pontbriant, who had worked at Loches and Amboise, took charge of the project. As work progressed, the original plans were altered and large sums of money were swallowed up but the king refused to cut corners. Even when the Treasury was empty and there was no money to pay the ransom for his two sons in Spain, when he was reduced to raiding the treasuries of the churches or to melting down his subjects' silver, work went on. It suffered only one interruption, from 1524 to 1525 when the King was a prisoner after the Battle of Pavia. In his enthusiasm the King even proposed in 1527 to redirect the course of the Loire so that it should flow in front of the château but in view of the enormity of this task a smaller river, the Cosson, was diverted instead.

By 1537 the major construction work was completed – the towers and body of the keep and the roof terraces; over 1 800 men had been employed under the direction of master masons Sourdeau and Trinqueau. Only the interior decoration remained to be done. In 1538 the King commissioned a pavilion linked to the keep by a two-storey building, and a second symmetrical wing to be added to the west side. The whole complex measured 117m by 156m (380ft by 510ft). In 1545 the royal pavilion was finished but François I, who until then had lived in the northeast tower, had little time to enjoy it as he died two years later. Henri II continued his father's work by building the west wing and the chapel tower while the curtain wall was completed. At his death in 1559 the château was still unfinished. Chambord château is a jewel of the Renaissance, the result of "a real mathematisation of architecture" (Jean Jacquart); it comprises 440 rooms, 365 fireplaces, 13 main flights of stairs and 70 backstairs.

Royal visits – In 1539 the King was able to receive **Charles V** at Chambord. A group of young women dressed as Greek divinities went to meet the Emperor and scattered flowers at his feet. The visitor, charmed by this reception and amazed by the château, said to his host: "Chambord is a compendium of human industry". Henri II continued his father's project. It was at Chambord, in 1552, that the treaty with three Germanic princes was signed, bringing the three bishoprics of Metz, Toul and Verdun to the French crown; this was ratified in 1648 by the Treaty of Westphalia. François II and Charles IX came frequently to hunt in the forest. Henri III and Henri IV hardly put in an appearance at Chambord, but Louis XIII reforged the royal link.

Sport of kings – The château estate was richly stocked with game and also lent itself to hawking. At one time there were more than 300 falcons. The royal hunt packs received unremitting care and attention, and for breeding purposes the best dogs were brought from the four corners of Europe to improve the strain.

Hunting was the favourite medieval sport and princes were brought up to it from their earliest days. Louis XII took 5m/16ft ditches on horseback without flinching. Despite his delicate constitution Charles IX used to hunt for as long as 10 hours at a stretch, exhausting five horses in the process and often coughing up blood such were his exertions. He it was who accomplished the feat of hunting down a stag without the help of the hounds.

La Grande Mademoiselle (17C) – Chambord was part of the county of Blois which Louis XIII granted to his brother, Gaston d'Orléans *(see BLOIS)*. Despite being a born intriguer, Gaston was nonetheless a good father: his daughter Anne-Marie-Louise, Duchess of Montpensier, nicknamed "La Grande Mademoiselle", relates that

Château de Chambord

her favourite game as a child was to make her father go up and down one of the double spiral staircases while she took the other, passing him in the opposite direction without ever meeting him.

Later on, it was at Chambord that La Grande Mademoiselle, an incorrigible supporter of the Catholic Fronde uprising who was later exiled by Louis XIV to St-Fargeau in Burgundy, declared her love to the Duke of Lauzun, a man of dubious repute whom she eventually married in a secret ceremony. She led him to a looking glass, breathed on it and wrote the name of the irresistible charmer with her finger.

Louis XIV and Molière – Under Louis XIV the property reverted to the crown. The King stayed at Chambord nine times between 1660 and 1685 and had considerable restoration work done.

Molière wrote *Monsieur de Pourceaugnac* at Chambord in a matter of a few days. During the première the King did not seem at all amused. Lully, who had written the music and was playing the role of apothecary, had an inspiration: he jumped feet first from the stage on the harpsichord and fell through it. The King burst out laughing and the play was saved.

Le Bourgeois Gentilhomme caused Molière renewed anguish. The King was icy at the first performance. The courtiers who were made fun of in the play were ready to be sarcastic. But after the second performance the King expressed his pleasure and the whole court changed their criticisms into compliments.

Maréchal de Saxe (18C) – Louis XV put the château at the disposal of his father-in-law, Stanislas Leszczynski, the deposed King of Poland. Then he presented the estate, with a revenue of 40 000 *livres*, to the Maréchal de Saxe as a reward for his victory over the Dutch and English at the Battle of Fontenoy in 1745. Was this a coincidence or a piece of mischief by the son-in-law? Maurice de Saxe was the natural son of Auguste of Poland, the lucky rival of Stanislas and the man who drove him from the throne.

The luxury-loving, proud and violent Maréchal filled the château with life and excitement. To satisfy his taste for arms he found quarters there for two regiments of cavalry composed of Tartars, Wallachians and natives of Martinique. These unconventional troops rode high-spirited horses from the Ukraine which were

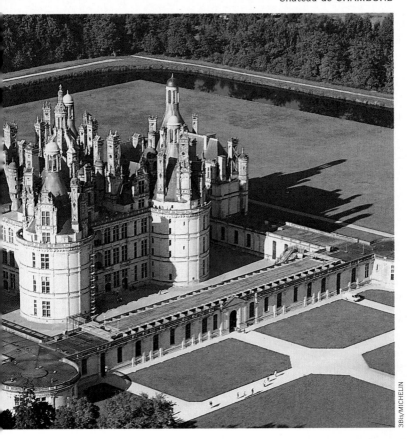

3Bis/MICHELIN

trained to assemble at the sound of a trumpet. The Maréchal imposed an iron discipline. For the slightest fault he hanged the culprits from the branches of an old elm.

More by terror than by courtship Maurice de Saxe won the favours of a well-known actress, Mme Favart, and compelled her to remain at Chambord. He re-erected Molière's stage for her amusement. Monsieur Favart played the triple role of director, author and consenting husband.

The Maréchal died at 54, some said, in a duel with the Prince de Conti whose wife he had seduced. Others ascribed his death to a neglected chill. Vainglorious even in death, Maurice de Saxe had given orders that the six cannon he had placed in the main courtyard of the château should be fired every quarter of an hour for 16 days as a sign of mourning.

From the Revolution to the Restoration – After the Maréchal's death the château was neglected and gradually fell into disrepair. What furniture was left was destroyed during the Revolution.

In 1809 Napoleon gave Chambord as an entailed estate to Berthier, Prince of Wagram. Berthier sold the timber and left the estate unoccupied. After his death the Princess was authorized to sell it.

It was bought by public subscription in 1821 for the Duke of Bordeaux, heir to the throne and posthumous son of the Duke of Berry who had just been assassinated. **Paul-Louis Courier** wrote such a trenchant pamphlet against the subscription that he was sentenced to two months in prison. He was so passionate in his politics that he even went so far as to propose that Chambord be demolished.

The Affair of the White Flag (1871-73) – In 1871 Henri, Count of Chambord and, since the fall of Charles X in 1830, legitimate heir to the French throne, was close to achieving his purpose. This was the year that, following the disruption of the Franco-Prussian war, the French elected a monarchist assembly in favour of the restoration of the monarchy. However, the monarchists were divided into two groups: the legitimists who supported the traditional absolute monarchy; and the Orléanists, more modern in their outlook, who upheld the principles of 1789. Eventually both parties agreed on the name of the heir: Henri V, the last of the Bourbon line. As he had lived in exile for 40 years, Henri was not well-informed

95

of the realities of French politics when he returned to his native soil. He went to live at Chambord where on 5 July 1871 he proclaimed his convictions in a manifesto which ended with these words: "Henri V will not give up the white flag of Henri IV".

The effect of this declaration on public opinion was a disaster: the royalists lost the partial elections. The Count of Chambord stubbornly refused to reconsider the matter and returned to Austria. Two years later in October 1873 a final attempt to compromise – a tricolour flag dotted with fleurs de lys – failed. The National Assembly accepted the situation and voted for the Republic. Henri did not succeed to the throne and died in 1883. Chambord château, which had witnessed the final hours of the monarchy, passed to his nephew, the Duke of Parma. In 1932 his descendants sold it to the State for about 11 million francs.

TOUR ⊙ *1hr 30min*

Visitors enter through the Porte Royale. Leaflets with a detailed ground plan of the château are available from reception.

Although the ground plan of Chambord is feudal – a central **keep** with four towers, which qualifies as a château in its own right, set in an enclosed precinct – the architecture is Renaissance and evokes no hint of war. The château is a royal palace built for pleasure. During the construction two wings were added, one containing the royal apartments and the other the chapel; the northwest façade is particularly impressive, its attractiveness deriving from the Italian influence in the sculptures and wide bays.

Chambord is the personal creation of François I. The name of the architect has not been recorded but the architecture seems to have been inspired by the spirit of Leonardo da Vinci who had been staying at the French court and died in the spring of 1519 just as work on the château began. François I never saw the finished château; it was Henri II who added the second storey of the chapel and Louis XIV who completed the building.

Main courtyard – From the entrance there is a fine view of the keep linked to the corner towers by two arcades surmounted by galleries. A gallery was added to the façade towards the end of the reign of François I at the same time as the two external spiral staircases in the north corners of the courtyard.

Double staircase – The famous double staircase stands at the intersection of the cross formed by the four guard-rooms. The two flights of steps spiral round one another from the ground floor to the roof terrace. The stonework at the centre and round the outside is pierced by many openings so that one can see from one flight across to the other and admire the splendid vaulting adorned with salamanders in the rooms which form a cross on the second floor. The pillars and capitals are beautifully decorated in the style of the early French Renaissance.

State apartments - The state rooms on the ground floor and on the first floor have been restored and refurbished to evoke memories of the kings and the many visitors to Chambord.

Ground floor: the Salle des Soleils, named after the sunbursts decorating the shutters, contains a number of interesting paintings, including the *Recognition of the Duke of Anjou as King of Spain* by Baron François Gérard, and the Brussels tapestry portraying the *Call of Abraham*. François I's Salle des Chasses (Hunting Room) is hung with a series of late-16C tapestries after cartoons by Laurent Guyot.

First floor: although at first François I had his rooms in the north tower of the keep, they were moved to the outer north tower when the chapel was added to the symmetrical west tower. In the King's bedchamber the bedspread and hangings are of gold embroidered velvet (16C Italian); it was on one of the window panes that the King is supposed to have engraved a melancholy couplet: *Souvent femme varie, bien fol est qui s'y fie* (Woman often changes, he who trusts her is a fool). In François I's dressing room the salamander, the King's emblem, and the letter F alternate in the coffers of the barrel-vaulted ceiling; the room was used as an oratory by Queen Catherine Opalinska, wife of Stanislas Leszczynski. The Chambre de la Reine (Queen's bedchamber) in the François I tower at the north corner of the keep is hung with Paris tapestries relating the *History of Constantine*, after cartoons by Rubens.

The King's suite, which follows, is decorated with tapestries and historic portraits; the rooms in the centre of the northwest façade of the keep were furnished by Louis XIV. The Royal or State Bedchamber, which was used successively by Louis XIV, Stanislas Leszczynski and the Maréchal de Saxe, has the original Régence style panelling fitted in 1748 for the Maréchal; the room next door at the exact centre of the building gives a remarkable view of the park. Maurice de Saxe left his mark in the King's Guard-room in the form of a huge porcelain stove. The Dauphin's Suite in the East Tower, contains many mementoes of the Count of Chambord: paintings, the state bed presented by his supporters, statues of Henri IV and the Duke of Bordeaux, the first and last Counts of Chambord, as children, and a collection of miniature artillery given to the young Prince for his amusement and instruction; the cannon fired shot which could pierce a wall. Also on display is his third manifesto dated 5 July 1871 in which he declared: "Henri V will not give up the white flag of Henri IV".

Second floor: the rooms are devoted to hunting: weapons, trophies and other related items; among the tapestries there is the *Story of Meleager* after cartoons by Lebrun (F. Sommer room) and the *Story of Diana* after cartoons by Toussaint Dubreuil (Diana room).

Roof terrace – *Photograph pp 46-7*. The terrace, a direct inspiration from castles such as Méhun-sur-Yèvre and Saumur, is unique: a maze of lanterns, chimneys, stairs and dormer windows, all intricately carved and curiously decorated with a sort of mosaic of inset slates cut in various shapes – lozenges, circles and squares – in imitation of Italian marble. The stair continues above the terrace in a single spiral enclosed in a magnificent lantern 32m/105ft high.

It was here that the court spent most of its time watching the start and return of the hunts, military reviews and exercises, tournaments and festivals. The thousands of nooks and crannies of the terrace invited the confidences, intrigues and assignations which played a great part in the life of that glittering society. One of the terrace pavilions contains a permanent **exhibition** of photographs and models explaining the history of the château.

Park – Since 1948 the park has been a national hunt reserve covering 5 500ha/13 591 acres of which 4 500ha/11 120 acres are forest; it is enclosed by a wall, the longest in France, 32km/20mi long and pierced by six gates at the end of six beautiful rides.

Walkers are admitted to a restricted area (520ha/1 285 acres) on the west side. Four observation hides have been built so that people can watch the herds of deer and wild boar browsing for food (before sunrise and after sunset).

A **display of horsemanship** ⓥ is held in the ruins of the former stables belonging to the Maréchal de Saxe. It is also possible to go for rides in **horse-drawn carriages** ⓥ.

Contemporaries of Chambord (1519-47)			
ENGLAND	**LOIRE VALLEY**		**PARIS REGION**
Bridewell Palace *	Azay-le-Rideau	Gué-Péan	Chantilly
Compton Wynyates	Beauregard	Talcy	(Petit Château)
Hampton Court	Blois	Valençay	Ecouen
Palace of Nonsuch*	Champigny-sur-	Villandry	Fontainebleau
St James	Veude*	Villesavin	Louvre
	Chaumont (décor)		(Vieux Louvre)
	Chenonceau		St-Germain-en-Laye
			(Château Vieux)

* Demolished or destroyed by fire

Château de CHAMEROLLES★

Michelin map 60 fold 20 or 237 fold 14

On the edge of the Beauce and the Gâtinais, on the edge of the Orléans forest, stands the **Château de Chamerolles** ⊙, a Renaissance building and its formal gardens recently restored to their former glory. The Dulac family moved here in the 15C, when Lancelot I (named after the hero immortalised in the story of the Knights of the Round Table) commissioned the construction of the present château. Lancelot, who was acquainted with Louis XII and François I, designed a medieval stronghold with very few apertures, but with an elegant, comfortable interior. Through their connections with Louise de Coligny, the Dulac family became unconditional supporters of the Protestant cause. Around the same period (1585), the **chapel** was converted into a Protestant church. Having belonged to the families of la Carre, Lambert and Jessé-Curely, the castle was bequeathed to the City of Paris by its very last inheritors. Having fallen into a sorry state of repair, it was finally donated, in 1987, to the regional authorities of the Loiret.

Promenade des Parfums – The new Chamerolles estate is given over to perfume and other olfactory delights. The south wing of the château contains a chronological exhibition of different smells, taking the visitor through the ages, from the 16C up to the present: each room contains objects, documents and items of furniture related to perfume. The tour ends with a "perfume organ" and a fine collection of remarkable flasks executed by Daum, Lalique and Baccarat for such prestigious perfume manufacturers as Guerlain, Lancôme, Roger et Gallet, Chanel etc.

A small bridge spanning the moat allows visitors to continue their aromatic exploration by visiting the **garden★**. The six flower beds have been painstakingly restored to the layout they would have had during the Renaissance, reflecting the threefold purpose of gardens in those days: ornamentation, leisure and utility. One has been conceived as an outdoor parlour where people engaged in conversation on grass banks. The others include an elaborate "embroidered flower bed" with boxwood edging, an "exotic patch" planted with many rare aromatic species used for making perfume, a "maze" and two vegetable gardens containing herbs, spices, fruit trees and vegetables common in the 16C and 17C. Beyond the dazzling sheet of water, a stroll through the park takes you to the bandstand, which commands a lovely view of the château.

CHAMPIGNY-SUR-VEUDE★

Population 859
Michelin map 67 fold 10 or 232 south of fold 34 – 6km/4mi north of Richelieu

Champigny lies in the green valley of the Veude and still has some 16C houses (rue des Cloîtres and route d'Assay). The most interesting sight, however, is the château chapel, with its fine Renaissance windows.

★ **Sainte-Chapelle** ⊙ – The chapel, which is a remarkable example of Renaissance art at its height, was part of a château built from 1508 to 1543 by Louis I and Louis II de Bourbon-Montpensier. The château itself was later demolished on the orders of Cardinal Richelieu who felt that its magnificence outshone his nearby Château de Richelieu. Only outbuildings remain but even these give some idea of the size and splendour of the château that was pulled down. The Sainte-Chapelle, which owed its name to the portion of the True Cross which was kept there, was saved by the intervention of Pope Urban VIII.

Louis I of Bourbon, who had accompanied Charles VIII to Naples, wanted the chapel to be in the transitional Gothic-Renaissance style.

The peristyle, which was built later, is decidedly Italian in character: the detailed sculptured ornament is based on the insignia of Louis II of Bourbon and includes crowned and plain Ls, lances, pilgrims' staffs, flowers, fruit etc. The porch has a coffered ceiling.

A fine wooden door dating from the 16C, carved with panels depicting the Cardinal Virtues, leads to the nave which has ogive vaulting with liernes and tiercerons. There also the visitor will see at prayer the figure of Henri de Bourbon, last Duke of Montpensier, carved by Simon Guillain at the beginning of the 17C.

★★ **Stained-glass windows** – Installed in the middle of the 16C, these windows are the chapel's most precious jewel. The windows all together form a remarkable example of Renaissance glasswork.

The subjects portrayed are: at the bottom, 34 portraits of the Bourbon-Montpensier House from the time of St Louis; above, the principal events in the life of St Louis; at the top, scenes from the Passion. The window in the centre of the chevet shows a poignant representation of the Crucifixion. The vividness and delicate combination of colours throughout should be noticed, particularly the purplish blues with their bronze highlights which are out of this world.

Pagode de CHANTELOUP★

Map 64 fold 16 or 238 fold 14 – 3km/2mi south of Amboise
Local map see Vallée de la LOIRE: Orléans-Chinon

The **pagoda** ⊙ standing on the edge of Amboise forest is all that remains of the splendid château built by the **Duke of Choiseul**, one of Louis XV's ministers, in imitation of Versailles. It was later abandoned and demolished in 1823 by estate agents.

When Choiseul was exiled to his estates to please Madame du Barry, he turned Chanteloup into an intellectual and artistic centre. He commissioned the pagoda (1775-78) from the architect, Le Camus, as a memorial to his friends' loyalty. This unusual building looks somewhat out of place on the banks of the Loire but it shows how popular anything with a Chinese flavour was in the 18C.

The **setting**★ of the pagoda evokes the sumptuous surroundings of Choiseul's exile; there is a plan of the whole structure inside the building.

The large fan-shaped pool, now overgrown, and the traces of the alleys in the park, which can be discerned from the balconies of the pagoda, help to resurrect the original design. The pagoda is 44m/144ft high and consists of seven storeys, each smaller than the one below.

From the top (149 steps) there is a fine **panorama** of the Loire valley as far as Tours and of the Amboise forest.

Chanteloup pagoda

CHÂTEAUDUN★★

Population 14 511
Michelin map 60 fold 17 or 237 fold 38
Local map see Vallée du LOIR: Bonneval-Vendôme

Châteaudun and its castle stand on a bluff, indented by narrow valleys called *cavées*, on the south bank of the Loir at the point where the Perche region joins the Beauce.

Fairs and markets – In the 18C and 19C Châteaudun was an important centre for the grain trade. The farmers came in from the Beauce with samples of their harvest which was sold and delivered to the grain merchants; they then sold it on to the millers, cattle farmers and horse dealers. On Thursdays the main square was a picturesque sight thronged with people conducting their business. Among the blue shirts, bonnets, light carts and sheep-dogs, moved the porters, wearing the plaque, the sign of their function, which they had paid for in gold. Traders and farmers feasted at the "Bon Laboureur" (Good Labourer) in rue Gambetta (no 61), where Zola, busy writing his novel *The Earth*, would go to watch them savouring the local cinder-covered Beauce cheese traditionally accompanied by a draught of beer.

Poppies from the Beauce were crushed in local presses to yield poppy-seed oil. Beauce sheep provided wool for the textile industry, as certain street names recall: rue des Filoirs and rue des Fouleries (spinning and fulling).

HISTORICAL NOTES

In the 10C Châteaudun was seized by Thibault the Trickster and so passed into the hands of the Counts of Blois. In 1392 the last of the Counts sold the counties of Blois and Dunois to Louis of Orléans, Charles VI's brother; Châteaudun passed by succession to Charles d'Orléans, the poet, who offered it to his half-brother John, the Bastard of Orléans, whose descendants, the Orléans-Longueville family, owned Châteaudun until the end of the 17C.

Birth of the Alexandrine metre – It was at Châteaudun in the 12C that the poet Lambert Licors was born. He was one of the authors of the *Story of Alexander*, a heroic poem inspired by the legend of Alexander the Great which was very popular in the Middle Ages. Its 22 000 lines were written in the heroic metre, with 12 feet or syllables to the line, which subsequently came to be known as the Alexandrine metre.

Dunois, the Bastard of Orléans (1402-56) – Handsome Dunois, the faithful companion of Joan of Arc, was the bastard son of Louis I of Orléans and Mariette d'Enghien. He was brought up by Valentina Visconti, Louis' wife, who loved him as much as her own children. From the age of 15 Dunois fought the English for several decades. In 1429 he rallied the army to the defence of Orléans and delivered Montargis. He took part in all the great events of Joan of Arc's career. Towards the end of his life, having won all the honours it is possible for one man to win, he retired to Châteaudun in 1457, where he founded the Sainte-Chapelle and received the poet François Villon.

Dunois was buried in the church of Notre-Dame at Cléry. He was well educated and well read and Jean Cartier, the chronicler, described him as "one of the best speakers of the French language".

A financier – **Dodun**, a local man, worked his way up from nothing to become Financial Controller under the Régence (of Philippe d'Orléans, 1715-23). In 1724 his portrait was painted by Rigaud; in 1727 Bullet built him a magnificent mansion in rue de Richelieu in Paris; the château and the marquisate of Herbault also came into his possession.

Dodun made up for his ill-gotten gains by finding the money to rebuild Châteaudun after the town burnt down in 1723. Reconstruction work was directed by Jules Hardouin, nephew of Jules Hardouin-Mansart; he was responsible for the part of the town which is laid out on the grid system.

A heroic defence – On 18 October 1870 the Prussians attacked Châteaudun with 24 cannon and 12 000 men. Confronting them were only 300 local members of the national guard and 600 free fighters, who managed to hold out all day behind their barricades, despite a heavy bombardment which lasted from noon to 6.30pm. Finally, they had to admit they were outnumbered and retreated. The Prussians promptly set fire to the town and 263 houses were burned down. In recognition of services to France, Châteaudun received the Legion of Honour and adopted the motto *Extincta revivisco* ("I rise again from the ashes").

★★ CHÂTEAU (A) ⊘ *1hr*

Châteaudun is the first of the Loire châteaux to come into sight on the road from Paris. It stands on a bluff rising steeply above the River Loir (there is an excellent view from the north bank at the level of an old mill near the bridge). The buildings, which date from the 12C and 16C, have been restored with care and good taste and the rooms have been provided with furniture and hung with sumptuous 16C and 17C tapestries.

Crude and fortress-like from the outside, the buildings resemble a stately mansion when seen from the courtyard. The keep, which is 31m/102ft high without the roof, dates from the 12C; it is one of the earliest round keeps, also one of the most impressive and best preserved.

The **basement rooms** which extend into the Dunois wing are always open *(entrance at the bottom of the Gothic staircase)*. Two large adjoining rooms, beautifully decorated with intersecting ribbed vaulting, housed the kitchens, each with a double fireplace extending the whole width of the room. The small rooms on the north side were occupied by the guards in charge of the exiguous prison cells, some of which have ogival vaulting.

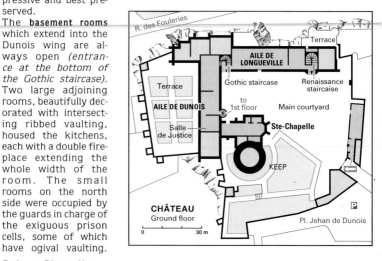

R. des Fouleries

Terrace

AILE DE LONGUEVILLE

Terrace

Gothic staircase

Renaissance staircaise

AILE DE DUNOIS

to 1st floor

Main courtyard

Salle de Justice

Ste-Chapelle

KEEP

CHÂTEAU
Ground floor

0 ⸺ 30 m

P

Pl. Jehan de Dunois

Sainte-Chapelle –

Dunois was responsible for this elegant 15C building; it is flanked by a square belfry and two oratories and the chancel ends in a three-sided apse. The upper chapel, which was provided for the servants, has a panelled wooden ceiling; the lower chapel has ogival vaulting.

The south oratory is decorated with a well-preserved 15C mural of the Last Judgement. The charming collection of 15 **statues**★★ is an excellent example of the work produced in the workshops in the Loire valley in the late 15C. Twelve of them are life-size and painted, and date from the time of Dunois; they represent St Elizabeth, beautiful St Mary the Egyptian, clothed only with her own hair, St Radegund with her sceptre, St Apollonia with forceps gripping a tooth, St Barbara with her tower, St Genevieve, St Catherine holding the wheel and the sword that killed her, a Mary Magdalene, St John the Baptist and St John the Evangelist, Dunois' patron saints, St Martha with a dragon at her feet and a majestic Virgin and Child. The Virgin Mary was the patron saint of Marie d'Harcourt, Dunois' wife. The three smaller statues are of Dunois himself, St Francis and St Agnes and were added by François d'Orléans-Longueville and Agnès de Savoie, son and daughter-in-law of the Bastard.

Aile de Dunois – This wing was begun in 1460 and is built in the true Gothic tradition, although the internal fittings suggest the desire for comfort which followed the Hundred Years War.
The huge living rooms have massive overhead beams and are hung with tapestries, including, on the first floor, a superb series from Brussels depicting the life of Moses. Visitors then come to the Salle de Justice (Court Room), where the Lord of the Manor gave judgement and which was panelled in the 17C and painted with the arms of Louis XIV from an occasion when the King visited Châteaudun. This room served as a Revolutionary tribunal in 1793. On the top floor a vertiginous parapet walk along the machicolations leads to the guard-room.

Aile de Longueville – In completing his father's work, François I de Longueville had a staircase built in the Gothic style; it rises through three floors and opens on to the main courtyard through a double bay like an Italian loggia; the decoration is in the Flamboyant style. The design is in transition between the medieval turreted staircase of the Dunois wing and the Renaissance at the east end of the Longueville wing.
The Longueville wing was built between 1511 and 1532 by François II de Longueville and then by his brother the Cardinal on foundations which date from the preceding century, but it was never completed. At roof level an Italian cornice supports a Flamboyant balustrade. The staircase at the east end is richly decorated with Renaissance motifs in a Gothic setting. The ground floor rooms, among them the Renaissance gallery, are hung with 17C Paris and Amiens tapestries. In the grand salon on the first floor there are carved 16C chests and, facing each other, two monumental chimneypieces, one in the Gothic and one in the Renaissance style.

ADDITIONAL SIGHTS

Vieille ville (A) – *To visit the old town follow on foot the route shown on the town plan overleaf.*
Rue du Château, which is lined by overhanging houses, opens into a charming little square with two old houses: the one with pilasters, beams and carved medallions is 16C, the other, much restored, is a corner house with a carved corner post showing the Virgin and St Anne (badly damaged).
Rue de la Cuirasserie, which contains a fine 16C house with a corner turret, opens into a square named after Cap-de-la-Madeleine, a town in the province of Quebec in Canada founded in the 17C by a priest from Châteaudun. On the right is the Hôtel-Dieu founded in 1092 and modernised in 1762; on the left is the Palais de Justice (Law Court) housed in a former Augustinian abbey, built in the classical style.
The church, **Église de la Madeleine**★ ⊙, is built into the ramparts; its north façade is topped by pointed gables, a common local feature. The interior is vast; it was built in the 12C to an ambitious plan and never completed owing to a lack of funds. The south door, overlooking a steep drop, is Romanesque with human figures and fantastic animals carved over the arch.
Continue down rue des Huileries to rue de la Porte-d'Abas; on the left, near the ruins of a Roman gate, stands the 16C Loge aux Portiers (Porters' Lodge) decorated with a carefully restored statue of the Virgin Mary.
Walk up rue St-Lubin with its central water channel to return to the front of the château. Go through the arch at the beginning of rue de Luynes and into impasse du Cloître St-Roch, then turn right into a narrow and winding street, venelle des Ribaudes, which opens into a small square on the edge of the bluff; from here there is a pleasant view of the Loir and the river valley. On the right of the square stands a 15C house with a Flamboyant door and mullion windows.

Take rue Dodun back to the château.

CHÂTEAUDUN

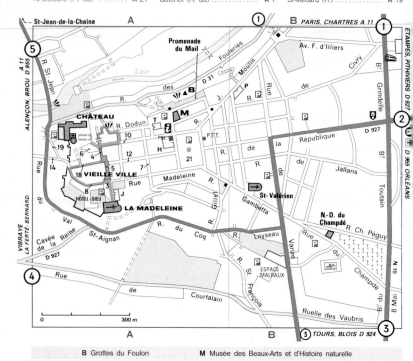

B Grottes du Foulon   M Musée des Beaux-Arts et d'Histoire naturelle

Promenade du Mail (A) – The mall walk, which runs along the edge of the bluff above the river valley, has been widened and turned into a public garden. The **view**★ stretches westward across the two branches of the Loir, the St-Jean suburb and beyond to the hillsides of the Perche region.

Musée des Beaux-Arts et d'Histoire naturelle (A M) ⊙ – This Fine Art and Natural History Museum is worth visiting for its fine **collection**★ of stuffed birds, mainly exotic species with shimmering plumage, although some also come from Europe. The room on the ground floor devoted to Egyptian archeology contains funerary objects from the early Dynastic Period (3100-2700 BC) discovered at Abydos in the late 19C by the French Egyptologist Amelineau. The same room also displays mummies and mummy masks. Local history and archeology are evoked by a display of exhibits excavated in the vicinity of Châteaudun, and by souvenirs of the 1870 war.

On the first floor, the section on Asian and Oceanian art presents French East India Company porcelain handed down by the Marquis of Tarragon in the 19C, together with a great many pieces belonging to the Wahl-Offroy collection: weapons from the Middle and Far East, Chinese jewellery, Buddhist statuary and Islamic miniatures.

Also displayed are a typical Beauce domestic interior, a series of 19C local landscapes and fragments of 16C polychrome wooden retables attributed to the workshops of Antwerp.

Église St-Valérien (B) ⊙ – The late 12C-early 13C church has a tall square tower and crocketed spire; on the south side there is a fine Romanesque multifoil doorway.

Chapelle Notre-Dame-du-Champdé (B) – All that remains of this funerary chapel, destroyed at the end of the 19C, is a Flamboyant façade with finely worked ornamentation; a delicate balustrade is supported by sculpted consoles at the base of the gable which holds an effigy of the Virgin Mary, to whom the chapel is dedicated.

Grottes du Foulon (A B) ⊙ – *35, rue des Fouleries.*
Lining the roadside like the many other caves in the area, and clearly visible, these caves owe their name to the activity of the fullers *(fouleurs)* who used to work here. Hollowed out in the Senonian limestone by the waters of the Loir, the cave roofs have flinty concretions which in places have been transformed into geodes of chalcedony or quartz by the effects of crystallisation.

Église St-Jean-de-la-Chaîne - *Exit ⑤ on the town plan.*
In the suburb of St John on the north bank of the Loir stands an early-16C ogee-arched gate at the entrance to the churchyard.
The **church of St-Jean** ⊙ was built mainly in the 15C but the apses date from the 11C and 12C.
From this side of the river there is a fine view of the north façade of the château.

EXCURSIONS

Lutz-en-Dunois - *7km/4mi on ②, towards Orléans.*
Lutz has a charming Romanesque **church** with a low bell-tower crowned by a saddleback roof. The interior is decorated with 13C **murals** in red and yellow ochre: those on the oven-vault above the apse depict Apostles and Bishop Saints; on the walls of the nave are Christ's Entry into Jerusalem, the Entombment, the Resurrection and the Descent into Limbo.

Abbaye du bois de Nottonville ⊙ - *18km/11mi on ②; take D 927 to Varize and then follow the signs.*
The 11C priory (restored in the 15C) belonged to Benedictine monks from Marmoutier. Note, in particular, the fortified doorway, the barn with a roof shaped like an inverted ship's hull, and the dovecot.

CHÂTEAU-GONTIER

Population 11 085
Michelin map 63 fold 10 or 232 fold 19
Local map see Vallée de la MAYENNE

On the border between Brittany and Maine, Château-Gontier is a picturesque old town, the capital of the Mayenne country. It was founded in the 11C by Fulk Nerra, Count of Anjou, who constructed a castle on the rocky spur overlooking the river and put it in the charge of one Gontier, an officer in his army. The area around belonged to the Benedictines of the abbey of St-Aubin at Angers, and it was they who built the 11C priory of St-Jean-Baptiste by the side of the castle.
The town suffered during the Hundred Years War (the castle was destroyed in 1368) and was one of the centres of Royalist resistance *(chouannerie)* to the French Revolution. The Royalist leader and friend of Cadoudal (leader of the Royalist rebels known as the Chouans), **Pierre-Mathurin Mercier**, was born the son of an inn-keeper in Rue Trouvée. Cadoudal and Mercier passed through the town in October 1793 with the forces of the Vendée. Mercier became a general and then Marshal of the Royal Armies in Brittany, meeting his death at the Battle of Loudéac in 1801, aged only 26.
Château-Gontier is divided into two distinct areas: the upper town bisected by Grande-Rue on the west bank of the river, and the suburb around St-Julien hospital on the east bank. The town has always been a great centre for fairs and markets, and every Thursday Parc St-Fiacre (**B**) hosts a market for sheep and calves, one of the most important of its kind in Europe.
The quaysides are a reminder of the days when Château-Gontier was a port on the canalised Mayenne *(for details of houseboat hire or boat trips on the Mayenne, see the Practical information section at the end of the guide).*

UPPER TOWN *1hr 30min*

Jardin du Bout du Monde (**A**) - These pretty gardens laid out in the grounds of the old priory are a pleasant place for a stroll and give glimpses of the river and the far bank.

Église St-Jean-Baptiste (**A**) - The church is built in flint and red sandstone. The **interior★** reflects a remarkably forceful yet pure Romanesque style. The nave has modern stained glass and irregularly-spaced columns supporting impressive arcades, while the crossing is roofed by an unusual dome resting on pendentives ending in colonnettes.
There are remains of 13C and 14C frescoes in the nave while those in the transepts date from the 12C: in the north transept they illustrate God's creation of the birds, domestic animals and Adam and Eve (the figures of the Three Wise Men can be discerned in St-Benoît chapel); in the south transept are representations of Noah and the Ark.
The beautiful crypt is roofed with groined vaulting supported on two rows of columns.
The walk down to place St-Just gives a glimpse of the steep rise known as montée du Vieux-Collège.

CHÂTEAU-GONTIER

Viewpoint – From under the elm trees on the terrace built on the old ramparts, downhill from the church, there is a fine view of the far bank of the river.

Go down montée St-Just to Grande-Rue.

At the corner of Grande-Rue and rue de la Harelle there is a fine 15C timber-framed house (**B L**) and, opposite, the old salt-store built in tufa and with a turret dating from the 16C.

Go up Grande-Rue and turn left into rue de Thionville, then right into rue d'Enfer.

This cobbled street is bordered on the left by the foundation structure of the church of St-Jean-l'Évangéliste.

To the right, rue Lierru leads to rue Jean-Bourré, a reminder of the fame that this son of the town acquired as Financial Secretary and Treasurer of France during the reign of Louis XI *(see Château du PLESSIS-BOURRÉ).*

Museum (**A M**) ⊘ – Housed in the lovely 17C Hôtel Fouquet, the museum has a number of good paintings and sculptures as well as Ancient Greek and Roman remains; an unfinished painting by Le Brun of the *Battle of Constantine and Maxentius*; 17C Dutch pictures; a fine wooden statue of St Martha (15C French) and a 14C marble Virgin Mary. Local artists are represented by engravings by Tancrède Abraham and watercolours by Louis Renier (19C).

Go up rue du Musée (note the building on the corner with rue Bruchemotte which has an elegant turret) and into rue Chevreul.

Hôtel de Lantivy (**A**) – This town house (no 26) has a particularly interesting 16C façade.

Take rue René-Homo to the left, then on the right rue Fouassier and rue de l'Allemandier to place St-Jean.

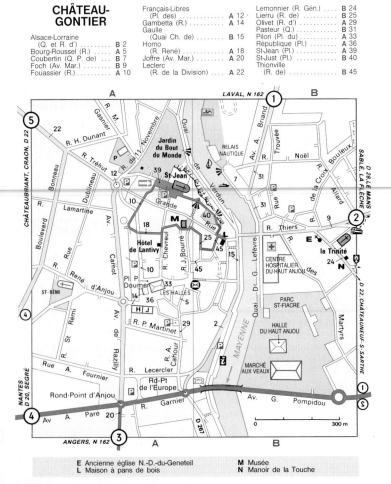

E Ancienne église N.-D.-du-Geneteil M Musée
L Maison à pans de bois N Manoir de la Touche

104

EAST BANK *30min*

There are fine views of the upper town from the Pierre-de-Coubertin quayside (**B 7**).

Église de la Trinité (**B**) ⊙ – This former Ursuline chapel was built in the 17C by Pierre Corbineau and his son Gilles, architects from Laval. A statue of St Ursula adorns the pilastered façade. Inside there is a monumental 18C altarpiece and the convent parlour grille.
To the right of the church is the elegant 15C manor house known as the **Manoir de la Touche** (**B N**).

Ancienne église Notre-Dame-du-Geneteil (**B E**) ⊙ – This austere little Romanesque church built of schist used to be a college chapel and is now used to house temporary exhibitions.

EXCURSIONS

Château de la Maroutière ⊙ – *3km/2mi on ③ on the town plan.*
Built in the 13C and 14C, the château is set in a superb park containing one of the last private racecourses.

Château de St-Ouen – *7km/4mi on ④ on the town plan.*
Just before **Chemazé** this 15C-16C château appears on the right of the road with a great square staircase tower bearing a tiara-like superstructure and dormer windows with sculpted gables.

Refuge de l'Arche ⊙ – *On ③ or D 267 south of Château-Gontier.*
Half-way between a zoo and a veterinary clinic, this sanctuary is committed to the shelter, care and protection of sick, wounded or abandoned animals (not including domestic cats and dogs). It has around 700 "house guests", fed and cared for mainly by children. When the animals have recovered, and if they are fit enough to survive on their own, they are returned to their natural environment. More exotic species remain at the sanctuary. The visit ends with a small open-air museum and an aquarium.

CHÂTEAU-LA-VALLIÈRE

Population 1 482
Michelin map 64 northwest of fold 14 or 232 fold 22

This calm, small town ideal for tourists seeking a quiet haven is situated in a wooded region interspersed with many stretches of water.

Louise de La Baume le Blanc (1644-1710), better known as the Duchess of La Vallière, spent her childhood at La Vallière manor, near the village of Reugny to the northeast of Tours.
Lady-in-waiting to Charles I of England's widow, Henrietta Maria, the gentle, gracious Louise captured the heart of the Sun King, Louis XIV, at Fontainebleau in 1662. She remained the royal mistress for five years before being ousted by the haughty Mme de Montespan. Following her fall from favour, she retired to the Carmelite convent in rue St-Jacques in Paris and eventually took the black veil from the hands of Queen Maria-Theresa; the preacher was Bossuet. For the 36 years of her convent life her piety, modesty and tolerance never failed her.

Étang du Val Joyeux – This vast stretch of water *(bathing and sailing facilities)*, formed by the River Fare, lies in an attractive wooded setting. The nearby hill is crowned by a church.

Forêt de Château-la-Vallière – The town is surrounded, except on the north side, by a vast forest of pines and oaks, interspersed with stretches of heath, which covers about 3 000ha/7 410 acres and is ideal for hunting.

Château de Vaujours – *3.5km/2mi.*
Standing in front of the romantic ruins of this château *(closed to the public)* are a fortified barbican and a rampart wall interrupted at intervals by round towers, one of which has survived almost in its entirety, complete with battlements. The courtyard is bordered by the remains of the chapel and main building dating from the 15C. Louis XI came to the château several times to stay with his half-sister, Jeanne, the daughter of Charles VII and Agnès Sorel. Louise de La Vallière also held the title of the Duchess of Vaujours but only visited the château once in 1669.

The towns and sights described in this guide
are indicated in black lettering on the local maps and town plans.

CHÂTEAUNEUF-SUR-LOIRE

Population 6 558
Michelin map 64 fold 10 or 237 fold 41 or 238 fold 6

On the site of the old fortified castle to which the town owes its name, where Charles IV, the Fair, died in 1328, Louis Phelypeaux de la Vrillière, Secretary of State to Louis XIV, built a small-scale imitation of the château of Versailles. After the Revolution the château was sold to an architect from Orléans who had it demolished; only the 17C rotunda and gallery, the outbuildings and the pavilions in the forecourt, some of which are used as the town hall, remain.

Château grounds – The park is bordered by a moat; the western section is filled with water and spanned by an elegant stone footbridge. It is at its best at the end of May or in early June when the exotic plants and giant **rhododendrons** are in flower.

Musée de la Marine de Loire ⊘ – The nautical museum on the ground floor of the château contains collections made up for the most part of donations from descendants of Loire boatmen, which testify to the importance of the great river through the ages. Among the displays are anchors and carpentry tools as well as furniture, clothes, jewellery and a beautiful collection of Nevers faience. There are also presentations on river floods and pack ice.

A documentation centre supplies detailed information about river navigation and transport on the Loire.

Faience adorned with a boat on the Loire

Église St-Martial – The church was built late in the 16C in the Gothic style but lost its nave in a fire in 1940; all that remains is a double arch through which the old market hall of St-Pierre can be seen. Inside stands the marble **mausoleum**★ of Louis Phelypeaux de la Vrillière who died in 1681. This imposing Baroque monument, framed by two skeletons acting as caryatids, was carved in Italy by a pupil of Bernini.

Halle St-Pierre – Next to the church stands this picturesque building supported on wooden columns; originally built as a boathouse, it became the corn market in 1854.

EXCURSION

Canal d'Orléans: Loire Reach – *The Seine Reach is described under LORRIS: Excursion.*
The Orléans canal, which links the Loire to the Loing just north of Montargis, was built between 1677 and 1692. The 79km/49mi long canal was the scene of intense activity, mainly the transport of timber and coal to Paris, for 250 years. The canal was closed in 1954 with the decline of river traffic on the Loire and the competition from the railways. Repairs are being carried out on the canal to make it navigable again for pleasure boats. The stretch between Fay-aux-Loges and Combreux is now open to boats and barges.

Take N 460 west (15km/9mi).

Chécy – This village was originally founded by the Carnutes, a Celtic tribe. The church of St-Pierre-St-Germain, with its 12C belfry-porch, offered hospitality to Joan of Arc on 28 April 1429, on the eve of the Orléans siege. Behind the church the small **musée de la tonnellerie** (Cooperage Museum) 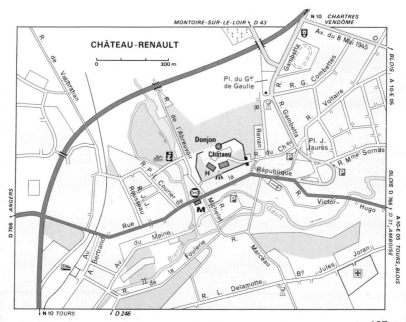 and a restored farmhouse remind visitors that in days gone by most of the local people were wine growers.

Take D 709 northeast (11km/7mi).

Fay-aux-Loges – This little village on the banks of the Orléans canal has a handsome low-roofed **church** (11C-13C). Despite its pointed vaulting, the building exudes the character and strength of a Romanesque church, an impression accentuated by the hard local stone used as a facing right up to the pyramidal spire. The modern stained glass blends well with the austere architecture. The fortified house behind the church is the vicarage.

Take D 9 east (14km/9mi).

Combreux – The town clusters on the picturesque south bank of the Orléans canal. On the north side of the town and the canal, east of the road (D 9), stands an eye-catching **château** (16C-17C), built of brick with stone dressings and surrounded by a moat.

Cross the canal to reach the reservoir and leisure park (2km/1mi west).

★ **Étang de la Vallée** – The reservoir which feeds the Orléans canal is on the eastern fringe of the Orléans forest in a wild setting of dense trees and tall reeds where ducks and moorhens can be heard cackling. There are facilities for swimming, fishing, windsurfing, sailing and picnics.

CHÂTEAU-RENAULT

Population 5 787
Michelin map 64 folds 5, 6 or 238 fold 1

Château-Renault was founded in 1066 by Renault, son of Geoffroi de Château-Gontier, on a tongue of land between the River Brenne and the River Gault at the point where they meet. The town has now extended well beyond its original limits. The main street runs in a large curve down to the river bank. Chemical and electronics industries have replaced the traditional activity of leather working.

Musée du Cuir et de la Tannerie (**M**) ⊘ – Housed in an old tannery, this leather and tanning museum displays the various stages of traditional manufacture with, among other things, a collection of old currying machinery.

Château – A 14C gate, surmounted by a hoarding (to enable the defenders to protect the entrance) leads onto the terraces shaded by lime trees, from where there is an attractive **view**★ over the town.

The top of the 12C **keep** *(donjon)* has been demolished. The town hall occupies the old 17C château. This belonged to the owners of the château in Châteaudun and then to two illustrious sailors: the Marquis of Château-Renault under Louis XIV and, under Louis XVI, the Count of Estaing who died under the guillotine in 1793.

EXCURSION

St-Laurent-en-Gâtines – *11km/7mi west.*
At the roadside stands a massive brick and stone edifice. Known for many years as "la Grand' Maison" (the Great House), it was once the residence of the abbots of Marmoutier, who owned the land of St-Laurent-en-Gâtines. The building was constructed in the 15C and converted into a church in the 19C: a spire was addded to the polygonal tower which housed the stairs and two large Flamboyant windows were inserted on one side.

Château de CHAUMONT-SUR-LOIRE★★

Michelin map 64 folds 16, 17 or 238 fold 14
Local map see Vallée de la LOIRE: Orléans-Chinon

The original fortress of Chaumont was demolished twice; it was rebuilt between 1465 and 1510 by Pierre d'Amboise, Charles I d'Amboise, the eldest of Pierre's 17 children, and Charles II, his grandson. The latter, thanks to his uncle, Cardinal Georges d'Amboise, who was in great favour with King Louis XII, became Grand Master of the King's Household, Marshal, Admiral of France and Lieutenant-General in Italy.
In 1560 Catherine de' Medici, the widow of Henri II, acquired the castle purely as a means of exacting revenge against **Diane de Poitiers**, the mistress of the late King. The Queen forced her rival to give up her favourite residence at Chenonceau in exchange for Chaumont. Diane de Poitiers never set foot in Chaumont, however, but retired to Anet where she died in 1566.

Catherine de' Medici's stay at Chaumont and the existence there of a room connected by a staircase with the top of a tower have given rise to plenty of speculation. The room has been said to be the study of **Ruggieri**, the Queen's Astrologer, and the tower the observatory from which Catherine and her master plotter consulted the stars. It was apparently at Chaumont that Catherine read in the future the grim fate awaiting her three sons, François II, Charles IX and Henri III, and the accession of the Bourbons with Henri IV of Navarre.

Mass-produced medallions – In the 18C one of the proprietors of the castle, Jacques Le Ray, Governor of the Invalides in Paris, retained the famous Italian artist **Nini**, a glass engraver and ceramicist, for 1 200 *livres* a year. Nini fitted out a workshop in the stables and an oven in an old dovecot. Using a hollow mould he reproduced many copies of medallions of more than a hundred famous people of the time, including Benjamin Franklin who spent some time at the château. Le Ray made a large profit from this new industrial method of portraiture.

Chaumont-sur-Loire

19C – Exiled from Paris by Napoleon, **Madame de Staël** spent some time in 1810 at Chaumont as a guest of Le Ray's son. She worked there, surrounded by her "court" which included Benjamin Constant and Madame Récamier. When her guests praised the landscape of the Loire, she replied sadly: "Yes, it's an admirable scene, but I so much prefer my gutter in the rue du Bac."

In 1875 the castle was bought by **Mlle Say**, heiress to an industrial fortune, who soon became the Princesse de Broglie; for Chaumont this was an era of luxury and magnificent festivities.

Since 1938 Chaumont has belonged to the French State.

TOUR *45min*

Chaumont château is as well sited as Amboise on the south bank of the Loire, overlooking the town and the river; the **view★** from the terrace is remarkable. The feudal austerity of the buildings is softened by the Renaissance influences and complemented by the magnificent stables, a reminder of coaching days.

The park ⊘ – A 10-minute walk uphill will bring you to the castle. This pleasant stroll is an opportunity to admire the fine landscaped gardens designed by Henri Duchêne. The paths wind their way through cedars, lime trees and redwoods.

The building – The outer west façade, which is the oldest, looks austere and military. Most of the windows that can be seen now did not exist originally. The two other façades, though they still have a feudal look, manifest the influence of the Renaissance.

At ground floor level there is a frieze bearing the interlaced Cs of Charles de Chaumont-Amboise, alternating with the rebus of the castle: a volcano or *chaud mont* (Chaumont). The emblem of Diane de Poitiers is carved in front of each machicolation on the fortress and the east wing: it consists of intertwined Ds or of the hunting horn, bow and quiver of Diana the Huntress.

The entrance gate is adorned with the arms of France and the initials of Louis XII and Anne of Brittany on a field of fleurs de lys and ermine in homage to the then reigning monarchs. The hat of the Cardinal d'Amboise is carved on the tower on the left, recalling that this prelate, a lover of the arts, oversaw the reconstruction of the château from the end of the 15C to 1509 on behalf of his nephew Charles de Chaumont-Amboise who had been held up in Italy by his duties as governor there. Charles's arms appear on the right tower of the fortress. These emblems are protected by small structures in a mixed Gothic and Italian Renaissance style.

On entering the courtyard go first to the terrace. This was built in the 18C on the site of the north wing, which had been demolished by an owner who liked the view. A magnificent view of the Loire countryside can be seen from it.

Apartments ⊘ – Note the room of the two rivals, Catherine de' Medici and Diane de Poitiers, and also Ruggieri's study and the Council Room, which is paved with 17C Spanish majolica tiles bought in Palermo, Sicily, by the Prince of Broglie. These apartments contain fine 16C and 17C tapestries, good furniture and a collection of the terracotta medallions made by Nini.

Stables ⊘ – *About 50m from the château.*

The size and luxurious fittings of these stables give an idea of the part played by horses in the lives of princely families.

Built in 1877 by the Prince de Broglie and fitted with electric lighting in 1906, the stables include stalls for the horses and ponies, boxes for the thoroughbreds, a kitchen, a remarkable harness room, horse-drawn carriages and a second courtyard known as the "guests' courtyard", in which there is a small riding centre. Note in a corner of the stables the unusual double-roofed tower, the former dovecot, transformed into an oven for Nini, which later became the riding school for the children at the château.

The stables organise trips in **horse-drawn carriages** ⊘.

Conservatoire international des Parcs et Jardins du Paysage ⊘ – The château farmhouse houses a permanent information and training centre offering thematic workshops aimed at enlightening visitors on the fascinating world of botany and horticulture. It also runs university-level studies in gardening and landscaping.

An important international **garden festival** is held here every summer, for which a specific theme is chosen each year and 30 plots of 250m²/300yd² are put at the disposal of landscape gardeners, who draw on their powers of imagination and originality in designing a garden. The purpose of the festival is to familiarise the general public with contemporary creations, new possibilities for garden layout and unusual, daring combinations of plants and flowers.

Château de CHENONCEAU★★★

The beautiful château of Chenonceau (*NB the town of Chenonceaux has an -x but not the château*) stretches across the River Cher in a harmonious natural setting of water, greenery, gardens and trees. To this perfection is added the elegance of the château's architecture, interior décor and magnificent furniture.

View of Chenonceau in 1850 *(Lithograph by Leroy)*

The château shaped by women – The first château was built between 1513 and 1521 by Thomas **Bohier**, Collector of Taxes under Charles VIII, Louis XII and François I. Bohier's acquisition of Chenonceau and the château's subsequent frequent change of ownership make up an eventful tale. For 400 years the main protagonists in this, both happy and sad, were women, be it royal wives, mistresses or queens.

Catherine Briçonnet, the builder – The Chenonceau estate, comprising a manor and a communal mill, belonged originally to the lords of Marques, who sold it in ruins to Bohier in 1499. An heiress exercising her hereditary right of repurchase bought it back, but Bohier refused to give up and patiently acquired all the adjoining fiefs and manors until the property was encircled. Finally, in 1512, Chenonceau was seized and put up for sale, whereupon Bohier bought it for 12 400 *livres*. Immediately he demolished all the old buildings except for the keep. As he was kept busy by his duties and often had to be with the army near Milan, he could not supervise the building of his new residence. It was his wife Catherine, from a family of great financiers in Touraine, who took charge and was the creative spirit behind the project. It is possible to detect a certain feminine influence and eye for convenience and comfort in the site chosen for the building and the simplicity of its layout, consistent with the requirements of someone used to running a household. The four rooms on each floor are arranged round a central hall and, another novelty, the flights of stairs rise in a straight line.

The new building was completed in 1521 but Bohier and his wife had little time in which to enjoy it as they died in 1524 and 1526 respectively. A few years later, Bohier's accounts were examined and he was shown to owe a large sum of money to the Treasury. In order to pay his father's debts, Antoine Bohier gave up the château in 1535 to François I who used it as a hunting lodge.

Diane de Poitiers, the everlasting beauty – When Henri II came to the throne in 1547 he gave Chenonceau to Diane de Poitiers. She was 20 years older than he but was still radiantly attractive. "I saw her," wrote a contemporary, "at the age of 70 (in fact she died at 67), as beautiful to look at and as kind as at 30. She had a very white skin and wore no make-up on her face". Diane was the widow of Louis de Brézé, for whom she had a splendid tomb built in Rouen cathedral, and in honour of whom she always wore black and white, the colours of mourning. Her influence over Henri II was such that, in addition to all the other favours she received, she made him wear mourning too, to the despair of the rejected and humiliated Queen.

Diane was an able manager and set out to exploit her estate and her position; she took an interest in agriculture, in the sale of wine, in her income from taxes and in anything else that earned money. She found an excellent source of revenue in

110

the 20 *livres* tax on bells, of which she received a good share; Rabelais said, "The king has hung all the bells of the kingdom round the neck of his mare". Diane was a woman of good taste; she created a beautiful garden and had a bridge built linking the château with the north bank of the Cher. She spent some happy times here with Henri II.

Diane made provisions for the future; the 1535 act by which Chenonceau became part of the royal estates was repealed and the château temporarily restored to Antoine Bohier, but as he was in debt to the crown it was seized automatically and put up for auction; Diane had only to buy it officially and thus became the legal owner.

Despite these precautions, when Henri II was killed in a tournament in 1599, Diane found herself face to face with Catherine de' Medici who was now regent. While her husband was alive the queen had been patient and dissembling and had accepted the situation, but now she wanted vengeance. Knowing that Diane was very attached to Chenonceau, she forced her to give up the property in exchange for Chaumont. After a brief attempt at resistance, Diane gave in, left the banks of the Cher and retired to Anet château where she died seven years later.

Catherine de' Medici, the extravagant – Catherine de' Medici satisfied her love of the arts and magnificence on a grand scale at Chenonceau. She had a park laid out, built a graceful two-storey gallery on the bridge and added extensive outbuildings. She held one magnificent feast after another, greatly impressing her contemporaries. She put on a huge party for the arrival of François II and Mary Stuart, and an even more sumptuous one for Charles IX. Young women disguised as mermaids would welcome visitors from the moats along the avenue leading to the château. Their singing would be matched by that of nymphs flitting out of the shrubbery. This graceful chorus would scatter at the arrival of a group of satyrs. No expense would be spared at these festivities, which would include banquets, dances, masquerades, fireworks and even a naval battle on the Cher.

Louise de Lorraine, the inconsolable (late 16C) – Catherine bequeathed Chenonceau to her daughter-in-law, Louise de Lorraine, wife of Henri III. After the King's assassination by Jacques Clément, Louise retired to the château and according to royal custom put on white mourning which she continued to wear until the end of her life, earning herself the nickname "White Queen" or "White Lady". Her bedroom, bed, carpets and chairs were covered with black velvet, her curtains were made of black damask; crowns of thorns and Franciscan girdles were painted in white on the black ceilings. For 11 years Louise remained faithful to the memory of her husband, passing her time by praying, embroidering or reading.

Madame Dupin, the intellectual (18C) – From Louise de Lorraine Chenonceau passed to her niece, Françoise de Lorraine, wife of César de Vendôme, the son of Henri IV and Gabrielle d'Estrées who had stayed at the château in 1598. In 1733 it became the property of Dupin, the farmer-general who was the tax collector. Madame Dupin held a salon which was attended by all the famous names of the period. **Jean-Jacques Rousseau** was her son's tutor and it was for the benefit of this boy that he wrote his treatise on education, *Émile*. In his *Confessions* the philosopher writes warmly of those happy days, "We had a good time in that beautiful place, we ate well, I became as fat as a monk."

Madame Dupin grew into old age encircled by the affection of the villagers, with the result that the château survived the Revolution unscathed. At her request she was buried in the park.

Madame Pelouze, the lover of antiquity (19C) – In 1864 Madame Pelouze bought Chenonceau and made it her life's work to restore the château to its former glory, albeit proceeding boldly with refurbishments in the somewhat debatable taste of the 19C. Catherine de' Medici had altered the main façade by doubling up the windows and having caryatids placed between them. The extra openings were now walled up and the caryatids removed to the park. A building which had been added between the chapel and the library was demolished.

Chenonceau château now belongs to the Menier family.

TOUR ⊙ *2hr*

Son et lumière – *See the Practical information section at the end of the guide.*

Approach – A magnificent avenue of plane trees leads to the château. Tourists who like to indulge their imagination can try to imagine the entry of Charles IX, among mermaids, nymphs and satyrs. Set back on the left, at the end of a path, are the caryatids removed from the façade by Mme Pelouze; the outbuildings erected after the plans of Philibert Delorme can be seen on the right, just after the path has passed between two sphinxes.

After crossing a drawbridge the path reaches a terrace surrounded by moats. To the left is Diane de Poitiers's Italian garden; to the right, that of Catherine de' Medici, bounded by the great trees in the park. On the terrace stands the keep of the original château remodelled by Bohier. It is adorned with the initials

Château de CHENONCEAU

"TBK" (Thomas Bohier and Katherine), along with the motto: *S'il vient à point, me souviendra.* The meaning of this motto is rather obscure; it may be, "If the building is finished it will preserve the memory of the man who built it."

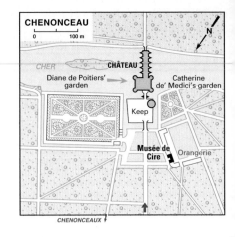

Château – The château consists of a rectangular mansion with turrets at the corners. It stands on two piers from the old mill, which rest on the bed of the Cher. The library and the chapel are corbelled out on the left. Catherine de' Medici's two-storeyed gallery stretches across the bridge over the river. This building by Philibert Delorme has a classical simplicity contrasting with the ornate and exuberant appearance given to the older section by the sculptures on the balustrades, roof and dormer windows.

Ground floor – The four main rooms lead off the hall which features ribbed vaults with keystones aligned along a zigzag axis. The old guard-room *(left)* is paved with majolica tiles and adorned with 16C Flemish tapestries; in the chapel is a 16C marble low-relief of a Virgin and Child; the fireplace in Diane de Poitiers's bedroom was designed by Jean Goujon; pictures and an Oudenaarde tapestry hang in Catherine de' Medici's Green Cabinet.

The great gallery overlooking the Cher is 60m/197ft long and has black and white chequered paving. Incorporated in its ceiling is the original ceiling of Louise de Lorraine's bedroom. During the First World War the gallery was converted into a military hospital and from 1940 to 1942 the demarcation line ran right through the middle.

François I's bedchamber contains paintings by Van Loo *(Three Graces)* and Il Primaticcio *(Diane de Poitiers as the Huntress Diana)*, and a handsome 15C Italian piece of furniture inlaid in ivory and mother-of-pearl. In a salon with a magnificent French-style ceiling are works by Rubens *(Jesus and St John)*, Mignard, Nattier *(Mme Dupin)* and a portrait of *Louis XIV* by Rigaud, in a sumptuous frame.

First floor – This is reached by a straight staircase, which at the time it was built was an innovation in France. From the vestibule, with its Oudenaarde tapestries depicting hunting scenes and Carrara marble statues of Roman emperors brought by Catherine de' Medici from Florence, walk through to Gabrielle d'Estrées' bedchamber, then the Royal or Five Queens' Bedchamber, then Catherine de' Medici's bedchamber and finally to that of César de Vendôme. All the rooms are furnished and adorned with fine Gobelins tapestries. A small convent for Capuchin nuns was set up in the attics, complete with a drawbridge which was raised at night to separate the nuns from the castle's other occupants.

Kitchens – There is an attractive dresser and a set of copper pots and pans.

Musée de Cire ⊙ – The waxworks museum is housed in the Dômes building, so called because of the shape of its roof. There are 15 scenes evoking life in the château and the personalities connected with it.

The park – This stretches along the banks of the Cher, offering picturesque views of the château.

ALONG THE CHER TO MONTLOUIS-SUR-LOIRE
Round trip of 50km/31mi – allow 1hr 45min

Leave Chenonceaux eastwards (towards Montrichard), immediately turn south across the Cher and take N 76 west towards Tours.

Bléré – At the entrance to Bléré, on place de la République, stands an elegant monument with particularly fine Italian style sculpted decoration; this is the **funerary chapel** (1526) of Guillaume de Saigne, Treasurer of the Royal Artillery under François I, all that remains of the old cemetery.

Château de Leugny ⊙ – This elegant château on the Cher was built by the architect Portier, a pupil of Gabriel, for his own use. It is furnished in the Louis XVI style.

Véretz – This smart little town tucked between the Cher and the hillside makes a charming picture from the north bank of the river: the houses and church lead the eye west to the tree-lined paths and terraces of the château. Among those who once strolled in the château grounds were the Abbé de Rancé (1626-1700) who reformed the Trappist order, the Abbé d'Effiat and Madame de Sévigné, the Princess de Conti and the Abbé de Grécourt who wrote light verse; Voltaire stayed at the Château de Véretz in his youth. In the village square stands a monument to **Paul-Louis Courier** (1772-1825), an officer under the Empire who bought the Chavonnière estate with its large house on the Véretz plateau in 1816 and settled there with his young wife. From his country retreat he began to harass the government with wittily caustic pamphlets, such as "A petty village tyrant under the Restoration". Despite his talent his quarrelsome and irascible temperament made him unpopular, and on 10 April 1825 he was assassinated in the Larçay forest in mysterious circumstances.

Take D 85 north across the River Cher to Montlouis.

Montlouis-sur-Loire – *See MONTLOUIS-SUR-LOIRE.*

Take D 751 east (to Amboise) and turn right onto D 40 to St-Martin-le-Beau.

St-Martin-le-Beau – The church has a finely-sculpted Romanesque doorway.
Return to Chenonceaux on D 40.

Many camp sites have shops, bars, restaurants and laundries;
they may also have games rooms, tennis courts, miniature golf courses, playgrounds, swimming pools...
Consult the current edition of the **Michelin** *Camping Caravaning France.*

Château de CHEVERNY★★★

Michelin map 64 fold 17 or 238 fold 15

Cheverny stands on the edge of the Sologne forest, not far from the châteaux of Blois and Chambord. Its classical façade is built of white stone from the Bourré quarries *(28km/17mi southwest)* and is crowned by a splendid slate roof. Built without interruption between 1604 and 1634 by Count Hurault de Cheverny, the château has a rare unity of style, both in its architecture and in its decoration.

The symmetric design and harmonious grandeur of the façade are characteristic features of the period of Henri IV and Louis XIII. On either side of the single bay containing the main entrance and staircase are steep-roofed central sections, themselves flanked by massive corner pavilions with square domes topped by open belfries. At first-floor level there are oval niches containing the busts of Roman emperors, while the Hurault coat of arms above the main doorway is surrounded by two concentric collars, one of the Order of the Holy Ghost, one of the Order of St Michael.

The interior is sumptuously appointed, with beautiful furniture, sculptures, gilt-work, marble, multicoloured panelling and much more.

APARTMENTS ⊘ *45min*

Son et lumière – *See the Practical information section at the end of the guide.*

Dining room – To the right of the hall is the dining room hung with a fine 17C Flemish tapestry and refurbished in the 19C when the passage and the chimneypiece with the bust of Henri IV were built. The room has retained its French-style painted ceiling and small painted wall panels depicting the story of Don Quixote; both are by Jean Mosnier (1600-56), a native of Blois. The walls are covered with Cordoba leather embossed with the Hurault coat of arms.

Private apartments in the west wing – Access to the west wing is via the splendid main staircase with its straight flights of steps and rich sculptural decoration. The private apartments consist of eight rooms, all magnificently furnished.

Armoury – The armoury is the largest room in the château. The ceiling, the wainscots and the shutters were painted by Mosnier, who also did the painting on the gilt wood chimneypiece, flanked by statues of Mercury and Venus. A collection of arms and armour from the 15C and 16C is displayed on the walls along with a tapestry from the Gobelins factory (1610) showing the *Abduction of Helen*.

King's bedchamber – The King's bedchamber is the most splendid room in the château. The ceiling is coffered in the Italian style, gilded and painted by Mosnier, as is the rich Renaissance chimneypiece, which is decorated with telamones, cherubs and plant motifs. The walls are hung with tapestries from the Paris workshops (1640) after Simon Vouet; beneath them are wainscots decorated with small pictures. The canopied bed is covered with Persian silk embroidered with flowers (1550).

Grand Salon – The ceiling of the Grand Salon on the ground floor is entirely covered, as is the wall panelling, with painted decoration enhanced with gilding. Among the paintings are, on either side of the mirror, a portrait of *Jeanne d'Aragon* from the School of Raphaël and, on the chimneypiece, a portrait by Mignard of *Marie-Johanne de Saumery*, Countess of Cheverny.

Château de Cheverny – Armoury

Gallery, Petit Salon, library – The **gallery** is furnished with magnificent Régence chairs and contains several paintings, including a canvas by François Clouet of *Anne de Thou*, Countess of Cheverny, a portrait of *Jeanne d'Albret* by Miguel Oñate and a self-portrait by Rigaud. The **Petit Salon** is hung with 16C, 17C and 18C paintings; the furniture includes a small gaming table inlaid with different types of Carrara marble. The **library** features some interesting woodwork and a beautiful parquet floor; it also contains some very fine bindings.

Tapestry room – The smaller salon, which follows, is hung with five 17C Flemish tapestries after cartoons by Teniers. Both rooms contain Louis XIV and Louis XV period furnishings, including a Louis XV Chinese lacquered commode and a Louis XV clock decorated with bronzes by Caffieri.

OUTBUILDINGS

Outbuildings – There is **kennelling** for a pack of 70 hounds, cross-breeds from English fox-hounds and the French Poitou, and the **trophy room** displays 2 000 deer antlers.
The château is still the home of the descendants of the Hurault de Cheverny family who have maintained the tradition of deer hunting; between autumn and Easter each year the hunt rides out in the surrounding woodland.

L'Orangerie – Some 200m from the northern steps, on the way out of the château grounds, stands a magnificent early-18C orangery, now entirely restored. Receptions are held here all the year round and, in summer, exhibitions.

Ballon captif ⊙ – This enormous **hot-air balloon** (22m/72ft diameter, 30m/98ft high, 5 500m³/194 230ft³ volume), securely fixed to terra firma, can carry 30 people at a time up to a height of 150m/492ft for an aerial view of Cheverny and its surroundings. What better way to admire such a vast panorama of the Sologne and Loire valley than this, free of noise and pollution?

Château de Cheverny

EXCURSION

Château de Troussay ⊙ – *3.5km/2mi west skirting the Cheverny park as far as D 52; turn left and take the first right fork.*
This small Renaissance château was refurbished in the late 19C by the historian Louis de la Saussaye with features from other historic buildings of the region then in a state of neglect. Note particularly the stone carving of a **porcupine**, the emblem of Louis XII, on the rear façade taken from the Hurault de Cheverny mansion in Blois and the beautiful **chapel door**★ carved with delicate scrollwork. The tiles on the ground floor date from the reign of Louis XII, the Renaissance windows came from the Guise mansion in Blois and the grisailles on the ceiling in the little salon are attributed to Jean Mosnier. The château, which is lived in, is furnished with fine pieces dating from the 16C to the 18C. The outbuildings round the courtyard house a small **museum** evoking past domestic and agricultural life in the Sologne.

CHINON★★

Population 8 627
Michelin map 67 fold 9 or 232 fold 34
Local maps see Excursions below and Vallée de la LOIRE: Orléans-Chinon

Chinon lies at the heart of a well-known wine region, surrounded by the fertile **Véron countryside** and beautiful **Chinon forest**. The well-preserved old houses of this medieval town are strung along the banks of the Vienne beneath the crumbling walls of its gigantic ruined fortress. A **medieval market** held here every year plunges visitors back into the atmosphere of the Middle Ages *(see Calendar of events)*.
The road approaching Chinon from the south gives the best **view**★★ of the spectacular setting of town and castle brooding over the River Vienne.
Park in quai Danton to take a closer look at the scene.
From the quayside, the differents parts of the castle can be clearly distinguished: on the left, the Fort du Coudray; in the centre, the massive Château du Milieu stretching as far as the slender clock tower with its roof and machicolations; on the right, the site where Fort St-Georges, now demolished, once stood.
One of the many pleasant activities Chinon has to offer is a walk along the banks of the Vienne, particularly to be recommended in the English-style landscaped garden, the **Jardin Anglais** (**B**), where flourishing palm trees are a testimony to the mild climate of the Loire valley.

Rabelais's childhood home – **François Rabelais** (1494-1553) was born near Chinon at La Devinière and grew up in Chinon where his parents had a house in rue de la Lamproie. He was the author of the spirited adventures of Pantagruel and his father Gargantua, two giants whose earthy realism always delights the reader. When Gargantua was born his first baby cry was for "A drink, a drink!"; fed on the milk of 17 913 cows, he grew rapidly and "became fat in the face with about 18 chins". The good-natured giants were fond of feasting and drinking and are freely invoked in the wine cellars of Chinon when the latest vintage is being sampled.

River Vienne at Chinon

HISTORICAL NOTES

Chinon was originally a Gallo-Roman camp and then a fortress belonging to the Counts of Blois. In the 11C it passed to their enemies, the Counts of Anjou, one of whom, **Henry Plantagenet**, built the major part of the present castle. In 1154 he became King of England but Chinon, at the heart of his continental possessions, was one of his favourite residences; he died there on 6 July 1189. However, it was during the Angevin period from 1154 to 1204 that Chinon really flourished.

John Lackland, dispossessed vassal – John, the youngest son of Henry II, inherited the Plantagenet kingdom on the death of his elder brother Richard the Lionheart, who was killed at Châlus in 1199. His deceitful character and his underhand plotting earned him many enemies. First he quarrelled with his nephew Arthur of Brittany who sought refuge at the French court. Then he abducted Isabelle d'Angoulême, the fiancée of the Count of La Marche, and married her at Chinon on 30 August 1200. Discontented with the behaviour of their overlord, the knights of Poitou appealed to the royal court in Paris. John refused to attend the hearing, at which he was condemned to forfeit his French fiefs.

John was reduced to being King of England only, and one by one Philippe Auguste recaptured all the former English strongholds in France; in 1205 Chinon passed to the French crown. John tried to fight back but in vain; after the truce of 26 October 1206 he was forced to give up. He sought, nonetheless, to exact revenge and in 1213 he took part in the Anglo-German coalition against Philippe Auguste. He was defeated the following year by the future Louis VIII at the Battle of La Roche-aux-Moines near Angers. The French victory was confirmed by the Treaty of Chinon on 18 September 1214. John, who had alienated all the knights in his kingdom and richly deserved his nickname of Lackland, died two years later.

The Court of the "King of Bourges" (early 15C) – With the accession of **Charles VII** Chinon moved into the limelight. France was in a desperate plight. Henry VI, King of England, was also "King of Paris"; Charles VII was only "King of Bourges" when he set up his little court at Chinon in 1427. The following year he called a meeting of the States-General of the central and southern provinces which had remained faithful to him. They voted 400 000 *livres* for organizing the defence of Orléans, then besieged by the English *(see ORLÉANS)*.

Joan of Arc at Chinon (1429) – Escorted by six men-at-arms, Joan travelled from Lorraine to Chinon, arriving on 6 March, without encountering any of the armed bands which were ravaging the country. The people took this as a clear sign of divine protection. Waiting to be received by Charles VII, Joan spent two days at an inn in the lower town, fasting and praying.

When the 18-year-old peasant girl was finally admitted to the palace, an attempt was made to put her out of countenance. The great hall was lit by 50 torches and 300 courtiers in rich apparel were assembled there. The King was hiding among the crowd while a courtier wore his robes. Joan advanced shyly, immediately recognized the real King and went straight up to him. "Gentle Dauphin," she said – for Charles, not having been crowned, was only the Dauphin to her – "my name

3Bis/MICHELIN

is Jehanne la Pucelle (Joan the Maid). The King of Heaven sends word by me that you will be anointed and crowned in the city of Reims, and you will be the Lieutenant of the King of Heaven, who is the King of France." Charles was consumed with doubts about his birthright as a result of the scandalous behaviour of his mother, Isabella of Bavaria. When Joan said to him, "I tell you in the name of Our Lord Christ that you are the heir of France and the true son of the King", he was reassured and almost believed in the courageous girl's mission.

His advisers were more stubborn, however. Joan was made to appear before the court at Poitiers. A tribunal of doctors and midwives was set up to decide whether she was inspired by God or the devil. For three weeks she was cross-examined. The simplicity and swiftness of her responses, her piety and her confidence in her heavenly mission convinced even the most sceptical and she was declared to be truly a "Messenger of God". She returned to Chinon, where she was given the necessary armed men and equipment. She left on 20 April 1429 to fulfil her miraculous and tragic destiny (*see map p 19*).

★★ OLD CHINON (VIEUX CHINON) (A) *45min*

Chinon was once surrounded by high walls which earned it the name Ville Fort (Fortified Town); the old town with its pointed roofs and winding streets lies tucked between the banks of the River Vienne and the castle bluff. There are numerous medieval houses with picturesque details: half-timbered houses with carved beams, stone gables with corner turrets, mullioned windows and sculpted doorways.

Start from place Général-de-Gaulle.

Take **rue Voltaire**, once called **rue Haute-St-Maurice**, which is the main axis of the old town.

Musée animé du Vin et de la Tonnellerie (M¹) ⊘ – Housed in a wine cellar, the Wine and Cooperage Museum uses life-size automata and a recorded commentary to present the work of a vineyard, the wine-making process and the cooper's art.

In a righthand turning, rue des Caves-Peintes, which leads up to the hillside, are the **Caves Peintes** where, according to Rabelais, Pantagruel drained many a glass of cool wine; the paintings have disappeared but since Rabelais's time these old quarries have always been devoted to the Sacred Bottle since it is here that the annual ceremony of the "Bons Entonneurs rabelaisiens" (the wine-growers' brotherhood) is held.

No 19 rue Voltaire is a 14C half-timbered house. Rue Jeanne-d'Arc climbs steeply up to the castle; a plaque marks the **well** where, according to tradition, Joan of Arc placed her foot when she dismounted from her horse on arriving in Chinon.

Hôtel Torterue de Langardière (18C) – *Rue Jeanne-d'Arc.*
The classical façade is enhanced by handsome wrought-iron balconies.

★★ **Grand Carroi (B)** – (*Carroi* = crossroads). Despite its restricted size, which hardly merits such a grand name, this was the centre of town in the Middle Ages, where rue Haute-St-Maurice, an old Gaulish road, intersected rue du Grand-Carroi which led down to the bridge over the Vienne. This is the setting for the annual "Medieval Market" (*see Calendar of events*).

The picturesque courtyards of the old houses are open to the public; the prettiest are not far from one another: no 38, called the **Maison Rouge** (Red House – 14C) is half-timbered with brick and an overhanging upper storey; another half-timbered house, no 45, is decorated with statues serving as columns; no 44, the **Hôtel des États-généraux** (States-General House) is a handsome 15C-16C brick building, which houses the Museum of Old Chinon, and the broad stone doorway of no 48, the 17C **Hôtel du Gouvernement** (Government House), opens into an attractive courtyard lined with elegant arcades.

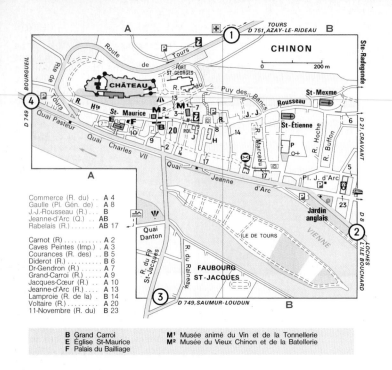

A   TOURS   B
D 751, AZAY-LE-RIDEAU

CHINON

Commerce (R. du) .. A 4
Gaulle (Pl. Gén. de) . A 8
J.-J.-Rousseau (R.).... B
Jeanne-d'Arc (Q.) .... AB
Rabelais (R.) .... AB 17

Carnot (R) .... A 2
Caves Peintes (Imp.) . A 3
Courances (R. des) .. B 5
Diderot (R.) .... B 6
Dr-Gendron (R.) ..... A 7
Grand-Carroi (R.) ..... A 9
Jacques-Cœur (R.) .. A 10
Jeanne-d'Arc (R.).... A 13
Lamproie (R. de la) . B 14
Voltaire (R.) .... A 20
11-Novembre (R. du) B 23

B Grand Carroi   M¹ Musée animé du Vin et de la Tonnellerie
E Église St-Maurice   M² Musée du Vieux Chinon et de la Batellerie
F Palais du Bailliage

Musée du Vieux Chinon et de la Batellerie (M²) ⊘ – The museum is housed in the Hôtel des États-Généraux, where Richard the Lionheart is said to have died in 1199 after being wounded at the siege of Châlus in the Limousin, and where the States-General – the French Parliament – met in 1428 at the request of Charles VII to provide him with the money to continue the war against the English.

The museum is devoted to the history of the town, as well as to river transport. The ground floor exhibits are mainly concerned with folk art and archeological finds. There are beautiful rooms: the main hall on the first floor has a full-length portrait of Rabelais by Delacroix; and the second floor, where the roof is in the form of a ship's hull, contains the collections of a local historical society. There are also ceramics including Langeais ware, St Mexme's cope brought back from the Holy Land during one of the Crusades, as well as Gothic chests and wooden statues of the Virgin Mary.

There are various exhibits connected with the traffic on the Vienne and the Loire and models of the different kinds of vessels: flat-bottomed barges, lighters and expendable pinewood boats *(see Vallée de la LOIRE)*.

Palais du Bailliage (F) – *No 73 rue Haute-St-Maurice.*
Walk round into rue Jacques-Cœur to admire the southern façade of this building which houses the Bailiff's Court and the Hôtellerie Gargantua with its pretty corbelled turret and crocketed gable.

Église St-Maurice (12C-16C) (E) – The high pointed vaulting in the nave and the chancel is in the pure Angevin style.
Further west in **rue Haute-St-Maurice** is the **Hôtel Bodard de la Jacopière** (no 81), a 15C-16C mansion with a town gateway (15C) in wood studded with nails; no 82 is a 16C building **(Hôtel des Eaux et Forêts)** with an interesting corner turret and elegant dormer windows.

★★ CHÂTEAU ⊘ *1hr*

It is best to approach the castle by the Route de Tours (D 751) which skirts the massive walls on the north side. Note the reconstructions of ancient fighting machines including a ballista (catapult for launching stones) and a trebuchet, used in siege warfare until the 14C.
Built on a spur overlooking the Vienne, this vast fortress (400m by 70m/1 312ft by 230ft) dates mostly from the reign of Henry II (12C). Abandoned by the court after the 15C and bought in the 17C by Cardinal de Richelieu, the castle was dismantled little by little until Prosper Mérimée undertook to preserve it. These majestic ruins evoke eight centuries of history.
The fortress consisted of three sections separated by deep dry moats.

Fort St-Georges – The eastern fort, which is now demolished, protected the vulnerable side of the castle which was accessible from the plateau.

Château du Milieu – The entrance to the Middle Castle is across the moat and through the 14C **Tour de l'Horloge** (Clock Tower) which is unusually shallow (only 5m/16ft deep). Inside, there are four rooms with displays evoking the great moments in the life of Joan of Arc. A bell, the Marie Javelle, which is dated 1399, sounds the hour from the lantern at the top of the tower. Visitors are free to stroll in the gardens and explore the ruined towers, in particular the recently-restored **Tour des Chiens** (Dogs' Tower). The south curtain wall commands a very picturesque **view★★** of the slate roofs of Old Chinon, the Vienne and the river valley.

Fort du Coudray – West of the gardens another bridge crosses the moat to the Fort du Coudray on the point of the rock spur. Coudray keep *(right)* was built by Philippe Auguste early in the 13C; the Templars *(see ARVILLE)* were imprisoned here by Philip the Fair in 1308 and it was they who carved the famous graffiti on the north wall of the present entrance. Joan of Arc was lodged on the first floor, now roofless, in 1429.

Logis Royaux – Joan of Arc was received in the great hall on the first floor, of which only the fireplace remains. The guard-room on the ground floor, hung with a 16C Flemish tapestry *(Bear Hunt in a Park)*, displays a large model of the castle as it was in the 15C. In the kitchens you can admire two 17C tapestries from Flanders belonging to the same series – *The Wedding of Thetis and Peleus* and *The Judgement of Paris* – flanked by four busts from Cardinal Richelieu's collection of antiques. The royal apartments also house an interesting 17C Aubusson tapestry, *The Recognition of the Dauphin by Joan of Arc*, and a small lapidary museum. The tour ends in the 13C **Tour de Boissy**, in a low vaulted room, once used as a chapel, where a map of France c 1420 is on show, along with the genealogy of the Capet, Valois and Plantagenet families, explaining the Dauphin's position at the time of Joan of Arc's arrival.

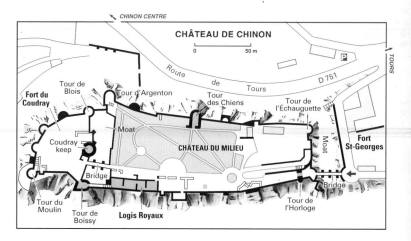

ADDITIONAL SIGHTS

Église St-Étienne (B) – This church was built c 1480 by Philippe de Commines and features a beautifully sculpted Flamboyant Gothic doorway carved with his coat of arms.

Rue Jean-Jacques-Rousseau (B) – Several picturesque medieval houses can be seen, especially nos 71 and 73 at the crossroads with rue du Puy-des-Bancs.

Église St-Mexme (B) ⊙ – Two imposing towers overlooking place St-Mexme and the nave and the narthex are all that is left of this 10C-11C church.

Chapelle Ste-Radegonde (B) ⊙ – *Access on foot up the steep path which begins northeast of the church of St-Mexme.*
The steep rise is bordered by troglodyte houses. In the 6C a pious hermit had his cell built in the cave. Radegund, the wife of King Clotair I, came to consult the hermit about her intention to leave the court and found the convent of the Holy Cross (Ste-Croix) in Poitiers – the cell was later enlarged into a chapel where the hermit was buried. A Romanesque portal leads into the chapel. On the left is a Romanesque fresco depicting a Royal Hunt; on the right 17C paintings recount St Radegund's life. Also of interest to visitors are the **cave dwelling**, adjoining the chapel, and the **Musée des Arts et Traditions populaires** (Folk Museum).

EXCURSIONS

Steam railway  – A steam train dating from the 1920s runs from Chinon to Richelieu via Ligré and Champigny-sur-Veude. *See RICHELIEU.*

Centre nucléaire de production d'électricité de Chinon ⊙ – *12km/8mi northwest on ④. Entrance near Port-Boulet bridge.*
It was here at Avoine, on the banks of the Loire, that the first of France's many nuclear power stations was put into service in 1963. EDF 1, nicknamed "the Bubble" (la Boule), was run by a subsidiary of Électricité de France (Uranium naturel-Graphite-Gaz) which has now ceased production. Electricity production is now carried out on this site by four 900mW generators which meet 40% of the demand in the Loire valley, Brittany and central France. "The Bubble" is open to visitors, as is the machine room of one of the active generators. The whole of the power station can be seen through the portholes at the top of the great sphere.

★ ① Vallée de la Vienne

Michelin map 67 folds 9, 10 or 232 folds 34, 35. *Round tour of 60km/38mi – about 3hr. Leave Chinon to the east on rue Diderot and D 21.*

The road follows the chalky hillside through the well-known vineyards of Cravant-les-Côteaux.

Vieux Bourg de Cravant – *1km/0.5mi north of Cravant-les-Côteaux.*
The church ⊙ in this old town is particularly interesting because of its age. The nave is a rare example of the Carolingian style (early 10C), built of characteristically small stones. The 11C south portal is adorned with a cable moulding; just at the entrance to the chancel two rectangular pillars have been adorned with Merovingian interlacing. These pillars used to support the roof of the south portal.
In the south chapel, added in the 15C, there are the remains of a fresco (on the west wall) depicting the chapel's donors, who were probably Georges de La Trémoille, Minister to Charles VII, Catherine de l'Ile-Bouchard, his wife, and their children. The church also houses a lapidary museum.

Follow D 21 to Panzoult and then take D 221 to Crouzilles.

Crouzilles – Built in the 12C and covered with Angevin vaulting in the 13C, the church is particularly interesting because of the way in which the statues have been incorporated into its structure. The buttresses on either side of the Romanesque door have been carved with a niche to hold a statue; in the apse, statues have been placed at the springing line of the vault: St Peter, the Virgin Mary, St John, St Paul and in the southeast corner of the south transept a figure known as the "beau Dieu de Crouzilles".

Take D 760 west to L'Ile-Bouchard.

L'Ile-Bouchard – *See L'ILE-BOUCHARD.*
The road passes in front of the church of St-Gilles, then crosses the Vienne to the other half of the town.

Take D 18 east to Parçay-sur-Vienne.

Parçay-sur-Vienne – This 12C church ⊙ has a fine Romanesque doorway flanked by blind arcades. It is decorated with carved archivolts representing bearded faces (33 in total), foliated scrolls and palmettes, and the ensemble is surmounted by a motif resembling fish scales. The capitals in the chancel are decorated with imaginary animals of quite astounding ugliness inspired by the Apocalypse of St John the Divine.

Return to L'Ile-Bouchard and take D 760 westwards along the south bank of the Vienne.

Tavant – The Romanesque **church** ⊘ here is of special interest because of the 12C **frescoes**★ which adorn the vaulting, apse and crypt. More markedly in the crypt than in the church, the figures embody a force of expression and a degree of realism extremely rare during the Romanesque period. Note the capitals in the chancel.

About 2 miles further on, beyond Sazilly, the road (D 760) passes the **Château de Brétignolles** *(left)*, a Louis XII-style building with turrets.

Turn left onto D 749.

★ **Château du Rivau** – *See Château du RIVAU.*

Return to Chinon on D 749 and ③ on the town plan.

② Rabelais country

25km/15mi leaving on ③ on the town plan. The road runs through a tunnel of tall plane trees to St-Lazare; turn right onto D 751ᴱ, an old Roman road; after 3km/2mi turn left onto D 759; then right onto D 24 and almost immediately fork right onto D 117.

La Devinière ⊘ – This farmhouse was the birthplace of **François Rabelais** (1494-1553). He was the son of a Chinon lawyer and after a studious childhood, he became a monk, fell in love with Ancient Greek and studied the humanists. He transferred to the secular clergy, studied medicine at Montpellier and became a famous doctor, under the patronage of such great names as Cardinal Jean du Bellay and his brother the Governor of Piedmont; in 1551 the Cardinal obtained the living at Meudon for Rabelais.

With the publication of *Pantagruel* in 1532 Rabelais, the distinguished Hellenist, revealed the humorous side of his character by choosing burlesque farce and every kind of comedy to express his philosophy.

At La Devinière visitors can see Rabelais's room and a small museum illustrating his life and work; there is an interesting study on the origins of his hero Gargantua.

Rejoin D 117 going south.

On the opposite side of the valley stands the beautiful **Château du Coudray-Montpensier** (15C) with its numerous roofs. In between lies **Seuilly-Côteaux**, a long straggling street of troglodyte houses.

It was in the abbey at Seuilly that Rabelais was educated; he used it as the setting for one of his characters in *Gargantua*.

Lerné – Picturesque village built of yellow tufa. In Rabelais' book this was the village from which the bakers *(fouaciers)* of a special sort of bread set out to sell their goods *(fouaces)* in Chinon market; it was a dispute between them and the shepherds from Seuilly that sparked off the comic Picrocholean War between Picrochole, king of Lerné, an aggressive fighter, and Grandgousier, the wise prince of Seuilly, who was Gargantua's father.

Return to Chinon along D 224 through Seuilly-Bourg at the bottom of the slope; near the junction with D 749 *(right)* stands **Château de la Roche-Clermault** which was taken by assault by Picrochole and his men in Rabelais's tale.

CHOLET

Conurbation 55 132
Michelin map 67 folds 5, 6 or 232 fold 30
Town plan in the current Michelin Red Guide France

Cholet is a spacious modern town, which thrives on its various industries: textiles, shoes, fashion, plastics, electronics, agricultural machinery and a Michelin tyre factory. The town is surrounded by the pastures of **Les Mauges** and is also an important cattle market.

Ravages of war – There is scarcely a building in Cholet which dates from before the Revolution since the town suffered sorely in the Vendée wars (Royalists versus Republicans). At the beginning of the peasant insurrection the town was captured by the Royalist Whites (15 March 1793) who regrouped before marching victoriously on Saumur and Angers. On 17 October Cholet was captured by Kléber after a bloody battle in which 40 000 Whites faced 25 000 Blues; the victor described it as a "battle between lions and tigers"; the dead numbered 10 000. On 10 March 1794 after vicious hand-to-hand fighting in the streets Stofflet won Cholet back for the Whites, but a few days later the "infernal columns" under General Turreau put Cholet to fire and the sword. On 18 March Stofflet returned once more but was soon driven out by General Cordellier, leaving the town of Cholet in ruins.

Cholet handkerchiefs

Weaving is a long-established industry in Cholet, where hemp and flax have been cultivated and spun since the 11C. In the 16C the handkerchief was introduced into France from Italy. In the 17C, as the practice of bleaching cloth became ever more widespread, local manufacturers came up with a whiteness for which Cholet was to become famous, by spreading their cloth out to bleach in the sun on green meadows where the damp clay soil prevented it drying out too much. In the 18C Cholet cloth was part of the cargo of manufactured goods which the shipowners of Nantes and La Rochelle traded on the coasts of Africa in exchange for slaves who were then sold in the West Indies, from where the rum bought with the profits was imported into France, in the infamous "trade triangle".

Despite the devastation wrought on the town during the revolutionary wars, Cholet was not destroyed; it re-established its crafts and tenaciously fostered its textile industry throughout the 19C. Cholet table and bed linen is now renowned for its high quality and as well known as the traditional red Cholet handkerchief, which is holding its own against stiff competition from abroad and from the disposable handkerchief industry. Many French department stores traditionally hold cut-price sales of table and bed linen in January – "le mois du blanc" – an idea which originated in Cholet!

SIGHTS

★ **Musée d'Art et d'Histoire** ⊘ – Installed in a building opposite the Hôtel de Ville, the Art and History Museum consists of two separate galleries.

Galerie d'Histoire – The History Gallery evokes Cholet in 1793, as well as the Vendée wars (1793-1796, 1815, 1832) and the chronological sequence of events which ravaged the city and plunged it into mourning during the period of revolutionary unrest (maps, arms, table coverings, everyday objects). Note *The Machecoul Massacre* by François Flameng, *The Rout of Cholet* by Girardet, *General Moulin's Suicide* by Benoît-Lévy and above all the series of famous full-length portraits of some of the leaders of the Vendée resistance, in particular those of *Henri de La Rochejaquelein* by Pierre Guérin and *Cathelineau (illustration under Les MAUGES)*, commissioned by Louis XVIII for the guard-room of the old Château de St-Cloud just west of Paris.

Galerie d'Art – The Art Gallery has a strong 18C collection with works by the local artist Pierre-Charles Trémolières (1703-39), Carle Van Loo, Hallé, Nattier, de Troy, Coypel and de Loutherbourg. Sculptures by Hippolyte Maindron and paintings by Troyon, Diaz de la Pena and Maufra represent the 19C. As far as the 20C is concerned, the main movement represented is Geometrical Abstraction with works by Vasarely, Gorin, Nemours, Herbin, Claisse, Gleizes, Valmier, Honegger, Magnelli and especially Morellet.

Musée du Textile ⊘ – This textile museum has been set up in an old bleaching-house by the Sauvageau river, a remarkable piece of 19C industrial heritage. The museum visit begins in an unusual modern building, modelled on Crystal Palace in London. This demonstration room, which shares some similarities with weaving factories (plenty of light, metal structure etc), houses four looms still in working order, the oldest of which dates from 1910. Next comes the steam-engine room in which the furnace and enormous machinery, no longer extant, generated the necessary energy for the entire factory. Other rooms contain a display on the history of textiles. Finally, a "textiles garden" has been laid out to show visitors some of the plants used in the manufacture and dyeing of cloth.

Old Houses – A pedestrian precinct has been created in the town centre, where place Rougé, rue du Devau and its continuation rue du Commerce have a number of old houses with rare 18C wrought-iron balconies. On the south side of the street the **Jardin du Mail** makes a pleasant garden setting for the Law Courts.

EXCURSIONS

Lac de Ribou – *3.5km/2mi southeast on D 20 (towards Maulévrier) and then D 600 to the right.*

This vast reservoir encircled by hills provides facilities for a variety of water sports (windsurfing, rowing, sailing etc) and fishing. The gently sloping, grassy shores are suitable for other sports such as archery, golf and riding. There is also a camp site.

The **Ferme de la Goubaudière** ⊘ is a farmhouse which has been converted into a museum on rural life, the **Musée de la Paysannerie**, showing a typical late-19C domestic interior from the Cholet region, with furniture, everyday articles and a collection of tools and farm machinery from 1900-50.

Lac du Verdon – *7km/4mi southeast.*
This lake lies immediately downstream from the Lac de Ribou and covers an area of 280ha/692 acres. One end of the lake stretches into the hills. The lake has become a nature reserve for the migratory birds that flock here in their thousands.

Maulévrier – *13km/8mi southeast (see MAULÉVRIER).*

Château du Coudray-Montbault ⊙ – *25km/16mi east on N 160 and D 960.*
The moated 16C château with its two massive round towers of brick and stone and green lozenge decoration was built on the ruins of a 13C castle. A ruined chapel in the park contains a recumbent figure and an Entombment.

CINQ-MARS-LA-PILE

Population 2 370
Michelin map 64 fold 14 or 232 fold 35 -5km/3mi northeast of Langeais

The place name is derived from a curious monument in the shape of a slim tower *(pile)*, dating from the Gallo-Roman period, which dominates the ridge east of the village. The structure is 5m/16ft square and 30m/98ft high and is topped by four small pyramids, one at each corner. It could be a funerary monument or a navigation light but it is most likely a mausoleum built in the 2C AD.

Château ⊙ – Two round towers (11C and 12C) on the hillside mark the site of the medieval castle where Henri d'Effiat, Marquis of Cinq-Mars, was born. He was the favourite of Louis XIII but was convicted of conspiring against Richelieu and beheaded in Lyon in 1642 at the age of 22.
Each tower contains three rooms, one above the other, roofed with eight-ribbed ogive vaulting. From the top there is an extensive view of the Loire valley. The surrounding **park**★ is particularly beautiful: here a romantic garden, there a complicated maze, elsewhere dense woodland. The bushes are clipped and the paths neatly edged but with a light touch that does not spoil the natural charm.

CLÉRY-ST-ANDRÉ★

Population 2 506
Michelin map 64 fold 8 or 238 fold 4
Local map see Vallée de la LOIRE: Orléans-Chinon

The present **church** had its origin in a humble chapel to which, in 1280, some ploughmen carried a statue of the Virgin Mary they had found in a thicket. Worship of this statue spread throughout the district, and the chapel, too small to accommodate the pilgrims, was transformed into a church served by a college of canons. This was destroyed in 1428 by the English commander Salisbury, during his march on Orléans. A popular **pilgrimage** is held on 8 September and the following Sunday.
Charles VII and Dunois supplied the first funds for rebuilding, but the great benefactor of Cléry was **Louis XI**. During the siege of Dieppe, while still only the Dauphin, he vowed to give his weight in silver to Notre-Dame de Cléry if he were victorious. His prayer was answered and he kept his vow. When he became King, Louis XI dedicated himself to the Virgin Mary and in doing so strengthened his attachment to Cléry. He was buried there at his request and the building was completed by his son, Charles VIII.
The house (now a school) in which Louis XI stayed during his visits to Cléry is on the south side of the church opposite the transept entrance.

★ BASILICA ⊙ 30min

Notre-Dame de Cléry basilica is a 15C building with the exception of the 14C square tower abutting the north side of the church which is the only part of the original church to have escaped destruction by the English. *Go in through the transept.*
The interior of the church is austere yet elegant; it should be imagined in the warm light of the stained-glass windows it once had, and with tapestries adorning the walls.

Tomb of Louis XI – The tomb stands on the north side of the nave and is aligned with the altar dedicated to Our Lady, so that it lies at an oblique angle to the axis of the church.
The marble statue of the King is the work of an Orléans sculptor, Bourdin (1622). It took the place of the original bronze statue, which was melted down by the Huguenots.

Funerary vault of Louis XI – Louis XI's bones and those of his wife, Charlotte de Savoie, are still in the vault which opens onto the nave near the tomb. The two skulls, sawn open for embalming, are in a glass case. Note the decorative mourning band *(litre)* which runs round the vaulting.

Tanguy de Châtel, who was killed during a siege while saving the life of Louis XI, is buried under a flagstone alongside the royal vault. Further to the right another stone covers the urn containing the heart of Charles VIII. The inscription on this urn is repeated on the nearest pillar.

★ **Chapelle St-Jacques** – *South aisle.*

The church dean, Gilles de Pontbriand, and his brother built this chapel, dedicated to St James, to serve as their tomb. The chapel's Gothic decoration is very rich. The vaulting is decorated with girdles and pilgrims' purses, for Cléry is on the pilgrimage route to St James's shrine in Santiago de Compostela, Spain. The walls are studded with ermines' tails and bridges (the arms of the Pontbriands). There are three fine statues: two in wood, of St James in a pilgrim's cloak (16C) and St Sebastian (17C); and one in stone of the Virgin Mary with very delicate features (16C). The Breton-style wooden grille in front of the chapel was donated by Louis XIII in 1622.

R. Mazin/DIAF

St James

Chapelle de Dunois – *From the Chapelle St-Jacques, the second door to the left.*

Dunois and his family are buried here *(see CHÂTEAU-DUN).* The church at Cléry was finished when this chapel was added (1464) so that the construction of the vaulting was complicated by the presence of a buttress.

Stalls – These were presented by Henri II. Their seats are carved with very varied human masks and the initials of the donor and his mistress, Diane de Poitiers (see cheekpieces of second row of stalls on the right).

Chancel – On the 19C high altar is a statue in wood of Notre-Dame de Cléry. In the central window a fine piece of 16C stained glass – the only one of this age in the church – represents Henri III founding the Order of the Holy Spirit.

Sacristy and Oratory of Louis XI – In the second ambulatory bay on the right is the beautiful door to the sacristy, in pure Flamboyant style. Above it, a small window opens into an oratory *(spiral staircase in the sacristy)* from which Louis XI could follow Mass.

CLOYES-SUR-LE-LOIR

Population 2 593
Michelin map 60 southwest of fold 17 or 237 fold 38
Local map see Vallée du LOIR: Bonneval-Vendôme

Cloyes, once a fortified town and staging post on the pilgrim road to Santiago de Compostela, straddles a bend in the Loir on the southern edge of the Beauce region. It is a welcoming town with several picturesque old houses and a church with a 15C belfry. In 1883 **Zola** stayed in Cloyes to study the local customs for his novel *The Earth* which is set in Cloyes and Romilly-sur-Aigre *(see below).*

The Children's Crusade – In 1212 a young shepherd from Cloyes, called Estienne, gathered a following of about 20 000 children on a pilgrimage to the Holy Land. Neither their parents nor their friends could deter them. The expedition was doomed to failure: some children died on the road, others perished at sea and some were even sold to the Saracens.

Chapelle d'Yron – *1km/0.5mi south on N 10 (towards Vendôme), then turn right onto D 8¹; entrance in the garden of the old people's home.*
This Romanesque chapel is decorated with well-preserved **mural paintings** in red and ochre tones. Those in the nave are 12C and depict the Flagellation and the Offering of the Magi *(left)*, the Kiss of Judas and a priest (St Bernard) *(right)* and the Apostles *(apse)* below a gentle-featured Christ in Majesty (14C) on the oven vault of the apse.

★ **Château de Montigny-le-Gannelon** – *2km/1mi north on D 23. See MONTIGNY-LE-GANNELON.*

VALLÉE DE L'AIGRE

Round trip of 20km/12mi. Leave Cloyes-sur-le-Loir on D 8 going east.
The road climbs onto a plateau overlooking the Aigre valley to the right.

Romilly-sur-Aigre – The quiet country village climbs the slope on the south bank of the Aigre. Above the village on the edge of the plateau *(D 83 towards Ouzouer-le-Doyen)* stands an unusual church adjoining a fortified building. Romilly appears in **Zola**'s novel *The Earth* under the name of Rognes; the large Beauceron farm described by Zola is probably based on La Touche about 500m beyond the church.
Return through the village to D 8; turn right.

La Ferté-Villeneuil – Drive through the village down to the banks of the Aigre where a fortified Romanesque church with a solid tower complements the charming scene.
Take the road back to Cloyes.

CORMERY

Population 1 323
Michelin map no 64 fold 15 or 238 fold 13

Cormery, which is famous for its macaroons, is prettily sited beside the Indre with inns on either bank. Near the bridge, half-hidden under the weeping willows is an **old mill**; downstream the river feeds the old washing place.

Abbey ⊙ – The Benedictine Abbey, which was founded in 791, was suppressed a thousand years later in 1791; the buildings were confiscated and sold by the French Republic and most were subsequently demolished. The few remains conjure up a picture of the complete abbey; the model shows it as it was in the 14C and 15C. Rue de l'Abbaye, which begins beside the town hall *(on N 143)*, passes under a tall ruined tower, the **Tour St-Paul**, the huge 11C bell-tower above the entrance to the church; note the Romanesque low-reliefs and the decorative effect below the upper windows. The **Logis du Prieur** (Prior's Residence) at the foot of the tower features an elegant staircase turret. In the street on the left are the arches of the old refectory (13C). Of the church itself, which would have been on the far side of the tower, nothing remains; the street follows the line of the nave. The elegant Gothic chapel (left) which was reserved for the Abbot was originally next to the apsidal chapel of the church and linked to the **logis abbatial** (Abbot's Residence) which has a turret and a half-timbered penthouse.

Notre-Dame-du-Fougeray – The church of Our Lady of Fougeray, which dominates the valley, is a Romanesque building with elements typical of the Poitou region: a large apse with three apsidal chapels, historiated brackets, a frieze and a dome on pendentives over the transept crossing.
In the cemetery opposite the church there is an altar and a 12C lantern of the dead.

Château de COURTANVAUX

Michelin map 64 fold 5 or 238 fold 1 – 2km/1mi northwest of Bessé-sur-Braye

The **château** ⊙, a Gothic building sheltering in the valley, was the seat of a marquisate held successively by the Louvois and Montesquiou families; one of the owners was Michel Le Tellier, Marquis de **Louvois** and Louis XIV's Minister for War. In 1815, when Napoleon fell from power, the château came to life again after 150 years of neglect and became the residence of the **Countess of Montesquiou** who had been the much-loved governess to the King of Rome, Napoleon's son by Marie-Louise.
An avenue of plane trees leads to the charming Renaissance gatehouse. The buildings have typical 15C and 16C features: tall roofs, mullioned windows and pointed dormer pediments. The courtyard is overlooked by two terraces. The main block, called the "grand château", has a suite of four rooms (47m/154ft long) on the first floor, which were redecorated in 1882.

CRAON

Population 4 767
Michelin map 63 fold 9 or 232 fold 18

Craon (pronounced Cran) is a quiet Angevin town on the River Oudon surrounded by woodland and pastures, devoted to arable farming and cattle raising. It is famous for its horse races (August and September).

Craon was the birthplace of **Volney** (1757-1820), a philosopher who enjoyed great fame in his lifetime.

Château ⊘ – Built c 1770 in the local white tufa, this elegant château has a curvilinear pediment and windows adorned with festoons characteristic of the Louis XVI period. The courtyard façade is in a severe neo-Classical style. Several 18C rooms with fine woodwork and Louis XVI furnishings are on show.

The pretty formal French **gardens** around the château and the fine landscape **park** (42ha/104 acres) in the English style running down to the river have recently been restored. Many of the trees can be identified with the aid of descriptive labels. There is a kitchen garden with its 19C greenhouses, a laundry building where clothes were "steamed" over wood-ash and an underground ice house, built in the 19C. In winter it was filled with ice and packed snow to serve as a cold chamber for the preservation of food in the summer.

EXCURSIONS

Cossé-le-Vivien – *12km/8mi northeast; on entering town take D 126 southeast*. In 1962, the painter and ceramicist **Robert Tatin** (1902-83), gave free rein to his architectural fantasies around the old farmhouse called La Frénouse. The result has now become the **Musée Robert-Tatin★** ⊘.

The museum is approached along an avenue lined with strange statues leading to the Giants' Gate and the figure of a dragon with jaws agape. Then come three major coloured structures made of reinforced concrete, representing Our Lady of the Whole World, the Moon Gate and the Sun Gate, which stand reflected in a pool shaped like a cross and lined by representations of the 12 months of the year. The architecture, painting and ceramics seem to have been drawn from experience of a symbolic, initiatory nature.

The museum as a whole, which has a certain affinity with Art Brut, takes the visitor into the fantastic world of this self-taught artist, whose naïve and visionary creations draw on Oriental, Pre-Colombian and even Celtic sources, fusing them into an art of universal significance – a bridge between East and West.

Renazé – *10km/6mi southwest*.
Having reached their heyday in the early years of the 20C, the quarries at Renazé continued to produce their finely-grained slate up until 1975. The Longchamp site has now been turned into a **musée de l'Ardoise** ⊘, with displays of slate-working tools and machinery, demonstrations of the slate-worker's skills and a slide-show *(15min)* evoking the dark world of the underground slate mines which have gradually replaced conventional quarrying.

Château de Mortiercrolles ⊘ – *11km/7mi southeast on D 25 and a track to the left*.
This beautiful château was built in the late 15C by Pierre de Rohan, Marshal of Gié. A broad moat surrounds the long curtain wall with its four corner towers, which is guarded by a remarkable **gatehouse★** with alternating courses of brick and stone and fine machicolations in tufa. In the courtyard the building containing the main apartments (right) is decorated with superb dormer gables. At the rear of the courtyard an elegant chapel of brick with stone courses was re-roofed in 1969: note the pretty Renaissance side door and the piscina adorned with shells.

*The chapter on art and architecture in this guide
gives an outline of artistic creation in the region,
providing the context of the buildings and works of art described
in the Sights section.
This chapter may also provide ideas for touring.
It is useful to read it before you leave.*

Église de CUNAULT★★

Michelin map 64 fold 12 or 232 fold 32 – 12km/8mi northwest of Saumur
Local map see Vallée de la LOIRE: Chinon-Champtoceaux

Cunault abbey was founded in 847 by monks from Noirmoutier fleeing from the Normans; in 862 they had to move from Cunault and take refuge further away in Tournus in Burgundy where they deposited the relics of St Philibert. Cunault therefore became a rich Benedictine priory dependent on Tournus abbey. The monastic church is a beautiful Romanesque structure dating from the 11C-13C. The huge 11C bell-tower has been extended by a 15C stone spire; the broad façade is simply decorated with arches at the base and three windows above. In contrast the tympanum over the door is richly decorated with a Virgin in Majesty in generous high relief.

Cunault – Virgin in Majesty on the church tympanum

Interior – On entering one is struck by the size and height of the pillars. Cunault church was built in the regular Benedictine style to provide for the liturgical ceremonies (seven per day in the Rule of St Benedict) and for the crowds which attended the pilgrimage on 8 September. The ambulatory with its radiating chapels which circumscribed the chancel and the side aisles were broad enough to take the traditional processions, and the raised chancel enabled the faithful to see the celebrant.

The church is impressive both for its clean lines and for the rich decoration (11C-12C) of its 223 **capitals**. Only two, at the entrance to the chancel, are visible without binoculars: *(right)* nine monks standing and *(left)* St Philibert welcoming a sinner. The ambulatory chapels contain *(starting on the left)* a 16C *Pietà*, a 16C ash vestment wardrobe (for stiff copes) and a rare 13C carved and painted **shrine** belonging to St Maxenceul who converted Cunault in the 4C. In the 15C the church was decorated with frescoes; a few fragments and a fine St Christopher remain. The four bells in the tower come from Constantine Cathedral in Algeria. Opposite the church stands the prior's lodging, an attractive 16C house.

Playing "Boules de Fort"

This boule game is typical of the Angers area (and, to a lesser extent, of the Indre-et-Loire, the Loire-Atlantique, the Mayenne and the Sarthe). Among the many legends that explain its origins, the most common one concerns the boatmen working on the Loire: when there was little or no wind, the ships would be moored along the banks of the river and the sailors would play with large weighted balls inside. The boule in its present shape and size was created in the early 19C.

Each boule is half-flattened, with an iron band circling its diameter: its has a "weak" side and a "strong" side (*fort* in French – hence the name). Originally fashioned from wood, they are now made with synthetic materials. As in all traditional boule games, the object is to roll the boule as close as possible to a smaller ball called the *maître*. The game opposes two teams made up of two or three players.

In the old days, these boule competitions were held on playing areas covered with soil taken from the municipality of Guédeniau – a mild, soapy type of clay which soaked up water without becoming sticky. Nowadays, however, the tracks, characterised by curved edges, are made with resin or flint. Playing areas are 21.5-24m/70-79ft long and about 6m/20ft wide; each boule weighs between 1.2-1.5kg/2.5-3.5lb.

DAMPIERRE-EN-BURLY

Population 915
Michelin map 65 fold 1 or 238 fold 7 – 13km/8mi west of Gien

The flat-tiled roofs of Dampierre present an attractive spectacle to anyone approaching from the west on D 952 from Ouzouer-sur-Loire; as the road crosses the tree-lined lake by a causeway, the ruins of a château come into view. Beyond what remains of the towers and curtain wall of the castle rises the church tower. In the square by the church stands one of the château gatehouses, an elegant early-17C building, in brick and stone, decorated with bossed pilasters beneath a pyramidal roof.

Centre nucléaire de production d'électricité (CNPE) ⊘ – *3km/2mi south; signposted.*
The four gigantic cooling towers (165m/541ft high and 135m/443ft diameter at the base) rising out of the flat Loire valley belong to the nuclear power station which, like those at Chinon and St-Laurent-des-Eaux, uses the river to supply water to the cooling system. The Dampierre complex, which was commissioned in 1980 and 1981, consists of four pressurized water reactors each with an output of 900mW.
The way in which the reactors work is described in the **information centre**, named after **Henri Becquerel** (1852-1908), physicist, whose family lived at Châtillon-Coligny 30km/21mi east.

DANGEAU

Population 742
Michelin map 60 fold 17 or 237 fold 38 (9km/6mi west of Bonneval)

The village square is bordered by old houses of brick and timber construction (15C).

Église St-Pierre – The church, which was built early in the 12C by monks from Marmoutier, is a vast, well-arranged structure in a very pure Romanesque style. The buttresses and facings are of ironstone. The door in the south porch is decorated with scrolls and strange symbols carved on the lintel: the cross appears between the sun and the moon which have human faces, avarice is shown as a demon holding a purse, luxury as a female figure.
The wooden ceiling in the nave is supported on archaic pillars. There are several statues in the aisles: the two figures on horseback are typical of popular 15C-17C religious art. The baptistery contains a marble triptych of the Passion and the Resurrection, dated 1536.

DESCARTES

Population 4 120
Michelin map 68 fold 5 or 232 fold 48

It was in Descartes, which used to be called La Haye, that **René Descartes** (1590-1650), the famous French philosopher, physicist and mathematician was baptised, although the family home was in the neighbouring town of Châtellerault. At the age of eight he was sent to the Jesuit College of Henri IV in La Flèche where he received a semi-military education, before joining the army under the Prince of Nassau. While pursuing his military career, he travelled widely in Europe, devoting most of his time to study, and the pursuit of his life's mission as it was revealed to him on 10 November 1619. In 1629 he went again to Holland where he stayed for 20 years, studying at various universities and writing and publishing some of his most famous works. In 1649 he accepted an invitation to the Swedish royal court, where he died on 11 February 1650.

Cartesian thought – Written in French rather than in the Latin of all philosophical or scientific works published hitherto, Descartes' *Discourse on Method* (1637) was intended to be accessible to everyone. Published four years after Galileo's condemnation by the Inquisition, this seminal work met with a quite different reception and was destined to confound the sceptics; it marked the beginning of modern thought and scientific rationalism. In it, Descartes broke with scholasticism and founded a way of thinking based entirely on reasoned methodology and the systematic application of doubt, even to the extent of querying one's own existence, which he however resolved in the following way: "I who doubt, I who am deceived, at least while I doubt, I must exist, and as doubting is thinking, it is indubitable that while I think, I am." Descartes' work gave birth to an intellectual revolution, one of whose first fruits was analytical geometry.

Musée Descartes ⊘ – *29 rue Descartes.*
This museum is the house where Descartes was born. Documents illustrating his life and works are on display.

EXCURSIONS

Balesmes - *2km/1mi to the northwest*. Standing amid this charming village with its houses roofed in rose-coloured tiles, the church features an attractive belfry above the transept crossing.

Ferrière-Larçon - *16km/10mi to the east.*

Château du Châtelier - Standing on a rocky outcrop, commanding the Brignon valley, this castle (rebuilt 15C and 17C) has preserved some of its medieval fortifications: moats, drawbridges and, to the east of its rampart, an imposing round keep with large window openings, some of which are mullioned.

Ferrière-Larçon - The picturesque tile roofs of this village climb haphazardly up the valley slopes. The **church** is an interesting mixture of styles with a narrow Romanesque nave (12C) and a vast, luminous Gothic chancel (13C). The elegant Romanesque bell-tower has an octagonal stone spire with rounded mouldings on the ridges and a pinnacle at each corner.

DOUÉ-LA-FONTAINE★

Population 7 260
Michelin map 67 fold 8 or 232 fold 32 – Local map see Vallée du LAYON

Doué and its outskirts are built on a chalk plateau which is riddled with caves; some are old quarries, others were excavated to provide housing or storage, as a wine cellar or a stable. The caves are invisible from the street since they were not hollowed out of the hillside as in the valley of the Loire and its tributaries, but were below ground level and opened laterally into a broad ditch forming a courtyard. Some are still in use but most were abandoned long since.

Doué still has a number of old houses with turrets and external stairs. The town's main activities are nursery gardening and rose growing; examples of these arts are on display at the famous flower show, **Journées de la Rose**, which takes place each year in mid-July in the arena, and at the **Jardin des Roses**, a large park on the Soulanger road. At the end of the park, some late-18C stables belonging to Baron Foullon have been converted into an open-air museum of old-fashioned shops *(see below)*.

A windmill marks the entrance to Doué in the Saumur road, the lone survivor of the many that used to cover the region.

★★ **Zoo de Doué** ⊙ – The zoo is situated on the western edge of Doué on the road to Cholet (D 960), in a remarkable troglodyte **setting**★. The old conchitic stone quarries, with their vast underground caverns and lime kilns, make an unusual habitat for the 500 or more animals which have their home here, more or less at liberty. The setting has been embellished with features such as waterfalls, rocky outcrops, acacias and bamboo to make it as natural an environment as possible for the various species, several of which are endangered. Breeding them in captivity in zoos such as this is an important contribution towards ensuring their survival.

Steelier-nerved visitors may like to go into one of the quarries which has been turned into a huge aviary containing about 20 vultures. Then there is the "Leopard Canyon", specially adapted to be home to three families of beautiful big cats: snow leopards, Sumatra tigers and jaguars. Recently, a colony of 35 penguins has been incorporated into the zoo. A number of hides have been set up around the zoo, so that visitors can observe and photograph the animals safely at close range.

Lemurs

There are several displays, including those in the **"Naturoscope"** on wildlife conservation and environmental protection, housed in an old farm. The importance of sound to animals is explained in an immense "sound cave". The "Faluna" gallery contains animal fossils from the park itself.

Musée des Commerces anciens ⊙ – The stables of Baron Foullon, the only remaining part of the château, provide a splendid setting for this museum of 20 or so old-style shops along two reconstructed streets. Covering about a century (1850-1950) of local retail trade, the museum includes an apothecary's, a clothier's, a corn chandler's, an ironmonger's, a barber's, a grocer's etc. Each shop has been reconstructed with great attention to detail and equipped with the relevant accessories (display counters, shop-windows, tills etc) for the period.

Arènes ⊙ – In the 15C an old quarry in the **Douces** district was transformed into an arena when terraces of seats were cut out of the solid rock. It is now used for theatrical and musical performances and the flower show *(see above)*. Beneath the terraces are vast caves which were for a long time inhabited, and kitchens and other rooms are still visible. Royalists were imprisoned here during the revolutionary wars.

Maison carolingienne – *Boulevard du Docteur-Lionnet, on the southern outskirts of the town near the road to Argenton-Château (D 69).*
This 9C fortified Carolingian house was later transformed into a keep.

EXCURSIONS

Village troglodytique de Louresse-Rochemenier ⊙ – *6km/4mi north on D 69 and D 177.*
The underground village of Rochemenier, an example of troglodytic settlement adapted to the conditions of the plain, was dug out of the marly deposit known as faluna. Though extending over a wide area, it is now hidden by the dwellings at ground level where the majority of the local people live. Two troglodytic farmsteads, abandoned around 1930, are open to the public.

Hameau troglodytique de la Fosse ⊙ – *5.5km/3mi north on D 214 (in Forges).*
Excavations in 1979 revealed this fine example of a type of rural architecture which was formerly unappreciated; the troglodyte hamlet used to house three families until it was abandoned in the 1940s. Like the *bories* of Provence it shows how the peasants adapted to living underground. The various chambers were hollowed out below ground around a sunken courtyard, similar to the troglodyte dwellings in Tunisia; only the chimneys protruded above ground level. Ovens and chimneys were dug straight into the earth, as were stores for grain and vegetables.

Caverne sculptée ⊙ – *5.5km/3mi north on D 69.*
This cave at **Denezé-sous-Doué** is most unusual; its walls are carved with hundreds of strange figures. From the attitudes and dress and musical instruments archeologists have dated the carvings to the 16C; they are probably the work of a secret society of stonemasons and depict their initiation rites. Guides are at hand to give a detailed explanation of the different scenes.

Château du Coudray-Montbault – *24km/15mi west on D 960. See CHOLET: Excursions.*

DURTAL

Population 3 195
Michelin map 64 fold 2 or 232 fold 20

Durtal occupies a charming site in the shelter of its château on the Loir. **Chambiers forest** on the southern edge of the town provides 1 300ha/5mi² of walks among the oak and pine trees; broad rides radiate from the Table au roy (King's table). The racecourse is a popular meeting place for the sporting fraternity.

Château ⊙ – This grand stronghold on the Loir belonged to François de Scépeaux, Marshal of Vieilleville, who was host to Henri II, Charles IX and Catherine de' Medici. It came through the Revolution relatively unscathed.
The six-storey keep and the round towers with machicolations and pepper-pot roofs are 15C and 16C. The sentry walk provides a view of the Loir valley and Chambiers forest. The main range and the other buildings are in the Louis XIII style. Note the tapered dormers framed with twisted columns in the courtyard. The tour of the interior includes the kitchens, the dungeons, the 15C round tower and the great hall which is decorated with frescoes.

Porte Verron – This 15C gate flanked by two turrets is part of the original curtain wall of the castle.

Old bridge – This old bridge commands a nice view of the River Loir, the watermills, the pointed roofs of the town and a medieval round tower upstream.

FAYE-LA-VINEUSE

Population 343
Michelin map 67 south of fold 10 or 232 fold 46 – 7km/4mi south of Richelieu

Faye-la-Vineuse stands on a rise once covered in vineyards overlooking the valley formed by a tributary of the Veude. During the Middle Ages it was a prosperous walled city of five parishes and 11 000 inhabitants. It was ruined during the Wars of Religion.

Église St-Georges ⊙ – The Romanesque church was once a collegiate church surrounded by cloisters and conventual buildings. It has suffered from excessive restoration but still retains some interesting features: a tall transept crossing with a cupola on pendentives, two side aisles typical of churches in the Berry region, a chancel with a very high elevation and an ambulatory, and fascinating carved capitals – apart from the many plant motifs and imaginary animals there are also battle scenes. The 11C **crypt** is unusually large and its vaulting high. Note the two carved capitals of the Adoration of the Magi and jousting knights.

La FERTÉ-BERNARD★

Population 9 355
Michelin map 60 fold 15 or 232 folds 11, 12 – Local map see Le PERCHE-GOUET

La Ferté-Bernard is a lively commercial town at the centre of an agricultural region. The old houses cluster round the church of Notre-Dame des Marais. The lush pastures of the Huisne valley are watered by this river, its tributary the Même and several smaller streams. The old fortified town, which grew up round the castle (ferté) was built on stilts in the middle of the marshes. It was distinguished by the name of the first feudal lord, Bernard, whose descendants held the domain until the 14C. Under Louis XI it was made the property of the Guise family; in the 16C it enjoyed a period of economic prosperity giving rise to some remarkable buildings which contribute to the charm of the town. After taking the side of the Catholic League and being defeated by the troops of Henri IV, La Ferté was sold to Cardinal de Richelieu in 1642 and was held by his heirs until the Revolution.

La Ferté-Bernard was the birthplace of the poet **R Garnier** (1544-90), whose best-known tragedy, *The Jews*, echoes Corneille and foreshadows Racine. His play *Bradamante* is an early tragi-comedy while his modernism links him to Voltaire.

The lambs of La Ferté – "It needs only two to strangle a wolf", it would appear. In 1590 the troops of Henri IV under the Prince de Conti laid siege to La Ferté which was defended by the supporters of the League commanded by a descendant of the Emperor of Byzantium, Drago Comnenos.

As food was in short supply, Comnenos decided to get rid of the surplus population and expelled a number of women to fend for themselves, to the great delight of the besiegers. Comnenos then disguised 200 of his ruffians as young women and expelled them. The besiegers approached with great expectations but when they came within range the "lambs" threw off their bonnets and petticoats and turned into hardened old troopers who put the gullible lechers to flight.

SIGHTS

★★ **Église Notre-Dame-des-Marais** (B) – This magnificent church is a fine example of the Flamboyant Gothic style with early touches of the Renaissance. The nave and transept and the square tower were built between 1450 and 1500; from 1535 to 1544 Mathurin Delaborde worked on the church and between 1550 and 1590 the Viet brothers were in charge of the construction of the spacious chancel (completed in 1596); the ambulatory serves the radiating chapels which have galleries, flying buttresses and solid buttresses topped with crocketed pinnacles.

Exterior – There are Renaissance motifs in the carved decoration of the chancel; the south side is ornamented with scrollwork and busts of Roman emperors in the spandrels; there are niches in the buttresses. The low gallery is supported on a carved cornice of shells and busts in relief between the corbels. On the balustrade stand some unusual little statues of the King of France and his 12 peers etc; in the spaces are the words "Regina Coeli". The upper gallery spells out the letters of "Ave Regina Coelorum". The height of the chancel compared with the original tower on the left side reveals the ambitiousness of the plans drawn up in the late 16C. The entrance is the Flamboyant south door.

Interior – At the west end are the original Renaissance holy water stoups; the nave contains the organ pipes supported on a Flamboyant corbel.
The skilfully constructed, elegant chancel consists of soaring arches, each one surmounted by a small statue on a dais, a light and simple Renaissance triforium and tall windows filled with light 16C and 17C glass.
The three **apsidal chapels**★ are particularly interesting. The right chapel has an astonishing ceiling of ogive vaulting meeting in a crown-shaped pendant; the windows, the delicate carved cartouches and the stoup are all 16C. In the central

chapel the spaces between the ribs are decorated with stalactites and honeycombs; the Renaissance window *(left)* shows the meal at Bethany with Mary Magdalene at Jesus' feet. The left chapel has an unusual ceiling. The altarpiece in the side chapel on the left of the chancel shows the instruments of the Passion.

Porte St-Julien (A) – This gate, which is protected by two round towers and machicolations, was built in the 15C under Louis XI; the moat was fed by the River Huisne. There was a postern and a double gate for vehicles guarded by a portcullis and a drawbridge.

Old houses – East of Porte St-Julien in rue de l'Huisne (**B 18**) are a few Renaissance houses (no 15 features a telamone).
There are several old houses in rue Carnot including a pilgrim inn (15C) on the road to Santiago de Compostela and a house (butcher's shop) decorated with painted telamones representing a pilgrim (ground floor) being stared at by a madman and a grimacing Moor and two people (first floor) stoning St Stephen. The tourist information office *(syndicat d'initiative)* in Cour du Sauvage is housed in the town's former salt store.

Halles (**B B**) – The market hall *(restored)* in place de la Lice and rue Carnot was built in 1535. The façade overlooking the square is decorated with Guise lions on each gable and an extensive tile roof pierced by dormers and supported by a splendid timber frame.

Fountain – The granite fountain (15C-16C) is fed by a spring in Les Guillottières district which is channelled beneath the Huisne.

Chapelle St-Lyphard (B) ⊘ – Thorough restoration work has revealed the former chapel of an 11C feudal castle that was built between two arms of the River Huisne and then partly demolished on the orders of Charles VI. The outbuildings *(private property)* also remain. The chapel, which was originally built against the main body of the castle and given a small side oratory in which a Virgin in Majesty may be seen, is decorated with modern stained-glass windows of Louis, Duke of Orléans, and his wife Valentina Visconti, lord and lady of La Ferté-Bernard to whom the castle was endowed in 1392.

EXCURSIONS

Ceton – *8km/5mi northeast.*
The **church of St-Pierre** (recently restored) derives its importance from the Cluniac priory to which it belonged from 1090. The tower is Romanesque, the Gothic nave and chancel were built in the 13C-16C. Each bay in the side aisles has its own roof at right angles to the nave in the Percheron manner. A touchingly naïve 16C Entombment stands out in the interior among the fine statues.

Le Perche-Gouet round trip – *See Le PERCHE-GOUET. From Ceton drive 5km/3mi east to Les Étilleux.*

La FERTÉ-ST-AUBIN

Population 6 414
Michelin map 64 fold 9 or 238 fold 5

The town extends north-south between the main road (N 20) and the railway line. A sawmill and a garment factory are the only remaining examples of the town's past commercial activity. The old district by the château has a few typical local houses: low, timber-framed constructions with brick infill and huge roofs of flat tiles.

★ **Château** ⊙ – Built on the banks of the Cosson in brick relieved with courses of stone, this is an impressive edifice, albeit an asymmetrical one; to the left is the "Little Château" still with its 16C diamond-patterned brickwork, to the right the "Big Château", built in the mid 17C with a classical façade topped by sculpted dormers. The centrepiece is formed by a pedimented portal flanked by domed pavilions.

Inside *(access via the ramp)*, the dining room and the Grand Salon have kept their 18C furnishings as well as a number of portraits including one of the *Marquis de la Carte* attributed to Largillière and another of *Louis XV* at the age of 54. The Marshals' Room is devoted to the memory of Maréchal de la Ferté, who distinguished himself at the Battle of Rocroi, and of Ulrich de Lowendal, a contemporary of Maréchal de Saxe, his neighbour at Chambord.

On the first floor of the right wing *(access on the right)*, are 17C, 18C and 19C state apartments and the guard-room with its fine French-style ceiling. On the second floor are a number of rooms with displays on traditional trades of the Sologne.

In the basement, are the spacious 17C kitchens with a display on traditional local cooking, explaining such deliciacies as *terrines* and *tarte tatin*.

The main courtyard is delimited by two identical buildings; that on the left houses the **stables** and the saddlery, and that on the right the orangery.

In the grounds is a **menagerie** with a little model farm. There are also 30ha/75 acres of English-style parkland with a network of islands and a small "enchanted house" for children.

Église St-Aubin – 12C-16C church. The tall tower over the entrance overlooks the Cosson valley.

EXCURSION

Domaine du Ciran, Conservatoire de la faune sauvage de Sologne – *7km/5mi east.*

This estate is a wildlife sanctuary incorporating a stretch of typical Sologne countryside: forest, scrubland, meadows, streams and pools. The château and the old storehouse contain a little **museum** ⊙ devoted to the Sologne and its former way of life.

La FLÈCHE★

Population 14 953
Michelin map 64 fold 2 or 232 fold 21
Local map see Vallée du LOIR: Vendôme-La Flèche

This charming Angevin town, pleasantly situated on the banks of the Loir, is renowned for its *Prytanée*, a military college which has trained generations of officers.

Market town for the varied fruit produce from the Maine, La Flèche has recently experienced an industrial expansion with the building of several large factories, including the printing works of the paperback publishers *Livre de Poche*.

Students tend to group around the Henri IV fountain (on the square of the same name); a stroll along the Boulevard Latouche and Carmes gardens is also pleasant.

Henri IV – La Flèche was given as part of a dowry to Charles de Bourbon-Vendôme, the grandfather of Henri IV of Navarre, of "Paris is well worth a Mass" fame. It was here that the young Prince Henri happily spent his childhood and where in 1604 he founded a Jesuit college, which was to become the *Prytanée*.

Cradle for officers – The Jesuit college grew rapidly and by 1625 there were 1 500 pupils. Carried away by their success, the good fathers started a dispute with the Governor of the town who wanted to prevent them fishing in their moat; the dispute became known as the "war of the frogs". Following the expulsion of the Jesuits from France in 1762, the college became a military school and then an imperial military academy *(prytanée)* in 1808, which produced some famous personalities *(see below)*.

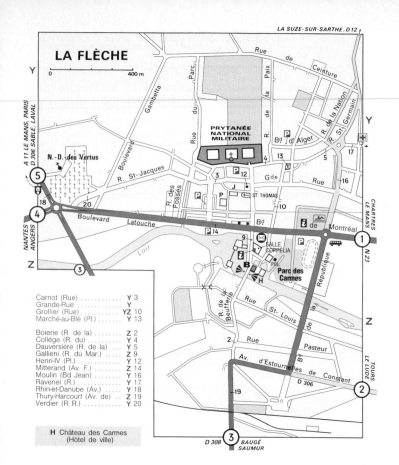

LA FLÈCHE

Carnot (Rue)		Y 3
Grande-Rue		Y
Grollier (Rue)		YZ 10
Marché-au-Blé (Pl.)		Y 13
Boierie (R. de la)		Z 2
Collège (R. du)		Y 4
Dauversière (R. de la)		Y 5
Gallieni (R. du Mar.)		Z 9
Henri-IV (Pl.)		Y 12
Mitterand (Av. F.)		Z 14
Moulin (Bd Jean)		Y 16
Ravenel (R.)		Y 17
Rhin-et-Danube (Av.)		Y 18
Thury-Harcourt (Av. de)		Z 19
Verdier (R. R.)		Y 20

H Château des Carmes
(Hôtel de ville)

Missionaries in Canada – **Jérôme le Royer de la Dauversière**, a native of La Flèche, was one of the founders of Montreal. The paganism of the Canadian Indians moved him to create the "society of Our Lady for the conversion of the Savages" which started a little colony in 1642, now the capital of Quebec. In 1646 several Jesuit priests from La Flèche, working as missionaries in the Huron country, were martyred by the Iroquois Indians: Jogues, Lalemant and Brébeuf. Another old pupil of the college in La Flèche, **François de Montmorency-Laval**, became the first bishop of Nouvelle-France in 1674.

Unhappy exile – Under the monarchy La Flèche was a peaceful town with nothing to offer by way of entertainment but a hairdresser's, two billiard halls and a café. The witty poet **Gresset** (1709-77) composed the heroic-comic masterpiece on the adventures of the parrot Ver-Vert, for which he is famous *(see Michelin Green Guide Burgundy-Jura)*, while in exile in La Flèche for indiscreet use of his tongue and his pen.

SIGHTS

★ **Prytanée national militaire** (Y) ⊘ – Located on the same site as the prestigious 17C Jesuit college, this military academy currently caters for a total of one thousand students, housed in two pavilions, named respectively after Henri IV and Gallieni. It is a state establishment offering an all-round education, open to all young French boys and preparing them for entrance to the national service academies *(grandes écoles militaires)*. The second part of the secondary curriculum is reserved for a limited number of beneficiaries admitted by competitive examination.
Founded four centuries ago to "introduce the younger generation to good literature and instil in them the love of science, honour and courage in order that they show even more dedication to the public", the college has remained loyal to the spirit of its illustrious founder, Henri IV, and over the years it has produced many great celebrities who have distinguished themselves in the service of their country: Charles Borda, René Descartes, Davout, Junot, Jourdan, Bertrand and Gallieni (who were all Maréchal de France), and more recently the astronauts Patrick Baudry and Jean-François Clervoy and the actor Jean-Claude Brialy. Not to mention also more than 1 500 generals and a number of government ministers. Among the alumni, 1 500 were killed in action.

134

A monumental Baroque doorway, surmounted by a bust of Henri IV, marks the entrance to the former Jesuit college. It opens into the main courtyard, also known as the Austerlitz courtyard; at the far end stands a Louis XVI-style house (1784) which houses the staff. The school has an excellent library of about 45 000 volumes, some of which date from the 15C.

★ **Église St-Louis** – 1607-37. The chapel is in the Sébastopol court where the architectural style is austere. It is laid out in the typical Jesuit manner: nave bordered by side chapels, large galleries, plentiful light. The Baroque décor is impressive, from the great retable on the high altar to the magnificent organ (1640) in its graceful loft. Set in an upper niche in the left transept is a heart-shaped lead gilt urn which contains the ashes of the hearts of Henri IV and Marie de Medici.

Chapelle Notre-Dame-des-Vertus (Y) – This is a charming Romanesque chapel with a semicircular-arched doorway and oven-vaulted apses. The wooden vaulting in the nave is completely decorated with 17C paintings (scrolls and medallions). The Renaissance **woodwork**★ came originally from the chapel of the Château de Verger; note the "Muslim warrior" on the back of the main door; the panels are Renaissance. The carvings in the nave include medallions and religious attributes.

Château des Carmes (Z H) – The 17C buildings erected on the ruins of a 15C fortress now house the town hall. The façade facing the Loir consists of a steep gable flanked by two machicolated turrets. The **Jardin des Carmes**, which is open to the public, stretches down to the river; from the bridge there is a fine view of the calm water reflecting the garden and the château.

J.-P. Langeland/DIAF

The Muslim warrior

EXCURSION

★ **Parc zoologique du Tertre Rouge** ⊙ – *5km/3mi east. Leave La Flèche on ② on the plan and turn onto D 104; the zoo is 1km/0.5mi after the third level crossing.*
The zoo covers 7ha/17 acres in a forest setting. There are mammals (big game, monkeys, deer, elephants etc), many birds and numerous reptiles housed in two vivariums (pythons, boas, crocodiles, tortoises etc). The **musée de Sciences naturelles** (Natural Science Museum) displays a diorama on regional fauna. The 600 stuffed animals in the collection of the naturalist Jacques Bouillault are on show in reconstructions of their natural habitats.

FONTEVRAUD-L'ABBAYE★★

Population 1 850
Michelin map 64 southwest of fold 13 or 232 fold 33
Local map see Vallée de la LOIRE: Chinon-Champtoceaux

Fontevraud abbey is on the borders of Anjou, Touraine and Poitou. Despite the ravages of history, it remains the largest group of monastic buildings in France. Major restoration work is now being carried out, including the gardens of the Bourbon Apartments. There is a good view of the abbey from the Loudon road on the south side of the village.

Foundation of the abbey (1101) – The monastic order at Fontevraud was founded by **Robert d'Arbrissel** (c 1045-1117) who had been a hermit in the Mayenne forest before being appointed by Urban II to preach in the west of France. He soon gained a large group of disciples of both sexes and chose this place to found a double community.

From the beginning the abbey was unique among religious houses in that it had five separate buildings accommodating priests and laybrothers (St-Jean-de-l'Habit), contemplative nuns (Ste-Marie), lepers (St-Lazare), invalids (St-Benoît) and lay-sisters (Ste-Marie-Madeleine). Each body led its own life, with its own church and cloister, chapter-house, refectory, kitchen and dormitory. Robert d'Arbrissel had ordained that the whole community should be directed by an Abbess chosen from among widows; she was later designated as "Head and General of the Order" and this female supremacy was to be maintained right up to the French Revolution.

In 1119 Pope Calixtus II came to bless the cemetery and consecrate the church.

The Order had dependent houses in both England and Spain. That at Amesbury in Wiltshire was founded by Henry II in 1177 in repentance for the murder of Thomas Becket.

An aristocratic Order – The success of the new Order was immediate and it quickly took on an aristocratic character; the abbesses, who were members of noble families, procured rich gifts and powerful protection for the abbey. The **Plantagenets** showered it with wealth and a dozen or so of their number elected to be buried in the abbey church. Henri II, his wife Eleanor of Aquitaine and their son Richard the Lionheart are buried in the crypt.

Later transfers to the crypt include the hearts of John Lackland and of his son Henry III, who rebuilt Westminster Abbey which in the 13C became the traditional burial place of English sovereigns.

The abbey became a refuge for repudiated queens and daughters of royal or exalted families who, voluntarily or under compulsion, retired from the secular world. There were 36 abbesses, half of whom were of royal blood including five from the House of Bourbon, between 1115 and 1789. Louis XV entrusted the education of his four younger daughters to the Abbess **Gabrielle de Rochechouart de Mortemart** (the sister of Madame de Montespan).

There were however periods of laxity caused by difficulties in recruiting nuns and the fact that the monks were disinclined to obey a woman, but an energetic abbess was always found to redress the situation. Marie de Bretagne (15C) was the first reforming abbess. Renée and Louise de Bourbon in the 16C and in the 17C Jeanne-Baptiste de Bourbon, daughter of Henri IV, and Gabrielle de Rochechouart de Mortemart, the "queen of the abbesses", made the abbey a spiritual and cultural centre of great renown.

In the 18C Fontevraud owned 75 priories and about 100 estates; the community consisted of 100 nuns and 20 monks.

Violation of the abbey – The Huguenots desecrated the abbey in 1561; in 1792 the Order was suppressed by the Revolutionaries who completely destroyed the monks' priory in the following year.

In 1804 Napoleon converted the remaining buildings into a state prison which was closed only in 1963.

Cultural vocation – In 1975 the Abbey embarked on a new vocation as a venue for cultural events: the **Centre Culturel de l'Ouest** (Cultural Centre of the West) ⓥ administers the buildings and organises concerts, exhibitions, seminars and lectures.

Accommodation for visitors is provided in the old St-Lazare priory, a short distance away from Fontevraud's other buildings.

★★ ABBEY ⓥ 2hr

Son et lumière – *See the Practical information section at the end of the guide.*

Among the buildings around the entrance court, most of which date from the 19C are, on the left, the vast 18C stables *(la fannerie)* and on the right, the 17C and 18C abbess's house adorned with garlands and low-reliefs. The entrance is situated in the former barracks which, during the last century, housed the military in charge of the prison (a standing exhibition presenting Fontevraud's history can be seen on the first floor).

★★ **Abbey church** – This vast 12C abbey church, divided into storeys at the time it served as a prison, has been restored to its original purity.

The wide nave with its delicately carved capitals is roofed by a series of domes, a characteristic of churches found in the southwest of France (Cahors, Périgueux, Angoulême etc). Fontevraud is the northernmost example of these curious domed churches and this can be explained by the important links between Anjou and Aquitaine during the Plantagenet reign.

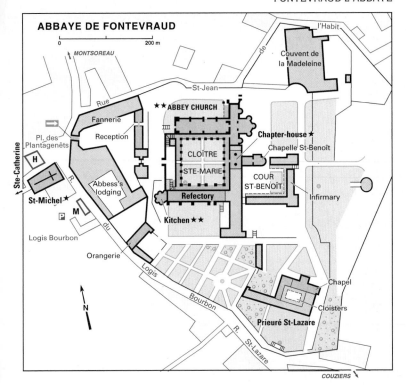

ABBAYE DE FONTEVRAUD

0   200 m

MONTSOREAU

St-Jean

l'Habit

Couvent de
la Madeleine

Rue

Fannerie

Reception

★★ ABBEY CHURCH

Chapter-house ★

Chapelle St-Benoît

Pl. des
Plantagenêts

CLOÎTRE
STE-MARIE

COUR
ST-BENOÎT

Abbess's
lodging

Infirmary

Ste-Catherine

St-Michel ★

Refectory

Kitchen ★★

Logis Bourbon

Orangerie

Logis

Bourbon

N

Chapel

Cloisters

Prieuré St-Lazare

St-Lazare

COUZIERS

Built several decades earlier than the nave, the transept and chancel resemble the Benedictine plan: an ambulatory and radiating chapels where the luminosity and repetition of vertical lines – slender columns, arcades, pillars – signify the aspiration to reach up to heaven.

The building houses **polychrome recumbent figures of the Plantagenets★**, representing Henry II, Count of Anjou and King of England, his wife Eleanor of Aquitaine, who died at Fontevraud in 1204, their son Richard the Lionheart and lastly Isabella of Angoulême, second wife of their son, King John of England. In the 16C these figures were laid in a funerary monument known as the *"cimetière des rois"* of which only the base still stands in the nave to the left of the chancel's entrance.

Cloître Ste-Marie – The cloisters in the nuns' convent have Renaissance vaulting except on the south side, which is Gothic-inspired. A richly carved doorway in the east gallery, paved with the Bourbon coat of arms, opens into the **chapter-house★** which has 16C murals representing some of the abbesses.

Cour St-Benoît – This 17C-18C courtyard leads to the infirmary. The north wing includes the 12C **chapelle St-Benoît**.

Refectory – This large hall (45m/148ft long) with its Romanesque walls is roofed with Gothic vaulting which replaced a timber ceiling in 1515.

★★ **Kitchen** – This is the only Romanesque kitchen in France to have been conserved over the centuries – despite its alterations. In many respects it resembles the abbot's kitchen at Glastonbury.

This most intriguing building is roofed with overlapping lozenge-shaped stones and topped by numerous chimneys, added in 1904 during restoration by the architect Magne. Originally, the building was free-standing, built on an octagonal plan and capped by an octagonal hood (27m/88ft high), and adjoined by eight auxiliary buildings, three of which were destroyed in the 16C, when the kitchen was attached to the Refectory. The kitchen's large size is commensurate with the size of the abbey and its community; it was also used as a smoke room for preserving meat and fish. Despite the technical and practical constraints imposed on the architect, he managed to design a room that is both aesthetically pleasing and functional.

Prieuré Saint-Lazare – This priory houses a hostelry but it also provides access to the chapel and its splendid 18C **spiral staircase**; in summer the small cloisters are used as a restaurant.

Fontevraud abbey kitchen

ADDITIONAL SIGHTS

★ **Église St-Michel** ⊘ – A low lean-to gallery was built against the walls of this parish church in the 18C, giving it an unexpected character and sheltering a beautiful 12C door with Romanesque paintings. Although the church was enlarged and remodelled in the 13C and 15C, an inner arcade with small columns and typical Angevin vaulting remain from the original Romanesque building. The church contains numerous **works of art**★. The high altar of carved and gilded wood was made at the behest of the Abbess, Louise de Bourbon, in 1621 for the abbey church. In a north side chapel is a 15C wooden Crucifix which somehow exudes an impression of both torment and peace, and an impressive 16C Crowning with Thorns by the pupils of Caravaggio. In a Crucifixion painted on wood in an archaic style by Étienne Dumonstier, the artist sought to portray the shameful waste of the struggles between Catholics and Protestants by depicting the protagonists at the foot of the Cross. Viewers can make out Catherine de' Medici as Mary Magdalene, Henri II as the soldier piercing the heart of Christ, and their three sons, François II, Charles IX and Henri III. Mary Stuart is the Holy Woman with a crown; the Virgin Mary has the features of Elizabeth of Austria. The modest nun in the foreground is the Abbess, Louise de Bourbon who was host to Mary Stuart in 1548, Charles IX in 1564 and Catherine de' Medici in 1567.

Chapelle Ste-Catherine – This 13C chapel stands in what was originally the churchyard; it is crowned by a lantern of the dead.

Gourmets...
The introductory chapter of this guide describes the region's
gastronomic specialities and best local wines.
The annual Michelin Red Guide France
offers an up-to-date selection of good restaurants.

Château de FOUGÈRES-SUR-BIÈVRE★

Michelin map 64 fold 17 or 238 fold 15 – 8km/5mi northwest of Contres

In the charming village of Fougères, surrounded by nursery gardens and fields of asparagus, stands the austere yet noble north façade of the feudal-looking **château** ⊘ of Pierre de Refuge, Chancellor to Louis XI. It is not too difficult to imagine the original moats, drawbridge and arrow slits – replaced in the 16C by windows – and the keep's battlements which disappeared when the roof was added.

The building was begun in 1470. Already, 20 years before, Charles d'Orléans had pulled down the old fortified castle at Blois and built a more cheerful residence in its place. The builder of Fougères did not follow the new fashion. He built a true stronghold round the square 11C keep.

However, when completed by his son-in-law, Jean de Villebresme, the château acquired a certain grace: the east wing in the main court has a gallery of arcades with lovely dormer windows; the attractive turreted staircase in the northwest corner with its windows flanked by pilasters with Renaissance motifs; the large windows added in the 18C to the south wing which made it ideal as a spinning mill in the 19C.

The size of the rooms seen from within is impressive; so are the wooden roof-frame of the main building which is shaped like a ship's hull, and the conical roof-frame of the towers.

EXCURSION

Le Château enchanté de Roujoux ⊘ – *5km/3mi east on D 7 towards Fresnes.*
The grounds of the Château de Roujoux, also known as the "magic castle", which was rebuilt by René de Maille in the reign of Louis XIII, are arranged for leisure activities with picnicking, games and mini-golf in a 7ha/17 acre park. Inside the château there is a historical **museum** where puppets re-enact the life of the château since the coming of the Vikings.

FRAZÉ

Population 489
Michelin map 60 fold 16 or 237 north of fold 37 – 8km/5mi northwest of Brou

Frazé is a little village in the valley beside the River Foussarde. Its origins are Gallo-Roman; later it was fortified and surrounded by water. The village square, place de la Mairie, provides a charming view of both the church and the château.
Frazé is a good starting point for an excursion into Le Perche-Gouet.

Château ⊘ – The château was begun to a square ground plan in 1493 and protected by a moat and a pool; it was completed in the 16C and 17C with the outbuildings which form an entrance porch.
The surviving buildings include a watchtower; two towers of which one stands alone and is decorated with machicolations and a moulding; a fort flanked by towers and ornamented with sculpted corbels; an interesting chapel with historiated ornaments. An old well, gardens, canals and terraces enhance the courtyard and the park.

Church – The church has an attractive Renaissance doorway supported by three atlantes.

GENNES

Population 1 867
Michelin map 64 fold 12 or 232 folds 32 and 33
Local map see Vallée de la LOIRE: Chinon-Champtoceaux

Among the wooded hills hereabouts are numerous megaliths including the **Madeleine dolmen** south of the Doué road. Discoveries including an aqueduct, baths, an amphitheatre and the figure of a nymph indicate the existence here of a Gallo-Roman shrine dedicated to a water cult. There is a small archeological museum (**musée archéologique** ⊘).

Amphithéâtre ⊘ – Discovered as long ago as 1837 and still being excavated, this is assumed to have been the structure serving as the local amphitheatre between the 1C and 3C. It is set into a terraced slope cut into on the northeast by a podium and has an elliptical arena whose principal axis measures 44m/145ft. On the north side is the boundary wall built of sandstone, tufa and brick paralleled by a paved drainage corridor.

Église St-Eusèbe  – This church, on a hill-top overlooking the Loire, has kept only its transept and tower from the 12C. From the tower there is a vast **panorama** over Gennes and the valley of the Loire from the Avoine nuclear power station to Longue and Beaufort. The churchyard has a memorial to the cadets of the Saumur Cavalry School who fell defending the Loire crossing in June 1940.

EXCURSIONS

Le Prieuré – *6.5km/4mi west on D 751, turn left in Le Sale-Village.*
The hamlet clusters around this charming priory whose **church** (12C and 13C) has a delightful square Romanesque tower and, inside, a fine painted wooden altar (17C).

Les Rosiers – *1km/0.5mi north.*
Linked to Gennes by a suspension bridge, this village has a church whose Renaissance tower was built by the Angers architect Jean de l'Espine; the staircase turret flanking it is pierced by pretty, pilastered windows. In the church square is a statue of Jeanne de Laval, second wife of **René of Anjou**.

Église de **GERMIGNY-DES-PRÉS**★

Michelin map 64 fold 10 or 238 fold 6 – 4km/3mi southeast of Châteauneuf-sur-Loire

The little church in Germigny is a rare and precious example of Carolingian art; it is one of the oldest in France and can be compared with the Carolingian octagon in the cathedral at Aachen.

TOUR ⊘ *30min*

The original church, with a ground plan in the form of a Greek cross reminiscent of Echmiadzin cathedral in Armenia, among other places, had four very similar apses. Visitors should try to imagine what it was like when the entire interior was sumptuously decorated with mosaics and stuccowork and the floor paved with inlaid marble and porphyry.

The east apse is the only original remnant. On its ceiling it has a remarkable **mosaic**★★ depicting the Ark of the Covenant surmounted by two cherubim flanked by two archangels; at the centre of the composition appears the hand of God. The use of gold and silver mosaic in the illustration of the archangels links this mosaic to the Byzantine art of Ravenna. This remarkable work of art was discovered under a thick layer of distemper in 1840 when some archeologists saw children playing with cubes of coloured glass which they had found in the church and decided to investigate.

Mosaic on the ceiling of the east apse

Theodulf, a dignitary at Charlemagne's court

Theodulf was a Goth, probably originally from Spain or the Ancient Roman province of Gallia Narbonensis (modern southwest France). This brilliant theologian, scholar and poet, well-versed in the culture of Classical Antiquity, came to Neustria after 782 and joined Charlemagne's erudite circle. After a long time spent journeying round the south of France as the emperor's missus dominicus, he was made Bishop of Orléans, then Abbot of Micy and of St-Benoît-sur-Loire.

Theodulf had a villa (country estate) not far from Fleury; all that now remains is the oratory, or Germigny-des-Prés church. The villa was sumptuously decorated, with murals depicting the Earth and the World, marble floors and superb mosaics in the oratory which date from about 806. On Charlemagne's death, Theodulf fell into disgrace, accused of plotting against Louis the Pious.He was deposed in 818, exiled and finally died in an Angers prison in 821. His villa was burned to the ground by the Vikings in the 9C. Much of the original rich décor of the oratory was destroyed by successive, clumsy restoration attempts in the 19C.

Other elements in the décor, such as the stucco blind arcades and the capitals, reflect a combination of several artistic influences: the Umayyads, the Mozarabs and the Lombards. In the centre, the altar is lit by a square lantern above the crossing fitted with panes of translucent alabaster (the technique for fitting glass panes was not then widespread). The present nave, which dates from the 15C, took the place of the fourth apse.

GIEN★

Population 16 477
Michelin map 65 fold 2 or 238 fold 7

Built on a hillside overlooking the north bank of the Loire, Gien, a small town with many a pretty garden, is well known for its glazed earthenware or faience. Respect for the traditional forms of regional architecture and a careful use of local materials have given the areas rebuilt after the last war an original and attractive appearance. From the bridge there is a lovely **view★** of the château, the houses along the quays and the Loire. Gien is a very old town which grew up round a castle, said to have been built by Charlemagne. It was here in 1410 that the Armagnac faction was set up in support of Charles d'Orléans against the Burgundians in the civil war which led up to the last episode in the Hundred Years War. The castle was later rebuilt by **Anne de Beaujeu** (1460-1522), the Countess of Gien, who was Louis XI's eldest daughter. Aged 23 when her father died, she was appointed regent during the minority of her brother Charles VIII (1483-91), a task which she performed with wisdom and firm control, revealing qualities of great statesmanship acknowledged by those around her.

In 1652 during the **Fronde**, the armed revolt mounted by the great princes (Condé, Beaufort and **Madame de Longueville**) against the King forced Anne of Austria, Mazarin and the young Louis XIV to flee from Paris. They took refuge in Gien while Turenne, at the head of the royal troops, defeated the Fronde insurgents at Bléneau (*25km/15.5mi east of Gien*).

SIGHTS

★★ **Musée International de la Chasse (Z M)** ⊘ – Gien **château★** stands on the eastern fringe of Orléans forest and the Sologne, a region abounding in game, making it an ideal setting for a hunting museum.

The château, which dominates the town, was rebuilt in 1484 of red brick with a slate roof. The decoration is restrained: a pattern of contrasting dark bricks and bands of white stone and a few stair turrets.

The rooms of the château with their beamed ceilings and fine chimneypieces make a worthy setting for the exhibition of fine art inspired by hunting: tapestries, porcelain, cut glass, paintings etc. The other displays are devoted to the weapons and accessories used in hunting since the prehistoric era: powder flasks, porcelain plates and jugs, decorated pipes, hunting knives, fashion plates, chimney plaques, crossbows, harquebuses, pistols and guns with detailed ornamentation.

Hunting scenes depict mythological and Christian legends: Diana surprised in her bath by Acteon whom she turned into a stag which was devoured by his own dogs; numerous portrayals of the legend of St Hubert. There are displays on the making of a pistol with Damascene decoration, while the falconry gallery explains the significance of the different coloured hoods.

Beneath its superb roof the great hall is devoted to the work of **François Desportes** (1661-1743) and **Jean-Baptiste Oudry** (1686-1755), great animal painters attached to Louis XIV; another room contains the uncluttered art of Florentin Brigaud (1886-1958), a sculptor and engraver of animals. The Daghilhon-Pujol Room displays a collection of jacket buttons decorated with hunting motifs. There is

Hunting hound by F. Desportes

also a collection of hunting horns and the trophy room contains the 500 antlers given to the museum by the great hunter, Claude Hettier de Boislambert.

From the château terrace there is an extensive **view**★ of the River Loire and the slate roofs of the town, reconstructed in the traditional style with pointed gables and diaper patterning in the brickwork.

On the north side of the château stands the **church of Ste-Jeanne-d'Arc**; it was rebuilt in brick in 1954 adjoining the 15C bell-tower which is all that remains of the collegiate church founded by Anne de Beaujeu. The slender round pillars of the interior create an atmosphere conducive to meditation, much like that found in Romanesque churches.

Faïencerie ⊘ – *West of the town (exit* ④ *on the plan). Access by quai or rue Paul-Bert.* When the faience (glazed earthenware) factory was founded in 1821 Gien was chosen because it was near the deposits of clay and sand needed for the paste, as well as having plentiful supplies of wood to fire the kilns, and because the Loire provided a means of transporting the finished product. Gien was well known for its dinner services and objets d'art, when at the end of the 19C it developed a new technique called Gien blue *(bleu de Gien)* which produced a deep blue glaze enhanced with golden yellow decoration. As well as continuing the old expensive handmade pieces, the factory produces modern services at reasonable prices. An old paste store has been converted into a **faience museum**; some of the very large pieces were made for the Universal Exhibition in 1900. There is also a display of current production and a shop.

GIEN

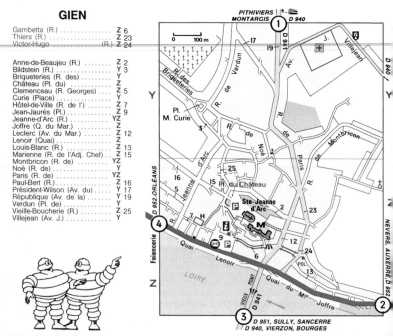

EXCURSION

St-Brisson-sur-Loire – *6km/4mi southeast.*
Here in the borderlands between Berry and the Orléans region stand the remains of a 12C hilltop **fortress** ⊙ minus its keep and crenellated south wall. The east wing and the staircase tower were restored in the 19C. The cellars of the old castle are open to the public, as is a suite of rooms with mementoes of the D'Estrades and Séguier families. In the library is a letter written by Rousseau. Replicas of medieval weaponry (mangonel, swivel gun) have been set up in the moat. Archery demonstrations are regularly staged in summer.

Take D 940 northeast, followed by D 43, to reach **La Bussière** *and the Château des Pêcheurs. This old fortress houses a museum on freshwater fishing.*

GIZEUX

Population 510
Michelin map 64 centre of fold 13 or 232 fold 34

Château ⊙ – East of the village, along a tree-lined avenue, stands this imposing château of the Angers area, which was the fief of the du Bellay, princes of Yvetôt, from 1330 to 1661 and has been occupied by the same family since 1786.

The central building, flanked by two perpendicular wings, was erected on the site of the old fortress in 1560. All that remains of the former building is the machicolated tower in the front of the court of honour. **Salle François I**[er] is decorated with paintings on wood executed by Italian artists. The **galerie des châteaux★** features 17C frescoes depicting royal châteaux (Chambord, Vincennes, Versailles). The interior boasts a fine set of Louis XV furniture.

The château is extended to the north by a series of interesting outbuildings dating from the mid 18C, with roofs reminiscent of Mansart's style.

Not far away stands the **church**, which contains 17C tombs of the Du Bellay family. On the right are two kneeling figures in white marble: René du Bellay (d 1611) in armour, and his wife Marie in an open-necked dress and bonnet. On the left is Martin du Bellay, their son, and his wife, both wearing ruffs.

EXCURSION

Vernantes – *12km/8mi west.*
Vernoil – The **church** has a massive bell-tower. Enter the priory yard *(right)* to see the solid octagonal turret and mullioned windows of the old prior's lodging.
Vernantes – A 12C tower marks the site of the **church** ⊙, of which only the chancel is still standing. The nave, destroyed by lightning in the 19C, has been replaced by a simple porch. A new church has been built on the other side of the square.

Le GRAND-PRESSIGNY

Population 1 120
Michelin map 68 fold 5 or 232 fold 48

Le Grand-Pressigny stands in a picturesque position facing the confluence of the Claise and Aigronne rivers. It was once protected by its hilltop castle.
The site is well-known in the field of prehistory on account of its many flint workshops where large numbers of blades were made at the end of the Neolithic era. These have been found far afield; some even in Switzerland.

★ **Musée départemental de la Préhistoire** ⊙ – The **castle** which provides a setting for this Prehistory Museum has retained characteristics of the medieval fortress of Guillaume de Pressigny: ramparts flanked by towers, fortified gateway, keep and late 12C underground gallery. Amid the carefully-tended gardens stands the 16C seigneurial home, which we owe to the renovation work carried out by Honorat de Savoie: the central gallery opens onto the court of honour through a pretty portico. At the top of the Vironne tower, the parapet walk affords an extremely pleasant **view** of the village and the Claise valley.
The **museum**, founded in 1910 traces the different stages of prehistoric evolution through displays of discoveries made in major sites in the Touraine.
There are special facilities for the blind.
Gallery 1 outlines the main periods of prehistory; Gallery 2, the very early and Lower Paleolithic Ages; there is a sample film of sediment from a sand quarry in Abilly. Gallery 3, exhibits from two sites in the Touraine, Roche Cotard in

Langeais and Reignoux in Abilly, represent the Middle Paleolithic era as does a model depicting the life of Mousterian hunters. Gallery 4 contains displays of the Upper Paleolithic era, particularly Solutrian hunters. Gallery 5 is devoted to the Neolithic Age, especially the late Neolithic period when knapped flint artefacts were widely used. Gallery 6 contains exhibits of the age of metals including a bronze seal from Azay-le-Rideau and presentations of sites in the Creuse valley.

The coachhouse, containing a section on paleontology, displays fossils from the Touraine, in particular those found in deposits from the Faluns Sea to the north and south of the Loire.

EXCURSION

La Celle-Guenand – *8.5km/5mi northeast.* La Celle-Guenand has a harmoniously proportioned church with a sober Romanesque façade. The covings in the façade's central doorway have been finely carved with masks and imaginary figures. In the transept crossing, which has a dome on squinches, note the interlacing work carved on the abacuses above the solid, rough-hewn capitals. To the right of the entrance, an enormous monolith decorated with masks serves as a stoup (12C).

Château du GUÉ-PÉAN

Michelin map 64 fold 17 or 238 fold 15 – 13km/8mi east of Montrichard

Gué-Péan château ⊘ is isolated in a quiet wooded valley. There is a picnic area in the grounds. The château was built as a country house in the 16C and 17C but the plan is that of a feudal castle: three ranges of buildings round a closed courtyard with a huge round tower at each corner, surrounded by a dry moat and reached by a stone bridge. The detail is more decorative; the tallest tower (the other three were never completed) is capped with a bell-shaped roof and delicate machicolations; the other buildings, with arcades and elegant windows flanked by pilasters, are roofed in the French manner.

Interior – The rooms are furnished in the style of Louis XV and Louis XVI; Germain Pilon designed the Renaissance chimneypiece in the Grand Salon. The library houses handwritten letters and historic souvenirs. Access to the sentry walk.

L'ILE-BOUCHARD

Population 1 800
Michelin map 68 north of fold 4 or 232 folds 34, 35
Local maps see CHINON: Excursions and Vallée de la MANSE

The ancient settlement of L'Ile-Bouchard, once one of the ports on the River Vienne, derives its name from the midstream island where in the 9C the first known lord, Bouchard I, is said to have built a fortress which was destroyed in the 17C. The estate was bought by Cardinal Richelieu and belonged to his descendants until 1789.

Prieuré St-Léonard ⊘ – *South of the town, signposted.*
The priory church stood on the lower slopes of the valley; little now remains standing: the 11C Romanesque apse in white tufa, an ambulatory and radiating chapels. The arcades were reinforced by additional arches a century later.

The church contains some remarkable **capitals**★ sculpted with narrative scenes depicting *(left to right)*:
1st pillar – Annunciation and Visitation, Nativity, Adoration of the Shepherds, Adoration of the Magi;
2nd pillar – Circumcision, Massacre of the Innocents, Flight into Egypt, Jesus in the midst of the doctors;
3rd pillar – Kiss of Judas, Crucifixion, Last Supper;
4th pillar – Jesus' Entry into Jerusalem, Descent into Hell, Beheading of St John the Baptist.

Église St-Maurice – 16C cathedra (detail)

Église St-Maurice ⊘ – The octagonal tower, dating from 1480, is capped by an open-work stone spire. The main church building is in the transitional Flamboyant-Renaissance style and supported on pilasters decorated with Renaissance medallions. The very beautiful replica of an early-16C **cathedra**★ (bishop's throne) in the chancel is adorned with most graceful Renaissance carvings portraying the Annunciation, the Nativity and the Flight into Egypt; the sculptors are shown on the cheekpieces.

Beside the church stands a charming early-17C manor house with pedimented dormers.

Église St-Gilles – This 11C church on the north bank of the Vienne was enlarged (nave) in the 12C and altered again (chancel) in the 15C. The two attractive Romanesque doorways have no tympanum but are decorated with plants and geometric figures. The dome on squinches over the transept crossing supports a Romanesque tower.

ILLIERS-COMBRAY

Population 3 329
Michelin map 60 fold 17 or 237 south of fold 26

Illiers, on the upper reaches of the River Loire, is a market town serving both the Beauce and the Perche regions.

"Combray" – It was under this name that **Marcel Proust** (1871-1922) portrayed Illiers in his novel *Remembrance of Things Past* in which he analysed his feelings and those of the people he had known.

Marcel Proust spent his holidays in Illiers where his father Dr Proust had been born; the impressions young Marcel experienced here, like the taste of madeleine cake dipped in tea, were later to become "that great edifice of memories".

The town is divided into the bourgeois district – *le côté de chez Swann* – facing the rich wheatfields of the Beauce, and the aristocratic district – *le côté de Guermantes* – overlooking the Perche region and its horses. In the novel the Loir becomes the Vivonne.

SIGHTS

Maison de tante Léonie ⊘ – *4 rue du Docteur-Proust.* Some of the rooms (kitchen, dining room) in this house belonging to Proust's uncle, Jules Amiot, are still as they were in the novel. The bedrooms have been arranged to match Proust's descriptions of them. The **museum** evokes the writer's life, work and relationships, and has portraits and mementoes as well as a number of photographs by Paul Nadar.

Pré Catelan – *South of the town on D 149.* Designed by Jules Amiot, the landscaped gardens, which include a "serpentine", a dovecot, a pavilion and some fine trees, make a pleasant place for a walk beside the Loir. The garden is evoked by Proust in *Jean Santeuil*, and its hawthorn hedge in *Swann's Way.*

Vallée de l'INDROIS★

Michelin map 64 folds 16, 17 or 238 folds 13 to 15

The River Indrois winds its picturesque way westwards through the clay and chalk of the Montrésor marshland *(gâtine)* to join the Indre. Its course is lined by willows, alders and poplars and lush green meadows. The sunny slopes are planted with fruit trees, in orchards or espaliers, and a few vines.

FROM NOUANS-LES-FONTAINES TO AZAY-SUR-INDRE

33km/20mi – about 2hr

Nouans-les-Fontaines – The 13C church in this village harbours a masterpiece of primitive art (behind the high altar): the **Deposition**★★, or *Pietà of Nouans*, by Jean Fouquet. This vast painting on wood (2.36m by 1.47m/8ft by 5ft) is one of the finest late-15C French works of art. The deliberately neutral colours employed, the resigned expressions of the figures and their majestic attitudes make this a moving composition.

Coulangé – At the entrance of this pleasant hamlet stands *(right)* the bell-tower of the old parish church (12C). On the opposite river bank are the remains of the fortifications of the Benedictine abbey of Villeloin.

★ **Montrésor** – *See MONTRÉSOR.*

Beyond Montrésor the road (D 10) offers scenic views of the lake at Chemillé-sur-Indrois and the countryside east of Genillé.

Genillé – The houses climb up from the river to the late-15C château with its corner towers and dovecot. The church has a striking belfry with a stone spire and, inside, an elegant 16C Gothic chancel.

St-Quentin-sur-Indrois – The town occupies one of the best sites in the valley. East of the village the road (D 10) offers a fine view south of Loches forest before joining the valley of the River Indre at Azay-sur-Indre.

Azay-sur-Indre – *See LOCHES: Excursions.*

INGRANDES

Population 1 410
Michelin map 63 fold 19 or 232 fold 30
Local map see Vallée de la LOIRE: Chinon-Champtoceaux

In the 17C and 18C Ingrandes was a major port on the River Loire. From the south bank of the river the low walls which protect the town when the river is in spate can be seen.

Its position just south of the Breton border made Ingrandes an important centre for smuggling salt. Anjou was subject to the salt tax *(gabelle)* which was particularly unpopular since salt was the only means of preserving food; Brittany, however, was exempt.

Church – The church was built on the site of a former church, which was razed in 1944. It is built of granite with a slate bell-tower; the huge glass bays were made by the Ateliers Loire after cartoons by Bertrand.

EXCURSION

Champtocé-sur-Loire – *6km/4mi east on N 23.*

On the northeast side of the town stand the ruins of the castle of **Gilles de Rais** (1404-40), a disturbing character who may have inspired Charles Perrault to write his story about Bluebeard. He was a powerful lord, a Maréchal de France by the age of 25 and the faithful companion of Joan of Arc whom he attempted to rescue from prison in Rouen. He left the king's service in 1435 and retired to Tiffauges, in Vendée, where for many years he terrorised the surrounding population, as he attempted to redress the massive debts he had run up with his profligate lifestyle, by dabbling in alchemy and reputedly sacrificing large numbers of children. When he was finally brought before the court in Nantes and charged with alchemy, raising the devil and the massacre of children, records suggest that – on pain of torture – he confessed his crimes in astoundingly great detail, hesitating only about the number of his victims: one hundred, two hundred or maybe more... On 26 October 1440 Gilles de Rais was hanged between two of his accomplices and his body then burned before an eager crowd. Nonetheless, the truth of the accusations levelled at De Rais is open to speculation; sceptics point out the Duke of Brittany's financial interest in De Rais's ruin, the irregularities of the proceedings and the incredible scope of his alleged crimes.

JARZÉ

Population 1 434
Michelin map 64 southwest of fold 2 or 232 southeast of fold 20

The countryside around Jarzé-en-Baugeois, once the fief of **Jean Bourré**, is equally divided between pasture, crops and woodland. The castle was built in 1500, burnt down in 1794 and restored in the 19C.

Church – This was originally a collegiate church built in the Flamboyant Gothic style on the foundations of an 11C building.

The seigneurial chapel *(right)* is covered with lierne and tierceron vaulting. The 16C stalls in the chancel are decorated with amusing carvings. A niche in a pillar on the right of the chancel contains a late-15C statuette of St Cyr, in robe and bonnet, holding a pear in his hand; St Cyr, the son of St Juliette of Tarsus, was martyred at the tender age of 3. The young child depicted here is more likely to be the son of Jean Bourré, reminding us that his father introduced the Bon-Chrétien pear variety into Anjou.

At the back of the apse are traces of a beautiful early-16C **mural** of the Entombment.

EXCURSION

Chapelle Notre-Dame-de-Montplacé ⊙ – *Round trip of 4km/2.5mi on D 82 north towards La Flèche; take the first turning on the right. Return to Jarzé on D 766.*

The chapel, standing in splendid isolation on its bluff, can be seen from some way off. The neighbouring farm buildings add a touch of the simple life to its elegant appearance. There is a fine 17C west doorway dedicated to the Virgin Mary.

In about 1610 the previous chapel on this site was being used as a sheepfold although it still contained an ancient statue of the Virgin. One day when the shepherdess brought in her sheep the statue was glowing. Next day the whole neighbourhood came to see; it was not long before miraculous healings were being reported on this site and it became the object of an ever-increasing religious fervour. Eventually, the generosity of pilgrims was such that the present chapel was built towards the end of the 17C. A tradition was established of making a pilgrimage to the Protector of the Baugeois region, and there is still a great annual Marian festival held on 15 August.

Entrance through the side door.

The three large altars are in the purest 17C style. In the niche in the left-hand altar is the ancient statue venerated by the pilgrims. It is a *Pietà* carved in walnut showing traces of its original colouring. The walls are hung with numerous votive offerings.

LANGEAIS★

Population 3 960
Michelin map 64 fold 14 or 232 folds 34, 35
Local map see Vallée de la LOIRE: Orléans-Chinon

The town's white houses nestle below the château's walls. Facing the château there is a lovely Renaissance house decorated with pilasters; the church's tower is also Renaissance.

Louis XI's château – At the end of the 10C Fulk Nerra, Count of Anjou, built a **donjon**, the ruins of which still stand in the gardens, which is thought to be the oldest surviving castle keep in France.

The château itself was built by Louis XI from 1465-69 as a stronghold on the road from Nantes, the route most likely to be taken by an invading Breton army. This threat vanished after the marriage of Charles VIII and Anne of Brittany was celebrated at Langeais itself in 1491.

★★ CHÂTEAU ⊙ *1hr*

The château was built in one go – a rare event – and has not been altered since – an even rarer event. It is one of the most interesting in the Loire valley owing to the patient efforts of M Jacques Siegfried, the last owner, who refurnished it in the style of the 15C.

From the outside it looks like a feudal fortress: high walls, round towers, a crenellated and machicolated sentry walk and a drawbridge over the moat. The façade facing the courtyard is less severe, suggesting a manor house with mullioned windows and pointed dormers decorated like the doors of the stair turrets.

The buildings consist of two wings set at a right angle; on the west side of the courtyard a terraced garden climbs to the keep, at the foot of which is the Siegfrieds' tomb.

★★★ **Apartments** – These apartments with their beautiful period furnishings exude an atmosphere which is much more alive than in most other old castles. They also give a very accurate picture of what aristocratic life was like in the 15C and early Renaissance. There are many fine tapestries, most of which are Flemish, but also including some *mille-fleurs*. Note the many examples of decorative motifs using the girdle of the Franciscan Tertiaries and the repetition of the interlaced initials K and A for Charles VIII and Anne of Brittany.

The guard-room, converted into a dining room by M Siegfried, has a monumental chimneypiece the hood of which represents a castle with battlements manned by small figures.

One of the first-floor bedchambers contains an early four-poster bed, a credence table and Gothic chest. The room where Charles VIII and Anne of Brittany celebrated their marriage is hung with a series of tapestries portraying the Nine Heroes, and there are also 15 waxwork figures clad in authentically reproduced costume, evoking the events which led to the union of Brittany with France. Charles VIII's bedchamber has a fine Gothic chest and a curious 17C clock with only one hand. The upper great hall, rising through two storeys, has a chestnut timber roof in the form of a ship's keel. The Creation is the theme of the Renaissance tapestries hanging here. The sentry walk, a covered gallery the length of the façade, offers views of the Loire and the town rooftops.

ADDITIONAL SIGHT

Musée de l'Artisanat ⊘ – *800m/0.5mi north, towards Hommes.*
Housed in the old church of St-Laurent, the exhibition displayed in this museum is devoted to traditional trades and crafts; there are the booths and workshops of coopers, farriers, saddlers, clog-makers, carpenters etc.

Musée R. Keyaerts, St-Michel-sur-Loire

Cadillac (detail)

EXCURSIONS

Cinq-Mars-la-Pile – *5km/3mi northeast on N 152. See CINQ-MARS-LA-PILE.*

St-Étienne-de-Chigny – *7.5km/4.5mi northeast on N 152; fork left onto D 76 and left again onto D 126 towards Vieux-Bourg. See ST-ÉTIENNE-DE-CHIGNY.*

Luynes – *12km/8mi northeast on N 152 and then left onto D 49. See LUYNES.*

St-Michel-sur-Loire – *Museum in the château de* **Planchoury** *(4km/2.5mi on N 152).*
A dedicated collector to the extent of having once negotiated the purchase of a Fleetwood Seventy-Five on a motorway, Robert Keyaerts has succeeded in bringing together around 80 Cadillac models, some 50 of which are on show in the **Musée Cadillac** ⊘. The most prestigious American car make, which saw the light of day in Detroit at the turn of the century, was named after the French founder of the town, Antoine de la Mothe Cadillac. Served by the exceptional talent of the designer Harley Earl, Cadillac became the pride and joy of General Motors during the "roaring twenties". After the war it came to symbolise the "era of glamour" with its 62-series coupés, its Eldorado cabriolet models with extravagant rocket-shaped fins, its daring "Dagmars" (bumper terminals shaped like bombs), its greedy radiator grills and its curved windscreens resembling a plane's cockpit. Renowned for its bold colour combinations (banana and mandarin in the case of the astonishing double windshield Phaeton of 1931) and its dazzling chrome accessories, Cadillac has also earned a worldwide reputation because of the stars who owned these magnificent machines (Gaby Morlay's 1928 V8 Imperial Sedan, Marlene Dietrich's 1933 V16 Town Cabriolet) and the films in which they featured *(The Great Gatsby, Le Corniaud)*.

Château de Champchevrier ⊘ – *12km/8mi north on D 15 then D 34; turn right when leaving Cléré-les-Pins.*
The château stands on the site of an old stronghold, which played a defensive role in the area for many centuries. The present building, dating originally from the 16C, was modified in the 17C and 18C. It has been occupied by the same family since 1728, testifying to the strong social and geographical attachment of these people to their land.
The château is completely surrounded by a late-17C moat. The interior is enhanced by the superb **Regency furniture**: the original upholstery, with fine colours which have remained intact, was woven in the Beauvais workshops. The huge tapestry called *Loves of the Gods*, which can be admired in several rooms, was executed by the Manufacture Royale d'Amiens after cartoons by Simon Vouet. The wood panelling of the wide staircase and its polychrome coffers were taken from the Château de Richelieu, demolished in 1805.
Located at the heart of a wooded area in which wolves roamed for many years, Champchevrier boasts the oldest pack of hounds in France. It perpetuates hunting traditions through its many trophies and collections; it also houses a series of kennels where visitors can make friends with 70 large dogs belonging to an Anglo-French pack.

LASSAY-SUR-CROISNE

Population 168
Michelin map 64 fold 18 or 238 fold 16 – 11km/7mi west of Romorantin

Lassay is a village in the Sologne, a region of woodland and vast lakes.

Église St-Denis ⊘ – This charming little 15C church has a beautiful rose window and a slender spire. In the left transept, above the recumbent figure of Philippe du Moulin, there is an attractive early-16C **fresco** of St Christopher; on the right the artist has painted Lassay church and on the left in the background the **Château du Moulin**.

★ **Château du Moulin** ⊘ – *1.5km/1mi west on a track beside the River Croisne.*
The Château du Moulin stands in a rural setting, its red-brick walls reflected in the water of the moat.
It was built between 1480 and 1506 by **Philippe du Moulin**, an important noble devoted to the service of Charles VIII and Louis XII, who saved the life of Charles VIII at the Battle of Fornoue in 1495. The original castle was built on the square ground plan typical of fortresses, surrounded by a curtain wall reinforced with round towers. Following the fashion of the 15C, the buildings are decorated with diaper pattern brickwork and bands of stone, giving an effect which is more elegant than military.
The keep or seigneurial residence has large mullioned windows and is furnished in the style contemporary with the period it was built: the dining room houses a 15C sideboard and a chandelier, both from the Sologne; there is a painted ceiling in the salon; the bedrooms contain tester beds and Flemish tapestries. However, 19C comfort is represented by the chimney plaques which provided central heating. Near the entrance, left of the drawbridge, is the vaulted kitchen with its huge fireplace; the spit was turned by a dog.

J. Becker/Château du Moulin

Château du Moulin

LAVARDIN★

Population 245
Michelin map 64 fold 5 or 238 fold 1
Local map see Vallée du LOIR: Vendôme-La Flèche

The crumbling ruins of Lavardin fortress are perched on a rocky pinnacle towering above the village and the River Loir, which is spanned by a Gothic bridge, making a picturesque scene which would tempt many a sketch-artist. The castle was the principal stronghold of the Counts of Vendôme in the Middle Ages and its strategic importance greatly increased as early as the 12C owing to its position between the kingdom of France under the Capets and the possessions of the Angevin kings. In 1188 Henry II of England and his son Richard the Lionheart besieged the castle, but in vain.
In 1589 the troops of the Catholic League captured the castle but the following year it was besieged by Henri IV's soldiers under the Prince de Conti and surrendered. The King ordered the castle to be demolished.

Château ⊙ – The path and flight of steps skirting the south side of the castle ruins offer a good view of the gatehouse and the keep. Although well worn by the weather and the passage of time, the ruins are still impressive and give a good idea of the three lines of fortified walls, the gatehouse (12C-15C) and the rectangular 11C keep (26m/85ft high) which was reinforced in the following century with towers of the same height. The innermost defensive wall is the best preserved.

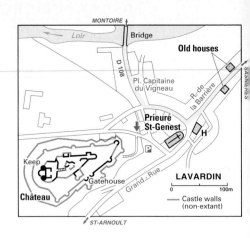

Prieuré St-Genest – The priory was built in an archaic Romanesque style with a square belfry porch. Low-relief sculptures have been reused in the structure; those in the apse represent the signs of the zodiac.

★ **Interior** – The church is divided into three parts by square piers capped by delicately-carved early-12C imposts. The chancel, which is entered through a triumphal arch, ends in an oven-vaulted apse, where curious Romanesque pillars, probably part of an earlier building, support roughly-hewn capitals. The windows in the north aisle are framed by delightful twisted Romanesque colonnettes.

The **mural paintings** date from the 12C to 16C. The oldest, most stylized and majestic ones are on the pillar at the entrance to the left apsidal chapel, depicting the Baptism of Christ and a Tree of Jesse. The well-conserved group in the chancel and apse shows scenes from the Passion *(right)* and the Washing of the Feet *(left)* on either side of a Christ in Majesty surrounded by the symbols of the Evangelists. In the right apsidal chapel note a St Christopher and Last Judgement (15C) where Paradise *(above)* and Hell are colourfully portrayed. On the pillars in the nave and aisles are 16C figures of saints venerated locally. Note the Martyrdom of St Margaret on the wall of the south aisle and the Crucifixion of St Peter on a pillar on the north side of the nave.

Old houses – One is 15C and half-timbered while the other is Renaissance with an overhanging oratory, pilastered, mullioned dormer windows and a loggia overlooking the courtyard.

The **mairie** (town hall – **H**) ⊙ contains two beautiful 11C rooms with handsome 15C vaulted ceilings; that on the ground floor is used for exhibitions.

The 13C **bridge** gives an attractive view of the lush green banks of the river.

This guide, which is revised regularly,
is based on tourist information provided at the time of going to press.
Changes are however inevitable owing to improved facilities and
fluctuations in the cost of living.

Vallée du LAYON

Michelin map 67 folds 6, 7 or 232 folds 31, 32

The Layon, which was canalized under Louis XVI, follows the trough which runs northwest between the Mauges schist terrain and the Saumur limestone escarpments, except between Beaulieu and St-Aubin where the river has cut across the ancient massif. In the clear air, the deeply incised meanders at times create the impression that the surrounding landscape is almost mountainous.

The region is a pretty one with vineyards, fields of crops interspersed here and there with fruit trees (walnut, peach, plum etc), hillsides crowned with windmills and wine-growing villages with graveyards in which dark green cypresses grow.

The "Coteaux du Layon" – The delicious mellow white wines of the Layon vineyards are produced by the *chenin*, often known as *pineau*, variety of grape. They are harvested in late September when the grapes begin to be covered with a mould known as "noble rot" *(pourriture noble)*. **Bonnezeaux** and **Quarts de Chaume** are two well-known wines from this area.

FROM CERQUEUX-SOUS-PASSAVANT
TO CHALONNES-SUR-LOIRE
72km/45mi – about 3hr 30min

Bisonland ⊘ – The grounds of a 19C Landes château in **Cerqueux-sous-Passavant** are home to a stock-breeding farm of buffaloes and fallow-deer. There is also an American Indian camp, "Tatanka", with reconstructions of typical dwellings of various American Indian tribes (tepee, lodge, wigwam) and traditional craftwork on show.

Follow the road towards Cléré-sur-Layon (D 54). At the entrance to the village turn left to Passavant.

Passavant-sur-Layon – This pretty village on the edge of a lake formed by the Layon, is enhanced by the eye-catching ruins of its castle. The church has a Romanesque chancel.

Take D 170 to Nueil-sur-Layon, turn right after the church onto D 77; after the bridge over the Layon bear left onto D 69 towards Doué-la-Fontaine.

The landscape at this point is still typical of the Poitou with its hedgerows, sunken roads and farmsteads roofed with Mediterranean-style pantiles. The vineyards are grouped on the exposed slopes and at Nueil the slate roofs more typical of northern France make an appearance.

Beyond Les Verchers bear left onto D 178 towards Concourson.

The road runs parallel with the Layon through fertile countryside; beyond Concourson it offers an extensive view of the river valley.

In St-Georges-sur-Layon take the road north towards Brigné, turning left onto D 83 to Martigné-Briand.

Martigné-Briand – This wine-growing village lies clustered round a château which suffered extensive damage during the Vendée War. It was built in the early 16C, and the north façade has glazed windows with Flamboyant motifs.

Take D 748 southwest towards Aubigné, turning right to Villeneuve-la-Barre.

Villeneuve-la-Barre – The road leads through this picturesque village with its numerous gardens to the **monastère des Bénédictines**, in a pretty setting with a welcoming courtyard. Visitors can ask to see the rather austere chapel, which occupies an old barn and has plain leaded glass windows with abstract motifs.

Aubigné-sur-Layon – This picturesque village still has several elegant old town houses. Near the 11C church stands an old fortified gateway where the remains of the portcullis and drawbridge can be seen.

Leave Aubigné on D 408 to Faveraye-Mâchelles and turn right onto D 120 through the village. After crossing D 24 bear left onto D 125.

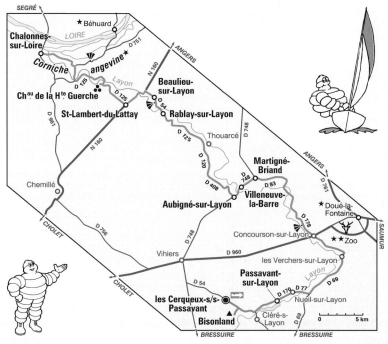

Rablay-sur-Layon – This pretty little wine-growing village occupies a well-sheltered site. In Grande-Rue there is a brick and half-timbered tithe house (15C) with an overhanging upper storey. A building dating from the 17C now houses artists' studios.

The road (D 54) crosses the Layon, then skirts a cirque with vine-clad slopes; from the plateau there is a broad view of the valley.

Beaulieu-sur-Layon – This wine-growing village *(viewing table)* in the midst of the Layon vineyards has attractive mansard-roofed houses. The town hall building was once the residence of the steward of the Abbess of Ronceray. There are 13C frescoes in the **church**.

To the west of Beaulieu *(to right of D 55)* is a wine cellar, **Caveau du Vin** ⊙, with a collection of old Angevin wine bottles and glasses.

The main road drops into the valley, past the steep valley sides riddled with caves and quarries. At Pont-Barré there is an attractive view of the narrow course of the Layon and a ruined medieval bridge, scene of a bloody struggle between Royalists and Revolutionaries on 19 September 1793.

St-Lambert-du-Lattay – A **Musée de la Vigne et du Vin d'Anjou** ⊙ was set up in the Coudraye wine cellars in 1978. Wine-growing and cooperage tools, illustrations, a collection of presses and commentaries embody the living memory of a people who have always been engaged in the cultivation of the grape. The room entitled "I'Imaginaire du Vin" appeals to visitors' senses of sight, smell and taste in a display on wine which emphasizes variety of bouquet and flavour.

The road to St-Aubin-de-Luigné winds its way up and down the slopes which produce Quarts de Chaume wine.

Before entering St-Aubin turn left onto D 106 and soon after turn right.

Château de la Haute-Guerche ⊙ – This castle was built in the reign of Charles VII and burned down in the Vendée wars; all that can now be seen from the valley are its ruined towers. There is an extensive view of the surrounding countryside from the site.

Rejoin D 125 and continue west to Chaudefonds; turn right onto D 121 which leads to Ardenay along a scenic cliff road.

★ **Corniche angevine** – *See Vallée de la LOIRE: From Angers to Champtoceaux.*

Chalonnes-sur-Loire – *See Vallée de la LOIRE: From Angers to Champtoceaux.*

Chartreuse du LIGET

Michelin map 68 north of fold 6 or 238 fold 14 – 10km/6mi east of Loches

On the eastern edge of Loches forest, by the edge of the road, stands the great wall of the **charterhouse** ⊙. The elegant 18C **gateway**★ is flanked by numerous outbuildings which give an idea of the size and wealth of the abbey just before the Revolution.

The abbey was founded in the 12C by Henry II of England in expiation, it is said, for the murder of Thomas Becket, Archbishop of Canterbury. It was sold as state property at the end of the 18C and mostly demolished. Nonetheless the few traces which remain suggest how large and impressive the abbey complex must have been.

Walk past the outbuildings (carpenter's shop, forge, locksmith's shop, baker etc) and walk down the central path.

In front of the house are the ruins *(left)* of the 12C church, behind which still stands one side of the great cloisters built in 1787. In the cell walls are the hatches through which the monks used to receive their meals.

Chapelle St-Jean ⊙ – *Return to the Loches road; 1km/0.5mi east turn left.*

Standing alone in the middle of a field is an unusual round 12C building where the first monks of the charterhouse probably lived. The interior is decorated with some Romanesque frescoes of the Deposition and Christ's Tomb.

La Corroirie – Eastwards towards Montrésor, at the bottom of a small valley, behind a screen of trees *(left)* stands another building belonging to the charterhouse which was fortified in the 15C. Clearly visible are the fortified gate and the square machicolated tower with drawbridge.

Le LION-D'ANGERS

Population 3 095
Michelin map 63 fold 20 or 232 fold 19 – Local map see Vallée de la MAYENNE

The town occupies a picturesque site on the west bank of the River Oudon just north Wof the confluence with the Mayenne. It is a horse breeding centre, particularly of half-breeds; the horse racing and competitions held here are famous throughout Anjou.

Église St-Martin ⊙ – The tracery decoration above the church door is pre-Romanesque, while the nave with its wooden vaulting is Romanesque. On the left wall of the nave above the entrance door are some 16C murals showing the Devil vomiting the Seven Deadly Sins, a Crucifix and St Christopher. In a recess there is a diptych of an Ecce Homo.

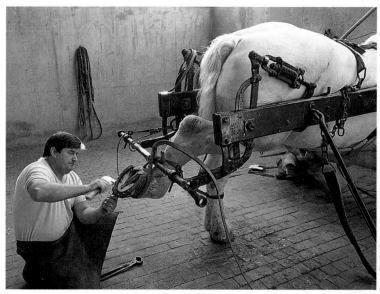

A Percheron being shod at the stud farm

★ **Haras national de l'Isle-Briand** ⊙ – *1km/0.5mi east of Le Lion-d'Angers.*
In 1971, the national stud farm, which used to be rather too near Angers city centre, was transferred to the Isle-Briand estate, where it now occupies an ultra-modern establishment. About 70 selected horses are stabled here. The tour of the stud farm includes the barns, the harness room, the forge (with oak flooring, more comfortable for the horses' hooves) and the riding school. The loose boxes are grouped according to the different types of horses: Normandy cob, Breton or Percheron draught horses, Anglo-Arabs, pure-bred Arabs, saddle horses, trotters and ponies. Horses which have won numerous prestigious races are brought here to pass on their genes, in the hope of producing another generation of winners.

Every year, the "Mondial du Lion" international race meeting is held on the third weekend in October; the elite of the racing fraternity from around 20 countries takes part in the event. See Calendar of events at the end of the guide for further details.

LIRÉ

Population 2 140
Michelin map 63 fold 18 or 232 fold 29 – 3km/2mi south of Ancenis
Local map see Vallée de la LOIRE: Chinon-Champtoceaux

The village of Liré in the Loire valley owes its fame to **Joachim du Bellay** (1522-60), the poet, who was born not far from here. Du Bellay, like his friends the poets of the **Pléiade**, was brought up on Greek and Latin poetry, and he sought to provide the French language with literary works of the same stature as those he admired in the Ancient Classical languages. He was the author of the group's manifesto, *The Defence and Illustration of the French Language*, which appeared in Paris in 1549. He signed it IDBA which stands for Ioachim du Bellay Angevin and shows his affection for his native province. In 1553 he went to Rome with his cousin, the Cardinal, and wrote his finest work *The Regrets*.

Musée Joachim-du-Bellay ⓥ – This museum occupies a 16C house *(restored)* in the middle of the town. Mementoes of the poet are displayed on the first floor; the ground floor is devoted to local traditions and customs.

> Plus que le marbre dur me plaît l'ardoise fine,
> Plus mon Loire gaulois, que le Tibre latin,
> Plus mon petit Liré, que le mont Palatin,
> Et plus que l'air marin la douceur angevine.
> *(I love thin slate more than hard marble,*
> *my Gallic Loire more than the Latin Tiber,*
> *my little Liré more than the Palatine Hill,*
> *and more than the sea air the sweetness of Anjou.)*
>
> **Joachim du Bellay** *Les Regrets*

LOCHES★★

Population 7 133
Michelin map 68 fold 6 or 238 south of folds 13, 14

Loches is a small town on the south bank of the Indre; its military past is most evident in the old town, which is huddled on the slopes of a bluff above the river and still resembles a medieval fortified town, with two of its original three defensive walls remarkably well preserved. From the entrance to the public gardens, there is a pretty **view**★ of the church of St-Ours, the imposing castle, and in the foreground the houses lining the banks of the river Indre.

Loches was the birthplace of the Romantic poet, **Alfred de Vigny** (1797-1863), whose mother's family had been closely involved with the town's history since the Renaissance. The poet left the town when only an infant.

A thousand-year-old fortress – Loches is built on a natural strongpoint which has been occupied since at least the 6C when Gregory of Tours made reference to a fortress commanding a monastery and a small town. From the 10C to 13C Loches was under the sway of the Counts of Anjou who altered the fortress by building a residential palace and a moated keep on the end of the promontory. Henri II of England reinforced the defences. On his death in 1189 his son Richard the Lionheart took possession of the land before leaving on crusade with Philippe-Auguste. In the Holy Land Philippe-Auguste, an artful schemer, abandoned Richard and hurried back to France (1191) where he plotted with John Lackland, Richard's brother, who agreed to give up the fortress (1193). When Richard was finally ransomed – he had been held captive in Austria – he hastened to Loches and captured the castle in less than three hours (1194), an exploit which was celebrated in all the chronicles of the day. When Richard died, Philippe-Auguste recaptured the castle by way of revenge but much less impressively: the siege lasted a whole year (1205). Loches was given to Dreu V de Mello, son of the victorious besiegers' leader, and repurchased by Louis IX in 1249.

Loches took on the role of royal residence for a succession of monarchs. In 1429, after her victory at Orléans, Joan of Arc rejoined Charles VII at Loches and insisted that he should set out for Reims.

Agnès Sorel – Agnès was the owner of Beauté castle (at Nogent-sur-Marne) near Paris and also a great beauty, so that her title, La Dame de Beauté, was doubly apt. She was born at Fromenteau castle in the Touraine in 1422. She became Charles VII's favourite, but left the court at Chinon, where the Dauphin, the future Louis XI, was making life impossible for her, to come and live at Loches. Her influence on the King was often beneficial – she cured him of his depression and encouraged him in his effort to save his kingdom – but her taste for luxury coupled with great generosity was a heavy burden on the slender royal purse. She died on 9 February 1450 at Jumièges where she had gone to be with Charles VII. Her body was brought back to Loches and buried in the collegiate church. Some years later the canons, who had benefited from her largesse, asked Louis XI to transfer her tomb to the castle. He agreed on condition that the gifts went too, whereupon the canons let the matter drop!

Louis XI's Cages (late 15C) – A tour of the castle will include the dungeons and barred cells, but not the cages in which Louis XI liked to confine his prisoners; these "monuments of tyranny" were destroyed by the inhabitants of Loches in 1790. The cages were made of a wooden framework covered with iron. The more comfortable measured 2m by 2m/6ft 7in by 6ft 7in on all sides but there was a shallower model in which the prisoner could only lie or sit. Legend has it that prisoners never came out alive; it seems however that the cages were used only at night or to transport prisoners. Cardinal Jean Balue, who is said to be the inventor of these cages, knew them well. He was greatly in favour under Louis XI who bestowed honour after honour on him, but he plotted secretly with the Duke of Burgundy; in 1469 he was discovered and imprisoned in Loches until 1480; he died 11 years later.

★★ MEDIEVAL TOWN 3hr

Park the car in Mail Droulin

★ **Porte Royale** (Z) – 11C. The Royal Gate had powerful defences; it was flanked by two towers in the 13C; the machicolations and the slots for the drawbridge chains are still visible.

Go through the gateway; turn left into rue Lansyer to reach the museums.

Musée Lansyer and Musée du Terroir (Z M) ⊘ – A visit to these two museums is also a way of taking a look at part of the inside of the Porte Royale. A local interior typical of the 19C has been set up in the old guard-room. Note the collection of paintings by the landscape artist **Maurice-Étienne Lansyer** (1835-93), a pupil of the great Courbet.

Musée Lansyer

Porte des Cordeliers and Château de Loches by M.-E. Lansyer

★ **Église St-Ours** (Z) – In 1802 the old collegiate church of Notre-Dame became the parish church dedicated to St Ours, a local apostle in the 5C. Its most characteristic features are the two octagonal pyramids between its towers: of the type commonly used for belfries, kitchens *(see Fontevraud)* or lavabos in monasteries, here they form the vaulting of the nave and, with the eight-sided dome surmounting the transept crossing, they evoke the silhouette of Aquitaine cupolas. The Angevin porch shelters a **Romanesque doorway**, richly decorated with unusual carved animals; the upper part (badly damaged) represents the Virgin Mary and the Three Wise Men. A holy water stoup has been hollowed out in a Gallo-Roman column.

The famous pyramid vaulting in the nave was built by Prior T. Pactius in the 12C. The transept, which was designed for a chapter of 12 canons, opens into the aisles (12C, 14C and 15C).

★★ **Château (Castle)** (YZ) ⊘ – The tour begins in the **Agnès Sorel tower** (B) which dates from the 13C and has been known since the 16C as the "Beautiful Agnès tower".

Son et lumière – *See the Practical information section at the back of the guide.*

Logis Royaux (Royal Apartments) – From the terrace, which provides a fine view of Loches and the Indre valley, it is clear that the château was built at two different periods. The Vieux Logis (14C), the older, taller building, is heavily fortified with four turrets linked by a sentry walk at the base of the roof. It was enlarged under Charles VIII and Louis XII by the addition of the more recent Nouveau Logis, in the manner and style of the Renaissance.

Enter the **Vieux Logis** through the room known as Charles VII's antechamber. The walls are adorned with a 16C tapestry of a lively allegorical depiction of music and a portrait of *Charles VII*, a copy of the painting by Jean Fouquet. Then enter the great hall with the large fireplace where on 3 and 5 June 1429 Joan of Arc came to urge Charles VII to go to Reims. She was accompanied at the time by

Recumbent figure of Agnès Sorel

Robert Le Masson, Chancellor of France, who died in 1443, Dunois and Gilles de Rais. Lovely tapestries are on display (*verdures* from Oudenaarde), together with a copy of the manuscript of Joan of Arc's trial.

The **recumbent figure of Agnès Sorel**★, placed in the Charles VIII room, is of special interest. During the Revolution, soldiers of the Indre battalions, whose historical knowledge was not equal to their Revolutionary zeal, took the favourite of Charles VII for a saint, chopped up her statue, desecrated her grave and scattered her remains. The monument was restored in Paris under the Empire and again on the occasion of its transfer to the Nouveau Logis. Agnès is shown recumbent, with two angels supporting her lovely head and two lambs – the symbol of gentleness and her name – lying at her feet. In the same room is displayed the portrait by Fouquet of the Virgin Mary, whose face is that of the beautiful Agnès, amid red and blue angels (the original is in Antwerp); the hairstyle, for which women had to have half their skull shaved to reveal a bare forehead, first became fashionable in Venice.

Another room contains an interesting **triptych**★ from the school of Jean Fouquet (15C), which originally came from the church of St-Antoine, with panels evoking the Crucifixion, Carrying of the Cross and Deposition.

The tour ends in Anne of Brittany's **oratory**, a tiny room decorated with finely worked motifs of the ermine of Brittany and the girdle of St Francis. The canopy opposite the altar originally stood over the royal pew and the only door was the one to the right of the altar. Executed in the pure Gothic style, this oratory was originally polychrome: a bright blue background with gilded cable moulding and silver-coated ermines.

Return to the church of St-Ours and, via rue Thomas-Pactius, make for the Mail du Donjon. Turn round, after a bend to the right, to get a view of the church.

★★ **Donjon** (Z) ⊙ – This keep was built in the 11C by Fulk Nerra to defend the fortified town from the south. It is a solid square construction which, together with the Ronde and Martelet towers, forms an imposing group of fortifications. Early in the 13C the promontory was defended by a moat, a rampart and the keep which comprised a residence and its outbuildings, a collegiate church and houses for the canons.

On the outside can still be seen the putlog holes in which the timbers supporting the hoardings rested. To the left of the entrance, in Philippe de Commines's dungeon, is an iron collar weighing 16kg/35lb.

The floors of the three storeys have vanished but three sets of fireplaces and windows can still be seen on the walls. A staircase of 157 steps leads to the terrace at the top of the keep from which there is a fine view of the town, the Indre valley and Loches forest.

Tour Ronde – This round tower was in fact another keep. Like the Martelet it was built in the 15C to complete the fortifications at the point where three walls met: the keep wall, the castle wall and the town wall.

One room is devoted to the casts of graffiti of various origins. A cell has been reconstructed to illustrate the incarceration of a prisoner in the late 15C. In the low vaulted cellar at the foot of the tower, a 1699 engraving by Gaignères depicts one of Louis XI's cages. A flight of 102 steps leads up to a terrace from which there is a view of the moat and, beyond, a vast panorama of Loches.

Martelet – The most impressive dungeons, occupying several floors below ground, are to be found in this building. The first was that of **Ludovico Sforza**, Duke of Milan, nicknamed the Moor, who was taken prisoner by Louis XII.

For eight years (1500-08) at Loches, he paid for his tricks and treachery. On the day of his release the sunlight was so bright and the excitement of freedom so great that he fell down dead. Ludovico, who was Leonardo da Vinci's patron, covered the walls of his prison with paintings and inscriptions. Next to the stars, cannon and helmets may be seen a phrase, hardly surprising in the circumstances: *celui qui n'est pas contan* (he who is not content).

Below, lit by a solitary ray of light, is the dungeon where the Bishops of Autun and Le Puy, both implicated in the change of allegiance to the Emperor Charles V by the Constable of France, Charles, Duke of Bourbon, found leisure to hollow out of the wall a small altar and a symbolic Stations of the Cross. In another cell was interned the Count of St-Vallier, father of Diane de Poitiers and one of the bishops' accomplices. He was sentenced to death and informed of his reprieve – thanks to the intervention of his daughter – only when on the scaffold.

On the same underground level as the dungeons, galleries open off to quarries, which in the 13C provided stone for the small fortified covered passageways *(caponiers)* flanking the ramparts.

Visitors who are pressed for time should turn right on leaving the Martelet to reach the Mail de la Poterie and their cars. For those with another hour to spare, we would recommend a walk round the outside of the ramparts.

★ **Walk round the outside of the ramparts and the old town** – *Turn left on coming out of the Martelet.*
This walk *(45min)* reveals that this medieval town was in fact an entrenched camp, complete with all its own defences. The perimeter wall is more than 1km/0.6mi long and is pierced by only two gateways.
Note first the three spur towers built in the 13C in front of the keep, then walk along the dry moat to Rue Quintefol before coming up onto the ramparts, from where there is a good view of the chevet of the church of St-Ours. This section within the second perimeter wall follows rue St-Ours past old houses built of tufa.

LOCHES

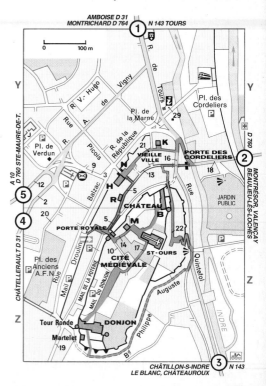

On emerging from the perimeter wall take one of the narrow pedestrian streets opposite which leads to the late-15C **Porte des Cordeliers★** (Y); this and the Porte Picois *(see below)* are the only two remaining gates of the town's original four. It was the main gate of the city on the road to Spain. Go through the gate to see its riverside façade lined with machicolations and flanked by bartizans.

Head north to the 16C **Tour St-Antoine** (Y K) one of the rare belfries to be found in central France; then on to the 15C **Porte Picois** (Y N), also with machicolations. This tower stands next to the **Hôtel de ville★** (Y H), an elegant Renaissance building with balconies bright with flowers in season. Continue to the **Chancellerie** (Y R), dating from the Henri II period (mid-16C), embellished with fluted columns, pilasters and wrought-iron balconies.

EXCURSIONS

Beaulieu-lès-Loches – *1km/0.6mi east on ② on the town plan. See BEAULIEU-LÈS-LOCHES.*

Bridoré – *14km/9mi southeast on ③ on the plan.*
The late-15C **church** here, dedicated to St Roch, contains a monumental 15C statue of the Saint *(nave right)*. The legend of St Hubert is evoked on a 16C low-relief sculpture. The **castle** ⊙, which belonged to Marshal Boucicaut in the 14C, was altered in the 15C by Imbert de Bastarnay, Secretary to Louis XI. It is an imposing complex, bordered by towers, caponiers and a deep dry moat on three sides.

★**Vallée de l'Indre**

27km/16mi northwest on ①, N 143 and D 17 – about 1hr

From Chambourg-sur-Indre to Esvres the road (D 17) follows a picturesque route beside the Indre which meanders lazily past here a windmill or there a boat moored in the reeds.

Azay-sur-Indre – Azay stands in a pleasant setting at the confluence of the Indre and the Indrois. Adjoining it is the park of the château that once belonged to La Fayette.

Reignac – Visible from the bridge over the Indre (on the road to Cigogné), is Reignac windmill, standing in a peaceful rural setting.

Cormery – *See CORMERY.*
Cross the Indre and follow N 143 towards Tours for 1km/0.6mi then bear left onto D 17.
The trip ends at Esvres, located in pretty surroundings.

Vallée du LOIR★★

Michelin map 60 fold 17 and 64 folds 2 to 7, or 232 folds 21 to 24, 237 folds 37 and 38 and 238 folds 1 and 2

The Loir winds placidly from the the Paris basin (Ile-de-France) to Anjou through a peaceful landscape delimited by gentle hills. Green meadows, smart towns and charming villages have earned the region the name "la Douce France" (Gentle France). From its source to its confluence with the Sarthe (350km/218mi) the Loir has made its way through chalky terrain, flowing under steep bluffs on the outside of its many bends. Since the Neolithic period people have hollowed caverns in these bluffs and these troglodyte dwellings are one of the charms of the valley.

Originally the river was navigable up to Château-du-Loir but now the only boats are occupied by fishermen who appreciate the variety and abundance of the fish and the beauty of the quivering poplars and silvery willows at the water's edge. This is a pastoral region devoted to raising cattle and poultry and growing grapes on the slopes *(Coteaux du Loir)* between Vendôme and Château-du-Loir.

In the Middle Ages pilgrims on the road to Santiago de Compostela followed the upper reaches of the river before turning south to Tours; their religious fervour has left its mark in numerous priories, commanderies, churches and chapels which are often decorated with frescoes.

UPPER REACHES

① From Bonneval to Vendôme *77km/47mi – allow one day*

Bonneval – *See BONNEVAL.*
Leave Bonneval to the south.
There are uninterrupted views of the surrounding countryside as the road crosses the plateau. Before **Conie** the road crosses the river of the same name and follows it (D 110) downstream to **Moléans** with its 17C castle. In the pretty village of **St-Christophe** the road rejoins the slow waters of the Loir which it follows (D 361) to Marboué.

Marboué – Once a Gallo-Roman settlement, the village is known for its tall 15C bell-tower and crocketed spire and for its bathing beach on the river.

★★ **Châteaudun** – *See CHÂTEAUDUN.*

★ **Montigny-le-Gannelon** – *See MONTIGNY-LE-GANNELON.*

Cloyes-sur-le-Loir – *See CLOYES-SUR-LE-LOIR.*

Leave Cloyes on D 81 east to Bouche-d'Aigre.

A picturesque road (D 145⁷) follows the east bank of the Loir south through **St-Claude** with its pointed church on the hill.

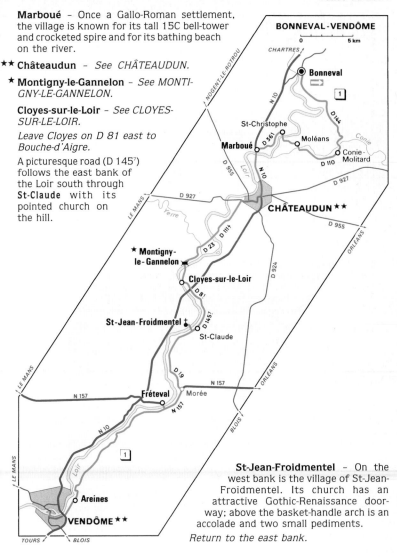

St-Jean-Froidmentel – On the west bank is the village of St-Jean-Froidmentel. Its church has an attractive Gothic-Renaissance doorway; above the basket-handle arch is an accolade and two small pediments.

Return to the east bank.

Only a row of poplars separates the road from the river. Between Morée and Fréteval there are fishing huts on the bank and one or two pretty riverside houses with flat-bottomed boats moored nearby.

Fréteval – The ruins of a **medieval castle** *(15min on foot there and back)* look down from their bluff on the east bank to Fréteval on the far bank which is a favourite rendezvous of fishermen.

Soon after this the signposted tourist road leaves the river bank to go past comfortable-looking houses and the odd pretty little church.

Areines – *See AREINES.*

★★ **Vendôme** – *See VENDÔME.*

MIDDLE REACHES

② **From Vendôme to La Chartre**

78km/49mi – allow one day – local map overleaf

★★ **Vendôme** – *See VENDÔME.*

Villiers-sur-Loir – The village overlooks the sloping vineyards opposite Rochambeau castle. The church is decorated with some very attractive 16C **murals**: on the left wall of the nave there is a huge figure of St Christopher carrying the child Jesus and the Legend of the Three Living and the Three Dead. The stalls date from the 15C.

Take the road towards Thoré. Immediately after crossing the Loir turn left.

159

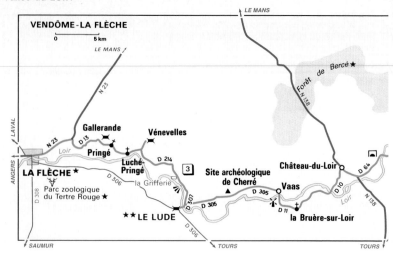

VENDÔME - LA FLÈCHE

Rochambeau – The road runs along the foot of the cliff through the semi-troglodyte village up to the castle where Maréchal de Rochambeau (1725-1807) was born; he commanded the French expeditionary force in the American War of Independence and is buried in Thoré.

Return to the west bank of the river and turn left onto D 5.

Le Gué-du-Loir – The hamlet was built where the Boulon joins the Loir amid lush meadows and islands ringed by reed-beds, willows, alders and poplars. On leaving the hamlet the road (D 5) skirts the wall of **manoir de Bonaventure**, which was probably named after a chapel dedicated to St Bonaventure. In the 16C the manor house belonged to Henri IV's father, Antoine de Bourbon-Vendôme who entertained his friends there, including some of the poets of the Pléiade. Later Bonaventure came into the possession of the De Musset family. The poet, **Alfred de Musset**, whose father was born at the manor, used to spend his holidays as a child with his godfather, Louis de Musset, at the Château de Cogners, since the manor had by then been sold.

Continue west on D 5 (towards Savigny); then take the second turning to the right (C 13) at a wayside cross.

A wooded valley leads to the picturesque village of **Mazangé** clustered round the pretty church with its Gothic door.

Return to Gué-du-Loir; turn right onto D 24 (towards Montoire-sur-le-Loir).

The road cuts off a large loop in the river where, in carving out its course, the Loir has uncovered a cliff face in which the inhabitants of Asnières hollowed out their troglodyte houses.

Turn right onto D 82 to Lunay.

Lunay – Lunay is grouped in a valley round the main square where some old houses have survived. The huge, Flamboyant Gothic **church of St-Martin** has an attractive doorway. The stones of the arch are carved with ivy and vine ornaments (pampres); in one of the niches which have decorated canopies is a charming little statue of the Virgin Mary and Child.

Les Roches-l'Évêque – The village occupies a long narrow site between the river and the cliff. The troglodyte dwellings are a well known feature of the region, their hen-houses and sheds half-concealed by festoons of wistaria and lilac in season.

Cross the Loir (D 917 – follow the signposts); turn right to Lavardin.

★ **Lavardin** – See LAVARDIN.

Take the pretty minor road along the south bank of the river to Montoire.

Montoire-sur-le-Loir – See MONTOIRE-SUR-LE-LOIR.

Soon Troo and its church appear on the skyline.

Troo – See TROO.

At Sougé turn left onto the signposted tourist road to Artins.

Vieux-Bourg d'Artins – The village is situated right on the river bank. The **church** has Romanesque walls with Flamboyant Gothic windows and a pointed-arched doorway.

From Artins take D 10 east; then turn right to l'Isle Verte; after 100m turn left onto a road which runs in front of the Château du Pin.

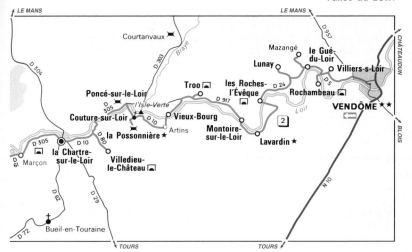

From the bridge opposite the château **l'Isle Verte** ("Green Island") can be seen a little way upstream where the Braye joins the Loir. It was here, where the row of poplars tremble in the breeze and the willows mark the edges of the meadows, that the poet Ronsard wanted to be buried; nowhere is more evocative of his genius.

Couture-sur-Loir – The church has a Gothic chancel with Angevin vaulting and 17C woodwork in the Rosary Chapel (on right of chancel). The recumbent figures in the nave are Ronsard's parents; note the costume detail.

In Couture-sur-Loir take D 57 south to La Possonnière.

★ **Manoir de la Possonnière** – *See Manoir de la POSSONNIÈRE.*

Return to Couture and continue north (D 57), crossing the Loir at the foot of the wooded hill on which Château de la Flotte stands.

Poncé-sur-le-Loir – *See PONCÉ-SUR-LE-LOIR.*

In Ruillé turn left onto D 80 which crosses the Loir.

The road is very picturesque, particularly south of Tréhet, where it runs along a hillside riddled with caves.

Villedieu-le-Château – This village has a pleasant **setting** in a valley with troglodyte dwellings hollowed out of the valley slopes. Houses, gardens, crumbling remnants of the old town wall and the ruins of the belfry of St-Jean priory all add to the charm of the scene.

Return to Tréhet and turn left onto D 10.

La Chartre-sur-le-Loir – On the north bank of the river, opposite this village, are Bercé forest and the Jasnières vineyard which produces a white dessert wine which ages well.

LOWER REACHES

③ From La Chartre to La Flèche

74km/46mi – half a day – local map above

La Chartre-sur-le-Loir – *See above.*

The road from La Chartre to **Marçon** (good wines) passes through peaceful countryside.

In Marçon turn right onto D 61 which cuts across the valley and crosses the river at the foot of the hillside on which the chapel of Ste-Cécile stands. Turn left onto D 64, which skirts the hillside with its numerous troglodyte dwellings.

Château-du-Loir – The keep in the public gardens is all that remains of the medieval castle to which this town owes its name. Underneath it are the old cells occupied briefly by the many convicts who passed through here bound for the penal colony of Cayenne via the ports of Nantes or La Rochelle. In the chancel of the **church of St-Guingalois** is a monumental 17C terracotta *Pietà*, in which the figure of the Virgin Mary has particularly expressive features. In the south aisle is a mounted figure of St Martin and in the north transept, a pair of Flemish Mannerist wooden panels showing the Nativity (15C) and the Resurrection (late 15C). Below the chancel there is a Romanesque crypt and, in the **presbytery** ⊘, a fine wooden group (16C) depicting the Scourging of Christ.

Leave Château-du-Loir on D 10 going south (towards Château-la-Vallière). After crossing the bridge in Nogent turn right immediately onto C 2.

La Bruère – The **church** here contains several interesting statues in the nave: St Fiacre holding his spade, St Roch and St Sebastian. The elegant chancel vaulting is in the Renaissance style and the stained-glass windows date from the 16C.

Leave La Bruère on D 11 towards Vaas and turn right onto D 30.

Vaas – On the left, just before you reach the bridge, stands an old corn mill, the **Moulin à blé de Rotrou** ⊙. The riverside, with its houses, tiny garden plots, church and washing place makes a delightful scene.

The road passes through meadows, nursery gardens and evergreen forests with clumps of gorse and broom.

Follow D 305, then turn right to Cherré archeological site.

Site archéologique de Cherré – This archeological site had already been identified in the 19C but it was aerial photography which speeded up research here in the 1970s. The Gallo-Roman settlement dates from the 1C and 2C AD and comprises a temple, baths, two other buildings and a theatre of pointed reddish sandstone which has been completely excavated. During the excavations a necropolis from the Hallstatt period (the protohistoric period – 8C to 5C BC) was discovered under the *cavea* (the seating area).

Carry on towards Le Lude along the south bank of the Loir.

★★ **Château du Lude** – *See Château du LUDE.*

Rejoin D 307 and drive towards Pontvallain, then, on the left, take the road to Mansigné.

Soon after the turn and before reaching the Château de la Grifferie there is a view over the valley which is laid out in fruit orchards, asparagus beds, potato fields and maize plantations.

Bear left onto D 214 to Luché-Pringé. After crossing the River Aune, turn right onto D 13 to the Manoir de Vénevelles.

Manoir de Vénevelles ⊙ – This 15C-17C manor house stands in a quiet valley and is surrounded by a broad moat.

Luché-Pringé – The exterior of the **church** (13C-16C) is quite unusual in appearance, with its many gables decorated with crockets and the row of tiny musician figures sitting on the edge of the roof on either side of the façade. Above the entrance door is a low-relief of St Martin on horseback.

The interior contains an early-16C *Pietà (right)* carved in walnut. The wide chancel (13C) ends in a square chevet; the Angevin vaulting is supported on tall slim columns in the traditional Plantagenet style. Next to the church stands an elegant priory (13C-15C) with an octagonal turret.

Pringé – The tiny Romanesque **church** ⊙ at Pringé was altered in the 15C. The doorway with arch mouldings in the façade is Romanesque. The interior is decorated with 16C murals depicting St Hubert, St George and St Christopher.

Château de Gallerande – *(Not open to the public, but it is possible to walk up as far as the gateway to the courtyard.)* The road (D 13) skirts the moat enclosing the inviting, peaceful park in which huge trees – cedars, limes and oaks – line the edges of the vast lawns. From the courtyard gate there is a fine view of the northeast façade of the château which has four machicolated round towers and an unusual octagonal keep.

★ **La Flèche** – *See La FLÈCHE.*

Vallée de la LOIRE★★★

Michelin maps 63, 64 and 65 or 232 and 238

The River Loire, sung by numerous poets since Ronsard and Du Bellay, was a lifeline for the surrounding countryside for centuries, but commercial river traffic now no longer plies this great waterway. Nonetheless, the river still overwhelmingly imbues the region with its character, enhancing many an already fine landscape with its long broad reaches and graceful meanders glinting in the sunlight.

GEOGRAPHICAL NOTES

The Loire, once a tributary of the Seine – The Loire is the longest river in France – 1 020km/634mi from its source at the foot of Gerbier-de-Jonc peak on the southern edge of the Massif Central to where it flows into the Atlantic Ocean at St-Nazaire. Only the middle course of it is described in this guide. Originally the Loire followed the present course of the River Loing and flowed into the Seine but, when an arm of the Atlantic penetrated inland as far as Blois, the river left its old bed and turned west. North of the loop thus formed extends the Orléans forest thriving on the granite sand carried down by the river from the Massif Central.

A capricious river – The Loire has an irregular and unpredictable regime. In summer, only a few rivulets *(luisettes)* trickle between the sand or gravel banks *(grèves)*, making the great river look for all the world like a river of sand. In autumn, during the rainy season, or at the end of winter, when the snow melts, the river is in spate and its swirling waters then run high. It sometimes bursts the dikes, known as *levées* or *turcies*, built to protect the countryside from floods. The flood waters then spread over the valley floor like a huge yellow blanket pierced here and there by a slate roof or the odd poplar tree. In many a village there are walls inscribed with the dates of great floods in memory of their tragic consequences: 1846, 1856, 1866 and 1910.

BOATS AND BOATMEN

Shipping on the Loire – Up to the mid 19C, in spite of various disadvantages – sandbanks, whirlpools, floods, mills and tolls – the Loire and its tributaries, particularly the Cher, were much used as a means of communication. As early as the 14C navigation was organised by a guild of mariners centred on Orléans who charged a toll and kept the channel clear. In the 17C-18C a canal was built from the River Loing to Orléans which developed into a large port with warehousing. In addition to merchandise – wood and coal from the Forez, pottery from Nevers, grain from the Beauce, wines from Touraine and Anjou – there was a great flow of travellers who preferred the river to the road. The journey from Orléans to Nantes by river took six days, and from 10 to 20 for the return journey with a good wind. Coaches and their passengers were transported on rafts.

The river traffic comprised flat bottomed barges (scows or lighters) with large square sails. **Toues**, barges without rigging, are still used today to transport hay and livestock; **sapines** with a greater capacity and crudely made of fir planks were destroyed at the end of the voyage; **gabarres** were much larger vessels with sails up to 20m/66ft high. The boats travelled in groups with a mother ship pulling two decreasingly smaller boats, one of which carried the bargee's cabin. The convoy was preceded by a wherry or punt to sound the river bed. The bargees had to be skilled on the upstream voyage to negotiate the bridges; the punt anchored beyond the

An "unexplodable" steam boat at Amboise

bridge and the barges were hauled through with their sails lowered. At Ponts-de-Cé and Beaugency, where the current flowed obliquely through the arches, ropes from the bridge were used to guide the boats.

The "Unexplodables" – In 1832 the first steamboat service was started between Orléans and Nantes. It caused a sensation. Only two days were needed for the journey. However, there were accidents, as boilers had a tendency to explode during the voyage. The initial enthusiasm died down. The appearance of new steamboats nicknamed "unexplodables" *(inexplosibles)* restored confidence, so much so that in 1843 more than 100 000 passengers were carried on the Loire and the Allier by the various steamboat companies which ran the services between Moulins and Nantes. With the development of the railway, navigation on the Loire declined. The last shipping company closed down in 1862.

The Loire Boatmen – Dressed in blue, with a red scarf and belt and gold earrings, the boatmen were a rough crew, given to regular bouts of drinking and teasing the barmaids. While waiting for a favourable wind they would consume with relish an eel stew and a glass or two of wine before embarking on a chorus of their favourite songs.

VIEWS OF THE LOIRE

The itineraries described below link some of the most famous sights of the Loire valley with

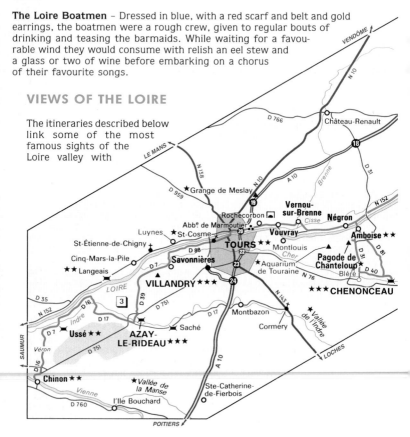

the most picturesque stretches of road. Car drivers should take care, however, not to allow the beauty of the countryside to distract them from the dangers of the – frequently winding – roads.

The road along the **north bank** (N 152) offers only the occasional glimpse of the Loire before Blois but after Blois the road follows the embankment closely and one lovely vista succeeds another as far as the outskirts of Tours. Between Tours and Angers the road continues to follow the river's course closely making an enchantingly pretty drive for most of this stretch.

Along the **south bank** there is no single road that follows the course of the Loire closely. Nevertheless, there are some pretty views from the road (D 751) along a stretch of a couple of miles downstream from Blois, where the embankment begins, and again between Amboise and Tours; also further downstream below Saumur and along the scenic road known as the Corniche angevine. The best views are to be had from the traffic-free country lanes parallel to the main road which follow the river bank more closely: D 88 west of Tours; D 16 downstream from Villandry; D 132 beginning at Gennes; and D 210 from Montjean-sur-Loire to St-Florent-le-Vieil.

★★ DOWNSTREAM TO BLOIS

[1] From Orléans to Blois

84km/52mi – about 6hr not including the St-Laurent-des-Eaux nuclear power station – local map above

★ Orléans – *See ORLÉANS.*

Leave Orléans on avenue Dauphine (south of the town plan).

Nursery gardens and rose gardens line both sides of the road. Cross the Loiret which flows between wooded banks.

Olivet – *See ORLÉANS: Olivet.*

In Olivet turn left onto D 14 which leads to La Source floral park.

★★ Parc floral de la Source – *See ORLÉANS: Olivet.*

Take D 14 westwards.

Neat little houses with pretty gardens line the road to Cléry.

★ Cléry-St-André – *See CLÉRY-ST-ANDRÉ.*

★ Meung-sur-Loire – *See MEUNG-SUR-LOIRE.*

Take N 152 to Beaugency; soon the large towers of the St-Laurent nuclear power station are visible on the horizon.

★ Beaugency – *See BEAUGENCY.*

Leave Beaugency on ③. Turn right just before St-Laurent-Nouan to the power station.

Centre nucléaire de production d'électricité (CNPE) de St-Laurent-des-Eaux – The nuclear power station is sited on a peninsula jutting out into the Loire. St-Laurent "A" station, using the natural uranium/graphite/carbon dioxide process, consisted of two units with a combined capacity of 500 mW. It was closed down in June 1992. St-Laurent "B" is of the pressurized water reactor type and consists of two units with an annual output of 10 billion kWh. The power station's waste water is used to heat an extensive area of greenhouses nearby.

St-Dyé-sur-Loire – Legend has it that this little place was founded in the 6C by St Deodatus (also known as St Dié or St Dyé). There are many reminders of the days when St-Dyé's riverside was busy with the activity associated with the construction of the great Château de Chambord; fortified walls looming above the quayside, little craftsmen's houses in rue de Chambord and a number of grander buildings of the 15C, 16C and 17C where their masters resided. The **church** ⊘, with

165

its impressive belfry-porch, contains the tombs of St Deodatus and his companion, St Baudemir, and has a Revolutionary inscription in the chancel.

The **Maison de la Loire**  in the 17C Hôtel Fonteneau houses the tourist information centre as well as exhibits relating to the Loire and its valley.

The road enters the walled Chambord estate (speed restrictions).

The stately façade of the Château de Chambord comes into sight suddenly at the end of an avenue making a striking impression.

★★★ **Château de Chambord** – *See Château de CHAMBORD.*

Take D 84 northwest to Montlivault on the banks of the Loire.

The road which follows the embankment offers beautiful **views★** of this green and leafy setting: poplars, fields of asparagus, tulips and gladioli. On the north bank stand the silhouettes of the Château de Ménars, then Blois with its basilica, cathedral and castle.

★★ **Blois** – *See BLOIS. Allow half a day.*

★★★ DOWNSTREAM TO TOURS

② From Blois to Tours

89km/55mi – about 4hr – local map previous pages

★★ **Blois** – *See BLOIS. Allow half a day.*
Leave Blois on ⑤, N 152.
This stretch of road offers numerous views of the Loire which is broken up in a number of places with sandbanks covered in greenery in summer. The Chaumont metal bridge leads to the Château de Chaumont on the south bank.

★★ **Château de Chaumont-sur-Loire** – *See Château de CHAUMONT-SUR-LOIRE.*
Return to the north bank.
Shortly after Le Haut-Chantier, the Château d'Amboise is visible from the road.

★★ **Amboise** – *See AMBOISE.*
Leave Amboise on D 81 then at Civray-de-Touraine bear left to Chenonceau.

★★★ **Château de Chenonceau** – *See Château de CHENONCEAU.*
Return towards Amboise along D 40; at La Croix de Touraine bear right onto D 31.

★ **Pagode de Chanteloup** – *See Pagode de CHANTELOUP.*
In Amboise cross the river and turn left onto N 152 which runs along the river bank towards Tours.

Négron – Standing below N 152 this village has a charming square overlooked by the church and a Gothic house with a Renaissance front.

Vernou-sur-Brenne – *See VOUVRAY: Excursion.*
The road (D 46) from Vernou to Vouvray passes beneath the TGV Atlantique line to southwest France.

Vouvray – *See VOUVRAY.*
Continue west along N 152 towards Tours.

On approaching **Rochecorbon**, a small town at the foot of a bluff riddled with troglodyte dwellings, note the **lantern**, a watchtower on the top of the hill. Further on, at the end of a long wall *(right)* stands an imposing 13C doorway, part of the **abbey of Marmoutier**, which was founded by St Martin in 372 and fortified in the 13C and 14C.

Enter Tours on ④ on the town plan.

★★ **Tours** – *See TOURS. Allow half a day.*

Y. Arthus-Bertrand/ALTITUDE

★★★ DOWNSTREAM VIA CHINON TO SAUMUR

③ **From Tours to Chinon**

61km/38mi – about 5hr – local map pp. 164-5.

★★ **Tours** – *See TOURS. Allow half a day.*

Leave Tours on D 88 going west.

The road runs along the Loire embankment passing gardens and vegetable plots and the **priory of St-Cosme★** *(see TOURS: Additional Sights)*. Fine views of the south bank of the river.

In L'Aireau-des-Bergeons turn left onto D 288 to Savonnières.

Savonnières – *See SAVONNIÈRES.*

★★★ **Villandry** – *See VILLANDRY.*
After Villandry take the road south (D 39) out of troglodyte country and into the Indre valley.

★★★ **Château d'Azay-le-Rideau** – *See AZAY-LE-RIDEAU.*

The road (D 17) runs west between Chinon forest *(left)* and the River Indre, which splits into several channels at this point. A charming but narrow road winds between hedges and spinneys with occasional glimpses of the river. A bridge spanning the Indre provides one of the best views of Ussé château.

★★ **Château d'Ussé** – *See Château d'USSÉ.*
After Rigny-Ussé, the road crosses the **Véron**, a tongue of highly-fertile alluvial soil at the confluence of the Loire and the Vienne. It yields grain, grapes and fruit in abundance; the plums used in the famous *"pruneaux de Tours"* are grown here.

★★ **Chinon** – *See CHINON. Allow 2hr.*

④ **From Chinon to Saumur**

38km/24mi – about 3hr – local map overleaf

★★ **Chinon** – *See CHINON. Allow 2hr.*

Leave Chinon on ③ on the town plan and then turn right onto D 751 to Saumur.

Just before entering Candes turn right onto D 7 across the bridge over the Vienne to enjoy a good view of the pretty **setting★** of this village at the Loire-Vienne confluence.

Return to the south bank of the Vienne.

Vallée de la LOIRE

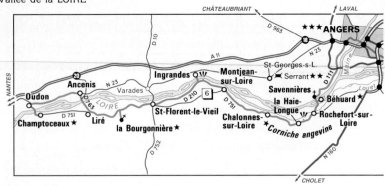

★ **Candes-St-Martin** – *See CANDES-ST-MARTIN.*

Montsoreau – *See MONTSOREAU.*

★★ **Fontevraud-l'Abbaye** – *See FONTEVRAUD-L'ABBAYE.*
Return to Montsoreau.

From the bridge over the Loire west of Montsoreau there is a fine view upstream of Montsoreau and Candes and downstream of Saumur château which is just visible. The road (D 947) is bordered by troglodyte dwellings and white Renaissance houses.

Small wine villages nestle between the road and the limestone cliffs, which are riddled with caves and old quarries, some of which are now used for growing mushrooms. At **Saut-aux-Loups** ⊙ just beyond Montsoreau on the Maumenière hillside, galleries display the different stages of mushroom cultivation and exhibit some of the rarer varieties, like the *pied-bleu* which smells slightly of aniseed or the pleurotus (oyster mushroom), which can be yellow or pink (the latter, also known as *"salmoneo straminens"*, has recently been cultivated on an experimental basis; its shape and colour make it look like some kind of flower). In season, it is also possible to taste the famous "somersault" mushrooms known as *"galipettes"*. These large button-mushrooms, picked when fully mature and cooked in bread ovens hollowed out of the tufa, probably owe their name to the fact that in the olden days they were grown in stacks and when they reached a certain stage of maturity fell to the ground, somersaulting as they went.

The sloping vineyards produce a dry or medium dry white wine, a Cabernet rosé called **Cabernet de Saumur**, and a red wine called **Champigny**.

Troglo"Tap ⊙ at Val-Hulin in the **Turquant** district is another example of local agricultural heritage. The art of dried apples *(pommes tapées)* has been revived in an enormous cave decorated with ancient farm implements. The apples are peeled, placed in flat wicker baskets, dried for five days in tufa ovens and when flattened for preservation may be kept for several months. They are eaten in a preparation made with local red wine flavoured with cinnamon. There is a slide presentation *(10min)*.

Continue along the D 947 to Saumur past the elegant church of Notre-Dame-des-Ardilliers *(see Saumur: Additional Sights)*.

★★ **Saumur** – *See SAUMUR. Allow 1hr 30min.*

★ **DOWNSTREAM TO ANGERS**

⑤ **From Saumur to Angers**
48km/30mi – about 3hr 30min – local map overleaf

★★ **Saumur** – *See SAUMUR. Allow 1hr 30min.*
Leave Saumur on ⑤ on the town plan.

Dried Apples

This technique for preserving fruit, which was in use at the time of the Revolution and continued until the beginning of 1914, reached its height in about 1880 when wine-growers, forced to abandon their vines in the wake of the phylloxera plague, turned to the drying of apples. With the advent of machines for peeling and drying, the activity developed from a craft into an industry and tons of dried apples were exported to Belgium, Great Britain and Sweden.

Historical archives on the Loire valley show that a similar method for preserving fruit was used at Rivarennes near Ussé, where the making of dried pears became a thriving industry.

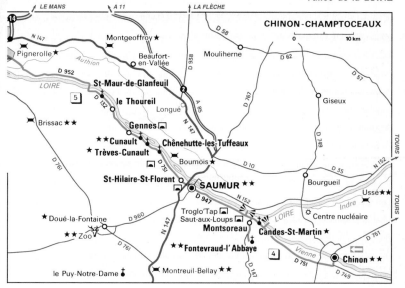

St-Hilaire-St-Florent - *See SAUMUR: Additional Sights.*
On the right stretch vast meadows bordered by trees and protected by dikes.

Chênehutte-les-Tuffeaux - The village **church** stands beside the road on the north side of the village. It is an attractive Romanesque building with a handsome doorway in the same style; the arch stones are carved.

Trèves-Cunault - A 15C crenellated tower is all that remains of the old castle. Tucked in beside it is the little **church★** of Trèves. It has a beautiful interior with great arches supporting the broad Romanesque nave; the chancel arch frames the rood beam on which there is a Crucifix. The holy water stoup by the entrance is of porphyry with primitive carvings; to the right is a recumbent figure; to the left stands a tall stone reliquary pierced with Flamboyant Gothic arches.

★★ **Église de Cunault** - *See Église de CUNAULT.*

Gennes - *See GENNES.*

Cross back over the bridge; turn right immediately onto D 132 along the south bank.

Le Thoureil - This quiet, spruce little village was formerly a very active river port for the handling of apples. Inside the **church**, on either side of the chancel there are two beautiful wooden reliquary shrines dating from the late 16C, which originally belonged to the abbey of St-Maur-de-Glanfeuil *(see below);* they are adorned with statuettes of Benedictine monks (Maurus, Roman) and saints who were popular locally.

Abbaye de St-Maur-de-Glanfeuil ⊙ - This ruined Benedictine abbey (now an international ecumenical centre as well as a religious community of Augustinians) is named after St Maurus, a hermit who came from Angers and founded a monastery in the 6C on the site of the Roman villa of Glanfeuil on the Loire.

Excavations in the first courtyard have revealed a 4C Gallo-Roman temple (nymphaeum) dedicated to female spirits of nature (nymphs). St Maurus converted the temple into a chapel; but the original column bases are clearly visible.

Follow the sign "chapelles" to the raised second courtyard. To the left are two chapels, St Martin's (13C) containing the tomb of St Maurus, and a modern chapel (1955), built up against the west front of the 11C abbey church, its austere appearance relieved by the use of sparkling stained glass. Follow the signposts to the second floor; carved into the gable of the old west front is a superb **Carolingian cross** with fine strapwork ornamentation.

★★★ **Angers** - *See ANGERS. About half a day.*

★ DOWNSTREAM TO CHAMPTOCEAUX

⑥ From Angers to Champtoceaux
83km/50mi – about 4hr – local map above

★★★ Angers – *See ANGERS. About half a day.*

Leave Angers on boulevard du Bon-Pasteur going west and turn left onto D 111 going south to Bouchemaine.

Beyond the riverside settlement of La Pointe the road leaves the Loire to wind through the vineyards to Épiré, before dropping into the valley of a stream which joins the Loire at Savennières.

Savennières – The attractive village **church** has a Romanesque south door, and chevet ornamented with modillions and carved friezes. The walls of the nave are built of schist decorated with a herringbone pattern in brick (10C). Two well-known, dry, white Savennières wines are "La Coulée de Serrant" and "La Roche aux Moines".

★ Béhuard – *See BÉHUARD.*

Rochefort-sur-Loire – Rochefort lies in a rural setting on the Louet, an arm of the Loire. The neighbouring slopes produce the famous **Quarts de Chaume**, a distinctive and heady white wine. There are several old houses, with turrets or watchtowers, in the main square below the road (D 751). A plaque in the church square commemorates the formation of the Rochefort Poetry School (École de Poésie) in 1941, which comprised a number of modern poets from the west of France.

★ Corniche angevine – From Rochefort to Chalonnes the road (D 751) along the south bank of the Loire twists and turns through many tight bends cut into the cliff face, making a scenic stretch known as the Corniche angevine. Beyond La Haie-Longue there are superb views of the riverside villages lying in the broad valley.

La Haie-Longue – In a bend in the road at the entrance to La Haie-Longue stands a chapel dedicated to **Our Lady of Loretto**, the patron saint of aviators. Legend has it that her house was carried by the breeze from Nazareth to the Dalmatian coast and thence to Loretto on the Italian coast where it is venerated as the Santa Casa (Holy House). Opposite stands a monument in honour of René Gasnier, a pioneer in aviation. Behind the monument is a viewing table. From here there is a remarkable **view★** of the River Loire and its backwaters glinting silver in the light; the turreted manor houses set amid meadows and sloping vineyards make a charming picture. The wine from these vineyards is known as "Coteaux du Layon".

Chalonnes-sur-Loire – Chalonnes, which was the birthplace of St Maurille, Bishop of Angers in the 5C, is pleasantly situated. From the quayside on the Loire there is a pretty view of the river. The old port now harbours more pleasure craft than fishing boats.

West of Chalonnes the road (D 571) skirts the edge of the plateau from which small streams flow north to join the Loire.

Montjean-sur-Loire – The narrow streets of Montjean (pronounced Montejan) are confined on a rocky promontory overlooking the Loire.
The buildings of the old forge house an interesting **museum** ⊙ devoted to traditional local commercial activities like the hemp industry, shipping on the Loire, lime-kilns, coal mining. From the terrace near the church there is a broad **view** of the Loire valley, of the suspension bridge over the river and of numerous villages with their grey slate roofs.

From Montjean to St-Florent take D 210.

The **road★** along the river embankment provides views over the Loire *(right)* and of the slopes rising to the south of the Thau, once a tributary of the Loire *(left)*. Beautiful **view** on reaching Ingrandes.

Ingrandes – *See INGRANDES.*

St-Florent-le-Vieil – *See ST-FLORENT-LE-VIEIL.*
West of St-Florent-le-Vieil the road (D 751) winds through gently rolling hills.

★ Chapelle de la Bourgonnière – *See Chapelle de la BOURGONNIÈRE.*

Liré – *See LIRÉ.*

Ancenis – The houses of Ancenis, built of schist and roofed with slate, stand in tiers on the north bank of the Loire overlooking the suspension bridge, which is 500m/1 640ft long. The town fortifications and the castle ramparts, now in ruins, once commanded the valley so that Ancenis was known as "the key to Brittany". The town used to be a busy port in the shipment of wine and was active in the sailcloth industry.

Ancenis is still an important agricultural market and has one of the largest co-operatives in France, the CANA (Cooperative Agricole La Noëlle à Ancenis), which is involved in many activities. The Vignerons de La Noëlle group of producers cultivates 350ha/865 acres of vineyards for the wines of Nantes and Anjou.

The vineyards of the district around Ancenis, Carquefou, Champtoceaux, Ligné, St-Florent-le-Vieil and Varades produce good wines including **Muscadet des Coteaux de la Loire** whites, and **Coteaux d'Ancenis Gamay** and **Coteaux d'Ancenis Cabernet** reds and rosés.

Leave Ancenis on ④ on the town plan, N 23 going west.

Oudon – The dominant feature of this town is the medieval keep, built between 1392 and 1415. From the top of the **tower** ⊙ there is a beautiful view of the valley.

★ **Champtoceaux** – Champtoceaux is built on an impressive **site**★ on the top of a ridge overlooking the Loire valley.

The terrace behind the church, **Promenade de Champalud**★★, is like a balcony above the Loire which divides into several channels round the islands in midstream *(viewing table)*.

Beyond the terrace are the ruins of the fortress which was demolished in 1420 and an old toll bridge over the river. The local white wines are to be recommended.

LORRIS★

Population 2 620
Michelin map 65 fold 1 or 237 fold 42 or 238 fold 7

Lorris is famous for the charter of freedom which was granted to it in 1122 by Louis VI. The town was a hunting seat for the Capet kings and a place of residence for Blanche of Castille and her son Louis IX of France. In 1215 it became the birthplace of Guillaume de Lorris, who wrote the first part of the *Romance of the Rose (Roman de la Rose)*, a poem of courtly love which influenced Chaucer in his writings.

★ **Église Notre-Dame** – The church is interesting not only for the purity of its architecture (12C-13C) but also for its furnishings. An elegant Romanesque door leads into a well-lit Gothic nave. High up in the nave are a **gallery** and the early-16C **organ loft**★, both ornately carved. The late-15C **choir stalls**★ are decorated with the Prophets and Sibyls on the cheekpieces and scenes from The Golden Legend, the New Testament and everyday life on the misericords. Above the old altar hang two 18C angels. Also worth a closer look are the polychrome statues in the ambulatory and an alabaster Virgin Mary (late-15C) near the font.

A **museum** dedicated to the organ and old musical instruments in general has been set up under the eaves.

Musée départemental de la Résistance et de la Déportation ⊙ – This museum is housed in the old station which has now been restored, against a backdrop of trees and greenery. Its rich collection of audio-visual documents relates the history of the Second World War and its consequences in this region. The course of events, from the underlying causes of the war until the liberation of France, is illustrated in detail with the aid of authentic documents, moving personal accounts, dioramas (the exodus of refugees and a reconstruction of a camp of members of the Resistance movement in a forest), figures in costume and a variety of other models.

Place du Matroi – The 16C **town hall**, built of brick with stone courses and heavily ornamented dormer windows, stands in the main street overlooking the huge town square; opposite is the **market** *(halles)* covered with an oak roof (1542).

CANAL D'ORLÉANS: SEINE REACH

For the Loire Reach of the canal see CHÂTEAUNEUF-SUR-LOIRE: Excursions. Round trip of 15km/9mi on D 44 to the northwest and then a left turn onto D 444.

Grignon – The hamlet is set deep in the countryside on the banks of the canal. It makes a most attractive picture with its towpaths, locks and lock-keeper's house.

Continue south to **Vieilles-Maisons** where the church has a timber-framed porch.

Étang des Bois – *Due south of Vieilles-Maisons.* This is another of the reservoirs associated with the Orléans canal. The little lake is fringed with oak, beech and chestnut trees and is a popular spot in summer (camp site, bathing, fishing, windsurfing, canoeing and picnic areas).

Château du LUDE★★

The Château du Lude lies on the south bank of the Loir which forms the border between Maine and Anjou. Since the first fort, La Motte, was built here the site has witnessed a thousand years of history. The Son et lumière entertainment, which was started in 1957, has proved a great attraction to visitors.

The 11C fortress of the Counts of Anjou was replaced in the 13C-14C by a castle which withstood several assaults by the English before it fell in 1425; it was recaptured two years later by Ambroise de Loré, Beaumanoir and Gilles de Rais. In 1457 the castle was acquired by Jean de Daillon, a childhood friend of Louis XI. His son built the present château on the foundations of the earlier fortress: it kept the traditional square layout with a massive tower at each corner but the large windows and the delicate decoration make it a country house in the fashion of its age.

Son et lumière – *See the Practical information section at the end of the guide.*

Tour of château ⊘ – The U-shaped early-17C courtyard was closed off in the late 18C by an arched portico.

Façades – Facing the park, to the right, is the François-Ier wing. Its façade is a mixture of the fortress style, with its round medieval towers, and Renaissance refinement: windows framed by pilasters, pedimented dormer windows, medallions and carved ornamentation. Overlooking the river, the Louis XVI wing in white tufa stone exemplifies the classical style: it is sober and symmetrical, its façade broken only by a central projecting section topped by a carved pediment. The north wing *(visible from rue du Pont which skirts the château)* is the earliest wing (early 16C); it was altered in the 19C when the stone balconies and equestrian statue of Jean de Daillon were added.

Interior – The Louis XII wing houses a large 19C library with 2 000 books that belonged to the Duke of Bouillon and a ballroom restored in the 15C and 16C style. The 18C building contains a fine suite of rooms including a splendid oval salon in pure Louis XVI style with carved woodwork and mirrors, an 18C bedroom and a 16C painting studio decorated with murals from the school of Raphael illustrating Biblical scenes and the *Triumphs* of Petrarch; note the ceiling painted in the Italian grotesque style. In the François-Ier wing a small library has a 17C Gobelins tapestry; in the dining room, where the window recesses reveal the thickness of the medieval walls, there is a vast chimneypiece with a carved salamander and ermine, while on the walls hang three Flemish tapestries including a *verdure* showing a red parrot.

The underground passages and 13C guard-room beneath the parterre of the former fortress are now open to the public *(access from the outside)*.

Maison des Architectes – *3 rue du Marché-au-Fil near the entrance to the château.*

The house, which was built in the 16C by the architects of the château, features ornamentation typical of the Renaissance period: mullioned windows, pilasters with Corinthian capitals decorated with roundels and lozenges and a frieze running between lower and upper floors *(not open to the public)*.

GENNETEIL TO LA BOISSIÈRE

Round trip of 28km/17mi – about 1hr 30min.

Leave Le Lude on D 257 going southwest.

Genneteil – The Romanesque **church** has a 13C bell-tower with a stair turret and a beautiful 11C doorway; the arch stones are carved with the signs of the zodiac and human faces. The left-hand chapel is decorated with Romanesque frescoes.

Take D 138 southeast.

Chigné – The fortified **church** (12C-15C) features an interesting façade flanked by a round tower. Above the triple-arched doorway note the line of carved brackets and the primitive carvings which have been incorporated, much altered, in the building.

Continue via les 4 Chemins to La Boissière.

La Boissière – *See La BOISSIÈRE.*

Take D 767 north; in La Croix-de-Beauchêne take D 138 right.

Broc – The attractive **church** has a squat Romanesque tower and a row of carved brackets on the chevet. The broad nave is roofed with lierne and tierceron vaulting; the Romanesque apse is decorated with 13C frescoes: Christ in Majesty *(on half-dome)*, the Annunciation *(left)* and the Virgin in Majesty *(right)*. On the nave wall is a very beautiful sculpted wood Crucifix of the Louis XIII period.

Return to Le Lude via La Croix-de-Beauchêne and D 307 to the right.

LUYNES

Michelin map 64 fold 14 or 232 folds 34 and 35
Local map see Vallée de la LOIRE: Orléans-Chinon

From the road running along the Loire embankment (N 152), there is a pretty view of this charming little town built in tiers up the hillside. Luynes still features numerous cellars hollowed out of the rock face, and a handsome timber-frame covered market hall, the **halles**, dating from the 15C, with a high roof of flat tiles. Visitors should also look out for one or two half-timbered houses, and in particular a house with carved corner pillars opposite the church (in rue Paul-Louis-Courier).

Leaving town on D 49, which climbs through vine-clad hillsides, there is a good view looking back of the medieval castle above the town.

Château ⊙ – This large medieval fortress perched on a rocky spur high above the little town was transformed in the 15C. It belonged to a crony of Louis XI, Hardouin de Maillé. Only three families have lived in the castle since the 11C, the Maillés, the Lavals and the Luynes. The castle is now occupied by the present Duc de Luynes. From the delightful inner courtyard there is a fine **panorama** of the Loire valley. The elegant residential block of the château, in brick and stone, was built during the reign of Louis XI, while the two wings date from the 17C. The interior houses sumptuous tapestries, paintings and antique furniture. The gardens are well laid-out, the harmony of their design reflecting a certain quest for the "good life". The tour of the château ends in the 15C canonesses' chapel.

Le MANS★★

Conurbation 189 107
Michelin map 60 fold 13 or 232 folds 10, 22
Plan of the conurbation in the current Michelin Red Guide France

Le Mans, a large modern city stands on the banks of the Sarthe at its confluence with the Huisne. It is a thriving provincial capital, its calendar packed with frequent fairs: the Spring Fair (end of March or early April); the Grand Exhibition called the Quatre-Jours (four days in mid-September); the Onion Fair (first Friday in September). It is also one of the most important insurance centres in France. Its industry is closely involved with the construction and racing of cars (24-hour Le Mans circuit, Bugatti circuit).

The citizens of Le Mans are fond of good food: potted pork *(rillettes)*, plump pullets *(poulardes dodues)*, capons *(chapons)* accompanied by sparkling cider and the famous local Reinette apple.

HISTORICAL NOTES

In the 4C the ancient town of Vundunum surrounded itself with ramparts to resist the barbarian invasions; this was the period when St Julian began to convert the people of the region.

The Plantagenet dynasty – The Plantagenet connections with this town were beneficial. When **Geoffrey Plantagenet**, Count of Anjou, married Matilda, the grand-daughter of William the Conqueror, he added Normandy and Maine to his estates. Geoffrey often resided at Le Mans and on his death in 1151 he was buried here. His son, who in 1154 became **Henry II** of England, was the founder of the Coëffort hospital and it was to Le Mans, his birthplace, that he retired in his old age only to be expelled by one of his rebellious sons **Richard the Lionheart**, then in alliance with the French king.

While on the Third Crusade Richard married Queen Berengaria of Navarre and it was to her in her widowhood that Philippe-Auguste gave the county of Maine which he had reconquered from Richard's younger brother, John Lackland. Berengaria founded Épau abbey *(see Excursions)* where she was buried. During the Hundred Years War Le Mans remained under English control until 1448.

The drama of 5 August 1392 – In the summer of 1392 King **Charles VI** of France launched a campaign against the Duke of Brittany, who supported the English. On 5 August the King left Le Mans with his troops and rode westwards. Suddenly, as they approached a leper house, an old man, hideously disfigured and with his clothes in tatters, blocked the King's path and cried "Don't go any further, noble king, you have been betrayed!"

Charles was deeply affected by this incident but continued on his way. A little later, when they were pausing to rest under the hot sun, a soldier let his lance fall against a helmet causing a strident clang in the silence. Charles jumped. Gripped by a sudden surge of fury and believing he was being attacked, he drew his sword and shouted out that he was being delivered to his enemies. He killed four men, gave his horse free rein and galloped wildly about for some while without anyone being able to intervene. Finally he wore himself out and one of his knights was able to mount behind and bring the horse under control. They laid the King in a wagon and tied him down; then they took him back to Le Mans convinced that he was about to die.

This terrible onset of madness in the middle of the Hundred Years War had serious consequences. Deprived of its ruler and a prey to princely rivalries, the kingdom grew weak. From time to time Charles VI would regain his reason only to sink again soon after into madness. Henry V of England was quick to take advantage of the situation: in 1420 he imposed the famous treaty of Troyes by which Charles VI disinherited his son and recognized Henry as his heir. Charles VI finally died in 1422, 30 years after the drama near Le Mans had begun.

The Comic Novel – The cathedral chapter in Le Mans had several members of note: Arnould Gréban, author of a *Mystery of the Passion* (c 1450) a poem of 30 000 lines; Ronsard, who was a canon in 1560; Jacques Pelletier, a friend of Ronsard; and Paul Scarron.

Scarron (1610-60), a poet, was an unordained canon of Le Mans

River Sarthe at Le Mans

cathedral by his mid-20s; this worldly cleric, who had a lively social life at court where he spent most of his time, enjoyed excellent health, a prebend and a house attached to the cathedral. Unfortunately for him, since he preferred city life, he was obliged to spend some time in Le Mans every now and then, where he consoled himself with the local food and wine. In 1638 Scarron fell victim to a noxious drug dispensed to him by a charlatan physician and found himself paralysed.

His hard lot was mitigated first by Marie de Hautefort, a former mistress of Louis XIII who had been exiled to Le Mans and who offered her friendship, and then by the Muse who inspired his *Comic Novel (Le Roman Comique)*, a burlesque work relating the adventures of a troop of actors in Le Mans and its neighbourhood. In 1652 Scarron married **Françoise d'Aubigné**, grand-daughter of the Calvinist poet Agrippa d'Aubigné, who said, "I would rather marry a cripple than the convent". When she was widowed she was elevated to the rank of **Marquise de Maintenon** before her secret marriage to Louis XIV (1683) over whom she had a great influence.

In the vanguard of progress – Before the Revolution, Le Mans had several flourishing industries: candle-making, tanning, making sailcloth from locally-grown hemp and weaving a coarse black woollen material used for clerics' and lawyers' gowns. A dozen merchants in the town controlled about 2 000 jobs across the surrounding district, producing 18 000 items of which two-thirds were exported. In the second half of the 19C the town entered the first rank of industrial centres when **Amédée Bollée** (1844-1917), a local bell-founder, began to take an interest in the infant motor car industry. His first car (*l'Obéissante*) was finished in 1873; it was a 12-seater vehicle with two engines each driving one back wheel; it weighed just over 4 tonnes empty and had a maximum speed of over 40km/25mi per hour. Later he built the *Mancelle*, the first car to have the engine placed in front under a bonnet and to have a transmission shaft. The Austrian emperor, Franz-Joseph went for a ride in the *Mancelle*.

Radiator of a 1912 Amédée Bollée

3Bis/MICHELIN

Bollée's son Amédée (1867-1926) devoted himself mainly to racing cars; they were fitted with Michelin tyres and reached 100km/62mi per hour. After the First World War he began to produce an early form of piston rings which became the main line of manufacture in his factory.

On 27 June 1906, the first prize on the Sarthe circuit was won by Szisz driving a Renault fitted with Michelin detachable rims.

In 1908 his brother, Léon Bollée, invited **Wilbur Wright** to attempt one of his first flights in an aeroplane at Les Hunaudières. When asked how the aircraft had performed Wright replied, "Like a bird". In 1936 Louis Renault set up his first decentralized factory south of Le Mans in the Arnage plain.

Le Mans 24 hour race – In 1923 Gustave Singher and Georges Durand launched the first Le Mans 24 hour endurance test which was to become a sporting event of universal interest and an ideal testing ground for car manufacturers.

The difficulties of the circuit and the duration of the race are a severe test of the quality of the machine and of the endurance of the two drivers who take turns at the wheel of each car.

The track has been greatly improved since the tragic accident in 1955 when several spectators died. Whether seen from the stands or from the fields or pine woods which surround the track, the race is an unforgettable experience: the roaring of the engines, the whining of the vehicles hurtling up the Hunaudières section at more than 350km/200mi per hour, the smell of petrol mingled with the resin of the pine trees, the glare of the headlights at night, the emotion and excitement of the motor car fanatics.

In May 1991, the 24 hour circuit was thoroughly modernised, with a new sports module and refuelling pits, making it one of the leading tracks of its kind in the world.

Every year there is also a Le Mans 24 hour motorcycle race and a Le Mans 24 hour truck race. There is also a Grand Prix de France motorcycle race held here regularly.

Course Records – The first 24 hour race in 1923 was won by Lagache and Léonard from Chenard and Walcker; they covered 2 209.536km at an average of 92.064km per hour; the fastest circuit time was achieved by Clément in a Bentley: 107.328km per hour. The most famous names in motor racing have taken part in the 63 trials held since then.

In 1971 when the track was 13.469km long Helmut Marko and Gijs Van Lennep covered 5 335.313km in a Porsche 917 at an average of 222.304km per hour; Siffert drove the fastest lap, also in a Porsche 917, at an average of 243.905km per hour.

Pit stop during the Le Mans 24 hour race

From 1972 to 1978 the circuit was 13.640km long; Didier Pironi and Jean-Pierre Jaussaud hold the course record with 5 044.530km in a Renault Alpine A 442 Turbo in 1978. The circuit was altered in 1979 (13.626km) and again in 1986 (13.528km). Between 1981 and 1987, Porsches had an uninterrupted run of victories.
In 1988 Jaguar put an end to Porsche's leadership and in 1989 it was the turn of Mercedes to carry off the first prize. In 1990 Jaguar won again. An important change was made to the track that year: for reasons of security, two slow sections were added to the Hunaudières straight, bringing the length of the circuit to 13.600km.
In 1991 it was Mazda (first victory of a Japanese firm and a rotary engine) that won. The year 1993 saw Peugeot's historic "hat trick": three cars on the starting line, three cars on the finishing line, and three cars winning laurels. As if that were not enough, they set a new track record on the longer circuit (13.600km) covering 5 100km at an average speed of 213.358km per hour.
In 1995 Porsche won their 13th victory at Le Mans in a Dauer 962 LM. In spite of the rain in 1995 the McLaren F1 GTR made an impressive entry onto the Le Mans scene by winning the very first time it participated.
However, the best 24 hour races at Le Mans are always those still to come!

★★ CATHÉDRALE ST-JULIEN 1hr

This magnificent cathedral, dedicated to St Julian the first Bishop of Le Mans, makes an impressive spectacle seen from place des Jacobins, where its Gothic chevet★★★ rises in a succession of tiers supported by an amazingly intricate system of Y-shaped two-tiered flying buttresses. The present building comprises a Romanesque nave, Gothic chancel and Rayonnant or High Gothic transept flanked by a tower. The interior is illuminated to show it to best effect.

Exterior – The south porch overlooking the charming place St-Michel has a superb 12C doorway★★ contemporary with the Royal Doorway of Chartres. A comparison of the two doorways shows that they feature the same sorts of figures: Christ in Majesty, the Apostles and a series of statue columns flanking the doorway. These portray St Peter and St Paul on the jambs, while the figures on the splay embrasures represent Solomon and the Queen of Sheba, a Prophet, a Sibyl and the ancestors of Christ. The Apostles occupy the niches of the lintel in serried ranks with Christ the King on the tympanum, surrounded by the symbols of the Evangelists, being censed by angels in the first recessed arch moulding. Among the other scenes on the arch mouldings are the Annunciation, Visitation, Nativity, Presentation in the Temple, Massacre of the Innocents, Baptism of Christ and the Wedding at Cana.
Looking to the right of the porch there is a good view of the transept with its immense window openings and the 12C-14C tower (64m/210ft high).
The west front, built in an archaic Romanesque style, overlooks place du Cardinal-Grente, its sides lined with Renaissance mansions. Clearly visible is the original 11C gable which was embedded in the gable added the following century when the new vaulting was being built.

At the right corner of the west front is a pink-veined sandstone menhir. Tradition has it that visitors should place their thumb in one of the holes to be able to claim that they have truly visited Le Mans.

Nave – The Romanesque main building rests on great 11C round arches which were reinforced in the following century by pointed arches. The convex or Plantagenet-style vaulting springs from splendid capitals with particularly finely worked detail.

In the side aisles are eight Romanesque stained-glass windows; the most famous one represents the Ascension (1). The great window of the west front, heavily restored in the 19C, depicts the Legend of St Julian.

Transept – The 14C-15C transept, with its boldly soaring elevation pierced by a triforium and immense stained-glass windows, has an ethereal quality in striking contrast to the nave. The south arm is dominated by the 16C organ-loft (2), while the north arm is suffused with light transmitted through the beautiful 15C stained glass. Three 16C tapestry hangings (3) illustrate the Legend of St Julian.

At the entrance to the baptismal chapel (Chapelle des Fonts), which opens into the north arm of the transept, are two remarkable Renaissance **tombs★★** opposite one another. The tomb on the left (4), that of Charles IV of Anjou, Count of Maine, the brother of King René, is the work of Francesco Laurana. The recumbent figure lies, in the Italian style, on an antique sarcophagus and the delicacy of the facial features recalls Laurana's talents as a portraitist. On the right the magnificent monument (5) to the memory of Guillaume du Bellay, cousin of the poet, shows the figure holding a sword and a book and reclining on one elbow in the Antique manner on a sarcophagus which is adorned with an attractive frieze of aquatic divinities.

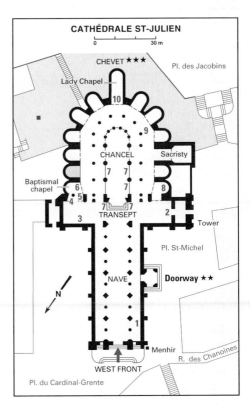

CATHÉDRALE ST-JULIEN

CHEVET ★★★

The tomb of Cardinal Grente (6) was placed here in 1965.

Chancel – "The sustained height of this almost detached choir is very noble; its lightness and grace, its soaring symmetry, carry the eye up to places in the air from which it is slow to descend" *(Henry James)*. The lofty Gothic chancel (13C), encircled by a double ambulatory with a circlet of apsidal chapels, is one of the finest in France – soaring 34m/112ft high (compare Notre-Dame in Paris 35m/115ft, Westminster Abbey in London 31m/102ft).

The massed ranks of the tall upward-sweeping columns support lancet arches showing a definite Norman influence. In the high windows of the chancel and first ambulatory and in the low windows of the chapels, the 13C **stained glass★★** is a blaze of colour dominated by vivid blues and reds. Binoculars are needed to identify the rather stylized and fierce-looking figures of the Apostles, bishops, saints and donors.

Hanging above the 16C choir stalls is the famous series of **tapestries** (7) of the same period depicting the lives of St Gervase and St Protase.

Chancel precincts – In the first chapel on the right (8) is a moving 17C terracotta Entombment. The sacristy door beyond used to be part of the 17C rood screen. The beautiful 16C woodwork, in the sacristy, originally formed the high backs of the choir stalls. The 14C Canons' Doorway (9) has a tympanum with an effigy of St Julian.

LE VIEUX MANS

B   Maison du Pilier Rouge
D   Maison canoniale
       St-Jacques
E   Maison du Pilier Vert
F   Ancien hôtel d'Arcy
H   Hôtel de ville
K   Tour du 14ᵉ siècle
L   Ancienne collégiale
       St-Pierre-la-Cour
M² Maison de la reine
       Bérengère (Musée)
N   Hôtel de Vignolles
Q   Maison de la Tourelle
R   Maison d'Adam et Eve
S   Hôtel d'Argoues
V   Hôtel de Vaux
W   Maison de Scarron
X   Grande poterne
Y   Maison des Deux-Amis
Z   Hôtel du Grabatoire

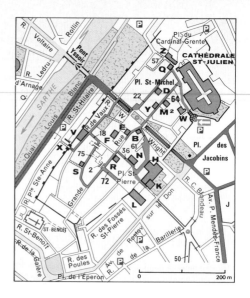

The Lady Chapel dates from the 13C; it is closed by a delicate 17C wrought-iron grille. The stained-glass windows date from the same period; they depict the Tree of Jesse (**10**) and the story of Adam and Eve.

The vaulting is covered with paintings dating from 1380. The scene, illustrating an Angels' Concert, is executed with skilled and refined draughtsmanship.

★★ MEDIEVAL TOWN *1hr*

The medieval town (Vieux Mans) is built on a hill overlooking the Sarthe. Restaurants and craft shops animate this picturesque group of winding streets, intersected by stepped alleys and lined with 15C half-timbered houses, Renaissance town houses and 18C *hôtels* graced by wrought-iron balconies. Clearly visible from all along the quays of the Sarthe, the well-restored **Gallo-Roman ramparts**★ in their typically pinkish hues are a truly unique landmark. The overall impression of elegance is created by the alternating layers of brickwork and black and white ashlar arranged in geometrical patterns. This 1 300m/4 270ft long military construction, interrupted by 11 towers, is one of the longest still extant in France.

From place des Jacobins follow on foot the itinerary indicated on the town plan below.

Place St-Michel – Standing in the cathedral precincts is the Renaissance house (**W**) where Paul Scarron lived during his period as a member of the cathedral chapter. The presbytery, at no 1 bis, still features its 15C staircase turret.

★ **Maison de la reine Bérengère** (**M²**) – *No 9 rue de la Reine-Bérengère.* This elegant house was built around 1460 for an alderman of Le Mans, over two centuries after the death of its namesake Queen Berengaria, wife of Richard the Lionheart. The decoration consists of an accolade above the door, beams supported on historiated brackets and sections of carved woodwork on the façade. The house at no 7, which dates from c 1530, is adorned with statues of St Catherine and St Barbara.

Musée de la reine Bérengère ⊙ – The Maison de la reine Bérengère is now a **museum of history and ethnography**. A Renaissance room on the ground floor contains a display of regional furniture.

On the first floor, the glazed pottery of the Sarthe region (Ligron, Malicorne, Bonnétable and Prevelles) makes a lively and imaginative display, with the strikingly fresh colours – yellow, green and brown – used lavishly on statuettes, altarpieces, chafing-dishes, pots, roof finials etc. On the second floor are paintings by 19C artists from the Sarthe region including Hervé-Mathé, Dugasseau and Gizard. *The third floor is currently being renovated.*

Maison des Deux-Amis (**Y**) – *Nos 18-20.*
The two friends *(deux amis)* are shown supporting a coat of arms. This mansion was built in the 15C and two centuries later was home to Nicolas Denizot, the poet and painter and friend of Ronsard and Du Bellay.

On the opposite side of rue Wilbur-Wright, which was cut through the hillside to relieve traffic congestion, is the **Maison du Pilier Rouge** (Red Pillar House) (**B**), a half-timbered house containing the tourist information centre and featuring a corner post decorated with a death's head.

At the beginning of the Grande-Rue stands *(right)* the **Maison du Pilier Vert** (Green Pillar House) (**E**) and further on the 16C Hôtel d'Arcy (**F**).
Return to the Maison du Pilier Rouge and turn right into the street of the same name which ends on place St-Pierre lined with half-timbered houses.

Hôtel de ville (**H**) – The town hall was built in 1760, within the walls of the palace of the Counts of Maine. Take the steps to rue Rostov-sur-le-Don from where there is a view of the old town's southeast ramparts; on one side of the steps is a 14C tower (**K**) and on the other the old collegiate church of **St-Pierre-la-Cour** (**L**) ⊙, now an exhibition and concert hall.

Hôtel de Vignolles (**N**) – This 16C mansion with tall French-style mansard roofs stands at the beginning of rue de l'Écrevisse on the right.

Maison d'Adam et Ève (**R**) – *No 71 La Grande-Rue.*
This superb Renaissance mansion was the home of Jean de l'Épine, an astrologer and physician.
At the corner of **rue St-Honoré** (**72**) a column shaft is decorated with three keys, the sign of a locksmith. The street is lined with half-timbered houses. The picturesque Cour d'Assé opens opposite rue St-Honoré. From here onwards Grande-Rue runs downhill between elegant classical mansions. Bear right into the less patrician rue St-Pavin-de-la-Cité; on the left is the Hôtel d'Argouges (**S**) which has a lovely 15C doorway in the courtyard. Carry on along the street and after a vaulted passageway turn left into rue Bouquet. At the corner of rue de Vaux a 15C niche shelters a statue of Mary Magdalene; the Hôtel de Vaux at no 12 (**V**) is a late 16C mansion. Further on to the left there is a view of the Great Postern steps (**X**), part of the Gallo-Roman ramparts.
Return along rue de Vaux to rue Wilbur-Wright; cross it and climb the steps turning left into rue des Chanoines. At no 26 stands St-Jacques canon's residence (**D**) built around 1560.

Maison de la Tourelle (**Q**) – This Renaissance mansion, with its windows and dormers decorated with delicate scrollwork, is named after the corbelled turret it features on the corner of the Pans-de-Gorron stepped alley.

Hôtel du Grabatoire (**Z**) – On the other side of the steps, opposite the Romanesque doorway of the cathedral, this 16C mansion stands on the site of what was originally the infirmary for sick canons, but which is now the episcopal palace. On its right stands the Maison du Pèlerin (Pilgrim's House) decorated with cockleshells, the symbol adopted by pilgrims who had visited the shrine of St James at Santiago de Compostela *(see Michelin Green Guide Spain).*

OUT AND ABOUT IN LE MANS

Entertainment – A small monthly magazine in French called *A l'Affiche* gives the full programme of exhibitions, discussion groups, shows and theatre performances on offer in Le Mans. Otherwise, contact the city's main entertainment venues direct: Centre Jacques-Prévert ☏ 02 43 24 73 85; Théâtre municipal ☏ 02 43 47 37 05; Théâtre du Radeau ☏ 02 43 24 93 60; Théâtre de l'Acthalia ☏ 02 43 23 42 87.

Local specialities – *Rillettes à l'ancienne* (potted pork strips), *diableries* (*rillettes* made of fish), *bugattises* (chocolate confectionery), wines from the Coteaux du Loir and Jasnières.

Dates for your diary – **April:** 24 hour motorcycle race; **May:** classical music festival at Épau abbey; **June:** Le Mans 24 hour motor race; **July:** "Scénomanies" (street theatre, music and dance); **August:** 24 hour go-carting race; **October:** 24 hour truck race, 24 hour book fair.

Markets – Marché des Jacobins on Wednesdays, Fridays and Sundays.

River trips on the Sarthe – Mini-cruises are organised on the Sarthe aboard *Le Mans*; lunch and dinner are available. Details from the Capitainerie, quai Amiral-Lalande, ☏ 02 43 23 83 84.

ADDITIONAL SIGHTS

★ **Musée de Tessé** (**BV**) ⊙ – This museum is housed in the old bishop's palace, which was built in the 19C on the site of the Tessé family mansion; its collections were seized in 1793 and its fine 19C paintings now form the nucleus of the museum.
Groundfloor – A small room *(left)* contains a superb enamelled copper plaque, called the **Plantagenet enamel**★, a unique piece depicting Geoffrey Plantagenet, Count of Anjou and Maine from 1129 to 1151, Duke of Normandy in 1144 and father of Henry II of England. Originally it adorned the tomb (no longer extant) of this powerful knight in the cathedral.

Le MANS

The Italian paintings include an interesting series of 14C-15C altarpieces with gold backgrounds, a delightful female saint with narrow, slanting eyes by Pietro Lorenzetti from Siena, two panels from a marriage chest by Pesellino of Florence (the Penitence of David and the Death of Absalom) and a very touching portrait of the Virgin Mary suckling the Infant Jesus.

In the Renaissance room there is a half-relief in enamelled terracotta from the Della Robbia workshop; also two panels by the Master of Vivoin, part of an altarpiece from Vivoin priory (Sarthe).

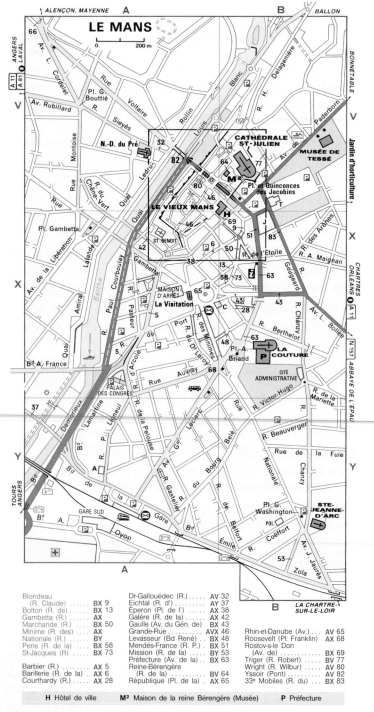

H Hôtel de ville	**M²** Maison de la reine Bérengère (Musée)	**P** Préfecture

There are classical paintings by Philippe de Champaigne (*The Dream of Elijah*, the famous *Vanity* exhibited in the Tessé room), Georges de la Tour (*St Francis in Ecstasy*) and Nicolas Tournier (*The Drinking Party* – in the entrance). The 18C room contains a superb bookcase by Bernard van Risenburgh.

First floor – The Northern school of painting is represented by Van Utrecht, Kalf (*Still Life with Armour*), several bambocciate (scenes of street life) and landscapes. A whole room is devoted to *The Comic Novel* by Scarron: as well as a portrait of the author there are paintings by Coulom and engravings by Oudry and Pater.

Second floor – This floor is reserved for temporary exhibitions of other collections belonging to the museum, as well as a section on Egyptian archeology.

Jardin d'horticulture (**BV**) – This beautiful horticultural garden with its rockery and cascading stream was designed in 1851 by Alphand, the landscape gardener responsible for the Bois de Boulogne and parks of Montsouris and Buttes-Chaumont in Paris. From the mall on the terrace there is a fine view of the cathedral.

Place and quinconces des Jacobins (**BV**) – The square, place des Jacobins, which is famous for its view of the chevet of the cathedral, was laid out on the site of a former Dominican convent. At the entrance to the tunnel through the old town stands a monument to Wilbur Wright by Paul Landowski and an unusual floral clock. Directly opposite, a modern concert hall has been built, the interior of which is decorated with a tapestry by Picart le Doux.

The quincunx, Quinconces des Jacobins, is made up of a series of terraced avenues of lime trees.

Pont Yssoir (**AV 82**) – This bridge affords a nice view of the cathedral, the old town, the Gallo-Roman fortified wall with its geometric decoration and a riverside walk past traces of medieval fortifications.

Close to the bridge on the north bank is the church of N.-D.-du-Pré.

Église Notre-Dame-du-Pré (**AV**) – In a square planted with magnolia trees stands the old abbey church of the Benedictine convent of St Julian in the Fields (St-Julien-du-Pré); the column capitals and chancel are Romanesque.

Église de la Visitation (**AX**) ⊙ – This church, which stands in the main square, place de la République, at the heart of the modern town, was originally a convent chapel; it was built in about 1730. The main façade, in rue Gambetta, is lavishly decorated with a portico of Corinthian columns sheltering a Rococo door; the interior décor, of the same date, is also Baroque.

★ **Église de la Couture** (**BX**) – This church, now in the centre of the town and next to the Préfecture housed in the old convent buildings (18C), was originally the abbey church of the monastery of St-Pierre-de-la-Couture (a corruption of *culture* which referred to the fields of crops that used to surround the church). The façade is 13C. The door is framed by the Apostles putting down the forces of evil; on the pediment is Christ, between the Virgin Mary and St John, presiding over the Last Judgement; on the arch stones, making up the Heavenly Host, are rows of Angels, Patriarchs, Prophets (1st row), Martyrs (2nd row) and Virgins (3rd row).

The wide single nave, built in the late 12C in the Plantagenet style, is lit by elegant twinned windows surmounted by oculi. Note in the first bay the forms of the Romanesque arches of the original nave on the blind walls of the great pointed arches which support a narrow ledge below the windows. To the left on entering is an interesting 11C pilaster sculpted with a Christ in Benediction. The enchanting white marble **Virgin**★★ (1571), on the pillar directly opposite the pulpit, is by Germain Pilon and originally came from the now-vanished retable of the high altar. The blind arcades are hung with 17C **tapestries** and 16C panels painted by one of the monks.

The massive round 11C columns of the chancel, with squat capitals showing Eastern influence in the decoration, support very narrow round arches. Above, the vaulting ribs spring from fine Plantagenet-style statues.

The 10C crypt, altered in 1838, has pre-Romanesque or Gallo-Roman columns and capitals; an inverted Antique capital serves as a base for one of the pillars. The 6C-7C shroud of St Bertrand, Bishop of Le Mans and founder in 616 of the monastery, is displayed at the entrance *(automatic time switch for lighting)*. The presumed burial place of St Bertrand is marked by a recumbent plaster figure in a wall alcove.

★ **Église Ste-Jeanne-d'Arc** (**BY**) – This church, on the site of the old Coëffort hospital, was founded c 1180 by Henry II of England in atonement, it is said, for the murder of his former Chancellor, Archbishop Thomas Becket in Canterbury Cathedral. The 12C great hall or ward for the sick is now the parish church. A similar institution, the former Hospital of St John in Angers was built by the same monarch. The plain façade, pierced by an arched doorway, above which are twinned windows, opens into a vast room divided into three naves of equal height. The elevation is elegant with slender columns topped by finely carved capitals, supporting Plantagenet vaulting. In the Middle Ages wide canopied beds for several patients at a time were aligned down the side aisles with an altar in the central passage.

MOTOR RACING CIRCUITS

To the south of Le Mans between N 138 and D 139.

Circuit des 24 heures – The 24 hour circuit (13.6km/8.5mi long) begins at the Tertre Rouge bend *(virage)* on N 138. The racetrack, which is about 10m/33ft wide, is marked in kilometres. The double bend on the private road and the Mulsanne and Arnage hairpin bends are the most exciting hazards on the 24 hour course. In

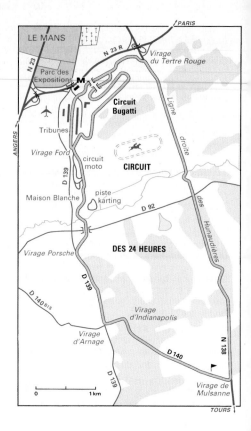

1972 the course was laid out to give the public a better view along a distance of 4km/2.5mi.

Within the confines of the circuit is Les Hunaudières racecourse for horses where Wilbur Wright made his first flight, commemorated by a stele.

From the main entrance to the track on D 139 a tunnel leads to the Bugatti circuit and the museum.

Circuit Bugatti ⊙ – Apart from being used by its school for racing drivers, the track (4.43km/2.75mi) is also a permanent testing ground for teams of racing car drivers and motorcyclists who use it for private trials.

★★ **Musée de l'automobile de la Sarthe (M)** ⊙ – *Access is through the main entrance to the circuit (D 139 north of D 921).*

Rebuilt in 1991, the new Motor Museum displays 115 vehicles in an extremely modern and instructive setting. With the help of video technology, interactive games and robots, a series of showcases and animated maquettes illustrate the Saga of the Automobile over the past hundred years. Tribute is paid to the "Bollée" models manufactured in Le Mans, as well as to the electrically-powered Krieger of 1908. The interwar period is represented by prestige cars: a Hispano-Suiza chauffeur-driven drop-head coupé (1929), a Voisin "aerodyne" (1935), a 1939 Bugatti, the 1931 caterpillar-track *Scarabée d'Or* Citroën that took part in the renowned *"Croisière Jaune"*. Note the only existing prototype of the 1952 gas turbine Socema Grégoire.

The section on racing cars, in particular those that won the Le Mans 24 hours, presents a superb collection of outstanding automobiles, including a 1924 Bentley, a 1949 Ferrari, a 1974 Matra, a 1983 Rondeau, a 1988 Jaguar, a 1991 Mazda and a 1992 Peugeot.

EXCURSIONS

★ **Abbaye de l'Épau** ⊙ – *4km/2.5mi on avenue Léon-Bollée (BX); turn right onto the ring road, cross the railway and follow the arrows.*

In 1229 a Cistercian abbey was founded on the south bank of the Huisne by **Queen Berengaria**, the widow of Richard the Lionheart, who spent her last days here. The monastic buildings were laid out around the cloisters, which were destroyed in 1365 by bands of mercenaries who were ravaging Maine. On the right is the **refectory** wing with the arcades of the washing place (lavatorium). Opposite are the monks' quarters, including the writing room (**scriptorium** – right) and the **chapter-house** (left) with elegant ogive vaulting and the tomb of Queen Berengaria; the first floor consisted of the monks' **dormitory** with wooden vaulting, which has been restored to its former appearance.

On the left is the **church**, which was built in the 13C and 14C and repaired after the ravages of 1365 early in the 15C; this is the date of the huge, delicately carved chancel window. The church was designed to the traditional Cistercian layout: a square east end with three chapels facing east in each arm of the transept. In the south arm, the square capitals are decorated with water-lily leaf motifs.

In recent years, the abbey has hosted the "Festival de l'Épau", a highly-esteemed festival of classical music.

Montfort-le-Gesnois – *20km/12.5mi east of Le Mans on avenue Léon-Bollée* (**BX**) *and N 23; after 16km/10mi bear left.*

Not far from **Connerré**, a small commercial town renowned for its *rillettes* (potted meat made from pork or goose), Montfort, resulting from the merging of Pont-de-Gennes and Montfort-le-Rotrou, lies in a peaceful, attractive site which developed from the Roman bridge over the Huisne river. The narrow humpback **bridge**, built with sandstone blocks in the 15C, spans the river at a point where it widens and flows among the trees. There is a pretty view of the 13C church of St-Gilles, a mill overgrown with Virginia creeper and surrounded by weeping willows, and a little weir where the water tumbles and races.

Bois de Loudon – *18km/11mi southeast on avenue Jean-Jaurès* (**BY**), *N 223 and D 304; fork left onto D 145ᴱ and turn left again onto D 145.*

Woodland tracks branch off to the right of the road (D 145) into the coniferous forest; in the autumn the sandy soil is covered with a thick carpet of heather.

Spay – *10km/6mi southwest on N 23 and D 51 turning near Arnage.*

The 9C-12C Romanesque **church** ⊙ (restored) has a richly decorated Baroque high altar and a very elegant 14C Virgin and Child. A valuable pyx (1621) is just one of the items in the church's treasury.

Vallée de la MANSE★

Michelin maps 232 fold 35 or 64 folds 14, 15 and 68 fold 4

The River Manse flows west through quiet picturesque countryside away from the main roads to join the Vienne at L'Ile-Bouchard.

L'ILE-BOUCHARD TO N 10 *27km/17mi – about 2hr*

L'Ile-Bouchard – *See L'ILE-BOUCHARD.*

Leave L'Ile-Bouchard to the north.

Avon-les-Roches – The 12C-13C **church** has a stone spire over the right transept. The arches of the porch and the door are decorated with archivolts and delicately carved capitals; an inscription in the porch *(left)* tells of the death of Charles the Bold.

Take the road east towards Crissay; after 1km/0.5mi turn left.

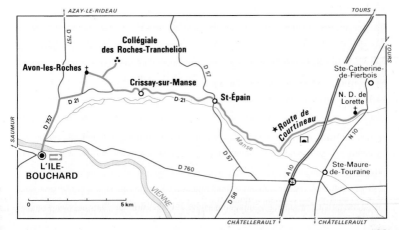

Collégiale des Roches-Tranchelion – The ruins of this Gothic collegiate church (1527) can be seen from some way off. *Car drivers can take the steep earth track which leads up to the church.* These ruins perched on a hill overlooking the surrounding countryside bear witness to past greatness. Little remains of the church vaulting but the elegant façade is still standing, decorated with delicate carving; note the seated figure above the great window under the triumphal arch, and the Renaissance decoration of pilasters and medallions representing the local feudal lords.

Crissay-sur-Manse – The ruins of the 15C castle *(left)*, the stone spire of the village church *(right)* and the several 15C houses with square turrets make up a charming scene.

St-Épain – The village church (12C, 13C and 15C) is capped by a 13C square tower. Adjoining it is a fortified gate, all that remains of the 15C curtain wall. Above the arch, the Hôtel de la Prévôté can be seen with its mullioned window and overhanging upper storey. Go through the doorway to admire the mansion's other façade, which is flanked by a round tower.
On the other side of the main street stands a house with a watch turret where the road bends southeast to Ste-Maure.
This road leads up the pretty Manse valley, green with vegetation.

After passing under the railway, bear left.

★ **Route de Courtineau** – This small scenic road winds between the stream hidden amid the trees and the cliff dotted with troglodyte dwellings. The Chapelle Notre-Dame de Lorette, a small 15C oratory, has been carved into the cliff face beside a small troglodyte dwelling of the same period.

Les MAUGES

Michelin map 63 folds 18, 19 and 67 folds 5, 6 or 232 folds 30, 31

The southern part of Anjou on the borders of the Vendée and Poitou, which is known as Les Mauges, is a peaceful, somewhat enigmatic region delimited by the Loire to the north, by the Layon valley to the east and the *départements* of the Vendée and Deux-Sèvres to the south and west. The terrain consists of schist rock, an extension of the Armorican massif culminating in the Puy de la Garde peak (210m/689ft). Les Mauges is a mixture of woodland and pasture used for cattle raising, where the Durham-Mancelle breed is fattened before being sold in its thousands at the markets in Chemillé and Cholet.
The straight main roads, which were laid down during the Revolution and under the Empire for political reasons, are superimposed on a network of deep lanes which were well-suited to the ambushes which played a prominent part in the Vendée War. The windmills which still crown the hillsides were often used by the Royalist Whites to send signals.

Memorials of the Vendée War – Throughout the region there are monuments to the events of 1793-96. At Maulévrier there is a pyramid commemorating Stofflet and a martyrs' cemetery *(see MAULÉVRIER)*.
At the crossroads on N 149 and D 753 near Torfou stands a column celebrating the victory of the Whites over the Mayence army (19 September 1793). Bonchamps was buried at St-Florent-le-Vieil. A cross was put up by the road to Nuaillé near Cholet where La Rochejaquelein fell on 29 January 1794.

Stained-glass windows – Many churches in Les Mauges and the Saumur region have stained-glass windows *(1)* that illustrate forcefully and realistically the Vendée War and relate the great deeds of its heroes. The windows, particularly in Vihiers, La Salle-de-Vihiers, Montilliers, Chemillé, Chanzeaux, St-Laurent-de-la-Plaine, Le Pin-en-Mauges and further north at La Chapelle-St-Florent, were mostly the work of local glass-makers including Clamens, Bordereau, Megen, and more recently, Rollo, who by both restoring and creating stained glass, has continued the tradition of this craft in Anjou.

SIGHTS *Local map p. 186; sights listed in alphabetical order*

Beaupréau – Beaupréau is a small town built on a steep slope on the north bank of the River Evre. In 1793 it was the headquarters of the Whites; their leader, D'Elbée, owned a manor at St-Martin, on the east side of the town, which now houses the public library. The 15C château overlooking the Evre (good view from

---

(1) For further information on stained glass in the Vendée area, read Les Vitraux vendéens et les maîtres verriers angevins by J.Boisleve (Maulévrier, Hérault) or enquire at the Mauges Environmental Centre (Carrefour touristique et culturel des Mauges) in St-Florent-le-Vieil.

The Vendée War (1793-96)

The execution of Louis XVI had profoundly shocked the rural French population, who were also not happy about the ensuing persecution of priests who refused to espouse Republican ideals. All that was necessary to provoke revolt, therefore, was the decision of the Convention in February 1793 to impose conscription. The cry went up, "Long live God and Long live the King!" and the peasants of the Vendée and Les Mauges, who were less than receptive of – indeed positively hostile towards – the new ideas, rose against the Republic and banded together under the white flag of the monarchy, hence their name, the Whites. They chose leaders from their own kind – **Stofflet**, the gamekeeper and **Cathelineau**, the pedlar – or from among the nobility – D'Elbée, Bonchamps, La Rochejaquelein and Charette. On 15 March they captured Cholet and it was not long before they held the region of Les Mauges. The Blues (blue was the colour of the Republican uniform) counter-

Cathelineau by Girodet-Trioson (1824)
(Galerie d'Histoire, Musée de Cholet)

Lauros/GIRAUDON

attacked and pushed the Roman Catholic and Royalist army back as far as the Sèvre; but the Whites regained the advantage and captured the whole of Anjou (June 1793). Alarmed at this turn of events, the Convention sent in the Armée de l'Ouest under Kléber and Marceau.

At first it was beaten at Coron, St-Fulgent and Torfou (19 September 1793) but then it was victorious at Cholet (17 October) after a bloody struggle in which the Whites were forced to retreat to St-Florent *(see ST-FLORENT-LE-VIEIL)*. The following day 60 000-80 000 Whites – panic-stricken men, women and children – crossed the Loire. In an episode (18 October to 23 December 1793) that became a byword for brutality in French annals, the survivors were massacred in their thousands, shot down or drowned in the Loire. General Westermann wrote a chilling account of events to the Convention: "There is no more Vendée; it has died under our sword of liberty... I have had the children crushed under horses' feet and the women massacred. I have not a single prisoner with which to reproach myself." Shortly afterwards, at the end of January 1794, the Convention sent in Turreau's **"infernal columns"** but the plans for total extermination failed. Insurrection flared up again in Les Mauges and in the Poitou marshes, manifesting itself as the revolt of the **Chouans**. The insurgents eventually weakened, however, and entered into a parley under General Hoche. A treaty was signed on 17 February 1795 but the resulting peace was precarious and often violated; it would only become permanent in 1800 under the Consulate.

the south bank) is now a clinic. Although it was set on fire in 1793, the entrance has retained its character: two large towers flanking a 17C pavilion which has a pyramidal roof flanked by two small slate cupolas.

Chemillé – This town, which spreads along the valley of the Hyrôme, is an important centre for stock-raising and for the production of medicinal plants (demonstration garden in the grounds of the town hall). In July 1793 Chemillé was the scene of a fierce struggle between Blues and Whites, in the course of which 400 Blues who had been taken prisoner were saved from death only by the intervention of General d'Elbée. In the place du Château there is a 13C doorway with honeycomb decoration, a vestige of the old citadel. The disused church of Notre-Dame has an interesting Romanesque **bell-tower** with blind arcading and two levels of richly decorated Romanesque window openings.

The 12C **church of St-Pierre**, which was thoroughly restored at the beginning of this century, has a fine stained-glass window (1917) by Jean Clamens. It illustrates the **Vendée Pater** incident when D'Elbée, one of the great leaders of the Vendée War, made his soldiers, who were pressing to kill their prisoners, recite the Our Father. They were thus encouraged to "forgive them their trespasses" and the men were spared.

About 3.5km/2mi east of Chemillé *(on the Saumur road then D 124)* stands the little **Chapelle de la Sorinière** ⊙, built in 1501

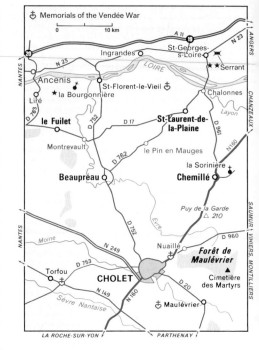

by the local lords of the manor. It still retains its interesting **murals★** dating from the beginning of the 16C. These are full of fascinating detail and depict the Nativity, the Adoration of the Magi and St Christopher. The altar has a Virgin Mary in Mourning, supported by St John (16C). In an adjoining room there are mementoes of the area's troubles during the Vendée War.

Cholet - *See CHOLET.*

Le Fuilet - Le Fuilet and the neighbouring hamlets - les Challonges, Bellevue, les Recoins etc - stand on an excellent clay soil which has given rise to numerous brickworks and potteries producing a variety of articles (ornamental, horticultural or artistic).

The potteries are open to the public during working hours: preparation and shaping of the clay by hand or by machine according to the work.

Maulévrier (Forêt de) - *See MAULÉVRIER below.*

St-Laurent-de-la-Plaine - A museum of traditional crafts, the **Cité des Métiers de Tradition** ⊙, is housed in a complex of several buildings, among them the 18C vicarage, one of the only two houses in the village which survived the ravages of the Republicans in 1794. About 50 trades are illustrated with implements collected from all over France (weaving equipment from St-Étienne, a saw from the Vosges, a paddle-wheel...). In addition to the traditional exhibition rooms (lace), a number of **workshops** - clog-maker, oil dealer, blacksmith, wax chandler, laundry - have been reconstructed inside a magnificent timber-built barn.

MAULÉVRIER

Population 2 650
Michelin map 67 fold 6 or 232 fold 30

The name Maulévrier is believed to date from the Merovingian period and means "bad greyhound" *(mauvais lévrier)*. Fulk Nerra built the first castle here in 1036 and set up a barony which, under Louis XIV, was passed on to Colbert's brother, whose descendants owned it until 1895. **Stofflet**, the famous Vendée leader, was gamekeeper to one of them in 1774. He is commemorated by a stele in the park. The castle, which was partly destroyed during the Revolution, was rebuilt to its original plan in the 19C. At the end of the century, a manufacturer from Cholet called upon the architect **Alexandre Marcel** to restore it and lay out an oriental-style park in the grounds.

Nowadays Maulévrier is well-known for its greyhound races.

Parc oriental de Maulévrier ⊙ – The terraces of Colbert castle overlook the oriental park of 28ha/70 acres that was laid out by Alexandre Marcel between 1899 and 1910. Like a Japanese garden, it was planned around a peaceful lake to represent the changing seasons and the progression of living things, with symbols of the life process from birth to death (rising and setting sun).

A path with Japanese lanterns leads around the lake through exotic species of shrubs and trees (Japanese maples, magnolia stellata, cryptomerias, flowering cherries and aucubas) to a pagoda and garden with a spring, the symbol of birth and light. There is also a Khmer temple (used by Buddhists) approached by steps adorned with lions, a red bridge leading to the Crane and Tortoise islands (symbols of paradise), a hill of meditation, a rise of azaleas, and so on.

Beyond the shadowy lanes of conifers are a bonsai exhibition and a Raku earthenware workshop.

The best times of year to visit the park are from mid-April to mid-May and from mid-October to mid-November.

Alexandre Marcel (1860-1928)

The Parisian architect Alexandre Marcel restored many old buildings before gaining recognition and becoming famous for his thermal baths *(Grands Thermes)* in Châtelguyon, private mansions in Paris and Cholet, and a magnificent palace for the Maharajah of Kapurthala.

His love for the Orient resulted in the "Pagoda" (now a cinema) in rue Babylone in Paris and acclaimed buildings for several international exhibitions. He designed the Round the World Panorama *(Panorama du Tour du Monde)* hall for the French shipping company Messageries Maritimes, and the Cambodian Pavilion, in which he reproduced parts of the Temple of Angkor Wat, for the Universal Exhibition in 1900.

Thanks to these constructions he was brought to the notice of King Leopold II of Belgium who asked him to rebuild, in Laeken Park (Brussels), the Japanese Tower and Chinese Pavilion which would otherwise have been demolished *(see Michelin Green Guides Brussels and Belgium/Luxembourg)*.

EXCURSION

Forêt de Maulévrier – The **cimetière des Martyrs** which is situated between Yzernay and Chanteloup beside the road (D 196), is surrounded by a forest of tall oak trees. During the Vendée War, **Stofflet** used its inaccessibility to conceal his headquarters where the wounded were brought for treatment. On 25 March 1794, however, the Blues penetrated the forest and massacred 1 200 of the Whites; two days later the latter took their revenge with a second massacre. The commemorative chapel standing alone in the forest is now a peaceful place.

Vallée de la MAYENNE★

Michelin map 63 folds 10, 20 or 232 folds 19, 31

The quiet Mayenne follows a picturesque and winding course between steep wooded banks as it flows south to join the Loire. The river was made navigable in the 19C when 39 locks were built between Laval and Angers and it is now ideal for pleasure craft.

The valley is too steep for any villages to be built beside the river so it has been preserved in its natural state. The route described below passes through the villages of low red stone houses with slate roofs which crown the top of the slopes. There are good views of the river, some from a bridge and some from the by-roads which lead down to a picturesque site on the river bank to a mill or an isolated château.

FROM CHÂTEAU-GONTIER TO ANGERS

71km/44mi – allow one day – local map below

Château-Gontier – See *CHÂTEAU-GONTIER*.

Daon – The village and its 16C manor house are superbly sited on a slope above the Mayenne. Daon was the birthplace of Abbé Bernier who negotiated the peace between the Chouans and the Republicans.

In Daon take D 213 east, then take the second turning on the left.

A long avenue of lime and plane trees leads straight to the attractive 16C moated **Manoir de l'Escoublère**.

Return to Daon and take D 22 southeast, bearing right onto D 190 to Marigné and D 78 to Chenillé-Changé.

Chenillé-Changé – This is one of the most attractive villages in the Segréen region with its fortified water mill, **moulin à eau fortifié** ⊘, dating from the turn of the century and still in use, as the white streaks of flour on the schist walls show. The old houses, 11C church and a **river boat centre** *(see Practical information section)* with small barges moored along the shady banks of the Mayenne, all add to the peace and beauty of the scene *(photograph p 257)*.

Take the road across the river to Chambellay and turn right onto D 187.

La Jaille-Yvon – The village is perched on the cliff above the river. From the east end of the church there is an extensive view of the fields and meadows in the valley.

Take D 189 west and turn left onto N 162 going south.

Shortly after the turning to Chambellay the imposing 15C-17C buildings of the **Château du Bois-Montbourcher** come into sight *(left)*, surrounded by lawns and woods on the edge of a vast lake.

Le Lion d'Angers – *See Le LION D'ANGERS.*

★ **Haras national de l'Isle-Briand** – Stud farm. *See Le LION D'ANGERS.*

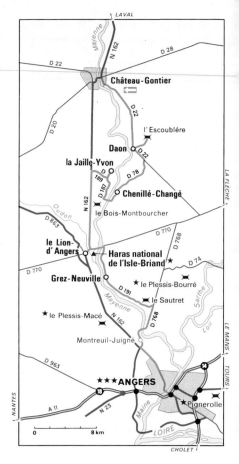

Grez-Neuville – This picturesque village in the heart of the Maine basin slopes gently down to the banks of the Mayenne, its slate-roofed bell-tower reflected in the water. Grez-Neuville is the departure point for **river cruises** *(see Practical information section)* along the Mayenne and Oudon. In season, a Percheron horse can be seen on the towpath pulling a boat for about 1km/0.5mi.

The road down the east bank (D 191) sometimes overhangs the river; it passes *(left)* **Château du Sautret**, an impressive building with a dry moat.

In Feneu take D 768 south across the river to Montreuil-Juigné.

★★★ **Angers** – *See ANGERS. About half a day.*

Château de MÉNARS★

Michelin map 64 fold 7 or 238 fold 3 – 8km/5mi northeast of Blois

This 17C château *(not open to the public)* on the north bank of the Loire was bought in 1760 by the **Marquise de Pompadour**, who had been Louis XV's mistress. She had extensive alterations carried out by the architect, Gabriel. The furniture and decoration she had fitted were of the very best, but the Marquise had little enjoyment of them since she died in 1764. Her brother, the Marquis of Marigny, who inherited the marquisate of Ménars, invited the architect Soumot to lay out the gardens.

All around the entrance court stand the **service buildings** which the famous Marchioness had built, their elegance belying their humble purpose. An underground passage enabled the servants to reach the château without crossing the courtyard.

Facing the Loire is the terrace, which in the Marchioness's time was the main entrance to the château; in the days before the road was built visitors arrived at Ménars by river. The steep slope between the château and the water is laid out in **terraces★** decorated with statues, vases, grottoes, fountains, temples of Venus and avenues of hundred-year-old trees.

MENNETOU-SUR-CHER

Michelin map 64 fold 19 or 238 fold 17

This medieval town is enclosed within its original ramparts.

Ramparts – These were built in the 13C, and three out of five towers as well as the three entrance gateways are still intact. On the side of town towards Vierzon, Bonne-Nouvelle gateway is supported by a round tower which used to flank a Benedictine priory. Only the church of this has survived. En-bas gateway, which can boast that Joan of Arc once passed through its portal, features pointed supporting arches, and its guard-room contains the original fireplace complete with hood. En-haut gateway is adorned with a twin window.

Old houses – Grande-Rue, the steep and winding main street, leads from Bonne-Nouvelle gateway to that of En-haut, past most of Mennetou's interesting old houses. These embody a variety of architectural styles, dating from the 13C (Gothic, with twin windows), 15C (half-timbered, with projecting upper storeys) and 16C (elegant mansions with pilastered façades).

MEUNG-SUR-LOIRE★

Population 5 993
Michelin map 64 fold 8 or 238 fold 4
Local map see Vallée de la LOIRE: Orléans-Chinon

This picturesque fortified village stretches from the Loire which laps at the roots of the tall trees lining the avenue up the slope to the main road (N 152) on the plateau away from the old town. From the **old market** a narrow and twisting street, **rue Porte-d'Amont**, climbs up to an archway; little lanes skirt **les Mauves**, a stream with many channels which runs between the houses (rue des Mauves, rue du Trianon). The town has put up a statue in honour of its most famous son, **Jean de Meung**. In about 1280 he added 18 000 lines to the *Romance of the Rose (Roman de la Rose)* which had been written some 40 years earlier by Guillaume de Lorris and consisted of 4 000 lines. The allegorical narrative was the greatest literary achievement of a period in which readers certainly had to have stamina. Chaucer translated part of the work and was much influenced by it throughout his poetic career.

The bridge at Meung was often fought over during the Hundred Years War; it was captured by the English in 1428 and retaken by Joan of Arc on 15 June 1429.

★ **Collégiale St-Liphard** – This plain church building with its bell-tower and spire dates from the 11C and 13C; the chevet is semicircular and the transept unusually has rounded ends to its arms. From beyond the chevet there is a good view of the church and the château.

Château ⊘ – This venerable building reflects a curious mixture of styles. The entrance façade (12C-13C), where there are still traces of the drawbridge which spanned the dry moat, is medieval; the main entrance was created on the opposite side in the 16C, when the medieval entrance was walled up, and altered in the 17C. The interior owes much to the 19C. After visiting the rooms in the château the tour goes **underground** to the 12C chapel with its palm-tree vaulting and the dungeons where prisoners were "put to the question".

Until the 18C the château belonged to the Bishops of Orléans, who administered justice in their diocese but who, being men of God, did not have the right to put people to death. Prisoners sentenced to lifelong confinement were lowered on ropes into an underground tower, the **oubliettes**, with a well at the bottom; every day they would be given the same quantity of bread and water, however many of them were down there, until they died of starvation or illness. The poet **François Villon**, who had powerful patrons, was the only one ever to come out alive; he suffered only one summer of imprisonment, for the theft of gold chalices from the church of Baccon, before Louis XI released him during a visit to Meung.

MIRÉ

Population 958
Michelin map 64 fold 1 or 232 fold 20 – 10km/6mi north of Châteauneuf-sur-Sarthe

Church – This is roofed with wooden keel vaulting decorated with 43 late-15C painted panels depicting the four Evangelists, angels bearing the instruments of the Passion and the Apostles presenting the Creed.

Château de Vaux ⊘ – *3.5km/2mi northwest on D 29 towards Bierné.*
The picturesque château stands well back from the road to the right. The ruined curtain wall enclosed an elegant building with a stair turret and mullioned windows. This manor house was built at the end of the 15C by **Jean Bourré**, Lord of Miré, whose main claim to fame is that he introduced a delicious fruit – *Bon-chrétiens* pears – to the Angevin orchards.

MONDOUBLEAU

Population 1 558

Michelin map 60 south of folds 15, 16 and 64 north of folds 5, 6 or 238 fold 1

Approached from the west, Mondoubleau can be seen clustered on the east bank of the River Grenne. Perched at a crazy angle on a bluff to the south of the road to Cormenon are the ruins of a red sandstone **keep**, the remains of a fortress built at the end of the 10C by Hugues Doubleau from whom the town has taken its name. Partly hidden among the houses and trees are the remains of the curtain wall which protected the keep and the several precincts of the castle.

Old houses – 15C. On the corner of rue du Pont de l'Horloge and the castle ramp.

Promenade du mail – Rue Gheerbrant leads to the post office and the square, place St-Denis; go through the public garden behind the post office to reach the Grand Mail, a long shady avenue providing a pleasant view of the valley.

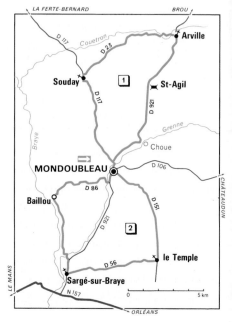

EXCURSIONS

① North of Mondoubleau

Round trip of 26km/16mi north on D 921 – about 1hr

Château de St-Agil ⊘ – This is an interesting château encircled by a moat. The part of the building dating from the 13C was altered in 1720. The early-16C entrance pavilion is flanked by two towers decorated with a diaper pattern in red and black bricks. The machicolations guard the sentry walk and the pepper-pot roofs. The main building has a dormer window with a medallion of the lord of the manor, Antoine de la Vove. The park was landscaped by Jules Hardouin-Mansart and transformed in 1872 in the English style. The splendid lime trees were planted in 1720.

Arville – *See ARVILLE.*

Souday – The nave of the **church** is extended by an interesting 16C two-storey chancel. Two flights of stairs, with wrought-iron railings which date from 1838, lead to the upper floor which is lit by Renaissance stained glass depicting the Passion and the Resurrection of Christ. The elegant ogive vaulting in the crypt springs from columns without capitals. The south transept is decorated with 16C paintings of St Joseph, St Joachim and four scenes from the life of John the Baptist; on the ceiling are the symbols of the four Evangelists.

② South of Mondoubleau

Round trip of 24km/15mi – about 1hr – leave Mondoubleau on D 151 going southeast.

Le Temple – All that is left of the Templar commandery is a 13C church with a squat bell-tower and a square chevet nestling pleasantly by a pool.

Turn right onto D 156.

Sargé-sur-Braye – The **church of St-Martin** ⊘ was built in the 11C and 15C. The painted wainscots date from 1549. The murals discovered in the nave are 16C (*Pietà*, St Martin) and in the chancel 14C (Christ in Majesty and the Labours of the Months; note the three faces of Janus symbolizing January).

Baillou – The little village is picturesquely clustered below a great 16C-17C château. The beautiful early-16C **church** ⊘ stands alone on a mount. The Renaissance doorway is flanked by scrolled pilasters, surmounted by figures of Adam and Eve.

Inside, the south transept contains a carved altarpiece (1618) depicting the death of the Virgin surrounded by the Apostles and the donor, a priest called Gaultier.

Take D 86 back to Mondoubleau. Fine view of the town on arrival.

Château de MONTGEOFFROY★

Michelin map 64 folds 11, 12 or 232 fold 32 – 24km/15mi east of Angers

The regular plan of this beautiful château can be appreciated from the entrance with its Rococo scrolls; it consists of an imposing central block linked by terraced pavilions to two wings set at right angles. The two round towers attached to the wings, the curvilinear moat defining the courtyard and the chapel to the right are the only remains of the original 16C building.

The Montgeoffroy estate came into the possession of Erasme de Contades in 1676; the buildings owe their present appearance to his grandson, the famous Marshal who commanded the German army in the Seven Years War and who was Governor of Alsace for 25 years. His architect was the Parisian Nicolas Barré.

The **château** ⊙ has remained in the family, and has consequently kept its original furnishings and décor, which combine to create an effect of great charm. There are signed pieces of furniture by Gourdin, Blanchard, Garnier and Durand (each in the place it was designed to occupy), pictures by Drouais, Rigaud, Pourbus the Younger, Van Loo, Desportes and Louis Vigée, together with tapestries and hangings from the 18C. The elegance of the château is enhanced by the charming flower arrangements which grace all the rooms, varying according to the season of the year. Documents bearing the signatures of Louis XV, Napoleon and Louis XVIII add to the interest, while in the kitchens is a display of 260 copper and pewter pots and pans.

The **chapelle Ste-Catherine** has Angevin vaulting and a 16C stained-glass window depicting the kneeling figure of the previous owner of Montgeoffroy, Guillaume de la Grandière.

In the **stables** is a collection of horse-drawn vehicles. The magnificent **harness room** fitted out in Norway spruce contains a collection of saddles, stirrups, bridles, whips and riding crops.

MONTIGNY-LE-GANNELON

Population 388
Michelin map 60 south of fold 17 or 237 fold 38 – 2km/1mi north of Cloyes-sur-le-Loir
Local map see Vallée du LOIR: Bonneval-Vendôme

This fortress on the north bank of the Loir can be seen from afar on the N 10. The name Montigny comes from Mons-Igny meaning Signal Hill; Gannelon evokes either the traitor who betrayed Roland to his enemies, or more likely the priest of Saint-Avit de Châteaudun who inherited the fortress in the 11C.

The small town, which lies between the river and the bluff, was once fortified; the Roland gateway (12C) still stands on the side facing away from the river.

★ CHÂTEAU ⊙

A second fortified wall with five gates used to enclose the château, which is now approached through the park, in full view of the highly composite west façade. The combination of brick and stonework is striking. Two towers – the Tour des Dames and the Tour de l'Horloge, with the coats of arms of the Montmorencys surmounting its portal, on the right, and of the Lévis, on the left – are the only remains of the Renaissance château which was rebuilt in 1495 by Jacques de Renty.

The château contains interesting information on the illustrious Lévis-Mirepoix family. To the right of a large Renaissance staircase adorned with portraits of Marshals of Lévis in medallions are the Gothic cloisters with a fine collection of 16C Italian faience plates. The richly-furnished rooms that follow contain numerous portraits and mementoes of the Montmorency and Lévis-Mirepoix families.

Salon des colonnes – Documents relate the founding of the town of Lévis-Lauzon in Quebec, which in 1861 was named after François-Gaston, Duke of Lévis, who had defeated the English at Sainte-Foy in 1760 *(see Michelin Green Guide Quebec)*. Another display evokes the high esteem in which the Prince de Montmorency, Duke of Laval, held Madame Récamier.

Salon des Dames – Portraits of the women of the family. Fine secret cabinet in the Italian Renaissance style.

Grand Salon – Portrait of Gilles de Montmorency-Laval, or de Rais, whose life remains shrouded in mystery and who is thought to have inspired Charles Perrault for his character Bluebeard *(see INGRANDES)*.

Salle à manger Montmorency – The Montmorency pavilion to the north of the Tour de l'Horloge was built as a dining hall in 1834 by the Prince de Montmorency, Duke of Laval, to house the full-length portraits of the rulers to whom he was attached as French ambassador as well as those of Popes Pious VII and Leo XII.

In the grounds, a colourful collection of ostriches, emus, nandus (a South American ostrich), waterfowl and pheasants (Amherst's and a splendid tufted monaul) roams through a cluster of trees over 150 years old. Hidden behind a screen of greenery is the former riding school and stables for coach teams, a vast shed on a frame of steel girders which was built at the same time as the Eiffel Tower. Today it contains old farm implements, carriages and stuffed animals.

ADDITIONAL SIGHT

Church ⊘ – This church, dedicated to St Giles and St Saviour, contains the shrine of St Felicity.

MONTLOUIS-SUR-LOIRE

Population 8 309
Michelin map 64 fold 15 or 232 fold 36 or 238 fold 13

Montlouis is built in terraces up a hillside of tufa which is riddled with caves. Its vineyards on the south-facing plateau between the Loire and the Cher produce a heady and fruity white wine made from the famous Pinot de la Loire grape. Beside the church stands a Renaissance mansion (now the priest's house) with dormer windows decorated with shell motifs.

The Babou family – In the 16C Montlouis was ruled by the Babous of La Bourdaisière, a turbulent family whose main residence, the **Château de la Bourdaisière** ⊘, lay a few miles to the south on the banks of the Cher. Montlouis was built c 1520 by Philibert Babou, silversmith to François I. His wife, Marie Babou, lived in it. She was known as "la belle Babou" and was the first to admit she had a roving eye; she boasted of having "known" François I, Charles V and many others. Gabrielle, the beautiful daughter born in 1573 to Antoine d'Estrées and Françoise Babou, also went on to enjoy royal favour: she was the mistress of Henri IV and when she died the King turned to another Babou for consolation.

Maison de la Loire ⊘ – *Quai A.-Baillet.* Exhibitions on the fauna and flora of the Loire region are displayed here.

MONTOIRE-SUR-LE-LOIR

Population 4 065
Michelin map 64 fold 5 or 232 fold 24 or 238 fold 1
Local map see Vallée du LOIR: Vendôme-La Flèche

Montoire developed round the priory of St-Gilles which was founded in the 7C. In the 9C Charles the Bald had a fort built to protect the country from Viking incursions.
Pilgrims making for Tours to pray at the tomb of St Martin used to stay the night in Montoire which was also on the route to Compostela in Spain. During this period leper houses were set up in Montoire and Troo.

A self-made man – In the 16C Montoire passed into the possession of the Bourbon family. Early in the 18C the Regent sold the manor of Montoire to Louis Fouquet, son of the Minister of Finance, who sold it in his turn to the Count of Les Noyers de Lorme. In fact the count's name was **Amédée Delorme** and his father was an innkeeper in Blois. Originally employed as a footman in Paris, he met the Regent in a brothel and lent him some money. He continued to serve the Regent as a moneylender and after making a tidy sum he increased it considerably speculating in rue Quincampoix, Paris, at the same time as John Law, a Scots financier, was founding a bank (1719) which crashed in 1720. Delorme went on to be appointed the first president of the Chamber of Audit at Blois.

SIGHTS

Bridge – There is a beautiful **view★** of the Loir flowing past old houses covered with wistaria where weeping willows trail their tendrils in the water among the fishing boats moored to the banks.

★ **Chapelle St-Gilles** ⊘ – At the beginning of the lane leading to the chapel stands a Renaissance house (Maison du "Jeu de Quilles" – **D**) which bears a plaque dedicated by a trade-guild to one of its members who came from Montoire. The main gate opens on to the apse of an elegant Romanesque chapel which belonged to a Benedictine priory of which the poet Ronsard was once head. He left in October 1585 to visit his other priories, Ste-Madeleine de Croixval and St-Cosme, near Tours, where he died two months later. The chapel and the prior's lodging are set against a pleasant backdrop of lawns and yew trees.

★★ **Mural paintings** – The paintings are to be found in the apse and transepts which are shaped like a clover leaf. Each half-dome roof vault bears a figure of Christ painted at a different date. The oldest (first quarter of the 12C) in the apse shows a very majestic Christ surrounded by angels; this is the **Christ of the Apocalypse.**

In the south transept is another 12C Christ, handing the keys to St Peter *(missing);* this figure shows Byzantine influence in the tight and symmetrical folds of the garments. The third figure in the north transept dates from the 13C and shows Christ with the Apostles at Pentecost; the more contrived attitudes and the colours –

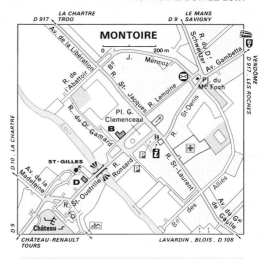

B, D Maisons Renaissance

white, ochre and the blue of the haloes – are typical of the early local school. Note too the paintings on the arches of the crossing, particularly the Battle of the Virtues and Vices on the western arch.

Castle – *Not open to the public.*
A stone fortified wall encloses the 11C keep which stands on a spur of rock.

Renaissance houses (B) – Two Renaissance houses stand side by side on place Clemenceau; the larger, with mullioned windows and high dormer windows, is also the older. There are two others in rue St-Oustrille (Maison du "Jeu de Quilles") and rue St-Laurent (Antoine-Moreau hospital).

Parc botanique de La Fosse ⊙ – *3km/1.5mi west on D 917, then D 94 going towards Fontaine-les-Côteaux.*
Created, refurbished, tended and embellished by the same family since the mid-18C, this undulating park covers an area of 25ha/62 acres. Depending on the season, visitors can admire the lanes lined with roses or hornbeams, the landscaped magnolia flower beds or the exuberant undergrowth with its floor of periwinkles. Several venerable trees deserve special attention on account of their age, their sheer size or their striking appearance: cedars of Lebanon dating from 1810, dark Corsican pine trees planted in 1820 or the *Acer griseum* and its unusual bark formation.

Hitler meets Pétain

In mid-October 1940 German uniforms began appearing in ever increasing numbers, convoys of machine guns roved the streets and anti-aircraft batteries were set up on the hills. Military patrols erected barbed wire barriers across the roads and made house-to-house searches in Montoire. The electricity and telephones were cut off and German railwaymen replaced the staff of the SNCF, while people living in houses beside the railway line were ordered to close their shutters and stay indoors. A squadron of Messerschmidts frightened the cattle in the fields and two armoured trains bristling with guns patrolled the line from Vendôme to La Chartre.
On 22 October Adolf Hitler and Pierre Laval met at Montoire station; in the event of an attack Hitler's train could have withdrawn into the tunnel at St-Rimay to the east. The following day the famous meeting between Hitler and Maréchal Pétain took place, in which the German Chancellor tried to persuade the French Head of State to declare war against the United Kingdom.

To choose a hotel, a restaurant or a camp site
consult the current edition of the annual Michelin Red Guide France
and the annual **Michelin Guide Camping Caravaning France**

Château de MONTPOUPON★

Only the towers remain of the original 13C fortress on this site. The main building, which has mullioned windows and Gothic-style gables, was built in the 15C, while the **entrance pavilion** ⊘, which is decorated in the Renaissance style on the rear façade, is early 16C.

Seen from the road, the whole complex exudes elegance. A visit to the château includes the entrance pavilion, as well as several rooms in the main building including the fine "chambre du Maréchal" (bedchamber).

The **outbuildings**★ contain an excellent demonstration of the way the castle was run in the last century. The kitchen, with its oven and copper pans, was still in use in 1978; the laundry displays delicate garments, decorated with pleats and edged with lace, such as were worn in the 19C.

A hunting museum, **Musée du Veneur**, set up in 25 rooms evokes the daily life of a gentleman-hunter as well as activities linked with hunting, such as forestry, animal breeding, crafts (manufacture of hunting horns, saddlery, farriery, manufacture of livery buttons etc). There are displays of hunting costumes and hunting souvenirs and on the history of the Montpoupon Hunt which was active from 1873 to 1949. Carriages are on display in the nearby stables, as is the equipment used by the château's owners in the saddle and harness rooms. A reconstruction of a huntsman's lodge gives an insight into his social life.

MONTRÉSOR★

The sloping site of Montrésor on the north bank of the River Indrois is reflected in the water. The old market in the town is a timber-frame construction and a handsome 16C house with a watchtower in the main street is now the police station.

★ **Château** ⊘ – The curtain wall with its ruined towers belongs to the fortress built by Fulk Nerra in the 11C; within it at the centre of a charming, romantic park stands the residence built in the early 16C by **Imbert de Bastarnay**, lord of Montrésor from 1493, adviser to several kings of France and grandfather of Diane de Poitiers. This building has mullioned windows on the south front facing the river, gabled dormers and two machicolated towers. In 1849 the château was restored by **Count Xavier Branicki**, a Polish émigré who accompanied Prince Napoleon to Constantinople during the Crimean War and tried to raise a Polish regiment.

The furnishings are as they were at the time of Branicki: his shooting trophies decorate the entrance hall; military souvenirs and medals and pictures by Polish and French painters are exhibited throughout. Also of interest are low-reliefs in wood depicting the battles of John III Sobieski of Poland (17C), a boudoir containing Italian primitives and gold and silver plate. From the curtain wall above the river there is an attractive view of the valley and the houses of the town.

Church – The church was built between 1519 and 1541 in the Gothic style – only the doorway is Renaissance; it was originally a collegiate foundation set up by Imbert de Bastarnay, who built the church to house his tomb. The **Bastarnay tomb**★ in the nave consists of three recumbent figures in white marble – Imbert, his wife and his son – resting on a base decorated with statues of the 12 Apostles. Of the same date are two windows and the choir stalls, the latter in Renaissance style and richly decorated with medallions and misericords. In the chancel chapel *(left)* is a painting of the *Annunciation* by Philippe de Champaigne (17C).

MONTREUIL-BELLAY★

The little town of Montreuil-Bellay occupies a charming **site**★ beside the Thouet on the border of the Poitou and Anjou regions. From the east bank of the river and bridge there are good views of the château and church. The gardens along the west bank are an agreeable place for a stroll as is the picturesque square, place des Ormeaux, in front of the château entrance.

Long stretches of the medieval wall are still standing: **Porte St-Jean**, a gate flanked by two large rusticated towers, dates from the 15C.

Recalcitrant vassals – In 1025 Fulk Nerra, Count of Anjou, gave this stronghold to his vassal **Berlay** (distorted into Bellay), who made it into a powerful fortress. A century later, safe behind their stout walls, his successors plotted and intrigued against their overlord. In 1151, one of them, Giraud, held out for a whole year before he capitulated to Geoffrey Plantagenet, who then razed the keep which he

Montreuil-Bellay

had just taken with the aid of an early incendiary bomb, made by sealing a vessel full of oil, heating it to burning point and firing it at the keep with a mangonel. When the Plantagenets acceded to the throne of England and thus became the main enemy of the king of France, the Berlays (who later became the Du Bellays) pledged their allegiance to their immediate overlord; Philippe-Auguste thereupon besieged their castle and demolished it.

SIGHTS

★★ **Château** ⓥ – Imposing walls, pleasant gardens and remarkable furnishings are the main features of Montreuil château. Behind the outer fortress, inside the fortified gateway, stands the graceful residence built by the Harcourt family in the 15C. From the courtyard terrace there are fine views of the church, the château and the grounds which dip in great steps down to the river.

The **medieval kitchen** with its central fireplace like the one at Fontevraud was slightly altered in the 15C and is still in perfect condition, with a set of copper pans and a kitchen range (18C) with seven fire boxes fuelled by charcoal.

The 15C **canons' lodge** has four staircase turrets with conical roofs serving four separate sets of rooms, each consisting of living rooms over a store-room (one was transformed into a steam-room) for the canons who served in the castle chapel.

The **château neuf** was built in the 15C. It features a beautiful staircase turret decorated with mullioned windows protected by delicately-carved mock balustrades. The loggia with its ogee arch is 19C; on its right stands a 12C-13C tower. In the vaulted **cellar** the brotherhood of the Sacavins holds its meetings; it was founded in 1904 by the then owner of the castle, Georges de Grandmaison, to advertise Anjou wine. The wine-press, into which the grapes were poured directly from the courtyard through a trapdoor, was still in use at the beginning of this century.

The rooms in the château are 7m/23ft high and fully furnished. The dining-room (49m²/527ft²) has painted ceiling beams. The little **oratory** decorated with frescoes is late 15C: the guide plays a recording of the motet depicted on the sheet music being played by the angelic musicians on the vaulting. Visitors see the bedchamber of the **Duchess of Longueville**, Prince Condé's sister, who was one of the main instigators behind the Fronde uprising and was exiled by Louis XIV to Montreuil where she lived in luxurious style. In the Grand Salon there is a Brussels tapestry and a German marquetry cupboard; in the small music salon there is a superb bureau made by the famous cabinet-maker Boulle (1642-1732), inlaid with copper and tortoiseshell.

Église Notre-Dame – The church was built as the seigneurial chapel between 1472 and 1484 and has astonishingly sturdy walls and buttresses. Note the black mourning band in the nave and the private oratory for the owner of the castle.

Maison Dovalle ⓥ – *69 rue Dovalle.*
The façade of this 16C house was altered in the 18C. The watchtower in the garden gives a fine view of the towers of the château, the Thouet valley and in the far distance, Puy-Notre-Dame. The building is named after the Romantic poet **Charles Dovalle** (1807-29) whose collected works *Le Sylphe* were published posthumously with a preface by Victor Hugo.

The attic floor, in which the original timber-work is visible, houses the **Musée Charles Léandre**. Originally from Normandy, Léandre (1862-1934), who lived in Montmartre, Paris, was a talented draughtsman, painter, pastellist *(Woman with a Dog)* and engraver, combining Classicism and Impressionism in his work. He is best known for the acerbic caricatures of his contemporaries which appeared in the satirical magazines of the Belle Époque like *Le Rire* and *L'Assiette au beurre.* He was also famous for his posters.

Les Nobis – Deep in the vegetation beside the Thouet are the ruins of the church of St-Pierre which was burnt down by the Huguenots in the 16C; the Romanesque apse is decorated with carved capitals. Nearby are two wings of some 17C cloisters.

EXCURSIONS

Moulin de la Salle ⊘ – *1km/0.5mi northeast on N 147 towards Saumur.*
This is the last water mill still in use on the River Thouet. The different stages for the conversion of wheat into flour are explained and a water-wheel which drives various grinding and sifting utensils may be seen in operation.

Ancienne abbaye d'Asnières ⊘ – *7.5km/5mi northwest.*
On the northern edge of Cizay forest are the evocative ruins of what was once an important monastery founded in 12C. The tall and graceful **chancel**★ with its delicately ribbed vaulting is, like the chancel of the church of St-Serge in Angers, a perfect specimen of Angevin Gothic art. The Abbot's chapel, which was added in the 15C, has a pointed recess decorated with trefoils and festoons and a 14C Crucifix.

MONTRICHARD★

Population 3 786
Michelin map 64 folds 16, 17 or 238 fold 14

From the riverbank and bridge over the Cher there is a good **view** of this town and its medieval houses clustered around the church below the crumbling keep.
The north bank above the town is pitted with quarries. **Bourré**, a village 3km/2mi to the east, has provided the stone used for the construction of the nearby châteaux. The quarries have now been transformed into troglodyte dwellings, caves for growing mushrooms and cellars for producing wine by the Champagne method.

SIGHTS

★ **Donjon** – The square keep which stands on the edge of the plateau above the River Cher is enclosed by the remains of its curtain wall and by a complex system of ramparts which protected the entrance. It was built c 1010 by Fulk Nerra, reinforced with a second wall in 1109 and then with a third in 1250. Despite having been reduced in height by 4m/13ft on the orders of Henri IV in 1589 for having fallen into the hands of the Catholic League at one stage, the keep still evokes its distant past. A museum – **Musée René-Galloux** ⊘ – retraces the archeological history of the town and the surrounding area.
The vestiges of the keep house a flock of around 60 large birds of prey, some of which have a wingspan of over 2m/7ft (eagles, condors, vultures, hawks, kites, lammergeiers); **flight demonstrations** ⊘ are organised twice a day.
Enjoy the fine **panorama**★★ of Montrichard and the Cher valley.

Église Ste-Croix – The church, which was originally the castle chapel, stands below the keep at the top of the flight of steps known as Grands Degrés Ste-Croix. The façade is decorated with elegant Romanesque arches; the arches of the porch are ornamented with a twisted torus. The elegant doorway is also Romanesque.
Jeanne de France, the daughter of Louis XI, and her young cousin, the Duke of Orléans, were married in this chapel in 1476. The 12-year-old bride, who was ugly and deformed, held no attraction for Louis d'Orléans who had been forced into the marriage by the King. Knowing that his daughter could not bear a child, Louis XI hoped in this way to bring to an end the Orléans line, a junior branch of the Valois family which chafed at royal authority.
Events, however, took a different course. In 1498 Louis XI's son, Charles VIII, died accidentally at Amboise leaving no heir since his sons had died in infancy. As the King's nearest relative Louis d'Orléans acceded to the throne as Louis XII. In his will Charles VIII had stipulated that the new King should marry his widow, Anne of Brittany.
Repudiated, Jeanne devoted herself to a life of good works; she withdrew to Bourges where she founded a religious order.

Old houses – There are several picturesque old façades up by the keep. **Hôtel d'Effiat** in rue Porte-au-Roi, which was built in the late 15C-early 16C, has Gothic décor with a few Renaissance elements. In the 16C it was the residence of Jacques de Beaune-Semblançay, Treasurer to Anne of Brittany and then to Louise of Savoy, the mother of François I. The mansion has retained the name of its last owner, the Marquis d'Effiat, who at his death (1719) presented it to the town to be converted into an old people's home.

There are two old timber-framed houses on the square, place Barthélemy-Gilbert, and on the corner of rue du Pont stands the **maison de l'Ave Maria** (16C) which has three gables and finely carved beams. Opposite are the Petits Degrés Ste-Croix *(steps)* which lead to some troglodyte dwellings.

Further on, at the corner of rue du Prêche, stands the 11C stone façade of the **Maison du Prêche** ("Sermon House").

Église de Nanteuil – *On the road to Amboise (D 115).*
This church is a tall Gothic building with a Flamboyant doorway; the apses are Romanesque decorated with carved capitals. The high, narrow nave has Angevin vaulting.

Above the entrance porch is a chapel built by Louis XI, which can be entered up internal or external flights of steps.

There is a long-established tradition of a pilgrimage to the Virgin Mary of Nanteuil on Whit Monday.

Caves Monmousseau ⊙ – These cellars used for maturing wine by the **Champagne method** are particularly interesting as they present age-old traditional methods as opposed to more modern techniques. The visit ends with a **musée des confréries européennes** (Museum of European Guilds) ⊙.

EXCURSION

Thésée – *10km/6mi east.*
West of the village stand the remains of the Gallo-Roman settlement of Tasciaca beside the Roman road from Bourges to Tours. During the 1C-3C it prospered from the making and selling of ceramic ware. Known as "Les Maselles", the settlement extended over the area of modern Thésée and Pouillé. The buildings were made out of the soft local limestone, their stone courses laid conventionally or in herringbone pattern and reinforced with brick at base and corners.

Musée archéologique ⊙ – Housed in the town hall (an 18C wine-grower's property in the middle of a splendid 7ha/18-acre park), the museum's archeological collection consists of objects excavated from the sanctuary *(fanum)* and from the numerous potteries unearthed on either side of the river. Ex-votos, statuettes, coins, jewellery, buckles as well as ceramics, some of them signed, all help to evoke the life of those who once dwelt here on the banks of the Cher.

MONTSOREAU

Population 561
Michelin map 64 folds 12, 13 or 232 fold 33
Local map see Vallée de la LOIRE: Chinon-Champtoceaux

Montsoreau is famed for its château which overlooks the confluence of the Loire and the Vienne.

Château ⊙ – The château was rebuilt in the 15C by a member of the Chambes family, famed for its bold warriors and enterprising women. One of the ladies of Montsoreau seduced the Duke of Berry, brother of Louis XI and through him formed the League for the Public Good (Ligue du Bien Public) which the King defeated only by the assassination of the pretender and his mistress. A century later one of the most active executioners in the massacre of the Huguenots on St Bartholomew's Day was a Chambes. An event in the history of the family and the château was used by Alexandre Dumas in one of his novels, *La Dame de Montsoreau*. The heroine was forced by her jealous husband to make a rendezvous with her lover, Bussy d'Amboise, at the Château de la Coutancière (on the north bank of the Loire) where the cuckold had him assassinated. After this outburst, husband and wife lived in perfect harmony until they died 40 years later.

The river front, which was once at the water's edge, is an impressive example of military architecture. The château houses the **Musée des Goums**, a museum on the conquest of Morocco, especially the French leader Marshal Lyautey and the history of the cavalry regiments *(goums)* recruited in Morocco. The collections, formerly in Rabat, were brought to France in 1956 when Morocco became independent.

Montsoreau

★★ **Panorama** – *1km/0.5mi along the road to the right of the château up the hill; follow the signposts.*
There is a lookout point at the heart of the vineyards on the clifftop, giving a good view downstream of the town, the château and the Loire valley, and upstream of the tree-lined confluence of the Loire and the Vienne.

Moulin de la Herpinière ⓥ – *1.5km/1mi southwest on V 3.*
Located in the municipality of **Turquant**, at the heart of a traditional troglodytic community, this windmill, in which the milling chamber is hollowed out of the tufa soil, dates back to 1514. Badly damaged in a storm in July 1992, it has been carefully restored in accordance with traditional techniques (wooden wheels, silex mill-stone). The windmill is now operational (on windy days, of course!) and visitors can buy flour ground here.

MOULIHERNE

Population 951
Michelin map 64 folds 12, 13 or 232 fold 33

Mouliherne stands on a rock on the north bank of the quiet Riverolle.

Church – The church, which is built on a mound, has a beautiful square 13C bell-tower with splayed windows and a twisting spire typical of the Baugé region. The vaulting of the interior, which ends in oven-vaulted apses, demonstrates the evolution of the Angevin style. The chancel is covered with pointed barrel vaulting, while the south transept features an early example of quadripartite vaulting. A more refined version of this is found again above the north transept and the transept crossing, supported on beautiful Romanesque capitals decorated with water lily leaves and fantastic animals. The wide Gothic vaulting above the nave, dating from the 12C-13C, is more refined still. The vaulting nearest the transept was redone in the late 15C. Behind the high altar in the chancel are 9C-10C Carolingian sarcophagi executed in conchitic stone with no ornamentation.

EXCURSION

Linières-Bouton – *5km/3mi east on D 62.*
This is a quiet village just off the main road. The **church** has a beautiful **chancel** built in the Plantagenet style; there is a painting of the Annunciation (1677), a huge Baroque cross in gilded wood and a sculpture of the Holy Family, probably 17C.

In this guide
town plans show the main streets and the way to the sights;
local maps show not only the main roads but also the roads recommended in a round tour.

MULSANS

Population 374
Michelin map 64 fold 7 or 238 fold 3 – 14km/9mi northeast of Blois

Mulsans is a small farming village on the edge of the Beauce, heralded by the village's traditional walled-in farmyards which are characteristic of this region. The charming **church** ⊙ has Flamboyant windows and a fine Romanesque bell-tower decorated with blind arcades and twin round-arched window openings. There is a Renaissance gallery supported on carved wooden columns extending the full width of the nave and incorporating the porch; this is a regional feature known as a *caquetoire* where people pause to talk after church.

NOYANT-LA-GRAVOYÈRE

Population 1 860
Michelin map 63 fold 9 or 232 fold 18

The Noyant-la-Gravoyère district, in the heart of the Segréen Upper Anjou region, once had a flourishing fine-slate industry for which the poet Du Bellay held great affection.

★ **La mine bleue** ⊙ – *Take D 775 towards Pouancé and then D 219.*
The St-Blaise slate quarries in La Gatelière, which overlook La Corbinière lakes, were closed down in 1936. Referred to locally as the "Blue Mine", they have since been pumped out and opened to the public.

A lift takes visitors (mining helmets must be worn) down the 130m/425ft into the bottom of the mine. Once at the bottom, a small train takes them through the cleared galleries to the enormous extraction chambers, some of which are 80m/260ft deep. There, a *son et lumière* show illustrates the life of miners in the 1930s, looking at the dangers to which they were exposed and the daily round of work at the bottom of the pit. The last chamber contains a display on the myths that the human imagination has conjured up about the world underground. Before leaving, there is a demonstration of a blast with explosives. A second tour of the underground chambers takes as its theme a "Voyage to the Centre of the Earth" after Jules Verne's novel.

Y. Monet

La Mine bleue

Back above ground, standing amongst birch-trees, are some restored **slate cleavers' huts**, once used by splitters or cleavers, who were also known as "lords of the hill". A slate cleaver gives a demonstration of the traditional way of splitting slate. The **musée de l'Ardoise** in the old boiler room relates the history of the slate industry, its operating methods and the technical progress made over the years thanks to improved machinery.

The birds of the Loire

The Loire, the "last wild river in Europe", with its islands, backwaters, long sand banks and grassy shores, is one of the natural regions in France where the flora and fauna are particularly abundant and diverse. Among the birds that build their nests along its banks are the common and little tern, the little ringed plover and the common sandpiper.

From March to the end of June, Parney Island below Montsoreau is home to over 750 pairs of gulls – black-headed, Mediterranean, common and Iceland – and common and little terns. Lastly, in August and September, among the many migratory species on the river is the osprey which makes spectacular dives into the slow waters.

ORLÉANS★

Conurbation 243 153
Michelin map 64 fold 9 or 237 fold 40 or 238 fold 5
Local map see Vallée de la LOIRE: Orléans-Chinon
Plan of the conurbation in the current Michelin Red Guide France

Orléans has always been an active business centre, trading in wheat from the Beauce, honey, poultry and potatoes from the Gâtinais, game from the Sologne and Loire valley wines. On the outskirts of town are several industrial zones such as Chapelle-St-Mesmin. These are interspersed with an unbroken network of garden centres, nursery gardens and market gardens which have made Orléans the "city of roses" and one of the focuses of the "garden of France" as the Loire valley is called.

Orléans is the capital of the Centre region of France (an economic division) and an important administrative and university town. These activities are mostly concentrated in the satellite town of **Orléans-la-Source**.

The **Fêtes de Jeanne d'Arc** every spring *(see Calendar of events in the Practical information section)* date back to 1435 and are the occasion of great merry-making on the part of the townspeople in celebration of their deliverance from the English.

From the Carnutes to Joan of Arc – The Gauls considered the land of the Carnutes to be the centre of their territory, Gaul; each year the Druids held their great assembly there and it was at Cenabum (Orléans) that the signal was given to revolt against Caesar in 52 BC.

A Gallo-Roman city soon rose from the Gaulish ruins. In June 451 it was besieged by Attila the Hun, but the inhabitants, inspired by their bishop, St Aignan, succeeded in driving off the invaders.

During the 10C and 11C Orléans was one of the focal points of the Capet monarchy.

THE SIEGE OF 1428-29

This memorable siege was one of the great episodes in the history of France; it marks the rebirth of a country and a people which were sinking into despair.

The forces engaged – From the early 15C the defences of Orléans had been set up to repel any English attack. The city wall was composed of two parts *(see plan)*; on the east side was the old square wall of the Gallo-Roman camp and on the west a longer wall, enclosing more ground, which was built in the 14C. There were 34 towers *(tours)* and the wall was divided into six sections each defended by 50 men. All the townspeople took part in the defence of the city either by fighting as soldiers or by maintaining the walls and ditches. In all about 10 000 men were involved under the orders of the Governor of Orléans, **Raoul de Gaucourt**, and his captains.

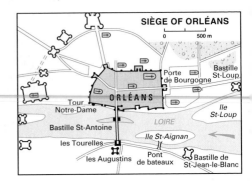

During the summer of 1428 the commander of the English army, the **Earl of Salisbury**, had destroyed the French strongholds along the Loire and gained control of the river downstream from Orléans, thus preventing the city from being relieved from the west. After the fall of Beaugency on 25 September Salisbury began to march on Orléans. His army consisted of 400 men-at-arms, 2 250 archers, together with 400 lancers and 1 200 archers recruited in France, in all over 4 000 men.

The struggle began on 17 October when the English began pounding the city with bombards and heavy cannon, although their chief aim was to cut the city off from any contact with the surrounding countryside. On the south side of the town there was a bridge spanning the Loire which was defended at its southern end by the fort of les Tourelles. The people of Orléans had earlier demolished all the buildings in this district to make the enemy's approach more difficult. On 24 October, the English nonetheless captured les Tourelles but as Salisbury was inspecting the grounds, he was killed by a cannon-ball thought to have been fired from the tower of Notre-Dame church. The French defenders blew up an arch and built a hasty wooden outwork in front of the Bastille St Antoine, a fort on an island in the river. By way of counteraction the besiegers demolished two arches in front of the fort of les Tourelles and built a high earth bank.

Orléans was now cut off from the rest of the French Kingdom. On 8 November the majority of the English forces withdrew to Meung-sur-Loire and the French took the opportunity to raze the other suburbs to prevent the English from

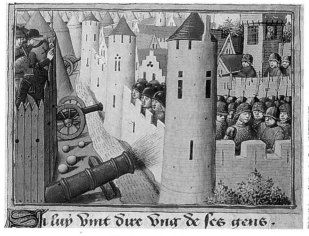

Bibliothèque Nationale, Paris/ARTEPHOT

The Siege of Orléans

re-establishing themselves there. The besiegers were not inactive, however. They surrounded the town with a series of trenches commanded by small forts, but their lines were not impenetrable – particularly in the northeastern sector where sorties were still possible. Count Jean of Dunois (also known as the Bastard of Orléans), who had arrived with his troops on 25 October, looked down from the top of the walls on the English forts without being able to intervene.

The two sides settled down to a war of attrition punctuated by skirmishes outside the gates. From time to time feats of arms raised the morale of the besieged. The prowess and cunning of Master-Gunner Jean de Montesclerc became legendary: he killed many English soldiers and would often pretend to die so that when he reappeared the dismay and alarm of the English were redoubled. Two bombards called Rifflart and Montargis rose to fame owing to their fire power and their range which caused great damage on the south bank of the Loire.

The months of misery and waiting seemed to grow longer and longer, however; food grew scarce and in February 1429 part of the garrison left. It seemed that the English were close to victory and in Orléans, Dunois was the only person to remain optimistic.

The Arrival of Joan of Arc – In April 1429 Joan of Arc persuaded the future **Charles VII** to rescue Orléans. She left Blois with the royal army, crossed the river and approached Orléans along the south bank, meaning to take the English by surprise, but the river was too high and the army had to return to the bridge at Blois. Meanwhile, Joan and a few companions crossed by boat a few miles upstream of Orléans at Chécy and entered the town on 29 April through the Porte de Bourgogne. She was greeted by an enthusiastic crowd and issued her famous ultimatum to the English, that they should surrender to her, the young girl sent by God to drive them out of France, the keys of all the French towns that they had captured.

The people of Orléans rallied and prepared for battle while Joan found herself up against the hostility of the captains and the Governor. On 4 May the royal army, which Dunois had rejoined, attacked the Bastille St-Loup without warning Joan. When she learned of it she made a sortie, raising her banner, and the French were victorious. The following day Joan, who had been excluded from the captains' council, suggested pressing forward the attack against the fort of les Tourelles and on the morning of 6 May, although her so-called companions-in-arms, tried to get her to make mistakes, Joan herself led the attack against the Augustinian monastery (les Augustins). For a second time her spirited intervention threw the English into confusion as they were engaged in pursuing the retreating French troops. This second victory increased her popularity and made the captains look ridiculous. The English troops grew alarmed. Joan called on them again to withdraw and when they refused she went on the offensive again on 7 May against the advice of the Governor who tried to bar her way. While fighting in the front line outside les Tourelles she was wounded in the shoulder by a crossbow bolt. The English thought she was done for and Dunois suggested postponing the attack until the following day but, having had the wound dressed and prayed to the saints, Joan returned to the attack with her standard raised high. With renewed vigour the French hurled themselves into the fray against the English defence, while the French who had remained in town made a sortie onto the bridge. The English garrison in the fort were caught in the crossfire; they were forced to abandon the fort and surrender. On Sunday 8 May the English withdrew from the last forts and raised the siege. Joan was carried back into Orléans in triumph after her victory.

This check to the English advance had wide-ranging repercussions. It threw their invasion plans into disarray, since they had counted on taking not only the town itself but also the bridge over the Loire, as its capture would have enabled them to join forces with the English troops stationed in central and southwestern France under the terms of the 1360 Treaty of Brétigny. It also weakened the position of the Duke of Bedford, the regent in England. But above all it gave new confidence to the Dauphin and his army. On 18 June the French forces won the Battle of Patay.

OUT AND ABOUT IN ORLÉANS

Tourist information – Ask at the tourist office for leaflets or brochures in English: place Albert-Ier, ☎ 02 38 53 05 95.

Entertainment – The cultural centre **Carré St-Vincent** comprises four sections for theatrical creation and performance: the Centre dramatique national, the Centre national de création (CADO), the Centre choréographique national and the Scène national d'Orléans. ☎ 02 38 62 75 30.

Local specialities – Olivet cheese, Cotignac (quince confection), Olivet William pear spirit, Orléans wines (auvernat, cabernet, gris-meunier), wine vinegar.

Dates for your diary – May: Joan of Arc festival; **late June, early July:** Orléans jazz, six evenings of jazz with international stars at the Campo Santo; **October and November:** three consecutive weekends of contemporary music as part of the Semaines musicales internationales d'Orléans music festival.

Markets – Halles de la Charpenterie (woodwork) on Tuesdays, Thursdays and Saturdays; Flower market at the place de la République on Tuesday, Thursday, Saturday and Sunday mornings; bric-a-brac market in boulevard Alexandre-Martin on Saturdays.

CITY CENTRE

★ **Cathédrale Ste-Croix (EY)** – This cathedral dedicated to the Holy Cross was begun in the 13C and construction continued until the 16C, although the building was partly destroyed by the Protestants in 1568. Henri IV, the first Bourbon King, being grateful to the town for having supported him, undertook to rebuild the cathedral, not in the style of the 17C, but in a composite Gothic style. The work went on throughout the 18C and 19C. The old Romanesque towers still standing before the Wars of Religion (1562-98) were replaced by pseudo-Gothic towers.

The **west front** has three large doorways with rose windows above them crowned by a gallery with open-work design. The skill of the masons can be seen in the unusually fine quality of the stonework. At the base of the two towers admire the delicacy of the spiral staircases, also with open-work design, at each of the four corners. The huge **doorway** has four gigantic statues of the Evangelists.

Interior – The vast main body of the cathedral comprises five aisles. On the north side of the chancel, in the chapel of St Joan of Arc, is the statue of Cardinal Touchet (1894-1926), who was instrumental in popularizing the worship of Joan of Arc as a saint. In the central chapel of the apse is a fine marble Virgin Mary by Michel Bourdin (early 17C), a sculptor born in Orléans.

Splendid early-18C **woodwork★★** adorns the chancel. It was made to the designs of Mansart, Gabriel and Lebrun by Jules Degoullons, one of the decorators of Versailles and designer of the stalls in Notre-Dame, Paris; the carved medallions and the panels of the high backs of the choir stalls are particularly impressive.

In the **crypt** ⊙ are traces of the three buildings which predated the present cathedral, and two sarcophagi; one belonged to Bishop Robert de Courtenay (13C) who collected the most precious items in the **treasury** ⊙. Among these are two gold medallions (11C) decorated with cloisonné enamel in the Byzantine manner, which used to adorn the gloves worn by the Bishop of Orléans for ceremonies and processions; 13C gold and silverware; and 17C paintings by Vignon and Jouvenet.

North transept and east end – In the north transept is a rose window with the emblem of Louis XIV at the centre. Excavations at the base have revealed the old Gallo-Roman walls and part of a tower.

The **east end** with its flying buttresses and pinnacles is clearly visible from the gardens of the former episcopal palace (**FY Q**), an 18C building which now houses the municipal library.

Campo Santo (EY) – To the left of the modern Fine Arts School (École Régionale des Beaux-Arts) is a graceful Renaissance portal and on the north side of this same building is a garden edged with an arcaded gallery. The garden was a cemetery outside the city walls in the 12C, the galleries were added in the 16C *(exhibitions)*.

★★ **Musée des Beaux-Arts (EY M¹)** ◷ – In the Primitives gallery of this fine arts museum is an outstanding 15C painting from the Sienese school, a *Virgin and Child* with two angels by Matteo di Giovanni. The 14C-16C sculptures include a marble Virgin and Child (1370) and a fine bust of Cardinal Morvillier by Germain Pilon. The Italian, Flemish and Dutch schools are represented by works by Correggio *(Holy Family)*, Tintoretto *(Portrait of a Venetian)*, Annibale Carracci *(Adoration of the Shepherds)*, Van Dyck, Teniers and Ruysdael. Velasquez's remarkable *St Thomas* (c 1620) dates from the period the artist spent in Seville.

On the first floor are works from the 17C-18C French school: vast religious paintings inspired by the Counter-Reformation, *St Charles Borromeo* by Philippe de Champaigne, *Triumph of St Ignatius* by Claude Vignon. The chiaroscuro technique is exemplified in *St Sebastian* from Georges de La Tour's studio. Among the 17C canvases are *Bacchus and Ariadne*, a rare mythological work by Le Nain, and *Astronomy* by La Hyre. Masterpieces from Richelieu's château include Deruet's graceful, imaginative *Four Elements* and his *Louis XIV as a Child.* The collection of 18C portraits includes: *Mme de Pompadour* by Drouais; *Moyreau*, the engraver, by Nonotte; the *Marquis of Lucker* by Louis Tocqué. Paintings by Hubert Robert *(Landscape with Ruined Tower, The Wash House)*, Boucher *(The Dovecot)* and Watteau (the unusual *Monkey Sculptor*) are also of interest.

In the Pastel Gallery there are 18C portraits including works by Perronneau, Quentin La Tour, Chardin *(Self-Portrait with Spectacles)* and Nattier as well as expressive busts by Pigalle and Houdon and French ceramics and medallions. The 19C is represented by artists such as Gros, Cogniet, Courbet *(The Wave)*, Boudin, Antigna, a Realist painter born in Orléans, and Gauguin *(Fête Gloanec)*. 20C art is illustrated by paintings by artists like Soutine, Rouault, la Fresnaye, Gromaire, Marie Laurencin and Max Jacob. There are sculptures by Bourdelle, Maillol, Zadkine, Charles Malfray and Gaudier-Breszka. The museum also houses a number of contemporary works.

Hôtel Groslot (EY H) – Built in 1550 by the bailiff Jacques Groslot, this large Renaissance mansion in red brick with diaper-work in black was subject to extensive remodelling in the 19C. Admire the delicate scrollwork on the staircase pillars and the two main entrances flanked by caryatids. This was the King's residence in Orléans: François II, who died here after opening the States-General in 1560, Charles IX, Henri III and Henri IV all stayed here.

On the other side of the building is the **garden** where the façade of the old chapel of St-Jacques (15C) has been re-erected. On the other side of the road stand the **Pavillons d'Escures (EY)**, town houses in brick with stone courses dating from the early 17C.

Place Ste-Croix (EYZ 139), a vast symmetrical esplanade, bordered by neo-Classical façades and arcades, was laid out c 1840 when rue Jeanne-d'Arc was opened up. On the south side of the square there is a bronze statue of the Loire holding the fruits of the river valley in the folds of her dress. The 15C **Hôtel des Créneaux (EZ R)** was the town hall from the 16C to 1790.

★ **Musée historique (EZ M²)** ◷ – This historical museum is housed in an elegant little mansion, **Hôtel Cabu** (1550), next to another Renaissance façade.

On the ground floor is the astonishing **Gallo-Roman treasure★** from Neuvy-en-Sullias *(31km/19mi east of Orléans)* which consists of a series of expressive statues, a horse and a wild boar in bronze as well as a number of statuettes which once graced a pagan temple.

The first floor is devoted to the Middle Ages and to the Classical period; there are sculptures from Germigny-des-Prés and St-Benoît-sur-Loire, souvenirs of Joan of Arc (15C German tapestry, 17C standard from the Joan of Arc Festival), as well as typical local ceramic ware. The second floor is occupied by local folklore, gold and silverware and clocks.

Place du Martroi (EY) – This square marks the symbolic centre of the town and is adorned with a statue of Joan of Arc by Foyatier (1855). The name of the square is derived from the Latin word *martyretum* which was used to refer to the 6C Christian cemetery. On the west corner of rue Royale stands the old **Pavillon de la Chancellerie** which was built in 1759 by the Duke of Orléans to house his archives. A pedestrian alleyway leads to an underground car park, where vestiges of the Porte Bannier still stand.

Rue Royale (EZ 125) – This broad street, lined with arcades, was opened up c 1755 when the Royal Bridge (**Pont George V**) was built to replace the old medieval bridge which had stood 100m upstream in line with rue St-Catherine, the main street of the old medieval city.

ORLÉANS

D   Centre Charles Péguy
E   Maison de Jeanne d'Arc
H   Hôtel Groslot
      (hôtel de ville)
K   Hôtel Toutin
L   Centre Jeanne-d'Arc
M¹ Musée des Beaux-Arts
M² Musée historique
M³ Muséum
P   Préfecture
Q   Ancien évêché
R   Hôtel des Créneaux
X   Ancienne Salle des Thèses

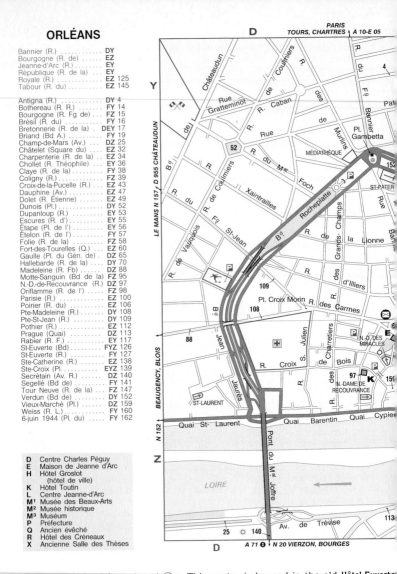

Centre Charles-Péguy (EZ D) ⊘ – This centre is housed in the old **Hôtel Euverte Hatte**, which is also known as Agnès Sorel House, because Charles VII's favourite may have lived there as a child. The present building was built later during the reign of Louis XII. The rectangular windows are framed with Gothic friezes; the Renaissance arcade in the courtyard was added during the reign of François I. The centre traces the life and career of **Charles Péguy** (1873-1914), poet and campaigner, who was born in Orléans and died on 5 September 1914 at the beginning of the Battle of the Marne. His writings reflect the causes he adopted and defended with intransigence: Dreyfus, socialism, patriotism, Catholicism. He wrote several works about the life of Joan of Arc, including a long play in 1897 and a series of mysteries in 1911-12. There is a library devoted to Péguy, his work and his literary, political and social environment including the background to the Dreyfus affair. The Péguy museum on the second floor contains manuscripts and memorabilia.

★ **Maison de Jeanne d'Arc (DZ E)** ⊘ – The tall timber-framed façade contrasts with the modernity of the square, place du Général-de-Gaulle, which was badly bombed in 1940. The building is a faithful reconstruction of the house of Jacques Boucher, Treasurer to the Duke of Orléans, where Joan stayed in 1429. An audio-visual show on the first floor recounts the raising of the siege of Orléans by Joan of Arc on 8 May 1429; there are reproductions of period costumes and weapons of war.

Centre Jeanne d'Arc (EY L) ⊘ – The centre's resources include a book library, a film library and microfilm and photographic archives (open to the public).
Beyond the house and the two adjacent Renaissance façades on the right there is an arch leading into Jacques-Boucher square. Standing alone in the garden is the **Pavillon Colas des Francs**, an elegant little Renaissance building, where

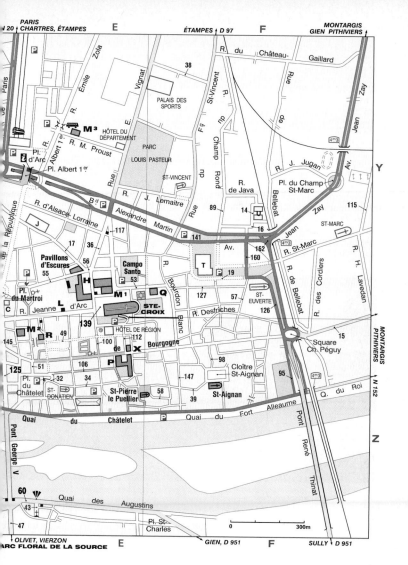

Boucher's grandson conducted his business; a room on the ground floor houses the archives, while another room upstairs was where the silver was kept.

Hôtel Toutin (DZ K) ⊙ – The house was built in 1540 for Toutin, manservant to François I's son. In the small courtyard is a double Renaissance arcade covered in Virginia creeper and a statue of François I.

Quai Fort-des-Tourelles (EZ 60) – Opposite a statue of Joan of Arc standing in a small square is a commemorative cross and an inscription on the low wall beside the Loire which mark the site of the southern end of the medieval bridge and les Tourelles fort in the 15C, the capture of which by Joan of Arc led to the defeat of the English and the lifting of the siege. Fine **view★** of the whole town.

Quai du Châtelet (EZ) provides a quiet shady walk beside the river. In Sully's time, early in the 17C, this was one of the busiest parts of town; it was from here that goods bound for Paris from the Loire valley and the Massif Central were transferred from river to road, and from here that the six-day voyage downstream to Nantes was begun.

Rue de Bourgogne (EFZ) – This was the main east-west axis of the old Gallo-Roman city. Now largely pedestrianised, it is ideal for window shopping. There are several old façades: no 261 is a 15C stone house with a half-timbered gable.

Along the street is the **Préfecture (EZ P)**, housed in a 17C Benedictine convent. Opposite in Rue Pothier is the façade of the old **Salle des Thèses** (Thesis Hall) **(EZ X)**, a 15C library, which is the only remnant of the University of Orléans where Jean Calvin, the religious reformer, studied law in 1528.

Collégiale St-Pierre-le-Puellier (EFZ) ⊘ – This 12C Romanesque collegiate church, now used to host **permanent exhibitions**, is at the heart of an old district of pedestrian streets.

Église de St-Aignan (FZ) ⊘ – The nave of this huge Gothic church, which was consecrated in 1509, was burnt down during the Wars of Religion leaving only the choir and the transepts. Note the 11C **crypt**.

★ **Muséum** (EY M³) ⊘ – The old museum, which has been completely restored and to which an extension has been added, now houses local and regional displays of a scientific and cultural nature.

Temporary exhibitions are held regularly on the ground floor. The four upper floors of the museum are devoted to the marine world, aquatic ecosystems (aquarium), reptiles and amphibians (vivarium), higher vertebrates (diorama on the Sologne region), mineralogy, geology, paleontology and botany (greenhouses of temperate and tropical plants on the top floor). There are simultaneous displays in scientific workshops and a geology laboratory explaining various techniques including the art of keeping aquaria, stuffing animals and pressing plants. Complementary information may be obtained from a library and audio-visual and computer aids.

Parc floral de la Source

★★ **Parc floral de la Source** ⊘ – This park was laid out in the wooded grounds of a 17C château to host the 1967 Floralies Internationales horticultural exhibition. It covers 35ha/86 acres and is home to a wide variety of garden layouts, including symmetrically arranged flower beds, rockeries, wooded parkland and evergreen and flowering shrubs. As the seasons change, so does the display: in spring, the flower beds are in bloom with tulips, daffodils, then irises, rhododendrons and azaleas; mid-June to mid-July is when the rose bushes are at their best; in July and August the gardens are bright with summer flowers; in September the late-flowering rose bushes come into bloom with the dahlias; and finally it is the turn of the chrysanthemums, which are displayed in the exhibition hall.

This park, a real showcase for local horticulture, is a delight for everyone, from people walking through it feasting their eyes on the display to amateur gardeners, for whom it is very instructive. From the "**mirror**"★, a semi-circular ornamental lake, there is a good view of the château and the dainty "Louis XIII embroidery" pattern adorning the lawns.

The **Loiret spring** ★, a short tributary of the south bank of the Loire, can be seen bubbling up from the ground. The spring is in fact the resurgence of the part of the river which disappears underground near St-Benoît-sur-Loire, some 58km/36mi upstream. Throughout the year, flocks of cranes and emus and herds of deer roam the park, while flamingoes stalk by the banks of the Loiret.

OLIVET

Like the southern suburbs of Orléans between the Loiret and the Loire, the greater part of Olivet is given over to growing flowers, roses and ornamental plants. It is also a pleasant summer resort on the south bank of the Loiret, composed of elegant houses and old water mills, where people come for the fishing and canoeing.

Promenade des moulins – *Round trip of 5km/3mi from the bridge by the side road along the north bank of the Loiret going west and returning on D 14 going east.*

At the far end of the loop, two old mills straddle the river over their mill-races between the wooded banks of the Loiret, while ducks and swans glide up and down on the quiet river.

EXCURSIONS

Gidy – *12km/8mi north. Take A 10 motorway and leave at the rest areas Aire d'Orléans-Saran heading Paris-Orléans or Aire d'Orléans-Gidy heading Orléans-Paris.*

Designed and created by the geological and mining research bureau (BRGM) the **géodrome** ⊙ is a garden of rocks representing an enormous relief map of the most remarkable geological features to be found in France. Eight hundred tons of rock have been laid out on a single hectare (2.5 acres) of land along with the vegetation typical of each French region. A huge painted frieze, 70m/230ft long, illustrates a cross-section of French soil from the Alps to the Armorican massif (Brittany).

Artenay – *22km/14mi north on N 20.*

The entrance to this large town in the Beauce region is marked by a windmill-tower with a revolving roof (19C). A restored farmhouse, **Ferme du Paradis**, houses a museum on travelling theatre, the **Musée du théâtre forain** ⊙. With its displays of costumes, equipment and accessories belonging to the Créteur-Cavalier troupe, who finished touring in 1974, the museum evokes the life of "collapsible theatre" from the 19C to the 1970s. Bits of scenery, puppets, posters and a costume wagon (containing the changing room, masks and disguises) all combine to reconstruct the social, professional and family life of these strolling players. A small theatre (200 seats) is home to a theatre ethnology workshop which puts on performances of works from the repertoire of travelling theatre.

In the sheep-fold there are two rooms on local archeology and paleontology.

Le PERCHE-GOUET

Michelin map 60 folds 15, 16

Le Perche-Gouet, which is sometimes known as Lower Perche, was named in the 11C after William Gouet who owned five baronies within the jurisdiction of the Bishop of Chartres: Alluyes la Belle, Brou la Noble, La Bazoche la Gaillarde, Authon la Gueuse and Montmirail la Superbe. Before the Revolution the administration of Le Perche-Gouet was divided between the authority in the Orléans district and that of the Upper Maine.

Le Perche-Gouet covers a sort of crescent between the Loir and the Huisne; the soil is composed of chalk marl and banks of sand or clay. Much of the immense forest which once covered the land has been replaced by fields and orchards. The eastern part of Le Perche-Gouet is very similar to the Beauce but is distinguished from it by its scattered farms and the abundance of hedges and trees. The western border is marked by a range of wooded hills, only 250m/820ft high, indented by a network of alluvial valleys and agricultural villages. Most of the streams flow east into the Loir; only the Rhône drains northwest into the Huisne at Nogent-le-Rotrou.

The farms hidden in the deep lanes were originally built of wattle and daub or within a brick framework. Their owners raise cattle, particularly dairy herds, which have replaced the breeding of the Percheron draught horses, their coats dappled grey, roan or black.

Maize is the modern crop grown for cattle fodder; its tall stems provide excellent cover for the game which used to shelter in the hedges before they were pulled up, to the alarm of the hunting fraternity.

ROUND TRIP STARTING FROM BROU

97km/60mi – about half a day

Brou – *See BROU.*

Take D 15 northwest.

Frazé – *See FRAZÉ.*

Thiron – The village has grown up on the south bank of the Thironne, which flows out of the Étang des Moines ("Monks' Pool") near the old abbey founded by St Bernard in 1114 and dedicated to the Holy Trinity. Tiron (spelt without an h in those days) abbey was especially prosperous in the 12C and 13C. Among the abbots in the 16C were Charles de Ronsard, the poet's brother, and Philippe Desportes, himself a poet. In 1629 the Benedictines of St-Maur moved in. The

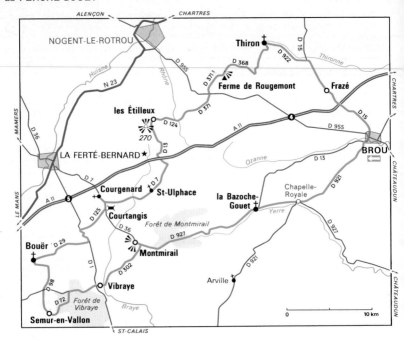

abbey church is still a huge building even though the chancel collapsed in 1817. Near the entrance *(left)* is the tombstone of John II of Chartres, Abbot of Tiron in the 13C; the old monks' stalls in the nave are 14C; the woodwork and stalls in the present chancel date from 1740. A few buildings from the 17C college still exist.

Ferme de Rougemont – From the road (D 371³) passing this farm there is an extensive **view** of the Ozanne river valley.

Les Étilleux – South of the village near a small farm on D 13 take the path (signposted) which climbs to the top of a mound (270m/886ft; at the foot of the television aerial) there are beautiful **views** of the Ozanne valley, the hills of Perche and the Huisne valley.

St-Ulphace – Halfway up the slope stands this church (15C-16C), with a powerful façade flanked by a tower and a Renaissance doorway.

Courgenard – In this small village with its pretty gardens, the door of the church ⊘ is carved with low-relief statues in the Renaissance style. The right wall of the nave is decorated with 16C murals depicting Hell and the Legend of the Three Living and the Three Dead; there is also an interesting Baroque altarpiece.

Château de Courtangis – Among the tall trees in an idyllically isolated valley are the turrets, dormers and steeply-pitched mansard roofs of a graceful early-16C manor house.

Bouër – Bouër is a tiny little village hidden in the hills overlooking the Huisne valley. The slate spire of the church is joined to the bell-tower by scrolls. There are two attractive wooden altars in front of the chancel.
From the terrace there is a fine view of the Huisne valley.

Semur-en-Vallon – This is an attractive village by a man-made lake. In the valley on the western edge of Vibraye forest stands a 15C moated and turreted **castle**. The entrance façade, which is flanked by round towers with lanterns, was altered in the 17C. Note the pretty, steeply pitched French roofs. The Decauville **tourist train** ⊘ runs on a 1.5km/1mi long circuit.

Montmirail – The little town of Montmirail, once strongly fortified, was built on a site with excellent natural defences. The **castle** ⊘, built in the 15C on top of a medieval mound, was altered in the 18C by the Princesse de Conti. It still has the original underground works dating from the 11C and 14C. On 9 January 1169, the castle was the scene of a memorable encounter between the Kings of England and France in the course of which the exiled Archbishop of Canterbury, **Thomas Becket**, reaffirmed the primacy of the Church. The apartments of the Princesse de Conti, including the Louis XV Grand Salon, are open to the public, as are the dungeons and armouries. The classical west façade, contrasting with the medieval south and east fronts, can be viewed from the terrace, which also gives a vast **panorama**★ over the countryside of Le Perche-Gouet.

The **church** (12C-16C) has a 16C stained-glass window in the chancel and a realistic early-17C painted sepulchre in the left aisle. Opposite is a carved stone which, until the Revolution, contained a reliquary.

A picturesque road (D 927) runs through Montmirail forest.

La Bazoche-Gouet – The **church**, 12C or 13C, was altered early in the 16C by the addition of Flamboyant windows in the side aisles; that on the south side is particularly interesting. The fine doorway features niches resting on spiral columns. Inside, a square tower supports the 16C bell-tower. The Renaissance windows in the chancel were the gift of the Bourbons-Conti, who owned the estate; the detail and realistic expressions are remarkable; the subject is the Passion copied from German engravings.

PITHIVIERS

Population 9 325
Michelin map 60 fold 20 or 237 fold 41
Town plan in the current Michelin Red Guide France

Pithiviers is situated on the border between the Beauce and the Gâtinais. Its main economic activities are related to local products – cereals and sugar-beet (sugar refinery at Pithiviers-le-Vieil) – but other industries are being introduced.
The rectangle containing the old town is enclosed on four sides by a shady tree-lined avenue. It is pleasant to wander along the quiet old streets which radiate from place du Martroi, an irregular triangle of open space in the shadow of the great tower of St-Salomon's church.

Musée des Transports ⊙ – The railway museum was founded by amateurs in a small station, the old terminus of the Tramways du Loiret line, which until 1951 used to deliver sugar-beet to the refineries and carry passengers between Pithiviers and Toury 32km/20mi to the west. The track is 0.60m/approximately 2ft wide, the same gauge as the prefabricated light railway developed by Decauville.
The museum contains several locomotives, some in working order, and various items of narrow-gauge rolling stock from a minute 2-axle machine built in 1870 (3 tonnes unloaded weight) to a powerful locomotive (1895) from the regional railway which was 1m/over 3ft gauge. There are many reproductions on display as well as items of equipment and uniform, old tickets, lamps and other railwayana.
Visitors can end their tour of the museum by taking a short trip (4km/2.5mi) in a train.

Musée municipal ⊙ – Predominantly local memorabilia are attractively displayed on the first floor of this municipal museum. The first room, on the South Sea Islands, adds a touch of the exotic. Another room is devoted to famous local people, to the more or less legendary origins of the culinary specialities of Pithiviers and to saffron, the strongly-coloured aromatic derived from the crocus, which the west Gâtinais was one of the first places in Europe to cultivate.

Château du PLESSIS-BOURRÉ★

Michelin map 63 fold 20 or 232 fold 19 – 20km/12mi north of Angers

Le Plessis-Bourré stands at the far end of a vista of meadowland dotted with copses. This white building beneath blue-grey slate roofs gives a very strong idea of what seigneurial life in the 15C would have been like.
Born in Château-Gontier **Jean Bourré** (1424-1506) first entered royal service under the Dauphin Louis, the son of Charles VII, whom he served faithfully. When Louis XI assumed the crown in 1461, Bourré was given the important post of Financial Secretary and Treasurer of France. In addition to building several châteaux – Jarzé and Vaux among others – he bought the estate of Plessis-le-Vent and in 1468 ordered work to begin on the new château. The design was inspired by the château at Langeais which he had supervised during its construction, and as Le Plessis was built in a single go it has a magnificent unity of style.
Among the many illustrious guests that Bourré welcomed to his new residence were Pierre de Rohan, Louis XI and Charles VIII.

Château du PLESSIS-BOURRÉ

Château du Plessis-Bourré

TOUR ⊘

On the outside Le Plessis, enclosed by a wide moat spanned by a long (43m/141ft), many-arched bridge, is plainly a fortress protected by a gatehouse with a double drawbridge and four flanking towers. The largest of these is battlemented and served as a keep. A 3m/10ft wide platform at the base of the wall provided for artillery crossfire. To the left of the gatehouse the chapel's slender spire rises above the roof.

On the inside of the entrance archway, Le Plessis is transformed into a country mansion with a spacious courtyard, low wings, an arcaded gallery, turret staircases and the high dormer windows of the seigneurial wing.

On the ground floor visitors will see the chapel of St-Anne and the Hall of Justice before going on to the splendid, richly furnished and decorated **state apartments**, from which there is a charming view of the gentle surrounding countryside.

The first floor boasts among other rooms a fine vaulted room with a monumental chimneypiece. The guard-room has a coffered wooden **ceiling**★★★ painted at the end of the 15C with such allegorical figures as Fortune, Truth, Chastity (a unicorn) and Lust, the Musician Ass etc. There are also humorous scenes with a moral, depicting for example the unskilled barber at work on a client, the overweening man trying to wring the neck of an eel and a woman sewing up a chicken's crop. The often quite crude realism of some of the scenes, which are accompanied by lines of verse, and their outstandingly fresh and graphic quality make them all the more striking and evocative.

The **cellars and attics** ⊘ are also open to visitors. The palm tree ceiling of the tower staircase rests on carvings inspired by alchemy which are just as striking as the paintings on the first floor. The attic under the beautiful chestnut keel **roof** leads out to the sentry walk.

The castle grounds have recently been laid out as a park and make a pleasant place for a walk.

EXCURSION

Manoir de la Hamonnière ⊘– *9km/6mi north via Écuillé.*
The architecture of this manor house, which was built between 1420 and 1575, shows the evolution of the Renaissance style. The buildings round the courtyard consist of a plain residential block *(right)* with a stair turret, a Henri III section *(left)* with a window bay framed by pilasters and capitals following the Classical progression of the orders, and at a right-angle a low wing with two twisted columns supporting a dormer window. To the rear stands the keep, probably the last addition made in the 16C, with a staircase turret running from ground level to the eaves and round-arched windows (unlike the rest).

Find the best routes in town using the plans in the Michelin Red Guide France which indicate:
  – through routes, by-passes, new streets, one-way systems, car parks...
All the necessary information, revised annually.

Château du PLESSIS-MACÉ★

Michelin 63 fold 20 or 232 fold 19 – 13km/8mi northwest of Angers

This château set apart from the village and hidden amid greenery is protected by a wide moat. Begun in the 11C by a certain Macé, the **château** became the property in the mid-15C of Louis de Beaumont, the Chamberlain and favourite of Louis XI, who transformed it into a residence fit to accommodate his royal master. The year 1510 saw the beginning of a 168-year-old ownership by the Du Bellay family.

TOUR ⊙

From the outside Le Plessis still has the appearance of a fortress with its tower-studded wall and rectangular keep, stripped of all its fortifications except the battlements and surrounded by a moat.

Once inside the great courtyard, the building has the appearance of a country residence: decorative elements in white tufa stone enhance the dark grey of the schist, while windows let in the light.

To the right are the outbuildings housing the stables and guard-room. To the left are the chapel, an unusual staircase turret which gets larger as it goes up and the main residential wing surmounted by pointed gables. In the corner with the main wing is a charming **hanging gallery**★ from where the ladies would watch jousting tournaments and other entertainments. A second balcony opposite, in the outbuildings, was reserved for the servants.

Le Plessis-Macé – The hanging gallery

The tour includes the dining room, the large banqueting hall, several bedrooms, one of which was the King's, and the **chapel**, which still features rare 15C Gothic **panelling**★ forming two levels of galleries, the first reserved for the lord and his squires, the second for the servants.

PONCÉ-SUR-LE-LOIR

Population 436
Michelin map 64 fold 5 or 232 fold 23
Local map see Vallée du LOIR: Vendôme-La Flèche

Beside the road (D 197) leading into Poncé from the east stands a Renaissance château. On the west side of the town, south of the main road and the railway line, is a **craft centre** ⊙ "Les Grès du Loir". This is housed in the 18C buildings of the old Pallard paper mill on the river bank and consists of the studios of several self-employed craftsmen: pottery, glassware, ironwork, weaving, woodwork and candle making.

Château ⊙ – This originally consisted of two pavilions flanking a central staircase tower, one of which was destroyed in the 18C and replaced by a rather characterless wing. Ionic pilasters flanking the windows and pronounced horizontal cornices give a balanced but geometrically severe appearance to the façade. The north façade, once the entrance façade, has an elegant Italian-style arcade which forms a terrace at first-floor level.

The stone **Renaissance staircase**★★ is one of the most remarkable in France; in front of it are the remains of a loggia. The coffered, white stone ceilings of the six straight flights are sumptuously sculpted, executed with a refinement, fluidity and mastery of the art of perspective rarely to be found. Over 130 decorative motifs portray real-life, allegorical and mythological subjects.

The well-tended **gardens**, with their highly effective symmetrical layout, make a pleasant place for a stroll: at the edges of the square lawn, a tree-lined walk makes a long vaulted path on one side, while on the other is a maze. Overlooking the entire scene runs a terrace with an avenue of lime trees.

The dovecot with its 1 800 nesting holes and revolving ladders for gathering the eggs is still intact. The outbuildings house a local folklore museum, the **musée départemental du Folklore sarthois**.

PONTLEVOY

Population 1 423
Michelin map 64 fold 17 or 238 folds 14, 15

Pontlevoy is a small town situated in the agricultural region to the north of Montrichard and can still boast a number of charming old houses with stone dressings.

★ ABBEY *1hr 15min*

The main interest of the **old abbey** ⊘ lies in its elegant 18C buildings (including two wings of the cloisters) and the 15C Gothic church. The abbey was founded in 1034 when, legend has it, Gelduin de Chaumont, vassal of the Count of Blois, established a Benedictine community here as a token of gratitude to the Virgin Mary for his surviving a shipwreck. In the 17C, when a reform of monastic life became essential, the abbey was entrusted to the Benedictines of St-Maur and the Abbot Pierre de Bérule, who opened an educational establishment in 1644 which made Pontlevoy famous until the 19C. Made an École Royale Militaire in 1776, the college added to the general education it offered the military training of scholarship students chosen by the King from among the lower nobility.

Abbey church – The abbey church, which was rebuilt in the second half of the 15C after being damaged during the Hundred Years War, consists solely of the chancel of an imposing building which was planned but never completed. It comprises two bays flanked by aisles where fragments of 15C wall-paintings have been uncovered.

In 1651 two large stone altarpieces with marble columns were added to the high altar and to the axial chapel where Gelduin de Chaumont and his immediate descendants are buried.

Conventual buildings – These 18C conventual buildings include the refectory which is adorned with a monumental Delftware stove, one of four which the Maréchal de Saxe had commissioned for Chambord, the remarkable staircase leading to the upper floor, and the majestic façade giving onto the gardens, decorated with emblazoned pediments at regular intervals.

Musée du Poids lourd ⊘ – Some 20 heavy goods vehicles built between 1910 and 1950 are displayed under the fine timber roof of the old riding school.

Musée municipal ⊘ – Housed in the west wing of the conventual buildings, the municipal museum is devoted to key themes of the early 20C in which local people played an important part.

The first theme is advertising, one of the pioneers of which was **Auguste Poulain**, born in Pontlevoy in 1825 and founder of the famous chocolate factory at Blois. There are old posters (among them examples signed by Cappiello and Firmin Bouisset), chromolithographs and other publicity items.

Then there are some hundred photographs from the collection of 10 000 plates taken by Louis Clergeau, a watchmaker with a passion for photography, and by his daughter Marcelle; they constitute a marvellous record of life in Pontlevoy between 1902 and 1960.

Finally, the heroic beginnings of aviation (1910-14), are evoked by models of the aerodrome and of four training aircraft as well as by photos from the Clergeau collection.

Manoir de la POSSONNIÈRE★

Michelin map 64 fold 5 or 232 west of fold 24 – 1km/0.5mi south of Couture-sur-Loir
Local map see Vallée du LOIR: Vendôme-La Flèche

When Louis de Ronsard, soldier and man of letters, returned from Italy in the early 16C he undertook to rebuild his country seat in the new Italian style. The result was La Possonnière characterized by the profusion of mottoes engraved on the walls.

The Prince of Poets – In 1524 **Pierre de Ronsard**, son of Louis, was born at the manor. He was destined for a brilliant future in the army or the diplomatic service and at 12 became a page at the court of François I. At the age of 15, however, an illness left him half deaf and he had to give up his ambitions. He took holy orders and turned to poetry and the study of the Ancients; Pindar in Greek and Horace in Latin became his models. He excelled in composing sonnets in which he described the beauty of Cassandra Salviati *(see TALCY)* and "Marie" *(see BOURGUEIL)*. He was the leader of the Pléiade group of poets and in 1558 was appointed Poet Laureate. However, he suffered from severe gout so chose to withdraw to his priories at Ste-Madeleine-de-Croixval *(6km/4mi southeast of la Possonnière)* and at St-Cosme-lès-Tours *(see TOURS: Additional Sights)* where he died in 1585 leaving a considerable body of work, including his famous collection of sonnets *Les Amours*.

★ **Manor** ⊙ – The manor house is built against the hillside on the northern fringes of the Gâtines forest and enclosed with a wall. The name comes from the word *posson* (*poinçon*, a measure of volume) and has sometimes been altered to Poissonnière under the influence of the Ronsard family coat of arms, three silver fishes *(poisson)* on a blue ground.
The main façade has mullioned windows in the style of Louis XII on the ground floor but the windows on the first floor are flanked by pilasters with medallions, clearly in the Renaissance style. Projecting from the rear façade is a graceful staircase turret adorned with an elegant doorway capped by a pediment decorated with a bust. The pediment dormer at the top of the turret bears the arms of the Ronsard family.

POUANCÉ

Population 3 279
Michelin map 63 fold 8 or 232 fold 17

Pouancé, in its protective ring of lakes, lies on the border between Anjou and Brittany. In the Middle Ages it played an important economic role owing to its iron foundries which were supplied with ore from the Segré basin. The surrounding woods provided shelter for the Chouans during the Revolution.

The main road (N 171) skirts the town, passing at the foot of the **ruined castle** ⊙ (13C-15C). The towers and curtain wall of dark schist are impressive and reinforced by a firing caponier linked to the keep by a postern.

EXCURSIONS

Menhir de Pierre Frite – *5km/3mi south on D 878, bearing left onto D 6 in La Prévière and then a track to the right (signposted).*
This menhir in woodland surroundings stands 6m/20ft high.

Château de la Motte-Glain ⊙ – *17km/11mi south.*
The red stone château with its strong lines was built late in the 15C by **Pierre de Rohan-Guéménée**, Counsellor to Louis XI and later one of the commanding officers of the armies of Charles VIII and Louis XII in Italy. A reminder of the château's location on the pilgrimage route from Mont-St-Michel to Compostela is given by the scallops and pilgrim's staff motifs decorating the courtyard façade. The gatehouse is flanked by two round towers.
In the chapel is a fresco from the early 16C representing the Crucifixion. 15C and 16C furniture and Renaissance fireplaces embellish the interior of the château, together with hunting trophies, most of them of African origin.

PREUILLY-SUR-CLAISE

Population 1 427
Michelin map 68 fold 6 or 238 fold 25

Preuilly, in which numerous interesting old houses have been conserved, rises in terraces on the north bank of the Claise. The town was once considered to be the leading barony of the Touraine region, held by such illustrious families as those of Amboise, La Rochefoucauld, César de Vendôme, Gallifet and Breteuil. Five churches and a collegiate church were barely enough to accommodate the town's worshippers in its heyday. A fortress used to stand above the town, but it has fallen into ruin and been replaced by a modern château. A few vestiges of the old castle (12C-15C) and of its church, the Collégiale St-Mélaine (12C), nonetheless remain standing.

Église St-Pierre – This old Benedictine abbey church is a Romanesque building in which traces of the architectural styles of the Poitou and Touraine regions are evident. Flying buttresses were added as structural reinforcement in the 15C. Architect Phidias Vestier carried out some excellent repair work in 1846, but the church was subsequently subjected to shoddy restoration in 1873, the year when the tower was built. The nave consists of five bays and is roofed by a barrel vault. The capitals are decorated with narrative scenes.
Next to the south transept, the priest's house is contained in a 15C building which also houses the chapter-house and monks' dormitory.
Near the church, there are several 17C mansions, one of which has been turned into a hospice (ancien hôtel de la Rallière).

EXCURSIONS

Boussay – *4.5km/7mi southwest.*
The château here combines such diverse elements as 15C machicolated towers, a wing in the Baroque style of Mansart, the architect who designed much of the château at Versailles, and an 18C façade. It stands in fine gardens laid out in the French style.

Le PUY-NOTRE-DAME

Population 1 322
Michelin map 64 fold 12 or 232 fold 32 – 7km/4mi west of Montreuil-Bellay

★ **Church** – The church is a remarkable example of Angevin architecture and was built in the 13C. The tower with its stone spire above the south transept is decorated with mouldings forming a recess containing a very beautiful statue of the Virgin (16C). On the north side of the church, enclosed in a cylindrical building, is the well.

In the Middle Ages people came from all over France to venerate the Virgin Mary's Girdle, a relic brought from Jerusalem in the 12C. The tall, narrow nave and aisles lend majesty to the interior; the vaulting in the chancel is rich with lierne and tierceron ribs. The carved stalls beyond the high altar are 16C.

RICHELIEU★

Population 2 223
Michelin map 67 southeast of fold 10 or 232 fold 46

Lying on the southern limits of Touraine, bordering on Poitou, Richelieu is a quiet town which comes to life on market days.

La Fontaine called the place "the finest village in the universe". It is a rare example of Classical town planning, the project of one man, the statesman and churchman **Cardinal de Richelieu**, who was eager to lodge his court near his château which was then under construction. The building of the town itself started in 1631 at a time when Versailles was still only an idea.

HISTORICAL NOTES

Cardinal de Richelieu – In 1621 when Armand du Plessis (1585-1642) bought the property of Richelieu it consisted of a village and manor on the banks of the Mable. Ten years later the estate was raised to the status of a duchy. On becoming Cardinal and First Minister of France Richelieu commissioned Jacques Le Mercier, the architect of the Sorbonne and Cardinal's Palace, now Palais-Royal, in Paris, to prepare plans for a château and a walled town. Built under the supervision of the architect's brother, Pierre Le Mercier, the project was considered at the time to be a marvel of urban planning which Louis XIV was to visit at the age of 12.

Determined not to have his creation outstripped in grandeur, Richelieu created a small principality around his masterpiece and jealously razed in whole or in part many other châteaux in the vicinity. He already owned Bois-le-Vicomte and was to add to his estates Champigny-sur-Veude, L'Ile-Bouchard, Cravant, Crissay, Mirebeau, Faye-la-Vineuse and even the royal residence of Chinon, which he was to allow to fall into disrepair. The great fortress of Loudon also suffered destruction at his hands, once its owner, Urbain Grandier, an arch enemy of the Cardinal, had perished at the stake.

Past splendour – One may call it retribution or the hazard of fate but little has survived of the Cardinal's magnificent residence.

An enormous park was once the setting for a marvellous palace filled with great works of art. Two vast courtyards surrounded by outbuildings stood in front of the château proper, which was protected by moats, bastions and watchtowers. The entrance porch was adorned with a statue of Louis XIII and surmounted by an allegorical figure of Fame, both the works of Guillaume Berthelot. The pavilion at the far end of the château's main courtyard was originally graced by obelisks, rostral columns (in the form of ships' prows) and Michelangelo's famous group, The Slaves, once intended for the tomb of Pope Julius II.

The apartments, gallery and chapel were hung with works by Poussin, Claude Lorrain, Champaigne, Mantegna, Perugino, Bassano, Caravaggio, Titian, Giulio Romano, Dürer, Rubens and Van Dyck.

The gardens were dotted with copies of Antique statues and artificial grottoes which concealed the then-popular water tricks (fountains or jets which would spring up unexpectedly, soaking unwary visitors). It was in these gardens that the first poplar trees from Italy were planted.

The dispersal of the riches gathered here began in 1727 when Maréchal de Richelieu, the Cardinal's great-nephew, transported some back to his Parisian town house and sold others. Confiscated in 1792 the château was visited by Tallien, a collector of silverware, and then Dufourni and Visconti who took all that was suitable for the Musée des Monuments français in Paris. After the Revolution the descendants of Richelieu ceded the château to a certain Boutron who demolished it for the sale of the building materials. The works of art were dispersed: the Louvre has *The Slaves* by Michelangelo, Perugino's paintings and a marble table encrusted with precious stones; the series of 12 paintings depicting the victories of Louis XIII are in Versailles; the local museums in Tours and Azay-le-Ferron have several paintings and sculptures; the Musée Ste-Croix in Poitiers has Berthelot's bust of Louis XIII. The Orléans Musée des Beaux-Arts has the work of Fréminet and Deruet in its Richelieu Gallery. The obelisks are now at Malmaison and the rostral columns in the Musée de la Marine, Paris.

SIGHTS

★ **The town** – The walled town which Richelieu planned at the gates of his château was in itself a fine example of the Louis XIII style designed by Jacques Le Mercier.

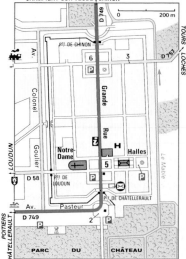

The town embodies the sense of order, balance, regularity and symmetry which characterised the 17C, or "Grand Siècle", in France. The rectangular ground plan (700m long by 500m wide/766yds by 547yds wide) was surrounded by ramparts and a moat. The impressive entrance gates are flanked by rusticated and pedimented gatehouses surmounted by high French roofs.

Grande-Rue – The main street crosses Richelieu from north to south. In addition to the gateways note the Louis XIII-style *hôtels* with the decorative elements in white tufa stone, especially no 17, Hôtel du Sénéchal, which has retained its elegant courtyard with busts of Roman emperors. There are two squares, one at each end of the main street.

Place du Marché (5) – In the southern square, opposite the church, stands the 17C **covered market**, its slate roof supported by a fine chestnut timber frame.

A **museum** ⊘ in the town hall (**H**), which was originally built as the Law Courts, contains documents and works of art pertaining to both the Richelieu family and the château.

The **church of Notre-Dame**, which is built of white stone in the classical, so-called "Jesuit" style, exudes a certain harmony and elegance. The niches in the façade contain statues of the Evangelists; the chancel is flanked by two towers topped with obelisks, a rare arrangement. The interior exhibits the same architectural features; note also the elegant 18C high altar.

Park ⊘ – A magnificent statue of Richelieu by Ramey stands at the southern end of the main street in front of the park (475ha/1 174 acres), which is criss-crossed by straight avenues of chestnut and plane trees.

Of the many splendid buildings to be found here once upon a time there remains a domed pavilion, once part of the outbuildings, which houses a small **museum** ⊘ containing models of the château and historical documents on Richelieu. The canals also remain as do two pavilions, the orangery and wine cellar, at the far end of the formal gardens *(southeast)*.

The old château entrance can still be seen from D 749 *(southwest)*.

EXCURSIONS

Steam trains in Touraine ⊘ – A genuine steam train dating from the turn of the century runs between Richelieu and Chinon via Champigny-sur-Veude and Ligré, covering a distance of 20km/13mi. The museum at Richelieu station displays ancient machinery: early 20C locomotives, saloon-carriages (1900) belonging to the company PLM, an American diesel engine (a relic of the Marshall Plan) etc.

Faye-la-Vineuse – *7km/4mi south on D 749. See FAYE-LA-VINEUSE.*

Abbaye de Bois-Aubry ⊘ – *16km/10mi east on D 757.*
The 12C Benedictine abbey in the middle of the countryside is heralded by its stone spire which may be seen standing on the horizon. The best-preserved feature of the ruins *(currently being restored)* is the square 15C bell-tower. Note also the 15C stone rood screen in Flamboyant Gothic style. The vaulting in the 13C nave has a keystone decorated with a carved coat of arms. There are 12 beautifully carved capitals in the early-12C chapter-house.

Gourmets...
The annual Michelin Red Guide France
offers a selection of good restaurants.

Château du RIVAU ★

Michelin map 67 fold 10 or 232 fold 34 – 11km/7mi north of Richelieu
Local map see CHINON: Excursions 1

The 13C **castle** ⊙ was fortified in the 15C by Pierre de Beauvau, Charles VII's chamberlain. Joan of Arc found horses for her soldiers here on her way to the siege of Orléans. Rivau is mentioned by Rabelais: Gargantua gave the castle to one of his knights after the Picrocholean War.

The interior of the castle is currently undergoing major restoration work and will be closed to the public during 1997.

Château de la ROCHE-RACAN

Michelin map 64 fold 4 or 232 fold 23 – 2km/1mi southeast of St-Paterne-Racan

The Château de la Roche-Racan stands perched on a rock *(roche)* overlooking the Escotais valley which, together with the nearby Loir, was a constant source of inspiration to the first owner and poet, **Racan**.
Born at Champmarin near Aubigné, Honorat de Bueil, Marquis de Racan (1589-1670), was a member of the well-known local family, the Bueils. Not really cut out for the life of a soldier and following a number of unlucky love affairs, Racan retired to his country seat for the last 40 years of his life, a period described in his work, *Stances à la retraite*.
There he was quite content to stroll by his fountains or hunt game or visit Denis de la Grelière, the Abbé of la Clarté-Dieu, who invited him to put the Psalms into verse. He brought up his children, pursued his lawsuits, grew beans and rebuilt his château.

Château ⊙ – In 1634 Racan commissioned a local master mason, Jacques Gabriel, a member of a long-established family of architects, to build this château. The main building was originally flanked by two pavilions only one of which remains standing, pedimented and adorned with a corner turret and caryatids. Long balustered terraces, above arcades decorated with masks, overlook the park and Escotais valley.

ROMORANTIN-LANTHENAY ★

Population 17 865
Michelin map 64 fold 18 or 238 fold 16

The point where the River Sauldre divides into several arms is the site of the former capital of the Sologne. Always an important market town, Romorantin-Lanthenay has gained a new impetus from modern industries such as electronics, refrigeration plants, high precision mechanics, sheet-iron and dehydration plugs. Matra, established in 1968, is the company which employs the most people in town; it now has three plants, where the "Renault Espace" model is assembled.

Royal associations – In the 15C Romorantin was the fief of the Valois-Angoulême branch of the French royal family and it was here that François d'Angoulême, later **François I**, spent his turbulent childhood and where his wife-to-be Claude de France, the daughter of Louis XII, was born in 1499. The king loved Romorantin and in 1517 he commissioned Leonardo da Vinci, then at Amboise, to draw up plans for a palace destined for his mother Louise of Savoy. Leonardo envisaged a palace astride the Sauldre, to be built with prefabricated units, but the death of Louise put an end to the project. Da Vinci also devoted some time to studying the possibility of creating a canal to link Romorantin to the Loire.
In France, the Feast of the Epiphany *(la Fête des Rois)* is celebrated by eating a cake *(la Galette des Rois)* which contains a bean. The finder of this bean is the bean king of Twelfth Night. On 6 January 1521, Epiphany, François I led a mock attack on the Hôtel St-Pol, where a bean king reigned. The occupants of the house were defending themselves when some ill-advised person threw out a glowing log which landed on the royal cranium. To dress the wound the doctors shaved his head, whereupon the King grew a beard. His courtiers promptly followed suit.

SIGHTS

★ **Old Houses (B)** – On the corner of rue de la Résistance and rue du Milieu stands **La Chancellerie**, a corbelled Renaissance house, of brick and half-timber construction, where the royal seals were kept when the King stayed in the town. The corner post features a coat of arms and a musician playing the bagpipes. Opposite stands **Hôtel St-Pol**, built of stone and glazed bricks with window mouldings.

ROMORANTIN-LANTHENAY

B   Maisons anciennes
E   Moulin-foulon
M¹ Musée de Sologne
M² Musée de la Course
    automobile
P   Ancien château royal
    (sous-préfecture)
V   Maisons à pans de bois

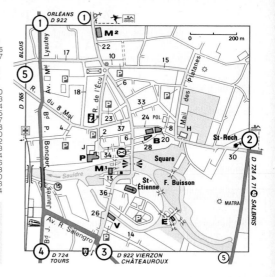

Standing at the junction of rue du Milieu and rue de la Pierre is the charming **Maison du Carroir Doré** ⊘ (archeological museum) with its remarkable carved corner posts showing the Annunciation *(left)* and St George killing the Dragon *(right)*.

★ **Musée de Sologne** (**M¹**) ⊘ – This museum is housed in three buildings by the river: the **Jacquemart tower** (the oldest building in Romorantin) which hosts temporary exhibitions; the little **Moulin de la ville**, a mill in the middle of the Sauldre which contains exhibitions on the history of the town; and the **Moulin du chapitre** (once two mills separated by a mill-course on the banks of the Sauldre) in which there is the museum proper. A fourth building, an old barn, is given over to a technical workshop.
The entrance to the museum complex is via the esplanade on quai de l'île Marin (with an allegorical statue of the Sologne by American artist Jean Lamore) which leads to the permanent collections. The museum's main themes are exhibited on four floors and include a presentation of the history, flora and fauna of the Sologne region; local society and architecture (in particular life in the châteaux and in the peasant community with reconstructions of 19C interiors); traditional rural economy (reconstructions of workshops and displays of tools for crafts which are no longer practised: clog-maker, cartwright, slate-splitter etc); contemporary economy (Matra, armaments, tourism, motor construction etc); and finally a display on the various aspects of hunting (to hounds, with guns and... poaching) backed up with costumes, literature, videos and other relevant items.

★ **View from the bridges** – From the north branch of the river there is a **view** of the **Château Royal** (**P**), opposite the Sologne museum complex, which dates from the 15C and 16C and now houses the sub-Prefecture. Along the narrow southern branch of the river there is a row of attractive half-timbered houses (**V**).

Public Garden (Square Ferdinand-Buisson) – This is a pleasant park with tall trees and footbridges over the river; there are pretty views of the river banks and the fulling mill (**E**).

Église St-Étienne – Above the transept crossing of the church rises a Romanesque tower with finely executed sculptures. Beyond the nave with its Angevin vaulting is the darker chancel which is also roofed with Angevin vaulting springing from powerful Romanesque pillars; each rib of the apsidal vault supports the statue of an Evangelist.

Chapelle St-Roch – This elegant chapel at the entrance to the St-Roch district is flanked by turrets with round-arched windows typical of the Renaissance.

Musée de la Course automobile ⊘ – This Motor Racing Museum displays an exhibition of Matra cars, including the Formula 1 car which was world champion in 1969, and a series of display cases tracing the technical developments in racing car construction. The museum also has a specialist library.

Tourists are asked not to visit a church during a service.

SABLÉ-SUR-SARTHE

Population 12 178
Michelin map 64 fold 1 or 232 fold 21
Local map see Vallée de la SARTHE

Situated at a point where two tributaries, the Vaige and the Erve, flow into the Sarthe, Sablé is dominated by the austere façade of its château, which once belonged to the Colbert family and now houses the National Library's restoration and book-binding workshops.

In the 17C the fief belonged to Laval-Bois-Dauphin, Marquis de Sablé. In 1711 Colbert de Torcy, the nephew of the great Jean-Baptiste Colbert, Louis XIV's Minister, rebuilt the château and radically changed the appearance of the town; many houses and the hospital date from this period. Since 1990 development on place Raphaël-Elizé has highlighted a fine group of 19C buildings in rue Carnot. The small port on the canalized part of the Sarthe used to receive sand-laden barges from the Loire. Nowadays it harbours about 20 craft for hire and there is also a **river boat**, for cruises along the Sarthe.

The town, which is famous for its shortbread biscuits (*sablés* in French), is the second largest economic centre in the Sarthe region. A favourable environment and pronounced dynamism have helped develop the foodstuff industry and diversify the local economy.

EXCURSIONS

Solesmes – *3km/2mi northeast. See SOLESMES.*

★ **Asnières-sur-Vègre** – *10km/6mi northeast. See ASNIÈRES-SUR-VÈGRE.*

Auvers-le-Hamon – *8.5km/5mi north.*
The nave of the church here is ornamented with 15C-16C **mural paintings** depicting a series of popular local saints and religious scenes: to the right St Mamès holding his intestines, St Martin on horseback, St Cénéré as a Cardinal, St Eutropius, St Andrew on his cross, St Luke riding a bull, the Nativity and the Flight into Egypt. To the left are a Dance of Death, St Avertin, St Apollonia whose teeth were pulled out by her torturers, St James and the Sacrifice of Isaac.

La Chapelle-du-Chêne – *6km/4mi southeast. In Les Noës turn left.*
The basilica of Notre-Dame-du-Chêne (Our Lady of the Oak) acts as a centre for religious activities as well as being the object of pilgrimages in honour of the Virgin Mary, who is represented by a 15C terracotta statuette. In the park there is a small-scale model of the Holy Sites of Jerusalem.

St-Denis-d'Anjou – *10.5km/6.5mi southwest.*
This village with its numerous pretty gardens has a 12C **fortified church** with keel vaulting and 12C and 15C **frescoes** which were discovered in 1947 and have been gradually restored. They depict St Christopher (west wall); the martyrdom of St John the Baptist and the legends of St Nicholas, St Giles and St Hubert on two levels. Opposite the church, which belonged to the Chapter of Angers, stands the 15C canons' house, which is now the town hall, and the 16C market, which has a very steep slate roof under which wine was bought and sold.

Chapelle de Varennes-Bourreau ⊘ – *6km/4mi southeast of St-Denis d'Anjou (D 615).*
This chapel nestles in the lush vegetation beside the River Sarthe; it is decorated with beautiful 12C and 15C frescoes: a mandorla surrounds Christ, whose hand is raised in blessing. The village of Varennes was formerly a small port engaged in the transport of wine to Angers before the vines were destroyed by phylloxera.

SACHÉ

Population 868
Michelin map 64 fold 14 or 232 fold 35 – 6.5km/4mi east of Azay-le-Rideau

Saché won a degree of renown through its association with the novelist **Honoré de Balzac** who stayed there on several occasions. A more recent famous resident was the American sculptor, **Alexander Calder** (1898-1976), who created mobiles and stabiles in abstract forms; one of his mobiles is displayed in the main square of Saché which bears his name.

Château de Saché ⊘ – The 16C and 18C château is set in a pleasant park. In the last century it belonged to M de Margonne, a friend of Balzac. The writer loved to escape to Saché from the bustle of Paris and the dunning of his creditors (he came here every year from 1828-38); in the peaceful surroundings of the château he wrote easily and the action of one of his novels, *Le Lys dans la Vallée*, is set in the Indre valley between Saché and Pont-de-Ruan. He found plenty of material locally for characters and places which appeared in his *Scènes de la vie* *de province*. The room where Balzac worked remains as it was in his lifetime. Other rooms in the château contain portraits, manuscripts, corrected proofs, first editions and various other souvenirs of the great writer.

Mobiles and stabiles

Having studied mechanical engineering, **Alexander Calder** turned to art, enrolling on a course in New York. He was a skilled draughtsman, able to capture a subject in a few swift strokes. Before long he had moved into making wire sculptures, initially of figurative, and later abstract subjects. From the early 1930s he began producing abstract constructions which moved, either by means of a motor or when touched. In 1932 Marcel Duchamp, a fellow member of the Abstraction-Création group in Paris with which Calder became associated at this time, coined the name "mobiles" for these, whereupon Arp came up with "stabiles" for Calder's non-moving sculptures. Calder is best known for the mobiles he made of tin shapes which were usually suspended or balanced in such a way as to move in response to draughts of air or even their own weight. Calder referred to them as his "four-dimensional drawings" and made no secret of the fact that his abstract geometrical creations were influenced in part by Mondrian.

Calder's reputation rests to no small degree on the fact that he was one of the first artists to include movement in sculptural art. Although he might be regarded as a precursor of Kinetic art, Calder was far more concerned with exploring free movement, rather than the more controlled motion produced by Kinetic artists. Most of Calder's works are in the United States (such as the enormous motorised mobile *Red, Black and Blue* hanging at Dallas airport), but there are others on show at the Tate Gallery in London and the Pompidou Centre in Paris.

ST-AIGNAN★

Population 3 672
Michelin map 64 fold 17 or 238 fold 15

St-Aignan stands on the south bank of the Cher at the heart of a region of woods and vineyards: Coteaux du Cher is the wine produced in Seigy and Couffy.

There is a picturesque view of the little town on its sloping site from the bridge or from the north bank on the road (D 675) north of Noyers. Both the church and the château are interesting; so too is rue Constant-Ragot which contains two Gothic houses and provides the best view of the chevet of the church. A stroll in the narrow streets and neighbouring square will reveal some 15C carved stone or half-timbered houses.

★ **Église St-Aignan** ⊘ – The collegiate church is a Romanesque building dating from the 11C and 12C with an impressive tower over the transept. A spacious tower-porch with delicately-carved capitals leads into the high, light nave; the capitals are finely carved into acanthus leaves and fantastic animals; the chancel and ambulatory have historiated capitals showing the Flight into Egypt *(north ambulatory)*, the Sacrifice of Isaac and King David *(south side)*.

★★ **Lower Church** – *Entrance in north transept*. Known once upon a time as the Church of St John or of the Grottoes, it was probably the early Romanesque church which was used as a stable or store during the Revolution. It is similar in plan to the chancel and decorated with **frescoes** (from the 12C to 15C): St John the Evangelist (15C) in the central chapel of the ambulatory; the legend of St Giles in the south chapel. A great Christ in Majesty in a double mandorla (1200) fills the half dome of the chancel and spreads his blessing through the mediation of St Peter and St James to the sick who are prostrate; the vault over the transept crossing shows the figure of Christ in Judgement resting on a rainbow.

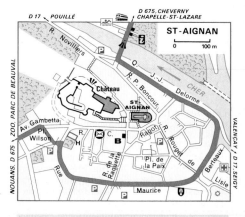

B Maison de la Prévôté

Château ⊙ – A great flight of steps starting from the church porch leads up to the château courtyard; pleasant view of the roofs of the town, one or two of slate among the tiles. The château consists of two buildings at right angles, mostly built in the 16C and backing on to the remains of the medieval fortifications on the east side of the courtyard. The elegant Renaissance dwelling has pilasters flanking the windows, carved dormer gables and a handsome stair in an octagonal turret terminating in a lantern. The terrace overlooks the turbulent Cher passing under the bridge.

Maison de la Prévôté (**B**) ⊙ – *On leaving the church cross the main street, rue Constant-Ragot.*
The 15C building is used for temporary exhibitions.

EXCURSIONS

Chapelle St-Lazare – *2km/1mi northeast on the road to Cheverny.*
On the north side of the road stands the chapel of St-Lazare, once part of a leper house, with a gable belfry.

★ **Zoo-Parc de Beauval** ⊙ – *4km/2.5mi south.*
The road downhill to Beauval zoological park offers a fine view of the local vineyards. A haven for both animals and flowers, this 11ha/27-acre park, built on undulating woodland, has been conceived as an old-fashioned rose garden (2 000 rose bushes), an African savannah and an Amazonian forest.
A visit to the zoo begins with its feathered residents. A 2 000m²/2 390yd² **aviary under glass** is home to several hundred exotic birds (including some tiny humming birds) free to flutter about in the lush environment of an equatorial forest complete with waterfalls and streams. Outside, there are about 2 000 more birds to be seen, including 400 or so parrots some of which are quite rare.
The next port of call is the section of the zoo given over to mammals. The zoo is home to several species of big cat, including some extremely rare white tigers with blue eyes. Numerous species of monkey and lemur are resident here as part of the European programme for the preservation of endangered species. Visitors will be fascinated by the intense, penetrating gaze and comical expression of small monkeys from the Congolese Basin or the Guinean heights, while the acrobatics of the athletic orang-utans and various gibbons who inhabit the magnificent huge **tropical hothouse**★ never fail to delight onlookers. The hothouse also contains a vivarium (with about a hundred snakes) and an aquaterrarium in which turtles and crocodiles are raised.
Several times a day during the tourist season, there is a half-hour opportunity to watch the underwater antics of a group of sea-lions. There are also half-hour flight demonstrations with 30 or so birds of prey, some of which have a wingspan of nearly 3m/10ft.
All the animals at Beauval were born in captivity.

Château de Chémery ⊙ – *13km/8mi northeast on D 675 turning right after St-Romain-sur-Cher onto D 63.*
The château (15C and 16C) is a mixture of medieval and Renaissance architecture. It was built on the site of a 12C fortress. In the grounds is a dovecot with spaces for 1 200 birds.

ST-BENOÎT-SUR-LOIRE★★

Population 1 880
Michelin map 64 fold 10 or 238 fold 6 – 10km/6mi southeast of Châteauneuf

The basilica of St-Benoît-sur-Loire is one of the most famous Romanesque buildings in France.

Foundation (7C) – According to Celtic tradition St-Benoît-sur-Loire was the place where the local Carnute druids assembled.
In 645 or 651 a group of Benedictine monks led by an abbot from Orléans came to this spot and founded a monastery which very soon gained the favour of the great as is shown by the gift of a shrine by a certain Mumma. In about 672 Mumma the Abbot of **Fleury**, as the monastery was called, learned that the body of St Benedict, the father of western monasticism who died in 547, was buried beneath the ruins of the abbey of Monte Cassino in Italy. He gave orders for the precious relic, a source of miracles and cures, to be transported to the banks of the Loire where it attracted great crowds of people and brought great success to the monastery.

Theodulf, Odo, Abbo and Gauzlin – Charlemagne gave Fleury to his adviser and friend, **Theodulf**, the talented bishop of Orléans, who founded two famous monastic schools, an external one for secular priests and an internal one for postulant monks. The scriptorium produced some beautiful work.

The death of Theodulf and the Viking invasions upset the courses of study and the smooth running of the monastery; discipline suffered as result.

In the 10C the situation underwent a spectacular change. In 930 **Odo**, a monk from the Touraine, became Abbot of Cluny; he imposed the Cluniac rule at Fleury and reopened the abbey school. St-Benoît regained its prosperity. Students flocked to the school, particularly from England, and the French king and princes offered gifts and patronage. The Archbishop of Canterbury, Odo the Good, received the Benedictine habit from Fleury.

The late 10C was dominated by **Abbo**, a famous scholar and teacher, who enjoyed the favour of the Capets. He entered Fleury as a child, studied in Paris and Reims where he was under the celebrated Gerbert, who had himself been at Fleury, and then returned c 975 to Fleury as head of studies. He added to the already extensive library and extended the area of study. During his reign as Abbot (from 988) the Abbey was at the forefront of western intellectual life with a particularly strong influence in England and the west of France. He was also a very able organizer of the monastic life of the Abbey. Abbo was very influential with Robert II and commissioned a monk called Aimoin to write a **History of the Franks**, which became the official chronicle expounding the "ideology" of the Capet monarchy. Abbo was assassinated in 1004 in a revolt.

The reign of Abbot **Gauzlin**, the future Archbishop of Bourges, early in the 11C is marked by the production of the so-called Gaignières **Evangelistary**, an illuminated manuscript – gold and silver lettering on purple parchment – which is the work of a Lombard painter, and by the construction of the handsome porch belfry.

The present church (crypt, chancel, transept) was built between 1067 and 1108; the nave was not completed until the end of the 12C.

Middle Ages to the present – In the 15C St-Benoît passed *in commendam*: this meant that the revenues of the abbey were granted by the monarch to "commendatory abbots", often laymen, who were simply beneficiaries and took no active part in the religious life of the community.

The monks did not always make such abbots welcome. Under François I they refused to receive Cardinal Duprat and shut themselves up in the tower of the porch. The King had to come in person, at the head of an armed force, to make them submit.

During the Wars of Religion (1562-98) one of these abbots, Odet de Châtillon-Coligny, the brother of the Protestant leader Admiral Coligny, was himself converted to Protestantism. He had the abbey of St-Benoît looted by Condé's Huguenot troops.

The treasure was melted down – the gold casket containing the relics of the Saint alone weighed 17.5kg/39lb – the marvellous library was sold and its precious manuscripts, about 2 000 in number, were scattered to the four corners of Europe. Some are now to be found in Berne, Rome, Leyden, Oxford and Moscow.

The celebrated Congregation of St-Maur, introduced to St-Benoît in 1627 by Cardinal Richelieu, restored its spiritual and intellectual life. The abbey was closed at the Revolution, its archives transferred to Orléans and its property dispersed. At the beginning of the First Empire the monastic buildings were destroyed and the church fell into disrepair. In 1835 it was registered as a historical monument, and it was restored on various occasions between 1836 and 1923. Monastic life was revived there in 1944.

The poet and painter **Max Jacob** (1876-1944) retired to the abbey in St-Benoît-sur-Loire, before he was arrested by the Gestapo in 1944. He died in the camp at Drancy and his remains are buried in the local cemetery.

★★ BASILICA ⊙ *45min*

This imposing basilica was built between 1067 and 1218. The towers were originally much taller.

★★ **Belfry Porch** – The belfry originally stood by itself, and is one of the finest examples of Romanesque art. It is well worth taking a close look at the richly carved capitals with their abaci and corbels beautifully carved in handsome golden stone from the Nevers region. Stylised plants and, more particularly, flowing acanthus leaves alternate with fantastic animals, scenes from the Apocalypse, and events in the life of Christ and the Virgin Mary. On the porch (second column from the left), one of the capitals is signed *Umbertus me fecit.*

Nave – This was completed in 1218 in the transitional Romanesque style. It is very luminous with its white stonework and high vaulting which lets in plenty of light. The organ loft was added c 1700.

Transept – Like the chancel, this was finished in 1108. The dome, built on superimposed squinches, carries the central bell-tower. Under the dome are the stalls dated 1413 and the remains of a choir screen in carved wood presented in 1635 by Richelieu, when he was Commendatory Abbot of St-Benoît. In the north transept is the precious 14C alabaster statue of Notre-Dame-de-Fleury. Max Jacob used to pray before this statue.

★★ **Chancel** – The very long Romanesque chancel was built between 1065 and 1108; note the décor of blind arcades with sculptured capitals forming a triforium. The ambulatory with radiating chapels is typical of a church built for crowds and processions; this floor plan can be found in most Benedictine churches.

St-Benoît-sur-Loire – Porch of the basilica (detail)

The floor is paved with a Roman mosaic which was transported from Italy in 1531 by Cardinal Duprat; it is similar to the style popular in the eastern part of the Roman Empire. The recumbent figure is that of Philippe I, the fourth Capet King, who died in 1108.

★ **Crypt** – This impressive masterpiece of the second half of the 11C has kept its original appearance. Large round columns form a double ambulatory with radiating chapels round the large central pillar containing the modern shrine of St Benedict, whose relics have been venerated here since the 8C.

ST-CALAIS

Population 4 063
Michelin map 64 fold 5 or 238 fold 1

St-Calais, on the border between Maine and the Vendôme region, is a market town dominated by the ruins of a medieval château. A few old gables still look down on the narrow streets.

Five bridges span the River Anille. The district on the west bank grew up round the Benedictine abbey which was founded in the reign of Childebert (6C) by Calais, a coenobite monk from Auvergne. The monastery was destroyed during the Revolution but the few 17C buildings which survived are now occupied by the library, the theatre and the museum.

Apple Turnover Festival (Fête du chausson aux pommes) – This great festival has taken place every year since 1581 (first weekend in September) to commemorate the end of the plague.

SIGHTS

Église Notre-Dame – Construction of the church began in 1425 with the chancel; the building is a mixture of the Flamboyant Gothic and Renaissance styles. The bell-tower is surmounted by a crocketed stone steeple.

The Italianate **façade★** was finished in 1549 and is typical of the second Renaissance. The carved panels of the twin doors portray scenes from the life of the Virgin Mary; above in the transom are two horns of plenty framed by a semicircular arch. The whole doorway is flanked by two Ionic pilasters. The charming side doors are surmounted by curvilinear pediments and niches. A pedimented window and an oculus are set in the upper part of the gable which is surmounted by five pinnacles ornamented with statues.

The first three bays of the interior are Renaissance; the vaulting with pendentives springs from majestic columns with Ionic capitals. The 17C loft came from the abbey and the organ itself is of the same date. Restored in 1974, it is the pride and joy of the church's organists. A Baroque retable adorns the high altar; a strong cupboard to the right of the chancel contains the "Shroud of St-Calais" which is made of Sassanid (6C Persian) material.

Riverside (Quais de l'Anille) – There are pleasant views of the riverside wash-houses, now covered in moss, and gardens of flowers against a background of picturesque roofs.

ST-CALAIS

Coursimault (Av.)	2
Dauphin (R. du)	3
Dr-Baudrillard (R. du)	4
Dr-Ollivier (R. du)	5

Guichet (R. du)	9
Image (R. de l')	13
Jean-Jaurès (Quai)	14
Maubert (R. H.)	17
Poignant (R. Fernand)	18
Sadi-Carnot (R.)	20

ST-ÉTIENNE-DE-CHIGNY

Population 1 164
Michelin map 64 fold 14 or 232 fold 35 – 13km/8mi northeast of Langeais

Set back from the village which is on the Loire embankment is the **Vieux Bourg** nestling in the Bresme valley, featuring several old houses with steep gables.

★ **Church** – The church was built in 1542 by Jean Binet, major-domo to François I and Mayor of Tours, whose arms appear both inside and out in the form of a mourning band. The nave is covered by a remarkable **hammerbeam roof**; the tie beams are carved with enormous grotesque masks and, in the chancel, Jonah in the belly of the whale. The 16C **stained-glass window** in the chevet shows the Crucifixion flanked by the figures of the donors, Jean Binet and his wife, Jeanne de la Lande. In the north transept hangs a 16C painting of the *Virgin and Child* by the French school; there is also a mural of St Clement, Pope and patron saint of boatmen. The font dates from the 16C.

ST-FLORENT-LE-VIEIL

Population 2 511
Michelin map 63 fold 19 or 232 fold 30
Local map see Vallée de la LOIRE: Chinon-Champtoceaux

The hill on which St-Florent is built can be seen from a distance. From the bridge over the Loire there is a good **view** of the town and its hilltop church.

The Mercy of Bonchamps – The revolt in the Vendée *(see Les Mauges)* began in St-Florent on 12 March 1793. The Whites were defeated at Cholet and retreated to St-Florent on 18 October with their prisoners and their wounded, including **Bonchamps** who was near to death. Incensed by the atrocities committed by Westermann and the Mayence Army, the Whites prepared to avenge their leader by massacring the Republicans imprisoned in the church. Hearing by chance of their impending fate, Bonchamps begged his cousin Autichamps to obtain a reprieve for the prisoners. Autichamps ran to the church shouting that Bonchamps wanted the prisoners to be spared and they were spared. Among their number was the father of David d'Angers, the sculptor, who in gratitude created the moving monument in the church.

Church – The church, once attached to the old Benedictine monastery, stands at the top of Glonne hill. It boasts towers and west front in a forthright Classical style. In one of the north chapels is the white marble **tomb of Bonchamps★** (1825) with David d'Angers's representation of the White leader as a hero of old. Like the chancel, the crypt was restored in the 19C; it has a 15C painted sculpture of the Virgin Mary.

PRISONNIERS !

Tomb of Bonchamps by David d'Angers

Esplanade – The tree-lined esplanade near the church ends in a column which was erected in honour of the Duchess of Angoulême, daughter of Louis XVI. From the terrace there is an extensive **view★** of the Loire valley.

Musée d'Histoire locale et des Guerres de Vendée ⓥ – This museum housed in the 17C Sacré-Cœur chapel contains documents, costumes (old-fashioned types of traditional headgear), uniforms and weapons mostly relating to the Vendée War and its leaders *(see Les MAUGES)*.

Ferme abbatiale des Coteaux ⓥ – The once-fortified buildings of this abbey farm now house the **carrefour des Mauges** (Environmental Centre) with thematic displays on the natural and man-made heritage of the Mauges region and aquariums containing varieties of fish found in the Loire.

ST-GEORGES-SUR-LOIRE

Population 3 101
Michelin map 63 folds 19, 20 or 232 fold 31
Local map see Vallée de la LOIRE: Chinon-Champtoceaux

St-Georges, on the north bank of the Loire, is situated not far from some famous vineyards, "La Coulée de Serrant" and "La Roche aux Moines", where some of Anjou's finest white wines are produced.

Abbey – The abbey was founded in 1158 by the Augustinian Order. Up to 1790 it was occupied by a scholarly community which emerged in 1635 as the result of an effort to bring together the different Augustinian communities: the Genovefans, who were regular canons belonging to the Abbey of St Geneviève in Paris.

The handsome building, which dates from 1684 and is occupied by the town hall, contains a grand staircase with a remarkable wrought-iron banister and the chapter-house with its original wainscoting where temporary exhibitions are held.

EXCURSION

★★ Château de Serrant – *2km/1mi on N 23 to Angers. See Château de SERRANT.*

ST-PATERNE-RACAN

Population 1 449
Michelin map 64 south of fold 4 or 232 fold 23

St-Paterne stretches out along the Escotais, which is bordered by riverside wash-houses and weeping willows.

Church – The church contains interesting works of art, some of which came from the nearby Abbey of La Clarté-Dieu. The 16C terracotta group to the left of the high altar portrays the Adoration of the Magi; at the centre is a charming **Virgin and Child★**.

In the nave, 18C polychrome statues represent the four great Latin Doctors of the Church – Ambrose, Augustine, Jerome and Gregory the Great – while in the south chapel a large retable (the Virgin of the Rosary) of the same period is accompanied by a 16C terracotta group of St Anne and the Virgin Mary.

EXCURSIONS

Château de la Roche-Racan – *2km/1mi south on D 28. See Château de la ROCHE-RACAN.*

St-Christophe-sur-le-Nais – *2.5km/1.5mi north on D 6.*
Also in the Escotais valley this village is the scene of a pilgrimage in honour of St Christopher (penultimate Sunday in July). The **church** is in reality composed of two separate buildings, an old 11C-14C priory chapel and the parish church with its 16C nave and belfry.
On the threshold of the nave a gigantic St Christopher welcomes the visitor. To the right in a recess is a reliquary bust of the saint. To the left of the chancel, the door leading to the prior's oratory is surmounted by a fine 14C statue of the Virgin and Child. Two Renaissance medallions adorn the church's timber roof.

Neuvy-le-Roi – *9km/6mi east on D 54.*
The **church**, which dates from the 12C and 16C, has a Romanesque chancel and a nave covered with Angevin vaulting; note in the north aisle the complex pattern of vaulting with projecting keystones (16C), and to the south of the chancel the elegant seigneurial chapel, also with projecting keystones.
On the outside of the north aisle there are many lateral gable ends, a feature frequently seen in the region.

ST-VIÂTRE

Population 1 063
Michelin map 64 north of fold 19 or 238 fold 17

This smart little town in the Sologne was formerly a place of pilgrimage containing the relics of St Viâtre, a hermit who retired here in the 6C and, so the legend says, made himself a coffin from the trunk of an aspen tree.

Church – The 15C transept gable is built of brick with a black diaper pattern and edged with spiral rosettes. A sturdy bell-tower porch shelters the 14C door.
At the chancel step stands a remarkable carved wood desk (18C) of surprising size. In the south transept are four **painted panels★** dating from the early 16C, giving a realistic evocation of the life of Christ and of St Viâtre.

Reposoir St-Viâtre – This small brick building (15C) at the north entrance to the village is a wayside altar.

STE-CATHERINE-DE-FIERBOIS

Population 539
Michelin map 64 southwest of fold 15 or 232 fold 35

The spirit of Joan of Arc hovers over this village which lies grouped round its church east of the main road (N 10).

Church – On 23 April 1429, following directions given by Joan of Arc, a sword marked with five crosses was found on this site. It was supposed to have been placed there by **Charles Martel** after his victory over the Saracens at Poitiers in 732. The chapel was rebuilt in 1479 and completed in the reign of Charles VIII, whose coat of arms appears on the building together with that of Anne of Brittany. The chapel, restored in 1859, is in the Flamboyant Gothic style with an interesting door beneath a pierced pediment.
The interior vaulting springs directly from the piers. Hanging under a glass cover on the north wall of the nave is a small but very realistic 15C Entombment. The south transept contains an unusual 15C altar; on it stands a 15C statue of St Catherine whose image is also carved on the front. Opposite is a rare confessional in the Flamboyant style, very delicately carved.

Maison du Dauphin – The door of this house (1415) to the left of the church is flanked by two sphinxes. Note the charming carving on the lip of the well in the courtyard.

Aumônerie de Boucicault ⊙ – *On the opposite side of the street to the Maison du Dauphin.*
Once a guest house with dormitories and a chapel dedicated to St James for pilgrims on the way to Santiago de Compostela in Spain, the almonry (1415) now houses a **museum** of local history.

STE-MAURE-DE-TOURAINE

Population 3 969
Michelin map 68 north of folds 4, 5 or 232 fold 35

This small town occupies a sunny site on a knoll commanding the Manse valley. The settlement, which is Roman in origin, developed in the 6C round the tombs of St Britta and St Maurus, and then round the keep built by Fulk Nerra. The Rohan-Montbazon family were the overlords from 1492 to the Revolution.

The town is known for its busy poultry markets and its local goats' milk cheeses. A national Cheese Fair is held annually in June.

Church – The church dates from the 11C but its original appearance was altered when it was restored in 1866. A chapel to the right of the chancel has an attractive 16C white marble statue of the Virgin Mary by the Italian school. In the central apse there are two painted panels, one depicting the Last Supper (16C), and the other, Christ on a gold background; the relics of St Maurus are venerated here. The crypt (11C and 12C) has a curious series of archaic Romanesque arcades and a small lapidary museum.

Covered market – The 17C covered market *(halles)* at the top of the town was built by the Rohan family.

Atelier de foie gras ⊙ – *1km/0.5mi south on N 10.*
Conceived as an introduction to the different stages in the fabrication of this prized delicacy, the centre seeks to reinstate *foie gras* locally, especially as Touraine was once an important region of production. The pyramid on top of the building is a reference to Egypt, the country where *foie gras* was born.

PLATEAU de STE-MAURE

Round trip starting from Ste-Maure *56km/35mi – about 1hr*

The plateau is dissected by the green valleys of two rivers – the Manse and the Esves – and bordered by three others – the Indre (north), the Vienne (west) and the Creuse (south). It is composed of lacustrine limestone which is easily eroded by running water; in the south there are bands of sand and shell, deposited during the Tertiary Era by the Faluns Sea and once used to improve the soil.

Leave Ste-Maure on D 59 going southeast.

The line of the road running through the valleys between limestone bluffs is often marked by a row of poplars.

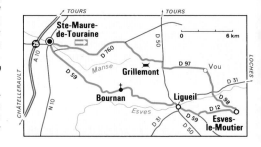

Bournan – The village church is Romanesque; it has a beautiful apse and a tower over the side chapel topped by a faceted spire.

Ligueil – Ligueil is a small town built of white stone; there are a few old houses. The decorated wooden washing place, now restored, is on the edge of the town on the road to Loches (D 31).

Esves-le-Moutier – The village, which lies on the south bank of the Esves, takes its name from a priory which was surrounded by a fortified wall. The **church** (10C-12C) has a massive square tower with bartizans. The interior contains a 17C wooden gilt altarpiece.

Château de Grillemont – The huge white château stands halfway up a slope overlooking an attractive **valley**★ of meadows round a lake; the slopes are capped by oak and pine woods. The huge round towers of the castle with their pepper-pot roofs were built in the reign of Charles VII for Lescoet, the governor of Loches castle; in 1765 the 15C curtain wall was replaced by magnificent classical buildings.

Admission times and charges for the sights described are listed at the end of the guide.
Every sight for which there are times and charges is identified by the symbol ⊙ in the Sights section of the guide.

Vallée de la SARTHE

Michelin map 64 folds 1 to 3 or 232 folds 20 to 22

The River Sarthe flows slowly southwest through the beautiful Maine countryside, cutting meanders into the soft soil of the Upper Cretaceous rocks. Around Sablé the water had to make its way through a granite outcrop. The river is navigable between Le Mans and the confluence with the Mayenne along lateral canals running parallel to it. The countryside through which it flows consists of woodland alternating with meadows and fields of cereals, potatoes and cabbages.

FROM LE MANS TO SABLÉ *73km/45mi – about 3hr*

★★ **Le Mans** - *See Le MANS. Allow a day.*
Leave Le Mans on N 23.

Spay - *See Le MANS: Excursions.*
Take D 51 to Fillé.

Fillé – The village is on the north bank of the Sarthe; the **church** ⊙, which was rebuilt after the Second World War, contains a large painted statue of the Virgin Mary (late 16C), glazed somewhat by the fire of August 1944.

La-Suze-sur-Sarthe – The bridge over the Sarthe provides a good view of the river, the remains of the castle (15C) and the church.
Leave La-Suze on D 79 going west through woods towards Fercé.

Fercé-sur-Sarthe – Attractive views from the bridge and from the road up to the church.
Return across the river and turn right onto V 5 to St-Jean-du-Bois; turn right onto D 229.

The road passes a troubadour-style castle *(left)* and provides several glimpses of the Sarthe before reaching Noyen.

Noyen-sur-Sarthe – Noyen is built in terraces on the sloping north bank overlooking the canal which at this point runs parallel to the broad Sarthe. From the bridge there is an attractive **view** of a weir, a mill, an island of poplars, a jumble of roofs and little gardens, the beach and another island.
Take D 69 north to Pirmil.

Pirmil – The **church**, a Romanesque building with buttresses, dates from 1165. The capitals are beautifully carved. The springers of the ogive vaulting are decorated with figures of a saint, a bishop and a priest and a grotesque head.
Return south through Noyen taking D 41 to Malicorne-sur-Sarthe.

Malicorne-sur-Sarthe – Malicorne is pleasantly situated at the water's edge. From the bridge there is a pretty view of a mill and the poplars along the bank. On the eastern side of the town, on the road (D 133) to Mézeray, there is a working **pottery** ⊙ which produces pieces in the perforated Malicorne style, as well as reproductions of period pieces. The 11C **church** contains a recumbent figure of one of the lords of Chaources (chapel on the right of the nave), a *Pietà* (south transept) and an attractive 16C piscina (left wall of the nave).
Downstream, set back from the south bank of the river in a beautiful park, stands the 17C **château** (altered) where Madame de Sévigné liked to stay, which belonged to the Marquise de Lavardin. The château has turrets and mansard roofs and is surrounded by a moat which is spanned by a charming hump-back bridge.

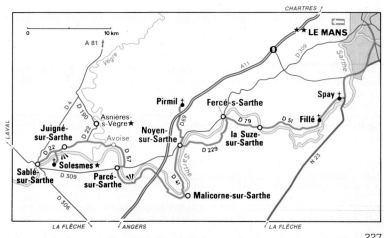

Take D 8 west towards Parcé, making a detour along a small country track (V 1) to the right via Dureil, which provides attractive glimpses of the River Sarthe before rejoining D 8.

Parcé-sur-Sarthe – Parcé is a charming little village grouped round a Romanesque tower with a mill on the river. The cypress-girt cemetery at the entrance to the village makes a peaceful setting for the chapel with its gable-belfry.

After crossing the river and the canal, turn left onto D 57. On leaving Avoise note, on the left, La Perrigne de Cry (private property), a 16C manor overlooking the river. Take V 4 to Juigné, cross the River Vègre and join D 22, turning left.

Juigné-sur-Sarthe – Juigné is a pleasant village set on a promontory which juts south across the valley. There are 16C and 17C houses and the 18C château which belonged to the Marquis of Juigné. From the church square there is a view of the river below and of Solesmes abbey downstream.

Solesmes – *See SOLESMES.*

Take D 22 alongside the canal and the old marble quarries to Sablé.

Sablé-sur-Sarthe – *See SABLÉ-SUR-SARTHE.*

SAUMUR ★★

Population 30 131
Michelin map 64 fold 12 or 232 fold 33
Local map see Vallée de la LOIRE: Chinon-Champtoceaux

Saumur is famous for its cavalry school, its wines – especially its sparkling wines – its medal makers and its mushrooms; local production of mushrooms represents 42% of the national figure. In recent decades, traditional industry in Saumur has diversified and become more modern, being joined by the manufacture of toys and by mechanical, plastics and electrical firms (Rocher, Barphone, Dalsouple). Saumur also has the largest factory making carnival masks in Europe (César-Masport). Every year a tattoo using horses and motor transport is given by the **Cadre Noir** on the vast Place du Chardonnet *(see Calendar of events)*, drawing large numbers of spectators. Repeat performances are given in the Riding School of the National Equitation Centre in Terrefort *(see below)*.

On summer evenings in July there are the **Tous aux Paradiableries** performances by strolling players in the streets. Local inhabitants dress in period costume in honour of famous figures who have helped to put Saumur on the map. Spectators are encouraged to join in.

An eventful history – Charles the Bald built a fortified monastery in the 9C to house the relics of St Florent who converted the region to Christianity in the 4C, but it was not long before it was destroyed by the Vikings. In the 11C Saumur was the subject of numerous conflicts between the Count of Blois and the Count of Anjou. In 1203 the town was captured by Philippe-Auguste. The castle was destroyed on several occasions and then restored or rebuilt. From the time of Louis IX (13C) Saumur shared the destiny of the House of Anjou.

In the late 16C and early 17C the town enjoyed its real heyday. It was one of the great centres of Protestantism. Henri III gave it as a stronghold to the King of Navarre, the future Henri IV, who appointed as Governor **Duplessis-Mornay**, a great soldier, scholar and fervent Reformer, who was known by the Roman Catholics as the Huguenot Pope. He founded a Protestant academy which won widespread renown. In 1611 a general assembly of the Protestant churches was held there to consolidate their organisation following the death of Henri IV and the departure of Sully. Louis XIII grew alarmed at the Protestant danger and ordered the town walls to be demolished in 1623. The Revocation of the Edict of Nantes in 1685 dealt Saumur a fatal blow; many of the inhabitants emigrated and the Protestant church was demolished.

École d'application de l'arme blindée et de la cavalerie (AY) – In 1763 the Carabiniers Regiment, a crack corps recruited from the best horsemen in the army, was sent to Saumur. The present central building was constructed between 1767 and 1770 as their barracks. It now houses the Armoured Corps and Cavalry School which trains the elite of the French cavalry and took its modern title in 1943. Distinct from the military school is the **École Nationale d'Équitation** (National Equitation Centre) which comprises the **Cadre Noir** (Black Squad) situated at St-Hilaire-St-Florent on the Terrefort and Verrie plateaux near Saumur.

Saumur Cadets – In June 1940 the officers and cadets of the Cavalry School made it a point of honour to defend the passage of the Loire. For three days, from 18 to 20 June, although inferior in number and having only training equipment, they performed many heroic feats and succeeded in holding the Germans in check on a 25km/16mi front between Gennes and Montsoreau.

3Bis/MICHELIN

Château de Saumur

★★ CHÂTEAU (BZ) ⓥ *1hr 30min*

The château is compact and solid, but the vertical lines of its pointed and ribbed towers lend it a certain grace. Despite being a fortress it is decorated as if it were a country house with sculpted machicolations and balustrades at the windows overlooking the courtyard. It stands high above the Loire valley on a sort of pedestal created by the star-shaped 16C fortifications.

A succession of fortresses has been built on the promontory. The present building, which succeeded Louis IX's castle, was rebuilt at the end of the 14C by Louis I, Duke of Anjou, and completed by Louis II. The interior was altered in the 15C by René d'Anjou and external fortifications were added at the end of the 16C by Duplessis-Mornay. Under Louis XIV and Louis XV it was the residence of the Governor of Saumur; it subsequently became a prison and then barracks and it now houses three museums. From the château terrace there is a fine **panorama**★ of the town and the valleys of the Thouet *(south)* and the Loire *(east, west)*.

★★ Musée des Arts décoratifs – The exhibits in this museum which include the Lair Collection, form a fine display of decorative works of art from the Middle Ages and the Renaissance period: Limoges enamels, alabaster and wooden sculptures, tapestries, furniture, paintings, church ornaments and a collection of faience and French porcelain (17C and 18C) together with furniture and tapestries from the same period. The 15C and 16C tapestries include the *Savages' Ball*, the *Return from the Hunt*, the *Coronation of Vespasian* and the *Capture of Jerusalem* (the last two make up part of a tapestry series on the *Story of Titus*).

★ Musée du Cheval – The equine museum depicts the history of the saddle horse and equitation in different countries down the years: collections of saddles, bits, stirrups and spurs, fine engravings referring to the Saumur Cavalry School, horse racing and famous thoroughbreds as well as splendid harness from the world over (Asia, North America and Africa).

Musée de la Figurine-Jouet ⓥ – The collection of old toys and figurines in the château's powdermill will delight both young and old not least because of the great variety of displays. Among them are the *Vertuni* series from the early 20C, made of plaster dipped in lead and representing the kings of France, *Lucotte* lead soldiers, late-19C toys made of plaster and flour, small unbreakable *Quiralu* soldiers dating from 1933 and various other items.

ADDITIONAL SIGHTS

★ Old town (BY) – The narrow twisting streets between the castle and the bridge still follow their original line; in some areas the old houses have been preserved while in others new constructions have been built in the medieval style or are resolutely modern but full of surprises (south of the church of St-Pierre).

Along the main shopping street, rue St-Jean, and in the square, **place St-Pierre (16)**, half-timbered houses and 18C mansions with wrought-iron balconies stand side by side. The new market in the corner (1982) blends with the older styles.

SAUMUR

H Hôtel de ville   M¹ Musée de l'École de cavalerie

★ **Église St-Pierre (BY)** – The church is Plantagenet Gothic except for the west front which collapsed in the 17C and was rebuilt. The beautiful Romanesque door in the south transept leads into the interior which is hung with two series of 16C **tapestries**★ *(these are currently being restored and are therefore not on display)*. Regular concerts of organ music are given here.

★ **Hôtel de ville (BY H)** – Only the left-hand section of the town hall is old (16C). Originally the Loire flowed past the foundations and the building was a bridgehead and part of the town walls, hence its military appearance. The façade facing the courtyard is in the Gothic-Renaissance transitional style with some fine sculpture.

★ **Église Notre-Dame-de-Nantilly (BZ)** – This is a fine Romanesque church. Louis XI, who had a great devotion to the Virgin Mary, added the right aisle; his oratory was used as a baptismal chapel. A pillar on the left in the same aisle bears an epitaph composed by King René d'Anjou for his nurse Tiphaine. Opposite stands the enamelled cross which belonged to Giles, Archbishop of Tyre and keeper of the Seals under Louis IX. The 12C painted wooden statue of Our Lady of Nantilly was placed in the apse on the right of the chancel. There is a tapestry depicting the Tree of Jesse in the left transept. In the nave, there are 18 interesting historiated capitals. The organ case, which is supported by telamones, dates from 1690.
There are fine **tapestries**★★ dating from the 15C and 16C except for eight in the nave which were made at Aubusson in the 17C and depict scenes from the lives of Christ and the Virgin.

★ **Musée de l'École de cavalerie (AY M¹)** ⊙ – *Entrance in avenue Foch.*
This museum's rich display of souvenirs, created in 1936 from Barbet de Vaux collections, traces the history of the school and the heroic deeds of the French cavalry and the armoured corps since the 18C.

The exhibits include ornamental swords inlaid with mother-of-pearl, ebony or tortoiseshell and engraved sabres which belonged to Egyptian Mamelukes or to marshals and generals of the French Empire: two damascened sabres which were the property of Kellermann, pistols which belonged to Augereau and Daumesnil, the baton of Brune and varius items of equipment used by Kléber and Bertrand. The uniforms of Napoleon's Grand Army and the Imperial Guard are illustrated by a collection of Sèvres and Meissen porcelain figures, and a series of helmets, cuirasses and sabres which were used by dragoons and hussars.

It is interesting to note the names of some of those men who served in the cavalry of the African Army between 1830 and 1962: Bugeaud, Gallieni (the saviour of Paris in 1914), Charles de Foucault, who was an officer before he became a missionary, Lyautey and de Lattre de Tassigny.

Musée des Blindés, Saumur

Finally the history of the French cavalry is traced from 1870 through the two World Wars and the Indo-Chinese and Algerian campaigns.

St-Chamond tank

★ **Musée des Blindés (AZ)** ⊘ – *Via boulevard Louis-Renault; follow the signposts.*

This new museum and information centre on tanks houses over a hundred vehicles (tanks, armoured vehicles, artillery equipment), many of which are in working order, coming from a dozen or more countries. It offers a survey of the history of the Armoured Corps and Cavalry from 1917 up to the present. The most prestigious or rare exhibits are the **St-Chamond** and the **Schneider** (the first French tanks), the Renault FT 17 (French tank used in the very last stages of the First World War), the Somua S 35, the B1bis (issued to the 2nd Armoured Division under General de Gaulle in 1940) and German tanks dating from the French Campaign until the fall of Berlin (Panzers III and IV, Panther, Tiger), the Comet A 34 (the British tank used in the Normandy landing), the Churchill A 22, the Sherman M 4 and AMX 13 and 30.

Besides examples of armoured tanks which played a part in the Allied landing of 6 June 1944 (practically all the different models are displayed), there are vehicles belonging to the UN peace-keeping forces, as well as numerous heavy and light tanks from a variety of nations (Germany, Russia, Britain, the United States, Sweden etc).

Several display windows and dioramas illustrate the way tanks are used in combat.

During the "Carrousel", in July, the Tank Museum exhibits several of these vehicles, which it has carefully restored, driven by trainees from the École d'application de l'arme blindée et de la cavalerie.

Église Notre-Dame-des-Ardilliers – *On the eastern edge of the city, Quai L.-Mayaud on ② on the plan, D 947.*

This beautiful 17C church building is one of the most popular places of pilgrimage in France. Devotion to Our Lady of Ardilliers began to develop in the reign of François I thanks to a miraculous statue a farm labourer was supposed to have discovered on this spot in the previous century, but it was to reach its height in the 17C when the number of pilgrims exceeded 10 000 a year.

ST-HILAIRE-ST-FLORENT *2km/1mi northwest on D 751.*

The village consists of one long street straggling at the foot of the hill beside the River Thouet. It is effectively a suburb of Saumur, which is given over mainly to the production of a famous sparkling white wine made by the Champagne method; all along on either side of the road there is one wine cellar after another.

Bouvet-Ladubay ⊘ – From its premises in galleries hollowed out of the tufa rock, this leading producer of Saumur Brut unveils the stages involved in the production of its wines, from the initial fermentation to the sophisticated design of its bottles. There is an outstanding collection of about 6 000 labels in specially designed display cupboards dating from the beginning of the 20C. A wine-tasting school is open to tourists, amateur wine-lovers and professionals alike.

Galerie d'art contemporain Bouvet-Ladubay ⊘ – This contemporary art gallery consists of nine rooms exhibiting works by artists of today, following their search for new directions to take in their various fields (architecture, sculpture, painting). There is also a section on journalism. A delightful little theatre founded in the late 19C to entertain staff has just been reopened.

Musée du Masque ⊘ – The Saumur-based company César has been in the business of making masks for carnivals, theatres and circuses since 1842. This museum presents visitors with a survey of their whole production, ranging from masks portraying the soldiers of Napoleon's guard and Punch and Judy type characters, fashioned from cardboard and papier-mâché around 1870, to the contemporary models made in synthetics for television and cinema. Familiar faces of today include Madonna, the racing driver Alain Prost, the actor Gérard Depardieu in the role of Cyrano de Bergerac, Belmondo and a number of French politicians.

D'après photo de l'Association «Les Amis du Cadre Noir»

Rider of the Cadre Noir performing the croupade

★ **École nationale d'équitation** ⊘ – The riding school was opened in 1972 on the Terrefort and Verrie plateaux. It is a modern establishment consisting of several units each comprising a granary where foodstuffs are stored, a large dressage arena that can seat 1 200 spectators and stabling for 400 horses with harness rooms and showers. One of the vocations of the school, which comes under the auspices of the French Ministry for Youth and Sport, is to maintain the level of French horsemanship and further its renown. The **Cadre Noir** (Black Squad) has been based here since 1984. A fundamental part of the school, it is involved in all its projects and gives its traditional repeat performances of *Manège* (dressage) and *Sauteurs en liberté* (jumps) in France and all over the world.

Musée du Champignon ⊘ – *2km/1mi west on D 751.*
Large areas of the old tufa quarries which pit the hillsides around Saumur are used for the cultivation of mushrooms which need humidity and a constant temperature (between 11°C and 14°C). Mushrooms have been grown in the quarries since the time of Napoleon I, but production has escalated to industrial scale and now takes up some 800km/497mi of galleries yielding some 200 000 tonnes per annum. This museum presents various methods of cultivation in a working environment; the oldest method of growing in mushroom beds is being replaced by more modern techniques using wooden crates, plastic bags, bales of straw and the trunks of trees. Apart from button-mushrooms, new types of cultivated mushroom such as shiitake, pleurotus (oyster mushrooms) and *pied-bleu* are also on show.
The visit ends with two exhibitions: "Forest Mushrooms" (over 200 varieties on show) and "Fossils from the Saumur Region".

EXCURSIONS

Bagneux – *South of Saumur on ③ on the plan.*
Bagneux, which lies at the heart of the oldest inhabited region of Anjou, is an old village on the banks of the Thouet.

Musée du moteur ⊘ – *No 18 rue Alphonse-Cailleau (second street on the left after Fouchard bridge).* The engines displayed in this museum have been collected by mechanics enthusiasts, most of whom attended the Saumur Industrial School and wish to preserve and restore old and contemporary engines.
Return to rue du Pont-Fouchard for a short distance. Beyond the town hall, bear left into rue du Dolmen.

Dolmen ⊘ – The Great Dolmen, situated in the centre of the village itself, is one of the most remarkable megalithic dolmens in Europe. It measures 20m long by 7m wide (66ft by 23ft) and consists of 16 standing stones (weighing about 500 tonnes) forming a passage and supporting a roof 3m/10ft high which is composed of four capstones.

★ **Château de Boumois** – *7km/4mi northwest on ① on the plan. See Château de BOUMOIS.*

St-Cyr-en-Bourg – *8km/5mi south on D 93.*
A visit to the **Cave des Vignerons de Saumur** ⊘ is a good way of learning more about the whole wine-making process, from the grape to the finished product, in a series of underground galleries reaching 25m/82ft below ground level; a motorised vehicle circulates in the galleries. There is a commentary and wine tasting in a special chamber.

SAVONNIÈRES

Population 2 030
Michelin map 64 fold 14 or 232 fold 35 – 2.5km/1.5mi east of Villandry
Local map see Vallée de la LOIRE: Orléans-Chinon

The church has a beautiful Romanesque doorway decorated with animals and doves.

Grottes pétrifiantes ⊙ – *On the western edge of the town on the road to Villandry (D 7).*
The petrifying caves were formed in the Secondary Era. In the 12C they were used as quarries and then partially flooded with water. The continuing infiltration of water saturated with limestone is slowly creating stalactites, pools and curtains. There is a reconstruction of prehistoric fauna and a **musée de la Pétrification** with lithographic stones and 19C copper matrices. There is also the opportunity to indulge in some wine tasting in the caves.

SEGRÉ

Population 6 434
Michelin map 63 south of fold 9 or 232 fold 18

The schist houses of Segré cascade down the slope to the river which is bordered by quays and spanned by picturesque bridges.
The town is the capital of the Segréen, a region of woods and meadows devoted to mixed farming and also known for its high-grade iron ore.

Old Bridge – The humpback bridge over the River Oudon offers pretty views of the old parts of the town.

Chapelle St-Joseph – There is a good view of the old town and the Oudon valley from this chapel.

EXCURSIONS

★ **Château de la Lorie** ⊙ – *2km/1mi southeast; after leaving Segré, take the road to Cholet.*
La Lorie is an imposing 18C château approached up a long avenue of trees which meet overhead. The château stands in a setting of formal French gardens.
A dry moat surrounds a square courtyard which is bordered on three sides by ranges of buildings with white tufa tiles; a statue of Minerva "the Bearer of Peace" adorns the central range, which was built in the 17C by René Le Pelletier, Provost General of Anjou; the château's imposing dimensions are due to the addition of the two wings and the symmetrical outbuildings (added in the late 18C).
The same nobility of line and form is to be found in the interior: the great gallery decorated with beautiful Chinese vases, the late-18C marble salon, the adjoining chapel and the 18C woodwork in the dining room. The great Salon is the most unusual; it is sumptuously decorated with Sablé marble and was designed by Italian artists in 1779; the musicians played in the overhead rotunda.

Le Bourg d'Iré; Nyoiseau – *Round trip of 21km/13mi – leave Segré on D 923 going southwest towards Candé; beyond the level crossing turn right onto D 181.*

Le Bourg d'Iré – *8km/5mi west.* This town stands in the valley of the River Verzée. From the bridge there is a most attractive **view** of the river.

Noyant-la-Gravoyère – *3km/2mi north of Le Bourg d'Iré on D 219. See NOYANT-LA-GRAVOYÈRE.*

From Noyant-la-Gravoyère to Nyoiseau (5km/3mi northeast), take D 775 towards Segré and then the first road on the left.

The road runs through a schist gorge, partially flooded by small lakes which make this the most picturesque section of the excursion. The land surrounding the two lakes – St-Blaise and La Corbinière – has been laid out as a **leisure park**.

Nyoiseau – The village – its name is a corruption of *Niosellum* meaning "little nest" – perched on the slopes of the Oudon valley has the remains of a Benedictine abbey for women, now used as a farm as well as housing the town hall. Along the road leading to L'Hôtellerie-de-Flée stands an old Gallo-Roman bridge.

Domaine de la Petite Couère ⊙ – *After leaving Nyoiseau north, follow the signposted route towards Renazé along D 71.*
A pleasant setting for country walks and leisure activities, this 80ha/198 acre park offers a fascinating combination of rural ethnography, animal collections and mechanical curiosities. Near the entrance stands a tractor museum, displaying around 60 vehicles from 1906 to 1950. Further on, there are around one hundred vintage cars, including a 1915 Brasier Phaeton and a B-type Peugeot tonneau dating from 1902. Another exhibition is the painstaking reconstitution

of a small village at the turn of the century with its chapel, school, town hall, café-grocery and various shops, in which each piece of furniture, each tool, each familiar object is accurately reproduced; this display is brought to life by dummies wearing costumes from the 1920s.

Visitors can also wander from one enclosure to the next and discover the animal park (emus, various types of deer, Poitou donkey etc) thanks to the various signposted paths (1-6km/0.5-4mi long). A small train makes a 15min trip from the picnic area to the village. Four luxury carriages belonging to the Compagnie des Wagons-Lits (three sleepers and one dining-car) are currently undergoing restoration and will be able to provide accommodation for around 50 people *(sleeping facilities plus breakfast)*.

D 271 north to Hôtellerie-de-Flée, then D 863 and D 923 south lead back to Segré.

Château de Raguin ⊘ – *8.5km/5mi southwest on D 923; in St-Gemmes-d'Andigné bear left onto D 183.*

The old 15C castle was replaced c 1600 by Guy du Bellay, son of Pierre du Bellay (cousin of the poet), with a Renaissance-style building.

Although a marshal in the King's army, Du Bellay had a taste for luxury and he made Raguin a luxurious and elegant château. When his son, Antoine, married in 1648, he had the first-floor salon and another room fitted with wainscots and had the walls and ceiling entirely redecorated; in the second room, "Chambre des Amours", the cherubs play with the initials of the newly-wed couple.

After the death of his father and then of his wife in 1666, Antoine du Bellay sold the château which then changed hands several times.

Château de Bouillé-Thévalle ⊘ – *11km/7mi north (D 923) in the direction of Château-Gontier: follow the signposted route at St-Sauveur-de-Flée.*

On the historical road of King René, this 15C castle, with its water-filled moat, still has an old stairway with cut-off corners. The attic houses a small costume museum. Note the carefully-reconstituted medieval garden.

SELLES-SUR-CHER

Population 4 751
Michelin map 64 fold 18 or 232 fold 16

Selles-sur-Cher is prettily situated in a bend of the River Cher, in which the towers of its castle are reflected. The town developed round an abbey which was founded by St Eusice, a hermit who lived in that spot. Only the abbey church now remains.

SIGHTS

Église St-Eusice – The church, which dates from the 12C and 15C, was burned down by Coligny in 1562; it was partially restored in the 17C and then more thoroughly in the last century. The façade, which is almost entirely Romanesque, has reused the columns and capitals from an earlier church which was destroyed by marauding Normans in about 903.

The **chevet**, which is well built, is ornamented with two friezes of figures; those below the windows are rough, simple and heavy but those above are better proportioned and more elegant. The lower frieze depicts scenes from the New Testament; the upper one illustrates the life of St Eusice.

Near the north wall are low-relief carvings of the Labours of the Months; higher up and further to the right there is a beautiful Visitation, protected by the transept chapel. It is however all very worn.

In the north wall, which was built late in the 13C, there is a charming door decorated with carved capitals supporting tori separated by a chain of flowers and wild rose leaves.

The crypt contains the tomb of St Eusice (6C).

Castle ⊘ – Hidden on the south bank of the Cher are the remains of an austere 13C fortress, within a rectangular moated enclosure, approached by four bridges. In contrast, framing the present entrance on the east side are two light 17C buildings joined together by a long arcaded wall, which is pierced by oculi and topped by a parapet walk. These were built by **Philippe de Béthune**, Sully's brother *(see SULLY-SUR-LOIRE)* who bought the castle in 1604.

Beyond the magnificent cedar and mulberry trees of the inner park, in the old part on the west side, is the gilded pavilion (**Pavillon Doré**), an elegant building, decorated in the Italian Renaissance style, which Philippe de Béthune introduced into the old 13C fortress. It has magnificent gilded chimneypieces, wall paintings and coloured coffered ceilings, all of which have retained their original lustre. Also on view are the study containing souvenirs of the **Count of Chambord** (1820-83), pretender to the French throne after the death of Charles X, the little oratory and the bedroom. While living in the gilded pavilion, Philippe de Béthune had a new château built in the contemporary style in red brick outlined in white stone. Here grandeur and generous proportions replace the more intimate charm of the gilded pavilion. The tour includes the guard-room with its great chimney, the bedroom of Maria Sobieska, the queen of Poland, in which the bed with its twisted columns stands on a dais, and the attractive games room.

Musée du Val de Cher ⊘ – A variety of exhibits is displayed in the Cher Valley Museum: documents about Selles's past, tools used by wine growers, basket-makers, coopers and watermen, and an interesting section on the preparation of gunflint, a thriving industry in the region from the middle of the 18C until the invention of the percussion cap *(see also Meusnes, described under Excursions below).*

EXCURSIONS

Châtillon-sur-Cher – *5km/3mi west on N 75 towards St-Aignan and a turning to the left.*
This little village stands on the north slope of the Cher valley. The **church of St-Blaise** contains *(left wall of chancel)* a **panel**★ by the school of Leonardo da Vinci depicting St Catherine between two cherubs: the treatment of the hands, a little mannered but very attractive, and the facial expression are typical of da Vinci's style. A statue of St Vincent, patron of wine growers, is surrounded by the batons of their brotherhood which are carried in their processions.

Meusnes – *6.5km/4mi southwest on D 956 briefly towards Valençay and then D 17 west.*
The **church** is in the pure Romanesque style. There is a triumphal arch in the transept surmounted by three charming open-work arcatures. Several beautiful 15C and 16C statues have been reinstated.
A small gunflint museum, **musée de la Pierre à fusil** ⊘, housed in the town hall, describes this industry which flourished in the region for 300 years.

Château de SERRANT★★

Michelin map 63 fold 20 or 232 fold 31 – 2km/1mi northeast of St-Georges-sur-Loire

Although built over a period of three centuries, 16C to 18C, this sumptuous moated mansion has great unity of style. Its massive domed towers and the contrast between the dark schist and the white tufa give it considerable character.
The **Château de Serrant** ⊘ was begun in 1546 by Charles de Brie, bought by Hercule de Rohan, Duke of Montbazon, in 1596, and sold in 1636 to Guillaume Bautru whose granddaughter married the Marquis of Vaubrun, Lieutenant-General of the king's army. On the death of her husband, who was killed beside Turenne at the Battle of Altenheim, the Marchioness continued construction work until 1705. She commissioned J.Hardouin-Mansart to build the beautiful chapel in memory of her husband, and Coysevox to design the white marble mausoleum. In 1749 her daughter, the Duchess of Estrées, sold the estate to an Irishman, Francis Walsh, who was made Count of Serrant in 1755 by Louis XV as a reward for his family's support for the Stuart cause – they provided the ship which carried Bonnie Prince Charlie to Moidart in 1745. Two generations earlier another Walsh had enabled James II to flee to exile in France. In 1830 the château came into the ownership of the Duc de la Trémoille, a forebear of the present occupant, Prince Jean-Charles de Ligne.

Tour – The **apartments** are magnificently furnished. Sumptuous Flemish tapes-tries hang in the dining room. Of particular interest are the great Renaissance staircase, the coffered ceilings on the first floor, the library with its 10 000 vol-umes and the state rooms where both Louis XIV and Napoleon were received. Numerous works of art on display include Flemish and Brussels tapestries, a very beautiful Italian cabinet, a bust of the Empress Marie-Louise by Canova and various portraits.

MICHELIN GREEN GUIDES
Art and Architecture
History
Geography
Ancient monuments
Scenic routes
Touring programmes
Plans of towns and buildings
A selection of guides for holidays at home and abroad.

SOLESMES

Population 1 277
Michelin map 64 folds 1, 2 or 232 fold 20
Local map see Vallée de la SARTHE

A few miles upstream from Sablé lies Solesmes which has won renown through its association with the Benedictine Order. From the north bank of the Sarthe and from the bridge there is an impressive view★ of the north front of the abbey, a dark wall, about 50m/164ft high, which was built at the end of the 19C in the Romanesque-Gothic style. The abbey buildings are reflected in the river, next to a less imposing, but rather more inviting-looking 18C priory.

Under the Rule of St Benedict – The Benedictine priory founded in 1010 by the Lord of Sablé was served by monks from St-Pierre-de-la-Couture in Le Mans *(see Le MANS: Additional Sights)*. It expanded rapidly and by the early 16C had become very wealthy; in the 17C it fell into decline and was taken over by the monks of St-Maur.

The Revolution brought ruin, but a new community was established in 1833 by a priest from Sablé, Dom Guéranger, and in 1837 the abbey became the headquarters of the Benedictine Order in France. In 1901 a law was passed expelling all religious orders from France but they returned when it was repealed 20 years later.

Since then the name of Solesmes has been linked with the restoration of the liturgy and the revival of the Gregorian chant in France. The abbey **services** ⊘ to which the public is admitted demonstrate the beauty of the liturgy celebrated in Benedictine monasteries.

★ **Abbaye St-Pierre** – *Only the abbey church (in the main courtyard) is open to the public.*

The **church** comprises the nave and transept which date from the 11C and 15C and the domical-vaulted chancel which was added in 1865. The famous sculpture groups, which are known as the "**saints of Solesmes**"★★, are in the transept.

The works in the south transept were commissioned by Prior Guillaume Cheminart: a monumental Entombment (1496) with a beautiful representation of Mary Magdalene at prayer; on the left a terracotta *Pietà* from an earlier period. The works in the north transept, which is dedicated to the Virgin Mary, were commissioned by Prior Jean Bougler between 1530 and 1556; the composition is rather crowded but the detail is interesting. The main scene is the Entombment of the Virgin; Jean Bougler is shown holding one end of the shroud; overhead are the four Fathers of the Church and the Assumption. On the sides are Jesus among the Doctors *(left)* and scenes from the life of the Virgin *(right)*.

La SOLOGNE

Michelin map 64 folds 8, 9, 18, 19 or 238 folds 3 to 7 and 16 to 19

The Sologne is a paradise for hunters and anglers. Its wide, flat expanses of picturesque heathland stretch as far as the eye can see covering an area of 4 900km²/ 1 892ni². The region, which is given over to farms, forests and a great many isolated lakes (accounting for 11 000ha/27 000 acres), is dotted with towns which add splashes of colour to the landscape with their red brick, stone and timber buildings.

Lying between the Loire and the Cher, the Sologne is delimited to the east by the Sancerre hills and to the west by a curved line running north from Selles-sur-Cher via Chémery, Thenay and Sambin to Cheverny.

The Sologne terrain, which is composed of clay and sand, slopes very gently westwards as indicated by the direction in which the main rivers – Cosson, Beuvron and Petite and Grande Sauldre – flow.

Development – In the past the region was a desolate wasteland ravaged by fevers caused by the stagnant water of its numerous lakes, but things changed radically for the better in the reign of Napoleon III who acquired the Lamotte-Beuvron estate and instigated a number of improvements. The Sologne Central Committee started to plant birch and Norway pine trees, dig canals, construct roads, clear and drain the lakes and improve the soil.

The fevers disappeared, the population increased and the Sologne took on something like its present appearance.

The Sologne countryside – The area under cultivation is about 140 000ha/345 940 acres. Fields of maize are widespread (about 21 500ha/53 130 acres); it is a particularly useful crop because it provides not only fodder for the livestock but also good cover for game, thus reconciling the interests of both farmers and hunters. The fodder produced feeds 35 000 cattle, 25 000 sheep and 10 000 goats. Many farms have taken up pheasant rearing or other activities connected with the provision of game. Wherever farmers have been able to drain the land, there are fruit orchards and also farms involved in the intensive rearing of cattle, sheep and goats.

The region round Contres produces vegetables and fruit which are sold locally or sent to the central markets or the canneries. The Sologne and the Loire valley near Blois form one of France's leading asparagus-growing areas. The cultivation of strawberries has become very specialised, leading to an increase in production. Along the Cher valley and in the neighbourhood of Blois the production of wine has improved owing to the introduction of the Sauvignon and Gamay grapes. Markets are held in certain small towns such as Gien, Sully, Romorantin-Lanthenay and Lamotte-Beuvron which is the geographical centre of the Sologne.

Traditional local industries (sawmills and packaging materials) have been joined by other manufacturers: porcelain at Lamotte-Beuvron, armaments at La-Ferté-Saint-Aubin and Salbris, commercial vehicles at Romorantin and the cultivation in the area of gladiolus bulbs, dahlias and yams.

The recent improvement in fish farming on the lakes has increasingly rationalised traditional methods of production. Pike, sauger, eel, carp and more recently merval (a freshwater catfish) are a delight to fishermen and gourmets alike.

Sologne forests – These form a unique region in central France. Their history and soil type, which is often sandy

Pheasant in the Sologne

and water-laden, are comparable to those of forests in Scandinavian countries. Forests cover an area of over 225 000ha/869mi², and with an afforestation rate of about 60% especially in the east, they have been spreading each year for a century and a half. Private landowners, who possess 90% of the wooded area and all the fallow land (400km²/154mi²), have improved the forests by introducing more suitably adaptable species such as the Scots pine, which has been a feature of the forests here for over 15 years, and, more recently, the larch and the Douglas fir. These conifers were originally intended for the pit-prop market which has now disappeared. They have gradually replaced the maritime pine which died out after the terrible winter of 1878-79, when ice destroyed more than 60% of the forest vegetation.

The trees are thinned out and used for the manufacture of paper pulp and chipboards. Recent development in the industry has led to the building of a large factory in Sully-sur-Loire and the modernisation of local sawmills where the sawn timber is now converted on the spot for packing, carpentry, joinery and furniture. The beautiful oak forests of the Sologne, Blésois and Cher produce high quality timbers which may be sliced (to make veneers), cut into planks for construction or made into parquet.

Stag in the Sologne

The thick cover provided by the forest, together with the general peace of the area and the presence of water, attracts a wide variety of fauna. The resident wildlife has to be regulated to protect the forest from the damage wrought by larger members of the Cervidae family as well as roe deer and rabbits in search of food. The region is also a favoured shooting ground on account of the abundance of migratory birds.

The Sologne is well described by Maurice Genevoix in *Raboliot*, the story of a poacher.

TOWNS AND SIGHTS *listed in alphabetical order*

The Sologne is at its most attractive in the early autumn, when the russet of the falling leaves mingles with the dark evergreen of the Norway pines above a carpet of bracken and purple heather, broken by the brooding waters of an occasional lake. One of the best ways to appreciate the natural beauty of the Sologne is by taking a walk.

However, the bursts of gunfire which announce the shooting season can detract a little from the charm of the region. Owing to the many enclosures, prohibited areas and animal traps it is definitely advisable to keep to the waymarked footpaths such as the GR 31 and the GR 3C *(see Practical information section)*. Another picturesque way of seeing the Sologne, and one which requires less exertion, is provided by the metric-gauge **railway** ⊘, operated by the "Compagnie du Blanc Argent", which runs between **Salbris** and Luçay-le-Mâle.
The "Sologne Scenic Road" (D 922) between Romorantin and La Ferté-St-Aubin passes through some typical Sologne landscapes.

Argent-sur-Sauldre - *See ARGENT-SUR-SAULDRE.*

Aubigny-sur-Nère - *See AUBIGNY-SUR-NÈRE.*

★ **Blancafort** - *See BLANCAFORT.*

Bracieux - Bracieux is a smart village on the border of the Sologne and the region round Blois. The houses are grouped round the 16C market on the south bank of the Beuvron which is spanned by a picturesque bridge.

Cerdon - *See ARGENT-SUR-SAULDRE: Excursions.*

★★★ **Château de Chambord** - *See Château de CHAMBORD.*

Chaumont-sur-Tharonne - The line of the old ramparts can be traced in the layout of the town which is picturesquely situated round its 15C-16C church on a bluff in the centre of the Sologne region.

★★★ **Château de Cheverny** - *See Château de CHEVERNY.*

La Ferté-St-Aubin - *See La FERTÉ-ST-AUBIN.*

Fontaines-en-Sologne - The **church**, which dates for the most part from the 12C, shows how widespread the Angevin style was: flat chevet, nave with remarkable domed vaulting. It was fortified in the 17C. Beside the church there are some pretty, half-timbered houses with roofs of small flat tiles, commonly found in the region.

Gy-en-Sologne - The typical Sologne cottage here, **Locature de la Straize** ⊘, dates from the 16C.

Lanthenay ⊘ - The **church** here contains a painting of the Virgin Mary between St John the Baptist and St Sebastian, dating from 1523 and attributed to Timoteo Viti from Urbino who influenced Raphael in his early days. There is also a 17C canvas of the dead Christ with the Virgin Mary and St John and 16C painted wooden statues of St Francis and St Clare.

Lassay-sur-Croisne - *See LASSAY-SUR-CROISNE.*

★ **Moulin (Château du)** - *See LASSAY-SUR-CROISNE.*

Neuvy - Neuvy is located on the southern edge of the Boulogne forest on the north bank of the River Beuvron.
The village **church** ⊘ stands on its own in its graveyard near a half-timbered farmhouse with brick infill on the opposite bank. It was partially rebuilt in 1525. The rood beam supports 15C statues; in the south transept there is a 17C painting of the dead Christ supported by two angels.

★ **Romorantin-Lanthenay** - *See ROMORANTIN-LANTHENAY.*

St-Viâtre - *See ST-VIÂTRE.*

Salbris - Salbris, on the south bank of the Sauldre, is a busy crossroads and a good centre for excursions into the forest.
The stone and brick **church of St-Georges** ⊘ was built in the 15C and 16C. The centre of the retable on the high altar is occupied by a *Pietà* (16C). The transept chapels have interesting coats of arms of the donors on the keystones of the vault and attractive pendant sculptures representing the Three Wise Men and the Virgin and Child *(south)* and the symbols of the Evangelists *(north)*.

Selles-St-Denis - This village lies on the north bank of the Sauldre. The **chapel**, which dates from the 12C and 15C and has side chapels and an apse in the Flamboyant style, is decorated with 14C murals of the life of St Genoulph to whom it is dedicated.

Villeherviers - The village is set among asparagus fields in the broad valley of the Sauldre. There is Plantagenet vaulting in the 13C **church** ⊘.

★ **Aliotis, l'Aquarium de Sologne** ⊘ - *East of Villeherviers on D 724; follow the signposted route as far as Moulins des Tourneux.*
This aquarium comprises eight different sections. The first, made up of 10 large 10 000-115 000 litre (2 200-25 300gal) tanks, is representative of the freshwater fauna found in France, coming from rivers, both small and large, waterways, lakes in mountains and plains, ponds, estuaries etc. Fifty additional

small tanks (50-500 litres/11-110gal) enlighten visitors on the myriad creatures living in deep water: frogs, leeches, various larvae. The second section comprises a huge 600 000 litre/132 000gal basin, home to some enormous fish from France and other European countries (note the rather intimidating catfish); two smaller basins contain a fine collection of Japanese Koi – a multicoloured variation of the carp. The two tanks in the third section are devoted to the sea: one houses the tiny organisms feeding off coral reefs, the other one, 10m/32ft long, is reserved for slightly larger species. The fourth section contains aquatic life from South America and includes two aquaterrariums which show life above and below the waters of a great South American river simultaneously. The fifth section is on Africa. The sixth is devoted to waterfalls. Section seven, "Ocean and Mirror", displays tropical fish. Finally, section eight explains life in lagoons. A laboratory is open to visitors eager to see more (microscopes etc).

Villesavin (Château de) – *See Château de VILLESAVIN.*

SUÈVRES

Population 1 360
Michelin map 64 southeast of fold 7 or 238 fold 3

The ancient Gallo-Roman city of Sodobrium hides its picturesque façades below the noisy main road (N 152) on the north bank of the Loire. The **church of St-Christophe** ⊘ beside the road is entered through a huge porch *(caquetoire)* where the parishioners could pause to engage in conversation. The stonework is decorated with various fishbone and chevron patterns characteristic of the Merovingian period.
The houses at no 9 and no 14bis in rue Pierre-Pouteau date from the 15C. Turn right into a picturesque cul-de-sac, rue des Moulins, running beside the stream which is spanned by several footbridges. Tamarisks and weeping willows are reflected in its waters. *Go back to the turning and cross the stone bridge.* The washing place is at the corner of rue St-Simon; on either side of the street are traces of an old fortified gate. Further on through the trees *(left)* emerges the two-storey Romanesque tower of the **church of St-Lubin** ⊘ with its attractive south door (15C).

SULLY-SUR-LOIRE★

Population 5 806
Michelin map 65 fold 1 or 238 fold 6

The Château de Sully commanded one of the Loire crossings. Its history is dominated by four great names: Maurice de Sully, Bishop of Paris who commissioned the building of Notre-Dame, Joan of Arc, Sully and Voltaire.

The determination of Joan of Arc – In 1429 Sully belonged to Georges de la Trémoille, a favourite of Charles VII. The King was living in the castle when Joan of Arc defeated the English at Patay and captured their leader, the famous Talbot, Earl of Shrewsbury. Joan hastened to Sully and at last persuaded the indolent monarch to be crowned at Reims. She returned to the castle in 1430 after her check before Paris, and there felt the jealousy and hostility of La Trémoille gaining influence over the King. She was detained almost as if a prisoner but escaped to continue the struggle.

Sully's capacity for work – In 1602 Maximilien de Béthune, the Lord of Rosny, bought the château and the barony for 330 000 *livres.* Henri IV made him Duc de Sully, and it was under this name that the great Minister passed into history.
Sully had begun to serve his King at the age of 12. He was a great soldier, the best artilleryman of his time and a consummate administrator. He was active in all the departments of State: Finance, Agriculture, Industry and Public Works. A glutton for work, Sully began his day at 3am and kept four secretaries busy writing his memoirs. He entitled them: *Wise and Royal Economies of State.* Fearing indiscretions, he had a printing press set up in one of the towers of the château and the work was printed on the spot, although it bore the address of a printer in Amsterdam. The old Duke had a mania for orderly accounts. Every tree to be planted, every table to be made, every ditch to be cleaned was the subject of a legal contract.
Sully had an awkward character and he frequently brought legal actions, especially against the Bishop of Orléans. Since the Middle Ages it had been the custom for the Lord of Sully to carry the Bishop's chair on the day of his entry into Orléans. The Minister, very much the ducal peer and a Protestant into the bargain, refused to comply with this custom. Finally he obtained permission to be represented at the ceremony.

Sully embellished his castle. The building originally stood on the Loire itself. He separated it from the river by an embankment, dug moats which he filled by deflecting a nearby river, laid out the park and entended the buildings.

Sully's career came to an end with the assassination of Henri IV in 1610. The Minister retired but he assured Louis XIII of his loyalty and encouraged his co-religionists to do the same. Cardinal Richelieu made him a Marshal of France.

The spirit of Voltaire (18C) – Exiled from Paris by the Regent for his cutting epigrams, Voltaire spent several seasons with the Duke of Sully who surrounded himself with philosophers and free-thinkers. Voltaire was 22. His gaiety and wit made him the life and soul of the castle. In the shade of the park among the trees which he described as "carved upon by urchins and lovers", young François-Marie Arouet (he had not then adopted his pen name) indulged in flirtations which he transferred to the stage. A theatre was built for him in the castle where he produced *Œdipus*, *Les Nuits Galantes* and *Artemis*, with his friends playing the roles.

Château de Sully-sur-Loire

★ CHÂTEAU ⊘ 45min

The castle is an imposing feudal fortress dating largely from before 1360. The keep, which faces the Loire, was built at the end of the 14C by Guy de Trémoille. It is rectangular with massive round towers at the corners. The upper part is equipped with machicolated sentry walks, loopholes and holes for cross-bows illustrating the evolution of military architecture during the Hundred Years War. The wing added to the living quarters by Sully dates from the 17C, but was remodelled in the 18C and 19C.

The tour of the château begins in the great lower hall in which six tapestries from the Parisian workshops, precursors of the Gobelins, are on display. They relate the stories of *Psyche*, *Venus* and *Cupid*.

The main hall, another enormous room (300m²/3 230ft²) on the first floor, was the part of the seigneurial residence used during the Middle Ages for dispensing justice and holding feasts. It was decorated by Maximilien de Béthune in the 17C. Portraits of the descendants of the first Duke of Sully and of his brother Philippe adorn the walls, which are hung with red fabric. This is the room where Voltaire performed his plays. In the window splays, the Grand Duke of Sully's ancestors are depicted in *trompe-l'œil*. An iron door hidden in the panelling leads to the old exercise room from where the guards operated the drawbridge and the trapdoor. Nowadays called the **oratory**, this room was also the duke's treasury in the 17C and houses an excellent copy of the funerary group of Sully and his second wife Rachel de Cochefilet (the original is at Nogent-le-Rotrou). The bed in the centre of the king's bedchamber has blue and gold curtains in honour of the Dauphin Louis XIV's stay here during the Fronde uprising. 17C tapestries and Louis XIII furniture make a complementary setting. Finally, on the second floor, there is the unique room with its famous timber roof. The visit ends with a tour of the sentry walk in view of the Loire.

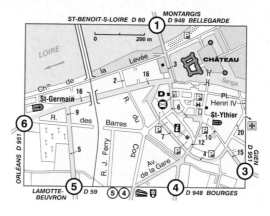

D Maison Renaissance

★★ **Timber roof** – The upper half of the keep has one of the finest timber roofs to have survived from the Middle Ages. It was built towards the end of the 14C by the master carpenters of Orléans and is impressive in size. Its good state of preservation is due to the infinite pains taken by its builders, both in treating the timber and in the way it was put together. Felled in winter under a waning moon, the trees were squared off, getting rid of the sap-wood, and sawn up following the grain. Immersion in water for a period of several months got rid of the sap. The wood was subsequently dried in the air over a period of many years, after which the precious material was smoked or cured to protect it from rot and decay. The final treatment consisted of coating it with an alum-based solution.

Petit château – This part of the château was built some years after the keep and houses the Duke of Sully's apartments, notably his bedchamber with a coffered ceiling adorned with mottoes and motifs related to his title of Grand Master of the Artillery (cannon balls, flashing explosions etc) and also reflecting the high esteem in which the duke held his king, Henri IV. The apartments contain some interesting pieces of furniture and paintings.

ADDITIONAL SIGHTS

Collégiale de St-Ythier – A chapel dedicated to Notre-Dame-de-Pitié was built in 1529 and enlarged in 1605, whereupon it became the collegiate church of St-Ythier. There are two 16C **stained-glass windows**: that at the end of the south aisle shows pilgrims on their way to St James's shrine in Compostela; the second, showing the Tree of Jesse with the Virgin Mary and the Infant Jesus, is in the central apse. In the north aisle there is a 16C *Pietà* above the high altar.

Renaissance house (D) – Above the façade decorated with medallions and pilasters, the roof features dormer windows with twin bays surrounded by caryatids.

Église St-Germain – The 13C church has been severely damaged several times over the centuries and is presently undergoing restoration *(so is not open to visitors)*. It has a remarkably fine spire, 38m/125ft high.

Château de TALCY★

Population 240
Michelin map 64 fold 7 or 238 fold 3

This **château** ⊙ on the borders of the Loire valley and Beauce region appears quite austere when seen from the outside. Once inside, however, visitors discover a charming, elegant manor house which, although dating from the Renaissance, nevertheless has none of the fancy decorative elements one would expect in a building of this period. From the moment it was built, the château has been at the centre of an agricultural estate as is still evident in its courtyards and gardens. The outbuildings, which have survived intact, comprise a barn, foot bath, dovecot and wine-press. Most unusually, the house itself has retained the interior décor and furniture it would have had in the 17C and 18C. The château also evokes some interesting literary associations.

The 13C manorial dwelling was bought in 1571 by a rich Florentine, Bernardo Salviati, a cousin of Catherine de' Medici. The Salviati family, who became famous in literary history, retained the estate until 1667. Bernardo was the father of Cassandra, to whom **Ronsard** *(see Manoir de la POSSONNIÈRE)* dedicated so many sonnets, and of Giovanni Salviati, whose daughter, Diana,

241

similarly inspired the young Agrippa d'Aubigné. Cassandra's daughter married Guillaume de Musset and one of her direct descendants was the great poet **Alfred de Musset** (1810-57).

Fine furniture (17C-18C) and Gothic tapestries adorn the guard-room, office, kitchen, bedrooms and salons which are roofed with French-style ceilings (with decorated exposed beams). The keep, part of which dates from the 15C has a double doorway (postern and carriage gate), two corner turrets and a crenellated sentry walk which looks medieval but dates from 1520. The fenestration at the first-floor level was modified in the 18C.

The first courtyard owes its charm to a graceful gallery and an attractive well. In the second courtyard is a large 16C **dovecot**, with its 1 500 pigeonholes in a remarkably good state of preservation. The old **wine-press** is still in very good working order.

TOURS★★

Conurbation 271 927
Michelin map 64 fold 15 or 232 folds 35, 36 and 238 fold 13
Local map see Vallée de la LOIRE: Orléans-Chinon

Tours, the capital of Touraine, is traditionally a centre for excursions into the châteaux country but it has many attractions of its own: its clear light, the orderly street plan, the squares and gardens, the churches, monasteries and museums.

HISTORICAL NOTES

Gallo-Roman metropolis – During the Roman period the settlement known as Turons became a prosperous free city with the name Caesarodunum (Caesar's Hill) and extended over a densely populated area of about 40ha/100 acres. Late in the 3C however, invasions obliged the inhabitants to take refuge in the present cathedral district which included the arena. A wall was built to enclose the city and traces of it can still be seen near the castle and in the nearby street, rue des Ursulines.

F. Joly/Bibliothèque municipale, Tours

St Martin cutting his cloak (14C Missal, Tours)

In 375 the town, which had reverted to its former name Turones, became the seat of government of the third Lyonnaise, a province comprising Touraine, Maine, Anjou and Armorica.

St Martin's city (4C) – The man who became the greatest bishop of the Gauls started as a legionary in the Roman army. At the gates of Amiens the young soldier met a beggar shivering in the cold wind. He cut his cloak in two with his sword and gave half to the poor man. The following night in a dream he saw Christ wearing half his cloak, so he got himself baptised and embarked upon his mission. At Ligugé in Poitou he founded the first monastery on Gallic soil. His faith and charity spread his fame far afield. In 372 the people of Tours begged him to become their bishop. Although Christianity had arrived in Gaul a century earlier, paganism was still rife. St Martin fought it with vigour; idols, statues and temples were systematically destroyed. The iconoclast was, however, also a builder and he covered Touraine with churches and chapels. The monastery of Marmoutier was built at the gates of Tours.

St Martin died in Candes in 397. The monks of Ligugé and Marmoutier quarrelled over his body; while the men of Poitou slept, the men of Tours transferred the saint's body to a boat and rowed hard upstream for home. Along the way a miracle occurred: although it was November, as the saint's body passed by trees turned green, plants burst into flower and birds sang – a St Martin's summer. In 471 a basilica was built over his tomb; it measures 50m×20m/164ft×66ft and has 120 columns, 32 windows in the apse and 20 in the nave.

A popular pilgrimage – In 496 or 498 **Clovis** came to St Martin's basilica to meditate and promised to be baptised if he defeated the Alemanni. He returned in 507 during the war against the Visigoths and commanded his army not to despoil the territory of Tours out of respect for St Martin. After his victory at Vouillé, near Poitiers, he did not forget to visit the basilica on which he bestowed many presents in thanksgiving. For the occasion he wore the insignia of the consulship which the Emperor of the East had conferred on him. These visits by Clovis were the beginning of the special protection which the Merovingians accorded to the prestigious sanctuary.

In 563 a young deacon in poor health, who was heir to a noble Gallo-Roman family in the Arverne (later Auvergne), visited St Martin's tomb. His name was Gregory. He was cured and settled in Tours. Owing to his piety and probity, coupled with the renown of several of his relatives (he was the great-nephew of St Nizier of Lyons) he was elected bishop in 573. **Gregory of Tours** produced many written works, especially the **History of the Franks** which has been the main source of information about the Merovingian period. He also wrote eight *Books of Miracles* and the *Lives of the Fathers*. Under his enlightened direction the town developed and an abbey grew up round St Martin's basilica. Gregory died in 594.

For many years pilgrims had been flocking to Tours for cure or counsel. The shrine of St Martin acquired a great reputation, which was assisted by skilful propaganda about the numerous miracles which had taken place round his tomb. Besides the ordinary pilgrims in search of the supernatural, kings, princes and powerful lords came seeking absolution for their many crimes and abuses. The sanctuary was also a place of asylum, an inviolable refuge for both the persecuted and the criminal. The popularity of the cult of St Martin brought the abbey great wealth; its estates, the result of many donations, extended as far as Berry and Bordelais. Royal favour was expressed in the abbey being granted the right to mint money.

Abbot Alcuin (c 735-804)

At the end of the 8C Tours added to its fame by becoming an intellectual and artistic centre under the influence of Alcuin, a monk of Anglo-Saxon origin, originally from York in England, who had met **Charlemagne** in Italy and accompanied him back to France.

The French King wanted to raise the level of learning in his kingdom and he opened a large number of schools to train a well-informed clergy capable in its turn of instructing the population. At his palace in Aix-la-Chapelle (Aachen) he organised a meeting of a group of scholars led by the great figure of Alcuin, inspirational behind the Carolingian Renaissance.

After serving energetically at court, where he set up a palace library, Alcuin decided to retire; Charlemagne offered to appoint him abbot of St-Martin of Tours (796). Although the community counted over 200 monks, it was not very active. Alcuin undertook to renew its prestige. He reformed the abbey school, creating two levels of study: one was elementary, the other consisted of the seven "liberal arts" (grammar, rhetoric, logic, arithmetic, geometry, music and astronomy). Students came from all over Europe. He revived the scriptorium where the copyists designed a new calligraphy for the illuminated manuscripts. He also produced a revised version of the **Vulgate Bible** which became the authorised text throughout the kingdom. He remained in close touch with **Charlemagne** who sought his advice and visited him just before his coronation in December 800. Alcuin died on Whit Sunday 804.

For 50 years after his death Tours continued to be a flourishing cultural centre. In 813 a council met in Tours and ordained that the clergy should comment on the Bible in French rather than Latin. In the 840s the **scriptorium** of St Martin's abbey produced some splendid masterpieces: the so-called Alcuin Bible, the so-called Moutier-Grandval Bible and the famous Bible of Charles the Bald. Artists from Aix-la-Chapelle and Reims renewed and enriched the illustrative technique of the abbey scriptorium.

From the early Capets to Louis XI – The Viking invasions reached Tours in 853: the cathedral, the abbeys and the churches were set on fire and destroyed. The relics of St Martin were removed and hidden in the Auvergne. The ancient abbey fell into decline and passed to the Robertians who were lay-priests. In 903, after further attacks, the abbey was surrounded by a wall and a new town grew up to the west of the old city; it was called Châteauneuf or Martinopolis.

The Robertians in charge of St-Martin's abbey held immense temporal power and the opportunity to pursue ecclesiastical careers; abbots, bishops and archbishops were appointed from among the 200 canons attached to the abbey. The surname "**Capet**" by which King Hugh was known at the end of the 10C comes from an allusion to the *cappa* (cloak) of St Martin, thus proving that the success of the new royal dynasty owed much to the famous monastery. One of Hugh Capet's vassals, Eudes I, Count of Blois and Tours, obtained from his King c 984 the neighbouring abbey of Marmoutier which was to acquire greater importance in the 11C.

In 997 a huge fire destroyed Châteauneuf and St-Martin's abbey which had to be completely rebuilt, including the basilica which dated from 471. The rivalry in the 11C between the houses of Blois and Anjou, whose domains met in Touraine, ended with victory for the Angevins.

When Pope Alexander III held a great council in Tours in 1163, Touraine belonged to the Plantagenets but in 1205 **Philippe-Auguste** captured the town which then remained French.

The 13C was a period of peace and prosperity; the **denier tournois**, the money minted in Tours and thereafter in other cities in the kingdom, was adopted as the official currency in preference to the *denier parisis*. Early in the 13C a monk from Marmoutier, John, author of the *History of the Counts of Anjou* and of the *Life of Geoffroi le Bel*, painted a very flattering portrait in his *In Praise of Touraine* of the citizens of Touraine and their wives. "They are always celebrating and their meals are of the very best; they drink from gold and silver cups and spend their time playing at dice and hunting. The women are astonishingly beautiful, they make up their faces and wear magnificent clothes. Their eyes kindle passion but they are respected for their chastity."

In 1308 Tours played host to the États-Généraux (French Parliament). Less welcome events soon followed; the arrival of the **Black Death** (1351) and the beginning of the Hundred Years War forced the citizens to build a new wall in 1356 enclosing Tours and Châteauneuf. Touraine, which had been coveted by the great royal vassals, was raised to a Duchy for the future Charles VII and he solemnly entered the town of Tours in 1417. In 1429 Joan of Arc stayed in Tours while her armour was being made. Charles VII settled in Tours in 1444 and on 28 May he signed the Treaty of Tours with Henry VI of England.

Under **Louis XI** Tours was very much in favour; the city acted as the capital of the kingdom and a mayor was appointed in 1462. The King liked the region and lived at the Château de Plessis-lès-Tours *(see below)*. Once again life became pleasant and the presence of the court attracted a number of artists of which the most famous was **Jean Fouquet** (born in Tours c 1415) who painted the magnificent miniatures in the *Great Chronicle of France* and *Jewish Antiquities*.

The Abbey once again enjoyed royal favour and recovered some of its former prestige. Louis XI died in 1483 at Plessis, whereupon the court moved to Amboise.

Silk weaving and Wars of Religion – Louis XI had promoted the weaving of silk and cloth of gold in Lyon but the project had not met with much enthusiasm so the weavers and their looms were moved to Touraine. The industry reached its highest output in the middle of the 17C when 11 000 looms were at work and there were two fairs each year.

In 1680 decline set in under the effect of competition from Lyon; in 1789 only 1 000 looms were at work in Tours. The silk industry has experienced a modest recovery in the 20C *(see below)*.

In this world of craftsmen, intellectuals and artists, the **Reformation** found its first supporters and Tours, like Lyon and Nîmes, became one of the most active centres of the new religion. In 1562 the Calvinists caused great disorder, particularly in St-Martin's abbey.

The Roman Catholics were merciless in their revenge; 10 years before Paris, Tours had its own St Bartholomew's Day massacre, with 200-300 Huguenots being drowned in the Loire. In May 1589 Henri III and the Parliament retreated from Paris to Tours which once again resumed its role as the royal capital. In the early 17C, a new wall, the layout of which may be seen in large boulevards such as Heurteloup and Béranger, doubled the space inside the city. In the latter half of the 18C, extensive town-planning by royal decree opened up a wide road on a north-south axis along which Tours was to develop in the future.

Nevertheless, in the 17C and 18C Tours lost its political and economic importance and in 1801 the population had dropped to only 20 000 inhabitants, less than Angers and Orléans. In the 19C development was slow; there was some building and improvement but little industry. The railway acted as a stimulant and the station at St-Pierre-des-Corps was the focus of renewed activity. In 1921 Tours had overtaken Orléans with a population figure of 75 000.

Wars – Owing to its communications facilities Tours was chosen in 1870 as the **seat of the Government for the National Defence** but three months later, in the face of the Prussian advance, the government withdrew to Bordeaux. In June 1940 the same chain of events took place but at greater speed. The town was bombed and burned for three days from 19 to 21 September. In 1944 the bombardments began again: 136 people were killed on 20 May. In all, between 1940 and 1944, 1 543 buildings were destroyed and 7 960 damaged; the town centre and the districts on the banks of the Loire were the most afflicted.

TOURS

Alouette (Av. de l') .... **X** 2
Bordiers (R. des) .... **U** 9
Boyer (R. Léon) .... **V** 10
Chevallier (R. A.) .... **V** 19
Churchill (Bd W.) .... **V** 20
Compagnons
  d'Emmaüs (Av. des) .. **U** 23
Eiffel (Av. Gustave) .... **U** 37
Gaulle (Av. Gal de) .... **V** 44
Giraudeau (R.) .... **V** 46
Grammont (Av. de) .... **V** 47
Grand Sud (Av.) .... **X** 51
Groison (R.) .... **U** 54
Marmoutier (Q. de) .... **U** 63
Monnet (Bd J.) .... **V** 69

Portillon (Q. de) .... **U** 81
Proud'hon (Av.) .... **V** 82
République (Av. de la) .. **U** 87
St-Avertin (Rte de) ..... **X** 89
St-Sauveur (Pont) ...... **V** 95
Sanitas (Pont du) ...... **VX** 96
Tranchée (Av. de la) ... **U** 98
Vaillant (R. E.) .... **V** 99
Wagner (Bd R.) ...... **V** 105

CHAMBRAY-LÈS-TOURS

République (Av. de la) . **X** 88

JOUÉ-LES-TOURS

Martyrs (R. des) .... **X** 64

Verdun (Bd de) .... **X** 102

ST-AVERTIN

Brulon (R. Léon) ...... **X** 14
Lac (Av. du) .... **V** 58
Larçay (R. de) .... **X** 59

ST-CYR-SUR-LOIRE

St-Cyr (Q. de) .... **V** 91

ST-PIERRE-DES-CORPS

Jaurès
  (Boulevard Jean) .... **V** 57
Moulin (R. Jean) ...... **V** 70

M⁵ Musée des Équipages militaires et du Train   **R** Château de Plessis-lès-Tours

TOURS, AN ECONOMIC CENTRE

Tours has now overflowed from its original site between the Loire and the Cher and consists of a huge conurbation. The course of the Cher has been straightened and canalised for 7km/4mi to provide two residential areas, an artificial lake (25ha/62 acres) and water sports facilities.

Tours has many light industries: a variety of processing plants, pharmaceutical laboratories, printing works. A tyre factory has been built by Michelin in Joué-lès-Tours on the southwest edge of the city. Tours has not abandoned its traditional livelihood: Jacquard still has looms producing silk and velvet cloth, which is exported throughout the world or used to refurbish the many châteaux and historic houses in France.

TOURS

Tours is an important centre for both road and rail traffic; it is also the economic centre for the west central region of France and a leading market for the wine and agricultural products of the area; there are two important fairs, in May and September. The varied cultural and intellectual life of the city is supported by the university with its 25 000 students, the Centre for Advanced Studies of the Renaissance, the National Conservatory of Music, the Regional School of Fine Arts, a National Centre for Urban Archeology and the various specialist institutes of higher education, including schools for business, information technology and management.

Out and about in Tours

Entertainment – Useful addresses include: Grand théâtre ☎ 02 47 05 33 71; Théâtre Louis-Jouvet ☎ 02 47 64 50 50; Le Petit Faucheux, for café-théâtre and jazz ☎ 02 47 39 29 34; the Vinci, international conference centre with three auditoriums ☎ 02 47 70 70 70.

Local specialities – Prunes stuffed with apple purée, prunes soaked in local marc (spirit), *muscadines* (pralines flavoured with Cointreau), *livre tournois* (dark chocolate, coffee and orange); *pavés de Tours* (biscuits); and last but by no means least, Touraine wines.

Dates for your diary – **May:** "Semaines musicales de Tours" (opera, symphony concerts); **June:** "Fêtes musicales en Touraine" (chamber music) in the setting of Meslay grange; **July:** "Le Chorégraphique" (dance); **26 July** (the feast of St Anne): garlic and basil fair.

Markets – Flower market on Wednesdays and Saturdays in boulevard Béranger; gourmet market on the first Friday of the month from 4pm to 10pm in place de la Résistance.

★★ OLD TOURS *1hr 30min*

The vast restoration work begun about 1970 around place Plumereau and the building of the Faculté des Lettres beside the Loire have brought the old quarter to life; its narrow streets, often pedestrian precincts, have attracted shops and craftsmen, and the whole quarter, near the university, has become one of the liveliest parts of town.

★ **Place Plumereau (ABY)** – This picturesque and animated square, once the hat market (Carroi aux Chapeaux), is lined with fine 15C timber-framed houses alternating with stone façades. On the corner of rue du Change and rue de la

Place Plumereau

Monnaie there is a lovely house featuring two slate-roofed gables and posts decorated with sculptures; closer examination of the corner post reveals a representation of the Nativity (15C). Continue down rue du Change to the corner of rue de la Rôtisserie where there is an old façade with wooden lattice-work. Retrace your steps to place Plumereau. To the north of the square a vaulted passageway opens on to the attractive little **place St-Pierre-le-Puellier (93)**, with its pleasant gardens. Excavations have uncovered, among other things, a 1C Gallo-Roman public building, 11C and 13C cemeteries and the foundations of the old church after which the square is named. Part of the nave is still visible on one side of the square and from the rue Briçonnet. To the north, a large ogive-vaulted porch opens onto a small square where four centuries of architecture are harmoniously represented together.

Rue du Grand-Marché (AY) – This is one of the most interesting streets in old Tours, with a great number of half-timbered façades embellished with bricks or slates.

Quartier du Petit-St-Martin (AY) – This pedestrian district features several craftsmen's workshops, especially near the **Carroi aux herbes (56)**.

Rue Bretonneau (AY) – At no 33 stands a 16C *hôtel* with pretty Renaissance carved foliage; the northern wing was added towards 1875.

Musée du Gemmail (AY M¹) ⊘ – *Entrance at no 7, rue du Mûrier.*
The **Hôtel Raimbault** (1835), a beautiful Restoration building with columns, contains a collection of non-leaded stained-glass windows graced with the luminosity of ordinary stained glass and the brilliance of precious stones. The 70 pieces on display were executed by master-craftsmen whose methods were similar to those of colourists working from cartoons. The 12C underground chapel is decorated with stained glass and a studio has been reconstructed in the old stables.

Rue Briçonnet (AY 13) – This charming street is bordered by houses showing a rich variety of local styles, from the Romanesque façade to the 18C mansion. Off the narrow rue du Poirier, no 35 has a Romanesque façade, no 31 a late-13C Gothic façade; opposite, at no 32, stands a Renaissance house with lovely wooden statuettes. Not far away, an elegant staircase tower marks the entrance to place St-Pierre-le-Puellier. Further north, on the left, no 23 has a classical façade. No 16 is the **Maison de Tristan (K)** ⊘, a remarkable stone and brick construction with a late-15C pierced gable: it is used as the premises of a modern languages centre, the Centre d'Études de Langues Vivantes. One of the window lintels in the courtyard bears the inscription *Prie Dieu Pur*, an anagram of the name of Pierre Dupui, who built the mansion.

Rue Paul-Louis Courier (BY 27) – In the inner court-yard, above the doorway of the 15C-16C Hôtel Binet (no 10) is an elegant wooden gallery served by two spiral staircases.

Place de Châteauneuf (BY 17) – There is a fine view of the **Tour Charlemagne (Q)**, and the remains of the **Ancienne basilique St-Martin** built in the 11C and 13C over the tomb of the great Bishop of Tours, after the Vikings had destroyed the 5C sanctuary. The new building was as famous as the old for its size and splendour. Sacked by the Huguenots in 1562 it fell into disrepair during the Revolution and its vaulting collapsed. The nave was pulled down in 1802 to make way for the construction of the rue des Halles. Since that time, the Tour Charlemagne, the tower which dominated the north transept, has stood alone. It collapsed partially in 1928, but after careful restoration, it has retained its original elegance. From the rue

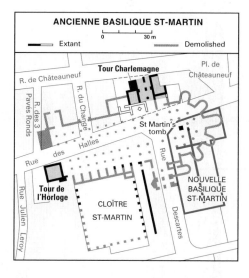

ANCIENNE BASILIQUE ST-MARTIN

Extant   Demolished

Tour Charlemagne

Pl. de Châteauneuf

R. de Châteauneuf

R. des 3 Pavés Ronds

R. du Change

St Martin's tomb

Rue des Halles

Rue des

Tour de l'Horloge

Rue Julien Leroy

CLOÎTRE ST-MARTIN

Rue Descartes

NOUVELLE BASILIQUE ST-MARTIN

des Halles, note a fine sculpted capital dating from the 12C. At the top of the tower a low-relief dating from the restoration work depicts St Martin sharing his cloak.

Opposite, the 14C ducal residence, **Logis des ducs de Touraine (E)**, houses a centre for military servicemen, the "Maison des Combattants", while the late-15C **church of St-Denis (D)** has been converted into a music centre. Further along rue des Halles stands the **Tour de l'Horloge (V)**, a clock tower marking the façade of the basilica which was crowned with a dome in the 19C.

The **Nouvelle basilique St-Martin**, built between 1886 and 1924 in neo-Byzantine style, houses the shrine of St Martin, still the object of pilgrimages, in the crypt.

Musée St-Martin (BZ M²) ⊙ – This museum in rue Rapin is housed in the 13C chapel of St-Jean, once an outbuilding of St-Martin's cloisters. Texts and engravings evoke the main events of the life of the saint and his influence on the Christian world borne out by the many churches dedicated to him not only in France, where about 4 000 bear his name, but throughout Europe. The museum also displays remains from the basilicas built in succession over the saint's tomb. Among them are carved marble items from the one built in about 470 as well as murals and mosaics from the 11C Romanesque basilica. There is also a model of the last building, showing what it looked like before it was destroyed between 1797 and 1802.

Before leaving rue Rapin, note the old houses, particularly that at no 6 which is the Centre for Advanced Studies of the Renaissance.

★ **Hôtel Gouin (BY)** ⊙ – This mansion, a perfect example of living accommodation during the Renaissance, is one of the most interesting of its kind in Tours. It was burnt out in June 1940, but the **south façade★** with its finely-sculpted Renaissance ornamental foliage and the north façade with its fine staircase tower were spared.

Tours – Hôtel Gouin

It houses the **museum** of the Touraine archeological society which has a very varied collection of exhibits from the prehistoric era through the Gallo-Roman, medieval and Renaissance periods to the 19C. Displayed against a background of 18C panelling are the instruments from the medicine chest at Chenonceau château designed by Dupin de Francueil and Jean-Jacques Rousseau as part of the education of Dupin's son. Exhibits include an Archimedes' screw, an inclined plane and a vacuum pump.

★★ CATHEDRAL DISTRICT (CDY) *2hr*

★★ **Cathédrale St-Gatien (CDY)** – The cathedral was begun in the mid-13C and completed in the 16C. It demonstrates the complete evolution of the French Gothic style; the chevet typifies the early phase, the transept and nave the development of the style and the Flamboyant west front belongs to the final phase. The first traces of the Renaissance are visible in the tops of the towers.

Despite the mixture of styles the soaring **west front** is a harmonious entity. A slight asymmetry of detail ensures that the façade is not monotonous. The foundations of the towers are a Gallo-Roman wall and solid buttresses indicate that the bases are Roman-

> It is a very beautiful church of the second order of importance, with a charming mouse-coloured complexion and a pair of fantastic towers. ... There are many grander cathedrals, but there are probably few more pleasing; and this effect of delicacy and grace is at its best toward the close of a quiet afternoon, when the densely decorated towers, rising above the little Place de l'Archevêché, lift their curious lanterns into the slanting light, and offer a multitudinous perch to troops of circling pigeons.
>
> **Henry James** *A Little Tour in France*

esque. The rich Flamboyant decoration was added to the west front in the 15C: pierced tympana, festooned archivolts, ornamented gables over the doorways. The buttresses, which rise to the base of the belfries, were decorated at the same period with niches and crocketed pinnacles.

The upper section of the north tower, which dates from the 15C, is surmounted by an elegant lantern dome in the early Renaissance style. The south belfry, which was built in the 16C on the Romanesque tower, is also surmounted by a lantern dome, here in the late Renaissance style.

The **interior** of the cathedral has a striking purity of line. The 14C and 15C nave blends perfectly with the older **chancel**, which is one of the most beautiful works of the 13C and is attributed to Étienne de Martagne, the architect who designed the Sainte-Chapelle in Paris.

The **stained-glass windows**★★ are the pride of St-Gatien cathedral. Those in the chancel with their warm colours are 13C. The rose windows in the transept are 14C; the south window is slightly diamond-shaped and the north one is divided by a supporting rib. The windows in the third chapel in the south aisle and the great rose window in the nave are 15C.

The chapel which opens into the south transept contains the **tomb**★ of the children of Charles VIII, an elegant work by the school of Michel Colombe (16C), mounted on a base carved by Jerome de Fiesole.

★ **La Psalette (Cathedral Cloisters) (CY)** ⊙ – This is an elegant Gothic-Renaissance building which once housed the canons and choir, hence the name La Psalette – the place where psalms were sung. The cloisters, which are on the north side of the cathedral, have three ranges: the west range (1460) supports the first-floor library while the north and east ranges (1508-24) are almost completely covered by terraces. A graceful Renaissance spiral staircase leads up to the scriptorium (1520) next to the library, a beautiful room with ogive vaulting and an exhibition of the 13C-14C frescoes from the church in Beaumont-Village.

★ **Place Grégoire-de-Tours (DY 52)** – This square gives a fine view of the east end of the cathedral and the Gothic flying buttresses; to the left is the medieval gable of the **archbishop's palace** (now the Musée des Beaux-Arts): the decisions of the ecclesiastical court were read out from the Renaissance gallery. Note, in rue Manceau, a 15C canon's house with two gabled dormers and, at the beginning of rue Racine, a tufa building with a 15C pointed roof which housed the Justice-des-Bains – the seat of jurisdiction of the metropolitan chapter. This had been built over the ruins of a Gallo-Roman amphitheatre which, during the Renaissance, was mistakenly believed to have been baths.

A little further along rue Racine is the **Centre de Création contemporaine (N)** ⊙ which organises temporary exhibitions of all forms of contemporary art.

Continue to place des Petites-Boucheries and take rue Auguste-Blanqui, then bear right into rue du Petit-Cupidon.

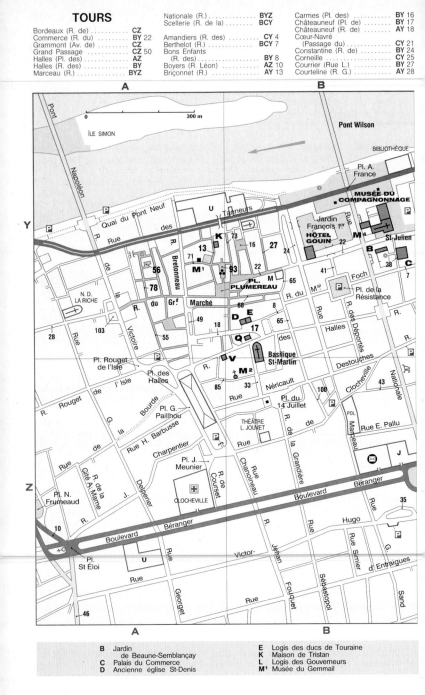

On the corner of rue du Petit-Cupidon and rue des Ursulines is an arched passage through buildings which leads into the garden of the Archives of the Indre-et-Loire *département*.

This spot contains the best preserved part of the Gallo-Roman walls and the ancient city of *Caesarodunum* with one of its defence towers, known as the Tour du Petit Cupidon and, carved out of the wall, the southern postern which would have been the entrance to a Roman road.

Further along the rue des Ursulines, on the left, is the 17C **Chapelle St-Michel** ⊙ in which Mary of the Incarnation is remembered. She was an Ursuline nun who left Tours to spread the Gospel in Canada and founded the first Ursuline convent in Quebec in 1639 *(see Michelin Green Guide Quebec).*

Continue to the end of the street to place François-Sicard.

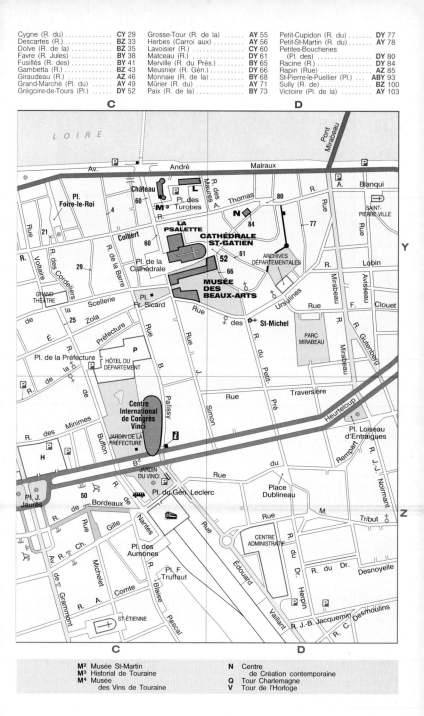

M² Musée St-Martin
M³ Historial de Touraine
M⁴ Musée des Vins de Touraine
N Centre de Création contemporaine
Q Tour Charlemagne
V Tour de l'Horloge

The square is named after the sculptor François Sicard who was born in Tours in 1862 and who made a number of sculptures for his home town. A statue of another artist from Tours, Michel Colombe, stands in the middle of the square.

★★ **Musée des Beaux-Arts** (CY) ⊙ – The fine arts museum is housed in the old archbishop's palace (17C-18C). Before going in, pause to admire the gigantic cedar of Lebanon, perfect in shape, which was planted in the main courtyard in 1804. The round tower *(left)* is recognizable as part of the Gallo-Roman wall from its alternate bands of brick and stone. From the formal garden there is a good view of the front of the museum and the cathedral. The rooms, which are decorated with Louis XVI panelling and silks made in Tours, make a perfect setting for the works of art, some of which used to adorn the châteaux of Richelieu and Chanteloup (now demolished) and the abbeys of

"Le Goût" after Abraham Bosse

Touraine: the Duke of Choiseul's desk, a lacquer commode, paintings by Boucher *(Sylvie fleeing from the Wolf she has wounded)*, Nattier and Rigaud, portraits and paintings of mythical figures by Largillière, Tocque, Perronneau and Vestier *(Bacchus holding a Glass of Wine*, influenced by Il Caravaggio). The "Salle de la Cheminée Louis XIII" is embellished with a fine "French style" polychrome wooden fireplace, typical of the early 17C. The walls are hung with a series of highly colourful anonymous paintings executed after engravings by **Abraham Bosse** (1602-1676), born in Tours. The work of this artist, who came to master the art of etching by adopting the techniques of Jacques Callot, can be seen in the Salle Abraham Bosse. His prints illustrate all the different strata of society and thus provide us with an interesting insight into how people lived in the 17C. Note sculptures by Le Moyne and Houdon, 17C Flemish and Dutch paintings include a famous ex-voto by Rubens and a *Flight into Egypt* by Rembrandt. Among the 14C and 15C paintings on the ground floor are some Italian primitives and the museum's masterpieces, *Christ in the Garden of Olives* and *The Resurrection*, both by **Mantegna**; both once belonged to the retable of San Zeno Maggiore in Verona (*see the current Michelin Green Guide Italy*). There is also a room devoted to Greek and Etruscan ceramics.

The second floor is devoted to 19C and 20C work: Delacroix, Chasseriau, Boulanger's portrait of Balzac, Impressionist canvases and a splendid collection of works heavily influenced by Oriental culture, in particular the mysterious and haunting *Femmes d'Alger* by Eugène Giraud, a painting encapsulating the trend towards anecdotal detail. One room is devoted to the contemporary painter Oliver Debré. There is also a display of ceramics by Avisseau (19C), from the Touraine: plates decorated with motifs in relief in the style of Bernard Palissy. Note the splendid collections of Langeais faience, highly valued throughout Europe in the 19C: the fine texture of the local clay, combined with kaolin, makes it possible to produce a great variety of shapes and the platinum glaze provides an unusual finishing touch.

Château (CY) – A tree-lined walk beside the Loire skirts the heterogeneous buildings of the castle, reminders of past ages. The **Tour de Guise**, with machicolations and a pepper-pot roof, was part of the 13C fortress; the tower owes its name to the young Duke of Guise who was imprisoned in the castle after the assassination of his father *(see BLOIS)* and then escaped. Next to it stands the **Pavillon de Mars**, which was built in the reign of Louis XVI and is flanked on the south side by a 13C round tower.

Aquarium tropical ⓥ – Located on the ground floor of the château, the aquarium is home to over 220 marine and freshwater varieties of tropical fish. The tanks, conceived as living tableaux, are in constant evolution thanks to the dedication of the aquarium staff, who endeavour to re-create the natural environment of the fish by carefully selecting suitable flora and fauna species.

★ **Historial de Touraine (CY M³)** ⓥ – The museum, which is housed in the rooms of the Pavillon de Mars and Tour de Guise *(see above)*, recalls the great moments in the history of Touraine in some 30 waxwork tableaux with 165 figures in sumptuous costumes. The most spectacular scenes show the marriage of Charles VIII and Anne of Brittany, the workshop of Jean Chapillon and his fellow trade-guild smiths, a ball at the court of the Valois etc.

On the quay stands the **Logis des Gouverneurs (CY L)**, a 15C building with gable dormers. At its base and running towards the Tour de Guise is the Gallo-Roman wall, composed of courses of brick alternating with small stones, typical of the period. On the second floor, the **Atelier Histoire de Tours** ⊘, which was founded in close collaboration with the National Urban Archeology Centre and Laboratory, contains archeological and historical documents as well as models and audio-visual presentations which explain the history of Tours and the development of its townscape. In conjunction with these permanent displays there are temporary exhibitions about living in Tours ("Vivre à Tours") which highlight its history.

★ ST-JULIEN DISTRICT (BCY) *1hr*

The streets near the bridge over the Loire suffered considerable bomb damage in the Second World War, but behind the regular modern façades in rue Nationale some picturesque little squares have still survived.

Pont Wilson (BY) – The stone bridge was built in the 18C when the route from Paris to Spain passed through Tours rather than Amboise. It was extensively restored after subsidence in 1978 and now spans the Loire for a distance of 434m/1 424ft.

Église St-Julien (BY) ⊘ – The 11C belfry porch is set back from the street in front of the 13C church. The sombre Gothic interior is lit through windows (1960) by Max Ingrand and Le Chevalier. Originally it had adjoining cloisters (now a garden) and conventual buildings. The Gothic chapter-house still exists, and the **Celliers St-Julien** (12C) is a huge vaulted chamber which now houses a local wine museum, the **musée des Vins de Touraine (M⁴)** ⊘.

★★ **Musée du Compagnonnage (BY)** ⊘ – *Entrance through a porch, 8 rue Nationale, and over a footbridge.*
The trade guild museum is housed in the Guest Room (11C) and the **monks' dormitory** (16C) above the chapter-house of the abbey of St-Julien. It traces the history, customs and skills of the trade guilds which provided training for their members and protected their interests. Both current and obsolete trades (stovesetter, ironmonger, smelter, nailsmith etc) are represented through their tools, historical documents and the many **masterpieces** which the **companions** (derived from *cum panis* and meaning someone with whom one shares one's bread) had to produce to become master craftsmen.

★ **Beaune-Semblançay Garden (BY B)** – *Entrance through a porch, 28 rue Nationale.*
The **Hôtel de Beaune-Semblançay** belonged to the unfortunate Minister of Finance who was hanged during the reign of François I. All that has survived the damage suffered by this Renaissance mansion is an arcaded gallery supporting a chapel, a beautiful façade decorated with pilasters and surrounded by plants, and the charming, finely carved **Beaune fountain**.
In rue Jules-Favre stands the sober and elegant façade of the chamber of commerce (**Palais du Commerce** – **BY C**) which was built in the 18C for the merchants of Tours; the courtyard is more elaborately decorated.

Rue Colbert (CY) – Before Wilson bridge was built, this street together with its extension, rue du Commerce, was the main axis of the city. The half-timbered house at no 41 bears the sign "A la Pucelle armée" (The Armed Maid); Joan of Arc's armour is believed to have been made by the craftsman living here in April 1429. Rue Colbert and rue de la Scellerie, which is reached via rue du Cygne, are full of antique dealers.

Place Foire-le-Roi (CY) – This was the site of the free fairs established by François I; it was also the stage for the mystery plays which were performed when the kings visited Tours. The north side is lined by 15C gabled houses. The beautiful Renaissance mansion (no 8) belonged to Philibert Babou de la Bourdaisière *(see MONTLOUIS-SUR-LOIRE)*. On the west side a side street leads into the narrow and winding "Passage du Cœur-Navré" (Broken-Heart Passage) which leads into rue Colbert.

ADDITIONAL SIGHTS

Musée des Équipages militaires et du Train (V M⁵) ⊘ – In 1807 Napoleon created a division of military carriages to remedy the problem of insufficient transport means: up to then, the army administration had resorted to using the services of various civilian companies, whose efficiency left something to be desired. The museum has been set up in the **pavillon de Condé** (the only vestiges of the abbey of Ste-Marie in Beaumont). Some 10 carefully laid out rooms retrace the history of trains (from the Latin *tranare* to drag along) used in a military capacity. On the ground floor, the "Empire" room explains how the first units of these trains were grouped together to form battalions. The "Restauration"

Centre International de Congrès Vinci

room evokes Marshal Bugeaud and his "flying columns" in Algeria; the "1914-1918" room is a reminder to visitors that the automobile network, functioning on an experimental basis in 1915, became fully operational in 1916, in particular along the *Voie Sacrée* running between Bar-le-Duc and Verdun *(see Green Guide Alsace-Lorraine in French)*. The first floor collections, displayed in rooms bearing the titles "Second World War", "Indochinese War" and "Algeria", are concerned more specifically with the modern train. Three adjoining rooms are devoted to the history of horse-drawn trains, military insignia and muleteers who hired out their animals as a public service.

Centre International de Congrès Vinci (CZ) – Looking for all the world like some gigantic crystal car-ferry, with its stern pointing to the station and its huge elongated hull nudging its way towards the cathedral, this international conference centre, the work of Jean Nouvel, heralds a new architectural style in Tours. The interior features three auditoriums (350, 700 and 2 000 seats) suspended in mid-air – a remarkable technical achievement unique in France. The complex consists of more than 3 500m^2/37 670ft^2 of exhibition space, 22 meeting rooms and an exceptionally advanced sound and image processing and transmission centre. The Vinci was opened on 17 September 1993 and had received more than 370 000 people for a variety of events (congresses, conventions, recitals, entertainment etc) by the end of 1995.

★ **Prieuré de St-Cosme (V)** ⓥ – *Town plan p 245. 3km/2mi west via quai du Pont-Neuf and avenue Proudhon, then along the riverside embankment.*
The priory, little more than a ruin, is situated in a peaceful location in the middle of well-cared-for gardens; there remain a few traces of the church at ground level, as well as the chevet wall, the chancel and the ambulatory (11C and 12C). The poet **Ronsard** was buried here in 1585. He was Prior of St-Cosme from 1565 until his death; a stone slab with a flowering rose bush covers his tomb.
In the monks' refectory, a large 12C building, note the reader's pulpit decorated with columns and sculptured capitals. The **Prior's lodging**, where Ronsard lived and died, is a charming little 15C house; in Ronsard's time an outside staircase led to the first floor of the residence, which only had one large room on each level. This staircase was pulled down in the 17C when the inside staircase was built. The "lodging" now houses a small **lapidary museum**, in which a collection of drawings, plans, photos, engravings and an audio-visual presentation evoke the poet's life.

Château de Plessis-lès-Tours (V R) ⓥ – *Town plan p 245. 1km/0.6mi from the Prieuré de St-Cosme along the avenue du Prieuré.*
This modest brick building is only a small part of the château built by Louis XI in the 15C, which consisted of three wings in a U-shape. The visit includes the room where Louis XI died, surrounded by linen-fold panelling, popular in the 15C. Various other rooms evoke the memory of Louis XI.
Son of Charles VII and Marie of Anjou, **Louis XI** was born in Bourges in 1423 and acceded to the throne in 1461. He spent a lot of time at Plessis-lès-Tours. Anxious to encourage the economic expansion of his kingdom after the ravages of the Hundred Years War, he developed industry and trade. His struggle with the Duke of Burgundy, Charles the Bold, who had designs on the crown, ended in the defeat and death of the Duke in 1477, and annexation of part of the Duchy in 1482. Louis XI's last years were clouded; fearing an attack on his life and imagining that he had leprosy, he lived in a fog of mistrust and superstition.

The betrayal of Cardinal **Jean Balue** came to light in this context: a favourite of Louis XI who showered him with honours, the cardinal secretly conspired with the Duke of Burgundy. He was unmasked in 1469 and imprisoned at Loches until 1480, but lived another 11 years after his release.

On the first floor there are paintings and sculptures recalling the memory of **St Francis of Paola**, a Calabrian hermit, whom Louis XI called to his side at the end of his life. St Francis was the founder of the ascetic Minim Order; he established his first French community on the royal estate at Plessis.

EXCURSIONS

★ **Grange de Meslay** ⊙ – *10km/6mi northeast on ② on the plan, N 10 and a road to the right.*
This former **fortified tithe farm** belonging to Marmoutier Abbey has a beautiful porch, the remains of a perimeter wall and a remarkable **barn**. The barn is a very good example of 13C secular architecture. The rounded main door is set in a pointed gable and the 15C timber roof is supported by four rows of oak heartwood pillars. Touraine music concerts *(see Calendar of events)* and art exhibitions are held in this barn.

Montbazon – *9km/5.6mi south.*
This is one of the 20 fortresses built by Fulk Nerra. From the ruined **keep** which dominates the village there is a good view *(rue des Moulins on the left of the town hall and a path on the right beyond the old gateway).*

Dolmen de Mettray – *12km/8mi northwest on ⑭ on the plan, N 138 turning right onto D 76 to Mettray.*
In a spinney in St-Antoine-du-Rocher to the north of Mettray on the right bank of the Choisille *(along a stone path: signposted)* stands the beautiful dolmen of the "Fairy Grotto", one of the most skilfully constructed megalithic monuments in France; it is 11m/37ft long and 3.7m/12ft high and consists of 12 evenly-cut stone slabs.

TROO

Population 320
Michelin map 64 fold 5 or 232 fold 24 or 238 fold 1
Local map see Vallée du LOIR: Vendôme-La Flèche

The bell-tower of Troo, which is perched on a steep-sided slope, can be seen from a long way off. The village still has numerous troglodyte dwellings. The houses are built in tiers, one above the other up the hillside, and linked by narrow alleys, stairways and mysterious passages. A labyrinth of galleries, called *caforts* (short for *caves fortes*), exists underground in the white tufa rock. In times of war these *caforts* served as hideouts.

SIGHTS

★ **La "butte"** – This is a feudal mound which provides a splendid **panorama** *(viewing table and telescope)* of the sinuous course of the River Loir and of the small church of St-Jacques-des-Guérets on the far bank.

Ancienne collégiale St-Martin – The collegiate church was built in 1050 and altered a century later. It is dominated by a remarkable square tower pierced by openings; the splays are ornamented with small columns in characteristic Angevin style. The windows in the Romanesque apse are Gothic. The nave and chancel are covered by a convex vault. The historiated capitals at the transept crossing are Romanesque. The choir stalls and communion table are 15C. The 16C wooden statue is of St Mamès who is invoked against all stomach ailments.

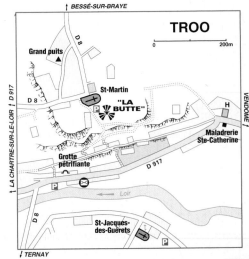

255

Grand puits – The great well is known also as the "talking well" because of its excellent echo; it is 45m/148ft deep and covered by a wooden shingle roof.

Maladrerie Ste-Catherine – On the eastern edge of the town on the south side of D 917 stands a 12C building with fine Romanesque blind arcades. Originally it was a hospice for sick pilgrims travelling to Tours or Compostela; there was also a leper-house to the west of Troo. When this disappeared the hospice took over its goods and its name.

Grotte pétrifiante ⊘ – The petrifying cave in which running water is a permanent feature contains stalactites and lime encrustations.

Église St-Jacques-des-Guérets – The services in this church were conducted by the Augustinians from the abbey of St-Georges-des-Bois southeast of Troo. The **murals★** were painted between 1130 and 1170 and reflect Byzantine influence; the draughtsmanship and the freshness of the colours are particularly pleasing. The most beautiful are in the apse: the Crucifixion, in which the half-figures represent the sun and the moon, and the Resurrection of the Dead *(left)*; Christ in Majesty, surrounded by the symbols of the Evangelists; and the Last Supper *(right)*. Statues of St Augustine and St George adorn the embrasure of the central window. On the right side of the apse appears the Martyrdom of St James who was beheaded by Herod, with Paradise above: the Heavenly Elect shelter in niches like pigeonholes. High up on the south wall of the nave is St Nicholas performing a miracle: the saint is throwing three gold pieces to three sisters whose father was about to sell them because he was too poor to give them a dowry; below is the Resurrection of Lazarus. Further on is a vast composition representing the Descent into Hell: a majestic figure of Jesus is seen delivering Adam and Eve. The left wall of the church was painted at different times from the 12C to 15C: Nativity and Massacre of the Innocents. In the church are two painted wooden statues (16C): in a niche *(left)* St James on a base which bears the arms of Savoy; in the chancel *(left)* St Peter.

Château d'USSÉ★★

Michelin map 64 fold 13 or 232 fold 34 – 14km/9mi northeast of Chinon
Local map see Vallée de la LOIRE: ①

The **château** ⊘ stands with its back to a cliff on the edge of Chinon forest, its terraced gardens overlooking the Indre river. Its impressive bulk and fortified towers contrast sharply with the white stone and the myriad roofs, turrets, dormers and chimneys rising against a green background. The best view is from the bridge, some 200m/220yd from the château, or from the Loire embankment. Tradition has it that when Charles Perrault, the famous French writer of fairy-tales, was looking for a setting for *Sleeping Beauty*, he chose Ussé as his model.

From the Bueils to the Blacas – Ussé is a very old fortress; in the 15C it became the property of a great family from Touraine, the Bueils, who had distinguished themselves in the Hundred Years War (1337-1453). In 1485, Antoine de Bueil, who had married one of the daughters of Charles VII and Agnès Sorel, sold Ussé to the Espinays, a Breton family who had been chamberlains and cupbearers to the Duke of Brittany and to Louis XI and Charles VIII. It was they who built the courtyard ranges and the chapel in the park. The château often changed hands. Among its owners was Vauban's son-in-law, Louis Bernin de Valentinay; the great engineer paid frequent visits to Ussé. The Countess de la Rochejaquelein left the estate to the Count of Blacas, whose descendants are its present owners.

TOUR

Exterior

The outside walls (15C) have a military appearance while the buildings overlooking the courtyard are more welcoming and some even carry an elegant Renaissance touch.

The courtyard is enclosed by three heavily-restored ranges: the east wing is Gothic, the west wing Renaissance and the south wing a combination of Gothic and classical styles. As in the case of Chaumont château, the north wing was pulled down in the 17C to open up the view of the Loire and Indre valleys from the terrace. The west wing is extended by a 17C pavilion. On the walk up towards the château, a lovely kaleidoscope of roofs and turrets can be glimpsed through the leaves of the stately cedars of Lebanon, said to have been planted by the great French author Chateaubriand.

Interior

Salle des gardes – In a corner of the building, the guard-room boasts a superb 17C *trompe-l'œil* ceiling and houses a collection of Oriental weapons. Note the delicately-painted ivory miniatures, each representing a famous sight. The small adjoining room presents porcelain from China and Japan.

Ancienne chapelle – The old chapel, which has been converted into a salon, has a fine set of furniture, including a Mazarin desk fashioned from lemon-tree wood and three 400-year-old Brussels tapestries, with colours which have remained vivid. Every year, this salon hosts an **exhibition of historic costumes** (mannequins, fashion accessories).

Grande Galerie – Linking the east and west wings of the château, the Great Gallery is hung with **Flemish tapestries★** depicting lively, realistic country scenes inspired by the work of Teniers.

Beyond the room devoted to hunting trophies, the wide 17C staircase (fine wrought-iron banister) leads to the rooms on the first floor: the library and the King's apartment. In the antechamber there is a splendid 16C Italian cabinet (admire the ebony marquetry inside, inlaid with ivory and mother-of-pearl).

Château d'Ussé
Flemish tapestry after Teniers the Younger

Chambre du Roi – As in all large stately residences, one of the bedrooms was set aside for the King in the event of his paying a visit to the château. This particular room was in fact never occupied by the sovereign.

It is hung with crimson silk furnishings, and contains a four-poster bed, a large Venetian mirror and a fine set of Louis XVI furniture.

The top of the **donjon** (keep) houses an extremely interesting **salle de jeux★** (recreation room) with china dinner services, toy trains and miniature furniture items from dolls' houses.

Dotted along the **wall walk**, several display cabinets illustrate the story of Sleeping Beauty: the wicked Fairy, Prince Charming and other popular childhood characters will delight visitors of all ages.

★ Chapel – Standing on its own in the park, the chapel was built from 1520 to 1538 in the pure Renaissance style. The west façade is the most remarkable. The initials C and L, to be found in other parts of the domain, are used as a decorative motif: they refer to the first names of Charles d'Espinay, who built the chapel, and his wife Lucrèce de Pons. Inside, the elegant and well-lit chancel is embellished with a hanging keystone and 16C carved stalls. The south chapel, supported by rib vaulting, houses a pretty Virgin Mary in enamelled earthenware attributed to Luca della Robbia.

Château de VALENÇAY★★

Michelin map 64 fold 18 or 238 fold 16

Geographically Valençay is in the Berry region but the château can be included with those in the Loire valley because of the period of its construction and its huge size, in which it resembles Chambord.

A financier's château – Valençay was built c 1540 by Jacques d'Estampes, the owner of the existing castle. He had married the daughter of a financier, who brought him a large dowry, and he wanted a residence worthy of his new fortune. The 12C castle was demolished and in its place rose the present sumptuous building. Finance has often been involved in the history of Valençay; among its owners were several Farmers-General and even the famous **John Law** whose dizzy banking career was an early and masterly example of inflation.

Charles-Maurice de Talleyrand-Périgord, who had begun his career under Louis XVI as Bishop of Autun, was Foreign Minister when he bought Valençay in 1803 at the request of Napoleon, so that he would have somewhere to receive important foreign visitors. Talleyrand managed his career so skilfully that he did not finally retire until 1834.

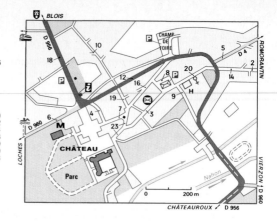

VALENÇAY

Blois (R. de) 4
Château (R. du) ... 7
Halle au blé (Pl. de la) 8
République (R. de la) 16

Abreuvoir (R. de l') 2
Auditoire (R. de l') . 3
Chabris (Rte de) .. 5
Châtaigniers (R. des) 6
Hymans (R. Max) .. 9
Marnières (R. des) . 10
Nationale (R.) 12
Princes (R. des) ... 14
Résistance (Av. de la) 18
St-Maurice (R.) 19
Talleyrand (R. de) . 20
Tournebride (R. du) 23

TOUR ⏱ 1hr

Son et lumière – *See the Practical information section at the end of the guide.*

The entrance pavilion is a huge building, designed like a keep but for show not defence with many windows, harmless turrets and fancy machicolations. The steep roof is pierced with high dormer windows and surmounted by monumental chimneys.

Such architecture is also found in the Renaissance châteaux of the Loire valley but here there are also the first signs of the classical style: superimposed pilasters with Doric (ground floor), Ionic (first floor) and Corinthian (second floor) capitals.

The classical style is even more evident in the huge corner towers: domes take the place of the pepper-pot roofs which were the rule on the banks of the Loire in the 16C.

West wing – The west wing was added in the 17C and altered in the 18C. At roof level mansard windows alternate with bulls' eyes (small circular apertures). The tour of the ground floor includes the great Louis XVI vestibule; the gallery devoted to the Talleyrand-Périgord family; the Grand Salon and the Blue Salon which contain many works of art and sumptuous Empire furniture including the famous "Congress of Vienna" table; and the apartments of the Duchess of Dino. On the first floor the bedroom of Prince Talleyrand is followed by the room occupied by Ferdinand VII, King of Spain, when he was confined to Valençay by Napoleon from 1808 to 1814; the apartments of the Duke of Dino and those of Mme de Bénévent (portrait of the princess by Élisabeth Vigée-Lebrun); the great gallery (with a *Diana* by Houdon) and the great staircase. Something of the spirit of the festivities organised by Talleyrand and his master chef, **Marie-Antoine Carême**, still lingers in the great dining room and the kitchens beneath.

Park ⏱ – Black swans, ducks and peacocks strut freely in the formal French gardens near the château. Under the great trees in the park deer, llamas, camels and kangaroos are kept in vast enclosures.

Musée de l'Automobile du Centre (M) ⏱ – The car museum, concealed in the park, contains the collection of the Guignard brothers, the grandsons of a coachbuilder from Vatan (Indre). There are over 60 vintage cars (the earliest dating from 1898), perfectly maintained in working order, including the 1908 Renault limousine used by Presidents Poincaré and Millerand; there are also road documents from the early days of motoring, old Michelin maps and guides pre-dating 1914.

VENDÔME★★

Population 17 525
Michelin map 64 fold 6 or 238 fold 2
Local maps see Vallée du LOIR: Bonneval-Vendôme and Vendôme-La Flèche

At the foot of a steep bluff, which is crowned by a castle, the River Loir divides into several channels which flow slowly under a number of bridges. Vendôme, which since 1990 is only 42 minutes away from Paris thanks to the new TGV line, stands on a group of islands dotted with gables and steep slate roofs. The industrialisation of the town and the surrounding area has produced such diverse activities as glove making (dating back to the Renaissance), printing, factory farming (Bel), household appliances (De Dietrich), electronics etc. The Communauté du Pays de Vendôme, grouping together the municipalities of Azé, Lunay, Marcilly, St-Firmin-des-Prés, St-Ouen, Thoré-la-Rochette and Vendôme, has been set up to act as a supervising body in charge of local economic development and town-planning.

A troubled history – Although the origins of Vendôme can be traced back to the Gaulish, and even as far back as the Neolithic periods, before the town received its name, Vindocenum, in the Gallo-Roman period, it only began to acquire importance under the Counts, first the Bouchard family, who were faithful supporters of the Capet dynasty, and particularly under the son of Fulk Nerra, **Geoffrey Martel** (11C), who founded La Trinité abbey.

Since the Count of Vendôme was a vassal of the Plantagenets, his estate was caught up in the Hundred Years War: its position on the border between the French and English possessions made it particularly vulnerable. In 1371 the royal house of Bourbon inherited Vendôme and in 1515 François I raised it to a duchy. In 1589 the town sided with the League but was captured by its overlord, Henri IV, and suffered for its disloyalty; the town was sacked and only the abbey church was left standing.

Henri IV's son, César – Henri IV gave Vendôme to César, his son by Gabrielle d'Estrées. César de Vendôme was often resident on his feudal estate while he involved himself with conspiracies, first during the minority of Louis XIII and then against Richelieu. He was imprisoned at Vincennes for four years before being exiled. He eventually lent his support to Mazarin's cause, before dying in 1655.

Balzac (1799-1850)

On 22 June 1807 the Collège des Oratoriens in Vendôme registered the entry of an eight-year-old boy, Honoré de Balzac. The future historical novelist was an absent-minded and undisciplined pupil. Balzac was to recall the severity of school discipline of those days in his writing. His general clumsiness and ineptitude at standard children's pursuits made him the frequent butt of his fellow pupils' jokes. He regularly got himself put into detention in order to read in peace. The harshness of the school regime eventually undermined his health and his parents had to take him away.

Balzac's early efforts at writing met with minimal success, so he embarked on a career in printing. However, the firm in which he was joint partner went bankrupt, leaving him at the age of 30 with debts which he was to spend the rest of his life attempting to pay off. He returned to writing and over the next 20 years produced a phenomenal number of novels (about 90), a vast collection which constitutes a richly detailed record of the society of his time, covering all walks of life and reflecting what he saw as people's overriding motivations at that time, mainly money and ambition. Typically, Balzac's novels contain keenly observed settings, peopled by characters exaggerated almost to the point of caricature by their creator's vivid imagination. Balzac's fascination by the contrast between life in the provinces and that in the glittering French capital is also reflected in his work.

Balzac retrospectively attached the label **La Comédie Humaine** to his life's work, giving some indication of the breadth of scope of the world he had tried to evoke – an ambitious project formulated after he had already written many of his most famous novels, but which was to remain uncompleted on his untimely death from overwork, just months after he had finally married Eveline Hanska, the Polish countess with whom he had maintained a passionate 18-year correspondence.

★ ABBAYE DE LA TRINITÉ *1hr*

One summer night, Geoffrey Martel, Count of Anjou, saw three fiery spears plunge into a fountain and decided to found a monastery which was dedicated to the Holy Trinity on 31 May 1040. Under the Benedictine Order the abbey grew considerably, becoming one of the most powerful religious foundations in France, to the extent that eventually the abbot was automatically made a cardinal. In the 12C this office was held by the famous Geoffroi of Vendôme, friend of Pope Urban II.

Until the Revolution pilgrims flocked to Trinité abbey to venerate a relic of the Holy Tear *(Sainte Larme)* – shed by Christ on Lazarus's tomb – which Geoffrey Martel had brought back from Constantinople. The knights of Vendôme would rally to the cry of "Sainte Larme de Vendôme". The relic was venerated on "Lazarus's Friday" and its curative powers were invoked in the case of eye diseases; this explains the repeated use of the theme of the resurrection of Lazarus in the decoration of the church.

★★ **Abbey church** – The abbey church is a remarkable example of Flamboyant Gothic architecture. The entrance to the abbey precinct is in rue de l'Abbaye. On either side of the wall stand the Romanesque arcades of the abbey granary which have been incorporated into more modern buildings; in fact from the 14C onwards the monks allowed the citizens to build their shops against the abbey walls.

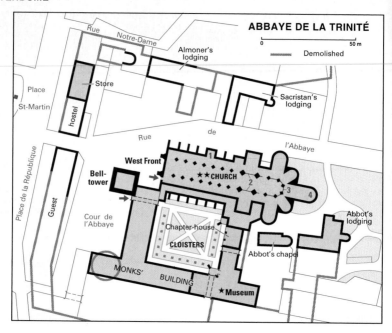

ABBAYE DE LA TRINITÉ

Romanesque bell-tower – To the right of the west front and set apart from it stands the 12C bell-tower, 80m/262ft high, which served as a model for the Old Bell-tower of the Cathedral of Notre-Dame at Chartres. An interesting feature is the way the windows and arcades, which are blind at ground level, grow larger as the embrasures also increase in size. The transition from a square to an octagonal tower is made by means of open-work mini bell-towers at the corners. The base of the first storey is decorated with grinning masks and animals.

West front – The astonishing Flamboyant west front, which is accentuated by a great carved gable, was built early in the 16C by Jean de Beauce, who designed the New Bell-tower of Chartres Cathedral. The decorative open-work, so delicate it looks like a piece of lace, contrasts with the plainer Romanesque tower.

Interior – The nave, which was started at the transept end in the middle of the 14C, was not completed until after the Hundred Years War; the transept, all that is left of the 11C building, leads to the chancel and ambulatory with its five radiating chapels.

The nave features a remarkably generous triforium and high windows. The transition from the 14C to 15C phase of construction was achieved without spoiling the overall unity of design: the capitals are phased out and the pattern of the frieze changes, as does the decoration of the triforium and the ribs. The baptismal chapel (1) in the north aisle contains a beautiful Renaissance font in white marble supported by a carved pedestal from the gardens of Blois château. The primitive capitals of the transept crossing are surmounted by polychrome statues (13C) of the Virgin Mary with the Archangel Gabriel, St Peter and St Eutropius who was venerated in the abbey church. The transept vaulting with its historiated keystones was altered in the 14C in the Angevin style; in the left transept are statues of St John the Baptist (14C) and the Virgin Mary (16C). The 14C chancel, which is lit through windows of the same date, is decorated with beautiful late-15C stalls★ (2). The misericords are decorated with naïve scenes illustrating daily life with various trades and zodiac signs. The choir screen (3) enclosing the chancel shows Italian influence. To the left of the high altar is the base of the famous monument of the Holy Tear, decorated with tears, with a small aperture through which the relic was displayed to the faithful by one of the monks.

The chapels radiating from the ambulatory are decorated with 16C stained glass which has been extensively restored: the best section, which depicts the meal in Simon's house, taken from a German engraving, is in the first chapel to the left of the axial chapel. This also contains a **window** dating from 1140 depicting the Virgin and Child (4).

Conventional buildings – Only the east side of the 14C cloisters exists in its entirety. In the 14C-15C **chapter-house** ⊘ a number of wall-paintings have been uncovered, depicting episodes from the life of Christ. The classical-style buildings now house a museum *(see below)*.

R. Mazin/TOP

Vendôme – 15C stalls in the abbey church

Take the passage through the south range of buildings to admire the monumental south front which was built between 1732 and 1742; the pediments bear the royal fleur-de-lis, the motto (Pax) and the emblem (Lamb) of the Order of St Benedict.

★ **Museum (M)** ⊙ – The museum collections are displayed in the abbey's monastic buildings which are reached up a majestic stairway.

The most interesting rooms on the ground floor are devoted to **mural painting**★ in the Loire valley and to **religious art**★ in the Vendôme area from the Middle Ages to the Renaissance. There are remains of the 16C tomb of Marie de Luxembourg and François de Bourbon-Vendôme, fragments of the funerary sculptures of Catherine and Jean VII de Bourbon, keystones from the cloister vaults, and an octagonal stoup which once formed part of the Holy Tear monument.

On the upper floors are the sections on archeology and natural history. Certain rooms are devoted to 16C-19C paintings and furniture and to earthenware; there is a superb late-18C **harp**★, the work of Nadermann, Marie-Antoinette's instrument-maker, together with contemporary sculptures by the artist **Louis Leygue**, from Naveil. Another room displays the tools used in the old local crafts and a reconstruction of a Vendôme rural interior.

ADDITIONAL SIGHTS

Jardin public – Running down to the riverside, the public garden gives a good view over the town, the abbey and the 13C-14C gateway, **Porte d'Eau** or Arche des Grands Prés.

From the open space on the opposite bank, place de la Liberté, there are views of the Porte d'Eau from a different angle as well as of the 13C **Tour de l'Islette**. Together with the **Porte St-Georges** *(see below)* these structures are all that is left of the old ramparts.

Parc Ronsard – Round this shady park are the Lycée Ronsard (originally the Collège des Oratoriens where Balzac was a pupil and now occupied by the offices of the town hall), the late-15C Hôtel de Saillant (now the tourist information centre) and the municipal library with its important collection of old books including 11 incunabula. A 16C two-storeyed wash-house (**L**) is sited on the arm of the river running through the park. The *Fallen Warrior* on the lawn is a bronze by Louis Leygue *(see above)*.

Chapelle St-Jacques – Rebuilt in the 15C, and subsequently attached to the Collège des Oratoriens, the chapel once served the pilgrims on their way to Compostela. It now houses temporary exhibitions.

Église de la Madeleine – The church bell-tower, which dates from 1474, is surmounted by an elegant crocketed spire.

Place St-Martin (19) – Until the 19C St-Martin's church (15C-16C) stood here; only the bell-tower remains. There is also a fine 16C timber-framed house called the "Grand St-Martin"; it is ornamented with figures and coats of arms and has a statue of Maréchal de **Rochambeau**.

Porte St-Georges – St-Georges gateway was the entrance to the town from the River Loir; it is flanked by towers largely built in the 14C although the front facing the bridge is decorated with machicolations and carvings of dolphins and Renaissance medallions which were added early in the 16C by Marie de Luxembourg, Duchess of Vendôme.

The gate was enlarged under the Empire to accommodate the passage of Napoleon's armies. Inside is the Council Chamber, in use since the 16C.

Castle ⊙ – *Access by car via St-Lubin district and Le Temple, a hamlet which grew up round a Templar commandery.* The ruined castle is set on the top of an outcrop – "la Montagne" – which overlooks the Loir. It consists of an earth wall and ramparts with 13C and 14C machicolated round towers at intervals; the great Poitiers tower (**F**) on the east side was reconstructed in the 15C. The early-17C Beauce gate (**K**) leads into the precinct which is now a huge garden. There are traces of the collegiate church of St-Georges which was founded by Agnès of Burgundy and where the Counts of Vendôme were buried: Antoine de Bourbon and Jeanne d'Albret, the parents of Henri IV, were buried here.

Promenade de la Montagne – From the terraces there are picturesque views★ of Vendôme and the Loir valley.

EXCURSIONS

Areines – *3km/2mi east on D 917 and the first turning left. See AREINES.*

Nourray – *11km/7mi south on N 10 and the third road on the left.*
The little **church** ⊘ which stands alone in the square has a row of Romanesque arcades beneath carved corbels on the chevet; note the polylobed arch of the central window. Inside, the ovenvaulted apse is surrounded by arcading with carved capitals.

Change (R. du)	5	Béguines (R. des)	3
Poterie (R.)		Bourbon (R. A.)	4
République (Pl. de la)	14	Chartrain (Fg)	6
St-Martin (Pl.)	19	Chevallier (R.)	7
Saulnerie (R.)	22	Gaulle (R. du Gén.-de)	8
		Grève (R. de la)	9
Abbaye (R. de l')	2	Guesnault (R.)	12
		St-Bié (R.)	15
		St-Jacques (R.)	18
		Verdun (Av. de)	23

F Tour de Poitiers   L Lavoir
H Hôtel de ville   M Musée
K Porte de Beauce

Villemardy – *14km/9mi southeast on D 957; turn left to Périgny and bear right to Villemardy.*
The **church** ⊘ dating from the 12C has a simple nave ending in a Gothic chancel. The interior decoration in carved oak is remarkably uniform; the high altar and tabernacle, which are surmounted by an altarpiece, are in the classical style, as are the two small symmetrical altars in the nave. The left wall of the chancel is decorated with a fresco (16C), the Adoration of the Magi, flanked by columns and a pediment in *trompe l'œil;* note the Virgin's head-dress which helps to determine the date of the work.

Rhodon – *19km/12mi southeast on D 917 (towards Beaugency); in Villetrun turn right to Selommes (D 111) and then left (D 161).*
The internal walls and Gothic vaulting of the **church** bear traces of 14C and 15C mural paintings: Christ in Majesty in the apse and the Months of the Year on one of the transverse arches of the nave.

Château du VERGER

Michelin map 64 south of fold 1 or 232 fold 20 – 3km/2mi north of Seiches

A great moat, flint towers with dressings and machicolations in white tufa, a gatehouse and imposing outbuildings *(private)* recall the huge residence which **Pierre de Rohan-Guéménée**, Maréchal de Gié, started to build in 1482 and where he received Charles VIII whose life he had saved at Fornoue. De Rohan was a marshal of France by the age of 25 and Louis XII's head of Council. In 1506 he unwisely intercepted the luggage of Anne of Brittany which he suspected of containing crown property, since the King was thought to be dying. The Queen had De Rohan banished to Verger. In 1776 Cardinal de Rohan ordered the château to be demolished; the precious works of art which it contained were dispersed.

The length of time given in this guide
– for touring allows time to enjoy the views and the scenery
– for sightseeing is the average time required for a visit.

Jardins et château de VILLANDRY★★★

Population 776
Michelin map 64 or 232 fold 35
Local map see Vallée de la LOIRE: Orléans-Chinon

Villandry is one of the last great Renaissance châteaux to be built on the Loire; it has features unusual in Touraine, like rectangular pavilions (instead of the previous round towers) as well as the layout of the esplanade and its moat.
Villandry's international fame is, however, based not so much on its château as on its gardens, which are among the most fascinating in France.

★★★ GARDENS ⊘ 1hr

The gardens at Villandry *(illustration pp 266-7)* are the most complete example in France of the formal Renaissance style adopted under the influence of the Italian gardeners brought into the country by Charles VIII; French traditions nevertheless assert themselves in many of the details.
When Joachim de Carvallo, founder of the French Historic Houses Association, acquired Villandry in 1906, he set about restoring the gardens to their original state, previous owners having altered them beyond recognition. The best overall **view** of the gardens is from the terraces to the rear of the château or from the top of the keep. There are three terraces one above the other: the highest, the water garden, has a fine sheet of water acting as a reservoir; below it is the flower garden, consisting of geometric designs outlined in box, one representing allegories of love, the other symbolising music; further designs are based on the Maltese, Languedoc and Basque crosses.
At the lowest level is the fascinating ornamental kitchen garden, a multi-coloured chequerboard of vegetables and fruit trees arranged in nine squares and enclosed by clipped hedges of box and yew. Between this and the church a herb garden has been laid out.
Canals, fountains, cascades, vine-covered pergolas, and the Romanesque village church all combine to make a charming background to the scene.
The flowers, shrubs and fruit trees known in the 16C were more or less the same species as today, though the potato had not yet arrived (introduced by Parmentier in the 18C). The art of gardening was already well-advanced, with pruning, grafting, the use of greenhouses and the raising of early vegetables.

★★ CHÂTEAU ⊘ 30min

Nothing remains of the early fortress except the keep, a square tower incorporated in the present structure which was built in the 16C by Jean Le Breton, Secretary of State to François I. Three ranges of buildings enclose the courtyard which is open on the north side overlooking the Cher and the Loire in the valley.
Joachim de Carvallo, a Spaniard, furnished the château with Spanish furniture and an interesting collection of paintings (16C, 17C and 18C Spanish schools). The great salon and the dining room on the ground floor have Louis XV panelling. The grand staircase with its wrought-iron banister leads to the picture gallery and to the room with the 13C **Mudéjar ceiling** which came from Toledo; the coffers are painted and gilded with typical Moorish motifs, an unexpected sight under northern skies; there are two 16C Italian paintings on wood (St Paul and St John) in lively colours and a portrait of the Infanta by the Velasquez school.
An audio-visual display in the picture gallery shows the astonishingly varied appearance of the gardens according to the season and the time of day.
From the keep there is a splendid view over the terraces of the gardens towards the Rivers Cher and Loire.

Château de VILLESAVIN

Michelin map 64 fold 18 or 238 folds 18, 16 – 3km/2mi west of Bracieux

Villesavin derives from Villa Savinus, the name of a Roman villa which stood beside the Roman road built by Hadrian which passed through Ponts d'Arian (Hadrian's Bridges) on the south side of the River Beuvron. The villa's existence is attested by the number of sarcophagi which have been found in the grounds, one of which is on display in the château.

The **château** ⊘ was built between 1526 and 1537 by Jean Le Breton, Lord of Villandry and superintendent of works at Chambord. It is a charming Renaissance building with certain classical tendencies and consists of a central block flanked by symmetrical pavilions.
The handsome dormer windows in the attics and the inscription on the rear façade add to the beauty of the château's harmonious proportions. The 16C white marble Italian **basin** in the courtyard is a very fine example of Renaissance decorative sculpture.

Château de VILLESAVIN

A collection of pewterware – plates, jugs etc – is on display in some of the furnished rooms. There are some vintage cars in the outbuildings.

To the left of the château stands a large 16C **dovecot** with 1 500 pigeonholes; it is in a good state of preservation, with its revolving ladder still intact.

Pigeons as a status symbol

The right to keep pigeons – held essentially by large landowners – was one of the privileges that disappeared with the Revolution. The size of the dovecot depended on the size of the estate: there was one pigeonhole containing a couple of birds for each acre of land. In the Middle Ages, dovecots were built to attract pigeons and doves for two reasons: not only did the birds provide meat, but their droppings were also highly prized as a fertilizer – though it was so rich in nitrates that it could be used only in the rainy season, when it would be naturally diluted. It is thought that the practice of keeping pigeons was brought back by the Crusaders from the Middle East where the land has always been fertilized with pigeon manure.

VOUVRAY

Population 2 598
Michelin map 64 fold 15 or 232 fold 36 or 238 fold 13
Local map see Vallée de la LOIRE: Orléans-Chinon

At the heart of the famous vineyard is the village of Vouvray which is set on the south-facing slopes of the hills that overlook the north bank of the Loire upriver from Tours. There are one or two old troglodyte houses in the village.

Vouvray boasts a statue of Gaudissart, the famous travelling salesman whom Balzac described in one of his novels. **Balzac** was born in Tours and often came to visit friends in Vouvray. The atmosphere and characters of 1830 have gone but the charm of the landscape described in his novels still remains.

Still or sparkling white Vouvray wines are some of the most famous of Touraine. Many wine producers and merchants have **caves** (cellars) open to the public.

Espace de la Vigne et du Vin ⊙ – This centre retraces the history of **wine-making** through various tools and pieces of equipment used through the ages up to the present. True to tradition, the centre organises a tasting session at the end of the visit, an opportunity to get acquainted with some delicious wines.

EXCURSION

Vernou-sur-Brenne – *4km/2.5mi east on D 46.* Vernou's picturesque old houses are surrounded by Vouvray vineyards against a hillside riddled with caves.

On leaving Vernou, take D 76 towards Jallanges.

The **Château de Jallanges** ⊙ comes into sight on a small ridge rising out of a sea of vineyards. It is Renaissance and has a 17C chapel.

YÈVRE-LE-CHÂTEL

Population 210
Michelin map 60 fold 20 or 237 fold 41 – 6km/4mi east of Pithiviers

Yèvre's site – on a promontory of the Beauce plateau overlooking the natural trench of the Rimarde, a tributary of the River Essone – cries out for a castle. The present ruins, the kernel of a fortified town, would appear to belong to a royal castle built in the 13C by Philippe-Auguste. A fortified gate under the elm trees in the main square opens into the outer bailey of the castle.

Château fort ⊙ – The fortress is diamond-shaped with a round tower at each corner containing hexagonal rooms with ogive vaulting.

The unprotected sentry walk linking the towers is dangerous.

Platforms in the northwest and south towers provide a **view** of the Beauce and the Gâtinais regions. On a clear day the spire of Pithiviers church is visible. To the south the treetops of Orléans forest darken the horizon.

Église St-Lubin – On the south side of the village among the tombstones stands the unfinished stone shell of a huge Gothic church. Its vast size seems to have been dictated by the need for a place of refuge rather than a place of worship. The church's great elegance and the speed of its construction (the first quarter of the 13C) suggest that the project had royal backing.

Rulers of France (until the Third Republic)

Ruler	Reign
Hugues Capet	987-996
Robert II "the Pious"	996-1031
Henri I	1031-60
Philippe I	1060-1108
Louis VI	1108-37
Louis VII	1137-80
Philippe II (Philippe-Auguste)	1180-1223
Louis VIII	1223-26
Louis IX (St Louis)	1226-70
Philippe III "the Bold"	1270-85
Philippe IV "the Fair"	1285-1314
Louis X "the Headstrong"	1314-16
Philippe V	1316-22
Charles IV "the Fair"	1322-28
Philippe VI	1328-50
Jean II "the Good"	1350-64
Charles V "the Wise"	1364-80
Charles VI "the Mad"	1380-1422
Charles VII	1422-61
Louis XI	1461-83
Charles VIII	1483-98
Louis XII	1498-1515
François I	1515-47
Henri II	1547-59
François II	1559-60
Charles IX	1560-74
Henri III	1574-89
Henri IV "Vert-Galant" *	1589-1610
Louis XIII	1610-43
Louis XIV	1643-1715
Louis XV	1715-74
Louis XVI	1774-89
French Revolution	1789-1804
Napoleon I (Emperor)	1804-14
Louis XVIII	1814-24
Charles X	1824-30
Louis-Philippe "the Citizen-King"	1830-48
Louis-Napoleon (Prince-President)	1848-52
Napoleon III (Emperor)	1852-70

* *Henri IV's nickname reflects his reputation as something of a ladies' man*

Practical
Information

Planning your trip

Passport – Visitors entering France must be in possession of a valid national passport. Citizens of one of the European Union countries can use a national identity card if they have one. In case of loss or theft report to your country's embassy or consulate and the local police. A leaflet entitled *Get It Right Before You Go*, on the do's and don't's of staying in France, is available from the French Tourist Office.

Visa – No **entry visa** is required for European Union, US, Canadian and New Zealand citizens as long as their stay in France does not exceed 3 months. Australians require a visa and should apply for one at the nearest French consulate. Citizens of other countries, check with a French consulate or travel agent.
US citizens should obtain the booklet *Your Trip Abroad* (US$1.25), which provides useful information on visa requirements, customs regulations, medical care etc. for international travellers. Contact the Superintendent of Documents, PO Box 371954, Pittsburgh, PA 15250-7954, ☏ (202) 512-1800.

Customs – Apply to the Customs Office (UK) for a leaflet entitled *A Guide for Travellers* on customs regulations and the full range of duty-free allowances. The US Customs Service, PO Box 7407, Washington, DC 20044, ☏ (202) 927-5580, offers a free publication *Know Before You Go* for US residents. There are no customs formalities for holidaymakers bringing caravans into France for a stay of less than 6 months. No customs document is necessary for pleasure boats and outboard motors for a stay of less than 6 months, but the registration certificate should be kept on board.

French tourist offices – For information, brochures, maps and assistance in planning a trip to France, travellers should contact the official tourist office in their own country:

Australia - New Zealand

French Tourist Office, BNP Building, 12 Castlereagh Street, Sydney, NSW 2000.
☏ (2)-9231-5244, Fax (2)-9231-8682.

Canada

Maison de la France, 1981 Av McGill College, Suite 940, Montreal, QUE H3A 2W9.
☏ (514) 288-4264, Fax (514) 845-4868/(416) 767-6755.

Eire

French Tourist Office, 35 Lower Abbey St, Dublin 1,
☏ (1) 703-40-46, Fax (1) 874-73-24.

United Kingdom

French Tourist Office, 178 Piccadilly, London W1V 0AL,
☏ (0891) 244123 (France Information Line, £0.45-0.50/min),
e-mail *piccadilly@mdlf.demon.co.uk*

United States

France On Call Hotline: ☏ 900-990-0040 (US$0.50/min) for information on hotels, restaurants and transportation.
East Coast: 444 Madison Avenue, 16th floor, New York, NY 10022.
☏ (212) 838-7800, Fax (212) 838-7855.
Mid-West: 676 North Michigan Avenue, Suite 3360, Chicago, IL 60611-2819.
☏ (312) 751-7800, Fax (312) 337-6339.
West Coast: 9454 Wilshire Boulevard, Suite 715, Beverly Hills, CA 90212-2967.
☏ (310) 271-2693, Fax (310) 276-2835.

When to go – Visitors to the Loire valley will be impressed by the beauty and variety of the landscape all year round. It is worth noting, when planning your visit, that the weather can be very hot and the various places of interest draw large crowds of visitors at the height of the summer (July-August).
Spring comes early to the Loire valley, especially in the western Loire which seems to enjoy its own microclimate creating a pocket of mild weather conditions. Trees come into blossom as early as the beginning of April in the Angers region and local plantlife burgeons in May and June, with green fields and orchards stretching away on either side of the roads. The river Loire is at its most scenic during this period.
By July, the river is reduced to a narrow stream in places, winding between golden sandbanks. Tempting although it is to go for a swim, bathers should first check that the riverbed is safe, as the sandbanks can be quite treacherous in some places.
The month of September, characteristically mild, heralds the wine harvest, in honour of which there are lively traditional harvest processions held throughout the Loire valley.

Travelling to France

By air – The various national and other independent airlines operate services to **Paris** airports (Roissy-Charles de Gaulle to the north, and Orly to the south). Daily connecting flights from both these airports to **Nantes** (flight time: 55min) are operated by Air Inter Europe (Air France Group).

There are daily direct flights from **London (Gatwick)** to **Nantes** (operated by Brit Air). Contact airline companies and travel agents for details of package tour flights with a rail or coach link-up as well as Fly-Drive schemes.

By rail – Eurostar runs via the Channel Tunnel between **London** (Waterloo International Station, ☎ (0345) 881881) and **Paris** (Gare du Nord) in 3 hours (bookings and information ☎ (0345) 303030). In Paris it links to the high-speed rail network (TGV) which covers most of France. Fast inter-city service from **Paris** (Gare Montparnasse) to **Le Mans** (50min), **Tours** (1hr) and **Angers** (1hr 30min) on the TGV. There are rail passes offering unlimited travel and group travel tickets offering services for parties. **Eurodomino Rover** tickets for unlimited rail travel over 3, 5 or 10 days are available in the UK, along with other kinds of tickets, information and bookings, from French Railways, 179 Piccadilly, London, W1V 0BA, 24hr brochure hotline ☎ (0181) 880 8161, bookings ☎ (0171) 203 7000 and from travel agencies. **Eurailpass, Flexipass** and **Saverpass** are options available in the US for travel in Europe and must be purchased in the US from Rail Europe Inc. ☎ (800) 438-7245.

Tickets bought in France must be validated *(composter)* by using the orange automatic date-stamping machines at the platform entrance (failure to do so may result in a fine).

A worthwhile investment is the **Thomas Cook European Rail** timetable, which gives train schedules throughout France (and Europe) as well as useful information on rail travel.

The French railway company SNCF operates a telephone information, reservation and prepayment service in English from 7am to 10pm (French time). In France call ☎ 08 36 35 35 39 (when calling from outside France, drop the initial 0).

By coach – Regular coach services between **London** and **Tours** or **Nantes**:

Eurolines (London), 52 Grosvenor Gardens, Victoria, London SW1W 0AU. ☎ (01582) 404511 (information), (0990) 143219 (ticket sales).

Eurolines (Paris), 28, avenue du Général-de-Gaulle, 93541 Bagnolet, ☎ 01 49 72 51 51.

By car – Drivers from the British Isles can easily travel to France and the Loire region by car, making use of the numerous **cross-Channel services** (passenger and car-ferries, hovercraft and SeaCat operating across the English Channel and St George's Channel and Le Shuttle via the Channel Tunnel). For details contact travel agencies or:

Brittany Ferries, The Brittany Centre, Wharf Road, Portsmouth, Hants PO2 8RU. ☎ (0990) 360360, Fax (01705) 873237.

Hoverspeed, Western Docks, Dover, Kent CT17 9TG. ☎ (01304) 240241, Fax (01304) 240088.

Irish Ferries, 50 West Norland Street, Dublin 2. ☎ (1) 6-610-511.

P&O European Ferries, Channel House, Channel View Road, Dover, Kent CT17 9TJ. ☎ (0990) 980980, Fax (01304) 223464.

Sally Line, Argyle Centre, York Street, Ramsgate, Kent CT11 9DS. ☎ (0990) 595522, Fax (01843) 589329.

Sea France Ltd, Eastern Dock, Dover, Kent CT16 1JA. ☎ (01304) 212696, Fax (01304) 240033.

Le Shuttle, Customer Services Centre, PO Box 300, Folkestone, Kent CT19 4QW. ☎ (0990) 353535.

Stena Line, Charter House, Park Street, Ashford, Kent TN24 8EX. ☎ (0990) 707070, Fax (01233) 202361.

To choose the most suitable route between one of the ports along the north coast of France and the Loire region, use the Michelin Motoring Atlas France, Michelin map 911 (which gives travel times and mileage) or Michelin maps from the 1:200 000 series (yellow cover).

Motoring in France

Documents – Nationals of the European Union countries require a full valid national **driving licence**. Nationals of non-EU countries should obtain an **international driving licence** (obtainable in the US from the American Automobile Association, cost for members: US$10, for non-members US$22). Motorists must carry with them the vehicle's **registration papers** (logbook) and a current insurance certificate. A nationality plate of the approved size should be displayed near the registration plate on the back of the vehicle.

Insurance – Insurance cover is compulsory and although an international insurance certificate (green card) is no longer a legal requirement in France for vehicles registered in Great Britain, it is the most effective proof of insurance cover and is internationally recognised by the police and other authorities. Most British insurance policies give the minimum third party cover required in France (check with your insurance company) – but be warned that this amounts to less than it would in the UK. Certain UK motoring organisations (AA, RAC) offer special accident insurance and breakdown service schemes for members, and the AA also has a scheme for non-members. Motorists should contact their own insurance company to enquire about special policies for foreign travel.
Members of the American Automobile Association should obtain the free brochure **Offices To Serve You Abroad.** The affiliated organisation for France is the Automobile Club National, 5, rue Auber, 75009 Paris, ☎ 01 44 51 53 99.

Highway code – The minimum age to drive in France is **18 years** old. Traffic drives on the right. It is compulsory for front-seat and back-seat passengers to wear **seat belts** where they are fitted. Children under the age of 10 should not travel in the front of the car. Full or dipped headlights must be switched on in poor visibility and at night; use side lights only when the vehicle is stationary. Headlight beams should be adjusted for driving on the right. It is illegal to drive with faulty lights in France, so it is advisable to take a spare set of bulbs with you.
In the case of a **breakdown** a red warning triangle or hazard warning lights are obligatory. Drivers should watch out for unfamiliar road signs and take great care on the road. In built-up areas **priority** must be ceded to vehicles coming **from the right**. However, traffic on main roads outside built-up areas (indicated by a yellow diamond sign) and on roundabouts has priority. Vehicles must come to a complete stop at stop signs and when the lights turn red at road junctions (where they may filter to the right only if indicated by a flashing amber arrow).
The regulations on **drinking** and **driving** (maximum permissible blood alcohol content: 0.05%) and **speeding** are strictly enforced – usually by an on-the-spot fine and/or confiscation of the vehicle.

Speed limits
Although liable to modification these are as follows:
- toll motorways *(péage)* 130kph/80mph (110kph/68mph when raining);
- dual carriage roads and motorways without tolls 110kph/68mph (100kph/62mph when raining);
- other roads 90kph/56mph (80kph/50mph when raining) and in towns 50kph/31mph;
- outside lane on motorways during daylight, on level ground and with good visibility; minimum speed limit of 80kph/50mph.

Parking regulations – In town there are zones where parking is either restricted or subject to a fee; tickets should be obtained from the ticket machines (*horodateurs* – small change necessary) and displayed inside the windscreen on the driver's side; failure to display may result in a heavy fine (and, in extreme cases, removal of the offending vehicle!).
In some towns there are "blue" parking zones *(zone bleue)* marked by a blue line on the pavement or a blue signpost with a P and a small square underneath. In this particular case motorists should display a cardboard disc which can be adjusted to display their time of arrival and which allows a stay of up to 1hr 30min (2hr 30min over lunchtime). These discs are on sale in supermarkets or petrol stations (ask for a *disque de stationnement*).

Route planning – The French road network is excellent and includes many motorways. The roads are very busy during the holiday period (particularly weekends in July and August) and to avoid traffic congestion it is advisable to follow the recommended secondary routes (signposted as *Bison Futé* or *itinéraires bis*). The motorway network includes rest areas *(aires)* every 10-15km/5-10mi and petrol stations, usually with restaurant and shopping complexes attached, about every 40km/25mi, so that long-distance drivers have no excuse not to stop for a rest every now and then.

Tolls – In France, most motorway sections are subject to a toll *(péage)*. This can be expensive especially if you take the motorway all the way (eg: Calais to Tours around 200F for a car). Tolls can be paid in cash or with a credit card (Visa, Mastercard).

Car rental – There are car rental agencies at airports, railway stations and in all large towns throughout France. European cars usually have manual transmission, but automatic cars are available on request (advance reservation recommended). It is relatively expensive to hire a car in France; Americans in particular will notice the difference and should consider booking a car from home before leaving or taking advantage of Fly-Drive schemes. Those who rent a car before leaving home should make sure that they inform the car hire company that they intend to take the car to France, so that their hire contract includes insurance for the car while on French soil.

Central Reservation in France:
Avis: 01 46 10 60 60   Europcar: 01 30 43 82 82
Budget: 01 46 86 65 65   Hertz: 01 47 88 51 51
Eurodollar: 01 49 58 44 44

Petrol

In France four different types of petrol (gas) are available:
    sans plomb 95 – unleaded 95 octane   *sans plomb 98* – unleaded 98 octane
    super – super leaded   *diesel/gazole* diesel
Petrol is more expensive in France compared to the USA and the UK. The French Tourist Office issues a map showing the location of cheaper petrol stations within a mile or so of motorway exits, usually in a hypermarket complex (send an SAE).

Tourist information

Local Tourist Offices – To find the addresses of local tourist offices throughout France, contact the **Fédération Nationale des Comités Départementaux de Tourisme**, 280 boulevard St-Germain, 75007 Paris. ☎ 01 44 11 10 20. Otherwise, contact local tourist offices directly to obtain useful brochures and information:

Comité Départemental du Tourisme du Cher, 5 rue de Séraucourt, 18000 Bourges.
☎ 02 48 67 00 18, Fax 02 48 67 01 44.

Comité Départemental du Tourisme de l'Eure-et-Loir, 10 rue du Docteur Maunoury, BP 67, 28000 Chartres Cedex. ☎ 02 37 84 01 00, Fax 02 37 36 36 39.

Comité Départemental du Tourisme de l'Indre, 1 rue St-Martin, BP 141, 36003 Châteauroux Cedex. ☎ 02 54 22 91 20.

Comité Départemental du Tourisme de l'Indre-et-Loire, 9 rue Buffon, BP 3217, 37032 Tours Cedex. ☎ 02 47 31 42 57, Fax 02 47 31 42 76.

Comité Départemental du Tourisme de Loire-Atlantique, place du Commerce, 44000 Nantes, ☎ 02 40 89 50 77, Fax 02 40 20 44 54.

Comité Départemental du Tourisme du Loir-et-Cher, 5 rue de la Voûte-du-Château, BP 149, 41005 Blois Cedex. ☎ 02 54 78 55 50, Fax 02 54 74 81 79.

Comité Départemental de Tourisme du Loiret, 8 rue d'Escures, 45000 Orléans.
☎ 02 38 62 04 88, Fax 02 38 77 04 12.

Comité Départemental de Tourisme du Maine-et-Loire, 11 place du Président-Kennedy, BP 2147, 49021 Angers Cedex 02. ☎ 02 41 23 51 51, Fax 02 41 88 36 77.

Maison Départementale du Tourisme de la Mayenne, 84 avenue Robert-Buron, BP 1429, 53014 Laval Cedex. ☎ 02 43 53 18 18, Fax 02 43 67 11 20.

Comité Départemental de Tourisme de l'Orne, 88 rue St-Blaise, BP 50, 61002 Alençon Cedex. ☎ 02 33 28 88 71, Fax 02 33 29 81 60.

Comité Départemental de Tourisme de la Sarthe, 2 rue des Maillets, 72072 Le Mans Cedex 09. ☎ 02 43 81 72 72, Fax 02 43 82 06 67.

Tourism for the Disabled – Some of the sights described in this guide are accessible to handicapped people and are indicated in the Admission Times and Charges section with the symbol ♿. For further information on museums which are accessible to the handicapped, contact the Direction des Musées de France. Service Accueil des publics spécifiques, 6 rue des Pyramides, 75041 Paris Cedex 01, ☎ 01 40 15 35 88. The **Michelin Red Guide France** and **Michelin Guide Camping Caravaning France** indicate hotels and camp sites with facilities suitable for physically handicapped people. Information is also available from the Comité National Français de Liaison pour la Réadaptation des Handicapés (236bis rue de Tolbiac, 75013 Paris, ☎ 05 53 80 66 66) and the Association France Handicaps (9 rue Luce-de-Lancival, 77340 Pontault-Combault, ☎ 01 60 28 50 12).

Useful organisations in the UK include RADAR (Royal Association for Disability and Rehabilitation, 12 City Forum, 250 City Road, London EC1V 8AF, ☎ (0171) 250 3222, Fax (0171) 250 0212) and Access Project (39 Bradley Gardens, West Ealing, London W13 8HE), who provide specialised practical information about on such matters as health insurance for disabled travellers.

Accommodation

Places to stay – The **Places to stay** map *(pp 8-9)* indicates recommended places for overnight stops and may be used in conjunction with the **Michelin Red Guide France**, which lists a selection of hotels and restaurants. **Loisirs Accueil** is a booking service that has offices in most French *départements* – contact the tourist offices listed above for further information.

A guide to good-value, family-run hotels, **Logis et Auberges de France**, is available from the French Tourist Office, as are lists of other kinds of accommodation such as hotel-châteaux, bed-and-breakfasts etc.

Self-catering accommodation – The **Maison des Gîtes de France** is an information service on self-catering accommodation in the Loire valley (and the rest of France). *Gîtes* usually take the form of a cottage or apartment decorated in the local style where visitors can make themselves at home.

Contact the Gîtes de France office in Paris: 59, rue St-Lazare, 75439 Paris Cedex 09. ☎ 01 49 70 75 75, or their representative, in the UK, Brittany Ferries *(address above)*.

Gîtes de France, Springfield Books Ltd and FHG Publications/World Leisure Marketing all publish listings of *gîtes* in France with details of how to book, or try contacting the local tourist offices which also send out lists of available properties.

Bed and Breakfast – Gîtes de France *(see above)* also publishes a guide to bed and breakfast accommodation *(chambres d'hôtes)* which consists of a room and breakfast at a reasonable price. Various other listings are available, either from bookshops or from the French Tourist Office.

Youth hostels – There are two main youth hostel associations *(auberges de jeunesse)* in France.

Paris:	Ligue Française pour les Auberges de la Jeunesse, 38 boulevard Raspail, 75007 Paris. ☎ 01 45 48 69 84, Fax 01 45 44 57 47. Fédération Unie des Auberges de Jeunesse, 27 Rue Pajol, 75018 Paris, ☎ 01 44 89 87 27, Fax 01 44 89 87 10, Minitel 3615 code FUAJ (1.01F/min).
Alençon:	1 rue de la Paix, 61250 Damigny, ☎ 02 33 29 00 48.
Le Mans:	23 rue Maupertuis, 72000 Le Mans, ☎ 02 43 81 27 55, Fax 02 43 81 06 10.
Nantes:	9 boulevard Vincent-Gâche, 44200 Nantes. ☎ 02 40 12 24 00, Fax 02 51 82 00 05.

Holders of an International Youth Hostel Federation card should contact the International Federation or the French Youth Hostels Association to book a bed. Hostelling International/American Youth Hostel Association in the US (☎ (202) 783-6161) offers a publication **International Hostel Guide for Europe** (US$13.95) – also available to non-members.

Camping – There are numerous officially graded sites with varying standards of facilities throughout the Loire valley. The **Michelin Guide Caravaning France** lists a selection of camp sites. An international Camping Carnet for caravans is useful but not compulsory; it may be obtained from motoring organisations or the Camping and Caravanning Club (Greenfield House, Westwood Way, Coventry CV4 8JH, ☎ (01203) 694995).

General information

Electricity – The electric current is 220 volts. Circular two-pin plugs are the rule. An electrical adaptor may be necessary (these are on sale at most airports).

Medical treatment – First aid, medical advice and chemist's night service rota are available from chemists/drugstores (*pharmacie* identified by a green cross sign).

It is advisable to take out comprehensive insurance cover as tourists undergoing medical treatment in French hospitals or clinics have to pay for it themselves. Nationals of non-EU countries should check with their insurance companies about policy limitations. Reimbursement can then be negotiated with the insurance company according to the policy held. All prescription drugs should be clearly labelled; it is recommended to carry a copy of prescriptions. American Express offers its cardholders only a service, "Global Assist", for any medical, legal or personal emergency: ☎ 01 47 16 25 29.

British and Irish citizens should apply to their local post office for **Form E111** (application form included in the brochure *Health Advice for Travellers* available from the post office). Form E111 entitles the holder to urgent medical treatment for accident or unexpected illness in EU countries. A refund of part of the costs of treatment can be obtained on application in person (recommended) or by post to the local French Social Security offices *(Caisse Primaire d'Assurance Maladie)*.

Tipping – Since a service charge is automatically included in the price of meals and accommodation in France, it is not necessary to tip in restaurants and hotels. However taxi drivers, bellboys, doormen, filling station attendants or anybody who has been of assistance are usually tipped at the customer's discretion. Most French people give an extra tip in restaurants and cafés (about 50 centimes for a drink and several francs for a meal). There is no tipping in theatres.

Currency – There are no restrictions on the amount of currency visitors can take into France. Visitors wishing to export currency in foreign banknotes in excess of the given allocation from France should complete a currency declaration form on arrival.

Notes and coins – *See illustration on page 277.* The unit of currency in France is the French franc (F), subdivided into 100 centimes. French notes are available for the values 50, 100, 200 and 500 francs (the old 20 franc note is being phased out). French coins come in the following values: 5, 10, 20, 50 centimes (all gold coloured except the 50 centime coin which is silver); 1, 2, 5, 10, 20 francs (all silver except the 10 and 20 franc coins which are silver with a gold border).

Banks and currency exchange – Banks are generally open from 9am to 4.30pm (smaller branches may close for lunch) and are closed on Mondays or Saturdays (except if market day). Some branches are open for limited transactions on Saturdays. Banks close early on the day before a bank holiday.

A passport is necessary as identification when cashing cheques (travellers' or ordinary) in banks. Commission charges vary and hotels usually charge more than banks for cashing cheques for non-residents.

By far the most convenient way of obtaining French currency is the 24hr **cash dispenser** or ATM (*distributeur automatique de billets* in French), found outside many banks and post offices and easily recognisable by the CB (Carte Bleue) logo. Most accept international credit cards (don't forget your PIN) and some even give instructions in English. Note that American Express cards can only be used in dispensers operated by the Crédit Lyonnais bank or by American Express. Foreign currency can also be exchanged in major banks, post offices, hotels or private exchange offices found in main cities and near popular tourist attractions.

Credit cards – American Express, Visa, Mastercard/Eurocard and Diners Club are widely accepted in shops, hotels, restaurants and petrol stations. If your card is lost or stolen, call the appropriate 24hr hotline:

American Express ☎ 01 47 77 70 00
Visa ☎ 01 42 77 11 90
Mastercard/Eurocard ☎ 01 45 67 84 84
Diners Club ☎ 01 47 62 75 50

You should also report any loss or theft to the local police who will issue you with a certificate (useful proof to show the credit card company).

Post – Main post offices open Monday to Friday from 8am to 7pm, and Saturdays from 8am to noon. Smaller branch post offices generally close at lunchtime between noon and 2pm and finish for the day at 4pm. Stamps are also sold in newsagents and cafés that sell cigarettes *(tabac)*. Stamp collectors should ask for *timbres de collection* in any post office (there is often a *philatélie* counter).

Postage via airmail:
UK: letter (20g) 3F
North America: letter (20g) 4.40F
Australia and NZ: letter (20g) 5.20F

Public holidays – The following are days when museums and other monuments may be closed or may vary their hours of admission:

1 January	New Year's Day *(Jour de l'An)*
	Easter Day and Monday *(Pâques)*
1 May	May Day
8 May	V E Day
	Ascension Day
	Whit Sunday and Monday *(Pentecôte)*
14 July	France's National Day (Bastille Day)
15 August	Assumption
1 November	All Saints' Day *(Toussaint)*
11 November	Armistice
25 December	Christmas Day *(Noël)*

Time – France is one hour ahead of Greenwich Mean Time (GMT), except between the end of September and the end of October, when it is the same.

When it is **noon in France**, it is

3am in Los Angeles
6am in New York
11am in Dublin
11am in London
7pm in Perth
9pm in Sydney
11pm in Auckland

R. Corbel

In France time is generally given using the 24hr clock, and "am" and "pm" are not used.

Shopping – Department stores and chain stores are open Monday to Saturday from 9am to 6.30pm-7.30pm. Smaller, more specialised shops may close during the lunch hour. Food stores (grocers, wine merchants and bakeries) are open from 7am to 6.30pm-7.30pm and some open on Sunday mornings. Many food stores close between noon and 2pm and on Mondays. Hypermarkets are usually open until 9-10pm.

Embassies and Consulates

Australia:	Embassy	4 rue Jean-Rey, 75015 Paris, ☎ 01 40 59 33 00, Fax 01 40 59 33 10.
Canada:	Embassy	35 avenue Montaigne, 75008 Paris, ☎ 01 44 43 29 00, Fax 01 44 43 29 99.
Eire:	Embassy	4 rue Rude, 75016 Paris, ☎ 01 44 17 67 00, Fax 01 45 00 84 17.
New Zealand:	Embassy	7 ter rue Léonard-de-Vinci, 75016 Paris, ☎ 01 45 00 24 11, Fax 01 45 01 26 39.
UK:	Embassy	35 rue du Faubourg St-Honoré, 75008 Paris, ☎ 01 42 66 91 42, Fax 01 42 66 95 90.
	Consulate	16 rue d'Anjou, 75008 Paris, ☎ 01 42 66 06 68 (visas)
	Consulate	L'Aumarière, 44220 Couëron, ☎ 02 40 63 16 02 *(just west of Nantes)*
USA:	Embassy	2 avenue Gabriel, 75008 Paris, ☎ 01 43 12 22 22, Fax 01 42 66 97 83.
	Consulate	2 rue St-Florentin, 75008 Paris, ☎ 01 42 96 14 88

Telephoning

Public telephones – Most public phones in France use prepaid phone cards *(télécartes)*. Some telephone booths accept credit cards (Visa, Mastercard/Euro-card; minimum monthly charge 20F). *Télécartes* (50 or 120 units) can be bought in post offices, branches of France Télécom, cafés that sell cigarettes *(tabac)* and newsagents, and can be used to make calls in France and abroad. Calls can be received at phone boxes where the blue bell sign is shown.

National calls – French telephone numbers have 10 digits. In Paris and the Paris region numbers begin with 01; 02 in northwest France; 03 in northeast France; 04 in southeast France and Corsica; 05 in southwest France. The French ringing tone is a series of long tones and the engaged (busy) tone is a series of short beeps.

International calls – To call France from abroad, dial the country code (33) + 9 digit number (omit the initial 0). When calling abroad from France dial 00, followed by the country code, followed by the area code and number of your correspondent.

International dialling codes:		
Australia: 61	Eire: 353	United Kingdom: 44
Canada: 1	New Zealand: 64	United States: 1

To use your personal calling card dial:

AT&T: 0 800 99-0011	BT: 0 800 99-0044
MCI: 0 800 99-0019	Mercury: 0 800 99-00 944
Sprint: 0 800 99 0087	Canada Direct: 0 800 99 0016

Telephone rates from a public phone are about 3F/min from France to the UK, and about 4.50F/min from France to the USA and Canada. Cheap rates with 50% extra time are available from private telephones to the UK on weekdays between 9.30pm and 8am, from 2pm on Saturdays and all day on Sundays and holidays. Cheap rates to the USA and Canada are from 2am to noon all week, and to Australia between 9.30pm and 8am Monday to Saturday and all day Sunday.

Toll-free numbers in France begin with 0 800.

Emergency numbers:
Police: 17
Fire (Pompiers): 18
Ambulance (SAMU): 15

Minitel – France Télécom operates a system offering directory enquiries (free of charge up to 3min), travel and entertainment reservations, and other services (cost varies between 0.37F-5.57F/min). These small computer-like terminals can be found in some post offices, hotels and France Télécom agencies and in many French homes. **3614 PAGES E** is the code for directory assistance in English (turn on the unit, dial 3614, hit the "connexion" button when you get the tone, type in "PAGES E", and follow the instructions on the screen). For route planning, use Michelin services **3615 MICHELIN** (tourist and route information) and **3617 MICHELIN** (information sent by **FAX**).

Cellular phones – In France these have numbers which begin with 06. Two-watt (lighter, shorter reach) and eight-watt models are on the market, using the Itinéris (France Télécom) or SFR network. Cell phone rentals (delivery or airport pickup provided):

Ellinas Phone Rental	☎ 01 47 20 70 00
Euro Exaphone	☎ 01 44 09 77 78
Rent a cell Express	☎ 01 53 93 78 00

International information, UK	00.33.12.44
International information, USA/Canada	00.33.12.11
International operator	00.33.12 + country code
Local directory assistance	12

Conversion tables

Weights and measures

1 kilogram (kg)	2.2 pounds (lb)	2.2 pounds
1 metric ton (tn)	1.1 tons	1.1 tons

to convert kilograms to pounds, multiply by 2.2

1 litre (l)	2.1 pints (pt)	1.8 pints
1 litre	0.3 gallon (gal)	0.2 gallon

to convert litres to gallons, multiply by 0.26 (US) or 0.22 (UK)

1 hectare (ha)	2.5 acres	2.5 acres
1 square kilometre (km²)	0.4 square miles (sq mi)	0.4 square miles

to convert hectares to acres, multiply by 2.4

1 centimetre (cm)	0.4 inches (in)	0.4 inches
1 metre (m)	3.3 feet (ft) - 39.4 inches - 1.1 yards (yd)	
1 kilometre (km)	0.6 miles (mi)	0.6 miles

to convert metres to feet, multiply by 3.28 . kilometres to miles, multiply by 0.6

Clothing

Women								Men
	35	4	2½		40	7½	7	
	36	5	3½		41	8½	8	
	37	6	4½		42	9½	9	
Shoes	38	7	5½		43	10½	10	Shoes
	39	8	6½		44	11½	11	
	40	9	7½		45	12½	12	
	41	10	8½		46	13½	13	
	36	4	8		46	36	36	
	38	6	10		48	38	38	
Dresses &	40	8	12		50	40	40	Suits
Suits	42	12	14		52	42	42	
	44	14	16		54	44	44	
	46	16	18		56	46	48	
	36	08	30		37	14½	14,5	
	38	10	32		38	15	15	
Blouses &	40	12	14		39	15½	15½	Shirts
sweaters	42	14	36		40	15¾	15¾	
	44	16	38		41	16	16	
	46	18	40		42	16½	16½	

Sizes often vary depending on the designer. These equivalents are given for guidance only.

Speed

kph	10	30	50	70	80	90	100	110	120	130
mph	6	19	31	43	50	56	62	68	75	81

Temperature

Celsius (°C)	0°	5°	10°	15°	20°	25°	30°	40°	60°	80°	100°
Fahrenheit (°F)	32°	41°	50°	59°	68°	77°	86°	104°	140°	176°	212°

To convert Celsius into Fahrenheit, multiply °C by 9, divide by 5, and add 32.
To convert Fahrenheit into Celsius, subtract 32 from °F, multiply by 5, and divide by 9.

Notes and coins

500 Francs featuring
scientists
Pierre and Marie Curie
(1858-1906), (1867-1934)

200 Francs featuring
engineer Gustave Eiffel
(1832-1923)

100 Francs featuring
Romantic painter
Eugène Delacroix
(1798-1863)

50 Francs featuring
pilot and writer
Antoine de Saint-Exupéry
(1900-1944)

20 Francs   10 Francs   5 Francs   2 Francs

1 Franc   50 Centimes   20 Centimes   10 Centimes   5 Centimes

Recreation

Information and brochures outlining the sports and outdoor facilities available in the region can be obtained from the French Government Tourist Office or from the organisations listed below.

ALONG THE RIVER

For information apply to the Syndicat Interdépartemental du Bassin de la Maine, place du Président Kennedy, 49000 Angers, ☎ 02 41 88 99 38.

Canoeing

This method of exploring local waterways need not be exclusively reserved for seasoned canoeing experts. Sometimes this sport can be a pleasant way to discover secluded spots inaccessible by any other means.

Canoeing trips of half a day, a whole day or more can be organised for individuals or a group (allowing for brief training and certain safety measures). The most suitable rivers are the Cisse, the Conie, the Cosson, the Huisne, the Indre, the Loir, the Sauldre, the Thouet and the Vienne. For information and bookings, contact the Loisir Accueil section in each *département*, and the Fédération française de Canoë-Kayak, 87 quai de la Marne, BP 58, 94340 Joinville-le-Pont, ☎ 01 48 89 39 89.

Fishing

Recent French surveys reveal that freshwater fishing is the second most popular national leisure pastime behind football! Swift-flowing or not, the waters of the Loire offer anglers numerous attractive possibilities.

All authorised types of fishing are open to the angler, whether fishing for gudgeon, roach and dace, or trying for pike or the striped mullet which come upstream as far as Amboise in summer, or going after the catfish, tench and carp which lurk in dips in the riverbed of the Loire, the Indre and the Loir and in the pools of the Sologne which are also full of perch.

Trout are to be found in the Creuse, the Sauldre, the streams of Anjou or the tributaries of the Loir, while the Berry, Briare, or Orléans canals are home to eels and sometimes freshwater crayfish which can be caught with a net.

For salmon and shad fishing it is necessary to have a flat-bottomed boat; the professionals have specialist equipment such as nets stretched across the river and held in place by poles fixed in the riverbed.

Regulations and open seasons – These differ according to whether the water is classified as first category (contains trout and salmon) or second category (coarse fish). Stricter rules apply to fish needing special protection, so salmon fishing in particular may be forbidden outright during some years, or permitted for a restricted period only between March and June.

Regional and national regulations should be observed. Anglers will need either to buy a special holiday fishing permit, valid for two weeks between June and September, or take out annual membership of an officially approved angling association. These offically stamped permits cover fishing with up to four lines on second category waterways administered by an angling association or one line on all public waterways. Only one line is allowed on first category waters and a supplementary tax is payable.

On private property, where the fishing rights belong to the owner of the bank, this owner's permission must be obtained. In the case of certain private lakes, which are excluded from the angling legislation, the owner's permission (annual, monthly or daily permit) is the only formality required and can be granted at any time of the year.

Minimum size of catch – National regulations state that anglers must return to the water any fish they catch below the minimum permitted length (50cm/20in for pike, 40cm/16in for pike-perch, 23cm/9in for trout, 50cm/20in for salmon, 9cm/4in for crayfish).

Useful brochures and folding maps *Fishing in France (Pêche en France)* are published and distributed by the Conseil Supérieur de la Pêche, 134, avenue de Malakoff, 75016 Paris, ☎ 01 45 02 20 20; also available from local angling organisations.

For information about regulations contact the Tourist Information Centres or the offices of the Water and Forest Authority (Eaux et Forêts).

Fishing organisations *(Fédérations de Pêche)*: 25 rue Charles-Gille, BP 0385, 37000 Tours, ☎ 02 47 05 33 77.

Fish of the Loire

Catfish *(Ictalurus melas)*

Eel

Rainbow trout

Pike-perch

Perch

Catfish *(Silurus glanis)*

Pike

River boating

Small private barges (*pénichettes*) can be taken on the following stretches of river:
the **Loire**: 84km/52mi between Angers and Nantes;
the **Maine**: 8km/5mi;
the **Mayenne**: 122km/76mi between the town of Mayenne and the Maine;
the **Oudon**: 18km/11mi between Segré and Le Lion d'Angers;
the **Sarthe**: 136km/85mi between Le Mans and the Maine.
The table below provides information on houseboats which can be hired – no permit necessary – for one or several nights in order to explore the Anjou region via its waterways. Day cruises on piloted boats are also available.
River cruising is possible all year round. However, before choosing an itinerary and the dates at which you will need to book the boat, it is essential to enquire about scouring periods or *écourues* (*see below*) and locks, which may close at certain times of the day or on public holidays. Remember that the cruising speed is 6 to 8kmph/3.7 to 5mph and that sailing is not permitted at night.
During the **scouring periods** when the water level is lowered for maintenance work, the river sections and canals concerned are closed to navigation. Work is usually carried out in autumn from 15 September to 30 October. In the Maine basin, work alternates from river to river, affecting the Sarthe one year and the Mayenne the next. Depending on the year, cruise companies move their pleasure boats to a different river during the scouring period.

River passenger boats

Trips on this type of boat, referred to as a *bateau-mouche*, usually leave at set hours (often at 3pm or 5pm); some trips include the passing of locks or a fascinating and instructive commentary on local birds species or water transport in the Loire region.
Discovering the tracks of small animals like beavers and bird spotting add to the pleasure of these charming, peaceful cruises.
Starting from **Briare**, along the canal on the *Bateaux touristiques*;
from **Chisseaux**, 1hr 30min cruise along the Cher aboard the *Bélandre*;
from **Fay-aux-Loges**, along the Orléans canal aboard the *Oussance*;
from **Montrichard**, 1hr 30min cruise along the Cher aboard the *Léonard-de-Vinci*;
from **Saint-Aignan**, 1hr 30min cruise along the Cher aboard the *Val-du-Cher*;
from **Olivet**, 1hr 30min cruise along the Loiret aboard the *Sologne*.

Chenillé-Changé – River boat centre

Departure points	Rivers	Boat companies
Angers	Mayenne Oudon Sarthe	Maine Réservations Place Kennedy, 49022 Angers Cedex 02 ☏ 02 41 23 51 30 Concord Plaisance Quai de la Savatte, 49100 Angers ☏ 02 41 87 93 50
Château-Gontier Morannes Entrammes	Mayenne Oudon Sarthe	Cap Rivières 53260 Entrammes ☏ 02 43 98 36 98
Cheffes-sur-Sarthe Mayenne	Mayenne Oudon Sarthe	Sarthe Fluviale 40, promenade de Reculée 49100 Angers ☏ 02 41 73 14 16
Angers Châteauneuf-s/Sarthe Chenillé-Changé Mayenne	Maine Mayenne Oudon Sarthe	Boat trips or house boats for hire Maine Anjou Rivières Le Moulin 49220 Chenillé-Changé ☏ 02 41 95 10 83
Daon	Mayenne Oudon Sarthe	France Mayenne Fluviale Le Port, 53200 Daon ☏ 02 43 70 13 94
Grez-Neuville	Maine Mayenne Oudon Sarthe	Anjou Plaisance Rue de l'Écluse, 49220 Grez-Neuville ☏ 02 41 95 68 95 Féerives Quai de l'Hirondelle, 49220 Gretz-Neuville ☏ 02 41 95 68 95
Sablé-sur-Sarthe	Mayenne Oudon Sarthe	Anjou Navigation Quai National, 72300 Sablé-sur-Sarthe ☏ 02 43 95 14 42

ON DRY LAND

Cycling

The Fédération Française de Cyclotourisme and its local committees recommend a number of cycling tours of various lengths.

The Loire countryside is fairly flat, so presents few difficulties to the average cyclist. The Indre valley, the Sologne, the numerous forest tracks and the banks of the Loire, away from the main roads, are particularly pretty. The ever-changing scenery and the rich heritage of the Loire valley add greatly to the pleasure of a cycling tour.

Contact the Fédération française de Cyclotourisme: 8 rue Jean-Marie-Jego, 75013 Paris, ☏ 01 45 80 30 21 for suggested itineraries covering most of France, with information on mileage, difficult routes and sights to see. There is an IGN map (1:50 000) of cycle routes around Orléans (1 000km à vélo autour d'Orléans).

Lists of cycle hire businesses are available from the Tourist Information Centres. The main railway stations also hire out cycles which can be returned at a different station.

For information on mountain biking (VTT, or vélo tout terrain) in the Layon region, apply to the Anjou tourist office in Angers.

Golf

For location, addresses and telephone numbers of golf courses in France, consult the map Golfs, Les Parcours Français published by Éditions Plein Sud based on Michelin maps.

Hunting

The varied terrain of the Loire countryside makes it very popular with hunters for stalking, beating, coursing or shooting. The plains of the Beauce and the meadows of Touraine and Anjou provide plenty of food for partridges, quails, thrushes and larks. Hares find cover in the copses and the fields of maize and sugar-beet. Wild rabbits and partridges breed in the sterile marshland while pheasants favour lakes and rivers. Red deer and roe deer are to be found in the thick woods around Baugé, in the forests of Château-la-Vallière and Loches and around Valençay. Wild boar favours the deep forest of Orléans and Amboise and the neighbourhood of Chambord. The islands and banks of the Loire provide nests for teal and mallard. The Sologne is a favourite haunt of game: duck, teal and woodcock on the lakes and rivers, pheasants by the roadside, wild boar in the marshy brakes and deer in the woods. Address all enquiries to St-Hubert-Club de France, 10 rue de Lisbonne, 75008 Paris, ☎ 01 45 22 38 90.

During the rutting season, from mid-September to mid-October, it is possible to watch the deer in action in Chambord forest – contact the Office national des Forêts for details, ☎ 02 54 78 55 50.

Riding and pony trekking

Not surprisingly, in view of the number of highly reputed local stud farms and the National Riding School at St-Hilaire-St-Florent near Saumur, the Loire region has numerous riding centres open to visitors. Some also serve as an overnight stop for those on pony-trekking holidays.

Guides indicating suitable routes and overnight stops are available from regional and national riding associations. Details of local equestrian centres can be obtained from the tourist information centres.

Contact the Délégation Nationale au Tourisme Équestre, 30 avenue d'Iéna, 75116 Paris, ☎ 01 53 67 44 44, which publishes an annual brochure on exploring France on horseback. Other useful contacts include:

Association Régionale de Tourisme Équestre Val de Loire-Océan; La Senserie, 44522 La Roche-Blanche, ☎ 02 40 98 43 66 (for the *départements* of Maine-et-Loire, Mayenne and Sarthe);

Association Régionale de Tourisme Équestre Val de Loire-Centre; Maison des Sports, 32 rue Alain-Gerbault, 41000 Blois ☎ 02 54 42 95 60 ext 411 (for the *départements* of Cher, Indre, Indre-et-Loire, Loir-et-Cher and Loiret).

Tourist trains

A number of charming old steam trains are operated along parts of the Loire valley, generally by groups of volunteers, with the result that they usually only run at weekends. It is therefore advisable to check details in advance.

From Chinon to Richelieu, a Mikado 1922

Pithiviers steam train (Loiret):
from Pithiviers to Bellebat. MTP ☎ 02 38 30 48 26 or Pithiviers tourist office.
Lac de Rillé historical railway (Indre-et-Loire):
trip round the lake of Pincemaille. AECFM ☎ 02 47 24 60 19 or 02 47 24 07 95.
Touraine steam train (Indre-et-Loire):
from Chinon to Richelieu. TVT ☎ 02 47 58 12 97 or 02 47 05 92 36.
Loir valley tourist train (Loir-et-Cher):
from Thoré-la-Rochette to Troo. ☎ 02 54 72 80 82 or Vendôme tourist office.
Compagnie du Blanc Argent (Loir-et-Cher):
trip through the Sologne from Salbris to Luçay-le-Mâle. ☎ 02 54 76 06 51 or Romorantin tourist office.
Sarthe steam train:
from Conneré-Beillé to Bonnétable. TRANVAP ☎ 02 43 85 05 03 or 02 43 89 06 17.
Semur-en-Vallon tourist train (Sarthe):
Narrow gauge railway operating on a distance of 1.5km/1mi. ☎ 02 43 71 30 36.

Walking

Short, medium and long distance footpath Topo-Guides are published by the Fédération Française de la Randonnée Pédestre (FFRP). These give detailed maps of the paths and offer valuable information to the rambler; they are on sale at the information centre: 64 rue de Gergovie, 75014 Paris, ☎ 01 45 45 31 02. For further information apply to: Comité de Touraine pour la Randonnée pédestre, Office de tourisme de Tours, 78 rue B.-Palissy, 37042 Tours, ☎ 02 47 70 37 35.

The Comité départemental du tourisme de l'Anjou has published five IGN maps (Institut Géographique National, 1:50 000) showing routes for ramblers. There is a network of long-distance footpaths *(sentiers de grande randonnée – GR)* covering the area described in the guide:

the **GR 3** along the Loire valley through the forests of Orléans, Russy and Chinon;
the **GR 3c** running westwards across the Sologne from Gien to Mont-près-Chambord;
the **GR 3d** through the Layon vineyards;
the **GR 31** linking Mont-près-Chambord, on the southeast edge of Boulogne forest, to Souesmes, south through Sologne forest;
the **GR 32** north-south through Orléans forest;
the **GR 335**, "from the Loir to the Loire", north-south between Lavardin and Vouvray;
the **GR 35** along the Loir valley;
the **GR 36**, the footpath from the English Channel to the Pyrenees route, crossing the region described in this guide between Le Mans and Montreuil-Bellay;
the **GR 46** along the Indre valley.

IN MID-AIR

Weather permitting, there are various ways of getting a bird's eye view of the Loire valley, from microlights (ULM, or *ultra-légers motorisés*), gliders, helicopters or light aircraft. Trips leave from the airport at Tours-St-Symphorien, flying over Chinon, Chambord, Chenonceau and Azay-le-Rideau, and from Blois-le-Breuil or Orléans aerodrome to fly over Amboise, Cheverny and Beaugency.

It is also possible to take a trip in a hot-air balloon (allow about half a day for 1hr-1hr 30min actually in the air, price about 1 200F per person).

Microlights

Aérodrome d'Amboise-Dierre, ☎ 02 47 57 93 91.
Aérodrome de Tours-Sorigny, ☎ 02 47 26 27 50.
Fédération française de planeur ultra-léger motorisé, 96bis rue Marc-Sangnier, 94700 Maison-Alfort, ☎ 01 49 81 74 43.

Gliders

Association vol-à-voile Léonard-de-Vinci, Tours, ☎ 02 47 54 27 77.
Fédération française de vol-à-voile, 29 rue de Sèvres, 75006 Paris, ☎ 01 45 44 04 78.

Helicopters

Acson hélicoptère, 49000 Angers, ☎ 02 41 76 24 24.
Aéro-club La Flèche Sarthe-Sud, Route du Lude, ☎ 02 43 94 05 24.
Blois-Hélistation, Pont Charles-de-Gaulle, on the D 951 at the Blois-Vienne exit, ☎ 02 54 74 35 52.
Jet Systems Hélicoptère Tours, Le Mans aerodrome, ☎ 02 43 72 07 70.
La Loire vue du ciel en hélicoptère, ☎ 02 54 78 55 50.
Touraine-Hélicoptère, BP 13, 37370 Neuvy-le-Roi, ☎ 02 47 24 81 44.

Light aircraft

Aéro-Club "Les Ailes Tourangelles", Amboise-Dierre aerodrome, 37150 Dierre, ☎ 02 47 57 93 91.
Bombard Balloon Adventures, 37400 Amboise, ☎ 02 47 30 11 82.
Tours Aéro Services, Tours St-Symphorien and Blois-le-Breuil airports, ☎ 02 47 48 37 27.

Hot-air balloons

Ballons de Bourgogne, 21630 Pommard, ☎ 03 80 24 20 32 or 02 47 30 11 82.
Bombard Balloon Adventures, 37400 Amboise, ☎ 02 47 30 11 82.
France Montgolfières, La Riboulière, 41400 Montou-sur-Cher, ☎ 02 54 71 75 40.
La Compagnie des Montgolfières, 15 rue du Bœuf-St-Paterne, 45004 Orléans Cedex, ☎ 02 38 54 51 07.
Loisirs-Accueils Loiret, rue d'Escures, 45000 Orléans, ☎ 02 38 62 04 88.
Sablé-sur-Sarthe tourist office (1hr 30min trips along the Sarthe valley), ☎ 02 43 95 00 60.

Leisure with a local flavour

HISTORICAL TOURIST ROUTES

Two associations for the preservation of national heritage, the Caisse Nationale des Monuments Historiques et des Sites and Demeure Historique, set up some historical tourist routes in 1975, the **Routes historiques**, on local architectural, cultural and traditional themes. There are now around 90 of these altogether, covering the whole of France. Local tourist offices can provide maps and leaflets for each itinerary, or contact the CNMHS, Hôtel de Sully, 62 rue St-Antoine, 75004 Paris, ☎ 01 44 61 21 50.

Each route is clearly signposted throughout. The main historical routes covering the Loire region are the following:

Route historique du roi René – Takes in the most important châteaux in the Anjou area; most of which are occupied, but nonetheless open to the public;

Route historique des Plantagenêts – Covers 11 routes between Rouen and Bordeaux; as far as the present guide is concerned, it includes the towns of Angers, Vendôme, Fréteval, Saumur, Fontevraud, Chinon, Loches and Montrichard;

Route historique de la Vallée des Rois – The route once used by the Kings of France, on the way from Gien to Saumur via Orléans, Blois and Tours;

Route historique des Dames de Touraine – Dedicated to the great ladies who showed both talent and determination in building, renovating, embellishing or simply enjoying their splendid estates, this route winds its way among the towns of Amboise, Beauregard, Montpoupon, le Grand-Pressigny and Azay-le-Ferron;

Route historique François-Ier – Runs from the Vendôme region down to the south of Berry, evoking the many visits François I and his retinue paid to the region;

Route historique Jacques-Cœur – This itinerary, which covers more ground in Berry than in the Loire region, runs from the Château of Bussière to the Château of Culan via the city of Gien;

Route historique des Hauts Dignitaires – This route dedicated to high court dignitaries includes the Châteaux of Chamerolles, Bellegarde, Sully-sur-Loire and Gien from this guide.

LOCAL INDUSTRY

The following workshops or factories are open to the public, giving an insight into local crafts and industry:

Chinon nuclear power station;

Gien potteries;

Montrichard, J M Monmousseau's champagne-method wine cellars;

Montsoreau Saut-au-Loup mushroom beds;

Poncé-sur-le-Loir arts and crafts centre;

St-Barthélémy-d'Anjou Cointreau distillery;

St-Cyr-en-Bourg Saumur cooperative wine cellar;

St-Hilaire-St-Florent Bouvet-Ladubay sparkling Saumur wines;

Turquant Troglo'Tap dried apples;

Vaas Rotrou corn mill;

Villaines-les-Rochers basketwork co-operative.

PARKS AND GARDENS

Route des Parcs et Jardins – The art of formal gardens which came to characterise French châteaux and parks was born in the Loire valley in the early 16C. This tourist route leads through some of the most beautiful and ingeniously-designed gardens from the Renaissance up to the present, including the château of **Chamerolles**, the château of **Villeprévost**, the floral park at **Orléans-la-Source**, the château of **Beauregard**, the château of **Chaumont**, the château of **Valmer**, the botanical gardens at **La Fosse**, the priory of **St-Cosme**, and of course the château and gardens of **Villandry**.

The Michelin Green Guide France.
Touring in France made easier with recommended five-day programmes
offering a wide choice of combinations and variations
which are easily adapted to personal tastes.

WINE COUNTRY

Like all wine-growers, the *vignerons* from the Loire region are extremely hospitable and eager to welcome visitors to their cellars and storehouses in order to offer tastings, talk about their profession, show their working equipment, explain wine-making techniques and... sell their wine.

The wine producers, merchants and co-operatives willing to accept visitors are too numerous for us to draw up a complete list. However, all the tourist information centres and the "Maisons du vin" (especially those in Amboise, Angers, Bourgueil, Chinon, Montlouis-sur-Loire, Saumur and Vouvray) will supply the necessary details: "La Maison du Vin de l'Anjou", 5bis place Kennedy, 49100 Angers, ☎ 02 41 88 81 13.

Conseil Interprofessionnel des Vins d'Anjou et Saumur (CIVAS), Hôtel des Vins La Godeline, 73 rue Plantagenêt, 49100 Angers, ☎ 02 41 87 62 57.

"La Maison des Vins de Nantes", Bellevue, 44690 La-Haye-Fouassière, ☎ 02 40 36 90 10.

"La Maison du Vin de Saumur", 25 rue Beaurepaire, 49400 Saumur, ☎ 02 41 51 16 40.

Comité Interprofessionnel des Vins de Touraine-Val de Loire (CIVTL), 16 square Prosper-Mérimée, 37000 Tours, ☎ 02 47 05 40 01.

The art of drinking wine

To identify and describe the qualities or defects of a particular wine, both wine buffs and wine experts use an extremely wide yet precise vocabulary. Assessing a wine involves three successive stages, each associated with a particular sense and a certain number of "technical terms":

The eye – **General impression:** crystalline (good clarity), limpid (perfectly transparent, no particles in suspension), still (no bubbles), sparkling (effervescent wine) or *mousseux* (lots of fine, Champagne-type bubbles).

Colour and hues: a wine is said to have a nice "robe" when the colour is sharp and clean; the main terms used to describe the different hues are pale red, ruby, onionskin, garnet (red wine), salmon, amber, partridge-eye pink (rosé wine) and golden-green, golden-yellow and straw (white wine).

The nose – Pleasant smells: floral, fruity, balsamic, spicy, flinty.
Unpleasant smells: corked, woody, hydrogen sulphide, cask.

The mouth – Once it has passed the visual and olfactory tests, the wine undergoes a final test in the mouth. It can be described as agreeable (pleasant), aggressive (unpleasant, with a high acidity), full-flavoured (rich and well-balanced), structured (well-constructed, with a high alcohol content), heady (intoxicating), fleshy (producing a strong impact on taste buds), fruity (flavour evoking the freshness and natural taste of grapes), easy to drink, jolly (inducing merriness), round (supple, mellow), lively (light, fresh, with a lowish alcohol content) etc.

Main wine-making events in Anjou, Saumur and Touraine

All year round, a great many wine fairs and wine festivals are staged at set dates in order to promote the different types of local "*appellations*".

Month	Event	Venue	☎
March	Wine fair	Bourgueil	02 47 97 75 02
April	Annual Saumur wine competition	Saumur	02 41 51 16 40
	Onzain wine fair	Onzain	02 54 20 72 59
May	Wine fair	Saumur	02 41 83 43 12
June	Champigny Biennial	Montsoreau	02 41 51 16 40
July	Wine harvest festival	St-Lambert-du-Lattay	02 41 78 30 58
	Vintage wine festival	St-Aubin-de-Luigné	02 41 78 33 28
August	Wine fair	Montsoreau	02 41 51 62 06
September	Saumur-Champigny festival	Varrains	02 41 88 81 13
November	Anjou-Villages competition	Brissac-Quincé	02 41 91 22 13
	Arrival of the most recent crop of Touraine wines *(primeurs)*	Montrichard	02 54 32 05 10

Quality control

French wines fall into various official categories indicating the area of production and therefore the probable quality of the wine. AOC *(appellation d'origine contrôlée)* denotes a wine produced in a strictly delimited area, stated on the label, made with the grape varieties specified for that wine and in accordance with local traditional methodology. VDQS *(vin délimité de qualité supérieur)* is also produced in a legally controlled area, slightly less highly rated than AOC. *Vin de pays* denotes the highest ranking table wine after AOC and VDQS.

The table below lists the main AOC wines produced in the region described in this guide (Anjou, Orléanais, Saumur and Touraine).

Appellation	Départements	Grape varieties	R red	r rosé	W white
ANJOU	Maine-et-Loire	*Cabernet Franc, Sauvignon*	R		W
ANJOU-GAMAY	Maine-et-Loire	*Gamay*	R		
BOURGUEIL	Indre-et-Loire	*Cabernet*	R	r	
CABERNET D'ANJOU	Maine-et-Loire	*Cabernet, Grolleau*		r	
CABERNET DE SAUMUR	Maine-et-Loire	*Cabernet, Grolleau*		r	
CHEVERNY	Loir-et-Cher	*Sauvignon, Chenin, Gamay*	R	r	W
CHINON	Indre-et-Loire	*Cabernet*	R	r	W
COTEAUX-DU-GIENNOIS	Loiret	*Sauvignon, Gamay*	R	r	W
COTEAUX-DU-LOIR	Indre-et-Loire	*Chenin, Gamay, Pineau d'Aunis*	R	r	W
COTEAUX-DU-VENDÔMOIS	Loir-et-Cher	*Chenin, Pineau d'Aunis, Pinot, Cabernet*	R	r	W
COTEAUX-DU-LAYON	Maine-et-Loire	*Cabernet Franc, Pineau*			W
CRÉMANT DE LOIRE	Indre-et-Loire	*Chenin, Chardonnay, Cabernet*		r	W
	Loir-et-Cher	*Pineau d'Aunis*		r	W
	Indre-et-Loire	*Sauvignon, Chenin, Pinot*			W
MONTLOUIS	Indre-et-Loire	*Chenin*			W
ORLÉANAIS	Loiret	*Pinot, Cabernet, Chardonnay*	R	r	W
SAUMUR	Maine-et-Loire	*Cabernet Franc, Sauvignon, Gamay*			W
SAUMUR-CHAMPIGNY	Maine-et-Loire	*Cabernet, Pineau d'Aunis*	R		
ST-NICOLAS-DE-BOURGUEIL	Indre-et-Loire	*Cabernet*	R	r	
TOURAINE	Loir-et-Cher	*Pineau, Gamay, Cabernet*	R	r	W
TOURAINE-AMBOISE	Indre-et-Loire	*Chenin, Gamay, Cabernet*	R	r	W
TOURAINE-AZAY-LE-RIDEAU	Indre-et-Loire	*Chenin, Grolleau noir*		r	W
TOURAINE-MESLAND	Loir-et-Cher	*Chenin, Sauvignon, Gamay, Cabernet*	R	r	W
VALENÇAY	Loir-et-Cher	*Sauvignon, Chenin*	R	r	W
VOUVRAY	Indre-et-Loire	*Chenin*	R		

MILLS OF ANJOU

The particular geographical and climatic conditions of Anjou account for the presence of many different mills in the region. Very early on, the extensive network of waterways encouraged the construction of a great many watermills of all kinds (barge-mills, bank-mills, mills with hanging wheels). But the region is furthermore exposed for most of the year to strong winds blowing from the southwest to the northwest – a fact which led to the proliferation of various types of windmill as early as the 13C. Some of these have been restored or converted and are still standing today.

For those who like to stray from the beaten track and get to know a particular region in more detail, it is fascinating to track down a few of Anjou's mills.

The Maine-et-Loire *département* – once home to more than 1 500 mills – still features around 20 such structures open to the public during the summer season or on request. They fall into three categories:

Turquant – Moulin de la Herpinière

Corn mills – characteristic of the Anjou landscape, the corn mill consists of a conical stone base called the "cellar", surmounted by a wooden cabin bearing the shaft and sails. The cellar was used for storing grain, flour and spare parts; in some cases, it also housed stables and a shed;

Post mills – the post mill was a huge wooden structure supporting the sails, the millstone as well as the whole mechanism. Unfortunately, because it was made entirely of wood, its age of glory was short-lived, either through lack of maintenance or because the shaft suffered damage;

Tower mills – by far the most common type of mill, the tower mill – built in stone – has remained comparatively intact over the centuries. The conical roof, with its rotating cap, carries the sails.

The following list mentions the mills open to the public, classified by category

Water mills:
Moulin au Jau on the Lathan at Breil; Moulin de Sarré on the Avort at Gennes; Moulin de la Salle on the Thouet at Montreuil-Bellay; Moulin de Bêne on the Ruisseau des Moulins at La Pommeraye;

Corn mills:
Moulin de la Herpinière at Turquant; Moulin Gouré at Louresse-Rochemenier; Moulin de la Pinsonnerie at Faye-d'Anjou; Moulin du Champ-des-Isles at Varennes-sur-Loire;

Les Rosiers – Moulin des Basses-Terres

Tower mills:
Moulin de l'Épinay at La Chapelle-St-Florent; Moulin de la Roche at La Possonnière; Moulin du Ratz at Challain-La-Potherie; Moulin des Basses-Terres at Les Rosiers;

Post mills:
Moulin de Patouillet at Charcé-St-Ellier

The Association des Amis des Moulins de l'Anjou (AMA) publishes brochures and organises visits to local mills. For information apply to 17 rue de la Madeleine, 49000 Angers, ☎ 02 41 43 87 36.

BIRDWATCHING

The Loire is frequently referred to as the "last untamed river in Europe". During the summer months, along some of its banks, the local climate can tend to resemble more that of African climes. This phenomenon, known as a topoclimate, favours the growth of many tropical plants. The Loire is also inclined to overflow, flooding the surrounding meadows and filling the ditches with water. When it eventually withdraws, leaving the gravel pits and sandbanks to dry out, it creates many natural niches and shelters, the perfect environment for myriad animal and plant species. Consequently, the banks of the Loire are home to a wide variety of birdlife attracted by the relative peace and calm of the river's waters, which are well stocked with food (water insects, larvae, tiny shellfish and amphibians etc).

More than 220 officially listed species of bird live in, nest in or migrate to the Loire valley every year. To get the most out of birdwatching, without disturbing the birds and while respecting their nesting places, visitors need to identify the particular habitat associated with each species. Along the banks of the Loire, suitable habitats include islets, gravel banks, tributary channels or *"boires"*, alluvial plains and marshes.

Islets and gravel banks

The islets, long sandbanks and high grasses found in midstream, provide safe refuges for the common heron, the kingfisher, the great crested grebe and the cormorant, who can rest peacefully, protected from intruders by a stretch of water. The irregular flow of the Loire appears to suit their reproductive pattern as it offers many open shores suitable for building nests. Downstream from Montsoreau, the **Ile de Parnay** (a protected site closed to the public from 1 April to 15 August) alone is home to more than 750 pairs of birds between March and late June, including black-headed gulls, common gulls, Iceland gulls, common terns and little ringed plovers. The Ile de Sandillon, 15km/10mi upstream of Orléans, is home to 2 500 such pairs.

"Boires"

This is the name given to the networks of channels filled with stagnant water which line either side of the Loire, and which flow into the river when it is in spate. These channels, rich in roach, tench and perch, provide shelter to the bittern, the moorhen, the coot, the garganey, and small perchers like the great reed warbler, which builds its nest 50cm/20in above the water, solidly attached to three or four reeds.

Alluvial plains

Alluvial plains – meadows and pastures which can sometimes be flooded after heavy rains – offer hospitality either to migratory birds like the whinchat and the gregarious black-tailed godwit, or to the more sedentary species such as the corncrake (from March to October).

Marshes and pools

Among the many migratory birds, the bald buzzard, which feeds on fish, had practically disappeared from French skies in the 1940s; fortunately, its population is now on the increase. It is indeed an impressive sight to see it hovering over the water while it looks for its prey, then darts forward, claws open, to pounce on a 30-40cm/12-15in long fish. The water rail is another breed which finds comfort in the long reeds and bulrushes surrounding the marshes.

The French national association for the protection of birdlife – Ligue pour la Protection des Oiseaux (LPO) – has its headquarters at La Corderie Royale, BP 263, 17305 Rochefort Cedex, ☎ 02 46 82 12 34. It is a non-profit-making organisation set up to protect species of wild bird as well as their environment. Its aim is to educate the general public and make people more aware of nature by organising visits, excursions and conferences on the subject of natural reserves.

The LPO Anjou (63bis rue Bara, 49100 Angers, ☎ 02 41 73 13 62) organises educational trips aimed at introducing people to the bird population of the Maine-et-Loire. Several weekends a year are devoted to the discovery of the environment and within this context the Carrefour des Mauges (a permanent body whose role is to provide information about the Loire and Mauges environment) stages a number of one-day programmes, including on-the-spot visits, during which you can identify the different bird species, study their behaviour and see them in their natural habitat *(telescopes and binoculars are supplied by the organisations)*.

Water-rail

Little ringed plover

Black-tailed godwit

Lapwing

Reed-bunting

Golden plover

Pochard

Calendar of events

In the *bouchons* (taverns) along the banks of the Loire, frequented by fishermen, old men can still be seen playing *alouette* or *bigaille*, a sailor's card game which requires a pack of 48. **Boules de Fort**, a version of boules particular to the Angers region, is played regularly by around 400 clubs belonging to the Fédération de l'Ouest, along the Loire river between Tours and St-Nazaire.

Naturally, the harvesting of crops, and of grapes in particular, is an occasion to celebrate in the Loire region, frequently calling for gargantuan banquets, washed down by liberal quantities of local wine.

Palm Sunday

Champagné. *(Michelin map 60 fold 14)* . . . . Lance festival.

Holy Saturday

St-Benoît-sur-Loire . . . . Great Easter Vigil (at 10pm).

March to November

Maulévrier . . . . Greyhound racing at La Tuilerie racetrack.

March to December

Fontevraud . . . . "Itinérances" music festival.

Star performers of the Cadre Noir

April to September

Saumur . . . . Public performance by the "Cadre Noir" in the dressage arena of the École nationale de l'Équitation.

April

Le Mans . . . . 24 hour motorcycle race.

Late April

Saumur . . . . International Horsemanship Competition.

Cholet . . . . Evening carnival parade.

7 and 8 May

Orléans . . . . Joan of Arc festival.

2nd week in May

Abbaye de l'Épau. . . . . Festival at the abbey. Rencontres Imaginaires (theatre).

Mid-May

Château-Gontier . . . . Horse show at Château de la Maroutière.

Châteauneuf-sur-Loire ...... Whitsun rhododendron festival.

Mid- to late June
Le Mans .... 24 hour race: motor racing on the 24 hour circuit.
Chambord .... Game Fair: national hunting and fishing festival.

Mid-June to mid-July
Sully-sur-Loire ....
Germigny-des-Prés .... Sully music festival: classical music, jazz, dance.

Late June
Grange de Meslay (Tours) ... Touraine music festival, in which international
artists take part.
Florilège vocal (Choral festival).
Choré-graphique (Contemporary dance festival).

July
Anjou .... Anjou festival in the impressive setting of the
châteaux of the Anjou region.

First weekend in July
Le Mans .... Les Cénomanies (street theatre) festival in Old Le
Mans.

1st July to 15 October
Chaumont-sur-Loire .... International Garden Show.

Mid-July
Doué-la-Fontaine .... Rose show in the amphitheatre.

15 July to 31 July
Loches .... Festival of musical theatre.

Fourth weekend in July
La Ménitré *(Michelin map 64* Head-dress parade with examples from the
fold 3) .... region's various folklores, modelled by a hundred
or so young women in traditional costume.

Last weekend in July
Saumur .... Military tattoo with mounted, motorised and
armoured divisions.

First weekend in August
Chinon .... Medieval market: reconstruction of Chinon in the
Middle Ages (period costumes, entertainers,
puppets, traditional crafts, sampling of old-style
dishes etc).

J.-P. Garcim/DIAF

Traditional Anjou costumes at La Ménitré

15 August

Molineuf *(Michelin map 64 fold 7)* . . . . Bric-a-brac fair; with antique-dealers, antiques enthusiasts and buyers.

Wednesday to Saturday in the last week in August

Sablé-sur-Sarthe . . . . Festival of Baroque music.

Early September

Château-Gontier . . . . Horse show at Château de la Maroutière.

Penultimate weekend in October

Le Lion-d'Angers . . . . International horse show. Demonstrations by the best riders in the world representing 20 nations, competing in three events (dressage, cross-country, jumping).

24 December

Anjou . . . . Messes des Naulets (held in a different country church every year). Groups in traditional Anjou costume sing Christmas carols in the local dialect.

St-Benoît-sur-Loire . . . . Christmas Eve vigil and Mass (at 10pm).

"Son et lumière"

These polished evening spectacles, which developed from an original idea of M. P. Robert-Houdin *(see BLOIS)*, were inaugurated as a feature of the Loire valley tourist season at Chambord in 1952.

By combining characters dressed in period costume with firework displays, illuminated fountains and image projection on huge screens, the *son et lumière* shed quite a different light on some of the Loire valley's most famous châteaux. Nocturnal illuminations enhance the architecture of the buildings, offering a different scene from that seen during the day. Special effects using film and staging techniques, laser beam projections and an accompanying soundtrack lend ancient walls a surprisingly different aura. From time to time the theme of the *son et lumière* is changed.

The information below describes only a selection of such events; it is advisable to check each programme with the local tourist information office.

Evening excursions leaving from Tours are organised for the "Son et lumière" at Amboise, Azay-le-Rideau and Le Lude. ☏ 02 47 70 37 37.

Amboise: *At the Court of King François* (A la Cour du Roy François)
This *son et lumière*, entirely written, staged and acted out by local volunteers, features around 400 jugglers, horsemen, fire-eaters and extras assisted by some highly sophisticated technology (fireworks, fountains, huge images projected onto the surroundings).The show evokes the building of the château, the arrival of Louise of Savoy, the childhood and adolescence of François I, the Italian campaign, as well as the daily life and festivities at Amboise to honour the King and his court.

Performances Wednesdays and Saturdays from 22 June to 31 August (1hr 30min). The show starts at 10.30pm in June and July and 10pm in August. 70-100F (30F for children aged 6-14 years). Contact "Animation Renaissance Amboise", ☏ 02 47 57 14 47.

Amboise – Son et lumière

Azay-le-Rideau: *The imaginary world of Azay-le-Château* (Les imaginaires d'Azay-le-Rideau). *Entrance from the square in front of the church.*
Visitor-spectators are free to walk round this *son et lumière* display in the park and château at their own pace. The illuminated façades, the music seeming to drift out of the surrounding woodland and the play of lights upon the water combine to create a fairy-tale atmosphere of this royal estate and summon up the spirit of that powerful surge of creativity seen here during the Renaissance.
Gates open daily at 10.30pm in May, June and July; at 10pm in August and September. Closes at 12.30am, last tickets sold at 11.45pm. Allow about an hour for the walk. 60F. ☎ 02 47 45 42 04 or 02 47 45 44 40.

Blois: *The Story of Blois* (Ainsi Blois vous est conté)
Alain Decaux of the Académie Française wrote the texts that retrace the history of Blois – "a thousand years' history spanning ten centuries of splendour" – and they are read by famous actors. Enormous projectors, combining photographs with special lighting effects, and the very latest in sound transmission systems make for a lively, entertaining and visually stimulating show, despite there being no live actors participating in the show.
Performances every evening between 9.30pm and 10.30pm (dusk) from 1 June to 6 September inclusive as well as at Ascension (Thursday, Friday and Saturday) and Whitsun (Sunday and Monday). 60F (half-price for children). ☎ 02 54 78 72 76.

Chenonceau: *The Ladies of Chenonceau* (Au Temps des dames de Chenonceau)
Under the influence of six women Chenonceau evolved from a fortified mill into an elegant residence where sumptuous parties were held.
Performances daily 1 July to 31 August at 10.15pm. 40F. ☎ 02 47 23 90 07.

Cheverny: *The river Loire down the ages* (Le Cours du Temps)
The "Association Louis XII" relates the story of Louise, daughter of a Loire boatman, whose life is bound up with the history of her country: tragic duels, hunting excursions, stories about the "Vibraye" hunt pack, rural scenes and historical events are presented, all taken from the great story book of the river Loire. Accompanying firework displays, along with horses and carriages, add a touch of realism.
Performances Fridays and Saturdays at 10.30pm from 8 July to 26 August; also on Tuesday and Wednesday during the first week in August. 80F (half-price for children). On some evenings, the performance includes dinner and a tour of the château. ☎ 02 54 42 69 03.

Abbaye de Fontevraud: *Imaginary encounters* (Rencontres imaginaires)
Son et lumière written and staged by Jean Guichard and Beate Althenn.
Show begins at 9.30pm from 9 August to 4 September (no performance 18 and 31 August). 80F. It is advisable to reserve seats in advance. Contact ☎ 02 41 38 18 17 or the tourist office at Saumur.

Loches: *Peau d'Ane*
"The Strange Story of Bélisane", an adaptation of one of Perrault's most famous fairy-tales, is staged here to the music of Lulli, Vivaldi and Rossini. The façade of the Logis Royal serves as a backdrop for a string of dream-like images, enhanced by over one hundred actors in superb costumes, horses, fireworks and... a donkey.
Performances Fridays and Saturdays from 12 July to the last weekend in August at 10pm. 70F (children: 40F). ☎ 02 47 59 07 98.

Le Lude: *Colours of the World* (Les Couleurs du Monde)
Lights, lasers, fireworks and illuminated fountains are used to evoke a journey around the world. The château is represented as holding a conversation with the sun, while projections of magnificent scenery clothe its façade.
Performances Fridays and Saturdays from 19 July to 17 August at 10.30pm (10pm in August). 85F. ☎ 02 43 94 62 20.

Semblançay *(Michelin map 64 fold 14)*: *Legend of the Spring* (Légende de la Source)
This live son et lumière is performed by 450 actors, jugglers and other members of the Association Jacques de Beaune. Little Benjamin and his grandfather bring to life the legend of the spring from the days of the Ancient Romans to the French Revolution.
Performance (1hr 45min) starts at 10.30pm on Saturdays in July, and at 10.15pm on Fridays and Saturdays until 17 August. 60F. ☎ 02 47 29 88 88.

Valençay: *Esclarmonde*
Numerous actors, with horses and carriages, recount the legendary tale of the mysterious princess of Byzantium, something of a magician and also in love with Roland...
Performances Fridays and Saturdays mid-June to mid-August at 10.30pm (July) and 10pm (August). 75F. ☎ 02 54 00 04 42.

Further reading

If works mentioned below are out of print, ask at a public library.

A Little Tour in France by Henry James

Art and Architecture in France 1500-1700 by Anthony Blunt (London, 1970)

Châteaux of the Loire by Marcus Binney (Penguin-Viking, 1992)

Châteaux of the Loire by Philippe and Gouvion (Thames & Hudson, 1986)

Companion Guide to the Loire by Richard Wade (Collins, 1984)

Eleanor of Aquitaine and the Four Kings by Amy Kelly (Harvard University Press, 1974)

Francis I by Robert Knecht (Cambridge, 1982)

History of French Architecture 1494-1661 by Sir Reginald Blomfield (London, 1911)

History of French Architecture 1661-1774 by Sir Reginald Blomfield (London, 1921)

Joan of Arc by Marina Warner (Penguin, 1983)

Loire Gastronomique by Hilaire Wolden (Octopus Books, 1992)

Loire Valley by J.J. and J. Wailing (Thomas Nelson Ltd, 1982)

Princely Gardens, the Origin and Development of the French Formal Garden Style by Kenneth Woodbridge (New York, 1986)

The Cathedral's Crusade, The Rise of the Gothic Style in France by Ian Dunlop (Hamish Hamilton, 1982)

The Loire by S. Jennett (Batsford, 1975)

The Loire Valley by Henry Myhill (Faber & Faber, 1984)

The Loire Valley and Its Wines by J. Selly (Lennard Publishing Ltd, 1989)

The following novels are set in the Loire region:

Alain-Fournier (Henri-Alban Fournier): *Le Grand Meaulnes*

Honoré de **Balzac**: *Eugénie Grandet, Le Curé de Tours, La Femme de Trente Ans, L'Illustre Gaudissart, Le Lys dans la Vallée*

René **Benjamin**: *La Vie Tourangelle*

Maurice **Genevoix**: *Raboliot*

Charles **Péguy**: *Jeanne d'Arc*

Marcel **Proust**: *A la Recherche du temps perdu, Jean Santeuil*

François **Rabelais**: *Gargantua and Pantagruel* comprising *Pantagruel, Gargantua, Tiers Livre, Quart Livre*

Émile **Zola**: *La Terre (Earth)*

Rabelais
(Orléans: Musée des Beaux-Arts)

Admission times and charges

As admission times and charges are liable to alteration, the information below is given for guidance only. In cases where it has not been possible to obtain up-to-date information, the admission times and charges from the previous edition of the guide have been given in italics.

The information applies to individual adults. Special conditions for groups are common but arrangements should be made in advance. In some cases there is no charge for admission on certain days, eg Wednesdays, Sundays or public holidays.

Churches are usually closed from noon to 2pm; tourists should not try to sightsee during services. Admission times are indicated if the interior is of special interest. Visitors to chapels are usually accompanied by the key-holder; a donation is welcome.

Most tours are conducted by French-speaking guides but in some cases the term "guided tours" may cover group visiting with recorded commentaries. Some of the larger and more frequented sights may offer guided tours in other languages. The symbol *indicates that tours are given by lecturers from the Historic Monuments Association (Caisse Nationale des Monuments Historiques et des Sites). Enquire at the ticket office or bookstall. Other aids for foreign visitors are notes, pamphlets or audio guides.*

Enquire at the tourist information centre 🛈 *for local religious holidays, market days etc.*

Every sight for which there are times and charges is indicated by the symbol ⊙ *in the alphabetical section of the guide. The entries appear in the same order as the sights.*

Sights which have comprehensive facilities for disabled tourists are indicated by the symbol &. *below.*

A

AMBOISE
🛈 quai Général-de-Gaulle, 37400. ☎ 02 47 57 09 28

Guided tour of the town – Apply to the tourist information office.

Château – Open (45min guided tours available) 1 July to 31 August from 9am to 8pm; 1 April to 30 June and 1 September to 31 October from 9am to 6.30pm; the rest of the year from 9am to noon and from 2pm to 5pm (or 5.30pm). Closed on 1 January and 25 December. 35F. ☎ 02 47 57 00 98.

Le Clos-Lucé: Leonardo da Vinci's Residence – &. Open 23 March to 12 November and on public holidays from 9am to 7pm (8pm in July and August); the rest of the year from 9am to 6pm. Closed on 1 January and on 25 December. 38F. ☎ 02 47 57 62 88.

Musée de la Poste – Open 1 April to 30 September from 9.30am to noon and from 2pm to 6.30pm; the rest of the year from 10am to noon and from 2pm to 5.30pm. Closed in January and on Mondays. 20F. ☎ 02 47 57 00 11.

Musée de l'Hôtel de ville – Open 1 July to 31 August (45min guided tours available) from 2pm to 6pm. The rest of the year by appointment only. Closed on Saturdays, Sundays and public holidays. Free admission. ☎ 02 47 23 47 23.

La Maison Enchantée – &. Open 1 July to 31 August from 10am to 7pm; 1 April to 30 June and 1 September to 31 October from 10am to noon and from 2pm to 6pm; the rest of the year from 2pm to 5pm. Closed on Mondays, except those in July and August, and all January. 25F. ☎ 02 47 23 24 50.

Mini-Châteaux – & Open 1 May to 31 October from 9am to 7pm; late-night opening until 10pm during July and August. Closed between 15 November and early February. 55F, or 95F for a combined ticket with Lussault aquarium or Mini-Châteaux, or 135F for a ticket for all three. ☎ 06 36 68 69 37.

Le fou de l'âne – & Open all year from 9am to 7pm; late-night opening until 10pm during July and August. 42F, or 95F for a combined ticket with Lussault aquarium or Mini-Châteaux or 135F for a ticket for all three. ☎ 06 36 68 69 37.

Excursion

Aquarium de Touraine – &. Open 1 April to 30 September from 9am to 7pm (10pm during July and August); 1 October to 31 March from 10am to 5pm. 46F, or 95F for a combined ticket with Lussault aquarium or "Le fou de l'âne", or 135F for a ticket for all three (children 25F, 60F or 85F). ☎ 06 36 68 69 37.

🛈 place Kennedy, BP 5157, or place de la Gare, 49051. ☎ 02 41 23 51 11

A combined Tourist Pass (*"billet combiné"* – valid until 31 December of the current year) is available for 50F, which includes admission to: the Château, the Galerie David d'Angers, the Logis Barrault (Fine Arts Museum), the Hôtel Pincé and the Musée Jean-Lurçat.

Guided tour of the town – 2 to 3hr tours available 1 June to 30 September daily except on Sundays (times vary depending on the day: 2pm, 5pm or 9pm). The rest of the year guided tours based on a particular theme on one Saturday every month. Apply to the tourist information office, which issues a programme of the different thematic lecture-tours.

Château – Open (Apocalypse gallery, gardens, ramparts and chapel; 1hr guided tours available of the Logis Royal and temporary exhibitions in the Logis du Gouverneur) 1 June to 15 September from 9am to 7pm; Palm Sunday to 31 May from 9.30am to 12.30pm and from 2pm to 6.30pm; the rest of the year from 9.30am to 12.30pm and from 2pm to 5.30pm. Closed on 1 January, 1 May, 1 and 11 November, and 25 December. 35F. ☎ 02 41 87 43 47.

Château d'Angers

Cathédrale St-Maurice – Open July and August daily (guided tours available on request) from 8.30am to 7pm; the rest of the year, open on Sunday afternoons only. ☎ 02 41 87 58 45.

Galerie David d'Angers – Open 15 June to 15 September daily from 9am to 6.30pm; the rest of the year from 10am to noon and from 2pm to 6pm. Closed Mondays 16 September to 14 June, and on all public holidays. 10F. ☎ 02 41 87 21 03.

Logis Barrault (Fine Arts Museum) – Same times and charges as for the Galerie David d'Angers. 10F. ☎ 02 41 88 64 65

Monastery buildings (Local Government Offices) – Open from 9am to noon and from 2pm to 6pm except when events are held at the Hôtel du Département. Free admission. For a guided tour call: ☎ 02 41 81 43 07.

Hôtel Pincé – Same times and charges as for the Galerie David d'Angers. 10F. ☎ 02 41 88 94 67.

Musée Jean-Lurçat et de la Tapisserie contemporaine – ♿. Open 15 June to 15 September daily from 9.30am to 6.30pm; the rest of the year from 10am to noon and from 2pm to 6pm. Closed Mondays and on all public holidays. 20F. ☎ 02 41 87 41 06.

Centre régional d'Art textile – Open Mondays, Tuesdays, Thursdays and Fridays from 10am to noon and from 2pm to 4pm. Free admission. ☎ 02 41 87 10 88.

Excursions

St-Barthélémy-d'Anjou: Distillerie Cointreau – ♿. Guided tours (1hr 30min) 15 June to 15 September Mondays to Saturdays at 10am, 11am, 2pm, 3pm, 4pm and 5pm, and on Sundays and public holidays at 3pm and 4.30pm; the rest of the year, Mondays to Saturdays at 3pm, and on Sundays and public holidays at 3pm and 4.30pm. Closed on 1 May and 25 December. 20F. ☎ 02 41 43 25 21.

St-Barthélémy-d'Anjou: Château de Pignerolle (Musée européen de la Communi-cation) – &. Open (2hr guided tours available) 1 July to 1 November from 10am to 12.30pm and from 2.30pm to 6pm; 1 April to 30 June at same times but closed on Mondays; the rest of the year Saturday afternoons and Sundays. Closed at Christmas. 45F. ☎ 02 41 93 38 38.

St-Sylvain-d'Anjou: Motte-and-bailey – Guided tours (1hr 15min) in July and August Tuesdays to Fridays from 2pm to 6pm, late-night opening Saturdays 2pm to 11pm, and tour with costumed actors on Sundays 2pm to 6pm. 25F. ☎ 02 41 76 45 80.

Trélazé: Musée de l'Ardoise – Guided tours (1hr) 1 July to 15 September from 2pm to 6pm (slate splitting demonstrations at 3pm); the rest of the year Sundays and public holidays from 2pm to 6pm. Closed on Mondays and from 1 December to 15 February. 30F. ☎ 02 41 69 04 71.

AREINES

Church – If church is closed during the week, the key can be obtained from the town hall (Mairie).

ARGENT-SUR-SAULDRE

Château: Musée des Métiers et Traditions de France – Open (1hr 30min guided tours available) April to November Mondays to Thursdays from 2pm to 6.30pm (doors close at 5.30pm), Fridays from 10am to noon and from 2pm to 7pm (doors close at 6pm), weekends and public holidays from 10am to 12.30pm and from 2.30pm to 7pm. 25F. ☎ 02 48 73 33 10.

ARVILLE

La Commanderie – Guided tours (1hr) 1 July to 15 September daily from 2pm to 6pm; Easter to 30 June and 16 September to 1 November at weekends and on public holidays at these times. 25F. ☎ 02 54 80 75 41.

ASNIÈRES-SUR-VÈGRE

Church – Open all year during the day. Guided tours Easter to 1 November on Sundays at 4.30pm. ☎ 02 43 92 40 47.

AUBIGNY-SUR-NÈRE   🛈 Ilot Ste-Anne, 18700. ☎ 02 48 58 40 20

Guided tour of the town – Apply to the tourist information office (during summer) or the Mairie ☎ 02 48 81 50 00 (the rest of the year).

Église St-Martin – Open Easter to 1 November daily from 2pm to 7pm (6pm in October). ☎ 02 48 81 50 00 (Mairie).

Ancien château des Stuarts: Musée Marguerite-Audoux – Open daily July to mid-September from 2.30pm to 7pm; Easter to late June weekends and public holidays from 2.30pm to 6pm; the rest of the year by appointment. Closed on 1 January and 25 December. Free admission. ☎ 02 48 58 40 20 (tourist office) or 02 48 51 50 00 (Mairie).

AZAY-LE-RIDEAU

Château – Open (1hr guided tours available) 1 July to 31 August from 9.30am to 6pm; 1 March to 30 June and 1 September to 31 October from 9.30am to 6pm; the rest of the year from 9.30am to 12.30pm and from 2pm to 5.30pm. Closed on 1 January, 1 May, 1 and 11 November, and 25 December. 32F. ☎ 02 47 45 42 04.

Excursions

Marnay: Musée Maurice-Dufresne – &. Open 1 May to 31 October from 9.15am to 7pm; the rest of the year 9.15am to 6pm. Closed January and February. 48F. ☎ 02 47 45 36 18.

Villaines-les-Rochers: Société coopérative agricole de Vannerie – &. Wickerwork displays and workshop open 1 July to 31 August daily from 9am to 7pm; the rest of the year from 9am to noon and 2pm to 7pm (16 October to 31 March Sundays from 2pm to 7pm). Closed on 1 January and 25 December. Free admission. ☎ 02 47 45 43 03.

B

BAUGÉ

Château – Open 15 June to 15 September from 11am to 12.30pm and from 2.30pm to 6pm. Closed Sunday mornings and Tuesdays (except in July and August). 15F. ☎ 02 41 89 18 07.

Chapelle des Filles-du-Cœur-de-Marie – Guided tours daily from 2.30pm to 4.30pm. No tours on Tuesdays, Whit weekend, 1st Sunday in July, 24-26 July, and 11-12 December. ☎ 02 41 89 12 20 or 02 41 89 75 49.

BAUGÉ

Hôpital public: Dispensary – For security reasons, this is currently closed to the public. ☎ 02 41 89 10 25.

Église St-Laurent – Open weekdays only from 9am to 5pm. ☎ 02 41 89 14 65.

Excursion

Pontigné: Church – If the church is closed, apply to the Bar-crêperie opposite.

BAZOUGES-SUR-LE-LOIR

Château – &. Guided tours (45min) 15 June to 15 September on Tuesdays from 10am to noon, on Fridays, Saturdays and Sundays from 3pm to 6pm; 1 April to 14 June open weekends and some days. 20F (gardens only: 5F). ☎ 02 43 45 32 62.

Church – Open in July and August from 10am to 6pm. Otherwise, apply to the priest's house, 5 rue du 8 mai, Bazouges. ☎ 02 43 94 88 44 or 02 43 45 32 20 (Mairie).

BEAUFORT-EN-VALLÉE

Excursion

Blou: Church – If church is closed, apply to the town hall in Blou or the priest's house in Longué. ☎ 02 41 52 10 28.

BEAUGENCY
🛈 Place de l'Hôtel de Ville, 45190. ☎ 02 38 44 54 42

Guided tour of the town – Apply to the tourist information office.

Musée Régional de l'Orléanais (Château Dunois) – Guided tours (45min) every half hour from 10am to noon and from 2pm to 5.30pm (4pm October to late March). Closed Tuesdays and on 1 January, 1 May and 25 December. 21F. ☎ 02 38 44 55 23.

Hôtel de Ville – Guided tours (15min) 1 May to 30 September at 11am, 3pm, 4pm and 4.30pm; the rest of the year at 3pm, 4pm and 4.30pm. Closed on all Sundays and public holidays, and additionally on Mondays and Saturdays from 1 October to 30 April. 9F. ☎ 02 38 44 54 42.

BEAULIEU-LÈS-LOCHES

Église abbatiale – Open May to October on weekdays from 10am to 6.30pm; November to April from 10am to 3pm. Closed at weekends. ☎ 02 47 59 06 64 (Mairie).

Château de BEAUREGARD

Open (45min guided tours – recommended) 1 July to 31 August from 9.30am to 6.30pm; 1 April to 30 June from 9.30am to noon and from 2pm to 6.30pm; 16 February to 31 March and 1 September to 31 December from 9.30am to noon and from 2pm to 5pm. Closed 1 January to 15 February, on Wednesdays between 1 October and 1 April, and on 25 December. 35F, walk in the park 15F, 45min guided tour "Jardin des portraits" costs an extra 10F; combined ticket to all three: 45F. ☎ 02 54 70 40 05.

BELLEGARDE

Hôtel de Ville: Salon Régence – Guided tours on request Mondays to Fridays from 8.30am to noon and from 1pm to 4pm, Saturdays from 9am to noon. Free admission. ☎ 02 38 90 10 03.

Forêt de BERCÉ

Guided tours (2hr) under the supervision of a guide from 14 July to 20 August. Daily departures (except Tuesdays) from the Chêne Boppe car park at 10am and 5pm. Sturdy walking shoes recommended. Tours can be arranged out of season by contacting the Office national des forêts, Direction régionale, 13 avenue du Général-de-Gaulle, 72017 Le Mans. 20F. ☎ 02 43 24 44 70.

BLANCAFORT

Château – Guided tours (45min) daily June to September from 10am to 7pm; October to May daily (except Tuesdays in October and November) from 10am to noon and from 2pm to 6.30pm. Closed mid-November to mid-March. 35F, children 25F. ☎ 02 48 58 60 56.

Excursion

Musée de la Sorcellerie - ♿. Open June to September daily from 10am to 7pm; Easter to May and October to 1 November from 10am to 6pm. 33F, children 25F. ☎ 02 48 73 86 11.

BLOIS   🛈 pavillon Anne-de-Bretagne, 3 avenue J.-Laigret, 41000. ☎ 02 54 74 06 49

Guided tour of the town 🅰 - 1hr 30min to 2hr tours in July and August on Saturdays at 2.30pm. 35F. Apply to the Château Conservation department, Service Animation du Patrimoine. ☎ 02 54 74 16 06 or 02 54 74 06 49.

Château - Open (1hr guided tours available) 15 March to 30 September daily from 9am to 6.30pm (8pm 1 July to 31 August); the rest of the year from 9am to 12.30pm and from 2pm to 5.30pm. Closed on 1 January and 25 December. 35F. ☎ 02 54 78 06 62.

Musée archéologique - Same admission times as for the Château. Joint ticket. ☎ 02 54 74 16 06.

Musée des Beaux-Arts - Same admission times as for the Château. Joint ticket. ☎ 02 54 78 06 62.

Pavillon Anne-de-Bretagne - Houses the Blois tourist information office. Open 1 May to 30 September on weekdays from 9am to 7pm and on Sundays and public holidays from 10am to 7pm; the rest of the year on weekdays from 9am to 12.30pm and from 2pm to 6pm, and on Sundays and public holidays from 11am to 1pm and 3pm to 5pm. ☎ 02 54 74 06 49.

Musée d'Art religieux - Open from 2pm to 6pm. Closed on Sundays, Mondays and public holidays. Free admission. ☎ 02 54 78 17 14.

Muséum d'Histoire naturelle - ♿. Open Tuesdays to Sundays from 2pm to 6pm. Closed Mondays and public holidays. 15F. ☎ 02 54 74 13 89.

Hôtel d'Alluye: courtyard - Visit by appointment only. Free admission. ☎ 02 54 56 38 00.

Cathédrale Saint-Louis: crypte Ste-Solènne - Guided tours with recorded commentary daily from 10am to 5pm.

Haras national - Guided tours 15 March to 15 November Mondays to Saturdays at 2.30pm. 30 F. ☎ 02 54 55 22 82 (Association Cheval et Culture).

Cloître St-Saturnin - Open 1 July to 31 August daily from 2pm to 6.30pm; Easter to 30 June and 1 September to 1 October at weekends and on public holidays from 2pm to 6.30pm. ☎ 02 54 78 06 62.

Excursions

Orchaise: Priory botanical gardens - Open 1 March to 31 October every Sunday from 3pm until nightfall. 25F. ☎ 02 54 70 01 02 or 02 54 70 03 92.

Maves: Windmill - Guided tours (30min) Easter to 1 November on Sundays and public holidays from 3pm to 6pm. Free admission. ☎ 02 54 87 35 17.

La BOISSIÈRE

Abbaye - Guided tours (30min) during Easter holidays and during August daily from 10am to noon and from 3pm to 6pm. 20F. ☎ 02 45 27 12 32.

BONNEVAL   🛈 2 place de l'Église, 28800. ☎ 02 37 47 55 89

Guided tour of the town - Apply to the tourist information office.

Excursion

Alluyes: Church - If closed, contact Mme Legrand. ☎ 02 37 47 28 00.

Château de BOUMOIS

Guided tours (1hr) 1 July to 15 August daily from 10am to 6pm. 39F. ☎ 02 41 38 47 27 or 02 41 38 43 16.

La BOURGONNIÈRE

Chapelle St-Sauveur - Leave the car in the car park and ring the bell at the Renaissance entrance, then take the avenue to the left up to the château. Open 1 July to 31 August from 9am to noon and from 2pm to 6pm, Sundays and public holidays from 2pm to 6pm; the rest of the year by appointment only. 15F. ☎ 02 40 98 10 18.

BOURGUEIL

Abbey – Guided tours (1hr) 1 July to 31 August daily (except Tuesdays and Wednesdays) from 2pm to 6pm; 1 April to 30 June and 1 September to 30 October on Saturdays, Sundays and public holidays at these times. 25F. ☎ 02 47 97 72 04.

Musée Van Oeveren – ♿ Guided tours 1 July to 1 September daily (except Mondays) from 2pm to 6pm; the rest of the year by appointment. 35F. ☎ 02 47 97 98 99.

Moulin bleu – Open 1 April to 30 September from 3pm to 7pm. Closed Tuesdays and Wednesdays. Free admission. ☎ 02 47 97 71 41.

Cave touristique de la Dive Bouteille – ♿ Guided tours (30min) 1 April to 30 September from 10am to 12.30pm and from 2pm to 6pm (7pm in July and August); in March and October open at weekends from 10am to noon and 2pm to 6pm. Closed Mondays except in July and August, as well as from 1 November to 28 February. 17F. ☎ 02 47 97 72 01.

Excursions

Les Réaux: Château – Only the château exterior is open to the public. 10F. ☎ 02 47 95 14 40.

Chouzé-sur-Loire: Musée des mariniers – Open 1 June to 31 August on Saturdays, Sundays and public holidays from 3pm to 5pm. 12F. ☎ 02 47 95 10 10.

Brain-sur-Allonnes: Site médiéval de la Cave Peinte – Open 15 April to 15 October from 10am to noon and 3pm to 6pm; guided tours (1hr 30min) 15 April to 15 October at 4.30pm. Closed on Sunday mornings and Mondays. 20F. ☎ 02 41 52 87 40.

Brain-sur-Allonnes: Museum – Open from 10am to noon and 3pm to 6pm. Closed on Sunday mornings and Mondays. 15F. ☎ 02 41 52 87 40.

BREIL

Château de Lathan – Apply for permission to visit by calling ☎ 02 41 82 55 06 or 02 41 82 55 21. Free admission.

BRIARE

Musée de la Mosaïque et des Émaux – ♿ Open June to September daily from 10am to 6.30pm; the rest of the year on weekdays from 2pm to 6pm, Sundays and public holidays from 10am to 12.30pm and 2pm to 6pm. Closed in January, February and on 25 December. 25F. ☎ 02 38 31 20 51.

BRISSAC

Château – Guided tours (45min) 1 July to 15 September from 10am to 6pm; 1 April to 30 June and 16 September to 31 October from 10am to noon and from 2.15pm to 5.15pm. Closed the rest of the year (except during school holidays) and on Tuesdays (except in July and August). 45F. ☎ 02 41 91 22 21.

Excursion

Centre Piscicole – Open 1 July to 31 August daily from 2pm to 7pm; 1 April to 30 June and 1 September to 31 October on Saturdays, Sundays and public holidays from 2pm to 7pm. 25F. ☎ 02 41 87 57 09 or 02 41 91 24 25.

BROU

Excursion

Yèvres: Church – If closed, contact M Boisserie, 9 rue de la Madeleinière. ☎ 02 37 47 03 52.

C

Château de CHAMBORD

Open (1hr 30min guided tours available) in July and August from 9.30am to 7.15pm; 1 April to 30 June and 1 to 10 September from 9.30am to 6.15pm; the rest of the year from 9.30am to 5.15pm. Last tickets sold 30min before closing time. Closed on 1 January, 1 May, 1 and 11 November, and 25 December. 40F (45F during exhibitions). ☎ 02 54 50 40 00. Lecture-tours are available but must be booked in advance.

Display of horsemanship – 45min show in July and August daily at 11.45am and 5pm; in May, June and September, shows at 11.45am, and at weekends also at 4pm. 45F (children 30F). ☎ 02 54 20 31 01.

Rides in horse-drawn carriages – It is possible to admire the grounds of Chambord château from a horse-drawn carriage (45min) between 1 May and 30 September. It is necessary to book first. 45F. ☎ 02 54 20 31 01.

Château de CHAMEROLLES

Open 1 April to 30 September from 10am to 6pm; the rest of the year open until 5pm. Closed Fridays, all January and on 25 December. 25F. ☎ 02 38 39 84 66.

CHAMPIGNY-SUR-VEUDE

Sainte-Chapelle – Open 1 April to 1 October from 10am to noon and from 2pm to 6pm. Closed Tuesdays. 16F. ☎ 02 47 95 71 46.

Pagode de CHANTELOUP

Open daily 1 July to 31 August from 9.30am to 8pm; in June and September from 10am to 7pm; in May from 10am to 6pm; the rest of the year from 10am to noon and from 2pm to 5pm (6pm in April and October). 30F. ☎ 02 47 57 20 97. It is possible to go for a stroll and have a picnic in the park of the Pagoda.

CHÂTEAUDUN
🛈 1 rue de Luynes, 28200. ☎ 02 37 45 22 46

Guided tour of the town – Group tours (1hr 30min). 10F. Apply to the tourist information office.

Château – Guided tours (45min) daily 1 July to 31 August from 9.30am to 6.30pm (tours of the keep at 11am, 2.30pm, 3.30pm and 4.30pm); 1 April to 30 June and during September from 9.30am to 6.15pm; the rest of the year from 10.10am to 12.30pm and from 2pm to 5pm. Closed on 1 January, 1 May, 1 and 11 November, and 25 December. 32F. ☎ 02 37 94 02 90.

Église de la Madeleine – Open daily May to September from 9am to 6pm; Saturdays and Sundays only in winter. ☎ 02 37 45 22 46.

Musée des Beaux-Arts et d'Histoire naturelle – Open 1 April to 30 September from 10am to 12.30pm and from 1.30pm to 6.30pm; the rest of the year from 10am to noon and from 2pm to 5pm (5.30pm Sundays and public holidays). Closed Tuesdays (except in July and August), and on 1 January, 1 May and 25 December. 17F. ☎ 02 37 45 55 36.

Église St-Valérien – Closed on Sunday afternoons and public holidays. ☎ 02 37 45 00 09.

Grottes du Foulon – &. Guided tours (1hr) 1 May to 30 September from 10am to noon and from 2pm to 6pm; the rest of the year from 2pm to 6pm only. Closed Mondays in winter, and from 5 to 25 January. 30F. ☎ 02 37 45 19 60.

Église St-Jean-de-la-Chaîne – Open Sundays only in summer. It is possible to ask for the key at the town hall. ☎ 02 37 45 22 46.

Excursion

Abbaye du bois de Nottonville – Open 1 May to 31 October on Saturdays and Sundays from 2.30pm to 6.30pm. 20F. ☎ 02 37 96 91 64.

CHÂTEAU-GONTIER
🛈 Péniche l'Élan, quai Alsace, 53200. ☎ 02 43 70 42 74

Museum – Open 1 July to 15 September daily from 11am to noon and 2pm to 6pm. Closed Mondays and Tuesdays. Free admission. ☎ 02 43 07 26 42.

Église de la Trinité – Open to sightseers weekdays only from 9am to 5pm.

Ancienne église N.-D.-du-Geneteil – *Open daily from 2pm to 6pm. Closed Tuesdays. Free admission.* ☎ *02 43 07 88 96.*

Excursions

Château de la Maroutière – Guided tours (30min) 15 July to 31 August on Wednesdays and Fridays from 2pm to 4.30pm. 20F. ☎ 02 43 07 20 44.

Le Refuge de l'Arche – Open 1 May to 31 August daily from 9.30am to 7pm; in March, April, September and October from 10am to noon and from 1.30pm to 6pm; in November, December, January and February from 1.30pm to 6pm. Closed on 1 January and 25 December. 25F, children 13F. ☎ 02 43 07 24 38.

CHÂTEAUNEUF-SUR-LOIRE
🛈 place A.-Briand, 45110. ☎ 02 38 58 44 79

Musée de la Marine de Loire – Due to building work, the museum is scheduled to be closed from October 1997 to April 1998. Otherwise, it is open 1 July to 31 August from 10am to noon and from 2pm to 6pm; in June and September on weekdays from 2pm to 6pm, Saturdays, Sundays and public holidays from 10am to noon and from 2pm to 6pm; 2 January to 31 March Sundays from 2pm to 6pm; in October Saturdays and Sundays from 2pm to 6pm; the rest of the year Sundays and public holidays from 2pm to 6pm. Closed on Tuesdays and on 1 January, 1 May, and 25 and 26 December. Last tickets sold 30min before closing time. 13.50F. ☎ 02 38 58 41 18.

CHÂTEAUNEUF-SUR-LOIRE

Excursion

Chécy: Musée de la tonnellerie – Open (1hr guided tours available) Palm Sunday to 1 November from 2.30pm to 5.30pm. Closed Mondays (except when the Monday is a public holiday). 10F. ☎ 02 38 46 60 51 or 02 38 91 32 64 (tourist office).

CHÂTEAU-RENAULT

Musée du Cuir et de la Tannerie – Open (1hr 30min guided tours available) 15 May to 15 September from 2pm to 6pm. Closed Mondays (including those which are public holidays, such as Easter Monday and Whit Monday). 12F. ☎ 02 47 56 03 59.

CHAUMONT-SUR-LOIRE

Château

Park – Open all year from 9am to sunset. Closed on 1 January, 1 May, 1 and 11 November, and 25 December. Free admission. ☎ 02 54 20 98 03.

Apartments – It takes 15min to reach the château, leaving from the car park. Elderly or physically disabled people can reach the château through the upper part of the park. Open (45min guided tours available) 15 March to 30 September from 9.30am to 6pm; the rest of the year from 10am to 4.30pm. Closed on 1 January, 1 May, 1 and 11 November, and 25 December. 32F (includes tour of stables). ☎ 02 54 20 98 03.

Stables – Same times and charges as for the Apartments.

Trips in horse-drawn carriages – In summer and during the Easter holidays, it is possible to book a horse-drawn carriage to visit the park and the vicinity of the château (25min). 30F. ☎ 02 54 87 57 62.

Conservatoire international des Parcs et Jardins et du Paysage – &. Open (1hr 15min guided tours available) daily 15 June to 20 October from 9am to sunset. 45F. ☎ 02 54 20 99 22.

Château de CHENONCEAU

Open 16 March to 15 September daily from 9.30am to 7pm; in spring and autumn the château closes at 6.30pm, then 6pm; in winter at 5.30pm, 5pm or 4.30pm depending on the time of year. 45F. Refreshments. In July and August there are boat trips along the Cher, a small electric train, and a garden with games and recreational activities for children (April to October). ☎ 02 47 23 90 07.

Musée de Cire – Same admission times as for the château. 15F (Waxworks Museum only).

Excursion

Château de Leugny – *Closed to the public at the time of going to press.*

Château de CHEVERNY

Open 1 June to 15 September from 9.15am to 6.45pm; the rest of the year from 9.30am to noon and from 2.15pm to 6.30pm (6pm from 16 to 30 September, 5.30pm in March and October). Guided tours available on request. Apply in writing to Château de Cheverny, 41700 Cheverny. Visitors can attend the "feeding of the hounds" between 1 April and 15 September at 5pm except on Saturdays, Sundays and public holidays; the rest of the year at 3pm except on Tuesdays, Saturdays, Sundays and public holidays. 32F (château and park); 57F (château, tour of park in tourist car and of the canal by electric boat); 79F (château and hot-air-balloon); 94F (combination of all options). ☎ 02 54 79 96 29.

Ballon captif – Daily flights (15min) 15 April to 10 November at same times as opening times of château. The hot-air balloon does not operate in strong winds. 79F (for visit to château, park and hot-air balloon trip), children of 7-14 years old: 45F, under-7s: 28F. ☎ 02 54 79 25 05.

Excursion

Château de Troussay – &. Guided tours (30min) 1 June to 31 August from 10am to 7pm (closes for lunch during June); in September and during Easter and autumn school holidays open daily from 10am to 1pm and from 2pm to 6.30pm; in May and October Sundays and public holidays from 10am to 1pm and from 2pm to 6.30pm. Closed the rest of the year. 24F (grounds and Musée de Sologne only 14F). ☎ 02 54 44 29 07.

CHINON   🚩 12 rue Voltaire, 37500. ☎ 02 47 93 17 85

A small tourist train with a historical commentary shows visitors round the town (45min). Operates 1 July to 31 August daily; from Easter to 30 June and from 1 to 30 September on Saturdays and Sundays. Departures every 45min from 2.30pm to 7pm from the Hôtel de Ville. 22F (children 18F). ☎ 02 49 22 51 91.

Guided tour of the town – Guided tours (1hr 30min) of the medieval district 15 April to 15 October on Tuesdays, Thursdays, Saturdays and Sundays at 10am. Leave from place de l'Hôtel-de-Ville. 20F. Enquire at the tourist office.

Musée animé du Vin et de la Tonnellerie – Guided tours (30min) 1 April to 30 September from 10.30am to 12.30pm and from 2pm to 7.30pm. Closed 1 October to 31 March. 23F. ☎ 02 47 93 25 63.

Musée du Vieux Chinon et de la Batellerie – Open 15 April to 13 October from 10.30am to 12.30pm and 2.30pm to 7pm. 15F. ☎ 02 47 93 18 12.

Château – Open 15 March to 30 September daily from 9am to 6pm (7pm in July and August); 1 to 31 October from 9am to 5pm; the rest of the year from 9am to noon and from 2pm to 5pm. Closed 1 January and 25 December. 27F. ☎ 02 47 93 13 45.

Église St-Mexme – Temporarily closed for restoration work. ☎ 02 47 93 53 00.

Chapelle Ste-Radegonde – Guided tours (30min) during school holidays from 10am to 7pm. Tours can be arranged by appointment on Mondays, Wednesdays and Thursdays from 3pm to 6pm with the "Amis du Vieux Chinon", 44 rue Haute-St-Maurice. ☎ 02 47 93 18 12.

The river Vienne at Chinon

Excursions

Steam railway – Operates 16 July to 14 August daily except on Tuesdays; 17 May to 15 July and 15 August to 28 September on Saturdays, Sundays and public holidays. Enquire at the tourist office at Chinon or Richelieu for timetable. 60F (return ticket), 30F (children 4-16 years old). ☎ 02 47 58 12 97.

Centre nucléaire de production d'électricité (CNPE) de Chinon – An "Information Centre" explains to visitors how a nuclear power station works with the help of various audio-visual aids. Open Mondays to Fridays from 8.30am to 12.30pm and 1.30pm to 5.30pm; April to November open also on Saturdays at these times. Visitors over 18 years of age are requested to show formal identification. Visits to be booked in advance by contacting the Mission Communication. Free admission. ☎ 02 47 98 77 77.

Cravant-les-Côteaux: Vieux Bourg de Cravant Church – *Guided tours (30min) from 2pm to 7pm. Closed Tuesdays.* ☎ 02 47 93 12 40.

Parçay-sur-Vienne: Church – To visit, contact the town hall ☎ 02 47 58 54 57.

Tavant: Church – Guided tours from 10am to noon and from 2.30pm to 6pm. Closed Tuesdays and 1 December to 1 March. 16F. ☎ 02 47 58 58 06 (Mme Ferrand) or 02 47 58 58 01 (Mairie).

La Devinière – Open (45min guided tours available) 1 May to 30 September from 10am to 7pm; 15 March to 30 April from 9am to noon and from 2pm to 6pm; the rest of the year from 9am to noon and from 2pm to 5pm. Closed 1 January and 25 December. 23F, combined ticket with St-Cosme priory and Saché: 46F. ☎ 02 47 95 91 18.

CHOLET

Guided tour of the town – Guided tours (1hr 30min) on various themes (Old town of Cholet, weaving, local history etc) mid-June to mid-September on Wednesdays at 6pm. 15F. Information and bookings from the tourist office.

Musée d'Art et d'Histoire – ♿ Open (1hr guided tours available) from 10am to noon and from 2pm to 6pm. Closed Tuesdays and public holidays. 15F (free admission on Saturdays between October and May). ☎ 02 41 49 29 00.

Musée du Textile – ♿ Open (1hr 30min guided tours available) 1 June to 30 September from 2pm to 6.30pm; the rest of the year from 2pm to 6pm. Closed on Tuesdays. 10F (free admission on Saturdays between October and May). ☎ 02 41 75 25 40.

Excursions

Ferme de la Goubaudière – Open 1 March to 31 October from 3pm to 6pm; the rest of the year from 2.30pm to 5.30pm. Closed Tuesdays and public holidays. Free admission. ☎ 02 41 71 25 94.

Château du Coudray-Montbault – Guided tours (1hr) 1 July to 8 September from 10am to noon and from 2.30pm to 6.30pm. Closed Monday mornings. 30F. ☎ 02 41 75 80 47.

CINQ-MARS-LA-PILE

Château – Open (30min guided tours available) from 9am to sunset (8.30pm in summer). Closed Mondays (unless they are public holidays), and the periods 15 February to 1 March and 15 October to 5 November. 12F or 20F (guided tour). ☎ 02 47 96 40 49.

CLÉRY-ST-ANDRÉ

Basilica – To visit the Chapelle St-Jacques and the funerary vault and oratory of Louis XI, apply to the sacristy or the presbytery at 1 rue du Cloître behind the east end of the basilica. Guided tours are organised 1 April to 1 November from 2.30pm to 6.30pm. ☎ 02 38 45 70 05.

CORMERY

Abbey – Guided tours (1hr) at about 10am and 3pm on request at the tourist office. ☎ 02 47 43 30 84.

Château de COURTANVAUX

Guided tours (1hr) Easter to 1 November weekdays and public holidays at 10am, 11am, 3pm, 4pm, 5pm and 6pm. Closed Tuesdays. 11.50F. ☎ 02 43 35 34 43.

CRAON

Château – The château grounds are open to the public 1 April to 1 November from 1pm to 7pm. Guided tours of the château interior (45min) in July and August only at these times. Closed Tuesdays. 25F (park); 35F (château and park). ☎ 02 43 06 11 02.

Excursions

Cossé-le-Vivien: Musée Robert-Tatin – Open daily from 10am to noon and from 2pm to 7pm; 1 October to 31 March closed Sunday mornings and open from 10am to noon and from 2pm to 5.30pm. Closed Tuesdays and 1 to 21 January. 40F (house and museum), 30F (museum only). ☎ 02 43 98 80 89.

Renazé: Musée de l'Ardoise – ♿. Guided tours (2hr) 2 May to 30 September Wednesdays to Sundays from 2pm to 6pm. Closed the rest of the year. 24F. ☎ 02 43 06 41 74.

Château de Mortiercrolles – Guided tours (1hr) of the outer walls and chapel 23 July to 31 August at 3.30pm and 4.30pm. 25F.

D

DAMPIERRE-EN-BURLY

Centre nucléaire de production d'électricité (CNPE) – Guided tours (2hr 30min) at 9am and 2pm on request. Apply 1 week in advance to the CNPE de Dampierre-en-Burly, BP 18, 45570 Ouzouer-sur-Loire. Visitors are requested to show formal identification. ☎ 02 38 29 70 04. Information Centre open daily from 10am to 12.30pm and from 2pm to 5.30pm. Closed on 1 January, 1 May, and 25 December.

DESCARTES

Musée Descartes – Open daily from 2pm to 6pm. Closed Tuesdays, and from 15 November to 15 January. 25F. ☎ 02 47 59 79 19.

DOUÉ-LA-FONTAINE   🛈 place du Champ-de-Foire, 49700. ☎ 02 41 59 20 49

Zoo de Doué – Open 1 April to 30 September from 9am to 7pm; the rest of the year from 10am to noon and from 2pm to 6.30pm. 60F (children aged 3-10: 30F). ☎ 02 41 59 18 58.

Musée des Commerces anciens – ♿. Guided tours (1hr 30min) 1 July to 31 August from 9am to 7pm; otherwise from 9.30am (10am in low season) to noon and 2pm to 7pm (6pm in low season). Closed on Mondays and Thursday mornings in low season as well as for the period Christmas to mid-February. 33F. ☎ 02 41 59 28 23.

Arènes – ♿. Guided tours (30min) 1 April to 31 October from 10am to noon and from 2pm to 6pm. Closed Mondays and 1 November to 31 March. 10F. ☎ 02 41 59 22 28.

Excursions

Louresse-Rochemenier: Village troglodytique – Open (1hr guided tours available) 1 April to 31 October from 9.30am to 7pm; the rest of the year on Saturdays and Sundays from 2pm to 6pm. Closed January and December. 22F. ☎ 02 41 59 18 15.

Forges: Hameau troglodytique de la Fosse – Open 1 June to 30 September from 9.30am to 7pm; 1 March to 31 May and 1 October to 30 November from 9.30am to 12.30pm and from 2pm to 6pm. Closed the rest of the year. 23F. ☎ 02 41 59 00 32.

Dénézé-sous-Doué: Caverne sculptée – Guided tours (30min) in June, July and August from 10am to 7pm; Palm Sunday to late May and 1 September to 1 November from 2pm to 7pm. 20F. ☎ 02 41 59 15 40.

DURTAL

Château – Guided tours (1hr) 1 July to 31 August from 9.30am to 12.30pm and 1.30pm to 7pm; 1 April to 30 June and 1 to 30 September from 10am to noon and 2pm to 6pm; the rest of the year from 2pm to 5pm. Closed on Tuesdays during all of January. 20F. ☎ 02 41 76 31 37.

F

FAYE-LA-VINEUSE

Église St-Georges – If the church is closed, or if you wish to visit the crypt, contact M Paul Baudu, ☎ 02 47 95 63 32.

La FERTÉ-BERNARD   🛈 15 place de la Lice, 72400. ☎ 02 43 71 21 21

Chapelle St-Lyphard – Open daily May to September, during exhibitions, otherwise contact the tourist office (guided tours several times a week). ☎ 02 43 71 21 21.

La FERTÉ-ST-AUBIN   🛈 rue des Jardins, 45240. ☎ 02 38 64 67 93

Guided tour of the town – Apply to the tourist information office.

Château – Open 1 March to 15 November daily from 10am to 7pm. Visitors are free to visit part of the château, the stables and the menagerie. Guided tours (45min) of the ground floor apartments also available at the same times. 40F. ☎ 02 38 76 52 72.

Excursion

Domaine du Ciran: Conservatoire de la faune sauvage de Sologne – ♿. Open (3hr guided tours available) daily from 10am to noon and from 2pm to 6pm (5pm 1 October to 31 March). Closed Tuesdays (in winter), on 1 January and 25 December. 30F. ☎ 02 38 76 90 93.

La FLÈCHE   🛈 Espace Pierre-Mendès-France, 72205. ☎ 02 43 48 53 70

Prytanée national militaire – Open during the summer holidays daily from 10am to noon and from 2pm to 6.30pm. Main entrance: rue Henri-IV. 20F. At other times of the year, group visits only can be arranged by appointment. ☎ 02 43 94 03 96 (extension 704).

Excursion

Parc Zoologique du Tertre Rouge – ♿. Open (3hr guided tours available) daily from 9.30am to 8pm (10am to 6pm in winter). 60F (children 35F). ☎ 02 43 48 19 19.

FONTEVRAUD-L'ABBAYE

Centre culturel de l'Ouest - For information call: ☎ 02 41 51 73 52 or 02 41 51 71 41.

Abbey - The various buildings are undergoing heavy restoration work which will last for several years. Open (1hr guided tours available) 1 June to the 3rd Sunday in September from 9am to 7pm; the rest of the year from 9.30am to 12.30pm and from 2pm to 6pm. Closed 1 January, 1 and 11 November, and 25 December. 32F. ☎ 02 41 51 71 41.

"Rencontres imaginaires" - Guided tours by actors in costume during August, every evening at 9.30pm. 80F. ☎ 02 41 38 18 17.

Église St-Michel - Open from 9am to 7pm (6pm during winter). ☎ 02 41 51 71 34.

Château de FOUGÈRES-SUR-BIÈVRE

Open (45min guided tours available) 1 April to 30 September from 9.30am to noon and from 2pm to 6.30pm; the rest of the year from 10am to noon and from 2pm to 4.30pm. Closed on 1 January, 1 May, 1 and 11 November, and 25 December. 25F. ☎ 02 54 20 27 18.

Excursion

Le Château enchanté de Roujoux - Open from last Sunday in March to autumn school holidays (late October/early November) daily from 11am to 6pm. 40F (children 20F). ☎ 02 54 79 53 55.

FRAZÉ

Château - Only the park is open to the public, from Easter to late September on Sundays and public holidays from 3pm to 6pm. 14F. ☎ 02 37 29 56 76.

Fontevraud-l'Abbaye
Recumbent figure of Henri II

G

GENNES

Musée archéologique - Open July and August from 10am to noon and from 2pm to 6pm; April, June and September Sundays and public holidays only from 3pm to 6pm. 16F (includes access to the Amphithéâtre). ☎ 02 41 51 83 33.

Amphithéâtre - Open (45min guided tours available) at the same times as above. 16F (tickets are sold at the museum; includes access to the museum). ☎ 02 41 51 84 14.

Église St-Eusèbe - Access to the tower daily 1 July to 31 August from 3pm to 6.30pm; the rest of the year on Sundays from 2pm to 5.30pm. 10F. ☎ 02 41 51 84 14.

GERMIGNY-DES-PRÉS

Church - Open (guided tours available if requested in advance) 1 April to 30 November daily from 8.30am to 8pm; the rest of the year from 9am to 7pm. ☎ 02 38 58 27 30 or 02 38 58 27 97.

GIEN   ▪ Centre Anne-de-Beaujeu, 45501. ☎ 02 38 67 25 28

Musée International de la Chasse - Open 1 May to 31 October daily from 9.30am to 6.30pm; the rest of the year from 9am to noon and from 2pm to 5pm. Closed from 25 December to 1 January. 25F. ☎ 02 38 67 69 69.

Faïencerie - The museum is open from 9am to 11.30am and from 2pm to 5.30pm; Sundays and public holidays from 10am to 11.30am and from 2pm to 5.30pm. Closed on 1 January, 1 and 11 November, and 25 December. 16F.
Visitors may join a group to visit the workshops Mondays to Fridays by appointment. 30F (includes visit to the museum). The shop is open daily except Sundays and public holidays. ☎ 02 38 67 89 92.

Excursion

St-Brisson-sur-Loire: Fortress - Guided tours (45min) Easter to 15 November from 10am to noon and from 2pm to 6pm. Closed Wednesdays. In summer archery demonstrations with medieval war machines are staged on Sundays at 3.30pm and 4.30pm. 22F. ☎ 02 38 36 71 29.

GIZEUX

Château – Open 1 May to 30 September daily from 10am to 6.30pm (Sundays from 2pm to 6.30pm). 35F. ☎ 02 47 96 50 92.

Excursion

Vernantes: Church – If closed, ask at the town hall. ☎ 02 41 51 50 12.

Le GRAND-PRESSIGNY

Musée départemental de la Préhistoire – Open (1hr 30min guided tours) 1 June to 30 September from 9.30am to 6.30pm; the rest of the year from 9am to noon and from 2pm to 5pm (6pm in April and May). Closed in January and December. 22F. ☎ 02 47 94 90 20.

Château du GUÉ-PÉAN

♿ Open (45min guided tours available) 15 March to 15 January daily from 9am to 7pm; the rest of the year on Saturdays, Sundays and public holidays from 9am to 6pm. 30F. ☎ 02 54 71 37 10.

I – J

L'ILE-BOUCHARD

Prieuré St-Léonard – Open from 8.30am to 6pm. The key is kept by Mme Page at 3 rue de la Vallée-aux-Nains. ☎ 02 47 95 26 68.

Église St-Maurice – *To visit the church, apply to Mme Page, 3, rue de la Vallée-aux-Nains.* ☎ *02 47 95 26 68.*

ILLIERS-COMBRAY

Maison de tante Léonie – Guided tours (1hr) 15 June to 15 September at 2.30pm, 3.30pm and 4.30pm; the rest of the year at 2.30pm and 4pm. Closed Mondays (except on public holidays), on 1 and 11 November, and from 15 December to 14 January. 25F. ☎ 02 37 24 30 97.

JARZÉ

Excursion

Chapelle N.-D.-de-Montplacé – To visit the chapel, apply to Mme d'Orsetti of the association for the preservation of the chapel. ☎ 02 41 95 43 01.

L

LANGEAIS

Château – Guided tours (1hr) 15 July to 31 August from 9am to 9pm; 1 April to 14 July and 1 to 30 September from 9am to 6.30pm; 1 October to 2 November from 9am to 12.30pm and from 2pm to 6.30pm; the rest of the year from 9am to noon and from 2pm to 5pm. Guided tours (1 hour) also available at the same times. 35F. ☎ 02 47 96 72 60.

Musée de l'Artisanat – Open 1 June to 15 September daily from 10am to 7pm; 1 April to 31 May and 16 September to 31 October from 10am to noon and from 2pm to 6pm; the rest of the year from 2pm to 6pm only. Closed in January and on 25 December. 28F. ☎ 02 47 96 72 64.

Excursions

St-Michel-sur-Loire: Musée Cadillac – ♿ Open 1 April to 30 September from 10am to 6pm. Closed the rest of the year. 39F. ☎ 02 47 96 81 52.

Château de Champchevrier – Open 1 July to 30 September from 11am to 6pm (45min guided tours available from 2pm to 6pm); 1 April to 14 June and 16 September to 30 September, open Sundays and public holidays at these times. 40F (château with tour), 30F (château without tour), 25F (grounds, kennels, kitchen, wash-house and temporary exhibitions). ☎ 02 47 24 93 93.

LASSAY-SUR-CROISNE

Église St-Denis – If the church is closed, the key can be obtained from M Martin (see note on church door).

Château du Moulin (Lassay-sur-Croisne) – Canopy bed

Château du Moulin – Guided tours (40min) 1 March to 15 November from 9am to 11.30am and from 2pm to 6.30pm (5.30pm in March and 1 October to 15 November). Closed the rest of the year. 30F. ☎ 02 54 83 83 51.

LAVARDIN

Château – Open 1 June to 21 September from 11am to 12.15pm and 3pm to 6pm. 20F. ☎ 02 54 85 07 74.

Mairie – Open Wednesdays from 2pm to 7pm, Fridays from 9am to noon and 2pm to 7pm and Saturdays from 8.30am to noon. Free admission. ☎ 02 54 85 07 74.

Vallée du LAYON

Les Cerqueux-sous-Passavant: Bisonland – Open 1 July to 31 August daily from 10am to noon and 2pm to 7pm; 1 May to 30 June and 1 to 30 September on Sundays and public holidays from 2.30pm to 7pm. 35F. ☎ 02 41 59 58 02.

Beaulieu-sur-Layon: Caveau du vin – Open 1 May to 1 October from 10am to 12.30pm and from 2.30pm to 7pm. Closed the rest of the year. Free admission. ☎ 02 41 78 65 07.

St-Lambert-du-Lattay: Musée de la Vigne et du Vin d'Anjou – Open 1 July to 31 August daily from 10am to 6.30pm; 1 April to 30 June and 1 September to 31 October from 10am to noon and from 2.30pm to 6.30pm. Closed Mondays outside high season. 24F. ☎ 02 41 78 42 75.

Château de la Haute-Guerche – Open 1 July to 31 August daily from 10am to noon and from 2pm to 6pm. Free admission. ☎ 02 41 78 41 48.

Chartreuse du LIGET

Charterhouse – ♿ Only the outside is open to visitors, from 9am to 7pm. 3F. ☎ 02 47 92 60 02.

Chapelle St-Jean – ♿. To visit, apply to Mme Arnould at the chapter-house. ☎ 02 47 92 60 02.

Le LION-D'ANGERS

Église St-Martin – If closed, contact the priest (M le Curé), ☎ 02 41 95 31 02.

Haras national de l'Isle-Briand – ♿. Open all year from 2pm to 5pm. Free admission. ☎ 02 41 95 82 46.

LIRÉ

Musée Joachim-du-Bellay – Open 1 February to 31 December Wednesdays to Sundays from 10am to noon and from 2pm to 6pm. Closed all January and on 25 December. Prices not released. ☎ 02 40 09 04 13.

🏛 place Wermelskirchen, 37600, ☎ 02 47 59 07 98

Guided tour of the town – Apply to the Pavillon du Tourisme.

Musée Lansyer and Musée du Terroir – Guided tours (1hr) 1 April to 1 October from 10am to 7pm; the rest of the year from 1.30pm to 5pm. Closed Tuesdays. 20F. ☎ 02 47 59 05 45.

Château – Open (45min guided tours available) 1 July to 15 September daily from 9am to 7pm; 15 March to 30 June and 16 to 30 September from 9am to noon and from 2pm to 6pm; the rest of the year from 9am to noon and from 2pm to 5pm. Closed 1 January and 25 December. 22F (château only), 30F (château and donjon). ☎ 02 47 59 01 32.

Donjon – Open (45min guided tours available) 1 July to 15 September from 9am to 7pm; 15 March to 30 June and 16 to 30 September from 9.30am to 1pm and from 2.30pm to 7pm; the rest of the year from 9.30am to 1pm and from 2.30pm to 6pm. 22F (donjon only), 30F (includes access to the Royal Apartments inside the castle). ☎ 02 47 59 07 86.

Excursion

Bridoré castle – Guided tours (1hr) 1 June to 30 September daily from 2pm to 6pm. 30F ☎ 02 47 94 72 63.

Vallée du LOIR

Château-du-Loir: Église St-Guingalois – Generally open daily. To see the "Scourging of Christ", apply to the presbytery, 2 rue Gendron. ☎ 02 43 44 01 28.

Vaas: Moulin à blé de Rotrou – Guided tours (1hr 30min) 1 June to 1 November Wednesdays to Sundays from 2.30pm to 5.30pm; Easter to 31 May and 1 to 31 October at weekends from 2.30pm to 5.30pm. Closed the rest of the year. 20F. ☎ 02 43 46 70 22.

Manoir de Vénevelles – The manor house is not open to the public but the gardens are. ☎ 02 43 45 44 60.

Pringé: Church – If closed, ask for the key from M and Mme Doyen, who live in a house to the left of the church.

Vallée de la LOIRE

Centre nucléaire de production d'électricité (CNPE) de St-Laurent-des-Eaux – Information Centre open daily from 9am to 6pm. Guided tours of the power station (minimum 2hr 30min) Mondays to Saturdays from 10am to 6pm by appointment. Visitors are requested to show national identity papers. Apply to the Service des Relations Publiques, BP 42, 41220 St-Laurent-Nouan. Closed on Sundays. Free admission. ☎ 02 54 44 84 09.

St-Dyé-sur-Loire: Church – If closed, consult the notice on the gate or call ☎ 02 54 81 65 45.

Maison de la Loire – Open (45min guided tours available) 1 July to 31 August daily from 2pm to 5pm (6pm on Sundays); the rest of the year from 10am to 12.30pm and from 3pm to 7pm. Closed Tuesdays, 1 January and 25 December and all of February. 15F. ☎ 02 54 81 65 45.

Saut-aux-Loups: Mushroom farm – ♿ Guided tours (45min) 1 March to 11 November from 10am to 6.30pm. 24F. Mushroom tasting sessions daily except Mondays. ☎ 02 41 51 70 30.

Turquant: Troglo'Tap – Open (45min guided tours available) 1 July to 31 August from 10am to noon and from 2.30pm to 6.30pm (except Mondays); 1 to 30 June and 1 to 30 September weekdays from 2.30pm to 6.30pm, Sundays from 10am to noon and from 2.30pm to 6.30pm; Easter to late May and 1 October to 11 November weekends only from 2.30pm to 6.30pm. Closed Mondays and 12 November to Easter. 26F. ☎ 02 41 51 48 30.

Abbaye de St-Maur-de-Glanfeuil – *The two chapels and the Carolingian Cross are open to the public in July and August from 10am to 6.30pm; the rest of the year open until 5pm. Closed January. Free admission.* ☎ *02 41 57 04 16.*

Montjean-sur-Loire: Museum – Open (2hr guided tours available) 1 April to 1 November from 3pm to 7pm (last visit at 5.30pm). Closed Mondays. 25F. ☎ 02 41 39 08 48.

Oudon: Tower – *Open (20min guided tours available) 1 July to 31 August daily from 10am to noon and from 3.30pm to 6.30pm; 1 May to 30 June and 1 to 15 September weekends and public holidays from 10am to noon and from 2.30pm to 6.30pm. 15F.* ☎ *02 40 83 60 17.*

LORRIS

près des Halles, 45260. ☎ 02 38 94 81 42

Musée départemental de la Résistance et de la Déportation – &. Open from 10am to noon and from 2pm to 6pm.Closed Tuesdays, Sunday mornings and on 1 January, 8 May and 25 December. 25F. ☎ 02 38 94 84 19.

Château du LUDE

Open 1 April to 30 September: the grounds from 10am to noon and from 2pm to 6pm; guided tours of the interior (45min) from 2.30pm to 6pm. 30F(guided tours). 15F (grounds only). ☎ 02 48 94 60 09.

LUYNES

Château – Guided tours (1hr) of the interior 15 March to 30 September from 10am to 6pm. 45F. ☎ 02 47 55 67 55.

M – N

Le MANS

hôtel des Ursulines, rue de l'Étoile, 72000. ☎ 02 43 28 17 22

Guided tour of the town 🅰 – In July and August daily at 3pm, leaving from the cathedral. Apply to the tourist information office.

Musée de la reine Bérengère – Open (1hr 15min guided tours available) from 9am (10am Sundays) to noon and from 2pm to 6pm. Closed public holidays. 16F (combined ticket with the Musée de Tessé: 25F). Free admission on Sundays. ☎ 02 43 47 38 51.

St-Pierre-la-Cour – Open during exhibitions from 9am to noon and 2pm to 6pm. ☎ 02 43 47 38 51.

Musée de Tessé – &. Same admission times and charges as the Musée de la reine Bérengère. 16F (combined ticket with the Musée de la reine Bérengère: 25F). No admission charge on Sundays. ☎ 02 43 47 38 51.

Église de la Visitation – Closed to sightseers on Sundays. ☎ 02 43 28 28 98.

Circuit Bugatti – &. Open 1 February to 30 November daily from 8am to 6pm except on racing days. Free admission. ☎ 02 43 40 24 24 or 02 43 40 24 30.

Musée de l'automobile de la Sarthe – &. Open 1 June to 30 September daily from 10am to 7pm; the rest of the year from 10am to 6pm. Closed on weekdays from 1 January to mid-February. 35F, 40F (during temporary exhibitions). ☎ 02 43 72 72 24.

Excursions

Abbaye de l'Épau – & Open from 9.30am to noon and from 2pm to 6pm (5.30pm in winter) by appointment. Guided tours (30min) also available by appointment at the same times – apply to the local tourist information office. The Abbey is sometimes closed to the public when cultural events are being staged. Closed 1 January and 25 December. 15F (exhibitions). ☎ 02 43 84 22 29.

Spay: Church – Open weekdays from 10am to 5pm (4pm in winter); Sundays from 11am to 5pm (4pm in winter). ☎ 02 43 21 82 43.

Les MAUGES

Chapelle de la Sorinière – Open 15 June to 15 September from 3pm to 6pm. 10F. ☎ 02 41 30 35 17 (town hall).

St-Laurent-de-la-Plaine: Cité des Métiers de Tradition – Open (2hr guided tours available) 15 March to 15 November daily from 10am to 12.30pm and 1.30pm to 7pm; 16 November to 14 March on weekdays only from 10am to noon and 1.30pm to 5pm. 30F (children 15F). ☎ 02 41 78 24 08.

MAULÉVRIER

Parc oriental – Open (1hr 30min guided tours available) 1 May to 30 September from 10am to noon and from 2pm to 7pm; the rest of the year from 2pm to 6pm. Closed 24 December to 31 January, all day on Mondays from October to April and on Monday mornings in May and September. 25F. ☎ 02 41 55 50 14.

Vallée de la MAYENNE

Chenillé-Changé: Moulin à eau fortifié – Guided tours (20min) April to October at 6pm and 6.30pm or by appointment. Closed at weekends and on public holidays. 20F. ☎ 02 41 95 10 83.

MEUNG-SUR-LOIRE ⊠ 42 rue de Jehan-de-Meung, 45130. ☎ 02 38 44 32 28

Guided tour of the town – Tours (1hr) available if booked in advance – contact the tourist information office.

Château – Guided tours (1hr) late March to mid-November daily from 9am to 6.30pm; the rest of the year from 10am to noon and 2pm to 5pm. 35F. ☎ 02 38 44 36 47.

MIRÉ

Château de Vaux – The château is currently undergoing restoration work and is therefore not open to the public at the time of going to press.

MONDOUBLEAU

Excursions

Château de St-Agil – The grounds are open to the public daily from 9.30am to 5.30pm. Guided tours (45min) of the interior are available for groups of 20 by appointment. Closed in January and December. 20F. ☎ 02 54 80 94 02.

Sargé-sur-Braye: Église St-Martin – Open on Sundays only. During the week the key can be borrowed from Boulangerie Desile, the bakery in Sarges.

Baillou: Church – Open Tuesdays and Fridays from 2pm to 6pm. The key is kept at the town hall. ☎ 02 54 80 81 23.

Château de MONTGEOFFROY

&. Guided tours (1hr) 15 June to 15 September from 9.30am to 6.30pm; 15 March to 14 June and 16 September to 31 October from 9.30am to noon and 2.30pm to 6.30pm. Closed the rest of the year. 45F. ☎ 02 41 80 60 02.

MONTIGNY-LE-GANNELON

Château – &. Open 15 June to 15 September: the park (free access) from 10am to 6.30pm, the château (1hr guided tours) from 2pm to 6.30pm; Easter to 1 November on Saturdays, Sundays and public holidays at these times. Closed in January, February and December. The château is floodlit every weekend between Easter and 1 November. 30F (château), 15F (park). ☎ 02 37 98 30 03.

Church – To visit the church, call at the château reception. ☎ 02 37 98 30 03.

MONTLOUIS-SUR-LOIRE ⊠ place de la Mairie, 37270. ☎ 02 47 45 00 16

Château de la Bourdaisière – Gardens open and 30min guided tours of the château available 1 May to 15 October daily from 10am to 7pm; 15 March to 30 April and 16 October to 15 November from 10am to noon and from 2pm to 6pm. 32F. ☎ 02 47 45 16 31.

Maison de la Loire – Open 1 April to 31 October from 2pm to 6pm. Closed on Mondays. 20F. ☎ 02 47 50 97 52.

MONTOIRE-SUR-LE-LOIR

Chapelle St-Gilles – To visit the chapel apply to 33bis rue St-Oustrille in Montoire. ☎ 02 54 85 38 63.

Fontaine-les-Côteaux: Parc botanique de La Fosse – Guided tours (1hr 30min) 1 July to 31 August on Wednesdays, Thursdays and Fridays (except if they are public holidays) at 3pm sharp and on Saturdays, Sundays and public holidays at 2.30pm and 4.30pm; Easter to 30 June and 1 to 30 September on Saturdays, Sundays and public holidays at 2.30pm and 4.30pm; in October and November on Saturdays, Sundays and public holidays at 3pm. 50F. ☎ 02 54 85 38 63.

Château de MONTPOUPON

Open (2hr guided tours available) 1 July to 31 August from 10am to 7pm; 15 to 30 June and in September from 10am to noon and from 2pm to 7pm; 1 April to 14 June and in October on Saturdays, Sundays and public holidays only from 2pm to 7pm. 35F. ☎ 02 47 94 30 77.

MONTRÉSOR

Château – Free access to the park and ramparts, guided tours (30min) of the interior July and August from 10am to 6pm; in April, May, June, September and October from 10am to noon and 2pm to 6pm. Closed from 3 November to 1 April. 32F. ☎ 02 47 92 60 04.

MONTREUIL-BELLAY

Château – Guided tours (45min) 1 April to 1 November from 10am to noon and from 2pm to 5.30pm. Closed Tuesdays. 40F. ☎ 02 41 52 33 06.

Maison Dovalle: Musée Charles Léandre – Open (1hr guided tours available) 1 July to 10 September from 2pm to 6pm; the rest of the year by appointment. 10F. ☎ 02 41 52 48 46.

Excursions

Moulin de la Salle – Guided tours (45min) 1 July to 31 August Mondays to Fridays from 3pm to 6.30pm by appointment. Closed at weekends. 18F. ☎ 02 41 52 30 62.

Ancienne abbaye d'Asnières – *Guided tours (30min) 1 July to 31 August from 2pm to 6.30pm. Closed Tuesdays.* ☎ *02 41 81 49 49.*

MONTRICHARD

Musée René-Galloux – Open daily during the spring holidays and 15 June to 17 September from 9.30am to noon and from 2.30pm to 6pm; Palm Sunday to 15 June and in September on Saturdays, Sundays and public holidays only from 9.30am to noon and from 2.30pm to 6pm. 8F. ☎ 02 54 32 05 10.

Birds of prey – These can be viewed from the spring holidays to late September daily from 10am to noon and from 2pm to 6.30pm. 20F (combined ticket giving access to the museums in the keep). **Flight demonstrations** at 3.30pm and 5pm. 45F. ☎ 02 54 32 01 16.

Caves Monmousseau – &. Guided tours (1hr) of the cellars 1 April to 30 November daily from 10am to 6pm. Closed the rest of the year. 15F. ☎ 02 54 71 66 66.

Musée des confréries européennes – Same times and charges as for the Monmousseau cellars.

Excursion

Thésée: Musée archéologique – Open 15 June to 15 September from 2pm to 6pm; Easter to 14 June and 16 September to 15 October at weekends and on public holidays from 2pm to 6pm. 15F. ☎ 02 54 71 40 20.

MONTSOREAU

Château – Open (1hr guided tours available) May to September from 10am to noon and from 2pm to 6.30pm; the rest of the year from 1.30pm to 5.30pm. Closed from 1 December to 28 February, 1 and 11 November, and on Tuesdays all year round. 29F. ☎ 02 41 51 70 25.

Turquant: Moulin de la Herpinière – Open (1hr guided tours available) 1 June to 31 August from 9.30am to 11.30am and from 3pm to 7pm; in May and September from 2pm to 6pm, closed on Wednesdays during these months; 1 March to 30 April and 1 October to 31 December open at weekends and on public holidays from 2pm to 6pm. Closed in January and February. 15F. ☎ 02 41 51 75 22.

MULSANS

Church – For guided tours, make an appointment for Tuesdays or Saturdays between 1.45pm and 5pm at the town hall (Mairie: Secrétariat), ☎ 02 54 87 34 73.

NOYANT-LA-GRAVOYÈRE

La mine bleue – Guided tours (2hr 30min) on a choice of theme, either an illuminated show with sound backing on life in the mine, or a show based on Jules Verne's novel *Voyage to the Centre of the Earth*. These are on offer Easter to 1 November daily from 10am to 5pm. Closed the rest of the year. The lift leaves every 15min (last trip down at 5pm). Temperature 13°C/55°F, so it is advisable to wear warm clothes and proper walking shoes. 75F, children: 50F. ☎ 02 41 61 55 60.

ORLÉANS

🛈 place Albert-Ier, 45000. ☎ 02 38 24 05 05

A small tourist train takes visitors round the streets on a tour of the city centre (45min). Departures from place Sainte-Croix, in front of the cathedral, 1 July to 31 August daily at 3pm, 4pm, 5pm and 6pm; 1 to 30 June at 3pm, 4pm and 5pm. 25F. There is a joint trip including the train ride and a tour of the cathedral's "upper limits" in July and August: 35F. For information apply to the tourist information office.

Guided tour of the town – All year on some Wednesdays and Saturdays at 2.30pm, leaving from the tourist information office. There are various tours on offer, focusing on different themes: 35F. Apply to the tourist information office.

Cathédrale Ste-Croix: Crypt – Guided tours (45min) 15 June to 15 September from 3pm to 6.30pm. Closed Fridays. 12F. ☎ 02 38 66 64 17 (M. Grandet).

Treasury – During restoration work, the treasury is closed to visitors until further notice.

Musée des Beaux-Arts – Open from 10am to noon and from 2pm to 6pm. Closed Tuesdays and on 1 January, 1 and 8 May, 1 November and 25 December. 18.50F. ☎ 02 38 53 39 22.

Musée historique – Same admission times as for the Musée des Beaux-Arts. Closed Tuesdays. 13F. ☎ 02 38 53 39 22.

Centre Charles-Péguy – Open from 2pm to 6pm. Closed Saturdays, Sundays and public holidays. Free admission. ☎ 02 38 53 20 23.

Maison de Jeanne d'Arc – Open (1hr guided tours available) 2 May to 30 September from 10am to noon and from 2pm to 6pm; the rest of the year from 2pm to 6pm. Closed Mondays and all public holidays. 13F. ☎ 02 38 52 99 89.

Centre Jeanne d'Arc – &. Open from 9am to noon and from 2pm to 6pm (4.30pm Fridays). Closed weekends and all public holidays. Free admission. ☎ 02 38 62 47 79.

Hôtel Toutin – Only the inner courtyard is open to the public from 10am to noon and from 2pm to 6pm. Closed Monday mornings, Sundays and public holidays and all August. Free admission. ☎ 02 38 62 70 61.

Collégiale St-Pierre-le-Puellier – &. Open only during exhibitions from 10am to 12.30pm and from 1.30pm to 6pm (Sundays from 2pm to 7pm). Closed Mondays. Free admission. ☎ 02 38 79 24 85.

Église de St-Aignan: Crypt – Open July, August and September from 1pm to 6pm. Guided tours only the rest of the year. Contact the tourist office for details.

Muséum – &. Open daily from 2pm to 6pm. Closed Saturdays and on 1 January, 1 May, 14 July, 1 November and 25 December. 21F. ☎ 02 38 54 61 05.

Parc floral de la Source – &. Open (1hr guided tours available) 1 April to 11 November from 9am to 6pm (7pm 16 June to 31 August); the rest of the year from 2pm to 5pm. 20F, 35F (with the butterfly greenhouse). A small tourist train operates from early May to mid-September every afternoon; mid-September to mid-November it operates afternoons of Wednesdays, weekends and public holidays. 7F. ☎ 02 38 49 30 00.

Excursions

Gidy: Géodrome – Open 28 June to 7 September from 10am to 8pm; 4 April to 27 June and 8 to 30 September from noon to 6pm. 10F. ☎ 02 38 64 47 06.

Artenay: Musée du théâtre forain – &. Open 1 June to 30 September from 10am to noon and 2pm to 6pm; 1 October to 31 May on weekdays from 2pm to 5.30pm, at weekends and on public holidays from 10am to noon and 2pm to 5.30pm. Closed Tuesdays, 1 January, 1 May, 1 November and 25 December. 20F. ☎ 02 38 80 09 73.

P

Le PERCHE-GOUET

Courgenard: Church – Can be visited by appointment made at the town hall. ☎ 02 43 93 26 02.

Semur-en-Vallon: Tourist train – Operates 1 July to 31 August on Saturdays from 4pm to 6pm, Sundays and public holidays from 2.30pm to 6.30pm; 1 May to 30 June and in September, on Sundays and public holidays from 2.30pm to 6.30pm (travel on weekdays can be arranged on request). 15F. ☎ 02 43 71 30 36 (at mealtimes).

Montmirail: Castle – Guided tours (45min) 7 July to 19 August daily (except Tuesdays) from 2.30pm to 6pm; 1 April to 7 July and 1 to 30 September Sundays and public holidays from 2.30pm to 6pm. 25F. ☎ 02 43 93 72 71.

PITHIVIERS

🚏 mail Ouest, Gare Routière, 45300. ☎ 02 38 30 50 02

Guided tour of the town – Group tours (1hr) available by appointment mid-May to late October Tuesdays to Saturdays. Apply to the tourist information office.

Musée des Transports – &. Open July and August Saturdays and Sundays from 2.30pm to 5pm; 1 May to 30 June and 1 September to 2nd Sunday in October Sundays and public holidays from 2.30pm to 6pm. 30F. ☎ 02 38 30 50 02.

Musée municipal – Open from 10am to noon and from 2pm to 6pm (5pm Saturdays). Closed Tuesdays and public holidays. 10F. ☎ 02 38 30 10 72.

Château du PLESSIS-BOURRÉ

Guided tours (1hr) 1 July to 31 August from 10am to 6pm; 1 April to 30 June and 1 to 30 September from 10am to noon and from 2pm to 6pm (except Wednesdays and Thursday mornings); 1 February to 31 March and 1 October to 30 November from 2pm to 6pm (except Wednesdays). 45F. The double drawbridge can be raised on request. ☎ 02 41 32 06 01.

Excursion

Manoir de la Hamonnière – Open to visitors by appointment only. 10F. ☎ 02 41 42 01 38.

Château du PLESSIS-MACÉ

Guided tours (1hr) 1 July to 31 August from 10.30am to 6.30pm; 1 to 30 June and 1 to 30 September from 10am to noon and 2pm to 6.30pm; early March to late May and in October and November from 1.30pm to 5.30pm. Closed Tuesdays (except in July and August) and on 1 and 11 November. 29F. ☎ 02 41 32 67 93.

PONCÉ-SUR-LE-LOIR

Craft centre – &. The workshops are open Tuesdays to Saturdays from 9am to noon and from 2pm to 6.30pm. On Sundays and public holidays only the display room and gift shop are open from 2.30pm to 6.30pm, but there is an audio-visual presentation of the different crafts practised in the workshops. Closed on Mondays, 1 January and 25 December. 30F. ☎ 02 43 44 45 31.

Château – Open 1 March to 10 November from 10am to 12.30pm and from 2pm to 6.30pm. Closed the rest of the year. 28F. ☎ 02 43 44 45 39.

PONTLEVOY

Abbey: Musée du Poids lourd and Musée municipal – Open 1 June to 31 August from 10am to noon and 2pm to 6pm; 30 March to 31 May and 1 September to 31 October from 10am to noon and from 2.30pm to 6.30pm. Closed Mondays (except in July and August) and from 1 November to 29 March. 30F. ☎ 02 54 32 60 80.

Manoir de la POSSONNIÈRE

&. Guided tours (45min) 1 July to 15 September daily (except Sunday mornings, Mondays and Tuesdays) at 10.30am, 2.30pm, 3.30pm, 4.30pm and 5.30pm; 1 April to 30 June and 16 September to 15 November Saturdays, Sundays and public holidays at same times. 30F. ☎ 02 54 72 40 05.

POUANCÉ

Ruined castle – Guided tours (1hr) 1 July to 31 August from 9am to noon and from 2pm to 6pm. The rest of the year, by appointment only. 12F. ☎ 02 41 92 45 86.

Excursion

Château de la Motte-Glain – Guided tours (30min) 15 June to 15 September from 2.30pm to 6.30pm. Closed Tuesdays. 28F. ☎ 02 40 55 52 01.

R – S

RICHELIEU

🚏 6 Grande-Rue, 37120. ☎ 02 47 58 13 62

Town Hall: Museum – Open (30min guided tours available) 1 July to 31 August daily from 10am to noon and from 2pm to 6pm (closed Tuesdays); the rest of the year from 2pm to 4.30pm (closed on Wednesdays). 10F. ☎ 02 47 58 10 13.

Park – Open May to mid-September daily from 10am to 7pm; late March to May and mid-September to late October Sundays and public holidays from 10am to 7pm. 15F. ☎ 02 47 58 10 09.

Excursions

Steam trains in Touraine – Operate 16 July to 14 August daily (except Tuesdays); 17 May to 15 July and 15 August to late September at weekends and on public holidays. Information about timetables and fares from ☎ 02 47 58 12 97.

Abbaye de Bois-Aubry – Open (30min guided tours available) daily from 10am to 5.30pm (ring on the day to arrange it). Free admission. ☎ 02 47 58 34 48.

Château du RIVAU

Outside open to the public 13 July to 8 September from 10am to noon and 1.30pm to 5.30pm. Closed Tuesdays. 15F. ☎ 02 47 95 77 56.

Château de la ROCHE-RACAN

Guided tours (45min) 5 August to 15 September from 10am to noon and from 3pm to 6pm. 25F. ☎ 02 45 77 97 80.

ROMORANTIN-LANTHENAY   🅱 place de la Paix, 41200. ☎ 02 54 76 43 89

Guided tour of the town – Guided tours (1hr 30min to 2hr) for groups of 20. Apply to the tourist information office.

Maison du Carroir Doré: Archeological museum – ♿ Open (30min guided tours available) 15 June to 15 September from 2.30pm to 6.30pm (except Sundays and Tuesdays). Closed 14 July and 15 August. The rest of the year by appointment only. 10F. ☎ 02 54 76 22 06.

Musée de Sologne – ♿ Open 1 April to 31 October from 10am to 6pm; 1 November to 31 March from 10am to noon and 2pm to 6pm. Closed Tuesdays, Sunday mornings and on 1 January, 1 May and 25 December. 25F. ☎ 02 54 95 33 66.

Musée de la Course automobile – ♿ Open 15 March to 15 November from 10am to 11.30am and 2pm to 5.30pm. Closed Tuesdays, Sunday mornings and on 1 January, 1 May and 25 December. 10F. ☎ 02 54 76 07 06.

SABLÉ-SUR-SARTHE

Excursion

St-Denis d'Anjou: Chapelle de Varennes-Bourreau – By appointment only on weekdays from 10am to noon and 3pm to 5pm. Apply to the Town Hall of St-Denis d'Anjou. ☎ 02 43 70 52 19.

SACHÉ

Château – Open (30min guided tours available) 1 July to 31 August from 9.30am to 6.30pm; the rest of the year from 9.30am to noon and from 2pm to 6pm (5pm out of season). Closed January and December. 23F, combined ticket with St-Cosme priory and La Devinière: 45F. ☎ 02 47 26 86 50.

ST-AIGNAN

Église St-Aignan – Tours with audio-commentary from 9am to 7pm (except Sunday mornings). In July and August it is possible to visit the tower. ☎ 02 54 75 01 33.

Château – The interior is not open to the public but visitors are allowed into the courtyard, which offers a lovely view of the Cher valley and the forest of Choussy. Apply to the caretaker.

Maison de la Prévôté – The rooms are only open for exhibitions (painting and sculpture), between Easter and September. Apply to the Town Hall. ☎ 02 54 71 22 18.

Excursions

Zoo-Parc de Beauval – ♿. Open all year daily from 9am to nightfall. Shows starring resident sea-lions and birds of prey are on offer from 1 April to mid-November. 60F (children 30F). ☎ 02 54 75 05 56.

Château de Chémery – Open 1 March to 31 December daily from 10am to nightfall; the rest of the year at weekends and on public holidays from 10am to nightfall. 28F. ☎ 02 54 71 82 77.

ST-BENOÎT-SUR-LOIRE

Basilica – Free access. Guided tours (1hr 15min) 1 March to 31 December at 10.30am, 3pm and 4.30pm (for groups of 10, and as long as there are no religious ceremonies in progress). The visiting times vary (see notice at entrance). No sightseeing on Sunday mornings or during Holy Week. Closed January and February, and on the 1st Friday of each month. 20F. ☎ 02 38 35 72 43.

ST-FLORENT-LE-VIEIL

Musée d'Histoire locale et des Guerres de Vendée – Open 1 July to 15 September daily from 2.30pm to 6.30pm; Easter to 30 June and 16 September to 2 November Saturdays, Sundays and public holidays from 2.30pm to 6.30pm. 15F. ☎ 02 41 72 63 32.

Ferme abbatiale des Coteaux – &. Open 1 July to 31 August from 10am to 12.30pm and 2.30pm to 7pm (Saturdays and Sundays 3pm to 7pm); 1 April to 30 June and 1 September to 31 October Sundays and public holidays from 3pm to 6.30pm. Closed 1 November to 31 March. Prices not available. ☎ 02 41 72 52 37.

STE-CATHERINE-DE-FIERBOIS

Aumônerie de Boucicault – Open 15 June to 15 September from 10.30am to 12.30pm and 4pm to 6pm. 10F. ☎ 02 47 65 60 61.

STE-MAURE-DE-TOURAINE 🖪 place du Château, 37800. ☎ 02 47 65 66 20

Atelier de foie gras – *Guided tours (1hr) from 9am to noon and 2pm to 5.30pm (Saturdays from 9.30am to noon and 2pm to 5pm). Closed public holidays, Sundays and in February. 35F. ☎ 02 47 65 50 50.*

Vallée de la SARTHE

Fillé: Church – Open weekdays only from 9am to 4pm. ☎ 02 43 87 14 10.

Malicorne-sur-Sarthe: Pottery – Guided tours (1hr 15min) of the workshops and museum Easter to 30 September from 9am to noon and from 2pm to 6.30pm. Closed Sunday mornings, Mondays and at Pentecost. 22F. ☎ 02 43 94 81 18.

SAUMUR 🖪 place de la Bilange, BP 241, 49400. ☎ 02 41 40 20 60

From 1 July to 31 August there are tours of Saumur (45min) in a horse-drawn carriage on Mondays to Fridays from 3pm to 7pm, leaving every 30min from the tourist office.

Guided tour of the town – Tours (1hr 30min) in July and August on Tuesdays at 3pm and Fridays at 9pm. 30F. Apply to the tourist information office.

Château – Free access to the Musée du Cheval, guided tours (1hr) of the Musée des Arts décoratifs 1 June to 30 September from 9am to 6pm; 1 October to 31 May (except Tuesdays) from 9.30am to noon and from 2pm to 5.30pm. There are evening tours in July and August on Wednesdays and Saturdays from 8.30pm to 10.30pm. Closed 1 January and 25 December. 35F. ☎ 02 41 40 24 40.

Musée de la Figurine-Jouet – Open (30min guided tours available) 15 June to 15 September daily (except Tuesdays) from 2pm to 6pm. 12F. ☎ 02 41 67 39 23.

Musée de l'École de cavalerie – Open Tuesdays, Wednesdays, Thursdays and Sundays from 9am to noon and 2pm to 5pm, Saturdays from 2pm to 5pm. Closed between Christmas and 5 January. Free admission. ☎ 02 41 83 93 06.

Musée des Blindés – &. Open 1 April to 31 October from 9am to noon and 2pm to 6pm; 1 November to 31 March from 10am to noon and 2pm to 5pm. Closed between Christmas and 1 January. 20F. ☎ 02 41 53 06 99.

St-Hilaire-St-Florent

Bouvet-Ladubay wine cellars – & Open 15 June to 30 September from 9am to 6pm; 1 October to 31 May from 8am to noon and 2pm to 6pm. 5F. ☎ 02 41 83 83 83.

Galerie d'art contemporain Bouvet-Ladubay – Open daily from 2pm to 6pm. Can be visited in the morning by appointment. 10F. ☎ 02 41 83 83 82.

Musée du Masque – &. Open Easter to 15 October daily from 10am to 12.30pm and from 2.30pm to 6.30pm; the rest of the year by appointment. 25F. ☎ 02 41 50 75 26.

École nationale d'équitation – &. Guided tours 1 April to 30 September: in the morning of the Cadre Noir in action (1hr 30min), departures between 9.30am and 10am, 30F; in the afternoon, guided tours of the facilities (1hr), departures between 2.30pm and 4pm, 20F. Not open to the public Monday mornings, Saturday afternoons and Sundays. On certain dates, the Cadre Noir performs to the public. The traditional public rehearsals of "Manège" and "Sauteurs en Liberté" are accompanied by a commentary. For further information, apply to Service des Visites, ENE, BP 207, 49411 Saumur Cedex. ☎ 02 41 53 50 60.

Musée du Champignon – &. Open (1hr guided tours available) 15 February to 15 November daily from 10am to 7pm. 35F. ☎ 02 41 50 31 55.

Excursions

Bagneux: Musée du moteur – ♿. Open 15 May to 30 September daily (except on Thursdays) from 2pm to 6pm; the rest of the year open to groups by appointment only. 25F. ☎ 02 41 50 26 10.

Dolmen – ♿. Open 15 March to 30 September from 9am to 7pm; the rest of the year from 9am to 6pm. 8F. ☎ 02 41 50 23 02.

St-Cyr-en-Bourg: Cave des Vignerons de Saumur – Guided tours (1hr) 1 May to 30 September from 8am (9am at weekends) to noon and 2pm to 7pm; the rest of the year visits stop at 6pm. Closed Sundays from 1 October to 30 April. 10F. ☎ 02 41 53 06 18.

SAVONNIÈRES

Grottes pétrifiantes – Guided tours (1hr) 1 April to 30 September from 9am to 6.30pm; 8 February to 31 March and 1 October to 15 December from 9am to noon and from 2pm to 6pm. Closed from 15 December to 8 February and on Thursdays between 12 November and 14 December and during February. 28F. ☎ 02 47 50 00 09.

SEGRÉ

Guided tour of the town – Guided tours (2hr to 2hr 30min) daily all year. To book, apply to the town hall. ☎ 02 41 92 17 83.

Excursions

Château de la Lorie – Guided tours (45min) 1 July to 15 September from 3pm to 6pm. Closed Tuesdays. 25F. ☎ 02 41 92 10 04.

Nyoiseau: Domaine de la Petite Couère – ♿ Open 1 June to 30 September daily from 10am to 7pm; 1 April to 31 May and 1 October to mid-November on Sundays and public holidays from 10am to 7pm. 60F. ☎ 02 41 61 06 31.

Château de Raguin – Guided tours (45min) daily 15 July to 15 September from 2pm to 6pm. Closed the rest of the year. 25F. ☎ 02 41 61 40 20.

Château de Bouillé-Thévalle – Guided tours (1hr 30min) Easter to 30 September from 2pm to 7pm. Closed Tuesdays. 38F. ☎ 02 41 61 09 05.

SELLES-SUR-CHER

Castle – Guided tours (45min) 1 July to 30 September from 10am to noon and from 2pm to 6pm; 1 October to 1 November at weekends and on public holidays from 10am to noon and 2pm to 5pm. 35F. ☎ 02 54 97 63 98.

Musée du Val de Cher – Closed for restoration work. ☎ 02 54 97 40 19.

Excursion

Meusnes: Musée de la Pierre à fusil – Open from 9am to 1pm. Closed Mondays, Sundays and public holidays. 5F. ☎ 02 54 71 00 23.

Château de SERRANT

Guided tours (1hr 30min) 1 April to 15 November from 10am to 11.30am and 2pm to 5.30pm. Closed Tuesdays except in July and August. 45F. ☎ 02 41 39 13 01.

SOLESMES

Abbaye St-Pierre: Religious services – Daily services: Gregorian mass at 9.45am, sext at 1pm, nones at 1.30pm, vespers at 5pm and compline at 8.30pm. ☎ 02 43 95 03 08.

The SOLOGNE

Salbris: Sologne railway – The metric-gauge railway line runs makes 15 stops between Salbris (Loir-et-Cher) and Luçay-le-Mâle (Indre). For all information regarding the dates, frequency and rates of tourist train rides, apply to the Compagnie du Blanc Argent, at the railway station of Romorantin-Lanthenay. ☎ 02 54 76 06 51.

Gy-en-Sologne: Locature de la Straize – Guided tours (1hr) 20 March to 15 November from 10am to 11.30am and 3pm to 6pm (4.30pm 15 October to 15 November). Closed Tuesdays, on 1 November and Palm Sunday. 18F. ☎ 02 54 83 82 89.

Lanthenay: Church – *If closed, apply to the inn, Auberge Le Lanthenay.* ☎ 02 54 95 33 95.

The SOLOGNE

Neuvy: Church – The church, located outside the village, is only open to the public during religious celebrations, or by prior appointment with Neuvy town hall. ☎ 02 54 46 42 69.

Salbris: Church of St-Georges – Open to sightseers weekdays only from 9am to noon and from 3pm to 7.30pm.

Villeherviers: Church – Open for sightseeing during the week; apply to the town hall. ☎ 02 54 76 07 92.

Aliotis, l'Aquarium de Sologne – ♿ Open 1 July to 31 August from 10am to 9pm; 1 April to 30 June from 10am to 7pm; the rest of the year from 10am to 5.30pm. Closed between 15 and 31 January. 46F, children: 32F. ☎ 02 54 95 26 26.

SUÈVRES

Church of St-Christophe – Open from 11am to 6pm. ☎ 02 54 87 80 28.

Church of St-Lubin – Guided tours by appointment. Apply to M Denis Jacqmin, château des Forges, 41500 Suèvres. ☎ 02 54 87 80 83.

SULLY-SUR-LOIRE   🛈 place du Général-de-Gaulle, 45600. ☎ 02 38 36 23 70

Château – Open (1hr guided tours available) 16 June to 15 September from 10am to 6pm; 1 May to 15 June and 16 September to 31 October from 10am to noon and from 2pm to 6pm; 1 March to 30 April and 1 to 30 November from 10am to noon and 2pm to 5pm. Closed 1 December to 28 February. 20F. ☎ 02 38 36 36 86.

T

Château de TALCY

Open (30min guided tours of the château, free access to outbuildings and park) 1 April to 30 September from 9.30am to noon and 2pm to 6pm; the rest of the year from 10am to noon and 2pm to 4.30pm (except on Tuesdays). Closed Tuesdays except in summer and on 1 January, 1 May, 1 and 11 November, and 25 December. 25F. ☎ 02 54 81 03 01.

TOURS   🛈 78 rue Bernard-Palissy, 37000. ☎ 02 47 70 37 37

A tourist pass (Carte Multi-Visites) is on sale at the tourist information office and at the entrance of most public museums, at a cost of 50F. It gives visitors the right to visit each municipal museum once. It is valid for one year and also entitles holders to attend a lecture-tour (on foot – 1hr 30min to 2hr). Various themes are on offer: Antique Tours, Renaissance Tours, St Martin and the Cathedral.

Guided tour of the town 🅰 – There are two different formulas: *general guided tours* (Cathedral and Plumereau districts, not including the interior of monuments) on Mondays, Wednesdays, Thursdays, Fridays and Sundays, and *lecture-tours* on Tuesdays and Saturdays following a set schedule distributed by the tourist information office. These pedestrian tours are usually led by the Guides-interprètes de Touraine. Apply to the Direction départementale du tourisme.

Musée du Gemmail – Open 15 March to 15 November from 10am to noon and 2pm to 6.30pm. Closed Mondays (except public holidays). 30F. ☎ 02 47 61 01 19.

Maison de Tristan – During school term, visitors have access to the courtyard Mondays to Fridays from 8.30am to 11.30am and from 1.30pm to 4.30pm. Free admission. ☎ 02 47 20 74 09.

Musée St-Martin – ♿ Open 15 March to 15 November from 9.30am to 12.30pm and 2pm to 5.30pm. Closed on Mondays and Tuesdays. 15F. ☎ 02 47 64 48 87.

Hôtel Gouin – Open (1hr guided tours available) 1 July to 31 August from 10am to 7pm; 15 March to 30 June and all September from 10am to 12.30pm and 2pm to 6.30pm; 1 February to 14 March and in October and November from 10am to 12.30pm and 2pm to 5.30pm. Closed January and December, and on Fridays in February, March, October and November. 20F. ☎ 02 47 66 22 32.

La Psalette – Guided tours (30min) from 9.30am to noon and 2pm to 6.30pm (5.30pm 1 October to 31 May), Sundays from 2pm to 6pm. Closed on 1 January, 1 May, 1 and 11 November, and 25 December. No sightseeing during religious services. 15F. ☎ 02 47 47 05 19.

Centre de Création contemporaine – ♿ Open Wednesdays to Sundays from 3pm to 7pm. Closed Mondays and Tuesdays, and on 1 January, 1 May, 24 and 25 December. Free admission. ☎ 02 47 66 50 00.

Chapelle St-Michel – Guided tours daily 15 June to 15 September from 3pm to 6pm. The rest of the year apply to the Communauté des Ursulines, 79 rue Blanqui, 37000 Tours. ☎ 02 47 66 65 95.

Musée des Beaux-Arts – &. Open from 9am to 12.45pm and from 2pm to 6pm. Closed Tuesdays and on 1 January, 1 May, 14 July, 1 and 11 November, and 25 December. 30F. ☎ 02 47 05 68 73.

Aquarium tropical – &. Open 1 July to 31 August daily from 9.30am to 7pm; 1 April to 30 June and 1 September to 15 November from 9.30am to noon and 2pm to 6.30pm (closed Sunday mornings); the rest of the year open from 2pm to 6.30pm. 30F. ☎ 02 47 64 29 52.

Historial de Touraine – Open 1 July to 31 August from 9am to 6.30pm; 16 March to 30 June and 1 September to 31 October from 9am to noon and 2pm to 6pm; the rest of the year from 2pm to 5.30pm. 35F. ☎ 02 47 61 02 95.

Atelier Histoire de Tours – Open 15 March to 15 December Wednesdays, Saturdays and Sundays from 3pm to 6.30pm. Free admission. ☎ 02 47 64 90 52.

Église St-Julien – Open daily 1 April to 30 September from 10.30am to noon and 2pm to 5pm. ☎ 02 47 05 61 85 or 02 47 64 42 03.

Musée des Vins de Touraine – Open daily from 9am to noon and 2pm to 6pm (5pm 1 October to 31 March). Closed Tuesdays and on 1 January, 1 May, 14 July, 1 and 11 November, and 25 December. 15F. ☎ 02 47 61 07 93.

Musée du Compagnonnage – &. Open 16 June to 15 September from 9am to 12.30pm and 2pm to 6pm; the rest of the year from 9am to noon and 2pm to 6pm. Closed Tuesdays out of season and on 1 January, 1 May, 14 July, 1 and 11 November, and 25 December. 25F. ☎ 02 47 61 07 93.

Musée des Équipages militaires et du Train – Open (1hr guided tours available) from 10am to noon and 1.30pm to 5.30pm (Fridays from 1pm to 4pm). Closed Saturdays, Sundays and public holidays, and during the period 20 December to 4 January. Free admission. ☎ 02 47 77 20 35.

Prieuré de St-Cosme – Open 1 June to 30 September from 9am to 7pm; the rest of the year from 9am to 12.30pm and 1.30pm to 6pm (5pm early February to mid-March and 1 October to 30 November). Closed in January and December. 23F, combined ticket with La Devinière and Saché: 45F. ☎ 02 47 37 32 70.

Château de Plessis-lès-Tours – Temporarily closed to the public at the time of going to press. ☎ 02 47 37 22 80.

Excursion

Grange de Meslay – &. Open Easter to 1 November on Saturdays, Sundays and public holidays from 3pm to 6.30pm. Closed 5 June to 10 July during the music festival (Fêtes Musicales en Touraine). 20F. ☎ 02 47 29 19 29.

TROO

Grotte pétrifiante – Open daily from 9am to 7pm. 5F. ☎ 02 54 72 52 04.

U – V – Y

Château d'USSÉ

Guided tours (45min) 14 July to 31 August from 9am to 6.30pm; Easter to 13 July from 9am to noon and 2pm to 7pm; 12 February to Easter and 1 October to 11 November from 10am to noon and 2pm to 5.30pm. Closed the rest of the year. 59F. ☎ 02 47 95 54 05.

Château de VALENÇAY

Château – Open July to August daily from 10am to 7pm; mid-March to June and September to mid-November from 10am to 6pm; the rest of the year at weekends and on public holidays from 10am to 12.30pm and 1.30pm to 5.30pm. 42F, children: 32F. ☎ 02 54 00 10 66.

Park – Joint ticket with the Château.

Musée de l'Automobile du Centre – Joint ticket with the Château.

VENDÔME
🛈 le Saillant, 47-49 rue Poterie, 41100. ☎ 02 54 77 05 07

Guided tour of the town 🅰 – Apply to the tourist information office, which organises visits (1hr to 2hr depending on theme) between 30 March and late October. 10F-31F depending on length of tour.

Abbaye de la Trinité: Chapter-house – Open daily from 10am to noon and 2pm to 6pm. Closed Tuesdays and 1 January, 1 May and 25 December. Free admission. ☎ 02 54 77 26 13.

Museum – Open from 10am to noon and 2pm to 6pm. Closed Tuesdays and 1 January, 1 May and 25 December. 15F. ☎ 02 54 77 26 13.

Castle – Open 1 April to 31 December from 9am to 6pm. For guided tours, apply to the tourist information office. Free admission. ☎ 02 54 77 26 13.

Vendôme – Stalls in the abbey church

Excursions

Nourray: Church – The key can be obtained either from the mayor, ☎ 02 54 77 87 95, or from M and Mme Geyer (who live near the church).

Villemardy: Church – Apply to Villemardy town hall or Selommes presbytery. ☎ 02 54 23 80 14.

Château de VILLANDRY

Gardens – Open 1 June to 31 August from 8.30am to 8pm; 1 April to 31 May and 1 to 30 September from 9am to 7pm; the rest of the year from 9am to sunset. 30F. ☎ 02 47 50 02 09.

Château – Open (45min guided tours available) 1 June to 31 August from 9am to 6.30pm; mid-March to 31 May and 1 September to 11 November from 9am to 5pm. 45F (château and gardens). ☎ 02 47 50 02 09.

Château de VILLESAVIN

Free access to grounds and guided tours (45min) of the interior 1 June to 30 September from 10am to 7pm; 1 March to 31 May from 10am to noon and 2pm to 7pm; 1 October to 20 December from 2pm to 5pm. Closed the rest of the year. 30F, 25F (exterior only). ☎ 02 54 46 42 88.

VOUVRAY
🛈 Mairie, 37210. ☎ 02 47 52 70 48

Espace de la Vigne et du Vin – Guided tours (1hr) mid-March to mid-October daily from 10am to 7pm; mid-October to mid-March from 2pm to 6pm. Closed the rest of the year. 29F. ☎ 02 47 52 76 00.

Excursion

Château de Jallanges – Open (45min guided tours available) from 1 March to 31 October from 10am to noon and 2pm to 7pm. 27F. ☎ 02 47 52 01 71.

YÈVRE-LE-CHÂTEL

Château fort – Open (1hr guided tours available) 1 May to 31 October from 2pm to 6pm. 10F. ☎ 02 38 34 25 91.

Tern

Useful French words and phrases

SIGHTS

abbaye	abbey		marché	market
beffroi	belfry		monastère	monastery
chapelle	chapel		moulin	windmill
château	castle		musée	museum
cimetière	cemetery		parc	park
cloître	cloisters		place	square
cour	courtyard		pont	bridge
couvent	convent		port	port/harbour
écluse	lock (canal)		porte	gateway
église	church		quai	quay
fontaine	fountain		remparts	ramparts
halle	covered market		rue	street
jardin	garden		statue	statue
mairie	town hall		tour	tower
maison	house			

NATURAL SITES

abîme	chasm		grotte	cave
aven	swallow-hole		lac	lake
barrage	dam		plage	beach
belvédère	viewpoint		rivière	river
cascade	waterfall		ruisseau	stream
col	pass		signal	beacon
corniche	ledge		source	spring
côte	coast, hillside		vallée	valley
forêt	forest			

ON THE ROAD

car park	parking		petrol/gas station	station essence
driving licence	permis de conduire		right	droite
east	Est		south	Sud
garage (for repairs)	garage		toll	péage
left	gauche		traffic lights	feu tricolore
motorway/highway	autoroute		tyre	pneu
north	Nord		west	Ouest
parking meter	horodateur		wheel clamp	sabot
petrol/gas	essence		zebra crossing	passage clouté

TIME

today	aujourd'hui		week	semaine
tomorrow	demain		Monday	lundi
yesterday	hier		Tuesday	mardi
			Wednesday	mercredi
winter	hiver		Thursday	jeudi
spring	printemps		Friday	vendredi
summer	été		Saturday	samedi
autumn/fall	automne		Sunday	dimanche

NUMBERS

0	zéro	10	dix	20	vingt
1	un	11	onze	30	trente
2	deux	12	douze	40	quarante
3	trois	13	treize	50	cinquante
4	quatre	14	quatorze	60	soixante
5	cinq	15	quinze	70	soixante-dix
6	six	16	seize	80	quatre-vingt
7	sept	17	dix-sept	90	quatre-vingt-dix
8	huit	18	dix-huit	100	cent
9	neuf	19	dix-neuf	1000	mille

SHOPPING

bank	banque	fishmonger's	poissonnerie
baker's	boulangerie	grocer's	épicerie
big	grand	newsagent, bookshop	librairie
butcher's	boucherie	open	ouvert
chemist's	pharmacie	post office	poste
closed	fermé	push	pousser
cough mixture	sirop pour la toux	pull	tirer
cough sweets	cachets pour la gorge	shop	magasin
entrance	entrée	small	petit
exit	sortie	stamps	timbres

FOOD AND DRINK

beef	bœuf	lamb	agneau
beer	bière	lunch	déjeuner
butter	beurre	lettuce salad	salade
bread	pain	meat	viande
breakfast	petit-déjeuner	mineral water	eau minérale
cheese	fromage	mixed salad	salade composée
chicken	poulet	orange juice	jus d'orange
dessert	dessert	plate	assiette
dinner	dîner	pork	porc
fish	poisson	restaurant	restaurant
fork	fourchette	red wine	vin rouge
fruit	fruits	salt	sel
sugar	sucre	spoon	cuillère
glass	verre	vegetables	légumes
ice cream	glace	water	de l'eau
ice cubes	glaçons	white wine	vin blanc
ham	jambon	yoghurt	yaourt
knife	couteau		

PERSONAL DOCUMENTS AND TRAVEL

airport	aéroport	railway station	gare
credit card	carte de crédit	shuttle	navette
customs	douane	suitcase	valise
passport	passeport	train/plane ticket	billet de train/d'avion
platform	voie	wallet	portefeuille

CLOTHING

coat	manteau	socks	chaussettes
jumper	pull	stockings	bas
raincoat	imperméable	suit	costume
shirt	chemise	tights	collants
shoes	chaussures	trousers	pantalon

USEFUL PHRASES

goodbye	au revoir	yes/no	oui/non
hello/good morning	bonjour	I am sorry	pardon
how	comment	why	pourquoi
excuse me	excusez-moi	when	quand
thank you	merci	please	s'il vous plaît

Do you speak English?	Parlez-vous anglais?
I don't understand	Je ne comprends pas
Talk slowly	Parlez lentement
Where's...?	Où est...?
When does the ... leave?	A quelle heure part...?
When does the ... arrive?	A quelle heure arrive...?
When does the museum open?	A quelle heure ouvre le musée?
When is the show?	A quelle heure est la représentation?
When is breakfast served?	A quelle heure sert-on le petit-déjeuner?
What does it cost?	Combien cela coûte?
Where can I buy a newspaper in English?	Où puis-je acheter un journal en anglais?
Where is the nearest petrol/gas station?	Où se trouve la station essence la plus proche?
Where can I change traveller's cheques?	Où puis-je échanger des traveller's cheques?
Where are the toilets?	Où sont les toilettes?
Do you accept credit cards?	Acceptez-vous les cartes de crédit?

Index

Notes

MANUFACTURE FRANÇAISE DES PNEUMATIQUES MICHELIN

Société en commandite par actions au capital de 2 000 000 000 de francs

Place des Carmes-Déchaux – 63 Clermont-Ferrand (France)

R.C.S. Clermont-Fd B 855 200 507

© Michelin et Cie, Propriétaires-Éditeurs 1996

Dépôt légal mars 1996 – ISBN 2-06-132204-2– ISSN 0763-1383

Printed in the EU 12-97/2

Compositeur : MAURY-Imprimeur S.A., Malesherbes.

Impression et brochage : KAPP LAHURE-JOMBART, Évreux

Illustration de la couverture Nathalie BENAVIDES

Notes

Route planning made Simple

internet
http : // w w w . michelin - travel . com

MICHELIN

Travel with Michelin

Maps, Plans & Atlases

With Michelin's cartographic expertise you are guaranteed easy-to-read, comprehensive travel and tourist information. And you can also be confident that you'll have detailed and accurate mapping, updated annually to make this collection the best travel companion for any motorist.

Red Guides

Each of these 12 titles, revised annually, offer a range of carefully selected hotels and restaurants rated according to comfort; From the friendly farmhouse to the luxury hotel, there is something to suit everyone.
Titles: Benelux, Deutschland, España/Portugal, Europe, France, Great Britain & Ireland, Ireland, Italia, London, Paris, Portugal, Suisse.

Green Guides

With over 160 titles covering Europe and North America, Michelin Green Guides offer independent travellers a cultural insight into a city, region or country, with all the information you need to enjoy your visit.
Each guide includes recommended main sights with detailed descriptions and colour photographs, accurate plans, suggested routes and essential practical information.

In Your Pocket Guides

These handy pocket-sized guides are designed for short breaks and are available to destinations all over the world. Drawing on Michelin's acclaimed expertise in this field, they offer essential cultural and practical information in an easy-to-read, colourfully illustrated format, to help the reader make the most of any visit.
Titles available in English, 'In Your Pocket" and French, "Escapade".

Michelin Route planner on the Internet

With Michelin's new website all you have to do is type in your start and finish points and your route is planned for you in a matter of seconds, with travel time, distances, road numbers, and tolls, for any destination in Europe
http://www.michelin-travel.com

MICHELIN

Michelin Green

Made in the USA
Middletown, DE
28 July 2019

As an account of the contemporary academic adjunct catastrophe, del Rosso's book should be required reading for full-time professors and their administrative bosses who are charged with maintaining the integrity of their institutions—of course, they'll likely flinch in the face of the reality that defines the life of the adjunct professor and that seems beyond redeeming and out of their control. It's not, and that's an important part of this story. However, what makes this rollicking, painful, smart, hilarious, and honest memoir required reading for all of us is its enormous heart: in adversity, del Rosso upholds and celebrates her students and her life—it is, in the end, a triumphant embrace.

—David Daniel, Co-founder and former president of the Affiliated Faculty of Emerson College; Associate Professor of Creative Writing at Fairleigh Dickinson University.

What is it about composition and writing classes that impels students and professors to bond, bitch, reveal, reflect, and often develop the closest of human bonds among one another? Lisa del Rosso's account of her years teaching at colleges, ranging from sublime to obscure, offers us a gritty account of America's hard-working, long-suffering, ever-exploited and ferociously committed professorial underclass. In so doing, she exposes the lesser-known peculiarities and exigencies of the teacherly life—experiences that all true teachers have experienced, whether they care to admit it or not.

—Jacques Berlinerblau, Professor, Georgetown University; author of *Campus Confidential: How College Works, Or Doesn't, For Professors, Parents, And Students*

Lisa del Rosso portrays the most accurate picture of academic life I've encountered. She goes beyond simply depicting the joy, humor, absurdity, heartbreak and satisfaction of working with students and shows what it's really like to be a part of their lives. After reading her book you may not want to quit your day job and become an adjunct professor, but you will understand why her students admire and respect her.

—Robert W. Kenefick, Ph.D., FACSM (Fellow of the American College of Sports Medicine)

Confessions

of an
Accidental
Professor

Lisa del Rosso

Serving
House
Books

ISBN: 978-1-947175-90-7

Cover art: a Roy Lichtenstein look-alike; not an original

Author photo by Elizabeth Slocomb

Serving House Books logo by Barry Lereng Wilmont

Published by Serving House Books

Copenhagen, Denmark, Florham Park, NJ

www.servinghousebooks.com

Member of The Independent Book Publishers Association

First Serving House Books Edition 2017

LdR note: Some names, especially those of departmental administrators, have been changed; however, many students were happy to allow use of their real names.

To Walt Cummins, Mary Folliet, Gerry Cavanaugh, Mrs. Elizabeth Hodges—the teachers who changed my life.

"I am a teacher! First, last, always!"

—Jean Brodie, *The Prime of Miss Jean Brodie*

"Professor del Rosso – Fuck, Yeah!"
Student Evaluation, Anonymous, NYU 2013

Table of Contents

Why Teach as an Adjunct Professor?

From an old student...

Subject:
From an old student...
Date:
May 15, 2012 8:05 PM

Hi Professor Del Rosso,

I took two semesters of your writing class my freshman year at NYU. Your class, Writing New York, was hands down the best course I took during my time in college. I wanted to let you know that it is because of you and your class that I fell in love with New York City, and decided not to transfer following my freshman year.

I struggled a lot as a freshman and was very close to quitting the university and the city. However, I remember you reaching out to me and offering to get me out of my neighborhood if I ever needed to talk to someone. You encouraged me to explore the city and to learn from it. I graduated from NYU today, and I'm going to continue to live and work here. I wanted to thank you for pushing me to become a better writer and for making me love this city.

Thank you,

Lianne Salcido

If You Change a Student's Life, Is It Worth It?

THERE ARE DOWNSIDES to being an adjunct. You will make
no money. You will likely be teaching at two or three different colleges to cobble together a living, and sometimes
you may teach at all three of those colleges on the same day.
You will need a roommate or two (or in my case, an ex-husband) because you will find, as you ask around, that though
you are armed with degrees and published, have spectacular
evaluations and observations and a chili pepper next to your
name on rateyourprofessor.com, a waiter (or, in my case, an
ex-husband who is a career waiter at an upscale restaurant)
makes three times the money you do. This is largely because
if you are part of an adjunct union to a large university like
New York University, and in April you receive your con-
tracted two courses for September (an adjunct cannot work
more than two courses at NYU) then there is no work in
the summertime because colleges are not in session, and
New York State decrees you cannot sign on unemployment
because to them, you are "on vacation" whether you want
to be or not, as those two courses wait for you in September. This is otherwise known as a Catch-22—bless Joseph
Heller! It also means that any money you would have saved
during the year you will spend—in June, July, and August—
on rent, student loan payments, bills, and health insurance
(that is, if you have health insurance, which I do not), ren-
dering you penniless by September. **Lastly, living this way
for a long period of time might be a wee bit stressful.**

I realize I have not answered the title question. I will,
in time.

The Accidental Professor

HALFWAY THROUGH THE INTERVIEW, I asked, "Do I have this job?"

The chair of the English Department, Michael Frew, answered, "Do you want this job?"

I have made all of the major decisions in my life, for better or worse, in under three seconds.

"Sure, why not."

"Great," Michael said.

"When do I start?" I asked.

"In a week," answered Michael, handing me the *Grassroots* book.

Then he said, "Don't tell the students this is your first time teaching. Put 'professor' on your syllabus. And get your BA as fast as you can. Don't tell anyone you don't have it."

I said, "Okay."

He said, "Good luck."

An hour later, I walked out onto East 43rd Street, in a daze, squinting in the blazing September sunlight. I had no idea why I had said yes, what made Michael hire me, or what on earth made me agree to show up for the interview in the first place.

I had always thought I would be a performer. I was a classically trained singer who studied in London and had performed in straight plays and musicals alike. When I moved to New York City, I planned on doing the same thing. But one Monday, on my way to a temp job, I blacked out on the Times Square-42nd Street subway platform. It was all

very dramatic and embarrassing. I had roughly a five-second warning before the blackout: it began with a complete body sweat, light-headedness, and once the tunnel vision began, I stepped away from the edge of the platform and got to a seat that I sort of keeled over onto. I was all dressed up and it was quite early in the morning. I am sure people thought I was some kind of yuppie drug user. No one paid attention (this is the subway at rush hour, after all). When I came to, sweaty and disoriented, I knew I didn't have the energy to get back to my sixth floor walk-up on West 44th Street. I got on the train and made it to Union Square. The building I worked in had a nurses' station. When I opened the door, the nurse on duty took one look at me and said, "You need oxygen." I tried to explain what happened and instead she put a mask over my face and said, "Breathe." After that, she gave me some juice and told me to lie down. Two hours later, I came to. She asked me what had happened, and I told her. She said, "I don't know what is happening to you, but I do know that the next doctor you see must be a neurologist. And you should try to see one as soon as possible."

It took a long time to diagnose, but I had epilepsy. I knew no other singers who had this condition, no actors (but recently did find out that the astonishing Cherry Jones has epilepsy). The meds I was put on, three times a day, induced only one thing: sleep. It took two years of firing doctors, trying various medications, dealing with side effects and finally consulting a homeopath in order for me to regiment my way of living, find the right drug, lessen my seizures and live a somewhat "normal" life.

Two years away from performing is a long time. I was also terrified I would have a seizure onstage, while singing… and I had to accept my body was not within my control. And what if I was across the country, far from my (next) neurologist?

So at twenty-eight, I stopped.

Having no other creative outlet open to me, I turned to writing, something I had always done but never taken seriously. I self-published a tiny "zine" ; a writer's colony in the Hudson Valley then invited me for a residency; I began writing theater reviews for *Time Out New York* and another small, city publication. As far as a degree was concerned, LAMDA, where I trained in London, is not an accredited school, so the credits did not transfer. Empire State College, down on Varick Street at the time, offered something called "life experience credit" which entailed writing extensive, detailed essays on what one learned in exchange for college credits, so a twenty-eight year-old woman wouldn't be starting her BA from scratch, as if she had not lived.

So in 2004, I began my BA in Creative Writing.

A gal needs money in this town, however, so I was also working coat check at Tao, an Asian-fusion tourist trap in midtown. My boss, Deb, was a crazy woman with an undisclosed medical condition that forced her to run outside periodically for marijuana breaks during a shift. She could be moody, cranky, sarcastic. But the job was fantastic in terms of cash, so I put up with her and the extremely drunk but exceedingly generous tipping crowd.

One night, Deb's brother came in. She introduced him. "Hey Steve, this is the new girl." To me, she said, "This is Steve, my twin. Irish twins, except we're Jews. Hahahah!!" Steve looked at her and rolled his eyes. We shook hands. Steve seemed calm, unlike his sister, with a pleasant, doughy face. He asked me a few background questions: where was I from, what was I doing. I told him about London, and he said what everyone says, which is, "Will you sing something?" I said, "Sure Steve, in the coatroom, in front of all these people, is what I live for." He laughed. Then Steve left, and Deb said

he was a professor at Berkeley College (a name stolen from Berkeley California), here in Manhattan.

The next night, Steve came back. He asked me a few more questions, about Empire State College, and the tutoring I was doing in the writing center—not because I wanted to (I didn't) or because I liked it (I didn't) but because my writing professor chose me. Steve nodded. I told him I didn't think I was very good at it, the one-on-one I found boring. The students who came in were adults and what I could do for them was minimal. Sometimes they would try to complain about their professors, which I was not having. Some had ESL difficulties that I was not equipped to deal with. And one man showed up daily for two weeks until he brought me a beautifully boxed amethyst earrings and necklace set, and asked me for a formal date. I said no. He refused to take back the jewelry. I gave the set to my Aunt Janet, who loves both the color purple and free stuff.

I really didn't care for the writing center at all.

A few days later, when I got home from school, there was a message from Steve on my answerphone (for those of you who do not know what an answerphone is, do feel free to Google.)

"Hi Lisa, this is Steve. The college I teach at is looking for a professor. I told my chairperson about you, so he's expecting a call. His number is 212-xxx-xxxx. His name is Michael Frew. Go in for the interview and mention me. Okay, see you later."

I was…a combination of furious and flabbergasted. How did Steve get my phone…oh, he asked Deb. That bitch! She didn't tell me. And he didn't even ask me first! He didn't ask me anything! And that is what I said when I called Deb, yelling. She said, "That's how my brother is."

Fantastic.

I called Steve.

"This is Steve."

"Are you out of your goddamn mind??"

"Who is this?"

"It's Lisa. Are you out of your goddamn mind?"

"Oh. What's the problem? I thought you'd be good at it, so go to the interview."

"Steve, I don't have a bachelor's degree! No master's, either! I've never taught before, were you smoking shit OR WHAT?"

"But you went to LAMDA, right? And you did graduate?"

"Yes, but…"

"And you're tutoring, right?"

"Yes, but…"

"Lisa, I don't have time for this, GO TO THE INTERVIEW FREW WANTS A CALL I ALREADY SET IT UP SO CALL HIM!"

And Steve hung up.

Hating everyone and feeling bullied, I called. My interview at Berkeley College was the following day.

Michael Frew was tall, dark, bespectacled. He reminded me of Clarke Kent and exuded calm. We sat down in his office, and he began explaining the course: Writing. He showed me the book, *Grassroots With Readings*. He told me there would probably be a lot of students but not to be alarmed. He told me a few of the problems that could come up, mentioned controlling the class, discipline and what the college would not tolerate with regard to student behavior. He asked very few questions. I asked fewer, due to shock.

When I say I knew absolutely positively nothing about college teaching, I mean I also knew nothing about how

colleges work, nothing about how one college can differ so widely from another, nothing about who gets to go to what college based on race, class, location, economic bracket, nepotism, etc…

Scratch that. I knew less than nothing.

After I had made my three-second decision and had the book in hand, Michael showed me around the college: classrooms, copy center, administrative offices, lounge. At the time, Berkeley College comprised mostly of Black and Hispanic inner-city students, very few white students and approximately 2% foreign students. The median age was about twenty-four years old. I assumed Berkeley, like Empire State College, was a state school, and that it was also, therefore, affordable. Later, when I found out I was completely wrong on all counts and that Berkeley was a for-profit college with a high tuition, I didn't understand how the students could afford it. I certainly couldn't. My bill from Empire State, after all was said and done, was about three thousand dollars. Right now, tuition at Berkeley College is approximately $24, 000 per year. Ten years ago, tuition was approximately $14, 000 per year. But many students do receive grants. And I was told Berkeley had a very high placement rate: that is, internships that lead to good jobs, or just jobs in general. That may have been true at the time, but as of April 2015, the New York City Department of Consumer Affairs was investigating Berkeley, "over concerns about students' drop-out and loan default rates, and the way students are recruited in the first place" (Harris 1/ *New York Times*/"New York Consumer Agency Investigating Four For-Profit College").

At the end of my tour, in the lounge I overheard a few male teachers talking about their class comportment. The conversation went like this:

Male teacher #1: You gotta be a real dick at the beginning of the semester, or the kids will think they can walk all over you.

Male teacher #2: A huge dick, a huge dick.

Male teacher #3: Oh yeah, you're right. Never let them know you're a human being for the first half of the semester.

Male teacher #4: I don't smile for the first three weeks.

Male teacher #1: Well, I don't smile for the first six weeks.

Male teacher #2: Well, I'm a Nazi for the first six weeks.

Male teacher #1: You have to be. You really do.

This was actually the best indirect advice I received, and it was particularly relevant as a woman. Michael said that in general, there are some male students who simply don't like a woman in charge, and he empathized with what some of his female teachers went through. So I decided I would be initially terrifying, then segue to tough but fair.

The first time I stepped out onstage, in a leading role, was as Ado Annie in *Oklahoma*. It felt easy. Like gliding on water. Like I belonged there. I had so much confidence at sixteen, and portraying a woman completely different from myself was very freeing. I liked the yellow-dotted Swiss dress the costume mistress had put me in for Act 1, the lavender gown with the huge skirt that flared out as Ali Hakim and Will spun me for Act 2, and how my hair had been rolled back and braided, which reminded me of Judy Garland's Dorothy in *The Wizard of Oz*. I felt in command and liked the audience's attention on me. I knew what I was doing. I could sing the crap out of the role, had a key to her character, had invented a background for her, and there was power in my assurance.

The first time I stepped into a classroom, in front of a

roomful of thirty-plus students, I thought I was going to have a heart attack. It was a shock how close the students were: almost right up my nostrils. Thirty-plus pairs of eyes watched me, and waited. I, in turn, sweated. Then I breathed.

Costumes can be a miraculous help in terms of stepping into a character: that first day, mine was a black suit. A top shelf, black, fitted, fine-wool-with-a-bit-of-stretch killer suit with a tailored jacket and slightly flared trousers by Elie Tahari, bought with my last 950 dollars of hard-earned coat check money. That suit became, very quickly, part of my professor "act," just like Ado Annie's dresses. The suit said the professor is smart, funny, attractive, knowledgeable, a leader, trustworthy, and takes no bull.   It also said this is the only suit I own, so I will be changing out the top, belt, shoes and jewelry, and will be wearing it to class every single day. That suit was my talisman. It gave me confidence. A strut. It made me stand up straight.

I looked out at all of the students seated in that large classroom, all of those eyes, waiting, and my LAMDA acting training kicked right in. In a big, booming voice, I said, "Hi. I'm Professor del Rosso. Welcome to Writing Class!"

Students' Lives - Part I

1. Berkeley and Adult Students

*"Professor del Rosso takes extra time, goes out of her
way to help students; including personal phone calls."*
    —Student Evaluation, Anonymous, NYU
    2011

"I am tired of getting the B+."
    —Student Comment, NYU 2012

IT WAS ON-THE-JOB-TRAINING at Berkeley: I taught the
students how to write, and the students educated me about
themselves. They were older than the typical seventeen or
eighteen year-old freshman, and adult students sometimes
brought with them adult problems. There was one young
man who had a very ill eight year-old daughter, and toward
the end of the term, she went into the hospital. The student
showed me her photograph, and kept me updated daily on
her progress. He was very worried. A few weeks passed,
class began as usual but he didn't come by my desk and
talk to me beforehand, which was unusual. He looked fine,
seemed fine. So while an in-class writing assignment was
going on, I pulled him into the hallway and asked him if
his daughter was all right.

He said, "She didn't make it."

Shocked, I said, "What?"

He said, "She didn't make it. She just, it just…took her."

This man, in my class, was funny and charismatic. He
drew people to him. He also had a beautiful smile. He was
trying to smile as we talked that day in the hallway, but he
was jumpy, like he couldn't stand to be inside his own skin.

I said, "I'm so sorry! What on earth are you doing here?"

He said, "I had to come. I didn't want to be absent for your class. I didn't want to miss anything."

I said, "Wait, but you know it would have been…fine…"

He said, "I had to come."

And he walked back into my classroom. I followed after him, and sat down, trying to keep it together. I looked at him, and he looked at me. If he could do it, so could I.

I think I gave him a card later on, and now wish I had asked if I could have attended the funeral. At the time, I thought it might be overstepping. Now, students ask me to get involved in their lives, so it's hilarious I even questioned asking. Regret number 1,000,006.

The experience with him hardened me in terms of absences, and I changed my attendance policy after that. The following term, on the first day of class, a female student asked about the number of absences allowed in a casual way, saying something like, "Suppose something comes up…" But what I heard was: how many absences can I get away with? My answer: Zero. I completely lost my cool, saying I had a student whose daughter died and if he could make it to class, so could she. She and the rest of the students were taken aback. Resentful. That lasted for most of the semester, and I blame myself entirely. But I would tell them the same thing again, albeit in a different way:I hate absences. That student came to class the day after his daughter died. I know he needed to come, not just for school per se. But unless there is a tragedy, there is no excuse not to come to class. There are only excuses.

Occasionally, there were male students in class—and they were without fail Greek or Italian—who did not want to follow my instructions, who initially thought I would be a pushover, or did not know what I was doing, or equated my feminine exterior with a soft interior. That was sorted quite early on, say, within two or three classes.

It is, of course, nothing new that there is a double standard when it comes to a strong woman at the front of a class vs. a strong man. But I did not care how I was perceived. I did not care what they thought of me and I did not care if they did not like me. I think I know why. I had superb examples to follow.

The best teachers in my life I never confused as friends. Their boundaries were clear. After I was no longer their student, that was different and some of my former teachers I am great friends with today. But not while I was in their classrooms. Some were formidable. Some still are. I respected them at the time and still do. I doubt they gave two thoughts about whether I liked them or not.

So I wanted my students to respect me and the rules of the class. I wanted them to try their best but it was preferable if they worked their asses off. I was in charge of the class. I was the one who gave out the grades. And if a young man didn't want to do the assignments as instructed simply because a woman told him to…he failed.

That did not happen often, though, and I can count the number of D's I have given out on one hand. But grading was never problematic for me, because my theory was and still is, I have to be able to sleep at night. The grade must be commensurate with everything that went on in the term: work, absences, attitude, mini-essays, participation… And, from the flip side, liking or disliking a student does not come into play.

Liking or disliking a student also does not figure into whom I remember, whose story stays with me, who becomes my friend, whom I mentor. When assigned to write about something that changed them, my students inevitably choose a negative experience. So after twelve years of expe-

riential learning, I can tell you that human beings tend to remember the worst rather than the best. I don't know why that is. I only know I am no exception.

2. The Worst Thing That Happened

"Engaging discussion class. Interesting topics and current affairs being debated in class. Mesmerizing professor: great sense of humor, great focus, incredible intelligence."
—Student Evaluation, Anonymous, NYU 2014

"I did not like the New York Stories."
—Student Evaluation, Anonymous, NYU 2013

THE FIRST TIME I EVER had a student-advocate awakening, it was the final class I taught at Berkeley. There was an overlap between the end of Berkeley and beginning at NYU, so I was going to be at two colleges at the same time with loads of papers still to correct. But there was one student in particular who haunted me, and I was glad to get away for a day during the holiday weekend. At least, I thought I was getting away.

I stepped off of the wooden walkway, my feet hitting chilly sand. Just ahead, the vast indigo ocean beckoned. Intoxicated by its beauty, I breathed in deeply and then exhaled. I could smell, could taste the fall coming, and it felt exhilarating. A few hours ago, the Long Island sun was overpowering and crowds of people impeded any walking I wanted to do. It seemed millions of rambunctious children were everywhere, watched over by cranky adults, disgruntled by too much sun, sea, and Labor Day beer. Now, the beach was all but deserted, save for what looked like a father and his three young daughters at the shoreline, still aching for a swim, their towels and things in a pile behind them.

This was the time I liked the beach best, just after dusk, with a fiery sinking sun to the west, and the leaching of all color, leaving only the palest shade of gray in the east. There is comfort for me in this particular kind of isolation, and I have never felt afraid on a deserted beach. I don't swim in the Long Beach waters at night, though, because the darker it gets, the more the waves resemble long, black, white-tipped fingers, eager to pull me down with their undertow.

We had arrived at the cabanas later than planned, which turned out to be a good thing. At a particular point in the late afternoon, suddenly everyone departed, off to other parties or barbecues. No more baseball games broadcast from radios. No more crying children. I could hear the gulls again. Sitting across from me at one of the sun-bleached picnic tables, Miguel, my brother-in-law and a school psychologist, asked what I would be teaching my writing students at Berkeley for the last two weeks of the quarter, now that I was decamping for NYU. I told him about the class's last topic, which was to write an essay about something that had changed them. There was one student in particular, Nina, who had joined the class quite late: a month into the quarter. She was a heavy woman, not very tall, Dominican, about twenty-five years old. She was a single mother with a two-year old daughter. Her essay described being sexually abused by her father from the age of two, which robbed her of the ability to speak for a number of years. This reminded me of the author Maya Angelou, but Angelou stopped speaking by choice, believing her voice was responsible for her rapist's death.

Months passed before her mother took Nina to a doctor, who discovered sores on her mouth and vagina. When he told Nina's mother he suspected abuse, she responded by saying that could not possibly happen in her house. So the abuse continued until Nina was three and a half, until the family moved to the United Sates, into an apartment so small, everyone slept in the same bed: her mother, father,

Nina and her younger brother. Still Nina did not speak. Her father had been selling drugs to support the family, and Nina still does not know exactly what happened, but one night her father was doing something behind the house, and when he came in, her mother screamed at him, slapped him in the face and threw him out. After many months passed, and Nina was sure he was not coming back, she began speaking, both in Spanish and English. She ended her essay with something like, "I can finally talk about it; I can finally speak."

Miguel cleared his throat. He had his arms folded and a pained look on his face.

I said, "I don't know, Miguel, but when I finished that essay, I wished I had a degree in another subject that would have been more helpful, or ..." I paused. "That I was you."

He laughed. "How did you respond to her?" he asked.

Nina had passed in her essay late, after the term had ended, so I critiqued her over the phone. It was extremely well-written, and I only asked for a few changes. Then, because I guessed the answer was no, I asked if she had sought counseling. Her friends had suggested it, and she knew the weight correlated to the abuse, blah, blah, blah, she said, but no. No counseling. I strongly suggested it as well, and from a specialist in sexual abuse and incest. I told her to keep writing, not as therapy but to make sense of what happened to her. She said she had been through a lot in her life, and I said it sounded so. It was her ambition to write a book before her life was over, and I said she definitely had one in her, she was a wonderful writer. And in a split second, two things occurred to me simultaneously: this was the first time in ten weeks Nina sounded confident, like she was on a path and she knew where she wanted to go; and that it was odd for her, at twenty-five, to use the words "before my life is over."

Then she said to me, "I tested positive."

"Positive for what," I said.

"HIV," she said, "I found out when I was pregnant."

I could not bring myself to ask whether her daughter was positive or not. Instead, I said something like ...

"Oh!" Miguel said.

I shrugged my shoulders. "That's right. 'Oh!' is exactly what I said. I got off the phone with her, and I just wanted ... I wanted ..." I shook my head. What I had done for Nina was nothing.

"Well," Miguel said, "You encouraged her to keep writing, and to get counseling. You gave her permission to write about it: a safe place where she can go to, yes, to make sense of what happened to her. Or, to just get it out so she doesn't have to hold onto it."

I was silent. To me, it sounded puny.

Miguel, clearly reading my thoughts, continued, "Believe me, in my job, I wish I had the power to do more than I can do. You know?"

It was then I went for a walk.

Standing on the shore, I tiptoed to the water, then raced back to the sand as the incoming tide chased me, a game I used to play as a child that made me breathless with laughter. It was coming in fast. A few feet away from me, the three girls, in the water now, were jumping up and down, splashing each other, shrieking, and appeared to be climbing all over their father intent on mock-drowning the poor man, who was laughing despite the fact that he was clearly outnumbered. Suddenly, I saw the pile of towels and clothes that the family had left once safely on shore slide by me, lifted up by water. One more wave, and their belongings would be gone. I raced in to save them and in the process, lost the game. The tide had won. But the girls, running toward me, squealed with gratitude. "Thank you! Thank you so much!"

"Thank you," their father said, sounding relieved.

"No problem," I replied.

As I turned to walk further on down the shore, I heard one of the young girls say to the other, "Wow, that would have been the worst thing ever, right? If we had lost our stuff?"

Yeah," the other girl said, "I don't care about the towel but my favorite tee shirt I just got and the other stuff, that would have been the worst."

I continued walking, my soaked shorts clammy against my skin. I thought about what the girls had said. I thought about Nina. I thought about fathers and daughters. The chill in the air had gotten sharper and there was a wind that no longer belonged to summer. I looked up. The stars were becoming visible, nudging out the red, bloody sky.

\

3. Discipline

"I didn't like the Sunday weekly postings, but they did make me think creatively."
—Student Evaluation, Anonymous, NYU 2010

"Workshops sometimes didn't seem very productive."
—Student Evaluation, Anonymous, NYU 2010

MOST STUDENTS AT BERKELEY, like Nina and the young man whose daughter died, are obviously adults already, so discipline problems were rare. Also, either the student or parents were paying or borrowing big bucks for them to be there and Berkeley, as I said, is not a state school and tuition, while not nearly as much as NYU, is not cheap. However, there were exceptions, and for those exceptions, I had backup.

Berkeley had a school disciplinarian, and though I never met him, I did hear him. The one time I complained about an obnoxious student, I got a call and the disciplinarian (who shall be referred to here as "The Big Man") put me on speakerphone so I could hear both him and my male student (who shall be nameless for these purposes). The disciplinarian sounded exactly like a drill sergeant crossed with a Baptist preacher. I imagined him eight feet tall, and in uniform, behind a pulpit. What followed sounded like this:

TBM: _____ WHAT WOULD YOU LIKE TO SAY TO PROFESSOR DEL ROSSO?

Student: I'm sorry.

TBM: AND WHAT IS IT THAT YOU ARE SORRY FOR, _____?

Student: I'm sorry for being disruptive in your class.

TBM: IN YOUR CLASS, WHAT? HOW DO YOU ADDRESS HER?

Student: I'm sorry for being disruptive in your class, Professor del Rosso.

TBM: AND?

Student: And I'll never do it again.

TBM: AND?

Student: I'm sorry I was disrespectful, Professor del Rosso.

TBM: AND? AND THIS IS NEVER GOING TO HAPPEN AGAIN, IS IT? BECAUSE I DON'T WANT TO SEE YOU IN MY OFFICE AGAIN, DO YOU UNDERSTAND? YOU DON'T WANT ME TO REMEMBER YOUR NAME, SON.

Student: Professor, it will never, ever happen again, I promise.

TBM: GOOD. DISMISSED!

Pause.

I heard footsteps, and then a door close.

TBM picked up the phone.

He said, "I don't think you will have any trouble with him again."

I said, "Oh no, neither do I."

And I never did.

I have had only one parallel discipline problem at NYU thus far. The student was male, and from India. The first thing he said in my class was, "I'm here because I did not get into Columbia."

So, off to a good start.

He did the opposite of everything I asked him to do, refused to use MLA guidelines, which every student in colleges across the country has to learn, lied about absences...

Students, let me tell you something. If you email the professor the day a draft is due and tell her how sick you are, so sick you cannot possibly make it to class; and then later the same day, she sees you walking down University Place smoking cigarettes with your friends, clearly well, then not only will she think you a liar and a fool, you had better practice groveling, for a D looms large in your future.

He got the D. But he was an anomaly.

The students at NYU are younger and wealthier (more on this in the "NYU Professor" essay), but the sums of money being spent by the parents for them to attend an extraordinarily expensive, elite institution means the cost of screwing that up plus the pressure to succeed, the stress, the competition (witness the suicide rate at NYU, for example) are all incentives to behave, at least in class. Outside of class? Please see chapter on New York Stories.

Camel's Back

—*Student Evaluation, Anonymous, NYU 2013*

"Not a lot of feedback or explination [sic] about my grades."

—*Student Evaluation, Anonymous, NYU 2013*

AFTER THREE YEARS AT BERKELEY, I felt restless. Maybe I had learned all I could learn. Maybe I needed another challenge. But Berkeley began to feel like hard work. Stressful. The difficulties outweighed the good: missed work, missed deadlines, and too many absences. It was exhausting chasing down so many students for their papers. Frustrated, I didn't know how to change it. I walked around in a state of perpetual annoyance.

At Berkeley, I checked my college mailbox before the day's classes began. There were hard-copies of emails circulated, text books from publishers to lure professors into using them for class, etc… And on one particular day, there was a Fedex envelope in my box. Why? From whom? I took it out, and read the return label. It was a Staten Island address, and I recognized the student's name. She was in my first class. I opened the envelope. It was her paper, due that day, with a note saying she couldn't make it to class. She didn't say why. She had spent money to Fedex me her

paper in lieu of being in class.

Incredulous is what I was. And personally insulted.

At that moment, I knew I couldn't teach there any longer. I'd quit, go back to coat-checking, sell ice cream out of a truck, I didn't care.

But in serendipitous fashion, NYU came along at the exact same time I had given up on Berkeley, and made me an offer I did not refuse. And because that story is long, involved and slightly scandalous, I'm skipping right over it to being a newbie at NYU, but have no fear! I will show and tell further on in the book (Pg. 126, for the impatient). I promise.

5. NYU Professor

"She's so BAD ASS! She commands respect!
She knows what she's doing. I love her."
—Student Evaluation, Anonymous, NYU 2011

"I wish they made del Rosso's for every subject."
—Student evaluation, Anonymous, NYU 2013

WHEN I BEGAN AT NYU IN 2008, I was told that for the first three terms, an NYU newbie is on a sort of "probationary period." After that, it was very difficult to get fired unless one did something incredibly stupid.

Despite the class load being less than Berkeley, the class size smaller and the pay higher, I was terrified. I wasn't sure I was supposed to be there. Maybe everyone would figure out I was a fraud and didn't know what I was doing? Maybe I didn't really know what I was doing? Which, after teaching for over three years and countless classes—the essay, poetry, drama, composition—was ridiculous.

Nevertheless...

Coming from Berkeley College to NYU felt a bit like whiplash; or stepping from a real world into an unreal one, the latter of which I knew little about. This was part of my learning curve: not only who gets accepted to a school like NYU, but also who can afford to attend a school like NYU even if one is accepted. At the time, students were mostly white, privileged, went to private or charter schools, had tutors, and every advantage one could think of. These students, in writing classes capped at fourteen or fifteen, were rarely absent, made all deadlines, completed all homework, asked for help, asked to do additional drafts, and com-

plained when they got a B+ instead of an A- (They still do. They still complain about the B+. A few have complained about the A-. They really have. They know who they are.)

The students were entirely different from what I was used to.

For example: my second semester, coming into spring break, a few of them asked what I would be doing with my time. I said I was going to Florida, it was the annual pilgrimage to my parents. Where? they asked. Sarasota, I said. One student said, "Oh, you should come to Miami and visit me on my father's yacht—we'd have so much fun and I've told him all about you."

She said this as casually as one would put on a soft, light-weight jacket. Linen, I think. White. Unlined.

I said, "Um… No, I will be spending the duration with my mother, but thank you so much for the invite."

She said, "Okay, another time."

NYU assigned a mentor—they do this for all incoming professors—a wonderful man who I will call the Gay Cowboy, because he wrote a fantastic book about gay cowboys. I liked him because he was smart, a writer, had outside interests other than NYU, lived with a professional jockey (I thought this the coolest thing ever) and was a no-bullshit sort of person. Case in point: a few other professors, also hired at the same time as I was, had said to me, "You should go full time!"

I asked the Gay Cowboy about it and he said, "Why would you want to go full time?" I said, "The money."

He proceeded to enlighten me on professors' salaries and said, "You think this is a lot of money?"

And actually, for what the full-timers have to do: attend meetings, sit on numerous committees, become academic advisors for countless students, have an office where students

can find them, etc…in addition to teaching three courses, it isn't.

The Gay Cowboy said, "If the money is the only reason for going full-time, don't do it. I was an adjunct for eight years before I went full-time. So think carefully."

The Gay Cowboy was instrumental in showing me the lay of the land. He observed my class and revealed a more effective way to run writing workshops, which surprised me because it was the same way they were run in my MFA program. I went to all the meetings, participated, attended the end of the term parties. I completed my three terms successfully.

Caveat: Completed three terms "successfully" yes, but I made many mistakes, all part of that learning curve. One was making students read the stories I assigned out loud, in class. This was a long-time practice at Berkeley because again, via experiential learning, the students did not read the homework. There were reasons, of course, and one student came to me and he explained, in detail, why there was "no quiet place in my house to read." So we read the text in class, and then no one could say they did not know the material when I gave a comprehension test. At NYU, it took me a while to trust that the students would do the work.

I did not know how to handle a student who stormed out in the middle of a class because she got a B+ on a paper while her best friend who sat next to her in the same class got an A. It was my first term. That had never happened to me before. I had no template. Her best friend was upset and texted her, looked at me, phone in hand. I was panic-stricken and so texted her as well, using the best friend's phone. The student who fled was unhappy with this and she was right.

Now, if a student stormed out in the middle of my class, I would barely raise an eyebrow.

Lianne, another student in that first term of teaching

at NYU, became a friend. When I was working on her seventeen recommendations for graduate school (no exaggeration), we had a series of conversations over a few dinners that she kindly treated me to as a gesture of thanks. I confessed her class was one of my first at NYU. She said, "I never knew. I'd never have known."

LAMDA acting training: the gift that keeps on giving.

It is now 2017, and after a one-term leave of absence, I am in my ninth year of adjuncting at NYU.

I think another conversation with the Gay Cowboy is overdue.

6. NYU vs. Berkeley College: a Mini-Version

"Phenomenal professor: inspiring, difficult, witty and effective."
—Student Evaluation, Anonymous, NYU 2009

"The room is a prison on planet bullshit. :(That is all."
—Student Evaluation, Anonymous, NYU 2010

THE YEAR AFTER I LEFT BERKELEY for NYU, I ran into a former student in a "real store," not my typical thrift shop because I was buying a birthday present for my sister. She came up to me and said, "Professor?"

We hugged. I was delighted to see her. She told me she had graduated, and I congratulated her on both graduating and the job. It was a good job, and I was pleased for her.

She said, "I'm pregnant." That is all she said, she gave no details.

I said, "That's great." She was young and unmarried. That is all I knew.

Then she said, "I heard you were at NYU."

I said, "Yes, I am."

She said, "I bet they're a lot smarter than we were, right?"

And the way she said it sounded like she thought:
BERKELEY = DUMB, NYU = SMART.

What I replied was idiotic, and not well-thought out. I still did not get it, was still oblivious to the haves and the have nots and the why that is.

I said to her, "No, actually, they're not smarter than you are. The difference between the students at Berkeley Col-

lege and the students at NYU is discipline: the discipline to do the homework, show up to class, hit the deadlines. Discipline is something you get from your parents: they are there to make you do your homework, make you study, make you show up, or there's trouble. There's punishment. There's consequences. And if you don't get it from your parents, or someone in the house who functions as a parent, you are at a disadvantage, because it's difficult to learn discipline once you're an adult, particularly when you are in college and working and have a life . . . So never think the NYU students are smarter than you are. They're not. It's discipline. And that has nothing whatsoever to do with smart."

She said, "Wow, I never thought of it that way."

And why did I think of it that way? Because that is the way I was raised by my one parent.

I relayed this conversation to my friend and longtime mentor, Walt Cummins, and he said, "It's more than that; it's also economics and coming from a culture of education."

As I said, at Berkeley, most of my students were Black and Hispanic. Many had jobs, some had families, responsibilities other than school. One of the myriad papers I assigned was titled "Something that Changed You," and I found that some of my students at Berkeley came from the following backgrounds: parents in jail, parents just gone, raised by their grandmother, raised by their gang, or they raised themselves, abuse, teen pregnancies... and I admired and respected my students, the ones who showed up, who persevered, who were determined to get the degree.

But it took me time—and reading and education and listening—to understand that a hand dealt to a child of color lacking in financial security, in geography, in housing, in discipline and with no culture of education was not so much circumstantial as it was both preordained and preventable.

Mainly, reading about their lives made me feel the same way as when I left an overnight shift at the Samaritans in London: lucky. Privileged. "There but for the grace of god go I."

This does not mean that, say, in the case of NYU, just because a student is born into wealth and privilege, he doesn't find countless opportunities to sabotage his good life and good fortune. He does find them, and frequently, he succeeds.

7. Tripping

What Features of this course were especially effective?

"The idea that Professor Lisa del Rosso should be NYU President."

Would you suggest any ways to improve this course?

"Make Professor Lisa del Rosso NYU President."

Additional Comments:

"Professor Lisa del Rosso should be NYU President."
    —*Student Evaluation, Anonymous, NYU 2011*

IT WAS THE WEEK of February 14th, 2014, the week when New York City had three major snowstorms, canceling school, delaying flights and stranding passengers. Among them was Sam, a friend of mine from LA who suddenly found himself in a winter wonderland for not two days but seven. Keeping him entertained was easy: Sam liked my company and I liked being taken out to dinner. On the Thursday evening of that week, I had my coat on and my hand had almost reached the doorknob when my phone pinged. A new mail. It was after 10 PM but I didn't hesitate in looking, as my response to my cell is Pavlovian: it pings, I must pick up, look, check, scroll.

This mail was from a student. Julio was from South America. He was in my freshman writing class for the second term in a row: an attentive, present, A-student, bilingual in Spanish and English who was also quite open about his obsession with the intricacies of extracting oil from marijuana leaves for the best possible buzz.

His mail read: Professor, I really really need to talk to

you right now I mean its okay if your not around but I really need to talk to you right now.

Damn it!

I replied: Julio, you have 5 minutes.

And I sent my number. Took my coat off. Paced. The cell rang.

"Hi professor."

"What's going on Julio?"

"Um…I'm at my father's….apartment on East 71st and….there are like a lot of people here? In the apartment. And….we made a lot of noise and the neighbor…downstairs…"

Julio was speaking in a slow, irritating way, very unlike him.

"Julio, are you on anything right now? Because you don't sound like you."

"Um…I'm having, like, a really bad acid trip…"

"That's just… fantastic."

"Yeah…it's never happened before…before tonight.."

I said, "So, your neighbor."

"Yeah, the neighbor…downstairs…complained? And this apartment….my father…it took him a long time to get the apartment…he's not an American citizen…and he…"

I said, "Okay, so it's a co-op and you woke the neighbor and you're afraid the neighbor will complain to the co-op board and your father will lose the apartment and then you'll be screwed. Is that close?"

"Yeah…I had…I'm sorry, there was no adult, I have no adult I can talk to here, and so you were the one that I…"

I said, "Julio, how many people are in your apartment?"

He said, "There are two people in the bathroom, and four in the kitchen and a few in the bedroom and I think someone is under the table in the main hall…"

"Okay Julio, this is what you're going to do. Are you listening?"

Julio said, "Yes. I am listening."

"Good. You're going to get all of those fucking people out of that apartment! All of them! Except one. You pick one friend to stay with you through your bad acid trip to make sure you don't decide to sail off the roof of your apartment building. Get it?"

"I would never throw myself off the roof, I wo-

"PICK SOMEONE, THE ONE WHO IS THE MOST SOBER, TO STAY WITH YOU! And get everyone else out."

Julio said, "Okay."

I said, "Good. The neighbor who complained: was it a woman?"

Julio said, "Yes."

I said, "Excellent. Tomorrow you are going to go out and buy the biggest, most beautiful bouquet of flowers you can find, and you are going to handwrite her a note. You are going to apologize for the noise and say that you and your friends were excited by the NYU snow day and didn't realize how loud you were. And before you go down and present those flowers to her, you are going to comb your hair so you look decent. And I promise it will be okay. But you have to do exactly what I tell you to do."

"Okay, okay professor. Thank you so-"

"Contact me when everyone's out of the apartment."

"Okay."

"Okay. I'm going to dinner now."

I hung up, put my coat back on and reached for the doorknob. The cell rang. It was Julio. It crossed my mind that I would have to use the words "murderous rage" in a future essay, or play, or short story, or something.

"WHAT NOW JULIO?"

"Um…professor? There are two friends out getting peet-za? Should I wait till they get back to tell them to go home?"

I said, "No, no, no! They have cell phones! You have a cell phone! Call and tell them not to come back!"

Julio said, "Oh. Yeah. Okay, I'll do that."

Fifteen minutes later, with a large glass of wine in front of me and the bottle nearby, I relayed the story to Sam.

He said, "Oh, well, if you need to go to his apartment, take me with you. I went through so many bad acid trips in the Sixties, I know exactly what to do."

I said, "I have never done acid, nor did I live through the Sixties. And we are not going to that apartment."

Sam said, "You saved a student tonight. Here's to you!"

I said, "I think that's a bit dramatic."

Sam said, "You did. Is he the first student who's contacted you with a problem?"

I said, "No."

Sam said, "More than a few? Many?"

I said, "Yes."

Sam said, "It doesn't surprise me. But NYU should really be paying you more, you know."

I said, "It's harder for the foreign students. Most of them have no one here: no family, no adult supervision, possibly an apartment to escape the dorms, a lot of money and Manhattan is their playground. At eighteen, nineteen years old. Sounds great. Total freedom. And it is great—until something bad happens."

Sam said, "And they contact you."

I nodded. "It's the part no one tells you about. Part counselor. I did tell one of the heads of the department, Kingsley, that I thought the best training I got for being a

college professor was volunteering at The Samaritans suicide hotline and counseling center in London."

"What did he say?"

"Kingsley said, 'Well, you're better equipped than the rest of us.'"

Sam said, "What?"

My cell pinged. "It's Julio," I said.

"Read it out loud."

"'Professor I did what you said and everyone is gone except two friends. I am okay and later we'll all go back to the dorms. You have no idea what you did for me tonight. Thank you.'"

Sam said, "You know exactly what you did for him! He should take you to dinner."

I said, "That's a brilliant idea! Wait…"

I replied to Julio: I know very well what I did for you tonight, and as my reward, you are taking me to dinner. Pick a Spanish restaurant that you like, where you won't complain about the food. It must serve wine. You will not be drinking, because you are underage. But I will be.

"Okay! I sent it."

Sam shook his head. "That's…that whole thing is crazy."

I poured myself another glass of wine. "It's an adventure."

The next day, I got a mail from Julio: Professor! The flowers worked! She said what a nice boy I was and of course she understood we were excited about the snow day and when my father comes to town, we should all have dinner together. She even wrote me a note back! I'll text it to you.

I replied: I told you it would work.

✱

Two weeks later, Julio and I were sitting across from each other at a Spanish restaurant in the Village. I had a glass of red wine in my hand. He had a glass of water.

I said, "Sorry you can't drink."

He said, "That's okay. I'll be drinking later on anyway."

I said, "Of course you will. Why didn't that occur to me?"

Julio said, "Do you like the food?"

I said, "I do. It's delicious."

He said, "I come here with my dad when he's in town. We're both Spanish food snobs, so it has to be good. Authentic. This place is good."

I said, "It is."

Julio said, "I told my friends I called you the night of the acid trip. They said, 'Are you out of your fucking mind, calling your professor?' I said, 'No, you don't understand. I called her because I knew I could.' Then I told them about you. Then they said, 'She sounds cool as shit! Can we take her classes?' I told them 'No, you can't. Her classes are all full. Too bad for you.'"

I laughed.

"Thank you," Julio said.

"You're welcome," I said.

8. NYU and FIT

> *"Professor del Rosso is very involved in the editing process of each essay, and she is very specific with her expectations. She truly devotes herself to each student and really cares about everybody's writing. The essay topics were challenging and pushed me out of my comfort zone."*
> —*Student Evaluation, Anonymous, NYU 2013*

AN ADJUNCT ALWAYS NEEDS more than one teaching job to make ends meet, even if one is employed by NYU. In 2010, I began teaching at FIT (Fashion Institute of Technology) in addition to NYU because my friend, Vasilios, an accessories and design professor, said that FIT needed to "kidnap me." I said they could do that on a part-time basis, of course, but my schedule at NYU came first. Vasilios was friends with then-Dean SS (now Dean and Provost at John Jay College), and put in a good word for me. I met SS at a nearby Starbucks (everyone at FIT goes to one particular Starbucks. It is always jammed with highly-strung people, and therefore, entertaining) where we talked about theater, books, music. A few days later, I met then-Chair Azra Dogan, who, after a brief but pleasant interview, hired me two days before the term began. That was the weekend of Hurricane Irene which turned out to be minor, but Monday, college was canceled, so I had three days to prepare instead of two. It didn't worry me. I was given writing classes, I had been teaching six years total by that time, and I knew what I was doing. But what I did not know about the state system was a lot. There were more students, which meant more papers; more students with more problems; and more work for less money.

9. FIT Therapy

"Her majesty's a very nice girl, but she doesn't have a lot
to say,

Her majesty's a very nice girl, and she changes from day
to day,

I wanna tell her that I love her a lot but I gotta get a
belly full of wine.

Her majesty's a very nice girl, someday I'm gonna make
her mine, oh yeah, someday I'm gonna make her mine."
—*Student Evaluation, Anonymous, NYU 2008*

I WAS IN CHAIR BENNETT'S OFFICE (he had replaced Chair Dogan and was the doppelgänger of Alan Bennett, so that is what I called him), trying to explain that increasingly, more and more students were coming to me with their problems and I was beginning to feel like a priest without the benefit of heavenly guidance. This because when the chair asks, "How are things going?" I assume he wants an honest answer.

He seemed confused. "What do mean? A student asked you for advice?"

It's really best to show, not tell, so I wrote down some of them for him. This particular semester, I had four classes, so roughly seventy students.

To: Chair Alan Bennett

A (partial) list of my current freshmen students:

Jill (18) has just gotten her first internship and is debating sleeping with her 30 year-old boss.

Alssa's mother is dying of lymphoma; her grandparents have moved into her house on Long Island and making matters worse, she had to get rid of her cat, Holmes, as one of them was allergic. Her mother receives treatment at NYU's Langone Medical Center.

Esme is battling anorexia, and after weeks of running 7 miles a day plus 5 cups of coffee and little food, had a hypoglycemic attack, could not breath and was rushed to the hospital. Is trying to eat regular meals with tea, no coffee. Hates all counselors.

Sal is Spanish, a singer, dorms and goes back to New Jersey on weekends to sell clothing; she is paying the rent on the house in which her father and brother live. She wants to sing and write, but primarily perform.

Sarah "came out" to me after class. Weeks later, she told me she was suffering from depression and suicidal thoughts.

Cate, Jack and Elizabetta also "came out" to me. Cate has told her parents. The other two, not yet.

Julie is in a borderline abusive relationship with a male student.

Suz is "kind of gay," drinks and does molly, or any other drugs she can find.

Penny's mother is angry she is in New York and is removing her to return to California next semester. Penny also likes to go on a website called "Seeking Arrangements," to troll for

men she believes will take her out, pay her for her company and sparkling wit and not want to have sex with her.

Jo has also gone on "Seeking Arrangements" and met random men for drinks.

Dee is perpetually depressed and not sleeping.

Alya lost her job, stopped passing in her papers, and skipped last class entirely.

Grace lied about going to The Tenement Museum, refuses to revise her Immigration paper and believes she will still pass my class.

Rodrigo wrote in his Writer's Paper how much he "liked older women" and detailed an affair. He asked me how to write the story of an immigrant friend of his, so I lent him *What is the What* by Dave Eggers. Rodrigo's father is an enormously successful drug dealer.

JL wants more feedback and guidance from me in addition to my comments, the workshops and the Writing Center, because his Korean is getting in the way of his writing a good essay in English.

Chair Alan Bennett's response: "Oh my God! You are their therapist!"

He went on to say something like, you can't be doing this, it's too much…but he didn't tell me how to handle it all, or what to do about it, and I was already in the middle of it. I had no idea it was going to get worse.

10. Super Woman!

"I want to be her when I grow up."
    —Student Evaluation, Anonymous, NYU 2012
"Too much reading."
    —Student Evaluation, Anonymous, NYU 2010

I SHOULD HAVE LISTENED more carefully, more closely, when my friend Mary Folliet, a retired professor, spoke about stress: environmental stress, what stress does to the mind, what it does to the body, and how it can manifest itself.

Because I had never taken stress seriously: what it does to the mind, the body, or how it can manifest itself, mainly because I did not think it affected me. I believed it was separate from my epilepsy, my health, my well-being. Yoga alternated with cycling plus a long bath with lavender oil before bed should be enough to put the day behind me.

Mary has always taken stress a little too seriously and says things like "It's the environmental stress" as a catchall for any ailment one may have at any given time, which in my head I coupled with her saying on countless occasions "Civilization is having a nervous breakdown." But they are not the same thing, and I should have listened.

The fact is, it never occurred to me I could not handle whatever came along, because I always had. Not always well. But handled, yes.

This could be from having an independent mother who pushed her daughter to be the same, or from going to live in a foreign country alone, at eighteen, forcing independence upon myself. My motto has always been, "I can do it myself."

Until I couldn't.

11. Rape and Sexual Assault, Spring Term 2013

"Professor del Rosso is concerned with each student as an individual. She actually cared when students were out sick, or had some sort of issue. She also makes her classes stay up to date on current events and news, which I think is incredibly important. She makes you examine the world in which we live. It's a life class as much as it's a writing class. I never wanted to miss a minute with her."

—*Student Evaluation, Anonymous, NYU 2013*

DISCLAIMER: The following is based on my experiences and those of my students. I claim to be neither an expert on this subject, nor have the last word.

So much has been written on rape and sexual assault, it's easier to begin with what is known: sexual assaults happen on every campus across the country. Whether they are reported or not is another matter entirely.

Out of the fourteen young women who have come to me, two have gone to the police and none have pressed charges. The reasons range from not wanting to relive every single moment of the sexual assault in open court; not wanting their sexual histories brought up in public (both of these statements make me think of the brilliant, harrowing memoir *Lucky* by Alice Sebold); and that somehow, they were partly or totally to blame. The ones that went to NYU directly for help did get the help they needed, and I have to say, NYU handled both the students and their situations in exemplary fashion. Note NYU is not on that long list of one hundred colleges being federally investigated. There is

a reason for that. Had they not helped the students, had their confessed rapists been allowed back on campus, had NYU protected its reputation rather than their students... But they didn't. In this regard, knowing the particulars, I am proud to work for such an institution.

In 2013, one of my freshman students at FIT missed a class, a deadline, and did not turn in the first draft of a major paper. This was unusual, so I sent her a stiff email and told her to get in touch, giving her a variety of options. It was the run-up to spring break and she was out of time.

She called me. She hadn't come to class because she was in the hospital. She said she had been raped. She did not know if she was going to press charges, but she did have a rape kit done. She didn't complete the assignment, but I no longer cared about the assignment.

It was horrible timing: the Friday before spring break began, so everyone—my chair, the dean, other professors —was gone. There was no one I could immediately talk to. My student, who I will call Elle, was set to go on a family vacation the following day. She still planned on doing so. I asked her to write down every single thing that had happened to her. Everything, while it was clear in her mind, so she didn't forget. I asked her to send me a copy. Before we got off the phone, I asked if she was going to tell her parents while she was on holiday. She said, "No."

And I really didn't understand why until she sent me her missive. Her mother had come to town and they had gone to a bar together. They had stayed there drinking till the early hours of the morning, and Elle confessed to her mother that she had a crush on the bartender. Her mother had flagged the bartender down, and told him. He was older, in his twenties, Australian, handsome. He and Elle exchanged

phone numbers. A week or so later, they arranged to meet up. He was not a student, so their meeting took place off campus, though, of course, Elle was still a freshman.

They met at his bar, then went to a party. The last thing Elle remembers was being handed a drink. After that, she came to stumbling on the Lower East Side, without her tights, or underwear, or handbag. She did have on her coat and because one of the pockets had a tear, her wallet had fallen through to the lining, so she still had that in her possession. She got a cab back to her dorm. Unfortunately, the security guard thought she had been drinking and reported her. Elle thought she had been date-raped. She was sore, so she went to the hospital. She was right about the alleged rape. She was told that unless she pressed charges, she could not find out about the toxicology screen, so she wasn't sure about being drugged.

She did call the Australian to ask him what had happened. He told her they had sex after the party, in a hallway, and then he had taken her back to her dorm. She told him that was unlikely.

Because Elle didn't want her mother to feel guilty or assume any blame, she did not tell her about the rape. She told no family members. The only person she really talked to, for the next six weeks, was me.

The Samaritans suicide hotline and counseling center experience did help, because mainly, it was listening to people talk about their problems. But nothing had prepared me for this.

After spring break, my chair was quite busy and seemed to have events every evening. Feeling increasingly hard done by because he did not have time to sit down and talk, while my schedule, running back and forth between NYU and FIT, was not flexible, I wrote him a letter of complaint and delivered it to him on a Saturday afternoon at a highbrow poetry reading I knew he would be attending. This is what

it said:

Chair Bennett, April 6, 2013

I regret that you were unable to make time to meet with me about my student, Elle, who was raped, and discuss her subsequent hearing and treatment by the FIT administrators with regard to her housing situation.

Elle has still not told her parents; she has only told me. So on Tuesday afternoon, April 2nd, when she asked me to be her witness and speak for her at her hearing, I said yes, because she has no one else. I called you and left a message because an upsetting situation had gone from bad to worse. Your response was nothing. No phone call, and no follow-up.

Earlier that same day, I came to your office and said I needed to speak with you about my student. You flipped through your calendar, said this week was bad, your daughter had a reading, and "next week would be better."

Because of what happened at that hearing, I will be meeting with Dean _____ next week. He, like my student and I, are minorities, and it will be of great interest to him what went on in that hearing room.

On a personal note regarding stress: I have dropped 12 pounds, skipped a period, and worried my friends considerably. I am not equipped to be the counselor for sixty students; I cannot do what I do alone, in a vacuum. My chairperson at NYU, _____ ,would have made time for me had I told her a student of mine had been raped. How do I know? The one time it happened, two years ago, she did.

You have a daughter. I just wonder, had she been the victim of a rape and a professor was doing everything she could to help her, yet the chairperson the professor answered to was too busy, how you would respond as a parent.

Sincerely,
Professor Lisa del Rosso

Within three seconds, I got a text from the chair, apologizing profusely. He came to that meeting with the (then) dean. We were talking about student problems and why students seem to feel more comfortable confiding in a writing professor than walking into an anonymous health center. The dean said he was happy Elle felt she could come to me, and then, as only a former writing professor could say, "We ask students to look into their hearts, to reach down into their souls and pour it out onto the paper. So there's a connection there immediately. Of course you would be the person to go to rather than confiding in a total stranger."

True. The "Something That Changed You" paper is not a 500-word, get-into-college essay. It's a seven-page (possibly longer) detailed paper. The students can go wherever they are comfortable, dark or light. I tell them not to go to places that make them uncomfortable.

I got Elle into counseling via the college, which she initially balked at, but in the end, found quite useful. She said, "I hated my previous counselor, but this woman I really like."

But let me go back to that FIT housing hearing referenced in my letter to the chair.

Because Elle had been accused of drinking and it was a second offense, she was being thrown out of the dorms, a decision she appealed. She needed a parent to stand up for her, but as no parent knew her situation, she called me.

"Will you come to this trial and stand up for me? I don't have anybody else…I can ask."

It took me a minute to answer. "I'll come if I can speak. If I can't speak, there's no point."

Elle said, "No, no, you can speak. You can speak."

I met her a few days later at the appointed place and time. Dressed up in a skirt, blouse, heels, with her hair down

and styled, my student looked quite beautiful and almost unrecognizable from the anonymous jeans/tee shirt/boots/ leather jacket student uniform she normally wore.

We were met by a woman wearing the most enormous, gleaming, silver crucifix on her chest that I have ever seen, short of the ones inside the homes of my Italian relatives. I thought, Oh no. Elle will be judged.

Elle introduced me and the first thing the woman with the crucifix said was, "You can't speak. You can be here but you can't speak."

I said, "Elle has written down every single thing that has happened to her, and I have that account with me. So when she needs help or forgets an important detail, I will prompt her with this account, and yes, I will be speaking."

Flummoxed, the woman stammered, "Oh, well, in that case..." and led us into a small, narrow room where Elle was to be judged by a jury of her peers and others.

Three plain, sullen-looking female students, all with their hair pulled back in severe fashion, sat at a table, hands folded, representatives of some sort of council, perhaps re-creating the tribunals of the Salem witch hunts. None of them looked like they had ever been on a date, much less had ever had sex. And Elle was beautiful.

The woman with the crucifix led the charge, and tried to blame Elle's behavior on what happened: if she hadn't gone out, if she hadn't been drinking, if, if, if. I, instead, tried to connect everything that happened: the bar with her mother, the bartender, the date rape, wandering home from the date rape, and the fact that it would be impossible for a security guard or anyone else to tell the difference between a young woman inebriated, and a young woman who had been slipped a date-rape drug. There was no proof, because Elle had decided not to press charges.

Why? Because she liked him. She agreed to go out with

him. She thought it was partly her fault. Hence, no toxicology report. Also, she had an active sexual history, some of which she shared in class via New York Stories.

Sidebar: Elle went on a website called "Seeking Arrangements." She was not the first of my students to do this and won't be the last. This site has gotten a lot of press, and we have discussed it in my classrooms, with some students saying, "Good for the young women," and others saying, "Sluts," and still others saying, "It's no different than a gold digger who becomes a housewife with children and never works again." On "Seeking Arrangements," college gals can meet up with older, wealthy men (Sugar Daddies) for "stability" and "redefine the expectations of a perfect relationship" (according to the website) and whatever else happens later is between two consenting adults. Elle went for one drink with one man, who told her he had lied on the site and was not single but married, in town for a conference. He paid her $300 to do so. She made sure a friend was at the venue with her, so she felt safe. He was nice enough, and it was only one drink and conversation. But Elle said he made it very clear that if they were to meet up again, it would be more than talk.

I have no idea how much of a woman's sexual history is brought up during a rape trial. I'd like to think that isn't done anymore. But I wouldn't bet my life on it.

In the end, the only thing the "judges" could agree on was this: blame the mother. And that boded well for Elle, since her mother was not under the college's auspices. Elle was placed on probation. No drinking, no friends in the dorm, or she was out. Elle promised to "be good."

Only when Elle told me she was making progress with her therapist did I relax. She still wouldn't tell her parents.

At the end of that same April, when I was home sweating on the bike (indoor bike, for recovery of a torn meniscus), I got a text from a student. She said she was taking a

"psych leave" and wouldn't be at college for the rest of the year. This student, I'll call her Jean: brilliant. Gifted. I asked her to ring me. Jean did, and told me she had been sexually assaulted in her dorm room by a fellow student. The particulars: Jean had known him since September. They had been watching a movie in her room. They were both drinking. Jean had either fallen asleep or passed out. When she came to, he was on top of her. He said what I have heard from female students before: well, you must have wanted this, or otherwise you wouldn't have passed out. Jean screamed, got him off her, and ran out of the room. She went to the university, then the police. The university contacted both for statements. The young man admitted what he did and NYU expelled him. Jean decided not to press charges because she did not want to relive what happened to her out loud in a courtroom. Against my advice, she did not seek counseling.

During those six weeks, I functioned as I normally did. I went to all of my classes, managed my sixty students, corrected all papers, never late, never sick, but dealt with my stress poorly. At first, it was not sleeping, which turned into not eating, followed by a fifteen-pound weight loss in total, and then my hair began falling out. It seemed beyond my control, and being unable to get it under control was mortifying. I could not figure out why the hair loss—I'm clearly slow on the uptake—and sought out my dermatologist, a wonderful woman, for answers. When I explained, she said, "You need to learn how to manage your stress or this is going to keep happening to you every time you go through a situation like this," and then prescribed Rogaine for a year.

I tried to find someone to talk to. I was reliably informed that though colleges used to have counseling services for the professors, both state and private universities had done away with these due to financial cutbacks. After going through one of the NYU health centers, and many people and many phone calls, I did find a therapist to help me deal with stress.

It was a great deal solely for professors: six sessions free for six months.

I began seeing her in June. On January 1st, my insurance changed from Aetna to Obamacare, because I could no longer afford Aetna; and January 1st is when I had to stop seeing the therapist because I could not meet the deductible, which was two thousand unforeseen dollars.

I kept using the Rogaine.

I received this missive from FIT almost at the end of the term, in May, well after my student was sexually assaulted, well after I needed help. Neither my chair, who was aware of the stress I was under, nor anyone else had told me this existed:

Subject: Fwd: EAP Program and Counseling Center
Date: May 14, 2015 4:04 AM

Begin forwarded message:
From: Miss Lymon/FIT
Date: October 9, 2014 7:24:32 AM PDT

Subject: EAP Program and Counseling Center

Dear Colleagues,

I wanted to let you know about two important resources at FIT. The first is the FIT/UCE Employee Assistance Program (EAP), which provides free and confidential counseling for all FIT employees. Their phone number is 212 217.5600. They also have programming on campus; current EAP program offerings can be found

by logging into MyFIT and clicking on the EAP link at the bottom of the page.

Secondly, please let your students know about the Counseling Center. They provide a variety of free services for students in any situation. Students who are going through a stressful time because of personal or family illness and emergencies, or simply need help balancing work and school responsibilities can find caring, confidential help there.

They are located in Room A212B and their phone number is (212) 217-4260. Their hours are Monday-Friday, 9-5, and Tuesday and Thursday evenings (by appointment only) from 5-7pm.

If you have a concern about a student and would like advice about referring them to the Counseling Center, please feel free to contact Alan Bennett or me.

Best,

Miss Lymon
Assistant Chairperson

12. Addendum: Thoughts on Alcohol

IN EVERY SINGLE CASE of rape or sexual assault that I have been contacted about, alcohol was a component. Either one party or the other or both had been drinking. At the beginning of each semester, I do give a brief speech to my freshman on the perils of underage alcohol consumption and how to protect one's self. This speech pertains to the young men in my class as well as the young women.

My foreign students tell me they don't understand this particular problem at all, but in France, England and most of Europe, etc…alcohol is part of the culture and is introduced early. I lived in London for ten years. I understand this. And I am not saying that these countries do not have problems with behavior pertaining to alcohol. What I am saying is now that sexual assaults on campus have reached epidemic proportions, it might be an idea to decriminalize alcohol by lowering the drinking age to eighteen, and subsequently, make the punishment for drunk driving much more severe. I personally like arrest, loss of license, and if the person continues to drive, jail time. But right now, I do not believe anyone can stop students from drinking, and colleges behave rather like speakeasies did during Prohibition—that is how well the drinking age is working on campuses thus far. If the student has been forbidden to touch a drop of alcohol at home, then college is manna from heaven, the holy grail of alcohol consumption. It can be acquired from so many people, places, parties, frats, bars; and on campus, fake ID's rule. Something's got to give, because the students think they're winning: hey, I'm bucking Authority! The parents think they're winning: hey, my underage kid wouldn't drink, not my kid! The colleges think they're winning: hey, we've abdicated our responsibility but we've got everything under control!

When in reality, everyone is losing.

13. M

"Prof. del Rosso is a little rough around the edges at times, but that's really a persona masking her fragile, caring heart. A rare case of a teacher actually giving a shit."

—*Student Evaluation, NYU Anonymous, 2016*

IN 2013, I HAD A TERRIFIC STUDENT in my freshman writing class I will call M. She exuded warmth, intelligence, and humor. A few weeks into the term, M asked to see me after class . Nervously, she confessed she was gay. We talked for a while. She had not yet come out to her conservative Michigan family, but I did tell her NYU was a very supportive environment: it has a large gay population, an LGBTQ student center, the Tisch School of the Arts ... and the city is more than welcoming. For a start, Stonewall is right down the street from Washington Square Park. In short, NYU in New York City is a very good place to be gay. M also had a crush on another student. I said to tell her.

This all worked out miraculously well. M's friends at NYU were wonderfully supportive. Her parents were in complete denial, but she had tried. That was all she could do. M professed her feelings for her crush, and her crush reciprocated. They made a ... dare I say it? They made a cute couple. They did! The kind of couple that finish each other's sentences. It didn't hurt that they were both articulate and well-read. About a month or so later, M came to me again after class. "What's going on?" I asked.

"I'm feeling ..."

"Yes?"

I am consolidating what was a very long conversation.

Pacing back and forth, M said, "I feel like I'm trapped in the wrong body. I've felt this way for a long, long time. As long as I can remember. I'm a man inside a woman's body and I feel like I want to kill myself."

I suppose the policy would have been to call someone, or escort M to the Wellness Center, where, if she had repeated that statement, M would have been confined to the NY Langone Medical Center Psych Ward until it was determined she was not longer a risk to herself. I actually did not know what the policy was at the time, but even if I had, it would not have changed what I did next.

I did not not call anyone, nor did I send M anywhere. I asked her to sit down. I asked her to look at me. I said, "You've come to the right person."

Where I get my healthcare in this city is a federally-funded LGBTQ primary care center in Chelsea: Callen-Lorde Community Health Center. They have been taking care of me for over twenty years. The staff there are exemplary human beings and that must be one of the prerequisites of the hiring process at Callen Lorde. My doctor at the time, Gal Mayer, on occasion called me personally and ordered me in for blood work, all to do with my epilepsy. When I told him I could not pay the bill, he said, "I do not do the billing. Don't worry about it. But you need to get that blood work done. When did you say you were coming?" That kind of thing.

When I asked Wendy Stark, Executive Director of Callen-Lorde, to describe the center, she said, "Callen-Lorde started as two grassroots, volunteer-staffed collectives, one formed in 1969 and the other in 1972, that provided healthcare to LGBTQ people outside of the mainstream healthcare system. Those two groups merged in 1983 in response to the burgeoning HIV epidemic. Today, the organization still has the same mission—to provide sensitive, quality healthcare services focused primarily on LGBTQ commu-

nities and people living with HIV, regardless of ability to pay —and is now a State-licensed, federally designated health center operating in three locations in New York City. Callen-Lorde is considered a global leader in LGBTQ health and a pioneer of the informed consent model of care for people of transgender experience."

Many years ago, I was walking by a construction crew working on a building next to Callen Lorde, en route to an appointment. One of the men stopped, looked at me and said, "Are you a man or a woman?" Clearly, he had heard about the riffraff next door.

"Wouldn't you like to know?" I said, grinning, and went right on in.

Callen Lorde is exactly where I sent M. I gave her the number. I told her to call and make an appointment with one of the counselors. I told her they were wonderful people who knew what they were doing and would help her make whatever decision she felt comfortable with. I promised she would be in good hands. M was very nervous about talking with someone. I asked her to trust me. Then I asked her to keep me posted.

Because M was still a teenager, she was able to get a grant for the gender-reassignment surgery at no cost to herself. She was so excited! And I was thrilled for her. M announced his name change on Facebook. For purposes of continuity, I'll say he changed it to Max.

Max is the happiest I have ever seen him.

Publicly, online he wrote:

> PdR kept me in school when I was seriously considering dropping out & was the 1st person I came out to as trans. I trusted her with sen-

sitive conversations at a time when I was too scared to talk to my family about them. She helped me process grief, anxiety, and depression without ever getting sappy.

My students have read and discussed trans teens, using an excellent, in-depth non-fiction piece in *The New Yorker*, "About a Boy" by Margaret Talbot, as a starting point. They have not yet been assigned an essay on that topic. I have, however, given them other hot-button topics to write about, most notably,

PORN

14. Porn and the Professor

What features of this course were especially effective?
"She really encouraged us to take an interest, the class was very interesting, she was very enthusiastic and it was clear she spent a lot of time on the class. It's clear when a teacher is interested and spends a lot of time on a class."
—*Student Evaluation, Anonymous, NYU 2008*

WHEN I WAS IN GRADE SCHOOL, my art teacher was my Aunt Janet. She had traveled around Europe, had had more than one boyfriend, been disowned by my grandfather twice for defying him, and drove a red convertible she gave me rides home in. There were a few in class who envied my "cool aunty."

Aunt Janet was married to my Uncle Joe. Uncle Joe was an organ tuner and an amateur race car driver, a good one. He smoked cigars and wore a jet-black toupee; everyone in the family knew but no one actually ever addressed the subject, though I stared at it many a time. But Uncle Joe was cool, too, in his way, and when my family went over to their house for holidays, sometimes—if the main bathroom was occupied—I used the more private bathroom off Joe and Jan's bedroom.

Next to the toilet, neatly arranged by month, was a tall stack of *Playboy* magazines. They were the first pornographic magazines I had ever seen, and truly I was fascinated. After the first time, I tried to use their bathroom as much as possible. Then, once I understood what the images were and what they were supposed to do, I asked my aunt if the magazines bothered her and if my uncle looking at the naked women

in the magazines bothered her. She shrugged. "It keeps him happy."

Around the same time, I accompanied my father and mother into the city so he could get a haircut. We arrived at a big, old barbershop, with lots of wood and red chairs and I could tell by the way my parents greeted the barber that they had all known each other for a long time. I was told to sit in a chair and read while the haircut was happening, and afterwards, they all went into a back room for a time, probably for some Sambuca.

I was a voracious reader, loved it more than anything. But there were no books next to the chair, only magazines. With pictures. So I dutifully read those, and when my parents came to get me, I was unfurling a centerfold of a naked lady lying down in a stream, water cascading over her body, and thinking I would really like to be doing that, too, because I loved the water and streams and rivers and the ocean. "Lisa!" my mother said. "What?" I said. My mother took the magazine from me. "'You're not supposed to be reading those." My father just laughed.

When I got older, in my teens, my maternal grandmother, who had Alzheimer's, was moved to a home because my grandfather could no longer look after her. He went to see her daily. I can no longer remember why I was in their bedroom, only that we had keys to their house in case of an emergency. I was looking for something, and in the bedside table bottom drawer, I found two porn magazines. On the cover of one of them was a photo of a woman in a tutu and nothing else; the other was a photo taken outside, and three people sat on a hill of some sort. There was a woman in the middle, a man on either side and all were naked: one man was black, the other white, and both were examining parts of her anatomy.

That discovery was kind of icky. By that time, I knew what porn was, so it made sense that my Uncle Joe had mag-

azines in his bathroom, and it made sense the barbershop kept them beside the waiting area chairs. But this was my grandfather.

That was the extent of my porn experience until I left home at seventeen. There was no computer in the house I grew up in. No cell phones (this is the late 1970s and early 80s). So the chasm between how porn influenced my life then and how porn influences my students' lives today is vast.

When I began teaching writing at NYU nine years ago, I had to find a topic for the Argument Paper, the second of three due for the term. I wanted to choose something that I would have wanted to write about at eighteen or nineteen, something that was relevant to me. Not wanting to repeat their high school experience with topics such as abortion and capital punishment, I came across a great article by Ross Douthat called, "Is Pornography Adultery?" in *The Atlantic*.

I thought, Great! My students can write about porn.

I get bored easily and assume my students do as well, so I change up my syllabus, bring in new material, ask students to focus on the city and world in which they live (presidential elections, mayoral elections, police brutality, protests, for example). I have also been known to add, subtract and change assignments at the last minute.

The Porn Paper never changes.

Here's why: porn is so ubiquitous, so easy to access, so benign now that it's not even outrage-worthy. The Douthat article was written in 2008. Another great piece, "The Porn Myth," by Naomi Wolf, came out in 2003. Can you think of the last time an inflammatory piece about porn came out? I can't, and I have searched. On September 21st, 2013, there was a piece titled "Intimacy on the Web, With a Crowd," by Matt Richtel in the *New York Times* Technology Section,

which was largely positive. An article on porn comes out in a major publication at least twice a year. Porn morphs, changes, spreads. It infiltrates my students' lives, but is no longer taboo.

Instead, porn has been appropriated by advertisers (and as my students know, sex sells), so you only need look at the American Apparel ads, or Victoria's Secret commercials, or Abercrombie and Fitch…the list is endless.

Want to write a bestseller? Just add porn. *Fifty Shades of Grey*? Soft-core porn sells! There are blogs, columns and memoirs devoted to strangers' sex lives. Apparently, we like to read about people we don't know having sex with other people we don't know.

This is what I have learned from my students: 99% of them have looked at porn. The young men typically have no problem with this, while the young women are of two minds. But what both genders mention (because I have them interview their peers— of both genders—for the papers as well) is that they are aware that porn not only demeans women but also depicts unattainable female standards of beauty they cannot live up to, or that their girlfriends cannot live up to. The young women feel they have to compete with skinny, blonde, long-legged, huge-breasted, manicured, coiffed, shaved, maquillage perfection.

And they say the advertising industry makes them feel the exact same way.

America really does have a bipolar relationship with women. Most women—myself, my friends, my students included—are raised to be modest, to wear appropriate clothing, and not dress provocatively. I don't mean modest in the sense of one's achievements, I mean modest in terms of dress. In my house, the word "classy" was a big compli-

ment from my mother, or "elegant." Sadly, these words seem
to have gone out of style. Out of fashion.

And yet, when a woman walks out of her door (at least,
in any major city) in a nice dress and heels, she is bombarded
with images of the exact opposite. "Nice" isn't what sells. "Nice"
isn't good enough. "Nice" will not get you noticed. Here's what
will: Two nearly naked women having a pillow fight in a jeans
ad. A woman holding up a satin sheet that barely covers her
nipple in a perfume ad, a strapping bare-chested man behind
her. A woman unzipping her hoodie, revealing a naked torso
in an apparel ad. Tight clothes, short dresses, push-up bras,
high heels, or better still, no clothes at all.

The mixed messages my female students are getting
equal a lack of self-esteem. Unless the young women have
ironclad egos (and at eighteen, this is unlikely) they are confused. They ask, what will make me attractive? Will I feel
okay if I don't recognize myself? It's the opposite of what I
learned at home, but…it seems to be what every ad is telling me. If I don't dress provocatively, will no man like me?
How will I be noticed, how do I compete? If I do, are there
consequences? Will I be judged? Will I be expected to act
the way I dress? Will people think I'm a slut?

I have many papers by young men and women that say
popular culture does more to demean women than porn ever
could. They say, at least porn is honest. And elective.

One of my students couched her paper in terms of role
models: she did not want to look for female role models in
porn, could not find them in advertising, and was unhappy
with the celebrity culture in which we live. I asked, who are
your role models? She said Lisa Ling.

And…? I said. She had no others that immediately
came to mind. She had to research.

If my female students, eighteen- and nineteen-year-old

women, future doctors, lawyers, entrepreneurs, and leaders (one hopes) cannot come up with role models for their generation, then we are doing a terrible job right now in terms of leading exemplary lives. In terms of how we portray women right outside our door. In terms of sex, sex, sex. Is that all there is, all that images of women are used for, to sell products, to consume? That enormous problem is not a porn problem—that problem is a Western problem.

So my students take the Douthat piece, connect to it, and write about porn: how it affects their lives, their relationships, their self-image, positively or negatively or somewhere in the middle. Whether they think porn is good, bad, indifferent, hilarious, or never going away so it's best to just accept it and move on. They interview their peers. They read up on both sides of the argument. In the unusual case of a student who has never looked at porn before, I tell them they have to, because you can't argue for or against something if you have never seen it (I do realize you can, but in this case, you really shouldn't). Some students have taken the bull by the horns and had "porn-viewing parties" where invitations were sent and the entire suite watched a porn film together. The students in question put the results of the parties in their papers: overall, the women laughed and the men were enthralled.

But for the very shy students who have never looked at porn and are terrified of typing a word into Google that accesses something they are not prepared for, this is my directive: take a friend and walk into a bodega. Go to the magazine section. Make sure your friend covers you, protects you, like a goalie protects the net during a hockey game. Pick up a *Playboy* magazine. Flip through it, for about a minute, maybe two. Put the magazine back and with your friend leading the way, leave the bodega. Congratulations! You have just looked at porn.

What I don't tell them is the kind of porn I remember

from my childhood, which is now the most benign, anachronistic kind of porn out there. *Playboy* is almost nostalgic, like that scene from Woody Allen's *Bananas* where he is in a Greenwich Village bodega and attempts to hide the porn mag in between the pages of Time and adds a couple of other highbrow magazines to his purchase. He gets to the counter and an older, grizzled male cashier starts to ring him up, stops when he gets to the porn mag, then shouts to another male coworker across the store: "Hey Ralph, how much is a copy of *Orgasm*"?

"What?"

Allen, red-faced and embarrassed, says, "Just put them in a bag."

But the cashier says it louder. "*Orgasm!* This man wants to buy a copy. How much is it?"

Allen, as a way of excusing his purchase, says, "I'm doing a sociological study of perversion up to advanced child molesting." Then he runs out of the store.

No one will ever be embarrassed in that way, for that reason, ever again.

15. Super Kids and Opportunity

"This was my favorite class; time flew in this class. God Bless the professor."

> —Anonymous Student Evaluation, OP Summer Intensive 2017

"No improvements needed, but you could hire her full time."

> —Anonymous Student Evaluation, OP Summer Intensive 2017

"del Rosso takes the time to listen to us and guides discussions excellently. She's always willing to help and lets us be creative. She also assigns relatable texts that are relevant to our lives."

> —Anonymous Student Evaluation, OP Summer Intensive 2017

NEW YORK STATE HAS a fantastic program that I had never heard of until I applied to teach in said program: HEOP (Higher Education Opportunity Program). HEOP benefits low-income inner-city teens who desire to go to college but cannot afford the cost. The program is sponsored through a grant from the New York State Education Department and in conjunction with NYU. What the HEOP program also does is *economically* diversify the college, which, like most colleges, it needs (and even this is, at best, a drop in the bucket: the latest statistic puts NYU fourth on the list of colleges with economic diversity at fourteen percent). Once accepted as an NYU/HEOP student, the next requirement is to pass a six-week intensive summer program in all dis-

ciplines, including writing. After passing, the student pays a fraction of the cost of NYU tuition. According to one of my gifted former students, KM, who comes from the Bronx and is now enrolled in the NYU nursing program, it was $3,000.00 for her freshman year, instead of $64,000.

In summer 2015, for the second time, I taught for HEOP. Also during that summer, an article came out in *The New York Times* by Julie Scelfo, "Suicide on Campus and the Pressure of Perfection," that caught my eye. It focuses on an increasingly despondent Penn student, Kathryn DeWitt, then segues to another brilliant Penn student, Madison Holleran, who leaped to her death from a parking garage on January 17, 2014. The students interviewed in the piece spoke of anxiety, depression, stress, fulfilling parental expectations… and the word "perfection."

When I was in school, I wanted to be the best I could be: in class, at play, at home, as a person. But I never felt the need to be "perfect." Perfect is a losing game. Perfect was also not something my mother expected of me.

I gave the piece to my thirty-six HEOP students. I wanted to know if they recognized themselves in the article, if this was familiar to them or not applicable.

This is what they said:

One half of the HEOP students, all young women, began losing their hair in the 10th grade or earlier. "I used to have this long, full hair, not like this," the HEOP student said, gently stroking both sides of her hair. "But every time I shower, clumps fall out."

And the first thing I thought was, "The same kind of stress I was under…temporarily? No no no! Not now! Not until you are in grad school!"

Some had ulcers. Skin conditions, like psoriasis. Gray hair.

One young woman said she stopped sleeping in tenth

grade, and gets about two hours of sleep a night. Now, she said, 'I can't sleep. I live on coffee."

Ninety-five percent of them get an average of four to five hours of sleep a night. Many get less.

About ten students admitted to using Adderall and other stimulants. But coffee was the drug of choice.

Most said they had some kind of "breakdown" or "I couldn't take it any more" moments, and had to go on antidepressants. One had a "time management consultant" who made things exponentially worse. Some therapists were helpful. But the stress remained.

What stressed them?

SAT's. Having a coach for SATs. Standardized testing. Grades.

Joining activities for the sake of activities because that is what colleges are looking for, "not because I like any of them."

Parents. The HEOP students are mostly Hispanic, Black and Asian. If at least one parent is an immigrant, the pressure is ON for the student.

"It's like, I came here for *you*; *you* are going to have a better life because *I sacrificed*; this theater and music you think you are doing is not serious, because after all I went through to come here, *you* are going to have a *future* with a *good job*, etc…" Tonio, a Dominican student, was holding his head. "That's my mother," he said.

All of the HEOP students were in the same pressure-filled boat. They had more to prove.

Friends, even if they are friends, are still the competition.

Social media makes everything worse. "Even though I had enemies in middle school and I hated them, I still looked up where they got into college and it made me so angry!"

Another student said the motto in her year was, "Pain is temporary, GPA is forever."

"How would you fix it?" I asked.

We should…we…

"No, fix the system. Because it's not you that is the problem."

Oh!

Take away standardized testing.

Get rid of all grades, so the system is pass/fail.

Less mandatory classes.

A more interesting curriculum with arts and science courses, more English courses.

My students come into class with the jumbo trough of coffee in hand and bags under their eyes. At any given time of the year, a number are ill with flu or hacking with bronchitis. I remind them not to spend the entirety of their college career going from class to study hall to part-time job/ internship to sleep—to wake up and do it all over again the next day. Four years gone, and no fun.

There was one student who was okay with everything: she had taken a "gap year." A gap year! My heart leaped with joy. Her parents had moved to the US from the UK when she was twelve. They not only understood the value of the gap year, they encouraged her to take it. She spent six months teaching English in Madagascar. No electronic devices. No social media. She said she felt more connected to people, and had more conversations, face to face, with no distractions, no looking down at a phone. At the end of her six months, she did not want to come home. And all of her students said, You must be dying to get home, you must miss it.

Because they have nothing, and all they want to do is come here.

Is there a happy medium, or do we as human beings only exist in extremes?

Also this past summer in HEOP, there was a disturbing development. Some students had been homeless, along with their families, or they had been through the New York City shelter system. They wrote about their situations: hiding from their fellow students that they were in a shelter or homeless; changing schools repeatedly; being unable to have friends; being unable to have something simple like a hair dryer because the shelter does not want anyone to get too comfortable. But none of them brought the essays up to present day. HEOP offers tuition and also housing for the student. I did not ask about the current housing situations of their respective families.

When I teach "On Dumpster Diving," by Lars Eighner (and that piece, I have to say, is another I won't stop teaching because homelessness is getting worse, not better), one of the things I ask students is: what were your thoughts on the homeless before you read this piece?

Some comments I have gotten over the years:

Layabouts.

They are all drug addicts and alcoholics.

Why can't they just get jobs?

They put themselves in that situation.

They have cellphones so they can work.

Dirty.

I try not to look at them.

Can't they go to a shelter?

They'll just use the money for drugs.

I realized, after summer 2015, that I would have to teach

that piece differently now. Because looking out at the faces of my students, I would never know if any one of them had been or still was homeless. And neither would their peers.

When I write about the stress I went through, it's fine because it is me and in the past. I'm an adult. I should have handled the stress in a better way, obviously. But when I write about student stress…they are not equipped to deal with it, because the brain is not yet fully developed (this is biology now, not opinion) and the formative years are so unbelievably important. Being a homeless child has to be the worst kind of environmental stress there is.

As a professor and as a person, I can read their essays, I can listen if they come to me. I can mentor. I can be there. I can empathize, not sympathize. It bothers me that is all I can think of to do, that I have come up with nothing else. So many of my students, regardless of economic background, want to make a difference in the world. Do I make a difference? Or rather, do I make enough of a difference?

The Teaching Life - Part II

1. NYU vs. FIT

Professor del Rosso brought in things from the outside world, out of literature, and turned all of it into something to write about.
—*Student Evaluation, Anonymous, NYU 2013*

FIT IS A STATE SCHOOL, and NYU is a private school. The writing classes at NYU are capped at 15, sometimes 14, which is sensible. That means every student will get individualized attention. There is the time to do so. The classes at FIT are capped at approximately 25. I think. I've not had more than 25.

Each of my classes is assigned three 5-7 page papers per semester (it used to be 7-10 pages), with three drafts of each that go under my purple pen. In addition, the students participate in peer workshops so they read and edit each other's drafts. But every draft of every of paper is corrected and finally graded by me.

Typically, I would teach two classes at NYU and two at FIT per semester. I hope you are doing the math. I can't do math, I only know it's a lot of papers.

At NYU, per course compensation is roughly $5760. Two courses a semester is $11,520. There is a small, automatic raise annually. But no matter how terrific the student evaluations, or how you rate in the department, there is no chance of earning more, or teaching any more courses as long as you are an adjunct professor. You have to wait until a full-time job opens up. Currently, there are 80 writing professors in LSP (Liberal Studies Program) where I teach at NYU. A full time job has not opened up since I was hired nine years ago.

At FIT, per course it is roughly $2500. That breaks down to a bi-weekly paycheck of $285 for the time you are in the classroom. Not the time you are correcting papers. But there are more students. More work for less pay. The time I spend correcting is approximately 105 hours for 2 NYU classes; 15 hours every other week for a 14-week term. Off weeks, we read from the course book and I comb the *New York Times*, *The Atlantic*, *The New Yorker*, anything that pops up on Facebook or Twitter for articles to send to my students, all in the interest of analysis and discussion. But as I said, I usually have four classes a term, and FIT classes are larger, so there is no "off" week. I simply stagger the workload. 4 classes = 210 hours correcting, approximately. If it's 3 classes, 160 hours correcting. I am paid for exactly none of that correcting time, and I'm not including research time.

At FIT, if you have 72 AOP (Academic Operating Procedures) hours (explanation of AOP hours: calculated not by hours of teaching but by the credit hours the class is worth. So if I taught a writing class and spent 45 hours in class during the term, what I accrue is 3 hours, because the course is a three-hour course. This is the most absurd, ridiculous and unfair way to not reward a professor that I have ever encountered), then you may join a union, but the pay does not go up. The only way to get on the tenure track is to either accrue a certain number of AOP hours and get some kind of permanent adjunct certificate; or, get a PhD. FIT stands for the Fashion Institute of Technology. The only department in the entire college that requires a PhD is the English and Communications Department. This for a college with no English major, no Creative Writing major, no writing major whatsoever. But making it so difficult sure does save money on a living wage salary and health insurance. Just hire an adjunct. Or eighty.

At FIT as an adjunct professor, I had to be observed once every single semester by a senior faculty member.

This was part of a "re-appointment process" state schools require, but really, part of making sure adjuncts don't suck.

Whenever I was observed, I always used the same material: the formerly mentioned "On Dumpster Diving" by Lars Eighner and "People Like Us" by David Brooks. I found the once-a-semester observations to be incredibly stressful, hateful, and demeaning. Also, what they can tell you is nothing, because the way students act (best behavior) and the way a professor acts (best behavior) when there is someone in the room observing her class is entirely different from the way the class is normally. As for myself, I am on edge, the students are wired (mainly because, to take the onus off me, I used to tell them *they* were the ones being observed) and it's uncomfortable for all involved. This is the same reason cameras in classrooms will never be allowed, and filming a classroom is a fiction: they can't tell the real story, nor paint an accurate picture.

Making the best of a heinous situation, I chose the two pieces that stir the most controversy, that get the students thinking not about the interloper in the room, but the subjects at hand. That way, I can forget about the observer as well. Even the observer forgets about being an observer. Win-win-win.

The first time I was observed by the new Chair Alan Bennett, my class rocked. Students were assigned the two essays, as usual: "On Dumpster Diving" and "People Like Us." They were instructed to: read; analyze the style and content of the piece; highlight parts that jumped out at them, made them think, surprised them or a turn of phrase they thought was interesting; and see if they could connect it to themselves and the world in which they live. They were told to come armed with thoughts and opinions. The upshot:

EVALUATION: Excellent

COMMENTS:
This was a high-energy class, on the part of both instructor and students. Members of the class obviously like Lisa a lot, and respond to her accordingly. For the hour I was there, the discussion was lively, incisive and enthusiastic. It was rewarding to watch that sustained level of engagement.

After I was given a copy of my evaluation, I met with Chair Bennett in his new office. He asked me to have a seat. He said, "Tell me what you want to teach and you can teach it. I can give you all kinds of courses...Writing about Architecture, Writing about Art and Design... you might like that because the students are older, juniors..."

All that sounded wonderful. And of course, I was pleased with the report. But here's the rub: I would have to teach four courses at FIT to make the money of two at NYU. So the most I could teach in any given term was four courses. Two at NYU and two at FIT equals roughly 70 students. Interestingly, a full-timer's course load at NYU is three classes. That is 45 students, full-time pay, with benefits.

So in the end, all of those brilliant recommendations, terrific student evaluations, rateyourprofessor.com comments or ratings, mean nothing. They don't even help you get a teaching job. All of my jobs have been by referral. If you publish a book, preferably one that sells, that is incredibly helpful.

If the goal is to teach at the highest level, get the best accolades, score well in the department, and you do all of those things yet still cannot make a living because none of those things translate into solvency, you start to wonder

why you are doing it at all. Why you are banging your head against a brick wall, waiting for it to move.

As of March 2017, the tuition + room at NYU is $71,000. Every time there is an (unannounced) tuition hike, I hear it from my students, and not in a good way. Of the most recent increase, one of them said, "Can they just keep raising it? I mean, is it ever going to stop, because it can't just keep going up, right? I mean, it has to stop sometime. Right?"

I had no answer to this.

At Tufts University, the tuition is $31,000 a year. In a 2014 landmark first union contract, Tufts voted to begin paying their adjuncts at least $7,300 a course, more if they have been teaching for eight years. They will also be compensated for non-classroom work, such as mentoring and advising. "The three-year agreement makes groundbreaking progress in job stability, includes a significant increase in per course pay and establishes new pathways for professional development" (Adjunct Action 1). This is certainly a start.

If Tufts values its staff, why not NYU? I can tell you: the tuition hikes pay for the 2031 plan, the 40% expansion of NYU into the Village. This is not about math. This is about misplaced priorities. It has been pointed out repeatedly by journalists and NYU professors in op-ed pieces in the *New York Times* and various other publications that the money flowing toward the expansion should rather be flowing toward the professors and financial aid for needy students. I concur.

As good as NYU is in comparison to FIT - and if I have not made it clear, the amount of money paid to adjuncts at FIT is both criminal and disgusting, though there are many, many other adjectives—adjunct compensation could be a lot better at NYU.

NYU wants to be a leader in so many ways: campuses in every major city around the world, a global, first-rate university with a recognized reputation. The expansion, and all of the press it has gotten (mostly negative) seems to be tarnishing NYU, rather than burnishing. If NYU really wants to stand head and shoulders above the rest, it should put its money where its talent lies: in their professors and their students, by attracting the brightest and the best to teach the brightest and the best. It is impossible to do that without paying a living wage, and impossible if only the elite can afford to pay the tuition. It is impossible if adjunct professors cannot afford to live in the city where they teach. Without supporting that talent, NYU is running on fumes. Eventually, it will run out of gas, along with that reputation it so desperately wants to hold onto.

As for FIT, the tuition is roughly $8,000. There is a tuition rise every few years. I have no idea where that money goes. The FIT campus is tiny. The buildings, for the most part, are old. Shabby. FIT is not looking to expand, although it certainly could, as it is over-subscribed and the most popular of all the state schools in the city. Many students apply to FIT and do not get in. But I still think the same applies to NYU as applies to FIT: if you want to attract the best and the brightest, because you also want to educate the brightest and the best, why are you unwilling to invest in your professors? On the sum of $285 every two weeks, no adjunct can afford to stay in that job. Unless FIT wants professors who consider teaching a "hobby," it's time to pay a living wage to adjunct professors that includes health insurance. Long past time.

ADDENDUM

The NYU adjuncts are protected by a union, which is rare. When I took a semester off from NYU, I was told by my union that I could take up to three consecutive terms of (unpaid) leave without losing my job. Wonderful! Except for the small matter of the "unpaid" part.

In a state school, such as FIT, adjuncts have no protection whatsoever.

None.

As of March 26, 2017, my union, ACT-UAW Local 7902, has been authorized and is prepared to strike because it has gotten nowhere with NYU in the collective bargaining contract negotiations. In layman's terms, NYU has refused every single thing the union has asked for: paid leave, healthcare, sick days, a pay raise.

If the union were asking for: a Lexus, weed, the keys to the city, I could understand NYU's hesitation.

But what the union is asking for are basics. Necessities. And NYU can afford to pay a living wage.

So, if ACT-UAW Local 7902 goes on strike, I will strike with them, not only because I voted for this, but also because the union in this case is right. As my mother said, "It's not like you are asking for extravagances here. Your grandfather and his crew went on strike for the same reason: the benefits and pay weren't enough. Workers who crossed the picket line were scabs. Sometimes you have to fight for what's right, or you don't get anything."

UPDATE: Despite its members chomping at the bit, ACT-UAW Local 7902 declined to strike. The contract that the union settled for looks exactly that: the union settled. No healthcare. No paid leave.

Subsidies for healthcare if you are on a family plan. If you are single, you are out of luck, friend. But there is money if an adjunct partakes in "course development."

It would be nice to be compensated for all of the hours I put in outside of class, never mind course creation. There is a tiny raise that is not reflected in my paycheck.

For two weeks pay, I currently clear $940.00 This is progress? I was out with a full-timer two nights ago and showed him that figure. He said, "That's not much more than I was making as an adjunct professor when I began twenty-seven years ago."

Again, this is progress?

2. Under the Radar

*"I do miss teaching, and students–some of them,
but mostly I miss drinking."*
—*Friend and former professor who shall remain
    nameless*

AT FIT AND NYU, one of the benefits of being an adjunct
is the ability to fly under the radar, undetected. I stay out of
office politics because I can, because in the scheme of things
I am a peon. I do not have to attend meetings. I have little
to no say in department matters and I can concentrate on
where I am needed most and what I do best: in the classroom, and teaching my students. Only once at NYU, when
I wrote a piece for the Modern Love section of *The New
York Times* about my unusual marriage/un-marriage/living
situation and a fellow professor recognized my name and
forwarded the piece to the entire department, did I make
a ripple. And even then, it was a good ripple, as I received
positive feedback, which was lovely.

The one time I was noticed at FIT, with no union to
protect me, ended poorly.

3. Avoid Being Stuck with a Lemon

*"Thank you. This course has made me reconsider what
I'm doing with my life. Now that's pretty fucking scary,
but also awesome."*
—Student Evaluation, Anonymous, NYU 2013

AT THE END OF MAY 2014, I got a call from the Chair
Bennett at FIT. I was on holiday with friends in Virginia at
the time. He said, "How would you like to teach Creative
Non-Fiction?" I said, "Yes, please!"

Creative Non-Fiction is what I do. It is where I have
had success publishing for the last ten years: in *The New
York Times, Serving House Journal, The Literary Traveler*,
and others. I teach it in my private writers' workshops but
never had the opportunity to teach it in a classroom setting,
because adjuncts at FIT are offered whatever courses are
leftover from what full-timers don't want. But a professor
had just retired, and I was on the FIT schedule to teach
only one course. So the chair gave me the CNF course. I
was deliriously happy. Until the emails began.

The assistant chair, Miss Lymon, was someone I had
always gotten along with. She had given me a terrific observation, I had gone to one of her poetry readings, we always
said hello and complimentary things when we ran into each
other in the main office.

But once she found out I had been given the CNF
course…well, this is how it started:

From: Miss Lymon
Sent: Monday, June 9, 2014 12:39 PM

To: Lisa del Rosso
Cc: Chair _____
Subject: Creative Nonfiction Syllabus

Hi Lisa,

Chair____ told me that you'll be teaching a section of Creative Nonfiction for us for the first time in the fall, and I thought it might be helpful to send you my most recent syllabus. I'm assuming he's already given you the departmental course of study from our "archives"? If not, I can email it to you when I'm in the office tomorrow afternoon.

The population of the course, and its position in the curriculum, have evolved quite a bit since I started teaching it in 2000. Creative Nonfiction, along with the other creative writing courses, is now an important requirement for students in the BFA programs in Fine Arts, Illustration, and some other majors.

I'd love to chat with you about it sometime. I am teaching online only this summer, but I am on campus a few times a week for the next couple weeks. I hope we can find a time that works to meet in person--or at least talk on the phone!

Cheers,

Miss Lymon
Professor and Assistant Chairperson
English & Speech Department
Fashion Institute of Technology-SUNY

Blindsided, I said yes. Then I thought about it and changed my mind.

From: Miss Lymon
Sent: Tuesday, June 10, 2014 9:10 AM
To: rossol
Subject: Re: Creative Nonfiction Syllabus

Hi Lisa,

It's truly wonderful that the department is able to offer the course to someone new, who is a writer working in the genre (and a very successful teacher in other courses)!

And what a great excuse for us to finally get together in person, if we can manage it. Are you free, by any chance, this Thursday early evening? I will be in late afternoon, so we could meet at the office and even go get a bite to eat somewhere, if you want. If not, next Wednesday or Thursday would work as well.

Let me know. I look forward to seeing you and chatting about CNF!

Cheers,
Miss Lymon
Professor and Assistant Chairperson
English & Speech Department
Fashion Institute of Technology-SUNY
New York, NY 10001

I put her off, because in fact, I felt uncomfortable about the whole thing. Also, I do not trust an overabundant usage of exclamation points.

In a panic, this is what I wrote to my chair:

Dear Chair Bennett,

Since Miss Lymon found out I was teaching CNF a little over a week ago, she has bombarded me with emails, suggestions, tips, her syllabus, her books, etc... and seemed concerned I had not taught it before. Because I resented being perceived as a novice, I sent her a mail back, saying I already had a book in mind, and a way to structure the course; also CNF is what I do, and where I have been published; in short, I know what I am doing. I was hoping I wouldn't hear from her again.

Wrong.

If I need help, I will ask for it. But she blindsided me and I didn't say that outright.

Furthermore, I am on vacation. I am an adjunct professor. I don't get paid to show up at FIT during summer.

Please get me out of this. Please help.

Lisa

Chair Bennett replied: "Don't do anything you don't get paid for."

Excellent! I thought. And I did not meet with her.

Miss Lymon continued to email. I continued avoidance. I told her I was teaching a summer course for NYU then leaving town on holiday, and did. July rolled by wonderfully and then I left for Provincetown, Massachusetts. On the day I got back, as my train was pulling into Penn Station on a Sunday night in late August, my cell pinged. It was an email from Miss Lymon.

On Sun, Aug 24, 2014 at 8:54 PM, Miss Lymon wrote:

Hello, Dear Lisa,

Summer has flown (yikes) and we are almost in the classroom again! Hope yours went well. Since we didn't have a chance to catch up in person and talk about the Creative Nonfiction course, maybe you would like to send yours to me by email? I promise to get back to you well before your first class meeting.

You've probably seen _____'s email on the subject, but as a reminder, we are required by the college to include the SUNY approved "learning outcomes" on our syllabi. For EN362 they are as follows:

On completion of EN362 students will:

· produce effectively written texts in a variety of nonfiction forms

· read and respond to a variety of texts in writing and speech

· develop an awareness of voice and audience

· use revision as a way to rethink and refine writing

· analyze written texts as a way to develop critical thinking skills

· utilize appropriate research methods to develop and support a point of view

Looking forward to seeing what you are doing with the class. Also, I will be in the office on Thursday, so please stop by when you get in and say hello!Cheers,

Miss Lymon

Professor and Assistant Chairperson
English & Speech Department
Fashion Institute of Technology-SUNY
New York, NY 10001

By now, I had been teaching writing for ten years total. My syllabus was completed and had included all of the "learning outcomes." If the chair had wanted to look over my syllabus, I would have sent it to him. But what he said to me was, "I have complete faith in you."

So I ignored her email.

She sent another one.

> Hi Lisa,
>
> Wondering if you missed this message (below) somehow. Hope your class went (is going) well--still offering to look over your syllabus before it's submitted to the department for our records.
>
> Also, hoping to have a chat about the class sometime soon, and to introduce you to Eugene Cross, who is teaching the other section of EN362.
>
> Take care,
>
> Miss Lymon
>
> Professor and Assistant Chairperson
> English & Speech Department
> Fashion Institute of Technology-SUNY
> New York, NY 10001

That September 2014, I was teaching four classes, running between two colleges, and juggling seventy students. I did not have time to meet the other professor (who my chair said was new, and also that "Miss Lymon made me give him the other section of CNF.") Also, I felt harassed. And stressed. No matter how I told Miss Lymon I did not need her help, she continued. My chair knew about all the emails, because I forwarded them to him. But he never stepped in

and asked her to stop. In desperation, I called my friend Ruth, whose sole motto for living is, "I don't have to do anything I don't want to—and neither do you." I asked her to help me fashion an email to get Miss Lymon to stop. She did, except she did not like the second half of the last line, which I added. Ruth was hardcore:

Miss Lymon,

It's kind of you to wish to help me; however, neither is it in my job description nor am I compensated for anything outside of my teaching at FIT. I am not in need of help, and to be honest, your persistent emails make me feel undermined rather than empowered.

Sincerely,
Lisa

Twenty-four hours passed. Miss Lymon sent me an apology email to which I did not respond.

I confess to having been close friends with Chair Bennett. So he had told me from the beginning that Miss Lymon was proprietary and jealous. I didn't understand: why? I am a peon in comparison. Teeny-tiny, in the scheme of things. An adjunct. She is tenured, assistant chair, etc...

He said, "Apparently, she thought she should have been 'consulted' before I gave you the course, but I don't have to do that. She wants to be consulted on everything: emails I send out that have nothing to do with her that she then goes back and follows up when there is no follow-up, and I have to go back and fix."

Okay.

"You are also younger. Attractive. Well-liked. Your students love you. They put chocolate boxes in your mailbox."

I never said Chair Bennett was not sexist. I doubt his

opinion on this had anything to do with why Miss Lymon was stalking me via email. And the chocolate box had only happened once.

The last words he said on the subject were, "She was really angry about that email you sent her. I told her to let it go."

And that was that.

I taught the CNF course. It was spectacular. Easily the most fun I had at FIT. A few became private students once it finished and many are now friends.

When the fall term concluded, I went on holiday to London to see my adopted family. I already had my two course schedule from NYU for spring semester, but the FIT classes were allocated much later. Chair Bennett had teased me, saying that there was one 8 AM course open he knew I would decline, as I never taught that early in the morning. I told him he was right. He laughed and said that other courses would open up and he would contact me. That was in December.

I returned to New York City in January. I heard nothing from FIT, which was a little odd. I contacted my chair and he said he was in the hospital, but did not tell me why. He also said that while he had been indisposed, Miss Lymon had "assumed programming responsibilities." When I asked about courses, he said, "Check with Miss Lymon."

And then I knew.

> Hi Lisa,
>
> Happy 2015 to you! _____ is on the mend, which is a great relief.
> Our schedule is all set for the semester; I wish you all the best with your teaching at NYU, and of course with your writing.
>
> Regards,

Miss Lymon

And because I had not acquired enough AOP hours to become a "permanent adjunct," as I am at NYU, there was nothing I could do. My chair could have stepped in and gone to bat for me, and didn't. This was unsurprising. He had to work with Miss Lymon every day, see her every day. Their offices were three doors away from each other. The lack of loyalty, however, was surprising, considering he had written the following on my last observation report in March 2014:

> Professor del Rosso is a gifted teacher, who elicits both interest and respect from her students. She is open and enthusiastic, and her classroom is one of the most dynamic I have ever observed. She challenges and encourages her students, and they respond with enthusiasm. This class was a pleasure to observe. We are fortunate to have Professor del Rosso as a member of our faculty.
>
> Alan Bennett English Chair,
> now Dean of English and Speech Dept.

Betrayal is never easy to accept. And that adage "The infighting in academia is so vicious because the stakes are so very low" does ring true. I was terribly hurt and more broke than ever, but there just wasn't time to wallow, and to be fair, I am not a wallower. I am more of a whisky drinker in situations such as these. My Scots friend Isobel, a frequent guest in my home, makes sure I am never out of Royal Lochnagar (The Glenlivet does in a pinch). She knows me well.

With NYU set to begin, classes to prepare for and students to teach, FIT, Miss Lymon, and sixty-eight dollars an hour were not worth wasting any more of my time or energy.

However, The Modern Love College Essay Contest was worth my time, and wouldn't it be swell and kind of sweet if one of my former FIT/CNF students got her piece published in *The New York Times*? A piece she had written in my class? Or, outside of my class but still under my tutelage?

4. Modern Love and Karma

"She (Ms. Lymon) got all up in your shit, didn't she?"
—A poet friend and teacher at Texas Tech with whom
I had dinner at Gennaro on 94th & Amsterdam. All
poets know each other, apparently.

ARLA KNUDSEN WAS ONE of my students in the Creative Non-Fiction class at FIT. She said she had never written anything before. She had only kept diaries but did like writing about herself and so decided, on a whim, to take my class.

Arla comes from Oklahoma City, Oklahoma. She has now graduated with her BA in Advertising and Marketing, but was twenty when she enrolled in CNF. Like many of the students who also took my class, she did not come in a natural writer. She had a lot to learn but worked very, very hard to improve.

Once the course ended (the term went from the end of August to mid-December 2014), Arla and five other students expressed their desire to continue with the writing, which thrilled me, and so they joined the long-running Scapegrace writers workshops I hold at my apartment. A revolving array of anywhere from three to ten students have met with me once every three weeks for the last seven years. The goal of the workshops is to complete and to publish (if possible). So many students leave work unfinished and then go onto the next piece that nothing is truly ever "done." They hate revision, but I tell them what I tell my students at NYU: every writer they loved as a child, every writer they love now, every writer that they will love in future have all revised countless times. And no writer does it alone.

Scapegrace was originally born because a few students came to me complaining about the high cost of writing workshops in the city (hundreds of non-refundable dollars) that they could not afford. One suggested I run my own workshop. I considered. I said yes, because though some of my students' parents may be wealthy, they are cash poor. But they want to learn, write and are eager to share their work with others. The work is on the whole excellent, and the atmosphere of the workshops is supportive yet constructive. It involves intense scrutiny and in-depth analysis of whatever the student wants to work on: essays, a memoir, a play, poetry, a novel.

I do love the intensity of the workshops, and the rewards are great in terms of seeing students thrive.

In February 2015, a college essay contest was announced for the Modern Love section of *The New York Times*. I have written for this section, and so sent the article and the prompt, written by the Modern Love editor Daniel Jones, to my students in my classes and in the workshop. It was to be about what external influences are affecting dating and love relationships now, what was going on with college students with respect to this now. I told my students that they should all write essays with a view to enter and I would help them with the revisions. This is how I motivated them:

"Don't let some asshole from Columbia win."

Columbia is the arch enemy of NYU in this town.

It worked.

Many of my students wrote essays and entered. But no student wanted it more, and no one worked harder, than Arla. We went through five or six drafts together, maybe more. I remember her in my sitting room, jumping up and down on my couch, clutching a sheaf of papers, saying, "I really, really, really, want to win this! In case you can't tell." I could. But wanting to win doesn't mean you will. I said,

"Submit and then forget it. Move on to something else entirely."

In the end, her Modern Love essay was unique, as is her background. I'm not going to explain it here, for one very good reason: you can read it yourself.

Arla placed second.

And who won? A Columbia student.

Arla's text: I have some crazy amazing news…I just got an email from Daniel Jones…I'm one of the top 5 finalists!!!!!!

That means Arla's essay was published in the *New York Times* May 2015, along with the four others. Not only that, but her piece was also chosen to be an animated short.

Me: I'm so proud of you, and so happy you are my student. You worked your ass off, and you deserve this. And so very pleased you took my CNF class!!

Arla: Me too. You have no idea. I would have never started writing if it weren't for you and your class!

Then I called her, yelling. Arla was laughing and yelling at the same time. All I can remember is saying, "Next time you call me with news like that" because a text is no match for the joy heard in Arla's voice.

Arla is now contemplating a very different future than the one she originally planned. She made a promise to herself that if she won, she would take the writing seriously and I'm glad. Arla should be writing, whether it's with me or with another teacher.

As Arla was still enrolled at FIT, she did want to inform them so they were not blindsided by the news:

(cc'd Miss Lymon)

Dear Dean ____,

As an FIT student who is two terms away from graduating and not affiliated with the English Department, I wanted to alert you to the fact that I placed as a finalist in the New York Times Modern Love Essay Contest, and my essay will be published in late May in the Styles Section of the NY Times. It is also being turned into an animated short, and I was interviewed on video as well, so you can also see my face in the NY Times, as well as my essay.

I am so thrilled, and I never would have written this essay, or written at all, really, had I not taken Professor Lisa del Rosso's Creative Non Fiction class last semester. Her mix of passion and tough love spoke to not just me, but everyone in our class.

I can't thank you enough for hiring Professor del Rosso. Her class was nothing short of life changing. I am considering options I have never considered, and none of this would have been possible without her.

I'm very proud to be able to represent FIT among the finalists from schools such as Columbia, Cornell and MIT. I hope this will be the first of many publications to come.

Best,
Arla Knudsen

Worth more than all the money in the world? You bet.

My Story - Part III

1. I Am First Generation/Second Generation/ Lucky

"Professor Del Rosso is the shit."
—*Student evaluation, Anonymous, NYU 2015*

NOT LONG AGO, in the context of a conversation about college, my ex-referred to me as "self-taught." Or, he said, "In geek-speak, a quasi-autodidact."

I came from a house with no culture and little tradition of education. In the parlor, a room which neither invited nor allowed play, there were bookshelves covered with knick-knacks, and in the center were a few books. Among them: *The Betsy* by Harold Robbins (dirty!), *Outrageous Acts and Everyday Rebellions* by Gloria Steinem (feminist!), *Death of a Salesman* by Arthur Miller (highbrow) and a couple by Sidney Sheldon (dirty! dirty!). I read all of them. If Freud were my analyst, he would have a field day with this divulgence. They were the only adult books in the house. Today, if you were to walk into my railroad apartment, you would find a small spare room where one could possibly raise children that instead is filled with hundreds of books. When James, my carpenter brother-in-law, lived in New York, I bribed him to build shelving in every apartment I moved into. The way to bookshelves was through a man's stomach, preferably with homemade Italian food.

I can trace back the reason I am anything today, have any education at all, to my mother's father: Achilles Nicoletti (once on these shores: Archie). I actually have just come into possession of his Italian passport. Italian, immigrated via Canada to the US in 1931 at the age of thirteen to live

with his aunt and cousins, when the US government decided Italians were of sub-par intelligence, closed off Ellis Island and told them they were no longer welcome.

The US government underestimated my grandfather.

I have no idea how he learned to read, write and speak English with no schooling, but he did. My grandmother, Maria Philomena (Phyllis for short; my grandfather nicknamed her Phil), was illiterate. But my grandfather read books and newspapers from cover to cover. He first apprenticed at an auto shop and learned everything there was to know about cars. Then he ran a construction crew and rolled tar on the highways of New England for thirty-three years. He married, bought land, designed and built a house—he was good at building—in a lower working-class, suburban neighborhood. He cultivated a terrific garden, and grew the best tomatoes, swiss chard, zucchini, mint. We even had a peach tree that yielded fruit in the backyard, I think because he willed it so. And, in true immigrant fashion, school was very important to him. His two daughters had to do better than he did because that was why he came to America. He'd make sure of it.

My grandfather was relentless and a taskmaster. He demanded straight A's from my mother and the day she got a B, the only B of her entire schooling, grades 1-12, she sat down and cried, knowing she would be punished (I initially did not believe this "straight A, one B" braggadocio until I looked up my mother's report cards. All A's. And that one B). My grandfather did not believe in corporal punishment, so she was grounded for two weeks. My mother had a very circumscribed social life which consisted of two chaperoned dates before she married my father, at twenty-one, as she did not go to college. So I am not really sure how much of a punishment "grounding" was.

I know that my mother began reading to me before I enrolled in school, because she told me. Consequently,

I began reading early and loved it. Literature came from school, or the library. *The Library*! This is the gift my mother gave me: reading + library card. She took me to the Tufts Library after school, on weekends and allowed me to take out as many books as I liked.

The Tufts Library was situated in the town square, in between a drustore and a photography studio. From the vantage point of adulthood, it was small, office-like. Perhaps shabby. But not at the time. At the time, it was a room full of thousands of windows waiting to be thrown open.

I entered every summer reading contest there was, thrilled at the growing number of silver and gold stars decorating my winning lists. The library was like a candy store to me, and I stuffed my head full of words. The first book I ever touched was Maya Angelou's *I Know Why the Caged Bird Sings*.

But as for culture, we never went to a museum (the MFA–Museum of Fine Arts in Boston, for example) or went into Boston, because my mother didn't like to drive into the city, nor did we take the trains. I never saw a professional opera or a symphony orchestra until I moved to London when I was eighteen. I did not hear classical music until I began singing it. Where the singing comes from, I have no idea.

My mother demanded of me the way her father had, but she was not as strict. She wanted me to have outside interests in addition to school, so we would negotiate: I could join the theater company as long as I maintained honor roll. I could take singing lessons as long as my grades did not drop, etc… When I got my report cards, I would show them to two people: my mother, and my grandfather.

I think if my biological father had remained in the house, then today I would be either a nun or a porn star. The former would have pleased him, for my chastity secured in perpetuity, the latter obviously would have been my rebellion.

My father was also an Italian immigrant, arriving from Italy via Ellis Island at approximately fifteen years of age. To my knowledge, he was too old to go through the American education system, so his reading and writing were rudimentary. He learned a trade and became a butcher. Like my grandfather, he could fix anything that broke, and was good at building. When he and my mother wed, my grandfather bought the plot of land next door. Together, he and my father built the house I grew up in, so my grandparents were right next to us. But being handy is where their similarities ended.

My father did not care about education, for one reason only: I was a girl. What possible use could it be when all that was expected of me was to marry and procreate?

Before my father immigrated to the United States, before he took that long voyage from Italy at fifteen with his sister and his mother on a ship called the Volcania into New York Harbor, he was a shepherd in the hills of Anversa degli Abruzzi.

Recently, I was in class and a student asked about my parentage. I told them. And it just struck me as… astonishing that my father was a shepherd in the mountains of Italy and I was sitting at the front of a classroom as a professor at NYU. That is a journey any immigrant father would be proud of. But I have achieved despite my father.

Due to his parentage and upbringing, I can forgive my father his patriarchy, his sexism, his cluelessness in a household full of women.

What I cannot forgive is his cruelty toward me, my sisters, my mother.

When I was ten, my parents divorced. When I was eighteen, about to leave for London, my father took me and my younger sisters out on his prescribed Sunday to the IHOP, a place that I now cannot pass without breaking into hives,

much less go in, and said the following to me: "If I were still in the house, you never would have gone to college, never would have left the state, never mind the country; you would have done a nice secretarial course, gotten married and had grandchildren."

I can still picture his face and the way he said it. Once I became an adult and no longer a child, one who could make my own decisions, he became adept at combining laughing at me and talking to me into one, with the desired result being humiliation.

So I said, carefully, because I was long past anger with him and no longer cared what he thought, as he had barely been in my life since the divorce, "Well, then I guess it's a good thing you're no longer in the house."

His face changed, and he sat back in the booth. "If we weren't at the IHOP, I'd rap you in the mouth."

Unlike my grandfather, my father believed in corporal punishment.

One of the reasons for the divorce was the clash over how to discipline the children, and my mother could not stand by while my father "hit little girls." His house, for it was his house until he left it, was a house of discipline and fear: I learned to be obedient, respectful, and finish all the food on my plate before I was allowed to leave the table. I learned to follow all of his rules to the letter. The one time I forgot to flush the toilet, at my grandmother's house one Thanksgiving, I remember looking up at him while he was yelling into my five-year-old face, with my Nana on one side of him, my mother on the other, begging him not to hit me because it would ruin the day. He did not listen.

My culture was almost entirely about family, food, loyalty, devotion, steeped in Italian-ese and in the end, totally claustrophobic. So it is not a surprise the title of Angelou's

book called to me.

When my friends say, "You are who you are because you went to London" part of what they mean is London took me and molded me in a similar way that Professor Henry Higgins does when he gets his hands on Eliza Doolittle. It was transformative.

Hearing that, what Walt said was, "You went to London because you are who you are." That, to me, was a revelation.

Incidentally, the only person who was happy for me on the day I left for London, the only person who was smiling, not crying, was my grandfather. I hugged him, and he said, "You do it now, while you're young. You do it now. Don't listen to anyone else." I took his advice.

I am the first in my family to get a degree, and also, an advanced degree. I did not come from poverty, but we didn't have much until my late teens, when my mother got a really good job. It didn't cross my mind why we didn't take vacations or why I didn't have name-brand clothes or sneakers because it's not like I knew anyone else in the neighborhood who took vacations or had any of those things, either. The clothes I eventually had to ask my mother to change because they became a magnet for bullies. Though I loved my blue Desert boots and white turtlenecks and loved shopping with my mother at the junky Building #19, I looked too different from everyone else, too weird, an anathema when one is between ten and thirteen and tween-girls are at their most vicious.

When it came time for college, what my mother could afford was two years for each of her three daughters. Because of scholarships, a huge grant and my audition, my first year at the Hart School of Music, Hartford University, in Connecticut, was free. As for LAMDA, we took out a parent-student loan. That's paid. I paid for the BA at Empire State myself and the MFA from Fairleigh Dickinson University is the only one I am still paying off. Though that debt is

troublesome, I have zero regrets about any of my schooling.

Any success I have had, I trace back to Achilles, and his daughter, my mother. My grandfather was a gruff man, devoid of sentimentality, so whenever I tried to thank him for anything, he'd give me the brush off. He didn't need the thanks. He enjoyed seeing me thrive. My mother I thank often, which she accepts. I try to imagine what or where or who I would be without them, and those thoughts make me glad I am not a fiction writer.

2. La Famiglia e la Madre

A FEW YEARS AGO, after hearing me describe how happy I was in the classroom, my mother said, "You should have begun teaching when you were twenty-two."

Oh, this is so typical of my mother! But what makes me happy now would not have made me happy at twenty-two.

I replied, "No, that is completely wrong. I would have had nothing to say to my students, nothing to teach them, nothing to bring to the table, no life experience, no stories, nothing."

And I believe that with my whole heart. I began teaching in my thirties, and didn't get my MFA until I was forty. By that time, I had plenty of experience, knowledge, and *cojones** to bring to the table.

So if my life has prepared me to teach, then the "training," as it were, began with the Samaritans.

---

cojones: So much better in Spanish than the English equivalent. Throughout my childhood, I remember my mother saying, when she was annoyed with one thing or another, "'Balls!' said the Queen, 'If I had two, I'd be King!'" So I have always been fond of this word, in all of its incarnations.

3. Samaritan

"Professor del Rosso was my hero for the semester."
—*Student Evaluation, Anonymous, NYU 2012*

DURING THE YEARS I lived in London, I volunteered for the Samaritans, a suicide counseling and hotline center. I volunteered for approximately two years. The shifts lasted three hours, once or twice a week depending on schedules, and an overnight shift once every two weeks. It remains one of the things in my life that I am most proud of doing. But not at the beginning. At the beginning, I was dragged to a volunteer workshop by my friend and lover, Paul, who was also a Samaritan. He told me I was spoiled and self-involved, had had a charmed life thus far (Paul was British and could say the word "thus" without me bursting into laughter) and that it was time to give back something of myself. He told me that I possessed the qualities it took to become a Samaritan: a good listener, and non-judgmental. At the time—I was in my early twenties—I thought, So what? Big deal. Everyone has those qualities.

Wrong.

There was an extensive screening process lasting six weeks. About one hundred people applied, and seven were eventually chosen. I went through one initial interview, two psychological interviews, and countless roleplays of mock situations similar to what I would be dealing with. All of this took place in front of the group of would-be volunteers.

Those of us chosen were told by the leaders we could guide or suggest, but never advise. The roleplays were certainly helpful, if only to illustrate how different people reacted in disparate situations. But nothing compared to

the reality of what went on in those counseling rooms and on those phones.

Ninety percent of the calls I took were not the calls of suicidal people. Mostly, people were lonely, or they had a problem and needed to talk to someone. People phoned the Samaritans because they knew their call would be taken, no matter what (except in the case of telephone masturbators—the directive was to issue a warning and then hang up.) My very first call was from a man who phoned from prison once a week. He had raped and murdered an eight-year-old girl in his tiny Welsh village, and everyone had disowned him: friends, family, everyone. I spoke with a widow who had lost her husband and after a year her friends were urging her to "move on" with her life, but she was not ready. I spoke with an army wife who said she had a terrific husband but in her isolation, she had fallen in love with a woman on the base. I spoke with a "flasher" who knew he should stop flashing the female cashiers at the local petrol stations but had not yet done so.

Samaritan volunteers were not allowed to give their opinions. That was not part of the job requirement. Mostly, I listened. I comforted people who needed comforting. I became more tolerant, and given the unsavory nature of some of the calls, remained firmly in neutral, feelings in check. I learned how to be patient (not one of my virtues) because one phone call could quite possibly take up an entire shift. I began to look at my life differently, and the opportunities I had been given.

These changes took place over the course of the two years. They were not immediate. There were many disturbing phone calls and face-to-face sessions. In fact, there were so many stories that I wrote a play based on my experiences at the Samaritans. Then there was one phone call that caused a shift in me. I listened to somebody take her own life. As a Samaritan, you are not allowed to end the phone

call. If the girl you are speaking with tells you she has taken an overdose, then you do your level best to coax her address out of her. If you obtain it, you can call an ambulance that speeds over containing medics and a few Samaritans tagging along. You are allowed to intervene in that instance. But you cannot trace the call, as the Samaritans are an anonymous organization. The girl I was speaking with told me her name, the colors of all the pills she had taken, but would not tell me her address. So we kept talking but gradually her voice began to slur and her speech became unintelligible. She asked me to stay with her and at one point, asked me to hold her. I was on with her until there was only labored breathing then two thuds then nothing. It sounded as if she had dropped the phone then hit the floor. For a time, I was incredibly angry with myself because I thought I had failed. I couldn't save her. Then later, during an alcohol-fueled evening, Paul told me that I had done what the caller had wanted me to do. I had stayed with her. I could not save her because she did not want to be saved. I have applied that knowledge more times in my life than I care to remember.

The Samaritans taught me tolerance and patience. Compassion. Before I got to them, I was an angry young woman, and I probably would have stayed that way, because my past was not as "charmed" as I had led Paul to believe. Before I began volunteering, I always knew that everyone had a story. But I learned that most people want to be heard, if they are only given the chance to talk to someone who is willing to listen.

When the student is ready, the teacher will appear.
—Buddhist proverb

4. Empire State

*"I love how much you love New York. I'm right there
beside you."*
—*Student Evaluation, Anonymous, NYU 2011*

IN 2002, WHEN I BEGAN at Empire State College, I was
assigned an advisor: Professor Mary Folliet. Before I met
her, I was confronted with a list of courses to choose from.

If you were not in New York City during 9/11, then it
is hard to describe the feelings that came afterwards, with
people fleeing for other states, with people badmouthing
my town, with concerned friends and relatives calling to
say, "Are you sure you want to keep living in that city?" They
couldn't even bring themselves to say its name.

I was just angry.

So when I looked at the list of courses, the only one that
jumped out and screamed at me was "Writing New York."
It was taught by Mary Folliet.

My intro to Mary was the following: students were
seated in a windowless classroom with "bad air." She wafted
in with a spritzer, sprayed it above our heads and directed
us to wave our arms in the air to disperse. She cared about
air quality long before those words hit *The New York Times*.
And the air certainly did smell better.

Her course was a revelation. There were roughly fourteen students, and we all sat around a long table. Opinions
and discussion were encouraged. She introduced me to Phil-
lip Lopate, the great essayist, and had copious, handwritten
notes on every single piece she assigned. She had the history
and the "tasty" tidbits on the writers. Her style was simulta-

neously relaxed and sharp. I attribute this to her long-time love of jazz. She could improvise with the best of them. And she was very, very tough on her students, necessarily so.

Unusually, for the two years I was at Empire State College, I managed to take all of my courses with Mary Folliet. Either no one one noticed this or no one cared, but I was delighted. So I got: Writing the Novel, Writing the Short Story, Writing the Essay, Writing the Novella. I took an independent study with her and wound up writing my first play, "Clare's Room" because she gave me the freedom to do so. "Clare's Room" went off-Broadway. Mary was there opening night, with bells on.

My classroom persona is built on the classes I took with her. I teach "Writing New York" because of her. I love Joan Didion, and have seen her read at 192 Books as well as Michael Ondaajte, and John Waters, and others accompanied by and because of Mary Folliet. We are both tremendous Vanessa Redgrave fans, not least because she has a real face; fans of the American Songbook; and huge theater goers. A diehard Francophile, she lived in Paris for many years and is more cultured than I will ever be. She brings her experience to the table of teaching, and that is also something I do. I had two years to observe her in action. She was teaching me in ways neither of us knew, and that I was unaware of until I began teaching myself.

After being at Empire State College for twenty-five years, first as an adjunct and then as a full-time professor, Mary was unceremoniously ousted at the age of fifty-eight. A new dean had come in and wanted the college to be more technological and business-oriented, and she seemed to be cleaning house. And a twenty-two year-old with not much experience can command a much lower salary than a full-time professor of fifty-eight.

I can't explain the entire story of how she was removed properly (or objectively), or the devastation she went

through, because it is not my story, it is hers. But if you ask Mary, I hope she will tell you.

She had a big leaving party at Empire State, in a room the size of an auditorium, because there were so many people wanting to cram themselves in. Jazz musicians played. And Mary closed the evening with this quote, from *The Prime of Miss Jean Brody*: "I am a teacher first, last and always."

I stood at the back—because only Mary would have a sold-out house and standing room only at her leaving party—choked up, and thought, That is exactly right. That is exactly who she is.

Mary never taught again in an academic capacity, though she does teach privately. This is a sin and a shame. All those students out there could have been staggered by her brilliance and the learning environment in her classroom. But they lost out.

She writes poetry. She edits others' books. She is the editor of an online publication I write theater reviews for. We usually go over the review once or twice before it's posted, and I continue to learn, and think, Why didn't I catch that? Damn, that sentence is so much better now. And I put down the cell and think, Yes. Mary is a teacher first, last and always.

5. Libidinous

MARY ALSO INADVERTENTLY INTRODUCED me to the man who was instrumental in terms of my introduction to NYU. I will win no morality awards here, but if I leave out this one particular story, my trajectory will not make sense. In any event, I can't blame Mary. I blame ... pheromones.

6. Out of Berkeley College and into NYU

*"PdR will definitely push you out of your comfort zone
- but in an awesome way!"*
—*Student Evaluation, Anonymous, NYU 2010*

"Grading was a little harsh."
—*Student Evaluation, Anonymous, NYU 2009*

So, HOW DID I get into NYU?

It was in the same sort of fashion as described in "The Accidental Professor," albeit the circumstances wildly differed.

In 2008, I was having a long-term affair with a bartender-web designer (while I was still married) at an Italian restaurant in Greenwich Village who had become friends with the very distinguished, very well-spoken, very British T.E., my not-yet-then chairperson She lives around the corner and loves their pizza. For every story she told him about her students at NYU, he told her one of mine (that I had told him about the students at Berkeley.)

After six months of swapping stories, T.E. said, "Do you think Lisa would like to teach at NYU?"

He said, "I don't know, you could ask her."

She handed him her card and said, "Tell her to call me."

He gave me the card. I jumped up and down, screamed, and then calmly called. She interviewed me at the bar (brunch, of course). In person, T.E. is tall, handsome, formidable. She is Cambridge-educated, absolutely first-rate mind, PhD, an intellectual, brilliant. She was also a wee bit intimidating, and I was a wreck. She asked about my

teaching style, literature, classes, authors I liked. I listed a few names as I felt my mind going into a white, blank slate of panic: Carver, Baldwin, Didion, the book *Random Family* by Adrian Nicole LeBlanc and explained my rationale. T.E. nodded. Then I said, "I love Junot Diaz, but his language is filthy." T.E. said, "Ohhh, I love filthy language," and I immediately thought, I could definitely teach for this woman.

T.E. was, in Anne Sexton's words, My Kind. She said she was letting two other professors go "…because I did not hand-pick them, and things don't go well when I do not hand-pick my people." She stared straight ahead while she said this, and looked as if she'd like to murder someone, and the thought of murdering that someone would give her great pleasure. At least, temporarily.

A couple of weeks later, I had another brief interview with the associate dean, and was hired as an adjunct professor at NYU.

7. Sex, School, and Sensibility

"Teacher made unwanted sexual advances. Just kidding!"
—*Student evaluation, Anonymous, NYU 2010*

IT WOULD BE DISINGENUOUS to write a book about being a professor and dealing with students without mentioning the topic of sex in the classroom. The following segue may not seem in keeping with that subject, but trust me, I will get to the sex.

One of my great pleasures is going to the theater. TDF, Theater Development Fund, is a fantastic organization that offers discount theater tickets to teachers via a small subscription fee. I love this city for its theater and I love TDF for making it possible for me to overdose on as much theater as I can take.

Because my classes finish after 6 PM, I often go right from class to the theater, and usually meet Mary beforehand. Once, when I had dashed from class and we were set to see a play at The Signature Theater, she stopped, took a moment to appraise my outfit and said, "You put your sexuality out there. You don't change it for the classroom, and I admire that."

That's the thing about smart friends. They force you to consider that which you had never considered.

Having left the threadbare Elie Tahari suit behind, I gravitated to and then fell in love with dresses, mainly because I am lazy and matching skirts or pants and tops is too time-consuming. Specifically, I love Diane Von Furstenberg wrap dresses. That iconic, patterned, medium-weight silk dress from the 1970's perfectly suits my body, is com-

fortable, practical and stylish, all at once. DVF has been lauded considerably recently, but I really need to continue extolling that dress's virtues.

I was wearing a DVF dress when Mary made her astute observation.

There were so many things to worry about and consider once I became a professor, but changing my style was not one of them. Not that I had the money for an entire new wardrobe (apart from that splurge on the only pantsuit I ever paid retail for) or knew what a professor was supposed to look or dress like. I just went with my own taste. I never liked "skirt suits," never considered wearing jeans or hoodies to class because that kind of garb is what my students wear to class. A few times at Berkeley I was mistaken for a student, and was not at all flattered. My theory has always been to dress better than my audience, as it were. I am certainly not the first, of course. Among many others, Steve Martin said this (and I paraphrase), hence his penchant for natty suits onstage early in his career. So that immediately rules out the very popular and inexpensive H &M, Forever 21, etc... because God forbid you show up in the same dress that is on a freshman in the front row of your class. I don't like sloppy, "relaxed fit," grungy, too-tight, too-short, and I hate the color brown. I like high-end clothes that fit well but I don't like what they cost.

So I shop on eBay. Almost exclusively. Also thrift shops, but there is a time factor involved. Not so eBay.

This is considered deeply unfashionable, said the professor who taught at the FASHION INSTITUTE OF TECHNOLOGY.

There is no handbook on how to dress like a professor. It's up to the person in question or if the institution in question has such rules.

New clothes in this town are impossibly expensive.

The cut-price stores Filene's Basement, Daffy's, and Loeh-mannn's are now gone. Granted, by the time they closed, people complained they weren't nearly as good as when they began, but I could still find something in at least one of them. In their place, TJ Maxx proliferated, and Marshall's, which TJ Maxx owns. There are a lot of cheap polyester garments taking up space, particularly in the dress world, because cotton is expensive to manufacture. But I refuse to buy polyester. Makes me sweat. Is sometimes slimy to the touch. And it exists because it is cheap to produce, not because the makers want you to look good in their clothes or be comfortable in them. TJ Maxx does have a "Runway Section" which is too expensive unless there is a sale, by which time all is picked over, and the selection is miniscule. TJ Maxx does not truck in the happy medium. A word about Macy's: because it feels like every person in the Tri-state area shops at Macy's, I cannot go in there. It's a hive on steroids: crammed with people at every hour, and there never seems to be an off-peak time, rather the way the subway is in the New York City of 2017. Bloomingdales is the upscale Macy's of the East Side. For a Westsider, it's also too far. Online, as many of today's brick-and-mortar shops are finding to their detriment, is just so much easier. There is far more variety. And, it is far less expensive.

So despite that deeply unfashionable eBay reputation, if you choose a couple of designers that suit you, know your size and fit, then you can have a fantastic wardrobe at a fraction of the cost of retail, simply because women get bored with their clothes. Or never wear what they've bought so it hangs in their closets until they watch or read something on "de-cluttering." Or change sizes. Or, Susan loved that beautiful red jacket until her partner broke up with her when Susan was wearing her red jacket, and now every time Susan looks at the red jacket, it's a constant reminder of pain and the red color just makes her want to commit murder so

Susan decides it's time for the jacket to go. For these reasons and more, woman decide to sell new or nearly new clothes. On eBay. Thousands of women, with exceptionally good taste. It does help to have a tailor, and if you add on tailoring costs, $10.00 to hem a $39.00 pair of Theory black flared or tapered or skinny trousers, it is still saving a ton of money. And no one will ever know where you got that Marc Jacobs bag, or Jil Sander coat, or Theory dress, or Burberry trench, unless you put that information in a book.

Which brings me back to the DVF wrap dress. That dress reveals just enough to not be boring. I don't like boring clothes. And eBay is a great place to get authentic, cut-price DVF dresses. Many of them, as a wardrobe staple.

I dress the way I dress because my clothes make me happy. I had always assumed that my students did not notice what I wore, because why would they? Which is why Mary's comment made me reconsider. So if my clothes are noticed, that's fine. If not, that's also fine. If they are noticed by my students in the way that Mary meant when she appraised my outfit that night at The Signature, then I stand by an adage of Ruth's: "What you think of me is none of my business." In other words, I prefer not to know.

…except students will tell you, with great delight, that you have a chili pepper on rateyourprofessor.com.

8. You Are Not Your Pepper

*"Professor Del Rosso's approach to every student and
every class is spot on. I have never had a teacher who
actively ensured everyone's participation and not only
got it but also managed to encourage everyone to WANT
to participate. And general daily discussion on anything
from recent news articles to (usually) controversial short
stories to the challenging but endlessly interesting essay
topics."*
—*Student Evaluation, Anonymous, NYU 2013*

NYU CHAIR T.E., BECAUSE SHE IS MADE of the strong stuff,
goes on rateyourprofessor.com , reads what students write
about her and then laughs about it. She says to me, "Never
go on there."

I say, "But you do!"

She says, "Yes, but I find them hilarious."

So I never have. Ever. Because willful ignorance is bliss.

One thing that never changes on my syllabus is the
last day of class: whatever date the last day of class falls
on, there is a MASSIVE FOOD PARTY. Every student
brings something, or makes something. Some students have
even persuaded their mothers to cook for the occasion. I
make gluten-free brownies or ricotta pie (my grandmother's
recipe). Though gluten-free, both are delicious, my former
students will tell you. In the past, students have brought a
vast array of goods: homemade rice and beans, homemade
empanadas, cheesecake, pizza, deep-fried Oreos ("You have
to try these professor!"), bacon-chocolate-chocolates, Cray-
ola-colored macaroons, a box of coffee (there must always be
coffee), macaroni and cheese, homemade guacamole (gone

in ten minutes) and tortilla chips, Atomic chicken wings, and one student, who was so obsessed with hot chocolate, she brought her own hot chocolate machine, plugged it in at the back of the room and made hot chocolate, cup by cup, for every person.

So on the last day of class, after students pass in their final drafts, they eat. And while they eat, they talk. And they tell me why they took my class. And they tell me that I terrified them on the first day of class but they decided to stay anyway. And then the subject of rateyourprofessor.com comes up.

There is no escaping the online, anonymous rating system, pervasive in so much of the online world today, not only via Yelp for restaurants, but virtually in every profession. I used to hate rateyourprofessor, but now consider it the law of averages: if enough students who liked your class go on to write you a good "review" with no incentive other than that, fine. Your rating goes up. And this is the go-to site for students when selecting their professors.

On the last day of class, my students insist on reading the (cherry-picked) comments aloud because they think they are funny. I would, too, if they were not about me.

A male student said, "Listen to this one! All the student wrote was 'HOT' in caps."

A female student said, "Oh yeah, you have a chili pepper next to your name!"

I said, "Nothing to do with the teaching, people, laugh all you like."

When the series "Weeds" was on, a male student said in front of the entire class, "Yeah, I was watching "Weeds" last night, and you remind me of her - Mary Louise Parker."

That time, I blushed.

A former male student said to me, "Nico told me to take your class because you were hot. So I took your class."

Now, that's a silly reason to take my class, as I am neither an easy teacher nor an easy grader. But this is part of the online deal: students respond however they respond then catalog it anonymously on rateyourprofessor and all of it is beyond my control. When my chili pepper is removed, I am sure a student will inform me.

In 2015, there was an article in *The New York Times* about Harvard University: they have now banned sexual relations between students and professors. Harvard stated its previously policy on dating between college professors and students was "strongly discouraged" in the past and now they were going to make it "against the rules."

We talked about this in my classes. The students' reactions ranged from "Ewww," to "It depends, because you don't choose who you fall in love with," to "All one person has to do is say it's rape and a career is over, especially if it's a grad student teaching," to "There is always a power imbalance," to "Except that Ethics teacher in Gallatin—his chili pepper is on fire."

Then they asked, what do you think, professor? And I told them I was surprised it wasn't against the rules to begin with. I said, "If I dated my students, you would look at me differently when you walked into my class. And then what would happen if I stopped seeing one student and dated another? Then there's gossip and details about the relationship going around. So no, I wouldn't do it. It would affect my reputation. It would affect the teaching. And besides, you all look so…young."

They really do and they really are. I would never, ever, ever date one of my students.

Caveat: unless a former student who is now twenty-five years old decides to contact me.

9. Sex, A Male Student, and Little Sense

"Professor del Rosso is the cat's pajamas."
—*Student Evaluation, Anonymous, NYU 2013*

THIS IS THE MOST HILARIOUS email I have ever received:

Mar 4, 2015 1:28 AM

Professor,
I was thinking about my past studenthood
today and found myself going back to the
creative writing class I had with you fall of '08.
I just wanted to randomly tell you how much
I enjoyed your class. Also, you are by far the
hottest teacher I have ever had, and would be
delighted to get a drink with you sometime.
You certainly do not remember me but am
shooting it out there anyways :) Btw i'm a tall
white guy. I can send a pic as well.

Logan

I had no recollection of this student whatsoever.

Logan, twenty-five, is in grad school up at Columbia. He has a year to go before he becomes a fully-fledged social worker. During one of the conversations when he was trying to jog my memory, he said, "I'm not like you. I'm not really passionate about what I do. But I think if you're going to do a job, you should be doing something to better the world."

That's nice, I thought.

He did send a photo of himself, in a bar, surrounded by his fellow grads. He was indeed tall, with a goatee, in a pink shirt, smiling. He himself looked a bit pink, despite goatee, and somewhat innocent.

In the next two photos he sent, he was not wearing a pink shirt. In the first, he was stripped to the waist in what appeared to be a bathroom with many toothbrushes. In the second, he was also stripped and the photo was cropped past his hipbone, past his pubic hair, just shy of his _____.

I did not notice toothbrushes or anything else.

"My chest is actually pretty defined," he explained, helpfully.

I begged him not to send me a dick pic. He didn't.

About that class discussion on professors not dating their students, the one that I was so vehement about. An ex-student doesn't count. An ex-student who is twenty-five and hotter than hot definitely does not count.

I said yes to a drink.

There was a three-week delay to our drink, because my spring break, which took me to Florida, interfered and I was swamped with work beforehand. So we talked on the phone. He was remarkably candid about himself and his experiences with women: candid, and blunt.

Logan had taken to answering ads on Craigslist. Sex ads. Sex ads of the unusual kind. One in particular he described was going to an address in Queens where he was told the door would be open. He went to the address, opened the door and went into a completely dark room. Once he closed the door, a woman whose face he could not see and who did not speak pushed him up against a wall, took down his pants, performed oral sex on him until he ejaculated, and when she considered him to be finished, zipped up his pants and pushed him out the door.

Because I was too busy visualizing, I did not respond

audibly.

"You still there?" he said.

"Yes. Sorry. I was just thinking if I had indulged in risky behavior when I was in my twenties ... and ... yes. But not like that."

"I was so turned on I went back and did it again."

"You went back?"

Logan said it was the thrill of not knowing that was so unbelievably exciting.

I said, "Sure, there's also the thrill that you could be murdered or never seen and never heard from again or gang-raped, right? Because that is high-risk behavior."

"Yeah, I know. I got out of control for a while but think I've calmed it down."

So perhaps he was a sex maniac. Or just liked walking on the wild side. Or both.

Changing tack, Logan asked, "So when was the last time you had sex?"

I said, "Um...January." It was December. I lied.

He replied, with a note of surprise, "January? But it's March!"

I said, "Um...right...How 'bout you?"

Logan said, "Two weeks ago."

I asked, "And? No seconds?"

Logan said, "She had a hairy ass."

I said, "That is easily taken care of."

Logan paused. "You're right. In certain positions she looked kind of ...mannish"

It could have been x-rated Seinfeld dialogue, really.

An hour later, after we got off the topic of sex, I wanted to know what kind of social work he was doing. It was the research end, apparently, like making sure prisons are taking

care of young offenders. For that he would actually go to the prison, but mostly it was not hands-on, he wasn't cut out for the hands-on kind. He asked me questions, about teaching and other students. "Have any other male students hit on you?"

"None that I was interested in," I said.

He wanted stories. So I told him stories. I asked about those photos he sent. I said, "Don't you worry about your future social worker self found naked online?"

He said, "Do you have any idea how many of those photos are out there? Millions."

Not worried. No big deal. Later, I asked Sam (who is fifty-eight, with college-age children) about the stripped to the waist photos. He said, "That's how they do things now!"

Logan did ask me for an "ass photo" while I was in Florida. As in, reciprocal pics. I said no, no, and never. I liked my job, I said. But I did send him a bikini photo. In the world right now, this would be rated G, below that of a Disney animated feature.

When we finally met, he turned up at my place in a suit. He had come from an interview for an internship. We actually went to a play: "Hand to God" a filthy, funny play that mines the nature of good and evil in us all. Afterwards, we went for a drink. Because it was pissing rain and neither of us was appropriately attired for the weather, we found ourselves at "Five Napkin Burger" which later Logan confessed he confused with "Five Guys" because he didn't expect the price of beer to be so high. I can't have gluten so therefore can't have beer, and didn't care. It was only one beer.

Logan ordered chicken and waffles, which he had never had before. He asked for everything separately. The waffle was terrible, he said. I suggested he eat it all together, as that really is how the dish is meant to be consumed. He did not. He ordered a second beer. He said, "You have no recollection of me whatsoever, do you?"

I laughed. "No, I don't."

Fortunately, he had a sense of humor.

We left in order to find "cheaper beer" and wound up someplace on 9th Ave in the 50's. Logan consumed a lot of beer, I think four or five pints. Then a whiskey. I had two drinks, and a whiskey. In between the drinks, there was kissing (I should add that I wanted to kiss him, sober or not), and I was thinking that this put me in the realm of *The Graduate*'s Mrs. Robinson, albeit without the "Mrs." or the children. The kissing was not unpleasant.

Logan suggested we go "uptown" to where I live.

About that apartment I share with my ex-husband: he is my roommate and actually very easy to live with, not only because he is an easy-going person, but also because we work completely opposite schedules. We have had a platonic status for eight years, since divorcing. He would not have been home at the time, had I chosen to bring Logan back with me. And Logan knew all this because he Googled my name and found that piece I wrote for the Modern Love section in *The New York Times* detailing my situation, which is how he found out I was divorced, which is why he contacted me.

Because "That's how they do things now."

But, in addition to the fact that it was the first time I had really met him (the classroom does not count) he drank a lot, more than I was comfortable with. Splitting a bottle of wine? Sexy. Five pints of beer and then a whiskey? Not sexy. Not to me. I never really did drunk sex, and I didn't want to begin now. Too much risk of being vomited on, too much risk of bad sex. How could the sex possibly be any good? Or be remembered, by either party?

So I went home alone, and Logan, who didn't look entirely happy, went back to Bushwick.

When I woke up the next morning, all I could taste and

smell was whiskey, and the story *Boys* by Rick Moody was going around in my head. That was about right, I thought.

Logan and I did not "hang out" again. I had thought we might become friends, but I don't believe he was interested in friendship.

I still have the photos.

Who is Teaching Whom? - Part IV

1. Methods of Teaching (Part I)

"If there is a way to be platonically in love with someone's personality, that's how I feel about Prof. del Rosso. I absolutely loved her class and her as a person. By far the favorite instructor I've ever encountered. Most certainly one of a kind."
—Student Evaluation, Anonymous, NYU 2010

"Class would be more effective if the room we were in had windows."
—Student Evaluation, Anonymous, NYU 2010

WE LIVE IN A 1ST PERSON POV world: Facebook, Snapchat, Instagram, Twitter. Memoir, memoir, memoir. Blogs. I, I, I. The essay is a perfect genre to be teaching. So it surprises me that students come into my class saying that they "weren't allowed" to have opinions in high school, that using "I" was forbidden in their papers.

They learn to find and express their opinions in my class. If they don't, how on earth will they get by in the world? Are we educating sheep? If and when my students do research, they have to have an opinion on that research, or it's not going in the paper. For example, I don't want an entire paper on the history and statistics of the homeless in New York City. I want students' thoughts on the homeless when they encounter them every day. What they think, feel. If they choose to see them, ignore them, interact. If they give money, or food, or nothing, and why. Their perceptions of the homeless, before and after they came to NYC. I would prefer the paper be divided into 70% of their own experience, 30% research. Otherwise, they are copying and pasting

and rearranging what they have read online, or paraphrasing. They are bored, I am bored, and all the papers read the same. Plus, it is too tempting for them to become little plagiarizers. So the essays segue into literary journalism. The paper still has to have a first-person point of view. I try to make the topics interesting, something everyone will have an opinion on. Like porn.

In 2005, I had a student at Berkeley College: Shajyre. I knew some of his background. His parents were out of the picture and he was being raised by his grandmother. The class he was in comprised thirty-three students, and they were a little difficult to control. I think that was also the class I had a felon, a stripper, a munitions specialist, and a very rich, wired, young, white man, prone to sudden outbursts. As for Shajyre, he used to put his baseball-hatted head down on his desk and attempt to sleep through my class. When that happened, I would stop whatever it was we were doing, walk over to his desk, tap on his baseball hat until he raised his head and say, "Shajyre, honey, you can't sleep through my class. If you don't want to come here, don't come; but you cannot sleep through my class." He'd groan, raise his head, slouch back in his seat.

This went on for a while.

Then one day, after the tapping commenced, he raised his head and said, "Miss, why do we have to read this boring old book? With stories by old dead white men?"

I thought about it. I didn't care for the book, which had been assigned to me and the class, either.

I said, "You don't. I'll find something else."

I got a book recommendation from a funny source, literally: David Sedaris. I went to a reading at the Union Square Barnes & Noble for his memoir/essay collection *Dress Your Family in Corduroy and Denim*" and before he began, he said

he didn't normally recommend other people's books, but his friend wrote this one, and Sedaris said it was brilliant, like watching a long, slow, train wreck. It was called *Random Family* by Adrian Nicole Leblanc. I became obsessed with this book, and he was right. It was brilliant. Harrowing. An in-depth biography of a two families in one section of the Bronx. It took LeBlanc ten years to write.

That's the book I brought to my students at Berkeley.

The first day, I copied chapters for them. I made up my own lesson plan, discussion questions, tests. The second day of teaching, most of the students had bought *Random Family* themselves. That's when I knew I had them.

They had opinions on everything in the book: drugs, sex, raising children, sexual abuse, violence, being a mother, being a father, is the main character a slut, is she a victim of circumstance… The discussions, which sometimes broke down along gender lines, were lively, loud, funny, sometimes angry.

Many students came to me after class and said they knew this area of the Bronx, that they lived there, or had lived there. They knew the streets that were in the book, recognized the area. They personally connected. And each day, I left that class in a state of exhilaration.

Random Family changed that class completely. My students were learning but it was fun so it didn't feel like LEARNING to them. They read and participated because they were invested, because they could connect the material to themselves.

Shajyre never fell asleep in my class again. At the end of the year, he wrote me a rap:

"I have chosen this topic because it's something I do on the regular. Professor del Rosso I would like to take the time out and write a rhyme for you. :)

How you doing there miss lady
to you I'm a baby
and that's why you nurture my mind
beautiful long hair light brown eyes
While I'm writing this I'm probably high as the sky
chill relax for a minute I was just playing
It don't look like it, but I do pay attention to what you sayin'
Just to let you know your teaching skills are so damn amazing
Dropped out of high school, started college didn't know what
I was face'in
Now it's kinda hard for me
look even my job trying to fire me
Always in my own world yeah something like ADD
I do try in this class, so pass me PLEASE

I'll never forget Shajyre, because he taught me a valuable lesson: if what you're doing is not working, find something else that connects with the students. Find it, try it, do it, do everything you can. It can change you, your students, the dynamic of the class. It can change everything.

2. I Really Didn't Mean To...

SOMETHING ELSE THAT CAN CONNECT with students and change the dynamic of a class is inadvertently including details of your personal life. And I do mean, change the dynamic not in your favor, even though all you did to deserve this was answer their questions honestly. Isn't honesty always the best policy?

Whoever taught me that should be fired.

3. On Having or Not Having Children

"Smart, Funny + Sexy. Made me a better writer!
Every time I hear "Lady Madonna" I think of you."
—*Student Evaluation, Anonymous, NYU 2010*

"Some of the articles we had to read, I did not enjoy very
much."
—*Student Evaluation, Anonymous, NYU 2010*

IN 2005, AT BERKELEY, IN ONE CLASS we were discussing the women depicted in *Random Family*. A fact that came up was that they all became pregnant multiple times. I asked them to find the word "birth control" in the text and they couldn't. That is because the word is absent from the text, to the women's detriment. We talked about the difference it makes to a woman's future if she has a baby, at what age, single or married or living with someone ("unwed mother" being an outmoded, derogatory term). If she has help, financial or other (childcare, etc..) from the father. We talked about a man's responsibility when it came to birth control, which provoked laughter from the men, and predictably, reactive anger from the women. The class was lively and loud. Then one of the young men raised his hand and said, "Professor, do you have kids?

I said, "No, I don't."

I cannot remember if I was next asked when I planned on having children, or if I volunteered the following information, but I do remember that I said these words:

"Actually, I don't want children."

The class went silent.

The same young man said, "Ever?"

I said, "Right."

He said, "Why?"

I said, "I just never have. I never wanted them."

After that, I came under a furious verbal assault, mostly from the men. A few:

"You're not a real woman.'"

"There must be something wrong with you."

"That's…that's…not normal."

Another young man raised his hand and asked, "What about your husband?"

Because, of course, I was married at the time so I had my wedding rings on. And because I had my wedding rings on, I must want children.

I said, "He doesn't want them, either. Do you really think I would marry a man who wanted children when I didn't? What do you think I am, some kind of idiot?"

The class was in an uproar. A student said, "It'll never last (the marriage)."

It didn't. But not because of the children issue.

I said, "Look, if we ever have any doubt as to whether we want children or not, this is what we do: we go to Mark's sister's house on Long Island and spend the weekend. She has three children. By the time Sunday night comes, we are so happy to get out of there and away from the *world of children*. Get it?"

"Not normal! Not a real woman!"

The forty-five minutes left of class felt like a referendum on my womb. I left battered.

To say I was astonished was an understatement, but when running this by Walt (and this is one of the main reasons I need him, because I am some kind of idiot and sometimes feel as if I know next to nothing), he pointed out it was also a cultural difference. These students had never

come into contact with an adult woman who had elected not to have children.

I have two younger sisters. Neither of them have children, also by choice. I did not think that was odd until someone said, "You don't think that's strange? That all three of you didn't want children?"

Well, no, because if you had lived in my house with my father, that would have made perfect sense to you.

But more than one person has commented on the statistical likelihood of three sisters in one family not having children. I leave that analysis to the Freudians (and to Chekov). All I can say is to all intents and purposes, my mother functioned as a single mother and then as a single, working full-time mother. It was not easy for her. So more than once, as a child and as a teen, I heard the following: "Remember, once you have children, your life is never your own. The child will always come first."

Now that we three sisters are grown ups and my mother is older, she complains that she has no grandchildren. I say one of the following, depending on my mood:

"Ask the other two, they're younger."

"Get a puppy."

"You can't be angry that we all actually *listened* to you."

In the adult world, away from my classrooms, comments on my elective childlessness range from interesting to insulting. And it's funny, most of the comments come from men (this immediately makes me think of Congress and men legislating on behalf of women's bodies, most of whom would really prefer they stop because if the congressional body comprised 98% women and the women periodically legislated on behalf of men's penises, men might feel a tiny bit hard done by but wouldn't that be an interesting sort of America?).

Comments such as these:

"If you had met the right man, you would have had children."

Really? I have met many "right men," many, many, many, in fact, and did not want to beget one single solitary child with any of them.

Once, during a "to baby, or not to baby" debate, I mentioned financial considerations, and the man in question said to me, "God will provide."

Regardless of any religious affiliation I do or do not have, I don't think God would like it if I behaved stupidly on purpose. To have a child with no money on purpose, for me, would be a stupid decision.

"A woman is supposed to want children."

Such an insulting assumption out of the mouth of a grown man, I couldn't dignify it with an answer.

I am quite sure every woman who has decided not to have children remembers what was said to her by someone each time, willfully or out of ignorance, as a commentary on her "lifestyle." On her seeming "selfishness." I am sure she can quote verbatim, as I can.

When I was diagnosed with epilepsy, at twenty-eight, I asked my neurologist at the time if it was possible for an epileptic to have a child. I have complex/partial seizures. I black out. I didn't know what happened to the body during a thirty-second to two-minute blackout.

My neurologist told me the following story: he had a patient who decided to have a child, and as he tells all of his female patients who are epileptics who want to have children, it's not impossible, but it can be tricky. The patient in question was in the sixth month of her pregnancy, and she was driving over the _____ bridge, when she had a seizure. Her van careened over the edge.

"And?" I said, nearly hyperventilating in his office.

"She lived. The baby died. So as I said, it's not impossible but it can be tricky."

If I had not wanted children by the age of twenty-eight, that story certainly didn't encourage me to change my mind.

I have a vivid memory of being at a family cookout, on my father's side of the family. It was before my parents divorced, so before the age of ten.

My very patriarchal family, directly from Anversa degli Abruzzi: very proud, very beautiful, very Italian, very traditional.

I remember looking around at all of the women, all of my Italian aunts, and to me, they looked unhappy. Each of them had more than one child, and at this particular cookout, they were the ones looking after their children. A few of them had jobs, but their lives centered around their families. I knew that one of my uncles ran around on his wife, because my father had told me. The women seemed… trapped. Then I looked over at the men. My uncles, standing and commingling with either a drink or a plate in their hands, were laughing. Talking, and telling stories. They seemed…free. Relaxed. Happy.

In hindsight, if I could have changed my gender at that moment, I would have. Instead, what I thought was, I never want to feel trapped. I want the same kind of freedom my uncles have. And that was the way I saw things, in my teeny-tiny mind, before the age of ten.

After that day at Berkeley College, the day when my student asked, "Professor, do you have kids?" I stopped wearing my wedding rings to class. I didn't want another public debate over my choice not to have children, and thought without the rings, no one would ever know if I was married

or not, so no one would assume I wanted children. But if I wanted to volunteer information about my personal life, that was different. Then it would be at my discretion.

No one ever asked me again.

However, I still referenced Mark in my classes—Mark now being my ex-husband/best friend/current roommate who is still part of my narrative, but no simple way to explain —and I referred to him as my "husband." This prompted one bold student to ask, "Professor, if you're married, then why don't you wear a wedding ring?"

That is a whole, other story, explained not here but, as I mentioned, most definitely by me in the Modern Love Section of *The New York Times*. And in my next collection of love essays.

4. LdR Profile

*"Professor del Rosso is a fabulous teacher who I love
and adore and she better work! All raggedy teachers can
learn from her."*
—Student Evaluation, Anonymous, NYU 2012

"You need to be a super genius to get an A."
—Student Evaluation, Anonymous, NYU 2010

WITH GREAT HESITATION, I submitted to an interview with
a former NYU student who, for a class, wrote a profile of her
most influential professor. Printed here with her permission:

ASHLEY MCHUGH-CHIAHPONE
LDR PROFILE

"Your mother is obligated to love you. I, however, am
not. So do what I say, or I might stop loving you," said Lisa
del Rosso, professor of writing at NYU and FIT, commanding a strong presence among a group of scared freshman.
*(LdR disclaimer: Wrongly attributed. I know I did not say this.
I envy the one who did).*

For many, this is the first class they have ever taken on
a college campus.

Through a clenched smile, del Rosso spelled out her
expectations. "If you don't want to learn, don't take my class,"
she said. "If you don't want to work, don't take my class. If
you only want an 'A,' don't take my class." As her students
listened, there was noticeable fear in their eyes. Before the
next time the class meets, at least one person from each section will drop the class.

Commanding a strong presence is commonplace for del Rosso, who has a naturally formidable personality. Having been classically trained as a singer at the London Academy of Music and Art, also known as LAMDA, she is used to being in the spotlight.

While her professional performing career is over, her energy and enthusiasm remains in tact. Now, she focuses all of her time on her writing and her students. This semester, she is teaching two creative nonfiction classes at FIT, as well as a mandatory writing class at NYU, albeit one of her own devising, entitled Writing New York.

Turns out, looks can be very deceiving. "The biggest misconception about me is that I'm terrifying," she admitted. Dressed in tight, black, form-fitting clothes, heeled boots, and with a mop of curly black hair, she embodies the quintessential New Yorker.

Not only does she look like a New Yorker, she acts like one. With a cool, confident attitude, there is not one topic she is afraid to speak about. She is open with all of her students and she is not afraid to reach out to them on a personal level. "She's very approachable, despite her exterior," said Isabelle Bank, an NYU sophomore and former student. "She really wants to know you, [no matter] whether you like her and her class or not."

Her class, which strives to hone the fundamental principles of writing, places a heavy focus on personal essay writing, short story readings and current events. The class is an open forum and everyone is free to voice their opinions. Any topic, from food to politics to hook-up culture, is fair game.

When she's not in the classroom, del Rosso spends her days writing for many publications. She has been featured in the *New York Times*, *Time Out New York*, *Young Minds Magazine*, among others. Most recently, she published a piece about the 9/11 Memorial Museum, a place she visited for the first time on her most recent birthday.

She's also had some success as a playwright, which is her self-proclaimed dream job. In 2006, her play, *Clare's Room*, was performed at the New York International Film Festival. In 2011, her play, *St. John*, was a finalist for the Eugene O'Neill National Playwrights Conference.

Despite her success, she has remained grounded and has become more invested in her work and students than ever before. Every semester, del Rosso gains 30 new pupils on which to impart her wisdom. With many, she develops deep, personal relationships.

And helping people is nothing new for her, either. After she graduated from the LAMDA program, she stayed in London for 10 years and became a Samaritan. Samaritans, found all across the world, are groups of people who volunteer their time and effort to help those in need. They operate 24-hour anonymous suicide call centers for those experiencing a crisis and have nowhere else to turn. Specifically chosen for this position, del Rosso spent years helping those who could not help themselves.

Today, del Rosso lives on the Upper West Side. A typical day for her involves strolls through Riverside Park, going to the theatre, grading papers, discussing current events and interacting with her students, both inside and outside of the classroom.

"For our first paper, the life event that changed you paper, she emailed me at 2 AM requesting my number and saying she had to speak with me immediately," recalls Grace Halio, a freshman journalism student. "I was so scared, but she called me and I guess I had a lot on my mind because we talked and talked for over two hours. It was so comforting to have a professor genuinely care about me."

Halio's experience with del Rosso is not an isolated one. Many of del Rosso's students have been personally contacted on her own time for a wide variety of reasons. Likewise, students actively reach out in order to discuss their various

issues.

"I'm from India and New York is very overwhelming. I had a lot of trouble adjusting to the city," said Pia Sharan, a sophomore at NYU. "Lisa was there any time I got lost or needed reassurance that coming here was the right decision for me. I'm grateful for that."

Del Rosso also maintains relationships with her students once they've left her classroom. Every other week, she hosts a writers workshop to help people looking to build their portfolios. For Thanksgiving, she hosts a misfits holiday party and invites anyone who can't, or won't, be spending time with his or her loved ones. During an average week, del Rosso will have lunch or grab a drink with a former student that she hasn't seen in a while.

"That's the thing about her. She wants to be there for you and she wants to make you feel important," said Julie Jeon, a sophomore at NYU. "And she always does."

5. Methods of Teaching (Part II) or, So Glad I Went to LAMDA (London Academy of Music and Dramatic Art)

> *"My entire schedule for this semester was chosen around this course. Professor del Rosso deserves a raise. And maybe her own building in NYC. We are all her monkeys, very willingly."*
> —Student Evaluation, Anonymous, NYU 2012

> *"the chairs were pieces of shit. and the play. Persephone. (at BAM) ew."*
> —Student Evaluation, Anonymous, NYU 2010

IT WAS BOTH APT AND SMART of Ashley to link LAMDA and the spotlight and being classically trained as things that connect me with teaching, rather than separating me from teaching.

Because I am an entertainer. Period.

This may sound silly to someone who has never taught or sat in on a freshman essay class, with fifteen blank faces staring back at you, waiting to see what you will do, say, ask.

My classes are billed as "lectures." Lecturing for seventy-five minutes does not remotely interest me. What does interest me are my students' opinions, thoughts, feelings on an essay I've given them: say, Brian Doyle's "Joyas Voladoras," or Joan Didion's "On Morality." I want to know what they think about style, form, content, yes. But I also want to know if the students can connect this piece to themselves, their lives, to the world in which they live. I try to do the

same with the piece, because the relationship between the students and me does become about sharing, about give and take.

I have a persona for the purposes of class:

PdR: Quintessential New Yorker. Fierce lover of the city. Opinionated. Funny. Hates children. Yankees fan. Anglophile. Hates tourists. Italian. Loves theater. Hates Times Square. Animated. Spirited. Cooks.

With this persona, I tell my students stories. For these stories, I also have a cast of characters distilled down just for class:

Jen: My youngest sister, the tattooed lady. Hippie chick, should have been born in the 1960's, so she could live in the woods, sit around a fire, singing and strumming a guitar to her heart's content. Ironically, she now lives in Portland, Oregon, where there are campgrounds galore. Fanatical, rabid Red Sox and Patriot's fan. Best not to bet against her when it comes to sports, unless you want your car Saran-Wrapped. Will throw you out into the snow during the Superbowl if you root against her team.

Kris: Middle sister. Cat person, prefers animals to people. Super-smart. Works in pharmaceuticals. Enviably tall. The only one in the family who wisely hates all sports.

Mark: My ex, which students may or may not know. A nice, secular Jew with a huge appetite and Woody Allen-ish, self-deprecating wit.

Libby: Mark's mother, now deceased. A big personality. Not a stereotypical Jewish mother, but a stereotypical Jewish mother x 10000. Sharp. Funny. Berated Mark for being a "bad Jew." It didn't work, he still didn't light the Menorah during Hanukkah.

Mom: Single mother, role model, Italian, taskmaster, demanding, supportive, lives in Florida, great cook. Fanatical, rabid Red Sox and Patriots' fan.

Father: "That jerk," said Libby.

Steve: Step-father. Fox News-watching Republican. Fanatical, rabid Red Sox fan. Also NY Giants.

JT: Actor. A pro. Also, St. Francis, reincarnated. Dogs and cats follow him down the street, birds land on his shoulders, squirrels scurry up his legs and sit happily on his lap.

Vasilios: Friend. FIT accessories and design professor. Greek. Loud. Insane, in a good way. Has a voice that resembles the possessed, demonic puppet in the Broadway play "Hand to God."

Ruth: My oldest, wisest friend. Actress. Difficult. Catchphrase: "I don't have to do anything I don't want to." What she said to me for over twenty years: "You don't have to do anything you don't want to." What I say now, to the consternation of everyone: "I don't have to do anything I don't want to, because Ruth said so." Brat.

Walt: Mentor. Wise. Oracle. Upon my graduation, after he handed me my MFA diploma, I made a speech and in it, I said, "Walt I would marry, if only to have an in-house editor. Alas, he is already wed."

Derek: My best friend. We have known each other since our teens. He is a Born-Again Christian, and I am a recovering Catholic/current Episcopalian/Humanist/searching. As we get older, I swing more and more to the Left, and Derek swings more to the Right. Our friendship has endured for nearly twenty-five years, and if we can get along and accept each other's differences, then I believe anyone can because the "I can" part is a choice.

Carol: Carol is Derek's spectacular wife and my friend—a beautiful actress, lover of animals, a wonderful mother. She is also highly opinionated, which thrills me. She is as honest a person I know.

Ian and Julia: Their children, who are equally spectacular. They call me "Aunty Lisa" or "Aunty del." If I had ever

wanted children, then when flipping through the "Children I Want" catalog, these are the children I would have pre-ordered. They are kind, smart, funny, polite, personable. They are good company. They have manners. I credit their parents, though Carol says she is sure some of it is "despite us." Nevertheless, they make it impossible for me to say I hate all children. What I do say is that I hate all children *except for them*.

All of these people, my people, are in the stories I tell to and for my students. Funny stories. Embarrassing stories. Interesting stories. Stories to make a point. Stories about London, nannying, my certifiable family members. New York Stories. Anything to make them laugh, think, to spur something in themselves they can contribute to the class discussion. To connect to the literature and their world. Seventy-five minutes isn't a lot of time. If you lose them, you're finished.

What I try to do is get them to care. Stories work. My stories, and theirs.

6. New York Stories

The weekly New York Stories:

> *First of all, the fact that the professor is very liberal with them makes them fun to write.*
>
> *Second, every week as something fun or interesting or funny happens, I immediately remind myself to write about it.*
>
> *And third, they work to create a type of diary of the most memorable events that happened throughout this semester that I otherwise might have forgotten.*
>
> *And finally, I love the fact that it's all a competition. The winner gets a little toy that at first sight might be considered useless, but what matters is the pride of receiving the toy in front of everyone. Also, watching as the collection of these prizes grows on your bookshelf is one of those small joys that make life that much more enjoyable."*

—Student evaluation, Anonymous, NYU 2014

NEW YORK STORIES WERE BORN out of laziness more than anything else.

NYU has a site, originally called Blackboard but now NYU Classes (NYUC) , like all colleges do, where students get class information, homework, announcements, etc…and then there is a Forum set up as well. The Forum requires a prompt. Professors were encouraged to post a weekly prompt for the students to respond to, so they would be writing on a regular basis. It was suggested that the prompt should be different each week. But at the time, I had four classes, seventy students, many papers to correct, and I just

could not add one more thing to my teaching "To Do" list. However, I did think the prompt an excellent idea for fostering weekly writing and possibly discussion…so why not have the content change rather than the prompt?

Hence, New York Stories was born.

This is the actual prompt:

Your weekly New York Stories: anything you have observed, witnessed, participated in. Anything funny, sick, baffling, unique, wonderful, terrible, offensive, inappropriate. Anything behaviorally out of the ordinary. I am only looking for a paragraph, 8 or 9 sentences. Photos/film/ video welcome. Post your stories by Sunday at 6 PM. The best New York Story wins a prize come Monday.

The forum itself is private, meaning only I and the students can read each other's posts. They do not go to my chair, the dean, the president…. and because of this, I give them carte blanche to write whatever it is that they want to write about, in any form—poetry or prose, for example—any language, any content. This is the "safe room" of my class.

Early on, a student raised her hand and said, "Professor, um…suppose we…want to write about something that we did….and it's illegal?"

The room went quiet.

I said, "You know, that question makes me really depressed, because you assume that I have never done anything illegal, which is not the case."

Everyone exhaled, laughing.

"You think I'm going to call the police? Write about whatever you want."

As a result, my students have been amazingly candid. I have read just about every drunken, debauched story you can imagine; hideous roommate stories ranging from one who

liked to arrange her toiletries in pentagrams (with photos for proof); to another who was bulimic, regularly vomited into a bathroom trashcan (or, nearly) and then left it while she went out for the evening, expecting others to clean up after her. Being "sexiled" is some kind of rudeness I still don't understand, nor do I understand having your boyfriend/girl-friend sleep over in your dorm room, in your bed, while your single, long-suffering roommate has to listen to you have sex. One guy built himself a sex cave out of his closet, and had a string of different women in and out of said cave for the duration of the term.

There were bad house parties. Bad raves. Bad break ups. Dropping a slice of pizza on a pizza parlor floor, cheese-side down, then picking it up and eating it (alcohol was involved). Good Samaritans who helped people who had fallen in the street. Bad Samaritans who did not help people who had fallen in the street. Female students who could not wait for the dorm toilet, and instead sat down and used the curb (alcohol was involved). Visits to other colleges in other cities and towns that could not compare to NYU or the Village as its campus. Being bearhugged by President John Sexton. Weird art exhibitions that were really art exhibitionists.

Hilarious subway stories: a video of the man dancing, Isadora Duncan-style, in either a black or a red sequined thong (depending on the day) and heels inside Union Square Station; a photo posted of a young man who decided he'd take a nap in the space underneath the subway seats, usually reserved for chewed gum, spit, spilled liquids and other detritus. The balloon man in Washington Square Park. The pigeon man in Washington Square Park. The sparkly pink crotchet lady in Washington Square Park, described as "weird but kinda hot." In a female student's dorm room, a photo taken of an unknown young man, passed out in a closet and discovered the next morning, naked save for a pair

of powder-blue boxer shorts. A video of ducks swimming somewhere in Prospect Park, Brooklyn, from a student who clearly missed nature.

I had a star basketball player's son as a student: CJ, Magic Johnson's son. He was wonderful. Tall, confident, witty and flamboyant, he had the best scarves and the best New York Stories, usually about a spa day at the Meridian or something else "fabulous" he had done. He did have a personal shopper at Bergdorf's, so there was a story about a leather jacket not arriving in a timely fashion, but other than that, no descriptions of conspicuous consumption. But people did often recognize him. They came up to him when he was out and about and asked him personal questions he usually found annoying. He was once in a club and a young, blonde woman came up to him and said, "Are you Magic Johnson's son?" Here we go, he thought. And he was so ready to tell her off, because he was just trying to have a good time. Until she said, and I paraphrase, Your father is such a role model to me because he has HIV and I do, too. Then she began to cry. CJ, shocked, took her aside, sat her down, calmed her and talked to her for most of the evening.

In the same class, there were two gals who tried to keep up with him: one a pathological liar, the other perpetually schlubby. Schlubby always looked like she had just rolled out of bed to come to my class. So it was surprising when she posted this as her NY Story, in the guise of the famous, heart-warming MasterCard commercial. I asked her to read it aloud to the class (I no longer have this in my notes and wish I did, so this is an approximation):

Friday:
Food: $500
Nightclub: $1000
W Hotel: $800
Saturday:

Food: $500
Nightclub: $1000
W Hotel: $800
Drugs: $250
Sunday:
Brunch: $150
Total Cost: $5000.00

Monday Morning: Credit card cut off, angry message from Mother on mobile.

Monday Afternoon: Angry message from Father on mobile.

Waiting to see what happens next despite awesome weekend: Priceless

She was the winner that week. Easily one of my favorite New York Stories.

Most of the time, students do not have time to read each other's posts, so I pick out the best ones, have the student describe the post, and then we briefly discuss. They all get to know each other this way, and I get to know them. Some students have divulged real problems and have asked the class for help or understanding. The class has usually stepped up and offered advice about how to get over a bad breakup, or deal with an obnoxious roommate. One young woman, Ali, confessed to being upset that she was rejected by a sorority, promoting comments such as, "You don't need them anyway," to "You are too good for them," to "Fuck them." Ali was smiling by the time they finished.

My students are searching, for who they are and what they want to do with their lives. This is their first time out in the world, and they make mistakes. I did too, when I was their age. I made many. But their candor is refreshing. Their

support of one another in the classroom gives me hope for humanity. They are smart and funny and they try, every day. And when I tell you I have the best students, that I have always had the best students, I really do mean it. They make me up my game. They bring the best of themselves to my class, and they make me want to come to class and try harder. And even then, I fail. Or get complaints. Usually about grading (eye roll).

7. Complaints

> *"I'm an English Major who frequently gets frustrated with sub-par writing courses. That was not the case with this course. It was phenomenal."*
> —Student Evaluation, Anonymous, NYU 2012

> *"Would have prefered to pick my own topic for the argument essay."*
> —Student Evaluation, Anonymous, 2013

THIS EMAIL WAS SENT TO ME at the end of the term, right before summer break, before Serge's final grade was posted:

> From: Serge
> To: Lisa Del Rosso
> Subject: Thank you
> Date: May 12, 2015 11:25 AM
> Dear Professor Del Rosso,
>
> I wanted to thank you once again for the super helpful/interesting/entertaining writing classes throughout the year. I enjoyed your classes a lot first semester and because you made me, as well as all of your students, feel so comfortable in your class, I've been able to enjoy even more the second part of the year. Thank you for the laughs. Thank you for being a class we looked forward going to. You are an awesome teacher.
>
> I look forward to seeing you next year,
> Have a wonderful summer,
>
> Serge

This email was sent to me at the end of the term, right at the start of summer break, immediately after Serge's grade was posted.

> From: Serge
> Sent: May 26, 2015 5:24 AM
> To: Lisa Del Rosso
> Subject: Follow Up
>
> Dear Professor Del Rosso,
>
> It is not really in my ethic to ask for a grade explanation. Tough this time I was a bit upset to see my grade unchanged compared to first semester as well as inferior to Ian's one. I really believed my English to be improved after one year of class spent with you. Also, I did not think that Ian fundamentally deserved a better grade than mine. Though if you think his work to be superior than what I provided to you I understand and I respect you judgment.
>
> I'd just like to understand the reason of this grade.
> Hope your summer is going well,
> Serge

I may have mentioned I have a reputation as a hard grader. This is fair. And complaints about this used to bother me, until I had a conversation with T.E., who backed me up completely.

So now when I get an email like this I think, really, tough shit.

I don't understand the point of an easy A. I don't understand the reward in that. I personally would feel a fake, and an unearned A is exactly that: unearned.

I teach college writing at an elite institution. It is supposed to be hard. It is supposed to be challenging. The goal is for students to improve: their participation, articulation, thinking, writing, expression, analysis, connection to the world in which they live. All of it, hopefully.

An A is hard to get in my class, but it is not impossible. Out of a class of fifteen, there are approximately six or seven A's. To me, that's great. Why the B+ is so abhorrent, I also do not understand.

This is what I would put on my syllabus for grade descriptions if I could:

A: Nothing more I can teach you about writing these kinds of essays. In addition to it being a technically perfect paper, you blew my mind with your original thinking and gorgeous writing combined.

A-: The same as above, but with either a few mistakes, or the thinking was not as original as I would have liked. It can also be a technically perfect paper.

B+: Very good, extremely well-written, with a few errors. A little bit more imagination required.

B: Very good, well-written, and could have pushed a bit more in the arena of proofreading.

C: This is my least favorite grade. It is the laziest grade. You did just enough work to pass, and that's it. Minimum effort. Why are you here?

D: is for Deserved it.

F: Fucking idiot for not coming to class, doing the work, and wasting an incredible opportunity.

This is the email I wrote back to Serge a month later:

To: Serge
Subject
Subject: Re: Follow Up

Date: Jun 12, 2015 12:55 AM
Serge,

My apologies for taking so long to get back to you; I've been traveling and just returned home. Your final paper was at my house, and I wanted to look at it again before responding.

I do not compare students, and wish you didn't, as it is ultimately unhelpful. However, because you referenced Ian in your email, I shall address him as well.

Yes, of course your English has improved. But I don't teach a language class; I teach a writing class. Your papers have also improved. But they also contain mistakes.

Ian: somewhere during the revisions of the second paper, the immigration paper, Ian decided he was going to revise until he had a perfect paper, a paper with no errors whatsoever. I did not ask him to do this, he did it of his own accord. I think he revised the immigration paper...6 times? Perhaps more.

For the landmark paper, he had an unusual idea: write about NYU only insofar as frats go, because he was pledging at the time. His source material was rich. He was directly connected to and invested in what he was writing about. That paper he rewrote maybe 12 times. He was hell-bent. A man on a mission.

The only mark on his final paper is mine: the grade at the top. There are no errors, and the writing is superb. If you'd like, I can sit down with you in September and you can read his paper. Then you can read yours. You can ask about the errors, which I will explain.

I have always wished there was a grade between an A- and a B+: that is how close some students have been. But there is not, and in the end, I make an assessment based on all your work, class participation, etc... and that is all I can do. Trust me, if the grade were just about how much I liked you and Ian, it would be AAAAAAAAAAAA. But grades don't work that way, and I have to be able to sleep at night.

I hope that provides you with some sort of explanation. If you want to talk further, in September I will make time for you. And by the way, a B+ is not a bad grade! Only NYU students complain about the B+. All over-achievers.

Best,
PdR

And just to balance out those complaint emails:

From: James Zhang
To: Lisa Del Rosso
Subject
Subject: Last assignment with you:(
Date
Date: May 3, 2014 12:37 AM
Message Body
Hi Professor,

Soooo on a Friday night i'm sitting here writing my essay reminiscing of all the good times i've had with you haha. I found out I'm not required to take writing anymore the other day when i

thought the whole time i'd be in your class most of the time at NYU:(

For the first time i'm not rushing to get "del Rosso" on Albert haha.

I wish writing were a requirement instead of cultural or social foundations. But I have to try and complete all the hard courses of my major before recruiting and interview season.

It's been a pleasure professor.

I hope i've shown you progress in the latter half of the class and have been fun to have around. I'm so happy for all the students that will get to have you as their prof in boring LSP. I will definitely write the sickest review on rate my professor haha.

Anyways, looking forward to the last week. Please don't tell anyone i said all this haha.

Oh and Donald Sterling might sue the nab... Hate that guy. But 6 game 7's this weekend... How are students supposed to study for finals..

Best regards,
James

8. To Teach, or Not to Teach? That is the Job

"This professor is absolutely amazing. Everything about her class is challenging but extremely beneficial to every student. The discussions we have after reading certain articles are unparalleled in any of my other classes. The prompts for our essays are also extremely interesting and provide all students with opportunities to go out and experience the city. This is an amazing class."
—*Student Evaluation, Anonymous, NYU 2015*

A JOKE:

A French student, an Icelandic student, and an Asian student walk into a classroom. The French student says to the Asian student, "What fresh hell is this?"

The Asian student says, "I don't know, we didn't do any of this last semester."

The French student says, "You're right, we didn't!"

The Icelandic student looks at both of them and says, "You're both wrong. It's not that we didn't do any of this last semester; it's that we didn't do anything last semester."

The Icelandic student is right.

By the time students come to choose classes for the spring semester (2nd semester) they have gotten to know how the land lies: what they do and do not want in a class, and they also know the professors or reputations of the professors. It is unusual for me to get new students who do not know anything about me coming in. Meaning, my reputation is hard but fair. What I actually say to students on the first day of class is the following: If you do not feel

like doing a lot of work this semester, please don't take my class. There are seventy-nine other professors you can take this class with and if you stay, don't complain mid-semester that I gave you too much work. Also, if you have to get the A, please don't take my class. An A is not a given, no matter where you come from. I don't care what you grades you got in high school, or what you did there. Everyone here is on a level playing field.

That little speech usually causes a few to drop, and others to take their places (students have two weeks to switch classes and find ones they like providing a space is available).

Good. Because I want students who want to be challenged, not ones who are looking for easy.

Second semester, 2015, I had my two usual classes at NYU, from 3:30-4:45 and 4:55-6:10, back to back, on Mondays and Wednesdays. In the second class, there were three new students, and after a few weeks, I heard through the grapevine (okay, from another student) that they weren't entirely happy. Normally, I could care less about this, but the students in question were bright, friendly and seemed eager to learn, so I wanted to find out why.

The first round of papers came in. I sat in on the peer workshops, and the paper that first alarmed me was that of an Icelandic-American student. He was born and raised in the US but Icelandic was his first language. In reading his paper, it was quite clear he had an ESL issue, a big one. I had a couple of conferences with him and asked a few questions, among them, the papers he worked on the previous semester.

"We didn't really do much writing," he said.

"How about revision?"

"Not really," he said.

"What did you write about?"

"Well…anything we wanted. But we never got papers back or anything," he said.

"Peer workshops?"

"No," he said.

"How many papers were assigned over the course of the semester?"

"One, due at the end of the term," he said.

"What was your final grade?"

"He gave everyone an A-," he said.

I said, "What was the name of your professor?"

"Professor _____," he said.

Containing my fury, I told my student he needed ESL tutoring, a suggestion he found completely insulting.

"I'd rather go to a regular tutor."

I didn't think I was wrong, but he wanted an opportunity to be right. "Okay. We'll try it your way, for now."

There was a backlog at the "regular" tutoring center, so my student couldn't see anyone for two weeks. I helped, but I am not an ESL teacher. His first paper, after three revisions, was riddled with errors and earned him a D. I said, "Now we do it my way."

He said, "I can look at a sentence a hundred times and still not see what's wrong with it."

I said, "I know. Leave it to me."

I began looking for ESL tutoring. I contacted Jim Short, the assistant of academic advising. I remembered there was a language program where ESL students got together weekly to talk, and work out problems. Jim was immensely helpful. He ran the program himself.

I then contacted my student's academic advisor, who didn't really understand what the problem was until I read her a few sentences from his final paper. She said, "Got it."

He was assigned an ESL tutor uptown, and attended

twice a week. Super-smart, he learned very quickly. He grew more confident in class, and asked if he could enter the Modern Love College Essay competition, and I said of course. The essay wasn't bad. His second paper was a B+. He thanked me and I said I was sorry it took so long to discover the ESL problem. He said, "You can thank my high school, too."

I said, "Granted, but you are paying a whopping sum to come here. It should have been caught earlier."

At the end of all this, I had another conversation with Jim Short. I said I was angry: angry that the ESL problem wasn't caught in September, angry that Icelandic was paying $71,000 dollars to learn...nothing? Angry on his behalf. He said I really needed to tell the chair what was going on, because she needed to know when things like this happened, so they did not happen again.

I dreaded doing that, because it felt like tattling. However, in the best interest of my student and any others who will be unfortunate enough to have this professor in future, I made an appointment with Chair T.E. It was weeks before I could get to her, which turned out to be a good thing.

Exactly a week after I had sorted out Iceland, I met with a French-American student to go over her paper. She was magnificently outspoken and articulate in class, but required more time to complete her work. That was fine, except more time did not translate into a flawless final draft, one that I knew she was capable of writing.

We sat down in the foyer after class and I went over my purple-inked comments with her, things that she didn't understand, things she didn't see.

She said, "I'm not a very good writer."

I said, "You are a very good writer; this is about learning and revision, that's all. That's what I'm here for."

She smiled.

I said, "Tell me kind of papers you did last semester. Who was your professor?"

She said, "He didn't teach."

I said, 'What?"

She said, "It was Dr. _____. He's very old. He didn't teach. He told stories for the seventy-five minutes. Some of the stories were entertaining. Sometimes he talked about his kidney transplant. But we didn't do any of this."

"Revision?"

"Yeah."

"What topics did you write about?"

"It was kind of like free-form."

"What does that mean?"

"We could write about whatever we wanted."

"How many papers did you pass in during the semester?"

"One, at the very end."

"And what was your final grade?"

She paused. "He gave everyone an A-."

I wanted to kill someone, but my teaching career would have been interrupted. Then again, I could always teach in prison.

She said, "I was actually really annoying and asked him questions all the time, because it was so frustrating to be in his class. And the Asian-American student, who sits in the front row? He was also in the same class with me. It was a little difficult."

I paused, thinking, searching for calm.

No wonder they didn't get my class. In comparison, it was regimented: we read and discuss pieces every other week from the assigned book everyone has to buy and the weeks we don't read, students are in peer workshops editing each other's papers. Three papers a semester, three drafts of each paper, and each draft goes through me. Inked, com-

mented on, handed back. All drafts of all papers = 75% of the grade. Class participation, mini-essays, attendance - 25%.

I said to her, "Revision is the point of the writing classes. Otherwise, you learn nothing. Every author you loved as a child, every author you love now, every author you will love in the future: they all revise! All of them. Over and over and over. And none of them do it alone. They have readers like the ones you have in your peer groups, and they have mentors. Revision is a process, and it's okay if you don't know where it's going, or how it's going to end or exactly what it is you're doing, but I promise you I will get you there."

What I did not say: It's time-consuming to correct fifteen or thirty papers that are seven-ten pages long (now five-seven pages). It's a pain in the ass. But it is part of the job.

My student looked at me with something like hope and said, "Thank you."

I met with T.E. and told her about these students. She was, naturally, unhappy. She said, "You can't not give students the building blocks in Writing 1 and then have them flailing around in Writing II. I'll take care of this. This one is new, I don't know him; but this one? Dr.____ ? He's been around for a long time. He should know better."

Before I left, I asked if they were full-time people, because when I told all this to my mother, she said, "After all you do? If they don't want to teach, tell your chair you'd be happy to take one of their full-time jobs." Alas, they were both adjunct professors.

At the end of the second semester, Icelandic student: B+, Asian-American student: B+, French-American student: A-. No joke.

If You Change a Student's Life, Is It Worth It?

*"SHE'S A KEEPER. How much do you pay these
people? Give her double that."*
—*Student evaluation, Anonymous, NYU 2011*

OF COURSE IT IS. But there's a caveat: Of course it is, but not
for the long-term. Because in the long-term, I can't afford
it, emotionally or financially.

I sat down and did my taxes on April 15th, 2015, waiting until the last day in the event of an unpleasant surprise.
And there it was: I made $350 more dollars than I had in the
previous year. That $350 that kicked me into a different tax
bracket, and the federal government decided I didn't really
need those Obamacare subsidies they helped me out with
per month for all those health insurance payments, and they
wanted them back. My tax bill? Over $2000.00

I am a happy person: genetically predisposed to hap-
piness. I have a positive, glass half-full outlook on life. My
mother is the same way, and I am grateful for this inheritance.

But for the twenty-four hours after I was handed my
tax bill on a platter, I mulled over the fact that if I were no
longer here, I would no longer be in debt. Not being able to
go to the doctors would suddenly be a moot point. I couldn't
even joke that I was worth more dead than alive, as I have
no life insurance policy.

Sam, the wonderful friend who lives in LA, responded
when I said I could not take his phone call, when I did not
seem like myself:

"Oy. Please don't kill yourself. Too much waste of beauty, wit, intelligence and hotness. Maybe it's easy for somebody who is relatively financially secure to say, but money isn't a measure of worth."

He was exactly right, but that is how I felt. Worthless.

On the 16th, I went to dinner with my friend Sylvia. I would have canceled, but the date had been made ages ago, she is eighty-four, I adore and did not want to disappoint her, so I made myself go. We talked for a long time. By the time I left, Sylvia had come up with many ideas, cheered me up and gave me much to think about.

Friday morning, I woke up and began writing this. I wrote without stopping for twelve days. I don't know if I will be able to continue teaching, so I wanted some sort of an account, a record, of all that being an adjunct professor entails. Of all that it has meant to me.

I have taught at various colleges for nearly fourteen years and it has almost never felt like just a job (the one time it did, I changed colleges). I love what I do and am effective at what I do, and that is how I know I am in the right profession. But my profession, educating and inspiring and mentoring the young minds of today who will be running my and your world tomorrow, is not sustainable. And there is really something wrong when I live with someone in the service industry who makes far and away more than I do, simply because he serves steak in an expensive restaurant.

It is that feeling—the love of students and the love of teaching—that universities now use against adjunct professors. It is that feeling that is gambled on for a low wage: for no heath benefits, no sick pay, no retirement fund, no job security. And the universities are winning. Now that more and more are run like corporations rather than institutions of higher learning, each year universities command higher

tuition, more administrative staff, lower pay for adjunct professors. More than 50% of all faculty appointments are part-time; there are other sources that put the figure as high as 70%. Why? Because I (we) love to teach, love my (our) students, and consider teaching a vocation.

But let me put this in starker terms, with none of my usual levity.

In the first few drafts of this book, I omitted my financials because I felt embarrassed, frankly. I didn't really want my students to know what I was making (or, not making) and under no circumstances did I want their pity. But my pride, well... has no place here.

At NYU, which again is the highest-paid adjunct job in the city, at the time of this writing (1/1/17), each course pays $5,760. I just signed a contract for $11,520—that is for two courses. Combining the fall and spring terms, that brings my annual salary to $23,040. Did I mention I live in Manhattan? I live in Manhattan. I have lived here for twenty-three years. I/we have a rent-stabilized apartment, and both of our names are on that lease, which is the only reason we can stay in this city. And the city is where the jobs are!

Trying to find another university job without knowing someone in another English department is almost impossible, unless you are a star writer.

How does this affect me on the daily? My ex pays three-quarters of the rent. He buys most of the groceries. He pays most of the bills. He also has health insurance, and I do not, so I pay out of pocket for doctor's appointments, blood tests and four monthly running prescriptions. Three out of four of those control my epilepsy. Every two weeks I get a paycheck: after credit card bills, student loan payments, rent, Metro card and my expenditures on food, I have

almost nothing left. Savings? Hilarious. Emergency fund? A scream. Retirement? My generation cannot afford to retire.

I am not an equal in the apartment in terms of finances. I try to make up for this deficiency by running writing workshops out of the apartment, year-round. I both sell and consign clothes and jewelry. When I shop, I either trade or buy via eBay or thrift shops. To extend the life of my clothes, I handwash to prevent fading, iron, and keep in excellent condition. Shoes are re-heeled and re-soled in lieu of the new. I belong to TDF (Theater Development Fund, for teachers and theater folk alike), so do get to see theater; I also write theater reviews for an English publication, so free press for the play means free admission for me and a friend. As for museums, I go only to The Met, which takes "Suggested Donations" rather than admission. I/we never go out to eat in restaurants so it is fortunate my mother taught me to be an excellent cook (to be fair, my ex is an excellent eater). I do not go to the movies. Vacations, if there are any, have to be planned well in advance (visiting my mother in Florida once a year on spring break, for example). For the last three years, I have taught the NYU/OP six-week summer course, which does bring in more money. The problem is it begins after July 4th, and with the first paycheck coming about July 21st, my last paycheck for the regular term is June 1st. By that time, I am late on bills, rent, and have to play catch-up.

I am extremely lucky to have lived in London via college in my late teens and twenties and was able to travel. During that time, through a nannying job, I was "adopted" by a well-off English family who think so highly of me from time to time they fly me from NYC to London for the pleasure of my familial company. For the love and generosity they have shown to me, I can never repay them.

Money is the only area where I have no confidence.

It's simple to say, Well, just move to a different place. My mother would say, Not without a job to go to. And starting

over totally in your 40's is different from doing it when you are in your 20's. For a start, I have pets.

Consider the following, from the point of view of having to obtain an MFA (a post-graduate degree) to teach college writing: I said NYU is the highest paid adjunct job in the city. That is because of my union. Most adjuncts don't have a union. The city colleges in the CUNY/SUNY system pay half of what NYU pays.

Half.

What is happening in this country is criminal. We have become a nation of contract workers, of part-timers, of cheap labor, through no fault of our own. All of us make up "the working poor." What percentage is that? 18.7% (I had to look that one up). That would be 28.19 million people. My friend is another one: a paraprofessional in a class full of disabled students, she is hired per term. The school she works for let her go just before Christmas, and then re-hired her in January, so they didn't have to continue to pay her throughout the holidays. So she remains part-time, insecure, no benefits. The same thing will happen in summertime.

This is the reality of my situation, hers, and so many, many others.

How does this affect the economy? We contribute less. We shop on eBay. We limit our vacations. We don't eat out in restaurants. We don't buy: cars, houses, apartments, gadgets, "the latest thing," museum subscriptions, theater subscriptions, cable, life insurance, health insurance. We stop with the Christmas presents, birthday presents, and send cards (old school, via snail mail. Not E-cards. I am, after all, a writing teacher) instead. We don't have children.

28.19 million of us. Anyone alarmed yet?

I wonder if any economist, or any conservative, liberal, Republican or Democrat in Congress will read this book. Because I am much more than a statistic. This is my life, the

way I live. Teetering on a high-wire. And as of right now, the beginning of 2017, just like last year, I have no health insurance whatsoever.

Not long ago, I was out with Arla and the subject of adjunct professors came up. She said, "Oh Lisa! It's in the zeitgeist! And it's all over my Twitter feed! You're the McDonald's employees of the college world."

If that is the yardstick, then we are all McDonald's employees, all 28.19 million of us. And counting.

Acknowledgements

I would like to give thanks to:

Achilles Nicoletti, my grandfather.

Joyce Bennett, my mother.

The Tufts Library and all of the wonderful, encouraging librarians steeped in the world of books, eager to share that world with young readers.

Mary Folliet, for seeing something in me that I could not.

Steve Streeter and Michael Frew for opening a door.

Fairleigh Dickenson University (FDU). Walt Cummins, for his editorial skill, his patience and for absolutely everything a writer could wish for in a mentor.

Elaine Tobin, for taking a chance.

Mark Lawitz, proofreader bar none.

My students.

Angela Neustatter, for believing and for reading and for writing and writing and writing.

David Daniel, RenéSteinke, Hans Balmes, Moira Young for their encouragement and help.

Lisa del Rosso originally trained as a classical singer and completed a post-graduate program at LAMDA (London Academy of Music and Dramatic Art), living and performing in London before moving to New York City. Her plays *Clare's Room*, and *Samaritan*, have been performed off-Broadway and had public readings, respectively, while *St. John*, her third play, was a semi-finalist for the 2011 Eugene O'Neill National Playwrights Conference. Her writing has appeared in *The New York Times*, *Barking Sycamores Neurodivergent Literature*, *Razor's Edge Literary Magazine*, *The Literary Traveler*, *Serving House Journal*, *Vietnam War Poetry*, *Young Minds Magazine* (London/UK), *Time Out New York*, *The Huffington Post*, *The Neue Rundschau* (Germany), *Jetlag Café* (Germany), and *One Magazine* (London/UK), for whom she writes theater reviews. She teaches writing at New York University. Some of the pieces in this book first appeared in other publications.